MRCS
Part B OSCES
Essential Revision Notes
Second Edition

Catherine Parchment Smith
BSc(Hons) MBChB(Hons) MRCS (Eng)

Julia Massey
MBBS MRCS(Ed)

PasTest
Dedicated to your success

© 2010 PASTEST LTD
Egerton Court
Parkgate Estate
Knutsford
Cheshire
WA16 8DX

Telephone: 01565 752000

First Published 2002, Revised edition 2006
Second Edition 2010

ISBN: 1 905635 559
         978 1 905635 559
A catalogue record for this book is available from the British Library.

PasTest Revision Books and Intensive Courses

PasTest has been established in the field of undergraduate and postgraduate medical education since 1972, providing revision books and intensive study courses for doctors preparing for their professional examinations.

Books and courses are available for:
Medical undergraduates, MRCGP, MRCP Parts 1 and 2, MRCPCH Parts 1 and 2, MRCS, MRCOG, DRCOG, DCH, FRCA, Dentistry.

For further details contact:
PasTest, Freepost, Knutsford, Cheshire WA16 7BR
Tel: 01565 752000   Fax: 01565 650264
www.pastest.co.uk   enquiries@pastest.co.uk

Project Manager Sue Harrison
Text prepared by Carnegie Book Production, Lancaster UK
Printed and bound in the UK by Page Bros (Norwich) Ltd

CONTENTS

ABOUT THE AUTHORS

Catherine Parchment Smith BSc (Hons) MBChB (Hons) FRCS (Eng)
Cathy did a degree in Biology at Warwick University and some research in Genetics at Dundee University before having a great time at Manchester Medical School. She did her BST in Manchester and was an SpR in Yorkshire. She was awarded the Association of Surgeons Gold Medal in her exit exam in General Surgery specialising in Colorectal surgery and is now a consultant Colorectal Surgeon in Pinderfields Hospital, Mid Yorkshire NHS Trust.

Julia Massey MBBS, MRCS (Ed)
Julia graduated from the University of Newcastle in 2003.
Following her House Officer year in Newcastle she completed the Basic Surgical Training Scheme in Leeds. She is now an ST4 in General Surgery in West Yorkshire.

Richard Young BSc (Hons) MBChB (Hons) MRCSEd
Richard completed his undergraduate training at the University of Leeds in 2006 and is currently a General Surgical trainee in Yorkshire. He has an interest in medical education and is an examiner for the University of Leeds.

Ryan Koshy Mathew MBChB (Hons) BSc (Hons) MRCS (Ed)
After reading medicine at Leeds, Ryan completed his foundation training in Yorkshire and is currently a Specialty Registrar in neurosurgery at Leeds General Infirmary. He has clinical experience in India, South Africa and Uganda. His primary research into tissue engineering led to placements at Harvard University and Massachusetts General Hospital in Boston.

Contributing authors to previous edition

Claire Ritchie Chalmers BA BM BCh MRCS

Karen Flood BMedSci, BM BS, MRCS (Ed)

ACKNOWLEDGEMENTS

I wrote this book in longhand on my kitchen table with my baby in a Moses basket on the floor next to me. I never imagined that we would still be selling hundreds of copies a year when my baby was buying skinny jeans and planning her first year in high school. I am grateful to all the trainees who have come up to me over the years saying that they found the book helpful – that was the plan, and I hope this new edition helps even more of you into a career which I have found exciting, stimulating and satisfying over those many years.

I am also grateful to my colleagues and patients at Mid Yorkshire who make it possible to continue enjoying this career, particularly Mark Rogers, Charles Morrison, Sivakumar Rangasamy, Gillian Faircliffe and Julie Crossley. Thanks also to my best mate Cath Hernon for always being there even when she was far away.

I am especially grateful to Julia Massey, a bright and energetic trainee who was able to give the time and energy to my book that I no longer have! I hope this means that the MRCS OSCE candidates will get as much use out of it in the future as other candidates have in the past. I would also like to thank Heather Harford for some of the photos, Sue and Cathy and all at PASTEST who have taken on working with me yet again, Rick who used his experience of the exam to help us out and everyone who contributed to this and the first edition.

I dedicate this book yet again to my family, Jon, for his support, Mum for her hard work and the children Bella, Ben and Zac who are still young enough to delight us all daily.

Cathy Parchment Smith

I would like to thank my wonderful family and friends who I have bored rigid about this book for all their support – especially my parents Rob and Mary Anne and my sister Louisa.

I also want to thank the people who have helped with this book including: Jonathan Smith and Bobby Bhartia for the new improved X-rays, Sue Harrison and Cathy Dickens at PasTest for all their help, and Richard Young and Ryan Mathew for being such reliable and excellent contributing authors. Huge thanks also to Cathy Parchment Smith for giving me the opportunity and encouragement and having faith in me to work on her brilliant book.

Julia Massey

We would also like to acknowledge the contributions made by **Claire Ritchie Chalmers** and **Karen Flood** to the previous edition of this book.

PERMISSIONS

Images on the following pages have been reproduced by kind permission of
The Wellcome Photographic Library, London.
Chapter 3: 58, 63(T), 66(BR), 68(M), 69(L), 71(T), 73(T), 77, 97(TR&B), 105, 107(L),
111(R), 115(T&BL), 121, 127, 128, 129, 131, 132, 133, 137(BL&R), 142(TL&R), 143.
Chapter 4: 207, 209, 211, 212, 213, 217, 219(R), 220, 221(TL&R), 226, 235(L), 237,
264, 269, 271(T), 275(L), 277, 279, 280, 283, 289, 291, 293(B), 299(T),
Chapter 5: 403, 405(B), 429, 445, 455, 456, 458, 459, 461, 463, 465, 467,
469(TL&R), 471(TR), 483, 487, 499, 500, 507(R), 509.

The following figures in this book have been reproduced from *ABC of Breast
Disease,* Dixon, 1st ed., 1997 by kind permission of the publisher BMJ Books
(Wiley/Blackwell).
Page 32 **(see page 227)**
Page 35 **(see page 221)**
Page 65 **(see page 228)**
Page 67 **(see page 228)**

The following figures in this book have been reproduced from *ABC of
Colorectal Diseases,* Jones DJ, 2nd ed., 1999 by kind permission of the publisher
BMJ Books (Wiley Blackwell).
Fig. 20.2   Page 76 **(see pages 337, 338)**

The following figures in this book have been reproduced from *ABC Urology,*
Dawson C and Whitfield H, 1st ed., 1997 by kind permission of the publisher
BMJ Books (Wiley/Blackwell).
Page 14 **(see page 285)**

The following figures in this book have been reproduced from *The New
Aird's Companion in Surgical Studies,* Burnand K et al., 2nd ed., 1998 by kind
permission of the publisher Churchill Livingstone.
Fig. 11.18   Page 317 **(see page 489)**
Fig. 16.6a   Page 259 **(see pages 115R, 115BL)**
Fig. 17.3   Page 305 **(see page 481)**
Fig. 17.20   Page 318 **(see page 491)**
Fig. 19.6   Page 419 **(see page 505)**
Fig. 25.13   Page 607 **(see page 123L)**
Fig. 31a,b,c   Page 741 **(see page 213)**
Fig. 49.5   Page 1356 **(see page 284)**
Fig. 49.11   Page 1360 **(see page 294)**

The following figures in this book have been reproduced from *Concise System of Orthopaedics,* Apley 2nd edition, 1994, by kind permission of the publisher Elsevier Science Ltd.

Fig. 19.21   Page 192 **(see page 387)**
Fig. 1922   Page 191 **(see page 387)**
Fig. 19.24   Page 193 **(see page 385(T)**
Fig. 20.15   Page 206 **(see page 397)**
Fig. 21.8   Page 216 **(see page .410)**
Fig. 24.10   Page 251 **(see page 431)**
Fig. 24.13.   Page 254 **(see page 431)**
Fig. 30.4   Page 320 **(see page 392)**
Fig. 30.6, 30.6c   Page 321 **(see page 393)**

The following figures in this book have been reproduced from *An Introduction to the Symptoms and Signs of Surgical Disease,* N Browse, 3rd ed., (Arnold 1997) by kind permission of the publisher Hodder Headline.

Fig. 2.7 A & B   Page 39 **(see pages 69B, 71)**
Fig. 3.4D   Page 77 **(see page 59B)**
Fig 3.5   Page 79 **(see page 63B)**
Fig. 11.12   Page 258 **(see page 113L)**
Fig. 11.5   Page 260 **(see page 111)**
Fig. 13.1   Page 311 **(see page 281)**
Fig. 16.19   Page 391 **(see page 257)**

The following figures in this book have been reproduced from *Clinical Signs,* Hayes C and Bell D, new edition, 1996, by kind permission of the publisher Churchill Livingstone.

Figs. 87, 88, 89, 90   Page 60 **(see pages 245, 246)**
Fig. 93   Page 62 **(see page 245)**
Fig. 104   Page 72 **(see page 303B)**

The following figures in this book have been reproduced from *Orthopaedics,* Hooper, 2nd edition, 1997, by kind permission of the publisher Churchill Livingstone.

Fig. 127   Page 84 **(see page 433)**
Fig. 169   Page 116 **(see page 326)**
Fig. 171, 172   Page 118 **(see page 435)**
Fig. 184, 185   Page 128 **(see page 395)**
Fig. 218, 219   Page 152 **(see page 444)**

The following figures in this book have been reproduced from *Surgery*, Corson J and Williamson R, 1ˢᵗ ed., 1991 by kind permission of the publisher Mosby.

Page 7.30.7	**(see page 215)**
Fig. 6.7	Page 4.6.5 **(see page 493)**
Fig. 7.28	Page 3.7.16 **(see page 243)**
Fig. 18.6b	Page 4.18.3 **(see page 477)**
Fig. 18.8, 18.9	Page 4.18.4 **(see page 478)**
Fig. 18.10, 18.11	Page 4.18.5 **(see page 479)**

The following figures in this book have been reproduced from *Clinical Anatomy for Medical Students*, Snell R, 6ᵗʰ ed. 2000 by kind permission of the publisher Lippincott Williams & Wilkins.

Fig. 3.27	Page 106 **(see page 185)**
Fig. 10.11	Page 527 **(see page 368)**
Fig. 10.18	Page 536 **(see page 468B)**

The following figures in this book have been reproduced from *Picture Tests in Surgery*, Stiff et al, 1ˢᵗ edition, 1996, by kind permission of the publisher Churchill Livingstone.

Fig. 29A	Page 17 **(see page 119)**
Fig. 54B	Page 35 **(see page 109)**
Fig. 82B	Page 54 **(see page 264R)**
Fig. 86	Page 57 **(see page 113)**
Fig. 94A & B	Page 63 **(see pages 272, 273)**
Fig. C	Page 70 **(see page 117)**
Fig. 107	Page 74 **(see page 271B)**
Fig. 141	Page 95 **(see page 285R)**

The following figures in this book have been reproduced from *Spot Diagnosis in General Surgery*, Ellis H, 2ⁿᵈ edition, by kind permission of the publisher Blackwell Science Ltd.

Fig.14.	**(see page 473TL&R)**
Fig. 30	**(see page 423)**
Fig. 32	**(see page 437T)**
Fig. 37	**(see page 127)**
Fig. 79	**(see page 245R)**
Fig. 85	**(see page 263)**
Fig. 86	**(see page 261)**
Fig. 101	**(see page 385T)**
Fig. 102	**(see page 287)**
Figs. A, B	Page 107 **(see page 95)**

The following figures in this book have been reproduced from *An Aid to the MRCP Short Cases*, Ryder REJ et al, 1991, by kind permission of the publisher Blackwell Science Ltd

Fig. 3.4 Page 141 **(see page 497)**
Fig. 3.15a Page 91 **(see page 502)**
Fig. 3.66a, b Page 195 **(see page 301)**
Fig. 3.82 Page 221 **(see page 297)**

The following figures in this book have been reproduced from *Clinical Anatomy*, Ellis H, by kind permission of the publisher Blackwell Science Ltd

Fig. 178a, b Page 262 **(see page485)**
Fig. 190 Page 287 **(see page 96)**

The following figure in this book has been reproduced from Oxford Handbook of Acute Medicine, edited by Remrakha PS, and Moore KP, 1997, by kind permission of the publisher Oxford University Press.
Insertion of a chest drain Page 87 **(see page 625)**

CHAPTER 1
INTRODUCTION

A THE INTERCOLLEGIATE MRCS EXAMINATION

From September 2008 the Intercollegiate MRCS examination has altered in order to reflect the new pattern of surgical training introduced in the UK in 2007. All new candidates must take this new exam.

The exam consists of two parts:

- **Part A – written component**
  This consists of two papers of multiple choice Single Best Answer and Extended Matching Items. Paper 1 focuses on Applied Basic Science and Paper 2 on Principles of Surgery-in-General. Each paper lasts 2 hours and both are taken on the same day.
- **Part B – OSCE (objective structured clinical examination)**
  This replaces the previously separate viva and clinical components and has been introduced in order for the MRCS to conform to PMETB (Postgraduate Medical Education Training Board) requirements.

To be eligible to apply for part B you must have passed part A. Candidates are currently allowed four attempts in which to pass the Part B OSCE.

B STRUCTURE OF THE OSCE

This is currently under regular review and, as such, the exact details of the examination might change. It is important to keep up to date by checking the website http://www.intercollegiatemrcs.org.uk. From May 2010 the exam regulations state:

- There will be 18 examined stations
- There will be 4 broad content areas
- There will be 4 domains
- 3 out of 4 specialties context stations must be chosen
- Domains will not be pass/fail but used to structure the exam and feedback

There may also be one or more 'preparation' stations and one 'pre-test' station. These will not contribute towards the final mark.

The OSCE consists of 18 examined stations and one or more rest/preparation stations. There may also be one 'pre-test' station. Each of the 18 examined stations are manned, some with two examiners and some with one.

The MRCS remains an examination for trainees in the generality part of their surgical training. However, in order to reflect new patterns of specialty training, six of the stations are specialty-orientated and 12 are generic.

Each station lasts 9 minutes and there will usually be four rest stations which means the total exam will last approximately 3 hours and 30 minutes.

The stations are divided into **four broad content areas**:

- Anatomy and surgical pathology
- Applied surgical science and critical care
- Communication skills in giving and receiving information and history taking
- Clinical and procedural skills

Specialty-orientated stations

There are six stations which are specialty-orientated. These stations are in the following content areas:

- Anatomy and surgical pathology (1 station)
- Communication skills (history-taking) (2 stations)
- Clinical and procedural skills (physical examination) (3 stations)

On the application form for the exam candidates are asked to specify their choice of a main specialty area which will be the focus of the anatomy and surgical pathology station, one of the two history-taking stations and one of the three physical examination stations. The second, different specialty will be the focus of the other of the two history-taking stations and one of the three physical examination stations. The third choice will be examined in one of the three physical examination stations.

The specialty areas are:

- Head and neck
- Trunk and thorax
- Limbs (including spine)
- Neurosciences

Domains

These 'domains' are areas of knowledge, skill, competencies and professional characteristics that a candidate should demonstrate. The OSCE covers four 'domains' which are assessed throughout the exam. Domains are specified in the candidate instructions and guidance notes as follows:

- **Clinical knowledge**: 'the clinical knowledge specified in the syllabus; the ability to understand, synthesise and apply knowledge in a clinical context.'
- **Clinical and technical skill**: 'the capacity to apply sound clinical knowledge, skill and awareness to a full investigation of problems to reach a provisional diagnosis; the ability to perform manual tasks related to surgery which demands manual dexterity, hand/eye coordination and visual-spatial awareness.'
- **Communication**: 'the ability to assimilate information, identify what is important and convey it to others clearly using a variety of methods; the capacity to adjust behaviour and language (written/spoken) as appropriate to the needs of differing situations; the ability actively and clearly to engage the patient/carer/colleague(s) in open dialogue.'
- **Professionalism**: 'the demonstration of effective judgement and decision-making skills; the consideration of all appropriate facts before reaching a decision; the capacity to think beyond the obvious and to maximise information efficiently; being alert to symptoms and signs suggesting conditions which might progress or de-stabilise; being aware of own strengths/limitations and knowing when to ask for help; the ability to accommodate new or changing information and use it to manage a clinical problem; to anticipate and plan in advance; to prioritise conflicting demands and build contingencies; and to demonstrate effective time management; patient safety.'

Marking

Each station is marked out of 20.

In addition to this mark out of 20, each station will also have a separate 'overall global rating'. This will be:

- Pass
- Borderline pass
- Borderline fail, or
- Fail

The candidate's overall mark for the OSCE is calculated from both the mark out of 20 and the mark they achieve from the 'overall global rating'. A minimum mark to pass the OSCE will be calculated. However, in order to pass the exam, candidates will have to achieve this minimum mark and achieve a minimum competence level in each of the four content areas and in each of the four domains. Statistics from the MRCS website show that the percentage of candidates who pass the OSCE has been around 60%.

C CANDIDATE INSTRUCTIONS FOR THE OSCE

Candidates are required to bring photographic identification to the exam, which includes your name and signature in addition to a photograph. A passport or photo driving licence would be appropriate.

Dress requirements require candidates to be bare below the elbow, with no jewellery except wedding rings. No tie is required. Polo shirts or T-shirts are unacceptable. Candidates with cultural or religious reasons for not observing these regulations at all stations need only follow this code in bays involving the physical examination of a patient or actor.

Mobile phones etc. must not be carried around during the examination.

All equipment required for a task will be provided, although you can bring your own stethoscope, measuring tape etc. if you want to.

If the task in a bay requires contact with patients or cadaveric equipment or a practical task, **candidates must use the hand gel provided.**

Each station will have instructions provided outside the bay with usually 1 minute to read these. The instructions will also be available in the bay in case you need to refer back to them during the course of the station.

In physical examination bays, the examiner will watch candidates, who will not be prompted and will not be required to give a running commentary.

If you finish your station before the 9 minutes is up you must remain there until the signal to move on is given.

Arrive in good time as there is nothing worse than running late and arriving flustered.

Good luck!

D HOW TO PREPARE FOR THE OSCE

Success in the OSCE is all about the three 'p's 'preparation', 'practice' and 'presentation'.

Preparation

- As stated earlier, the structure, timing, regulations and requirements for the MRCS are constantly changing as the exams are updated. The outline given in this chapter is accurate at the time of writing, but you should not rely on this or on any other printed or verbal information as it could be out of date by the time it reaches you. You must be certain that you understand what you are being tested on and how the exam will be run and marked to allow you to revise effectively.
- The best way to keep up to date currently is by regularly checking the website 'http://www.intercollegiatemrcs.org.uk'. This contains information on:
  - Announcements
  - Examination dates
  - Regulations
  - Application forms
  - Guidance notes
  - Candidate feedback
  - Syllabus
  - Domain descriptors
  - Annual report
- A helpful approach to revising for the clinical skills stations is to make a list of common cases or scenarios you might expect to see. Plan a systematic history and examination approach for each. Be sure you are aware of the basic facts and the principles of investigation and management of cases you are likely to see. Then practise, practise, practise until this becomes second nature.

Practice

- Use this book in sections to help you. Read a chapter and then practise in groups. For clinical and communication skills, practise in groups of three with people who are also sitting the exam. One of you can be the candidate, one the patient and the third the examiner. Try to keep the conditions as 'exam like' as possible. Use the summary cards for the clinical skills stations you practise. This provides the 'examiner' with a list to check through to ensure that all parts are completed.

- Once you have got slick at this you can try and reproduce mock cases. This is best done in pairs. The 'patient' selects a case at random from the book and reproduces the symptoms/signs. At the end the candidate can present their findings and guess the diagnosis.
- If you practise a structured approach to these skills you will be amazed how relieved you feel in the exam, both when the cases you have prepared for come up and also when a more obscure case presents itself.

Presentation

- **Be smart** (within the confines of the 'bare below the elbow' and 'no ties' rules). The candidate guidance notes suggest either a conventional short-sleeved shirt/blouse, open at the neck, or a long-sleeved shirt/ blouse with the sleeves rolled up throughout the examination. T-shirts and polo shirts are not acceptable dress.
- **Be prepared** (again!). You will be nervous but try to thoroughly read the instructions for each station. Briefly think how you will approach the case before you are called in. There is nothing more flustering than getting the wrong end of the stick and being asked to start again (and you lose valuable time).
- **Be professional**. Imagine you are in the environment of the scenario, e.g. outpatient clinic, ward, theatre. Look your examiners in the eye. Do not mumble or mutter. They do not often want to waste time shaking your hand, so unless a hand is offered, a polite smile, nod, and 'Good morning' is the correct response to their introduction. The right tone to strike is friendly, efficient and businesslike.
- **Be kind**. Depending on your response to stress you may either be nervous and flustered or arrogant and overconfident. Make sure you greet each patient and introduce yourself. During examinations never hurt the patient. If there are any signs of discomfort, apologise immediately with 'I'm sorry, was that tender? I'll be more gentle,' acknowledging the fact. Ignoring it or continuing to cause the pain and you risk failing.
- **Be keen**. The examiners want to see an enthusiastic trainee who is doing their best to put on a good performance for them. The hardest part of this exam is to keep persevering brightly and politely when all seems to be going wrong. Don't let one disastrous station put you off. It might not have gone as badly as you thought; try to forget it until the end of the exam.

E SURVEY OF PAST CANDIDATES

The lists in this section are not exhaustive, but reflect previous candidates' experiences of the exam.

GENERAL ADVICE FROM PREVIOUS CANDIDATES

WHAT WERE THE EXAMINERS LIKE?

- *Some stony and others enthusiastic – seemed to respond if you tried to work things through using the old faithful 'first principles', as I had to a few times!*
- *NO feedback from the examiners at all! I could see them ticking some boxes, which is as close as I got to any feeling of whether my questions were relevant or not.*
- *The examiners were friendly and instructions clear but sometimes a bit long – I messed up one station completely because I rushed through reading the instructions.*
- *I got asked to go back out and read the instructions again – I got the wrong end of the stick entirely and tried to examine on a history station but got back on track thanks to the orthopaedic consultant.*

WHAT WAS THE EXAM LIKE?

- *More core 'non-specialty context' knowledge was assessed than I expected! Specialty choices did make a difference but I still got asked questions on wide range of topics.*
- *All reasonable stations but my main problem was running out of time.*
- *The written stations are tough! Time is limited and the free text answers made it difficult to know what level of detail to give in the answer.*
- *Warning bell at 6 minutes was a life-saver. Knew when to shut up, present and then face the dreaded questions from the examiners.*
- *The timetable at the beginning was useful to see what order I'd be doing things in. Started on a rest station – typical!*
- *Felt very, very rushed.*
- *The exam was well organised and ran on time. Everything is provided but I am glad I took my own stethoscope for cardiovascular assessment.*

🖥 **TOP TIPS FOR THE OSCE?**

- *You wait around for AGES! Eat a good breakfast or lunch or you will regret it.*
- *Completely thrown at first when* **asked to examine and take a history at the same time**. *Sounds stupid but I would definitely practise this before the exam.*
- **Don't forget to gel your hands** *before and after examining the patients – I did it once and then completely forgot for the rest!*
- *There are no 'killer' stations, so just keep going no matter what you just did in the previous stations.*
- *Don't worry about the examiners – concentrate on the patients.*

On arrival at the exam you'll be required to register with the documents and identification stipulated by the college. You will receive a badge with your candidate number on which must be clearly displayed. You will also receive a timetable setting out the order in which you will sit the OSCE. You will then wait with your fellow candidates until everybody has registered before receiving a briefing from the examiners.

Use the timetable and this time to prepare for what lies ahead. Having a clear idea of what your first couple of stations are will help to focus your thoughts and allow you to hit the ground running.

You will visit 18 examined stations in total. There will be a comfort break halfway through the exam. When the examination starts, a bell is sounded to signal the start of the exam. On arrival to each station you have 1 minute to read the printed instruction sheet before a bell sounds again to signal that you may enter the station and begin. The next bell sounds at 6 minutes, which serves as a warning that you have just 3 minutes remaining and in some stations also signifies the time for the examiners to stop you and begin questioning. The final bell is at the end of the station, at which point you leave and the minute to read your next instruction sheet begins. The timing is extremely strict – you will be dragged out while furiously trying to finish answering your last question! The examiners will literally stop mid-sentence when the bell goes and ask you to leave.

Examples of potential OSCE stations

The examination has been run officially three times at the time of writing. Examples of potential OSCE stations are detailed in Chapter 12, Mock OSCE examinations. The full detail of how to approach the stations is given in later chapters; the idea of this section is to give a realistic insight into what you could perhaps expect to face and any comments from previous candidates.

F FOCUS OF THIS BOOK

The main focus of this book is on the clinical, communication and procedural skills areas covered in the MRCS Part B. The remaining two areas of 'Anatomy and surgical pathology' and 'Applied surgical science and critical care' are mainly covered in the *Essential Revision Notes for Intercollegiate MRCS: Books 1 and 2*. However, we cover OSCE examples from these two content areas at the end of the book.

The book is arranged in four sections:

Section 1: Clinical skills in history taking and physical examination
Section 2: Communication skills
Section 3: Surgical skills and patient safety
Section 4: Surgical science, critical care, anatomy and pathology

The 'Clinical skills in history taking and physical examination' section of the book has been divided into the four specialty areas for ease of use. Within each specialty area, both history taking, clinical examination skills and common OSCE cases will be covered.

Some of the stations ask for you to take a focused history while simultaneously examining a patient. This requires a certain level of discipline in order to remain systematic and focused in your examination, picking up any salient clinical signs while at the same time asking relevant questions and summarising your findings succinctly at the end. Again, the 3 'p's are the key to success here. We provide you with examples of a full history and full examination and, in addition, we have provided a 'combined assessment box' in case you have to combine both skills. We have also provided an example of a 'pre-assessment history' (pg 24), which you can use if asked to assess fitness for anaesthesia and surgery while examining a patient.

SECTION 1: CLINICAL SKILLS IN HISTORY TAKING AND PHYSICAL EXAMINATION

CHAPTER 2
OVERVIEW OF CLINICAL SKILLS STATIONS

A HISTORY TAKING – A 'GENERAL FORMULA'

Taking a relevant, concise and accurate history is an essential skill for a surgeon because it is during the history that you will be able to make most diagnoses.

There is a general structure for taking a surgical history with which you should already be familiar. Once you have this basic structure you will find you can usually 'fine tune' it to a specific situation. It is especially important to have a basic structure to rely on in the stressful situation of the exam. However, on the day it is appropriate to structure the history according to the topic you are given. An example of a 'general formula' is given overleaf. This book will then concentrate mainly on the 'presenting complaint' and the 'history of the presenting complaint' for the different topics.

A 'general formula' for taking a surgical history

1. Introductions and demographics

Introduce yourself and explain what you are doing. Check who they are, their relationship with anyone they may have bought with them, how old they are and what they do for a living (if appropriate).

'Hello, I'm Dr Parchment Smith the Surgical CT2 with Mr White's firm. Are you Mrs Jones?' (Smile and shake hands with the patient. If they have someone accompanying them it is important to find out who they are and what relationship they have, but do not make assumptions – this can be very embarrassing if you are wrong – instead ask an open question such as**...) 'Who have you brought with you today?' 'According to the letter I have here from your GP you are 70 and used to work as a receptionist in the hospital. Is that correct?'**

2. Presenting complaint

In order to determine a 'presenting complaint' such as 'change in bowel habit for 6 months' or 'right loin pain for 2 hours' you need to initially ask them an open question such as **'What has caused you to come and see me today?'** If they list a vast array of concerns and you remain slightly unclear as to the main problem, ask them **'What is the thing that's bothering you most at the moment?'**

Try and illicit the duration of the problem. Again, if they are a bit vague, asking them when they were last well can help. **'When did this all start?'** or **'When were you last well?'**

3. History of presenting complaint

This is the story of the complaint as they describe it from when they were last well. **'Tell me what's being happening?'** Gather details of the presenting complaint.

For example, if it is pain, a systematic way to approach this is using SIROD CASP:

Site: **'Where is the pain?'**
Intensity: **'Can you rate the pain on a scale from 1 to 10. 1 being no pain and 10 the worst pain ever,'** (this is subjective and it is more important to know how it affects their life, i.e...) **'Does it keep you off work?', 'Does it wake you at night?'**
Radiation: **'Does the pain move anywhere else?'**
Onset: **'Does the pain come on suddenly or gradually?'**
Duration: **'How long does the pain last?'**

Character: **'What is the pain like?'** (if they require prompting, ask if it is sharp, dull, burning, colicky?)
Alleviating and exacerbating factors: **'Does anything make the pain better, or worse?'**
Symptoms associated with the pain: **'Do you notice anything else when you get the pain?'** (e.g. jaundice, vomiting, change in bowels)
Previous episodes: **'Have you had a pain like this before?'** (if yes…) **'What did you do then?'**

If the complaint is not pain, you can still ask sensible, specific questions targeted to their problem. Each section below goes over common presenting complaints in each specialty area. If you get stuck, use the 'combined assessment boxes', which give you a few key questions and allow you to get back on track and not miss the essentials.

Review the relevant system/s: for the example of abdominal pain this may include a GI, gynaecological and urological history but not the other systems unaffected by the presenting complaint. This requires direct questioning about every aspect of that system and recording of the positives and negatives.

Relevant medical history: for instance with abdominal pain this would include any previous episodes of pain, any abdominal surgery or investigations.
Risk factors associated with the presenting complaint: for example with rectal bleeding a family history of IBD/colorectal cancer, anticoagulants, smoking.
Risk factors associated with having an anaesthetic (if appropriate): e.g. previous anaesthetics, family history of problems under anaesthetic, limiting co-morbidities, exercise tolerance, anticoagulant medication.

4. Past medical and surgical history
All the previous medical history of illnesses, operations, investigations not mentioned as relevant to the history of the presenting complaint.

5. Medication and allergies
List of all drugs taken, doses and timings of these. List allergies and the nature of the reaction. Ask directly about medications that may have to be stopped pre-operatively such as the oral contraceptive pill, antiplatelet medications e.g. aspirin or clopidogrel, and warfarin.

6. Social history

- Smoking – current, ex or never and how many per day for how long.
- Alcohol – current, ex heavy drinker or teetotal and number of units per week.
- Recreational drug use (if appropriate).
- Where they live (nursing home, residential home, sheltered accommodation or own home – bungalow or stairs).
- Who they live with – are they a carer for someone else?
- Who cares for them and whether they have social service input, how much they can manage on their own (if appropriate)?

7. Family history

Any relevant family history not ascertained earlier, for instance a family history of diabetes in a patient with an abscess.

8. Full review of non-relevant systems

This includes all systems not relevant to the presenting complaint. Depending on the time you have left, you may be able to do a quick systems review. You should have already thoroughly reviewed the systems relevant to the presenting complaint in the history of the presenting complaint section earlier on. There might be an important fact to pick up on that the examiners want you to find.

Cardiovascular:	Chest pain
	Dyspnoea
	Palpitations
	Paroxysmal nocturnal dyspnoea
	Orthopnoea
	Ankle oedema
	Claudication
Respiratory:	Cough
	Sputum
	Shortness of breath
	Exercise tolerance
	Haemoptysis
	Wheeze

GI tract:	Appetite	BOWELS:
	Weight loss	Frequency
	Dysphagia	Blood/slime
	Indigestion	Diarrhoea/constipation
	Abdominal pain	Melaena
	Haematemesis	Tenesmus
		Urgency
		Incontinence
		Passing flatus

Genitourinary:	Incontinence
	Dysuria
	Haematuria
	Nocturia
	Frequency
Men:	Prostatic signs: dribbling, hesitancy, flow rates
	Impotence
	Urethral discharge
Women:	LMP/menopause
	Pregnant?
	Discharge

| Sexual activity: | Protected/unprotected sex |

Neurological:	Headaches
	Fits
	Faints
	Weakness
	Hearing
	Vision

Locomotor:	Pain
	Stiffness
	Function
	Swelling

| Thyroid: | Hyper: Hot, sweaty, diarrhoea, tremor, weight loss, palpitations |
| | Hypo: Cold, depressed, tired, constipated, deep voice |

9. Summary

A summary allows you to check you have understood what the patient has been telling you and ensure that you have not missed anything essential.

'So, Mrs Jones, you have said you have had 3 months of bleeding from the back passage. You also noticed that you have lost some weight during this time and your appetite is not as good as it used to be. Are there any other problems that I have missed?'

10. Differential diagnosis

'From what you've told me today there could be a few reasons for the bleeding that you've been having. It could be your piles but with the weight loss as well it is sensible to do some investigations to make sure something else isn't going on.'

11. Conclusion

Explain plan for after consultation. 'I need to examine you today and then we will need to send you to have some blood taken and a telescope test to have a look at your bowel. Is that OK with you? Is there anything you would like to ask me?'

Check that the actor doesn't have any outstanding issues. 'Have we covered everything that you are concerned about? Are there any other problems that you've been having that we haven't covered today?'

Summarise plan. 'Today we need to take some blood from you before you leave the clinic. You'll get a letter through the post with a date for the telescope test and then we'll arrange to see you back in clinic with the results.'

Offer future contact. 'If you have any problems in the meantime then just phone Mr White's secretary and she'll be able to contact one of us regarding the problem.'

Departure, stating next point of contact. 'Goodbye, we'll see you next week for the telescope test.'

SUMMARY: HISTORY TAKING – A 'GENERAL FORMULA'

1. Introduction and demographics
2. Presenting complaint
3. History of presenting complaint
   a) The story
   b) Details of complaint
   c) Relevant medical history
   d) Review of relevant system
   e) Risk factors for presenting compliant
   f) Risk factors for surgery
4. Past medical and surgical history
5. Medication and allergies
6. Social history
7. Family history
8. Full review of non-relevant systems
9. Summary
10. Differential diagnosis
11. Conclusion

B HISTORY TO ASSESS FITNESS FOR SURGERY

You may be asked to assess a patient's fitness for surgery or anaesthesia while performing an examination. A thorough history is given above which would cover everything you need to know. However, it would be very difficult to cover all this while performing a decent clinical examination. Therefore, below is a focused 'pre-assessment history' which will allow you to assess your patient's fitness for surgery but (with practice!!) will also allow you to examine them simultaneously.

> Examine this patient's right groin and ask him some questions to allow you to make an assessment of his fitness for anaesthesia and surgery

Proceed with 'Examination of the groin' (pg 200).

'Can I ask how old you are sir?' (While age should not be a reason not to operate on someone, usually increasing age brings increasing co-morbidities)
'Have you had much trouble with your right groin' (in the case of a groin hernia you would be particularly interested to ask 'Is it always reducible?', 'Has it ever got stuck out and become painful?', 'When this happened did you get any other problems? (e.g. vomiting, constipation, abdominal pain?)' (Their response to these questions would help you determine the urgency, or not, of repair, which you can then balance against the risk of the surgery for that patient.)
'Have you had any other medical problems?' (in particular) 'Have you ever had any trouble with your heart or lungs?' (This is key and if they respond positively you must explore this further.)
'Do you have any other symptoms currently? For instance, shortness of breath or chest pain?' (This allows you to assess how symptomatic they are from any diagnosed co-morbidities they may have told you about but will also bring to light any undiagnosed problems.)

'How far can you walk on the flat without stopping?', 'Can you climb a flight of stairs?' 'Can you dress yourself without getting SOB/chest pain?' (Assessing their exercise tolerance is also vital in determining whether you think they will get through an operation. For instance, if they are too short of breath due to cardiac failure to lie flat for 30 minutes, it is unlikely they will manage to get through a groin hernia repair, even if it is under regional or local anaesthesia, and a better option might be a supportive truss).

'Have you had an anaesthetic before?' (If yes, determine what type, e.g. general, regional, local, when they had it and did they have any problems with it?)

'Do you take any regular medication?' (especially warfarin or antiplatelet agents?)

C HOW TO PRESENT A HISTORY

It is important to practice presenting histories, either to your consultant/other colleagues at work, friends or family. By doing this, your presentation will become precise and accurate.

Presentation

The presentation to the consultant should follow a logical structure, contain appropriate clinical language (if the patient is no longer present), pick out the key points and should cover the information obtained thoroughly but succinctly.

Questions

You may be asked:

- What differential diagnosis would you suggest at this stage based on the history you have taken?
- What signs would you specifically look for when examining this patient?
- What investigations would you request for this patient?

When presenting, make sure that you are sitting up straight, looking the examiner in the eye and speaking in a clear, measured voice.

1. Introductory Sentence

Name, age and occupation.

'I would like to present Matthew Hardy, a 47-year-old chemistry teacher.'

2. Presenting Complaint

In one or two words state the MAIN COMPLAINT that has caused the patient to be referred to the hospital and the time that they have been suffering from it. **'His presenting complaint is a 3-month history of weight loss and bloody diarrhoea.'**

3. History of the Presenting Complaint

A.   The story:

>   Background to the illness
>   When last well
>   What exactly happened, including timescale
>   Treatment given/GP seen

'The history of the presenting complaint: Mr Hardy is a gentleman who was fit and well until 3 months ago. The first thing he noticed was that he started to open his bowels three to four times per day, having previously only opened them once a day. He initially thought it might pass, but it continued and he became worried when he noticed what looked like blood mixed in with the loose stool. During the last 2 weeks he's been experiencing some lower abdominal pain. He's lost about a stone in weight during this time and when his symptoms didn't settle he went to see his GP.'

B.   Details of the complaint

>   If it's a pain – SIROD CASP

'The pain was described as a gradual-onset, intermittent, colicky ache specific to his left iliac fossa. At worst he scored it 8/10 and it is normally aggravated when opening his bowels and relieved by taking co-codamol. The pain lasted up to 3 hours and had made him nauseous. He hasn't experienced a pain similar to this before.'

C.   Relevant medical history

'Mr Hardy has had no previous problems with his bowels apart from having occasional trouble from haemorrhoids.'

D. Review of the relevant system (GI tract in this case)

'In addition to his weight loss, Mr Hardy has noticed a decrease in his appetite. He has no problems with swallowing and doesn't suffer from indigestion. Although he has had increased frequency of his motions he doesn't complain of tenesmus.'

E. Risk factors for the presenting complaint

'He is an ex-smoker and has a strong family history of bowel cancer, with his father dying at the age of 51 from it.'

F. Risk factors for surgery

'He has no risk factors for surgery, being in good general health and having had one previous uncomplicated general anaesthetic.'

4. Past Medical and Surgical History

A. Operations
B. Hospital admissions
C. Major illnesses
D. Question directly about: Diabetes

                                         Heart attack

                                         Stroke

                                         Hypertension

                                         Epilepsy

                                         Asthma

                                         Bronchitis

                                         Tuberculosis

                                         Rheumatic fever

                                         Childbirth (women!)

                                         PE/DVT

'Apart from an appendicectomy performed 5 years ago, Mr Hardy has never been in hospital.'

5. Medication/Allergies

List all the tablets the patient is currently taking. You may have to remind women about the pill or HRT, which they often don't include as medication.
'Mr Hardy does not take any regular medication and has no known allergies.'

6. Social History

A. Smoking/drinking
'Mr Hardy used to smoke 30 cigarettes a day, but gave up five years ago. He only drinks a few pints of beer at the weekend.'
B. Home
'Mr Hardy lives with his wife and one daughter, aged 5.'

7. Family History

'Apart from his father's bowel cancer, there is no other family history of note.'

8. Review of Non-relevant Systems

'There is nothing of note on review of his cardiovascular, respiratory or other systems.'

9. Summarise

Summarise the main points of the history in one short sentence.
'In summary, Mr Hardy is a 47-year-old man, normally fit and well, who presents with a 3-month history of increased frequency of bowel motions, rectal bleeding and significant weight loss.'

10. Differential Diagnosis

'The differentials I would like to exclude are bowel neoplasia (if presenting in front of the patient)/cancer (if presenting in private) or inflammatory bowel disease. Other possibilities are infective diarrhoea or diverticular disease.'

D TOP TIPS IN HISTORY TAKING AND CLINICAL EXAMINATION

TOP TIPS FOR HISTORIES

- Try and establish a good rapport with the 'patient'
- Let them do the talking initially
- Ask 'open' questions rather than leading the patient with 'closed' questions
- Check you have understood the patient by summarising at appropriate intervals
- Try to elucidate a set of differential diagnoses via targeted questions
- Use a list of 'red flag' symptoms for any given presenting complaint which are focused and a useful fallback if things are going badly
- Also try to elicit the patient's ideas, concerns and expectations or 'ICE'
- Avoid medical jargon and explain terms as required

TOPS TIPS FOR EXAMINATIONS

- Introduce yourself and wash your hands with alcohol gel
- Ask if the patient has any tenderness
- Demonstrate a systematic approach
- Show your handling is gentle and respectful
- Demonstrate satisfactory inspection and palpation
- Identify and interpret key clinical signs
- Present findings logically

You are not required to give a running commentary in the exam and in certain stations you may be required to take a focused history simultaneously. However, you must explain to the patient anything that you are doing to them.

CHAPTER 3
HEAD AND NECK

A The Histories   33

B The Examinations   43

C The OSCE Cases   57

Lumps

Thyroid

CONTENTS

A THE HISTORIES

NECK LUMP/S

If you are asked to take a history from a patient with a neck lump you need to initially ask questions about the lump to whittle down the potential differential diagnoses. You should then ask about relevant associated symptoms or risk factors that fit in with your differential. Obviously, if you can see a lump, the position of this might help you (see diagram pg 46). If you run into problems in the OSCE remember the essential points in the 'Combined Assessment Box' to get you back on track.

Introductions

'Hello, my name is Dr Parchment Smith. Please can I check your details? Would you mind if I asked you some questions about your neck lump?'
Ask about demographics.
'May I ask how old you are?'[1]
'What do/did you do for a living?'[2]

Presenting complaint (open question!)

'What has caused you to come and see me today?'

History of presenting complaint *(the patient may volunteer the following information but questions you need to cover about the lump/s include)*
'How many lumps have you noticed?'[3]

---

[1] Some neck lumps are commoner in certain age groups. Age can therefore give you a clue as to the differential diagnosis:
- Child: cystic hygroma, congenital dermoid cyst (see case on pg 62)
- Young adult: branchial cyst (see case on pg 106)
- Adult: carotid body tumour (>30 usually) (see case on pg 112)
- Older adult: malignant neck nodes due to laryngeal/pharyngeal carcinoma (see case on pg 98), pharyngeal pouch (>50 usually) (see case on pg 110)

[2] For instance a publican may have drunk alcohol/smoked and be at a higher risk for head and neck carcinoma. Someone who has worked abroad may have a greater risk of TB.

[3] If one, possibilities include cystic hygroma, carotid body tumour, carotid artery aneurysm, submandibular gland stone/tumour, parotid gland stone/tumour, pharyngeal pouch (left side), branchial cyst, thyroglossal cyst, single thyroid nodule, goitre.
If bilateral, possibilities include chronic parotitis due to stones, mumps, Sjögren/Mikulicz syndrome.
If multiple, possibilities include sebaceous cysts, lipomata, lymph nodes (infective, malignant), multinodular goitre.

'Where do you notice the lump/s?'[4] (*This may be obvious from observation and therefore it may be more appropriate to check you are both talking about the same lump: 'Is it the lump I can see on the left there that you are concerned about?'*)

'How long have you noticed the lump?'[5]

'Has it been getting bigger, smaller or remaining the same?'

'Is the swelling present all the time or does it come and go?' (*Intermittent swelling can be caused by salivary gland stones; these tend to be related to food. Therefore if the answer is yes, ask about precipitating factors:* **'Have you noticed anything that brings the lump on?'**

'Has the lump/s ever been painful?' (*If the answer is yes, investigate further with questions about onset, duration, precipitating*[6] *and relieving factors.*)

You need to ask about associated symptoms that may either help you reach a diagnosis or be distressing to the patient and need treatment. The relevance of these questions depends on what you think is going on.

'Have you been getting difficulty with swallowing?' (*If yes, questions which may help you work out what kind of neck lump they have include*)

'Is it painful when you swallow?'[7], **'Does your neck bulge or gurgle on swallowing?'**[8])

'Have you had any difficulty with your breathing?'[9]

'Have you had a cough lately?' *If yes,* **'Have you been coughing anything up?**

'Have you seen any blood?'[10]

'Have you noticed any change in your voice?'[11]

'Have you lost any weight?'

'Have you had any problems with temperatures/sweating at night?'

---

[4] Side of the neck: possibilities include sebaceous cyst, lipoma, lymph nodes (infective, malignant), cystic hygroma, carotid body tumour, carotid artery aneurysm, submandibular gland stone/tumour, parotid gland stone/tumour, pharyngeal pouch (left side), branchial cyst, thyroid nodule.
Midline: thyroglossal cyst, dermoid cyst, thyoid mass.
Bilateral: see above.

[5] Lump/s which have been present for <3 weeks could be attributable to lymphadenopathy from a self-limiting infection.

[6] Salivary gland stones will often cause intermittent pain and swelling which is related to eating.

[7] Constant painful dysphagia suggests neck nodes associated with laryngeal/pharyngeal carcinoma.

[8] This is associated with pharyngeal pouch. Other clinical features of pharyngeal pouch include: regurgitation of food, weight loss, hoarseness, aspiration pneumonia, recurrent sore throat, left-sided neck lump and halitosis.

[9] You are unlikely to see someone with stridor in the exam. However, it is important to determine that they have no problems with their airway.

[10] A pharyngeal pouch can predispose to aspiration pneumonia. A bronchial carcinoma may cause metastatic cervical lymphadenopathy.

[11] Hoarseness can be caused by carcinoma of the bronchus, oesophagus, thyroid or pharynx, which could all lead to metastatic cervical lymphadenopathy.

Other questions to ask if you are concerned about head and neck cancer include **'Have you had any ear pain?'**[12], **'Have you had a sore throat?'**[13] *If you think the patient may have a thyroid lump you need to ask about symptoms caused by hyper/hypothyroidism (see Thyroid history on pg 36)*

Past medical and surgical history

In particular, what investigations have they had of the neck lump. Have they had any operations/radiotherapy/chemotherapy. **'Have you had any tests to investigate the lump?'**, **'Have you had any treatment for the lump?'**

Medication and allergies

'Do you take any regular medication?', **'Do you have any allergies?'**

Social history (smoking and drinking) *It is important to ask about smoking and alcohol as these are common risk factors for head and neck carcinoma.*[14] **'Are you a current or ex-smoker?'** *If yes, ask about smoking habits,* **'What do you smoke?'**, **'How many do you smoke a day'**, **'How long have you smoked for?'**[15]
'Do you, or have you ever, drunk alcohol?' *If yes,* **'What type of alcohol do you drink?'** *(e.g. spirits, wine, beer)* **'How much do you drink per week?'** *(convert this to units per week).* **'How long have you drunk for?'**

Combined Assessment Box – NECK LUMPS

Ask:
- Where is the lump? How long has it been there for?
- Are there any associated symptoms, e.g. hoarseness, difficulty swallowing, cough, pain
- Do you smoke?
- Have you lost any weight?

Examine:
- Inspect the neck
- Ask patient to swallow
- Ask patient to stick their tongue out
- Palpate the lump
- Palpate the regional lymph nodes

---

[12] Otalgia: referred ear pain can occur with pharyngeal and laryngeal carcinoma. Remember the old saying 'Beware the hoarse patient with the painful ear'.

[13] Sore throat can occur with oropharyngeal carcinoma.

[14] Less common risk factors include:
- Nasopharyngeal carcinoma: patients from China/Hong Kong, EBV infection
- Oropharyngeal carcinoma: dental sepsis, ionising radiation
- Laryngo/hypopharyngeal carcinoma: Plummer-Vinson syndrome, pharyngeal web, radiotherapy, asbestos/ nickel exposure

[15] You can use this information to calculate the number of 'pack years' a patient has smoked. A 'pack year' is 20 cigarettes per day for 1 year, so if a patient has smoked 10 cigarettes a day for 20 years this equates to 10 'pack years'.

THYROID STATUS

You may be asked to take a history of a patient's thyroid status, in which case follow this guide, or you may be asked to take a history of a patient with a neck lump, in which case follow the neck lump history on pg 33. Then, when it becomes obvious it is a thyroid lump, ask the following questions. If you run into problems in the OSCE remember the essential points in the 'Combined Assessment Box' to get you back on track.

Introductions
'Hello, my name is Dr Parchment Smith. Please can I check your details? Would you mind if I asked you some questions?'
Ask about demographics.
'May I ask how old you are?'
'What do/did you do for a living?'

Presenting complaint (open question!)
'What has caused you to come and see me today?'

History of presenting complaint *(the patient may volunteer the following information but questions you need to cover include)*
'Do you prefer a warm or cold room?'[16]
'Have you gained or lost any weight recently?' *If yes,* **'How much and over how long?'**[17]
'Has your appetite increased recently?'[18]
'Has your bowel habit changed?'[19]
'Have you noticed a change in your mood?'[20]
'Have you noticed any palpitations or chest pain?'[21]
'Have you noticed a change in your periods?'[22] *(female patients only!)*
'Have you noticed a change in your appearance?'[23]
'Have you had a change in your vision?'[24]

---

[16] Cold = hyperthyroid, warm = hypothyroid.
[17] Weight loss = hyperthyroid/carcinoma, weight gain = hypothyroid.
[18] Yes suggests hyperthyroidism
[19] Diarrhoea = hyperthyroidism, constipation = hypothyroidism.
[20] Increased anxiety = hyperthyroidism, depression = hypothyroidism.
[21] Palpitations/angina = hyperthryroidism.
[22] Altered menstruation can occur with hyperthyroidism or hypothyroidism.
[23] Hypothyroidism can cause weight gain, thinning hair, loss outer third eyebrow, neck lump (see case on pg 86). Hyperthyroidism can cause weight loss, sweatiness, neck lump (see case on pg 88).
[24] Eye disease (exophthalmos, lid lag) in Graves' disease can cause visual symptoms, including double vision and discomfort.

'Have you noticed a lump in your neck?' *If yes,* **'Does it cause you any problems?'** *Local complications of a goitre may include stridor, SVC obstruction, dysphagia, sudden painful enlargement (haemorrhage into cyst).*

Past medical and surgical history

'Do you have any other medical conditions?'[25]
'Have you had any operations on your thyroid or radiotherapy to your neck in the past?'

Medication and allergies

'Are you on any medication for your thyroid? Do you have any allergies?'

Combined Assessment Box – THYROID STATUS

Ask:
- Have you noticed any change in your weight?
- Do you prefer a hot or cold room?
- Has there been a change in your bowel habit?
- Have you noticed any change in your appearance?

Examine:
- Inspect neck
- Ask patient to swallow
- Ask patient to stick out tongue
- Palpate lump
- Palpate regional lymph nodes
- Assess thyroid status (hands/pulse/face/eyes)

---

[25] Associated diseases include: hypothyroidism – depression, carpal tunnel syndrome. Associated autoimmune diseases: pernicious anaemia, haemolytic anaemia, diabetes, Addison's disease, rheumatoid arthritis, Sjogren syndrome, ulcerative colitis, lupoid hepatitis, systemic lupus erythematosus, hypoparathyroidism.

DYSPHAGIA

Dysphagia refers to difficulty (not pain) when swallowing; pain on swallowing is called odynophagia. Dysphagia can be caused by diseases you will encounter in both the 'head and neck' section and in 'trunk and thorax'.[26] *If you run into problems in the OSCE remember the essential points in the 'Combined Assessment Box' to get you back on track.*

A THE HISTORIES

Introductions
'Hello, my name is Dr Parchment Smith. Can I check your details please. Would you mind if I asked you some questions?'
Ask about demographics.
'May I ask how old you are?'
'What do/did you do for a living?'

Presenting complaint (open question!)
'What has caused you to come and see me today?'

History of presenting complaint *(the patient may volunteer the following information but questions you need to cover include)*
'Have you been getting difficulty with swallowing?' *(Given the subject, hopefully the answer will be yes!)*
'How long has this been going on for?'
'Is it constant/intermittent?'
'Is it painful to swallow?' *(i.e. odynophagia rather than dysphagia)*
'Is the pain constant or intermittent?'[27]
'Does any particular type of food or drink cause the pain?'[28]
'Has it been getting progressively worse?'[29]
'Can you swallow solids, liquids, your saliva?'
'Can you drink fluid as fast as you used to?'[30]

---

[26] **Causes of dysphagia** can be divided into anatomical and functional causes. Anatomical causes include: oesophageal/pharyngeal malignancy, cricoid web, peptic stricture, GORD, extrinsic pressure from lymphadenopathy or bronchial carcinoma. Functional causes include: motor neurone disease, post-CVA, globus, diffuse oesophageal spasm, scleroderma.
Causes of odynophagia include: reflux oesophagitis, peptic oesophageal ulceration, thrush, pharyngitis, diffuse oesophageal spasm, oesophageal/pharyngeal malignancy.
[27] Constant odynophagia suggests laryngeal/pharyngeal carcinoma.
[28] Odynophagia caused by hot liquids is associated with GORD.
[29] Progressive dysphagia from solids to liquids suggests oesophageal carcinoma. This can assist your management decision regarding need for nutritional/fluid supplementation.
[30] If yes suspect a stricture, if no consider a motility disorder.

'Is it difficult to make a swallowing movement?'[31]

'Does food seem to get stuck anywhere in particular?'

'Do you ever bring food back up?' *(reflux of food is effortless, it is not vomiting)*[32]

'Do you get a sensation of a lump in your throat?'[33]

Associated symptoms to enquire about include:

'Have you ever noticed a lump on your neck?' *If yes, possibilities include metastatic lymphadenopathy from oesophageal or laryngeal/pharyngeal carcinoma or a pharyngeal pouch (see case on pg 110); if this is a possibility enquire* 'Does your neck bulge or gurgle on swallowing?'

'Have you noticed a change in your voice?'[34]

'Have you noticed any problems with your breathing?' *(As mentioned earlier you are very unlikely to see a patient with stridor in the exam but you need to be seen to be asking about their airway.)*

'Have you noticed any weight loss?' *(If yes, try to quantify how much and over what time period. This could obviously be caused by the dysphagia itself as well as by the underlying cause for the dysphagia.)*

'Have you developed a cough?'

'Have you got any pain elsewhere?' *(epigastric pain/heart burn – GORD; otalgia – referred pain from pharyngeal carcinoma)*

Past medical and surgical history

In particular, what investigations have they had for the dysphagia?[35] *Have they had any operations/radiotherapy/chemotherapy? Are they requiring nutritional supplementation; if yes, what kind?*

'Have you had any investigations for your difficulty in swallowing?'

'Have you had any treatment for your difficulty in swallowing?'

Medication and allergies

Do they take any medication for reflux/GORD? 'Are you on any medication?
Do you have any allergies?'

---

[31] If it is difficult for them to swallow suspect neurological causes, e.g. post-CVA, especially if they cough after swallowing.

[32] Reflux of food is found in patients with a pharyngeal pouch.

[33] A sensation of a lump in the throat when not swallowing suggests globus.

[34] Hoarseness together with dysphagia can be caused by pharyngeal carcinoma.

[35] Investigating dysphagia: upper GI endoscopy is usually the first investigation. If this is normal they may proceed to a barium swallow. An abnormal Upper GI endoscopy may lead to biopsy of lesion/CT if external compression. If barium swallow is normal consider manometry and pH studies.

Social history (smoking and drinking)

It is important to ask about smoking as this is a risk factor for GORD.
'Are you a current or ex-smoker?' *If yes, ask about smoking habits,* **'What do you smoke?', 'How many do you smoke a day', 'How long have you smoked for?'**
'Do you, or have you ever, drunk alcohol?' *If yes,* **'What type of alcohol do you drink?'** *(e.g. spirits, wine, beer)* **'How much do you drink per week?'** *(convert this to units per week).* **'How long have you drunk for?'**

Combined Assessment Box – DYSPHAGIA

Ask:
- Is swallowing painful?
- Can you swallow solids/liquids/your saliva? (i.e. is it progressive?)
- Have you lost any weight?
- Do you smoke/drink?

Examine:
- Oral cavity for thrush etc.
- Neck for lumps
- Chest for signs of bronchial malignancy or chest infection due to impaired swallowing
- Abdominal examination for signs of oesophageal carcinoma (e.g. Virchow's node)

HOARSENESS

Hoarseness is caused when a vocal cord does not properly oppose with its counterpart. There are many causes, some are due to organ pathology and others due to misuse of healthy organs of phonation.[36] If you run into problems in the OSCE remember the essential points in the 'Combined Assessment Box' to get you back on track.

Introductions

'Hello, my name is Dr Parchment Smith. Please can I check your details? Would you mind if I asked you some questions?'

Ask about demographics.

'May I ask how old you are?'

'What do/did you do for a living?'[37]

Presenting complaint (open question!)

'What has caused you to come and see me today?'

History of presenting complaint *(the patient may volunteer the following information but questions you need to cover include)*

'How long has it been going on?'[38]

'Is it getting better or worse?'

'Did anything in particular bring it on?'[39]

---

[36] **Causes of hoarseness** include: vocal cord nodules (singers' nodules due to vocal abuse caused by vascular congestion at the midpoint of the cord), vocal fold haemorrhage (due to intermittent severe vocal abuse e.g. football fans), vocal cord cysts, leukoplakia, hyperkeratosis, CIS/SCC, acute/chronic laryngitis (usually secondary to smoking), vocal cord paralysis due to: cancer (of the bronchus, oesophagus, lymphoma, thyroid, pharynx), trauma (including post thyroid, cardiac, lung or carotid surgery), idiopathic, inflammatory (TB or RA in which there is cricoarytenoid joint fixation), neurological disorders (including Parkinson's disease, diabetes, MS – in which the intrinsic muscles are damaged).

[37] This is especially important as their profession may be a **cause** of hoarseness, e.g. teachers (see above). It is also important to ascertain what **impact** hoarseness will have on the patient's life as they may lose their means of making a living.

[38] Persistent progressive hoarseness over 3 weeks, especially in a smoker, requires exclusion of pharyngeal/laryngeal carcinoma.

[39] Hoarseness can be caused by trauma. If the hoarseness started after thyroid, cardiac, lung or carotid surgery this suggests that recurrent laryngeal nerve injury at surgery may be the cause.
The vocal cords are supplied by the recurrent laryngeal nerve, but the external laryngeal nerve supplies cricothyroid, which is the only adductor of the cords. Vocal cord injuries can therefore be divided into
a) recurrent laryngeal nerve injuries, which can be unilateral incomplete, unilateral complete, bilateral incomplete, bilateral complete, or
b) external laryngeal injuries.
The left cord is more commonly affected than the right due to the longer course of its recurrent laryngeal nerve.

'Does anything make it better or worse?'[40]
'Do you use your voice frequently, e.g. amateur actor/singer?'[41]
'Have you lost any weight recently/night sweats?'
'Do you have any problems with your breathing?'[42]
'Have you developed a cough?' *If yes,* 'What have you been coughing up?'[43]

Past medical and surgical history

'Do you have any other medical conditions?'[44]
'Have you had any investigations or treatment for hoarseness?'[45]

Medication and allergies

'Do you take any medication? Do you have any allergies?'

Social history (smoking and drinking)

'Are you a current or ex-smoker?' *If yes, ask about smoking habits* 'What do you smoke?', 'How many do you smoke a day', 'How long have you smoked for?'[46]
'Do you, or have you ever, drunk alcohol?' *If yes,* 'What type of alcohol do you drink?' *(e.g. spirits, wine, beer)* 'How much do you drink per week?' *(convert this to units per week).* 'How long have you drunk for?'

Combined Assessment Box- HOARSENESS

Ask:
- Did anything bring the hoarseness on?
- Do you use your voice regularly?
- Have you lost any weight?
- Do you smoke/drink?

Examine:
- It is most unlikely that you would be asked to perform nasendoscopic examination of the patients larynx in the exam
- You may get asked to examine their neck for lumps or chest for signs of scarring from the operation which lead to their iatrogenic hoarseness

---

[40] Hoarseness which is more apparent towards the end of the day suggests vocal cord paralysis.

[41] They may use their voice in ways not associated with their job but which are important to them. This again can point to the cause of hoarseness.

[42] Stridor can occur in vocal cord palsy if the abductors are affected.

[43] Poor cough/aspiration can be caused by vocal cord paralysis.

[44] Hoarseness can be caused by granulomatous disorders, e.g. TB, sarcoid, Wegener's, vocal cord paralysis due to cancers of thyroid, oesophagus, bronchus or carotid body tumour, endocrine disorders (acromegaly, Addison's disease, myxoedema)

[45] **Investigating hoarseness**
Initially, laryngoscopy to look at the vocal cords. Idiopathic vocal cord paralysis should be investigated with CXR, CT (skull-base to diaphragm), endoscopy, barium swallow.

[46] Smoking can cause acute/chronic laryngitis, bronchial carcinoma or pharyngeal carcinoma, which can lead to vocal cord paralysis.

B THE EXAMINATIONS

EXAMINATION OF A LUMP

This is a guide to examine any lump on the body, not just one in the neck and can therefore be used in the other specialty areas too.

Introduction and SITE
'Hello, my name is Dr Parchment Smith. Can I check your details please? Could I have a look at that please? Is it tender at all?' [47]

WASH/GEL YOUR HANDS BEFORE YOU TOUCH THE PATIENT

Feel its SIZE[48], SHAPE[49], SURFACE[50] and EDGES[51].
Test for CONSISTENCY[52] and do a definite test of FLUCTUANCE[53].
Then hold the lump still to assess PULSATILITY[54].
Next press the lump into the underlying structures to assess COMPRESSIBILITY[55] and REDUCIBILITY[56].
Assess LAYER OF ORIGIN[57], FIXITY[58] and TETHERING[59]. Move the skin.

---

[47] If the pathology is obvious you could give your diagnosis now. However, in the OSCE it is more likely the examiners will want a full examination, so we suggest you go through this logical examination of the lesion.
[48] Think in three dimensions: width, length and depth or thickness.
[49] Think in three dimensions: 'hemispherical' not 'circular'.
[50] Smooth or irregular?
[51] Clearly defined or diffuse?
[52] Consistency includes stony-hard (not indentable), rubbery (hard to firm but slightly squashable), spongy (soft and squashable with some resilience) and soft (squashable with no resilience).
[53] Fluctuation can only be elicited by feeling at least two other areas of the lump while pressing on a third. If two areas on opposite aspects of the lump bulge out when a third area is pressed in, the lump fluctuates and contains fluid. This is best achieved by holding two opposite edges of the lump, e.g. between finger and thumb of one hand, and pressing on the surface of the lump with the finger of the other. Note that lipomata often show fluctuance due to the low density of fat, although not strictly a fluid.
[54] Lumps may be pulsatile because they lie adjacent to an artery. Aneurysms and vascular malformations tend to be expansile, i.e. a finger placed on either side of the lump will be forced apart with each pulsation.
[55] Some fluid-filled lumps can be compressed until they disappear and then reform when the compressing hand is removed (e.g. venous malformations). This is not the same as reducibility – technically, the reducible lump will not spontaneously reappear after reduction but has to have a force such as gravity or coughing exerted upon it.
[56] Reducibility is a feature of herniae. The lump will be felt to move to another place when it is gently compressed. If you ask the patient to cough, the lump may return, expanding as it does so (cough impulse).
[57] It is important to determine the relationship of the lump to deep (usually muscle) and superficial (usually skin) tissues.
[58] Attachment to deeper structures can be difficult to decide. If there is an organ in the vicinity of the lump, moving the organ (deep breaths for a liver mass, swallowing for a thyroid lump, sticking out the tongue for a thyroglossal cyst) will help decide if the lump is fixed to it.
[59] If the lump is tethered to the skin, the skin will pucker when you try to move the skin over the lump. This is a bad sign in breast lumps, which only tend to invade the skin if malignant.

Does the lump move with the skin[60], or does the skin move over the lump[61]? Does the skin pucker when the lump under it is moved[62]?

Move the lump in the direction of the fibres of the underlying muscle. Ask the patient to **'tense that muscle against my hand'** *while you provide appropriate resistance, e.g. pushing the elbow down in the case of a shoulder lump, and move the lump in the direction of the muscle fibres and at right angles to them.*
Does the lump become immovable when the muscle is tensed? Does the lump become less easy to feel?[63]
Inspect and feel the OVERLYING[64] and SURROUNDING[65] skin.
Feel for the LOCAL LYMPH NODES.[66]
'I'm just going to feel in your armpit/groin. Have you noticed any lumps or bumps here yourself?'

Present your findings to the examiners:
'There is a non-tender lump on the right shoulder. It is about 3 cm in diameter, hemispherical in shape, with a lobulated surface and diffuse edges. It is soft, fluctuant, non-pulsatile, non-compressible and non-reducible. The lump lies superficial to the muscle, and the skin moves easily over it. It therefore arises from the subcutaneous tissues and is not tethered or fixed. The overlying and surrounding skin is normal; not red, discoloured, inflamed or warm. My diagnosis is a …'

If asked by the examiners whether you would like to examine anything else:
'A full examination of a lump[67] traditionally includes transillumination, listening for a bruit and examining the distal arterial and nerve supply.'

---

[60] This suggests the lump arises from the skin, e.g. sebaceous cyst, basal cell carcinoma.

[61] This suggests the lump arises from the subcutaneous tissue or deeper and is not tethered to the skin.

[62] This suggests tethering to the skin.

[63] These features indicate that the lump is tethered to, lies within or deep to the muscle. If tensing the muscle makes no difference to mobility, or makes the lump more prominent, the lump probably lies superficial to the muscle.

[64] Is the lump ulcerating through the skin, causing excoriation, or does it have increased vasculature? Is there pus or fluid pointing?

[65] The surrounding skin may show evidence of ischaemia (which would make any planned excision more problematic), venous insufficiency, oedema (e.g. peau d'orange in breast cancer) or inflammation.

[66] This is advised in all but the most straightforward and obvious benign lumps.

[67] Any of these examinations should be carried out if there is an obvious indication (e.g. feel for pulses in an obviously ischaemic foot with a ?malignant melanoma (this is relevant for post-op healing). Transilluminate testicular or obviously fluid-filled lumps. Listen for a bruit over pulsatile or vascular compressible lumps. However, do not go through the motions brainlessly and automatically. You will look very stupid listening for a bruit over a squamous cell carcinoma, or trying to transilluminate it!

EXAMINATION OF A NECK LUMP

'Hello, my name is Dr Parchment Smith. Would you mind if I examined your neck? Could you sit on a chair away from the wall with the buttons of your blouse undone (in a lady)/your shirt off (in a man)?'

WASH/GEL YOUR HANDS BEFORE YOU TOUCH THE PATIENT

Stand back, your hands behind your back, and look from in front.
On general inspection look for any evidence of myxoedema, hyperthyroidism or plethoric facies.[68] Look at the neck – can you see a lump? – if so, where is it and roughly how big is it?

Offer the patient a drink.
'Could you take a sip and hold it in your mouth until I ask you to swallow?'
Step back again.
'Could you look up slightly? Now swallow please.'
You need to assess whether the lump moves/does not move with swallowing, or whether there is no lump seen on swallowing.

'Could you stick your tongue out?' [69]
Does the lump move or not when the patient extends their tongue? Or can you see no lump on extending the tongue?
Next palpate the neck from behind.
'Is the neck tender anywhere? Have you noticed any swellings or lumps yourself? Right, I'll be gentle.'
If you identify a thyroid lump proceed with the thyroid lump examination (see pg 48). If you feel a lump elsewhere, palpate it, feeling for and describing its tenderness, site, size, shape, surface, edges, composition, consistency, fluctuance, pulsatility[70], compressibility, reducibility, layer of origin, fixity, tethering and overlying and surrounding skin, as described in Examination of a lump (see pg 43).

---

[68] Due to superior vena cava obstruction (commonly due to lymphadenopathy).
[69] This is to exclude thyroglossal cyst (see pg 94).
[70] If a lump is pulsatile it should be auscultated for a bruit, and gently compressed to see if it shows compressibility.

Next examine the lymph nodes[71] *(the parotid, mastoid, occipital, superficial cervical, deep cervical, submandibular, submental and anterior cervical).*

Present your findings to the examiners:
'My differential diagnosis is....'[72]

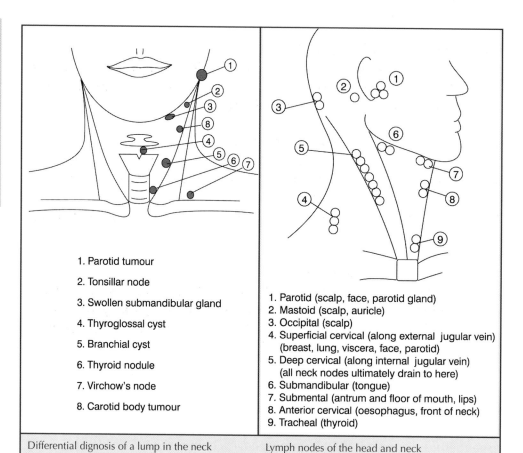

1. Parotid tumour

2. Tonsillar node

3. Swollen submandibular gland

4. Thyroglossal cyst

5. Branchial cyst

6. Thyroid nodule

7. Virchow's node

8. Carotid body tumour

1. Parotid (scalp, face, parotid gland)
2. Mastoid (scalp, auricle)
3. Occipital (scalp)
4. Superficial cervical (along external jugular vein) (breast, lung, viscera, face, parotid)
5. Deep cervical (along internal jugular vein) (all neck nodes ultimately drain to here)
6. Submandibular (tongue)
7. Submental (antrum and floor of mouth, lips)
8. Anterior cervical (oesophagus, front of neck)
9. Tracheal (thyroid)

Differential dignosis of a lump in the neck | Lymph nodes of the head and neck

---

[71] Lymph nodes are felt as subcutaneous swellings.
Enlarged lymph nodes may be:
- Separate – reactive hyperplasia
- Infective mononucleosis (glandular fever)
- Lymphoma
- Matted – neoplastic (metastatic or lymphoma), tuberculous
- Mobile – a good sign
- Fixed – to skin or deep tissues (more worrying)
- Rubbery – Hodgkin's
- Hard – neoplastic

If enlarged lymph nodes are felt, you should at least offer to examine the axillae, groins, spleen and liver.
[72] See figures above for sites and causes of a lump in the neck.

EXAMINATION OF THE THYROID

This is traditionally a very common case. It can be approached in one of three ways depending on what the examiners ask. Decide immediately which one of the following to do:

Is it an examination of a thyroid lump?
If the instructions tell you to 'examine this patient's thyroid gland' or 'examine this neck lump' in a patient with an obvious thyroid lump, you should carry out the 'examination of a thyroid lump' (see pg 48).

Is it an examination of a neck lump of unknown origin?
'Examine this patient's neck' in the 'head and neck' station means something different from the same instruction in the 'limbs including spine station' (see pg 343). If it is not obvious where the lump arises from (or indeed, you cannot see a lump) then you should carry out the examination of a neck lump (see pg 45).

Is it a general thyroid status examination?
If the instructions tell you to 'examine this patient's thyroid status' or if, after you have examined the neck lump, the examiners ask you, 'Can you tell if she is hyper/hypo/euthyroid?' you should follow the examination scheme for examination of thyroid status (see pg 50).

EXAMINATION OF A THYROID LUMP

'Hello, my name is Dr Parchment Smith. Would you mind if I examined your neck? Could you sit on a chair away from the wall with the buttons of your blouse undone (in a lady)/your shirt off (in a man)?'

WASH/GEL YOUR HANDS BEFORE YOU TOUCH THE PATIENT

Stand back, your hands behind your back, and look from in front.
Look for any swelling in the anterior triangle of the neck. Is it more prominent on one side than the other?

Hand the patient a glass of water (which should be available).
'**Could you take a sip and hold it in your mouth until I ask you to swallow?**'
Step back again.
'**Could you look up slightly? Now swallow please.**'
Look to see whether the lump moves with swallowing.

'**Could you stick out your tongue?**'[73]
Look to see whether the lump moves on sticking out the tongue.

Next palpate the lump.
Move to behind the chair.
'**Just point out the area which concerns you.**[74] **Ah, I see, there on the right? Is it tender at all? I'll be gentle then.**'
Place one hand flat against the abnormal (e.g. right) lobe of the thyroid, pushing it gently towards the midline. This will make the left side more prominent and allow you to examine this normal side first. Keep the right hand still, and gently palpate the left side in a few brief but systematic movements, trying to feel the upper, lower, medial and lateral borders and the surface. Ask the patient to swallow.[75] Repeat this for the right side, asking them to swallow again.

---

[73] This is to exclude a thyroglossal cyst (see pg 94).

[74] It is sometimes impossible to see the lump, and asking the patient will save a lot of embarrassing fumbling around, but is a risky tactic. Asking outright might be construed as cheating by some examiners, but few could object if you combine it with an enquiry about whether the lump is tender (as your motive is then avoiding any undue distress). If you have reservations about this approach, go with your conscience and do not try to ask, as cheating results in an automatic fail.

[75] The thyroid gland and any lumps arising from the thyroid move on swallowing but not on sticking out the tongue.

Next examine the LYMPH NODES in the neck.[76] *Feel the eight groups of neck nodes quickly (parotid, mastoid, occipital, superficial cervical, deep cervical, submandibular, submental and anterior cervical) (see pg 46).*

Stand back and say to the examiners:

'There is a swelling on the right lobe of the thyroid. It feels firm but not craggy and is not tethered to the overlying skin. It is non-tender, about 2 cm in diameter, round with a smooth surface. It is not pulsatile or reducible. The overlying skin is normal. There is no enlargement of the regional lymph nodes clinically. If this were a diffusely enlarged thyroid rather than a prominent lump I would PERCUSS for retrosternal extension and AUSCULTATE for a Graves' bruit. To complete my examination I would like to formally assess this patient's THYROID STATUS.'[77]

---

[76] The thyroid drains chiefly into the deep cervical lymph nodes along the internal jugular vein, but one would be concerned about any palpable nodes in a neck with a thyroid swelling as thyroid cancer can metastasise via the lymphatics.
[77] See pg 50, Examination of thyroid status.

EXAMINATION OF THYROID STATUS[78]

'Hello, my name is Dr Parchment Smith. Would you mind if I examined you? Could you sit on a chair away from the wall with the buttons of your blouse undone (in a lady)/your shirt off (in a man)?'

B THE EXAMINATIONS

WASH/GEL YOUR HANDS BEFORE YOU TOUCH THE PATIENT

Stand back and look.
Is the patient comfortable at rest? Look for signs of hyperthyroidism such as tremor, restlessness, wasting, signs of hypothyroidism such as myxoedema facies, a dull aspect or periorbital puffiness. In addition look for goitre or scars in the neck.

'Can I start with your HANDS please?'
Take the patient's hands, look at them and feel the pulse.
In a hyperthyroid patient you might see sweaty, warm palms with a tachycardic or irregular pulse. Look for acropachy. In a hypothyroid patient you might see dry, cool and pale hands with rough, inelastic skin and non-pitting puffiness. They might be bradycardic. *Ask the patient* '**Do you get any tingling or numbness in the hands?**[79]

Next look at the face.
'Just look ahead please.'
Look at their face from in front.
In Graves' eye disease you would expect to see exophthalmos, lid retraction and signs of corneal irritation.
'Can you follow my finger with your eyes please, keeping your head still?'
Move your finger up and then down.
Look for lid lag. In a hypothyroid lady look for thinning, dry, brittle hair, loss of the outer third of the eyebrows and a sallow complexion.

---

[78] **Causes of hypothyroidism (details on pg 86)**
1. Iatrogenic (90%)
2. Primary idiopathic myxoedema
3. Hashimoto's disease
Causes of hyperthyroidism (details on pg 89)
1. Graves' disease
2. Toxic multinodular goitre
3. Toxic solitary adenomas
[79] Carpal tunnel syndrome is associated with hypothyroidism.

Next examine the NECK for a goitre or a thyroid lump.
Carry out thyroid lump examination (see pg 48).

'Finally I would like to check ANKLE REFLEXES[80] **and ask the patient some QUESTIONS.'** [81]

---

[80] Hypothyroid patients have **slow-relaxing reflexes**, best demonstrated if you ask the patient to stand next to a chair and put one knee on it, supporting him/herself on the back of the chair and allowing the foot to hang off the chair. A tap on the Achilles tendon should show the gastrocnemius plantar-flexion reflex that would be brisk in a hyperthyroid patient, but the foot would be slow to return to the normal position in the hypothyroid patient.

Because this is quite awkward to do, just offer to do it in the exam, but make sure you practice it so that if they call your bluff you can perform it smoothly. The normal patellar tendon reflex that is more easily done in a sitting position has the confounding effect of gravity pulling the leg back into position.

[81] **See Thyroid status history pg 36.**

EXAMINATION OF A PAROTID LUMP

If asked to examine a subcutaneous lump at the angle of the jaw the chances are that this is arising from the parotid gland.[82] Alternatively you may be asked directly to examine the parotid gland.

'Hello, my name is Dr Parchment Smith. Would you mind if I took a look at this lump?'

WASH/GEL YOUR HANDS BEFORE YOU TOUCH THE PATIENT

Look for any obvious swelling visible over the angle of either side of the jaw. To the examiners:
'Is it tender at all? Can I feel it?'
PALPATE it, feeling for and describing its tenderness, site, size, shape, surface, edges, composition, consistency, fluctuance, pulsatility, compressibility, reducibility, layer of origin, fixity, tethering and overlying and surrounding skin, as described in Examination of a lump (see pg 43). Mention also if the rest of the gland is enlarged or feels normal. The findings will depend on the pathology (see individual cases of parotid on pg 118–125).

Next examine the LYMPH NODES… the parotid, mastoid, occipital, superficial cervical, deep cervical, submandibular, submental and anterior cervical.

---

[82] **Lumps arising from the parotid gland include:**
1. Benign pleomorphic adenomas (3/4 of all parotid adenomas). Contain epithelial and mesothelial stroma. Occur in middle-aged men and women as a slow-growing painless lump (see case pg 118).
2. Benign monomorphic adenomas (1/4 of parotid adenomas). No sign of stroma. Includes adenolymphoma, *also known as* Warthin's tumour, that contains epithelial and lymphoid tissue.
Together adenomas account for 90% of salivary gland neoplasms.
3. Intermediately malignant tumours (such as acinic cell tumours, mucoepidermoid tumours).
4. Carcinomas (adenocarcinomas, squamous cell carcinomas, undifferentiated carcinomas), very malignant with local invasion along nerve sheaths, sinuses, blood vessels, into base of skull. Also widespread metastases (see pg 122).
A lump at the angle of the jaw not arising from the parotid could be:
Arising from the skin: sebaceous cyst, basal cell carcinoma, squamous cell carcinoma, malignant melanoma. Subcutaneous: lipoma, dermoid cyst, lymphoma or a metastatic deposit from an extraparotid primary.
A generally enlarged parotid gland is caused by (details on pg 124):
- Chronic parotitis
- Mikulicz syndrome
- Sjögren syndrome
- Drugs
- Sialadenosis
- Acute parotitis

'Have you noticed any other lumps or sores on your scalp sir?'[83]
'I would now like to take a look INSIDE THE MOUTH. Is there a glove and pen torch available?'
Look inside the mouth.
'Open wide! Lift your tongue please? Move it to the left… to the right… thank you.'
Look for obvious ulcers or tonsillar swellings in the mouth.[84]

'Can I just feel the inside of your cheek with my gloved finger, sir?'[85]
Feel for a stone in the parotid duct.
Withdraw your finger and take off the glove.

'Let me just take another look at your FACE sir.'
Look for any obvious lesions on the face.
'Could you show me your teeth please sir, like this… now raise your eyebrows like this… and scrunch your eyes tight closed.'
You are assessing whether the FACIAL NERVE is intact.[86]

Stand up and face the examiner and give your diagnosis (see cases: Pleomorphic adenoma pg 118, Parotid carcinoma pg 122, Chronic parotitis pg 124).

---

[83] Be aware that the lump over the angle of the jaw could itself be an enlarged lymph node secondary to a malignant lesion elsewhere. Parotid lymph nodes typically drain from the scalp, face and parotid gland.

[84] Malignancies here can drain to neck nodes, causing lumps in the parotid area.

[85] Gently slide the index finger into the side of the mouth that the lump is on. With the other, ungloved hand, feel the lump from the outside. The parotid gland cannot be palpated bimanually because it lies behind the anterior edge of the masseter muscle and the vertical ramus of the mandible. A pleomorphic adenoma in the deep part of the parotid can push the tonsil and the pillar of the fauces towards the midline. From the inside feel for the parotid duct, which drains opposite the second upper molar tooth. A stone will feel sharp or like a piece of grit on the inner cheek.

[86] Facial nerve infiltration is a sign of malignancy, so carcinoma of the parotid gland should be suspected.

C THE OSCE CASES

HOW TO USE THIS SECTION

Common history or examination cases you might see in the exam appear in this section.

For each case, you will be given an example 'history question' and an example 'clinical examination question' which you could expect to find outside a station in the examination. Following each of these is an example of how to present a 'typical patient' with this complaint. You can then use these examples to practise with friends/colleagues. One of you should be the candidate and use the basic history and examination schemes to start you off. A second person should pretend to be the patient in the example given. A third person could be used as the examiner to check that all the questions or examination steps from the basic schemes are completed. The candidate can then present their findings at the end and have a guess at a differential diagnosis. At the end of the 'station' the 'examiner' can then use the 'What you should know' section to ask the candidate some questions about the case. Try and time yourselves so you get an idea of how long 9 minutes is.

In the actual exam you could be asked to examine a patient, just to take a history, or to 'assess' the patient (i.e. do both). You therefore need to be flexible. Use the 'Combined Assessment Boxes' in the History and Examination sections if you get stuck.

Following this are photograph/s of the condition in the 'What you should see' section so that if you don't get a chance to see a particular case in all those outpatient clinics you will be attending before the exam at least you will have an idea of what it will look like!

Take a history from this patient with a neck lump

(see pg 33)

LIPOMA

'I would like to present Mrs W, a 40-year-old office worker. She has had a non-tender lump on the right side of her neck for several years. She has not noticed that it has grown particularly and she has no associated symptoms. She finds it unsightly and it rubs on her collar. She had a similar lump on her arm that was removed under local anaesthetic 5 years ago. She is otherwise fit and well, takes no regular medication and has no known allergies. She is a non-smoker and does not drink alcohol. She lives with her husband.

I think this lady has a lipoma but my differential diagnosis includes a lymph node, a sebaceous cyst, a liposarcoma[87], a thyroid lump etc. I would like to examine the lump to confirm my diagnosis.'

WHAT YOU SHOULD KNOW

[87] **Definition**: lipomata are hamartomas (overgrowth of cell types normally found in that organ). A lipoma is a cluster of mature fat cells that have become overactive and distended with fat.

Presentation: patients usually present because it is unsightly, inconvenient, or they are worried about the diagnosis.

Treatment: simple excision under LA or GA due to cosmetic reasons, or if unduly large or suspicious of a liposarcoma.

Liposarcoma: does not arise from lipoma but de novo from different sites, deeper tissues and in the retroperitoneum. Tend to affect older patients. Firmer and more vascular than lipomata. Need urgent excision.

Lipomatosis: a condition of multiple contiguous lipomata causing enlargement and distortion of the subcutaneous tissues. Usually occurs in the buttocks, occasionally the neck (see below).

[88] Common sites, but can occur anywhere where there is fat. Tend not to occur on the palm, sole of the foot or the scalp because in these areas the fat is contained within dense fibrous septa.

[89] Can be of any size.

[90] Lipomata are roughly spherical but are usually compressed between skin and deep fascia so become discoid or hemispherical.

[91] Although the soft fat in a lipoma is not liquid, it can be jelly-like and larger lipomata may fluctuate. Most small lipomata are soft and yielding but do not truly fluctuate like a fluid-filled cyst would.

[92] Subcutaneous lipomata are not usually attached to superficial or deep structures and can be moved freely in all directions. Some lipomata, however, arise from the fat within muscles (intramuscular lipoma), are fixed to the muscle and, unlike the usual lipoma, become less prominent on contracting the muscle rather than more prominent.

[93] May be stretched and translucent with visible veins. There may be a scar from previous excision as recurrence is common.

[94] Lipomata rarely transilluminate unless they are extremely large and prominent. There is no fluid thrill, no bruit and they are dull to percussion. They rarely disrupt the distal circulation, venous drainage or neurology, although an extremely large intramuscular lipoma may do.

[95] People with one lipoma may have others. Dercum's disease is a familial syndrome of multiple lipomata.

Examine this patient's lump

(see pg 43)

LIPOMA

'There is (in this adult of any age) a non-tender lump on the back/shoulder/neck/trunk/forearms.[88] It is 4 cm in diameter[89], hemispherical in shape[90] with a lobulated smooth surface. The edges are also lobulated and slip away from the fingers (the slip sign). It is soft and fluctuant/but does not fluctuate[91], non-pulsatile, non-compressible and non-reducible. The skin moves over it and it appears/does not appear to be fixed to the deep tissues[92], as it becomes less distinct/more distinct on contraction of the underlying muscle. The overlying skin is normal[93] and the regional lymph nodes are not enlarged.[94] This is a lipoma. I would like to ask if the patient has noticed any others.'[95]

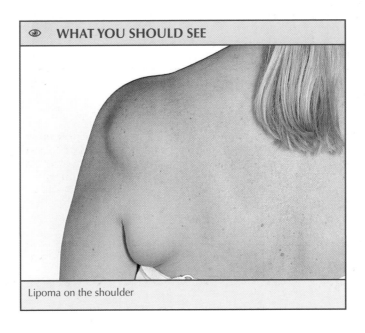

👁 WHAT YOU SHOULD SEE

Lipoma on the shoulder

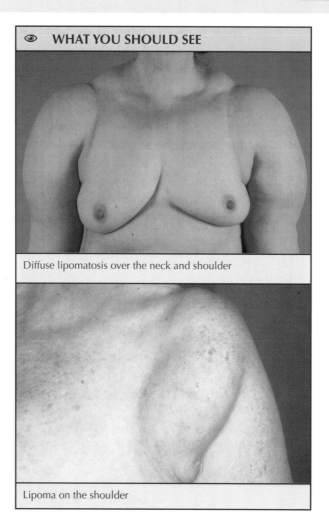

👁 **WHAT YOU SHOULD SEE**

Diffuse lipomatosis over the neck and shoulder

Lipoma on the shoulder

SEBACEOUS CYST/ EPIDERMAL CYST

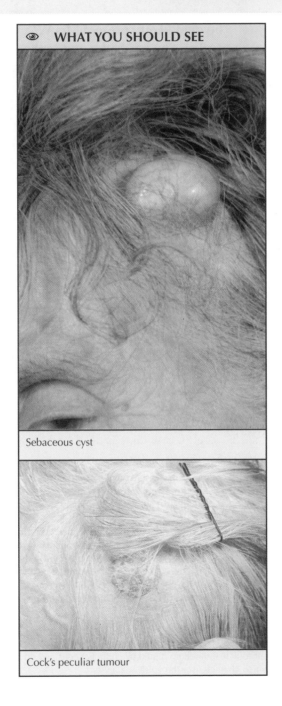

👁 **WHAT YOU SHOULD SEE**

Sebaceous cyst

Cock's peculiar tumour

Take a history from this patient with a neck lump (or could be anywhere else in the body)

(see pg 33)

SEBACEOUS CYST/ EPIDERMAL CYST

'I would like to present Mrs W, a 40-year-old office worker. She has had a non-tender lump on the right side of her neck[97] for several years. She has noticed it has gradually got larger. About 6 months ago the lump became red and painful and her GP gave her some antibiotics, which settled things down. She has no other associated symptoms. She finds it unsightly and it rubs on her collar. She is otherwise fit and well, takes no regular medication and has no known allergies. She is a non-smoker and does not drink alcohol. She lives with her husband.

I think this lady has a sebaceous cyst, which became infected 6 months ago. My differential diagnosis would include a lymph node, a lipoma, a thyroid lump etc. I would like to examine the lump to confirm my diagnosis.'

✍ WHAT YOU SHOULD KNOW

Also known as: epidermoid cysts, epidermal cysts, trichilemmal cysts, pilar cysts. They occur in all age groups but are rare in children. They are slow growing and usually asymptomatic apart from being unsightly or catching on the hairbrush when on the scalp, they can then get infected, when they become suddenly enlarged, red, painful and can discharge offensive purulent contents. There are two main types (neither derived from sebaceous glands):

1. Epidermal cysts
Pathology: arise from infundibular portion of hair follicles. Histologically, comprise keratinous debris lined by keratinising squamous epithelium with a distinct granular layer.
Complications: infection, discharge of foul-smelling, cheesy contents.
Malignant change has been reported (McDonald 1963) but is extremely rare.
Multiple cysts occur in Gardner syndrome.
Treatment: complete surgical removal of entire cyst and its contents intact with an ellipse of overlying skin including the punctum. Recurrence occurs if even a small portion of the cyst lining is left behind. Can be done under local anaesthetic but large, multiple cysts may be removed under GA. Beware bleeding during excision of scalp lesions; have diathermy available, shave area for good access, use a local anaesthetic with adrenaline and close with mattress sutures to aid haemostasis. Mattress sutures are useful on the scalp but should be avoided on areas where cosmetic result is important.

2. Trichilemmal cysts
Clinically identical to epidermal cysts but not as common; 90% on scalp; 70% multiple. Genetic predisposition (autosomal dominant)
Pathology: derived from hair follicle epithelium. Lined by epithelial cells and do not have the granular layer from the epidermis which characterises the epidermal cysts.
Treatment: as for epidermal cyst.
Complications: calcification (not seen in epidermal cysts).

Examine this patient's lump

(see pg 43)

SEBACEOUS CYST/ EPIDERMAL CYST

'There is a large non-tender[96] lump on the right side of the scalp.[97] It is 3 cm in diameter[98], spherical with a smooth surface and a well-defined edge. It is hard in consistency, not compressible or pulsatile. It moves with the skin freely over the underlying deep structures and although the surrounding skin is normal, the overlying skin shows signs of hair loss, excoriation and inflammation. There is/is no evidence of a punctum/scar from previous excision/current infection and discharge. This is a sebaceous cyst.'

📋 **WHAT YOU SHOULD KNOW (CONT)**

Pilar tumour
Proliferation of epithelium lining cyst.
Ulceration and proliferation: may resemble a squamous cell carcinoma (Cock's peculiar tumour, see fig on page 59).
Malignant transformation: reported but rare.
Treatment: as for epidermal cyst.

[96] Tenderness is a sign of infection.
[97] Most sebaceous cysts are found in the hair-bearing parts of the body, especially the scalp, scrotum, neck, shoulders and back. They can occur wherever there are sebaceous glands (i.e. not the palms of the hands or soles of the feet).
[98] They can vary from a few mm to upward of 4 cm in diameter.

Take a history from this patient with a neck lump (or could be anywhere else in the body. For common sites see below)

(see pg 33)

DERMOID CYSTS

'I would like to present Joey W, a 4-year-old boy. His mum tells me that he has had a lump in the midline of his neck since he was born. He doesn't complain of it being painful and he has no other associated symptoms. However, his mum is worried that it is unsightly and that Joey has recently been upset by other children teasing him about it. He is otherwise fit and well, takes no regular medication and has no known allergies. He lives with his mum and dad and has just started school.

I think this boy has a congenital dermoid cyst. I would like to examine the lump to confirm my diagnosis.'

WHAT YOU SHOULD KNOW

A dermoid cyst is a cyst, deep to the skin, that is lined by skin. Skin can become trapped in the subcutaneous tissues either during fetal development (**congenital dermoid cyst**) or following an injury which forces skin into the deeper tissues (**acquired/implantation dermoid cyst**).

Congenital dermoid cyst
Definition: congenital subcutaneous cysts caused by developmental inclusion of epidermis along lines of fusion.
Histology: cysts lined by stratified squamous epithelium but, unlike the epidermal (sebaceous) cyst, the wall also contains functioning epidermal appendages such as hair follicles, sweat and sebaceous glands.
Sites: occur at sites of fusion of skin dermatomes, typically the lateral and medial ends of the eyebrow (external and internal angular dermoid), the midline of the nose (nasal dermoid), sublingually, the midline of the neck and at any point in the midline of the trunk, typically the perineum and sacrum.
Complications: may create a bony depression and penetrate down to the dura. Meningeal penetration is only a problem with midline dermoids along the cranio-spinal axis but does not occur with internal/external angular dermoids. A nasal dermoid may look like a small superficial pit but can be an extensive cyst that passes between the nasal bones towards the sphenoid sinus.
Treatment: rarely troublesome and rarely get infected so can be left alone. Needs experienced surgeon in case of deep extension. May need CT scan and skull X-ray pre-operatively.

Acquired/implantation dermoid cyst
Definition: a cyst formed after the survival of a piece of skin forcibly implanted into the subcutaneous tissues by an injury such as a small deep cut or stab injury. The patient might not remember the injury. The histology is similar to the congenital dermoid.
Sites: occur in areas subject to repeated trauma (such as fingers) so tend to be troublesome, interfere with function, and can become painful and tender.
Management: excision. It is commonly confused with a sebaceous cyst, but the presence of a scar and history of an old injury is helpful in differentiating them. Dermoid cysts, unlike sebaceous cysts, rarely become infected.
[99] May transilluminate but more commonly will not as it is filled with a thick, opaque mixture of sebum, sweat and desquamated epithelial cells.
[100] Unlike sebaceous cysts (arising from the skin) and implantation dermoid cysts (tethered to skin).

Examine this
patient's lump

(see pg 43)

DERMOID CYSTS

'There is a non-tender lump at the outer aspect of the left eyebrow. It is about 2 cm in diameter, ovoid in shape with a smooth surface and well-defined edges. It is soft and fluctuant but does not transilluminate.[99] It is dull to percussion, is not pulsatile, compressible or reducible. It arises in the subcutaneous tissues and is not attached to the skin[100] but appears to be fixed to the deeper structures. The overlying and surrounding skin and regional lymph nodes are normal. This is a congenital dermoid cyst.'

👁 WHAT YOU SHOULD SEE

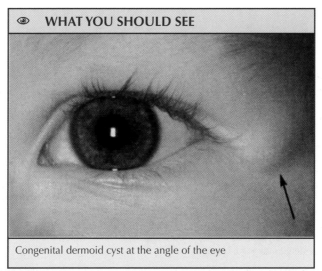

Congenital dermoid cyst at the angle of the eye

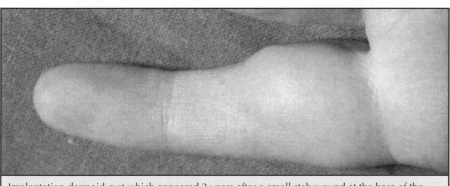

Implantation dermoid cyst which appeared 2 years after a small stab wound at the base of the finger

Take a history from this parent whose child has a lump

(see pg 33)

HAEMANGIOMA

'I would like to present Sophie W, a 3-year-old girl. Her mum tells me that she has had a lump on her neck since a few weeks after she was born. It is red and sticks out and her mum says it looks a bit like a strawberry! She doesn't complain of it being painful and has no other associated symptoms. However, her mum is worried that it is unsightly but has been relieved that it seems to have been getting a bit smaller and paler recently and wants to know if this will continue. Sophie is otherwise fit and well, takes no regular medication and has no known allergies. She lives with her mum, dad and older brother.

I think this girl has a congenital intradermal haemangioma, or strawberry naevus. I would like to examine the lump to confirm my diagnosis.'

⌨ WHAT YOU SHOULD KNOW

Definition: haemangiomata are hamartomas – an overgrowth of a cell type normally found in that organ. A haemangioma (or vascular naevus) is an abnormal proliferation of the embryonic vascular network. Most display arterial, venous and lymphatic elements. Angiogenic and hormonal factors may be responsible. They are more common in females. They occur in 1–2.6% of newborns, 20% of whom have more than one lesion. All types can ulcerate and induce hyperkeratosis in the overlying stratum corneum. They hardly ever undergo malignant change.

Types of haemangioma
1. Strawberry naevus (congenital intradermal haemangioma or cavernous haemangioma): bright-red, lobulated lesion that stands proud of the skin and does, indeed, look like a strawberry. Formed by a network of capillaries radiating from an artery. Present at a few weeks of age, they often regress spontaneously within months or years. It is not associated with any other congenital vascular malformation apart from other haemangiomata.

2. Port-wine stain (*also known as* naevus vingus, intradermal haemangioma): a congenital extensive collection of dilated venules and capillaries just below the epidermis, it is similar in histology to the strawberry naevus but does not stick out from the surface of the skin. It also does not tend to regress as the baby grows, but may fade in colour. They are common on the face and at the junction between the limbs and the trunk and are very noticeable and disfiguring due to their deep purple-red colour. Occasionally, small vessels within the stain become prominent and bleed. It can present as part of a more extensive vascular abnormality. Sturge–Weber syndrome is a port-wine stain in the distribution of the first and/or second division of the trigeminal nerve associated with ipsilateral intracranial haemangiomata and a history of epilepsy and/or learning difficulties. In general, however, there are no associated neurological abnormalities and the main symptom is deformity.

Examine this patient's lump

(see pg 43)

HAEMANGIOMA

'There is (in this young child) a non-tender lump on the right side of the forehead. It is dark red in colour, 2 cm in diameter, hemispherical and protuberant with well-defined edges and a smooth, pitted surface giving it a strawberry-like appearance. It is soft and compressible; gentle pressure empties the lump leaving it colourless and collapsed. It is not pulsatile. It arises from the skin and moves with it freely over the underlying structures. The surrounding skin is normal and the regional lymph nodes are not enlarged. This is a congenital intradermal haemangioma, or strawberry naevus.'

WHAT YOU SHOULD KNOW (CONT)

3. Vin rosé patch (salmon patch, naevus flammeus neonatarum): another congenital intradermal haemangioma in which mild dilatation of the subpapillary dermal plexus gives the skin a pale-pink colour. It is often associated with other vascular abnormalities such as extensive haemangiomata, giant limbs due to arteriovenous fistulae and lymphoedema. The vin rosé patch can occur anywhere and causes no symptoms. Unlike the port-wine stain, it is not dark enough to be disfiguring and has often been accepted by the patient as a birthmark and forgotten about.

4. Spider naevus: a solitary dilated skin arteriole feeding a number of small branches that leave it in a radial manner. It is an acquired condition and is often associated with liver disease. In general > 5 are pathological.

5. Telangiectasis: a dilatation of normal capillaries. Tend to arise after irradiation. Occurs on internal mucosal surfaces as well as the skin, and can lead to gastrointestinal haemorrhage, epistaxis, haematuria and intracerebral bleed.

6. Hereditary haemorrhagic telangiectasia (Osler–Weber–Rendu syndrome): a Mendelian dominant genetic condition with incomplete penetrance affecting 1–2/100 000. Tiny capillary haemangiomata scattered over mucous membranes and skin gives rise to bleeding (haematemesis, melaena, haematuria) and iron deficiency anaemia.

The patient has telangiectasia on the face, around the mouth, on the lips and on the tongue, the fingers and the buccal and nasal mucosa. In some variants pulmonary arteriovenous aneurysms are common and increase in frequency with age (as do the telangiectases). Telangiectasia of the face also occurs in the CREST syndrome of Calcinosis, Raynaud Syndrome, Oesophagitis, Sclerodactyly and Telangiectasia.

7. Campbell de Morgan spot: very common, well-defined, uniformly brilliantly red capillary naevus, 2–3 mm in diameter. Develops on the trunk in middle age. No clinical significance.

Treatment of haemangiomata

Apart from the strawberry naevus and the port-wine stain, patients with the haemangiomata described above do not often seek treatment. Reassurance and waiting for natural regression is the best line of management initially for the strawberry naevus, as premature treatment may lead to scarring which natural regression will not. Large, ulcerating or persistent lesions may need treatment that is difficult and controversial. Cryotherapy, laser photocoagulation, radiotherapy, sclerosants, electrolysis, steroids and excision with reconstruction have all been used. The port-wine stain may fade but does not tend to regress, and many of the above methods have been used, with laser therapy currently the treatment of choice for most specialists. It is usually combined with conservative methods such as camouflage creams.

👁 WHAT YOU SHOULD SEE

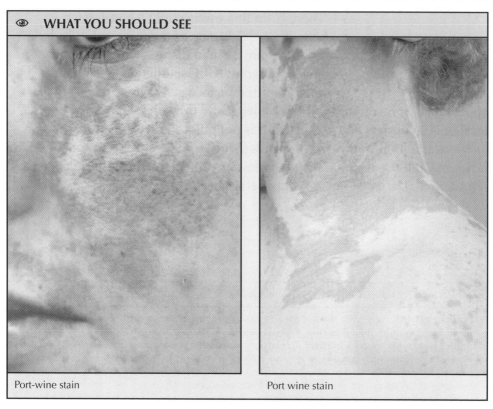

Port-wine stain

Port wine stain

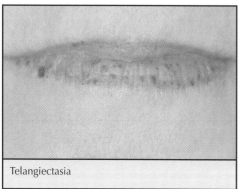

Telangiectasia

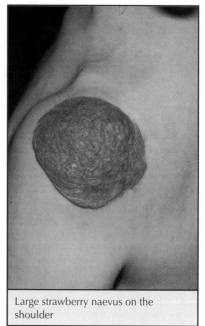

Large strawberry naevus on the shoulder

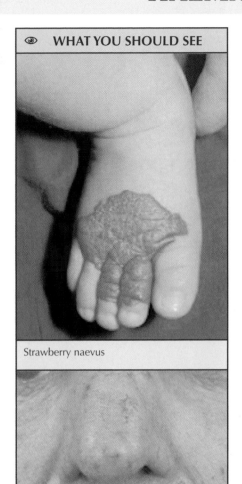

👁 **WHAT YOU SHOULD SEE**

Strawberry naevus

Osler–Weber–Rendu syndrome

HAEMANGIOMA

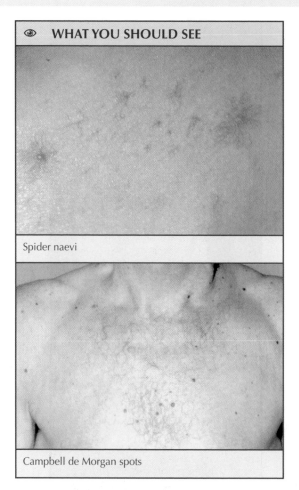

👁 **WHAT YOU SHOULD SEE**

Spider naevi

Campbell de Morgan spots

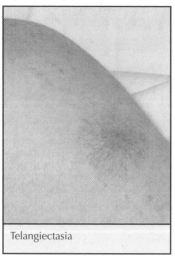

Telangiectasia

OTHER BENIGN SKIN LESIONS

✎ WHAT YOU SHOULD KNOW

Other benign skin lesions

Seborrhoeic keratosis (*also known as* senile wart, seborrhoeic wart, verruca senilis, basal cell papilloma) is a benign overgrowth of the basal layer of the epidermis containing an excess of small, dark-staining basal cells. They occur in both sexes and are more common in the elderly (almost ubiquitous in over-70s). They become more prominent and are often multiple if the skin is not regularly and firmly washed (hence they are common in inaccessible areas such as the back of elderly patients). Colour varies from normal skin colour to grey or brown. Appear as raised plates of hypertrophic greasy skin with a distinct edge and a rough, papilliferous surface. Distinguishing feature is that it can be picked or scraped off, leaving a pale-pink patch of skin that may bleed slightly. No other skin lesion behaves like this. Generally do not need treatment but if they catch on clothes or become a nuisance they are easily scraped off. If infected they can look like a pyogenic granuloma, epithelioma or malignant melanoma.

Warts are patches of hyperkeratotic overgrown skin whose growth has been stimulated by the presence of a papilloma virus. They are commonest in children and young adults and may be present for months, most typically on the hands or feet (verrucae), but also on the knees, face and arms. They are greyish brown, hemispherical, only a few millimetres in diameter and frequently multiple. They have a rough, hyperkeratotic surface, are hard and non-compressible. Verrucae (plantar warts) look slightly different because they are pushed into the skin, causing a 'punched out' appearance of a pit containing a wart, surrounded by hardened, thickened, tender skin.

◉ WHAT YOU SHOULD SEE

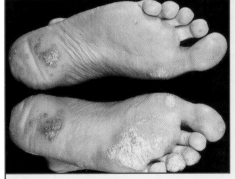

Veruccae (plantar warts)

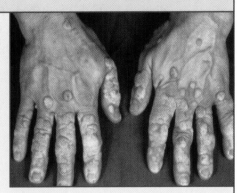

Warts

Seborrhoeic keratoses on the back

69

Take a history from this patient with a neck lump (or could be anywhere else in the body. For common sites see below)

(see pg 33)

BENIGN PAPILLOMA (SKIN TAG)

'I would like to present Mr W, a 60-year-old man. He has a number of very small lumps on his neck, which he has had for several years. They had not bothered him until he caught them on his shirt collar 2 months ago and after this they became red and swollen for a few days.[101] This settled spontaneously but after this he became worried about the lumps and decided to seek advice. He has no associated symptoms. His previous medical history includes a replacement metallic aortic valve 2 years ago and he therefore takes warfarin. He is on no other medication and has no allergies. He has just retired from his job as a postman and lives with his wife. He has smoked for 60 pack years and drinks 4 units of alcohol a week.

My diagnosis is that this man has skin tags on his neck, which became inflamed following rubbing from his collar. I would like to examine him to confirm my diagnosis. If this confirms that these are benign papillomata/skin tags I would discuss with him the risks versus benefits of excising the tags, particularly as he would need to stop his warfarin and start heparin pre-operatively.'

🗒 WHAT YOU SHOULD KNOW

[101] **Definition**: simple overgrowth of all layers of the skin. It is not a benign neoplasm (it is a skin tag). Can occur at any age but is more frequent with advancing age. Also known as fibroepithelial papilloma, soft fibroma.

Complications: can catch on clothes. May become injured, red, swollen, ulcerated or infarct. Spontaneous ulceration is rare. The skin that forms a papilloma contains sweat glands, hair follicles and sebaceous glands, all of which can become infected and make papillomata swollen and tender. If the granulation tissue that forms in response to the infection becomes exuberant, the swelling can look like a carcinoma.

Treatment is simple excision with a pair of sharp scissors under a local anaesthetic. Occasionally a single suture is needed to control bleeding from the feeding vessel.

[102] Can be single.

[103] Can be pigmented.

[104] They can be sessile.

Examine this patient's lump

(see pg 43)

BENIGN PAPILLOMA (SKIN TAG)

'There are multiple[102] non-tender, discrete, skin-coloured[103] tags around the neck and axilla. They are less than 5 mm across, pedunculated[104], papilliferous polyps. They arise from the skin and move with it, not invading deeper structures. They are soft, solid, and non-compressible. The surrounding skin and lymph nodes are normal. These are benign papillomata/skin tags.'

👁 WHAT YOU SHOULD SEE

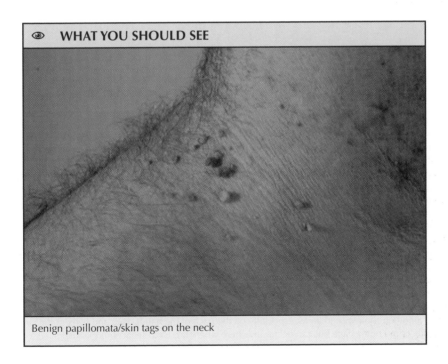

Benign papillomata/skin tags on the neck

Take a history from this patient with a lump on his right cheek (or could be elsewhere on the body. For common sites see below)

(see pg 33)

KERATOACANTHOMA

'I would like to present Mr W, a 75-year-old man. He noticed a lump on his right cheek 4 weeks ago.[105] It has gradually got larger during this period, which has worried him. It is non-tender and he has not noticed any other lumps. The lump has been itchy on occasion but has not bled. He has no other associated symptoms. His previous medical history includes hypertension. He is therefore on an antihypertensive medication but has no allergies. He is a retired office worker and lives with his wife. He has an aversion to flying and therefore has never left the North of England so he has had limited sun exposure. He is an ex-smoker who stopped 10 years ago and smoked a total of 20 pack years. He is teetotal.

The differential diagnosis includes keratoacanthoma, solar keratosis or squamous cell carcinoma. I would like to examine him to try and delineate between these, although the diagnosis should be confirmed by an excision biopsy.'

✐ WHAT YOU SHOULD KNOW

Also known as adenoma sebaceum, molluscum pseudocarcinomatosum, molluscum sebaceum.
Definition: a self-limiting overgrowth of hair follicle cells producing a central plug of keratin with subsequent spontaneous regression. Cause unknown – may be self-limiting benign neoplasm or an unusual response to infection.
Epidemiology: occurs in adults; 2–4 weeks to grow, 2–3 months to regress. Normally single lesions. More common in males.
Presentation: usually occurs on the face. The central core is hard and eventually separates. The lump collapses, leaving a deep indrawn scar. Often mistaken for squamous cell carcinoma. Unlike a keratoacanthoma, a squamous cell carcinoma grows more slowly, does not have a dead central core, and gradually becomes an ulcer.
Treatment: should be excised to confirm diagnosis and to prevent depressed scar.
Differential diagnosis: solar keratosis. A premalignant condition predisposing to squamous cell carcinoma.
Usually found on sun-exposed areas, especially on the back of the hands, face and helix of the ears.
[105] Usually found on the face but can occur anywhere where there are sebaceous glands.

Examine this patient's lump

(see pg 43)

KERATOACANTHOMA

'There is a non-tender lump on the right cheek.[105] It is a skin-coloured hemispherical nodule, about 2 cm in diameter, with a black sloughy centre. It has well-defined edges, is firm and rubbery, but the central core is hard. It is not fluctuant, pulsatile or compressible. The lump arises from the skin and moves freely with it over the underlying structures. The surrounding skin and regional lymph nodes are normal. Clinically this is a keratoacanthoma rather than a squamous cell carcinoma but this should be confirmed by an excision biopsy.'

👁 WHAT YOU SHOULD SEE

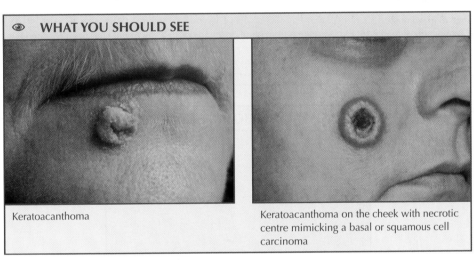

Keratoacanthoma

Keratoacanthoma on the cheek with necrotic centre mimicking a basal or squamous cell carcinoma

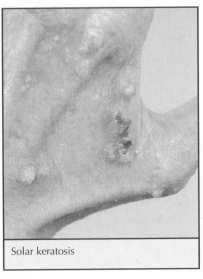

Solar keratosis

Examine this patient's lump

(see pg 43)

RHINOPHYMA

'There is (in this elderly man) a marked overgrowth of the skin and subcutaneous tissues of the nose. This is rhinophyma.'

✍ WHAT YOU SHOULD KNOW

Definition: thickening of the skin over the tip of the nose caused by hypertrophy and adenomatous changes in its sebaceous glands. Probably a severe degree of acne rosacea. The nasal cartilages and bones are spared.

Aetiology: not associated with alcohol abuse, mostly occurs in old age. Twelve times more common in men than women.

Complications: malignant transformation (into basal or squamous cell carcinoma) has been reported but is extremely rare.

Treatment: surgical planing of the nose as far as the base of the sebaceous glands, trying to avoid full-thickness debridement. Methods include scalpel, skin graft knife, laser, electrocautery, cryotherapy.

👁 WHAT YOU SHOULD SEE

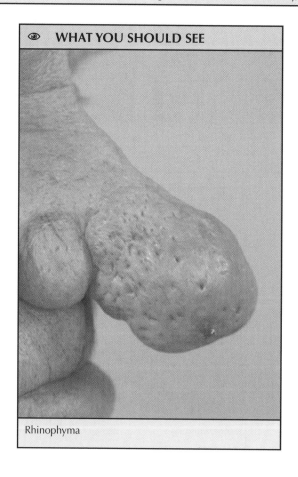

Rhinophyma

THE THYROID OSCE CASES

The thyroid is traditionally a common case. If you see a patient with a goitre proceed to history of a neck lump (see pg 33) or examination of a thyroid lump (see pg 48) and, if appropriate, proceed to history of and/or examination of thyroid status (see pgs 36 and 50).

Bear in mind the patient could be:
- Euthyroid
- Hyperthyroid
- Hypothyroid

And have:
- No goitre
- A diffuse goitre
- A multinodular goitre
- An apparently solitary thyroid nodule

> Take a history from this patient with a neck lump
>
> (see pgs 33 and 36)

DIFFUSE GOITRE

'I would like to present Mrs W, a 30-year-old woman. She became aware of a lump on her neck 3 months ago that has slowly enlarged. She has no symptoms of local pressure from the lump and no symptoms of hyper- or hypothyoidism. She is particularly concerned as she is 5 months pregnant and also because she does not like the cosmetic appearance. She has no significant previous medical history and in particular has had no problems in the past with her thyroid. She is on no medication and has no allergies. She is a housewife who has recently moved to the UK from the Andes! She has never smoked or drunk alcohol.

This lady from the Andes has developed a neck lump during her pregnancy that would be consistent with a diffuse goitre due to dietary iodine deficiency and the increased physiological demands of pregnancy. She is clinically euthyroid, which I would expect. I would like to examine her to confirm the diagnosis.'

✎ WHAT YOU SHOULD KNOW

Definition: a non-toxic simple goitre diffusely involves the whole gland without producing nodularity and is not associated with hypo- or hyperthyroidism. It is a compensatory hypertrophy and hyperplasia secondary to a reduction in T3 and T4 output which causes an increase in thyroid-releasing hormone and thyroid-stimulating hormone which in turn cause thyroid enlargement. It may revert to normal, may stay as a simple goitre or may progress to a multinodular goitre (see case on pg 78), which may be toxic or euthyroid.

Causes of diffuse non-toxic simple goitre
1. Physiological goitre: due to increased demands for thyroid hormone e.g. in pregnancy and puberty.
2. Dietary iodine deficiency: now uncommon but traditionally the cause of goitres in areas far from the sea such as the Alps, Himalayas and Andes, or even closer to home (Derbyshire neck).
3. Dietary goitrous agents: such as uncooked brassicas (cabbage, turnips), calcium or fluoride in drinking water, para-aminosalicylic acid (PAS), lithium, phenylbutazone, thiouracil, carbimazole.
4. Hereditary congenital defects (in thyroid metabolism): very uncommon and do not usually require treatment but may account for familial goitre. Include iodine transport defects, de-iodinase deficiency, iodotyrosine coupling defects and thyroglobulin synthesis defects.
5. Treated Graves' disease: associated with a smooth, small- to moderately-sized symmetrical goitre, hypervascularity, a bruit and typical facial signs (see pg 92). If untreated it is associated with hyperthyroidism.
6. Other rare causes of diffuse goitre: lymphoma, anaplastic carcinoma, autoimmune (Hashimoto's) thyroiditis, de Quervain's thyroiditis, thyroid amyloidosis.
Treatment of diffuse non-toxic simple goitre: if small, no treatment needed apart from reassurance and possibly iodine supplements. For cosmetic reasons subtotal thyroidectomy may be required.

Examine this patient's lump. Her GP is concerned that she has an enlarged thyroid gland

(see pgs 47 and 50)

DIFFUSE GOITRE

'There is a smooth, firm, diffusely and symmetrically enlarged thyroid gland. It is non-tender, moves on swallowing and there is no evidence of retrosternal extension or bruit. The patient is clinically euthyroid and there is no evidence of Graves' disease or enlarged regional lymph nodes. This is a diffuse goitre.'

👁 WHAT YOU SHOULD SEE

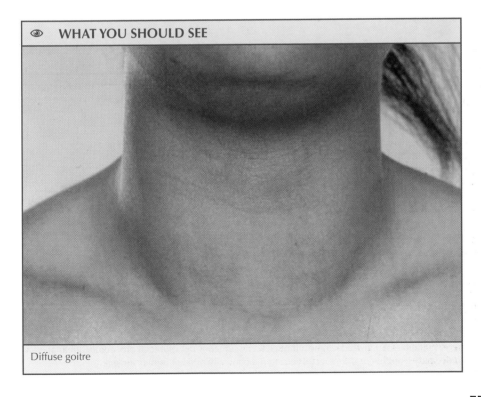

Diffuse goitre

Take a history from this patient with a neck lump

(see pgs 33 and 36)

MULTINODULAR GOITRE

'I would like to present Mrs W, a 45-year-old woman. She became aware of a lumpy area on her neck 5 months ago that has slowly enlarged. She has no symptoms of local pressure from the lump and no symptoms of hyper- or hypothyroidism. She does not like the cosmetic appearance and both she and her GP want to exclude a cancer. She has no significant previous medical history and in particular has had no problems in the past with her thyroid. She is on no medication and has no allergies. She is a housewife who has never smoked or drunk alcohol.

This middle-aged lady is clinically euthyroid and has developed what she describes as a 'lumpy area' on her neck, I therefore think the most likely diagnosis is a multinodular goitre. My differential diagnosis would include cervical lymph nodes, a diffuse goitre or a solitary thyroid nodule. She is clinically euthyroid, which I would expect. I would like to examine her to confirm the diagnosis.'

✎ WHAT YOU SHOULD KNOW

Definition: a non-toxic multinodular goitre occurs when a diffuse simple goitre progresses to a larger (up to 2 kg) goitre with multinodular focal hyperplasia. The majority are euthyroid but some are hyper- or hypothyroid.

Causes of non-toxic multinodular goitre
1. Progressive enlargement of diffuse goitre caused by any of the factors listed on pg 76.
2. Sporadic multinodular goitre predominantly affecting middle-aged women.

Complications:
Local symptoms: stridor, SVC obstruction, dysphagia, cosmesis, retrosternal enlargement.
Toxicity (<50%): mild hyperthyroidism in the absence of Graves' disease: Plummer syndrome.
Malignant change: 5% of untreated multinodular goitres.
Haemorrhage into cyst: can lead to sudden, painful enlargement.
Treatment: thyroxine may prevent progression (should reduce TSH levels).

Indications for surgery of a multinodular goitre
- Local symptoms, e.g. significant or symptomatic retrosternal extension, dysphagia, tracheal deviation or compression
- Enlarging dominant nodule (unless unequivocally benign)
- Recurrent laryngeal nerve palsy
- Cosmesis
- Hyperthyroidism

Surgery should be total thyroidectomy although some surgeons do a subtotal procedure. Subtotal thyroidectomy leads to the risk of recurrence and technically difficult further surgery.

MULTINODULAR GOITRE

Examine this patient's lump. Her GP is concerned that she has an enlarged thyroid gland

(see pgs 47 and 50)

'The thyroid gland is nodular and asymmetrically enlarged, the right lobe more so than the left. It is non-tender, moves on swallowing and there is no evidence of retrosternal extension or bruit. The patient is clinically euthyroid and there is no evidence of Graves' disease or enlarged regional lymph nodes. This is a multinodular goitre.'

👁 WHAT YOU SHOULD SEE

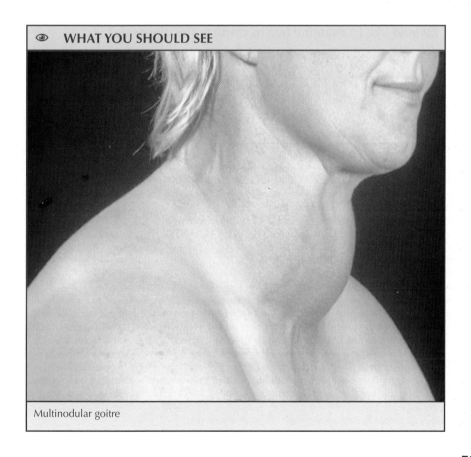

Multinodular goitre

79

> Take a history from this patient with a neck lump
>
> (see pgs 33 and 36)

THYROID NODULE

'I would like to present Miss W, a 30-year-old woman. She became aware of a lump on her neck 5 months ago that has rapidly enlarged. It is non-tender, but she has noticed some discomfort on swallowing. She gives no history of hoarseness or stridor. She has no symptoms of hyper- or hypothyroidism. She does not like the cosmetic appearance and both she and her GP want to exclude a cancer. She thinks she had irradiation to her neck as a child although she is unsure what this was for. Currently she is on no regular medication and has no allergies. She works as a solicitor and lives with her husband. She has never smoked but does drink 2 to 3 units of alcohol per week.

In this young woman with a rapidly enlarging neck lump and a history of irradiation I am concerned about a solitary thyroid nodule due to a papillary carcinoma. However, my differential diagnosis includes a prominent nodule in a multinodular goitre, other causes of a solitary thyroid nodule such as an adenoma, cyst or thyroiditis, or other causes of neck lumps such as a lymph node. I would like to examine her to confirm the diagnosis.'

☝ WHAT YOU SHOULD KNOW

[106] Only tracheal sarcomas and abnormal lymph nodes adherent to the thyroid can be mistaken for thyroid lumps, and these are both uncommon. Parathyroid adenomas are almost invariably impalpable.

[107] **Differential diagnosis of a thyroid nodule**:
- 5% of the adult population can be found to have a thyroid nodule
- In 50% this is a LARGE NODULE IN A MULTINODULAR GOITRE
- In 50% this is a TRUE SOLITARY NODULE
- Of the true solitary nodules, 80% are ADENOMAS
- 10% are cancer (mostly papillary)
- 10% are cysts, fibrosis or thyroiditis

Investigations: the two most sensible and universal investigations to mention in an examination situation are **thyroid function tests (autoantibodies)** and an **ultrasound scan** (to see if the lump is a prominent nodule in a multinodular goitre, a solitary nodule or a cyst). **FNA** is required by NICE and BTA guidelines although it has been controversial, as it can miss follicular carcinoma. FNA should be requested if malignancy is suspected in a lump that would not otherwise need surgery. All true solitary nodules must either be excised or definitively shown to be benign by FNA aspiration. **Core biopsies** should be taken only from large or inoperable thyroid masses because they risk haemorrhage and damage to surrounding structures, even when performed under ultrasound control. A **technetium isotope scan** is indicated if TSH is decreased to assess if there is a solitary hot nodule. **CT** or **MRI** are indicated if potential technical difficulty is suspected in surgery (e.g. large retrosternal element).

THYROID NODULE

Examine this patient's lump. Her GP is concerned that she has an enlarged thyroid gland

(see pgs 47 and 50)

'There is a non-tender lump in the anterior triangle of the neck. It is about 2 cm in diameter, hemispherical, smooth with diffuse edges. It is firm, not fluctuant, pulsatile or compressible or reducible. It arises deep to the skin that moves over it, but moves on swallowing with the thyroid gland from which it is most likely to arise.[106] The overlying and surrounding skin and draining lymph nodes are normal. The patient is euthyroid. My diagnosis is a solitary thyroid nodule, or a prominent single nodule in a multinodular goitre.'[107]

⌲ WHAT YOU SHOULD KNOW (CONT)

Management of a true solitary thyroid nodule: ask the following two questions:
1. **Hot** (i.e. functioning) **or cold** (i.e. solid or partly cystic non-functioning) nodule?
Hot: almost invariably benign – can be observed. Treat if patient becomes hyperthyroid.
Cold: may be neoplastic. Tissue diagnosis essential either by excision or FNA (see below).
2. **Needs removal clinically?** (e.g. pressure symptoms, cosmesis, patient wishes, suspicious of malignancy):
Yes: total lobectomy or subtotal thyroidectomy (if centrally placed or isthmic nodule). Never subtotal lobectomy for a true solitary nodule.
If frozen section histology during surgery confirms malignancy the surgeon should proceed to total thyroidectomy and adjuvant treatment. The exception is papillary carcinoma confined to the thyroid, in which case total hemithyroidectomy plus isthmectomy is an acceptable minimum if the other lobe is palpably normal.
No: FNA needed (if definitely benign no further treatment needed). If definitely malignant, proceed with surgery as above. If follicular (?benign ?malignant), total hemithyroidectomy and await result of paraffin section histology.
CONTINUED on pg 82

📖 **WHAT YOU SHOULD KNOW (CONT)**

Thyroid cancers
70% papillary adenocarcinoma – seen in younger patients, often with a history of irradiation to the neck. Most are TSH-dependent, some are multifocal. Treatment is total thyroidectomy, including level 6 nodes, with thyroxine. A lobectomy may be performed if the papillary carcinoma is <1cm and unifocal and confined within the thyroid capsule and with no nodal involvement. Ten-year survival is 90%.
20% follicular carcinoma – unifocal treated by total thyroidectomy. FNA results unreliable. Ten year survival is 85%.
5% medullary carcinoma – tumour of calcitonin secreting 'C' cells. Familial tendency can be part of the MEN (multiple endocrine neoplasia) syndrome. Can be multifocal. Treatment total thyroidectomy including level 6 nodes.
<5% anaplastic carcinoma – seen in older patients. Worst prognosis. Treatment is debulking surgery and external beam radiotherapy. Poor 5-year survival.
CONTINUED on pg 84

THYROID NODULE

👁 **WHAT YOU SHOULD SEE**

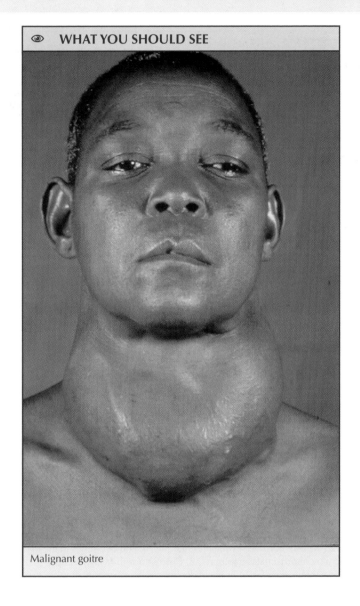

Malignant goitre

83

✎ WHAT YOU SHOULD KNOW (CONT)

Thyroid Surgery

Pre-operative assessment and preparation

Thyroid status: TFTs (T3,T4,TSH), thyroid autoantibodies. Must treat/reduce thyroid activity pre-op. with carbimazole and beta-blockers because operating on thyrotoxic patients can precipitate a thyroid crisis.

Vocal cord check: by ENT surgeon to ensure no pre-existing damage is present.

For anaesthetist: ECG, c/spine X-ray (due to neck extension needed on table), thoracic inlet X-ray, chest X-ray (to check for tracheal deviation). Occipital CT for large goitre to assess airway and extent of nodules behind sternum and larynx.

Frozen section: if histology alters operation, e.g. follicular carcinoma.

Consent should include:

Nerve damage: recurrent laryngeal → hoarseness. May need Teflon injections.

External laryngeal → weak voice, only a problem for singers.

Post-operative oral thyroxine for life if total thyroidectomy (and a risk in subtotal).

Others: bleeding, thyroid crisis, recurrent thyrotoxicosis, hypocalcaemia, scar, abandoning tumour if inoperable.

Positioning: supine, head up, head-ring, prep. from lower lip to nipples.

Incision: transverse 2 cm above suprasternal notch in existing skin crease beyond medial border of sternocleidomastoid.

Procedure

1. Elevate upper flap (with platysma) as far as upper thyroid cartilage and lower flap as far as the sternal notch.
2. Vertical midline incision between strap muscles through pretracheal fascia. Mobilise thyroid identifying important structures:
3. Superior thyroid artery and vein (transfix and ligate as the upper pedicle NEAR TO THE GLAND avoiding external laryngeal nerve).
4. Recurrent laryngeal nerve must be identified in the tracheo-oesophageal groove (more laterally on the right).
5. Middle thyroid vein ligated and divided entering internal jugular.
6. Inferior thyroid artery – beware as it crosses the recurrent laryngeal nerve just over the parathyroids – ligate the artery in continuity laterally FAR FROM THE GLAND to avoid nerve damage. Traditionally by now many take branches on the gland avoiding recurrent laryngeal nerve and preserving parathyroid blood supply.
7. Ligate lower thyroid vein to free lower pedicle.

For subtotal thyroidectomy: mobilise other lobe and isthmus, cut through thyroid leaving lateral sliver in front of parathyroids and recurrent laryngeal nerve. Suture thyroid remnants to trachea.

For total lobectomy: identify and preserve recurrent laryngeal and parathyroids and dissect the thyroid free from these structures. Dissect isthmus from trachea and take the isthmus with the lobe, or subcuticular suture. Divide while oversewing and suturing cut end of isthmus to the trachea.

Closure: suction drains, approximate strap muscles, close skin with Michelle clips.

Post-operative: nurse semi-sitting for 24 hours to decrease venous pressure. Beware expanding haematoma. Check serum calcium daily for 2 days. Drains out after 24 hours. Alternate clips out day 3, final clips out day 4.

Complications of thyroid surgery:

Bleeding from	Torn middle thyroid vein
	Dissection in wrong plane
	Slipped tie on superior pedicle (always doubly ligate)
Nerve injury	Recurrent laryngeal → hoarseness
	External laryngeal → weak voice – problem for teachers who need to shout
Retrosternal goitre	Rarely needs sternotomy
Anaplastic tumour	Biopsy, decompress and close
Hypocalcaemia	+/– tetany / carpopedal spasm
Recurrent thyrotoxicosis	Radioactive iodine or medical treatment may be sufficient
Hypothyroidism	Need thyroxine for life

THYROID NODULE

◉ THYROID SURGERY PROCEDURE

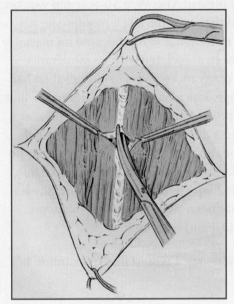

1. Division of pretracheal fascia

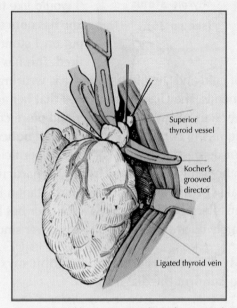

Superior thyroid vessel

Kocher's grooved director

Ligated thyroid vein

2. Transfix and ligate superior thyroid artery and vein as upper pedicle

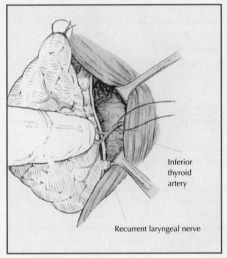

Inferior thyroid artery

Recurrent laryngeal nerve

3. Ligating thyroid artery away from recurrent laryngeal nerve

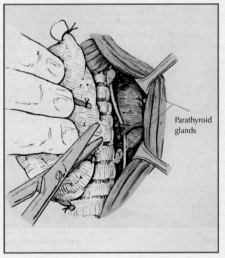

Parathyroid glands

4. Total lobectomy

85

Take a history from this patient. Her GP thinks she may have an alteration in her thyroid status

(see pg 36)

HYPOTHYROIDISM/ MYXOEDEMA

'I would like to present Miss W, a 50-year-old woman. She has noticed that over the last 6 months she has put on 1 stone in weight and has become increasingly tired. This has been associated with an intolerance of cold and she often finds she is wearing many more layers of clothes than her friends. They have commented that her appearance has altered, particularly that her hair seems drier, thinner and more coarse. On direct questioning she also admits to constipation. She has not noticed a neck lump. She is being treated for depression by her GP and has pernicious anaemia but other than this has no other previous medical history, in particular none relating to her thyroid. She takes an antidepressant and has vitamin B12 injections every 3 months. She has no allergies. She works as a solicitor but has been struggling to get into work lately due to tiredness. She has never smoked and is teetotal.

My diagnosis is primary idiopathic myxoedema. I would like to examine her to confirm the diagnosis.'

✍ WHAT YOU SHOULD KNOW

[108] Thickened coarse facial features, periorbital puffiness and pallor.

[109] A Hashimoto's goitre is symmetrical, firm and finely micronodular.

[110] Evidence of previous Graves' disease suggests previous surgery (scar often difficult to see) or radioactive iodine treatment which has resulted in hypothyroidism.

[111] **Causes of hypothyroidism**

1. Iatrogenic (90%) due to previous total or subtotal thyroidectomy, radioactive iodine treatment for hyperthyroidism or exogenous irradiation for nearby neoplasm (e.g. lymphoma). No goitre but may have scar from surgery or signs of previous Graves' disease.

2. Primary idiopathic myxoedema usually autoimmune associated with other autoimmune diseases such as pernicious anaemia. TSH-blocking autoantibodies so serum TSH is high but T4 is low. More common in women. No goitre.

3. Hashimoto's disease autoimmune disease – cytotoxic Tc cells and antibody action on follicular cells. Firm symmetrical enlarged goitre.

Associated autoimmune diseases:

Pernicious anaemia, Addison's disease, rheumatoid arthritis, Sjögren syndrome, ulcerative colitis, lupoid hepatitis, systemic lupus erythematosus, haemolytic anaemia, diabetes mellitus, Graves' disease, hypoparathyroidism.

Treatment of hypothyroidism

Oral thyroxine for life.

[112] See pg 36, History of thyroid status for list of questions.

[113] Should be slow-relaxing (see pg 51, Examination of thyroid status).

Examine this patient's thyroid status

(see pg 50)

HYPOTHYROIDISM/ MYXOEDEMA

'On initial inspection the patient (who is a middle-aged lady) is overweight with myxoedematous facies.[108] The hands are dry, cool and pale, with rough, inelastic skin and non-pitting puffiness. She has/denies symptoms of carpal tunnel syndrome. She is/is not bradycardic. On inspection of the face there is thinning, dry, brittle hair, loss of the outer third of the eyebrows and a yellowish complexion. There is/is no evidence of a goitre[109] or any evidence of previous Graves' disease such as exophthalmos.[110] The diagnosis is myxoedema.[111] I would like to ask her some questions[112] and check her reflexes.'[113]

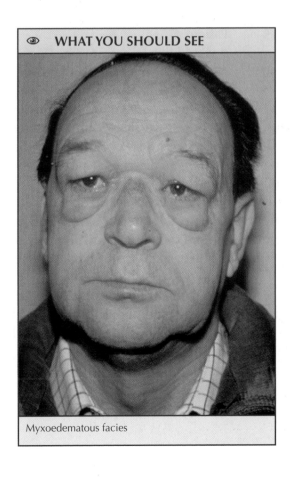

👁 **WHAT YOU SHOULD SEE**

Myxoedematous facies

THYROTOXICOSIS
AND GRAVES' DISEASE

Bear in mind the patient could be:

- **Patient A** – thyrotoxic without Graves' disease
- **Patient B** – thyrotoxic with Graves' disease
- **Patient C** – euthyroid (due to surgery or treatment) with residual signs of Graves' disease
- **Patient D** – hypothyroid (due to surgery or treatment) with residual signs of Graves' disease

Take a history from this patient. Her GP thinks she may have an alteration in her thyroid status

(see pg 36)

THYROTOXICOSIS

Patient A

'I would like to present Mrs W, a 50-year-old woman. She has noticed that over the last 6 months she has lost 1 stone in weight despite a marked increase in her appetite and has become increasingly restless. This has been associated with an intolerance of heat and she often finds she is wearing fewer layers of clothes than her friends. On direct questioning she also admits to diarrhoea, a tremor and palpitations. She has/has not noticed a neck lump and has had no problems with her eyes. She has no medical history/she has had an operation on her thyroid for similar problems in the past. She takes no medication and has no allergies. She works as a secretary (but has found this difficult lately due to the tremor) and lives with her husband. She has never smoked and is teetotal.

This patient appears thyrotoxic but has no signs of Graves' disease. The presence of a goitre suggests toxic multinodular goitre/the absence of a goitre suggests a solitary toxic adenoma/the evidence of previous thyroid surgery suggests a recurrent toxic multinodular goitre.'

THYROTOXICOSIS

Examine this patient's thyroid status

(see pg 50)

Patient A
'On initial inspection this (middle-aged female) patient is thin and restless, with a visible tremor. The hands are warm and sweaty with thyroid acropachy[114] and there is an irregular pulse.

There is no exophthalmos, lid retraction or signs of corneal irritation. The lid lag test is positive. There is[115]/is no[116] sign of a goitre or a scar in the neck. This patient appears thyrotoxic but has no signs of Graves' disease. The presence of a goitre suggests toxic multinodular goitre/ the absence of a goitre suggests a solitary toxic adenoma/the evidence of previous thyroid surgery suggests recurrent toxic multinodular goitre.'

✏ WHAT YOU SHOULD KNOW

Causes of hyperthyroidism (5% of all women)
1. Graves' disease (an autoimmune disease caused by stimulation of TSH receptors by autoantibodies which also cross-react with eye muscle and skin antigens. Commoner in women and associated with other autoimmune diseases such as diabetes and pernicious anaemia. The hyperthyroidism can be corrected in the usual way but the eye signs usually persist).
2. Toxic multinodular goitre (multinodular focal hyperplasia). Less than half are thyrotoxic. Usually moderate thyrotoxicosis.
3. Toxic solitary adenomas (benign, solitary, discrete encapsulated nodules. Usually non-functioning but can cause mild hyperthyroidism).
The above three disorders account for 99% of cases. Rarer causes of hyperthyroidism includes thyroiditis, carcinoma, choriocarcinoma, hydatidiform mole, teratomas, pituitary adenoma (TSH-secreting), neonatal thyrotoxicosis (associated with maternal Graves'), iatrogenic (iodide- or thyroxine-induced).

Treatment of hyperthyroidism
Anti-thyroid drugs such as carbimazole.
Surgery: for malignancy, pressure or cosmesis; 10% become hypothyroid, 5% have recurrent hyperthyroidism.
Radioactive iodine: almost always results in hypothyroidism.
[114] Thyroid acropachy resembles finger clubbing. New bone formation appears on X-ray as 'soap bubbles' on the bone surface with coarse spicules. Sometimes the new bone formation in acropachy is both visible and palpable along the phalanges.
[115] In the case of a toxic multinodular goitre.
[116] In the case of a toxic solitary adenoma/nodule (rarer).

👁 WHAT YOU SHOULD SEE

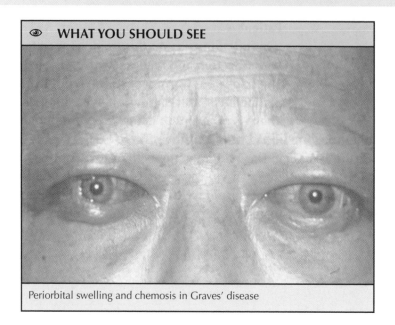

Periorbital swelling and chemosis in Graves' disease

👁 WHAT YOU SHOULD SEE

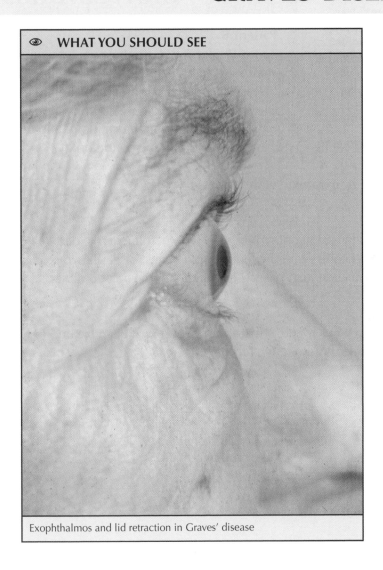

Exophthalmos and lid retraction in Graves' disease

Take a history from this patient. Her GP thinks she may have an alteration in her thyroid status

(see pg 36)

GRAVES' DISEASE

Patient B
As for Patient A but usually a young woman with symptoms of hyperthyroidism and features of Graves' disease, including symptoms relating to Graves' eye disease, e.g. chemosis, ophthalmoplegia and diplopia[117] and a small neck lump. She may have a previous medical history of another autoimmune condition.

'This patient is thyrotoxic with Graves' disease.'

Patients C/D
Clinically euthyroid/hypothyroid (see Hypothyroidism/myxoedema case, pg 86 for symptoms) with the features of Graves' disease (symptoms relating to Graves' eye disease, e.g. chemosis, ophthalmoplegia and diplopia and a small neck lump).

'She has a previous medical history of hyperthyroidism treated in the past by thyroidectomy or radioactive iodine.'

⟳ WHAT YOU SHOULD KNOW

[117] Graves' exophthalmos is due to cross-reaction of autoimmune anti-thyroid antibodies with intra-orbital muscles. The proptosis (bulging eyes or exophthalmos) is due to increased retro-orbital fat and enlarged intraorbital muscles infiltrated with lymphocytes and containing increased water and mucopolysaccharide. It may develop in the absence of hyperthyroidism and remit, persist or develop further despite successful treatment of hyperthyroidism. Complications of exophthalmos include chemosis, ophthalmoplegia and diplopia.
[118] Pretibial myxoedema tends to develop after the hyperthyroidism has been treated, especially with radioactive iodine.

Examine this patient's thyroid status

(see pg 50)

GRAVES' DISEASE

Patient B

As for Patient A but with the features of Graves' disease, including exophthalmos[117], pretibial myxoedema[118], and a small diffuse goitre with a bruit.

'This patient is thyrotoxic with Graves' disease.'

Patients C/D

The features of Graves' disease (exophthalmos, pretibial myxoedema +/– goitre or scar of thyroid surgery) in a clinically euthyroid patient.

'This patient has Graves' disease and is clinically euthyroid/hypothyroid. It is likely that she has had hyperthyroidism treated in the past, either by thyroidectomy or radioactive iodine (look for scar).'

Take a history from this patient with a neck lump

(see pg 33)

THYROGLOSSAL CYST

'I would like to present Miss W, a 20-year-old woman. She noticed a lump in the midline of her neck 2 months ago.[119] Initially it was non-tender, but over the last week it has become painful and larger and the overlying skin has become erythematous. She has no symptoms of local pressure from the lump and no symptoms of hyper- or hypothyroidism. On direct questioning she has noticed that the lump elevates on protruding her tongue. She does not like the cosmetic appearance. She has no significant previous medical history, is on no medication and has no allergies. She is a sociology student who has never smoked but does drink approximately 30 units of alcohol a week.

This woman has a thyroglossal cyst that has become infected in the last week. I would like to examine her to confirm the diagnosis.'

✎ WHAT YOU SHOULD KNOW

[119] They can in fact lie anywhere from the chin (suprahyoid) to the second tracheal ring (pretracheal). The cyst can slip to one or other side of the midline, especially if it develops in front of the thyroid cartilage.
[120] Varies from 0.5 to 5 cm in diameter.
[121] Some cysts are too tense or too small to fluctuate but most do.
[122] The contents of the cyst are usually opaque because of desquamated epithelial cells, they may transilluminate if large.
[123] The thyroglossal duct is always closely related, and usually fixed, to the hyoid bone. When the hyoid bone moves the cyst also moves. The hyoid bone moves when the tongue is protruded. This is occasionally evident on observation (and is part of the inspection of the neck examination pg 45 which you should have performed on examining this lump) but more commonly can be felt as a tugging sensation during palpation. Ask the patient to open her mouth and keep her lower jaw still. Hold the cyst with your thumb and forefinger. Ask the patient to stick her tongue out. If the cyst is fixed to the hyoid bone you will feel it tugged upwards as the tongue goes out. This sign is absent with many thyroglossal cysts, however, especially those below the level of the thyroid cartilage.
[124] The overlying skin is usually normal.
[125] The overlying skin is inflamed if infected.
[126] A thyroglossal **sinus** is an acquired sinus which arises following rupture or surgery for a thyroglossal cyst. Unlike branchial fistulae these are never true fistulae, as they do not connect to the mouth. The physical signs include a sinus opening, usually in the midline, +/– a previous scar, often surrounded by a crescentic skin fold. The cyst may or may not be palpable.
[127] Whenever there is an abnormality of thyroid gland development, examine the base of the tongue for ectopic (lingual) thyroid tissue, which looks like a flattened strawberry sitting on the base of the tongue. This is rare, but it may be the only thyroid tissue present if seen, so an USS neck to look for a normal thyroid is recommended.
CONTINUED on pg 96

Examine this patient's neck lump

(see pg 45)

THYROGLOSSAL CYST

'There is (in this young person) a non-tender lump in the midline of the neck at the level of the thyroid cartilage.[119] It is 2 cm in diameter[120], spherical and smooth with well-defined edges. It is firm but fluctuates[121] and does not transilluminate[122]. It is not pulsatile, compressible or reducible. It is tethered to deep structures, and can be moved sideways but not up and down. It moves on extending the tongue, suggesting attachment to the hyoid bone.[123] The overlying skin is normal[124]/inflamed[125]/shows signs of a sinus[126] and the surrounding skin is normal. The regional lymph nodes are not enlarged. The base of the tongue shows no ectopic thyroid tissue.[127] This is a thyroglossal cyst.'

👁 WHAT YOU SHOULD SEE

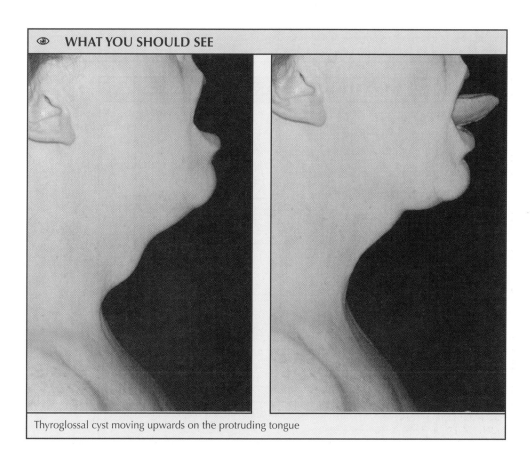

Thyroglossal cyst moving upwards on the protruding tongue

✐ WHAT YOU SHOULD KNOW (CONT)

Definition: a portion of the thyroglossal duct which remains patent.

Embryology: the **thyroglossal duct/tract** is the (normally obliterated) remnant that marks the developmental descent of the thyroid gland. The thyroid appears as a midline diverticulum at the fourth week of gestation and descends ventrally from what will become the foramen caecum of the posterior third of the tongue down between the second branchial arches (see diagram showing descent of thyroid during development). The **thyroglossal cyst** is a dilatation along the thyroglossal duct, the rest of which may or may not be obliterated.

Histology: lined with stratified squamous epithelium or ciliated pseudostratified epithelium. May have thyroid or lymphoid tissue in the wall (site of ectopic thyroid which may develop a malignancy – usually papillary carcinoma).

History: they can appear at any age but generally between 15 and 30, more often in women. They are usually a painless lump, but can become painful, tender and enlarged if infected. They are removed for cosmetic reasons, discomfort or the risk of infection.

Differential diagnoses: congenital dermoid cyst, sebaceous cyst, enlarged lymph node, subhyoid bursa, pyramidal lobe of thyroid, thyroid nodule.

Complications: infection, thyroglossal sinus, malignancy (papillary thyroid cancer).

Treatment: surgical excision. Pre-operative assessment: ultrasound to confirm diagnosis and define a patent thyroglossal duct passing superiorly. Confirm normal thyroid function pre-operatively.

Surgical procedure: transverse incision over cyst, dissect cyst out, look for downward tract (rare) and excise it, then follow main tract upwards to hyoid bone. Excise middle third of hyoid bone and excise rest of duct to its apex in continuity. Beware damage to thyrohyoid membrane and entering mouth via mucosa of foramen caecum (risk of infection, must close defect with absorbable sutures). Post-op. complications: haematoma, infection, recurrence.

✐ WHAT YOU SHOULD KNOW

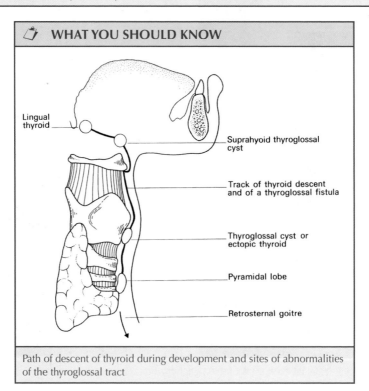

Lingual thyroid

Suprahyoid thyroglossal cyst

Track of thyroid descent and of a thyroglossal fistula

Thyroglossal cyst or ectopic thyroid

Pyramidal lobe

Retrosternal goitre

Path of descent of thyroid during development and sites of abnormalities of the thyroglossal tract

THYROGLOSSAL CYST

👁 WHAT YOU SHOULD SEE

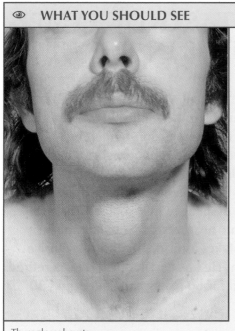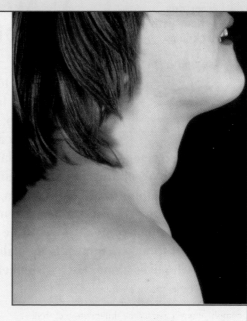

Thyroglossal cysts

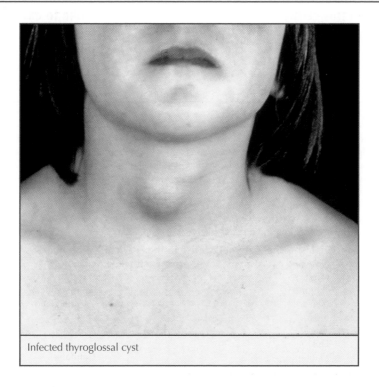

Infected thyroglossal cyst

Take a history from this patient with a neck lump

(see pg 33)

A: METASTATIC LYMPH NODE/S IN THE NECK

'I would like to present Mr W, a 70-year-old man. He noticed a lump on the right side of his neck 2 months ago. The lump is non-tender, but he has also noticed an ulcer on the right side of his tongue, which is tender. He also complains of otalgia. He has lost weight as he has noticed his clothes are looser but he is unable to quantify how much. He has no symptoms of abdominal pain, dysphagia, hoarseness, stridor or cough. He has hypertension and ischaemic heart disease and has angina attacks approximately twice a week. He takes aspirin, an antihypertensive and his GTN spray when he gets the pain. He has no allergies. He is a retired publican who lives alone. He has smoked for 60 pack years and drinks 30 units a week.

It would be important to exclude metastatic lymphadenopathy from a tongue carcinoma in this gentleman.[128] Therefore, next I would like to examine his neck and buccal cavity.'

⌂ WHAT YOU SHOULD KNOW

The commonest causes for cervical lymphadenopathy are **metastatic deposits** (in adults), **Hodgkin's and non-Hodgkin's lymphoma** in children and young adults and **tuberculous lymphadenitis** in young immigrant adults. Reactive lymphadenopathy secondary to **infection** (e.g. URTI, tonsillitis, glandular fever, toxoplasmosis) is also common, especially in babies, children and young adults. **Sarcoidosis** is another cause.

[128] **Metastatic deposits** of cancer cells in the cervical lymph nodes are the commonest cause of cervical lymphadenopathy in adults. The possible sites of primary cancer are legion (see below) but are most often in the buccal cavity (tongue, lips and mucous membranes) and larynx.

Sites of primary neoplasms that can metastasise to the cervical lymph nodes:

Head:	Nose and nasopharynx	Arms and trunk:	Glands:
Scalp	**Mouth:**	Arms	Parotid
Face	Tongue	Chest wall	Submandibular
Ears	Gums	Breast	Thyroid gland
Neck	Mucosa	Lung	
	Tonsils		**Abdomen**
	Lips		
	Mandible		**Genitalia**

Examine this
patient's neck
lump

(see pg 45)

A: METASTATIC LYMPH NODE/S IN THE NECK

'There are (in this middle-aged/elderly man) a group of non-tender swellings at the anterior border of the sternocleidomastoid on the right side of the neck.[129] The lumps are matted together, and form an irregular-shaped mass around 5 × 2 centimetres, with the long axis running down with the muscle. Some of the lumps are smooth and discrete, but the main mass is lobulated and craggy with indistinct edges. They are stony-hard, not fluctuant, pulsatile, compressible, reducible or transilluminable. They are fixed to deep structures but not to the skin, which moves over the lumps.[130] They can be moved slightly in a transverse direction but not vertically.

This is a group of enlarged lymph nodes and I would want to exclude metastatic disease.[131] Other lymph nodes in the neck (say which) are also enlarged/not enlarged. If I saw this patient in clinic I would like to ask him some questions, examine him for a primary lesion and arrange some urgent investigations[132] which would include a full ENT examination.'

📝 **WHAT YOU SHOULD KNOW (CONT)**

[129] Lesions above the hyoid tend to drain to the upper deep cervical nodes (see diagram of neck nodes, pg 101). The larynx and thyroid tend to drain to the middle and deep cervical nodes. An enlarged supraclavicular node commonly indicates intra-abdominal or thoracic disease (Virchow's node, Troisier's sign).

[130] In later stages tumour can invade the overlying structures and become tethered to the skin.

[131] Be careful how you say you think it is malignancy in front of the patient. It is insensitive even if you are right, and can be terrifyingly misleading for the patient if you are wrong. One way to say this is, 'It is important to exclude a malignancy', which has the advantage of sounding professional, not being scary and hedging your bets!

CONTINUED on pg 100

☞ WHAT YOU SHOULD KNOW (CONT)

[132] **What you need to do before you can biopsy a lymph node in the neck**

History: most head and neck cancers occur in patients aged over 50 years. Symptoms depend on the primary, e.g. sore ulcer on tongue, hoarse voice, weight loss, cough, dyspepsia, abdominal pain. Most commonly patients are asymptomatic and present with a painless, steadily enlarging lump in the neck. Ask if they are smokers.

Examination of the head, scalp, face, ears, neck. Look in the nose. Look in the mouth at the tongue, gums, mucosa and tonsils. Palpate the parotid, submandibular and thyroid glands. Examine the arms and chest wall, especially the breasts. Examine the abdomen and genitalia.

Investigations: full ENT examination under general anaesthetic, including air sinuses, oropharynx, nasopharynx and buccal cavity. Chest X-ray (or CT if worrying signs or symptoms).

Principles of management of an enlarged neck node: If primary found, en bloc dissection or other appropriate treatment usually advised by relevant specialist. If no primary found, excision biopsy of the lymph node must be performed to confirm benign nature of the node. If a biopsy of a lymph node is carried out without a full exclusion of a head and neck tumour, curative en bloc resection may be compromised if the node is found to be metastatic.

◉ WHAT YOU SHOULD SEE

The patient presented with hard enlarged lymph glands in the neck. The primary lesion was the insignificant-looking mole above his right eyebrow

LYMPH NODE/S IN THE NECK

✎ WHAT YOU SHOULD KNOW

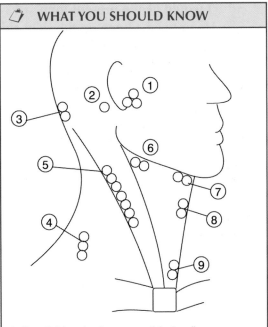

1. Parotid (scalp, face, parotid gland)
2. Mastoid (scalp, auricle)
3. Occipital (scalp)
4. Superficial cervical (along external jugular vein)
   (breast, lung, viscera, face, parotid)
5. Deep cervical (along internal jugular vein)
   (all neck nodes ultimately drain to here)
6. Submandibular (tongue)
7. Submental (antrum and floor of mouth, lips)
8. Anterior cervical (oesophagus, front of neck)
9. Tracheal (thyroid)

Lymph nodes of the head and neck

Take a history from this patient with a neck lump

(see pg 33)

B: LYMPHOMA

'I would like to present John, a 15-year-old boy. He noticed a lump on the right side of his neck 2 months ago, which is non-tender. He also complains of general malaise and aching joints, together with night sweats. He has lost 1 stone in weight over the last month.[136] He is asthmatic but has never required hospitalisation for this. He only takes a salbutamol inhaler as he needs it. He is allergic to penicillin and says the reaction he got after taking it was facial swelling. He is at school, in the first year of his GCSEs. He does not smoke or drink alcohol. He lives with his mother and father.

It would be important to exclude lymphoma as a cause for this young man's cervical lymphadenopathy, but a differential diagnosis would include infective lymph nodes. Next, I would like to examine his neck.'

✏ WHAT YOU SHOULD KNOW

Lymphoma (Hodgkin's and non-Hodgkin's) is a huge topic worthy of a textbook in itself. If it appears in a surgical history/examination the main aims will be a thorough history/examination of the neck (see pgs 33 and 45), identifying the features of a neck lump caused by a primary neoplasm of the lymph nodes (see pg 98) and understanding of the principles of managing any suspected enlarged lymph node in the neck (see pg 100, Metastatic lymph node).

[133] Any of the cervical lymph nodes can be affected. Lymphoma is one of the few conditions apart from infection that often causes lymphadenopathy in the posterior triangle.

[134] The nodes can be enlarged to any size.

[135] In Hodgkin's disease the lymph nodes remain separate and distinct, even when enlarged, unlike tuberculous nodes, which quickly become matted together and indistinct.

[136] History: children and young adults, males more than females, will present most commonly with a painless lump in the neck. Associated symptoms include malaise, weight loss, pallor, night sweats, aching bones and pruritus.

[137] If asked 'Would you biopsy this lesion?', remember the principles of managing any lump in the neck (see Metastatic neck lump pg 98). A primary source of malignancy must be excluded before en bloc dissection is compromised by biopsy unless other evidence of lymphoma (e.g. on blood tests, chest X-ray or CT) is found.

B: LYMPHOMA

Examine this patient's neck lump

(see pg 45)

'There is (in this young adult) a non-tender lump in the posterior triangle of the right side of the neck.[133] It is 3 cm in diameter[134] ovoid, smooth with discrete edges.[135] It is firm and rubbery, not fluctuant, pulsatile, compressible, reducible or transilluminable. It arises deep to the skin and the skin moves easily over it. Although not fixed (the lump can be moved from side to side), it is tethered to nearby structures. The overlying and surrounding skin is normal. The surrounding lymph nodes are not/are (say which ones) also enlarged. This is an enlarged lymph node. In a patient of this age it would be important to exclude a primary lymphatic malignancy. In the clinical setting I would take a full history[136], perform a general examination, looking especially at the liver, spleen, lymphadenopathy in the axillae or groins, and request a full blood count and chest X-ray in the first instance.'[137]

👁 WHAT YOU SHOULD SEE

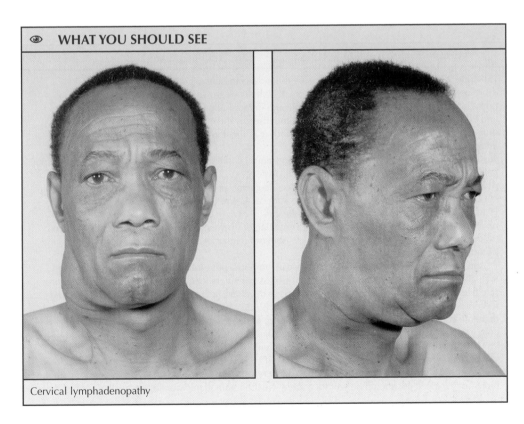

Cervical lymphadenopathy

Take a history from this patient with a neck lump

(see pg 33)

C: TUBERCULOUS LYMPHADENOPATHY

'I would like to present Mahmoud, a 15-year-old boy. He noticed a lump on the right side of his neck 2 months ago, which is non-tender. He also complains of general malaise and night sweats. He has lost his appetite and has lost 1 stone in weight over the last 2 months. He has no history of cough. Of note he has recently moved to the UK from India/Pakistan and has a positive family history of TB in his mother and sister. He is asthmatic but has never required hospitalisation for this. He only takes a salbutamol inhaler as he needs it. He is allergic to penicillin and says the reaction he got after taking it was facial swelling. He is at school in the first year of his GCSEs. He does not smoke or drink alcohol. He lives with his mother, father and sister.

I think this young man is most likely to have tuberculous lymphadenopathy, but an important differential diagnosis would be lymphoma. Next, I would like to examine his neck.'

WHAT YOU SHOULD KNOW

The upper deep cervical nodes of the neck are the most commonly affected.

TB is less common in the UK because most people who have grown up here have been immunised. Immigrants from countries where TB is endemic and immunisation not widespread such as India and Pakistan commonly present in Britain with the disease. There is also a resurgence of TB, often drug-resistant, in adults from deprived backgrounds (e.g. the homeless, drug addicts) and in the immunocompromised (e.g. HIV patients).

History: anorexia, weight loss (systemic symptoms unusual in the young), respiratory symptoms, previous history of TB, immunisation, family history, social history.

Atypical mycobacterial lymphadenitis usually cervicofacial, affecting children. The children it affects are not usually immunocompromised. Treatment is surgical as it responds very poorly to antibiotics.

[138] In the early stages the nodes are firm, discrete and 1–2 cm in diameter. As caseation increases the nodes necrose, coalesce, become matted and grow larger. The deep cervical chain is usually involved (so the lumps lie along the line of the sternocleidomastoid muscle) and the mass can become very large, distorting the neck.

[139] A mass of tuberculous lymph nodes can caseate, turn into pus and become a **tuberculous abscess** that, although not typically warm, may make the mass painful, tender and fluctuant, with the overlying skin becoming discoloured. If a tuberculous abscess develops, tachycardia, anorexia, weight loss and fever may be clinical features. A collar-stud abscess is one which has burst through the deep fascia and therefore consists of two collections of pus, one deep and one superficial, the contents of which can be compressed one into the other through a narrow connection.

[140] Once again, the principles of management of an enlarged lymph node in the neck (see pg 100) should be followed, with a biopsy only undertaken if TB is diagnosed by some other means or a primary malignancy which might have metastasised to the cervical glands is excluded. When it is performed, the biopsy or aspirated pus should be sent for a Ziehl–Neelsen stain to microbiology as well as for histology.

Examine this patient's neck lump

(see pg 45)

C: TUBERCULOUS LYMPHADENOPATHY

'There is (in this patient of any age, perhaps from India or Pakistan) a large lump along the upper half of the anterior border of the right sternocleidomastoid. The whole irregular-shaped swelling measures about 7 × 3 cm, with the long axis extending along the line of the sternocleidomastoid muscle.[138] It is an indistinct, firm mass consisting of several discrete, smooth lumps that seem to be matted together in the centre. It is not fluctuant, pulsatile, compressible, reducible or transilluminable. It arises deep to the skin, which moves easily over it, and is tethered to the deep structures. It moves slightly from side to side but not vertically and appears to arise deep to the muscle. The overlying skin is normal[139] and there are no/are (say where) other enlarged lymph nodes nearby. These are enlarged lymph nodes, and I would be keen to exclude tuberculosis.'[140]

👁 WHAT YOU SHOULD SEE

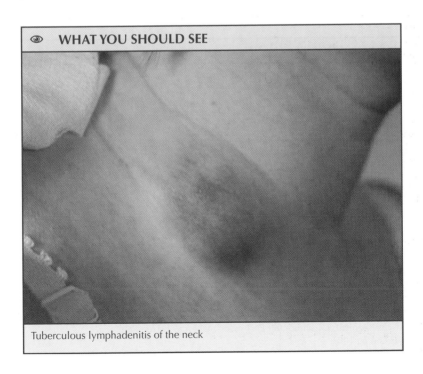

Tuberculous lymphadenitis of the neck

105

Take a history
from this
patient with a
neck lump

(see pg 33)

BRANCHIAL CYST

'I would like to present Mr W, an 18-year-old young man. He noticed a lump on the right side of his neck 2 months ago, which is non-tender. He has no associated symptoms. He has no previous medical history, takes no regular medication and has no known allergies. He is studying history at the local university. He lives in halls of residence. He has smoked for 2 pack years and drinks 21 units of alcohol per week.

I think this young man is most likely to have a branchial cyst but my differential diagnosis would include lymphadenopathy (lymphoma or tuberculous). Next, I would like to examine his neck to confirm my diagnosis.'

✐ WHAT YOU SHOULD KNOW

[141] Most branchial cysts are 5–10 cm in diameter.

[142] Most cysts are hard, but a lax cyst feels soft.

[143] This sign is difficult to elicit in the neck, especially if the cyst is small and the sternocleidomastoid muscle is thick.

[144] The contents of the cyst are usually opaque because of desquamated epithelial cells but if large and filled with fat globules and cholesterol crystals secreted by the lining sebaceous glands the cyst may transilluminate.

[145] Which differentiates it from a carotid body tumour (see pg 112) which is also situated slightly lower in the neck than a branchial cyst.

[146] From which it arises (not a sign of malignancy).

[147] Depending on whether it is infected or not.

[148] Examine carefully for evidence of an external communication, which appears as a dimple along the anterior border of the sternocleidomastoid low down in the neck.

[149] If the surrounding lymph glands are enlarged, reconsider your diagnosis in favour of a tuberculous abscess (see pg 104).

[150] **Differential diagnoses**: malignant cervical lymph node (pg 98, not fluctuant unless cystic degeneration has occurred), pharyngeal pouch (pg 110, older patient, different history), carotid body tumour (pg 112, pulsatile, lower in neck), parotid lump (pg 118, branchial remnants can occur here and require parotidectomy for their removal).

Pre-operative assessment: CT and/or full ENT assessment may be required.

CONTINUED on pg 108

Examine this patient's neck lump

(see pg 45)

BRANCHIAL CYST

'There is (in this young or middle-aged patient) a non-tender swelling arising from the anterior edge of the upper third of the right sternocleidomastoid muscle, bulging forwards. It is ovoid, with its long axis running forwards and downwards, about 8 cm × 5 cm in size.[141] It has a smooth surface with distinct edges and is hard/soft[142] and fluctuant[143]. It does not transilluminate.[144] It is dull to percussion, is not pulsatile[145], compressible or reducible. The bulk of the mass is deep to the sternocleidomastoid muscle and it is fixed to the deep structures.[146] The overlying skin is normal/red and inflamed.[147] The surrounding skin is normal with no signs of external sinus openings lower in the neck[148] and the draining lymph nodes are not enlarged.[149] This is a branchial cyst, but I would like to order some investigations to exclude my differential diagnoses.'[150]

👁 WHAT YOU SHOULD SEE

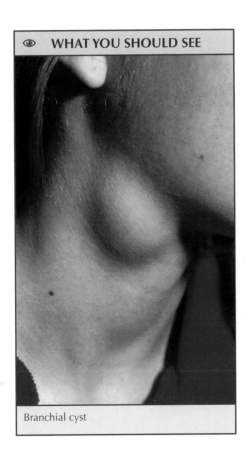

Branchial cyst

✎ WHAT YOU SHOULD KNOW (CONT)

Definition: a remnant of a branchial cleft – usually the second. Branchial cysts are rare; branchial sinuses are common.

Development: second branchial arch grows down to cover the remaining arches. It leaves a temporary space lined with squamous epithelium. Usually disappears but can persist and distend with cholesterol-containing fluid.

History: present at birth but do not distend and cause symptoms until adult life. The majority present between 15 and 25 years but may present in early middle age. It affects males and females equally. It is a painless swelling at the anterior border of the sternocleidomastoid muscle. It may become painful and swollen if it becomes infected.

Histology: lined with squamous epithelium but there are patches of lymphoid tissue in the wall, which are connected with the other lymph tissue in the neck and which can become infected.

Complications: infection causes pain and swelling. A **branchial fistula** is a variation of the branchial cyst which occurs if fusion fails to occur distally, leading to a persistent sinus which appears as a small dimple in the skin intermittently discharging clear mucus (or pus if infected). This external opening is situated at the junction of the middle and lower thirds of the sternocleidomastoid, or even lower at the suprasternal notch. If the upper end of the branchial tract is obliterated, this is a **branchial sinus**. If the whole branchial cleft has stayed patent, this is a true branchial fistula, connecting the skin with the oropharynx just behind the tonsil. Swallowing accentuates the openings on the skin.

Treatment: surgical excision. If not excised a branchial sinus or fistula will invariably become infected.

Pre-operatively: exclude differential diagnoses (see pg 106), treat an acutely inflamed or infected lesion with antibiotics and electively excise it when it has settled. Incision and drainage may be necessary, but subsequent surgery is made more difficult. Examine carefully for an external opening low in the neck suggesting a branchial sinus or fistula (see above). This may be tiny and is usually along the anterior border of the sternocleidomastoid muscle.

Operative technique and hazards: transverse incision over cyst (or elliptical incision around external opening if a sinus), expose cyst, free from carotid sheath and continue dissection cranially until the upper limit or oropharyngeal opening. Beware the mandibular branch of the facial nerve, hypoglossal nerve, accessory nerve, carotid sheath. Try not to rupture cyst. Complications include recurrence if inadequately excised, wound haematoma and infection, nerve palsies.

Pre-auricular sinus: remnant of the first arch, most commonly seen as a tiny pit in front of the ear.

BRANCHIAL CYST

👁 WHAT YOU SHOULD SEE

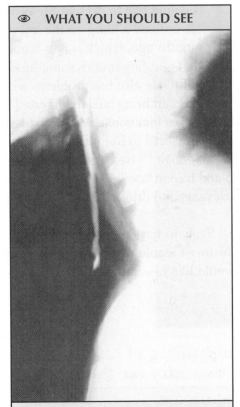

Sinogram showing contrast material that has been injected through an opening on the skin surface. The fact that the contrast fails to empty into the tonsillar fossa suggests that this is a sinus and not a fistula

Take a history
from this
patient with a
neck lump

(see pg 33)

PHARYNGEAL POUCH

'I would like to present Mr W, a 50-year-old man. He noticed a lump on the left side of his neck 6 months ago, which is non-tender.[165] He has noticed that gurgling sounds sometimes come from the lump. He also has problems with regurgitation and can bring back undigested food at any time, including at night, which makes him choke. He has had a recurrent sore throat and his wife has complained to him that he has halitosis! He has not lost any weight and has no cough.[151] He has no previous medical history, takes no regular medication and has no known allergies. He works in an office and has smoked for 20 pack years and drinks 30 units of alcohol per week.

I think this man is most likely to have a pharyngeal pouch but given his smoking and alcohol history I would need to exclude a metastatic cervical lymph node. Next, I would like to examine his neck to confirm my diagnosis.'

✐ WHAT YOU SHOULD KNOW

[151] **Definition**: a pulsion diverticulum of the pharynx through the gap between the lowermost horizontal fibres and the higher oblique fibres of the inferior constrictor muscle.

Cause: uncoordinated swallowing in which the lower sphincter-like fibres of the inferior constrictor do not relax, the weak unsupported area just above these fibres (Killian's dehiscence) bulges out. Eventually the bulge develops into a sac that hangs down (usually to the left side) and presses against the side of the oesophagus.

History: appears in middle to old age, more commonly in men. Long history of halitosis (bad breath) and recurrent sore throat. Common symptom is regurgitation of food that is undigested and comes up into the mouth at any time (no bile or acid taste). Regurgitation at night causes aspiration; nocturnal choking and coughing can lead to aspiration pneumonia and lung abscesses. It can also cause dysphagia and gurgling sounds and eventually malnutrition and weight loss.

Investigations: barium swallow. Careful endoscopy by experienced endoscopist.

Treatment is by surgical excision. Starve for at least 24 hours. Beware inhalation during induction of GA (Mendelson syndrome). NG tube (difficult but advised).

Endoscopic stapling is becoming the treatment of choice, however, and is replacing surgical excision.

[152] Most pouches are not palpable below 5 cm and rarely enlarge to be bigger than 10 cm.

[153] A pouch can occasionally be emptied manually by compression (this may cause regurgitation) and the pouch will not recur until the patient eats again (hence compressible but not reducible).

[154] A pharyngeal pouch lies deep to the deep fascia, behind the sternocleidomastoid muscle. On palpation it can be appreciated that it originates from behind the trachea and is fixed deeply (in fact to the pharynx, but this attachment cannot be felt).

[155] Look for aspiration pneumonia, collapse of a lobe or a lung abscess.

[156] The diagnostic investigation of choice.

Examine this patient's neck lump

(see pg 45)

PHARYNGEAL POUCH

'There is (in this middle-aged/elderly patient) a non-tender bulge behind the sternocleidomastoid muscle below the level of the thyroid cartilage. The lump is a deep structure with an indistinct shape and edges, but appears to be about 7 cm in diameter.[152] It has a smooth surface and is soft and compressible but not reducible.[153] It is dull to percussion, is not pulsatile and does not fluctuate or transilluminate. It arises from the deep structures in the neck, to which it is firmly attached, and cannot be moved freely.[154] The overlying and surrounding skin is normal and the regional lymph nodes are not enlarged. This is a pharyngeal pouch. I would like to see the chest X-ray[155] and barium swallow[156].'

WHAT YOU SHOULD KNOW

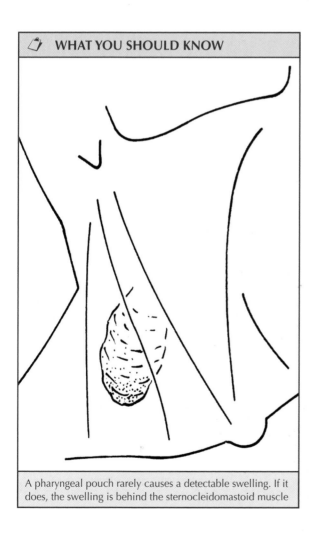

A pharyngeal pouch rarely causes a detectable swelling. If it does, the swelling is behind the sternocleidomastoid muscle

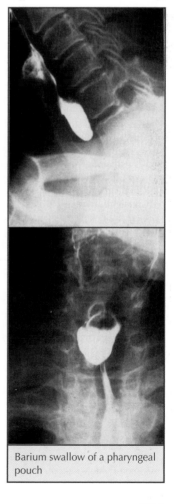

Barium swallow of a pharyngeal pouch

Take a history from this patient with a neck lump

(see pg 33)

CAROTID BODY TUMOUR

'I would like to present Mr W, a 50-year-old man. He noticed two lumps bilaterally on his neck six months ago.[157] They are non-tender and slowly enlarging. When he touches the lumps he has noticed that they have a pulse. Of note he recalls that his father had similar lumps. He has no symptoms that might suggest TIAs.[157] He has no previous medical history, takes no regular medication and has no known allergies. He works in an office and has never smoked and only drinks at New Years.

This man is likely to have bilateral carotid body tumours but with no evidence of pressure on the carotid artery causing TIAs. I would like to examine his neck to confirm my diagnosis.'

🔖 WHAT YOU SHOULD KNOW

[157] A rare tumour of the chemoreceptors of the carotid body (a chemodectoma). It is usually benign but has malignant potential (5–10% of untreated tumours develop metastases within 10 years). It is more common in high altitude areas such as Peru and Mexico.
History: a painless, slowly growing, pulsatile lump in a patient aged 40–60 years. There may be associated transient ischaemic attacks due to pressure on the carotid artery.
Investigations: carotid arteriography by catheter, needle or intravenous digital subtraction arteriography shows a splayed carotid bifurcation containing a highly vascular tumour and gives information on cerebral circulation and potential collaterals (unlike USS and CT).
Treatment: surgical excision is strongly recommended due to risk of malignant transformation and progressive enlargement, making surgery more risky. The procedure may require sacrifice of the external carotid artery and/or bypass, vein grafting or shunting of the internal carotid. Pre-operative embolisation may be used in larger tumours. Older patients may decline surgery, as there is a risk of mortality (1–2%), hemiplegia and nerve injury. Radiotherapy may be an alternative for these patients.
[158] Vary from 2 cm to 10 cm in diameter.
[159] Often called 'potato tumours'.
[160] Either transmitted pulsation by virtue of close association with the carotid bifurcation, or true expansile pulsatility due to vascularity of the tumour itself.
[161] It may indeed be compressible if it is very vascular but is more often solid.
[162] Due to attachment to the carotid sheath.
[163] In 20% of cases.
[164] A third of familial and 10% of non-familial carotid body tumours are bilateral.
[165] 30% are incorrectly diagnosed on clinical examination. If a tumour is found unexpectedly at operation, further dissection should be abandoned without a biopsy being taken.
[166] See pg 98. Only distinguishable from carotid body tumour by virtue of the relationship with the carotid arteries.
[167] See pg 106.
[168] Carotid artery aneurysms: rare; symptoms and signs include neck swelling, TIA/CVA, local pressure symptoms; rarely rupture.

Examine this patient's neck lump

(see pg 45)

CAROTID BODY TUMOUR

'There is (in this middle-aged patient) a non-tender lump in the upper part of the anterior triangle of the neck at the level of the hyoid bone on the right. It is irregular but basically round in shape, about 5 cm in diameter.[158] It is hard, solid[159], dull to percussion, non-fluctuant and non-transilluminable. It is pulsatile[160] but not compressible[161]. The skin moves over the lump freely, and the lump can be moved from side to side but not up and down.[162] The lump is deep to the cervical fascia and beneath the anterior edge of the sternocleidomastoid muscle. It does not move on swallowing or extending the tongue. The common carotid artery is palpable below the mass and the external carotid artery passes over its superficial surface. There is a bruit on auscultation.[163] There are no regional enlarged lymph nodes palpable, and there is no similar lump on the other side.[164]

This is likely to be a carotid body tumour, but my differential diagnosis[165] is an enlarged lymph node[166], a branchial cyst[167] or a carotid artery aneurysm[168].'

👁 **WHAT YOU SHOULD SEE**

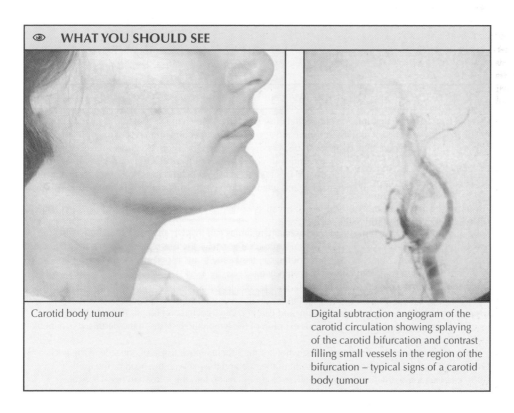

Carotid body tumour

Digital subtraction angiogram of the carotid circulation showing splaying of the carotid bifurcation and contrast filling small vessels in the region of the bifurcation – typical signs of a carotid body tumour

113

Take a history from this child (and their parent) with a neck lump

(see pg 33)

CYSTIC HYGROMA

'I would like to present Joey W, a 3-year-old boy. His mother says he has had the lump on the right side of his neck since birth and that she was initially very upset as it was so large and disfiguring. However, it does not trouble Joey and he has not had any treatment on it as yet.[169] She thinks that it may gradually be getting smaller. He has no previous medical history, takes no regular medication and has no known allergies. He lives with his older sister and mother.

This young boy has a cystic hygroma which has been present since birth. It sounds as though it may be beginning to regress.'

✎ WHAT YOU SHOULD KNOW

This is a type of **lymphangioma** – a congenital cluster of lymphatic channels that forms a lymph cyst.
[169] The majority are present at birth but some are aggravated by infection and present in adult life. The only symptom is disfigurement, which can be very distressing in a newborn. Regression by the age of 4 years is possible and therefore a watch-and-wait policy avoids surgical scarring or nerve damage. Persistence into adolescence may be treated by attempts at aspiration and injection of sclerosing agents. Surgical excision is technically demanding and often incomplete, risking collateral damage and lymph leaks.

Other types of lymphangioma
Solid or diffuse lymphangiomas and lymphohaemangiomas can involve any part of the body and are usually present at birth. Growth usually occurs at the same rate as the rest of the body, but they may be associated with local overgrowth of surrounding soft tissue and bone, especially in the face and neck. It is diffuse, difficult to excise and prone to recurrence.
Cutaneous lymphangioma presents as small, multiple, transparent or red vesicles of skin and mucosa that present at birth or in childhood. They can occur alone or with solid lymphangiomas and lymphohaemangiomas. They are disfiguring and can become infected and bleed. They are treated by local diathermy or extensive subcutaneous excision of the lymphatic cisterns in the dermis. It is difficult and recurrence is common.
[170] It can be very extensive and involve the whole of the subcutaneous tissue of one side of the neck. Lymph cysts typically occur near the junction of the arm and the leg with the head or the trunk.
[171] An examination of the oropharynx would exclude extension into the retropharyngeal space.

Examine this child's neck lump

(see pg 45)

CYSTIC HYGROMA

'There is (in this child/young person) a large non-tender mass at the base of the neck in the posterior triangle.[170] It is about 10 cm in diameter, lobulated and flattened with an indistinct surface and edges. It is soft, fluctuant and dull to percussion. Of note, it transilluminates brilliantly, emphasising its superficial nature and its clear, fluid content. It is not reducible. It arises from the subcutaneous tissues deep to the skin but is not fixed to skin, and is superficial to the underlying muscles.[171] There are no enlarged lymph nodes in the region or local lymphoedema. This is a cystic hygroma.'

◉ WHAT YOU SHOULD SEE

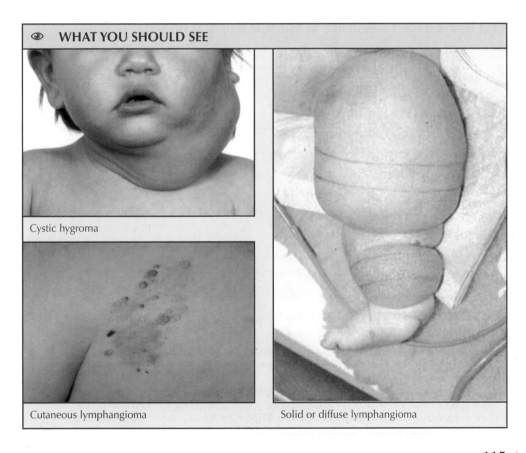

Cystic hygroma

Cutaneous lymphangioma

Solid or diffuse lymphangioma

115

Take a history from this patient with a neck lump

(see pg 33)

SUPERIOR VENA CAVA OBSTRUCTION

'I would like to present Mr W, a 75-year-old man. Over the last 3 weeks he has noticed that his head, neck and arms have become progressively more swollen. His wife has commented that he is going blue and has noticed enlarged veins on his chest which are new. He has a long-standing cough which is productive of yellow sputum and blood. He is getting progressively more short of breath and is now breathless at rest.[172] Other associated symptoms he has noticed include a headache and dizziness.[173] His previous medical history includes COPD and he was diagnosed with lung cancer 5 months ago. He is on home nebulisers and oxygen. He has no known allergies. He lives with his wife who is his main carer. He is an ex-smoker of 60 pack years who gave up 5 months ago when he was diagnosed with lung cancer. He does not drink alcohol.

I think this gentleman with known lung cancer has developed superior vena cava obstruction. I would like to examine him to confirm my diagnosis.'

✍ WHAT YOU SHOULD KNOW

Causes of SVC obstruction:

Acute obstruction	Chronic obstruction	Iatrogenic
Carcinoma bronchus	Retrosternal goitre	Central TPN
Thymoma	Slow-growing mediastinal tumour	
Lymphoma	Constrictive pericarditis	
Carcinoma thyroid	Mediastinal fibrosis	

Investigations:
Chest X-ray, chest CT may show lung or mediastinal tumour.
Bilateral brachial vein injections of contrast to determine extent of occlusion.

Management:
Exclude terminal disease.
Obtain tissue diagnosis.
Treat underlying cause (e.g. by radiotherapy).
Caval bypass to right atrium.

[172] Tinnitus, epistaxis, a cough and dysphagia are all related symptoms that can be attributed to the underlying cause, the effects of venous congestion, and direct pressure effects of a mass in the neck or mediastinum.
[173] These symptoms are caused by obstruction of venous return to the heart.
[174] For goitre, central line scars or lymphadenopathy.
[175] For pulmonary effusion due to carcinoma bronchus.

Examine this patient's neck lump

(see pg 45)

SUPERIOR VENA CAVA OBSTRUCTION

'The patient has a markedly swollen head and neck, which are suffused and cyanosed. The neck veins are distended and do not collapse on elevation or with respiration. He is short of breath at rest. The diagnosis is superior vena caval obstruction. I would like to ask the patient about associated symptoms, examine his neck[174] and listen to his chest[175].'

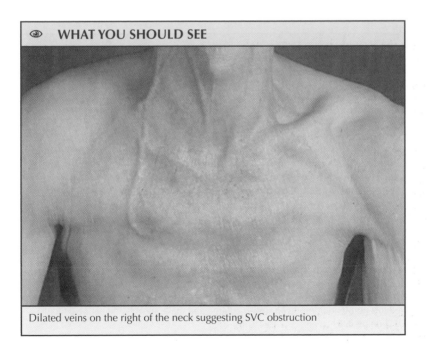

👁 WHAT YOU SHOULD SEE

Dilated veins on the right of the neck suggesting SVC obstruction

117

PLEOMORPHIC ADENOMA OF PAROTID/ADENOLYMPHOMA/ WARTHIN'S TUMOUR

> Take a history from this patient with a neck lump
>
> (see pg 33)

'I would like to present Mr W, a 40-year-old man. He presents with a 6-month history of swelling at the angle of the jaw. It has slowly increased in size and is non-tender. He has no facial weakness. He has no previous medical history, takes no regular medication and has no known allergies. He lives with his wife and works in an office.

This man has a pleomorphic adenoma of the parotid. The differential diagnosis includes a Warthin's tumour (although this usually occurs in men aged over 50 and is occasionally bilateral) or a parotid gland malignancy (again these tend to occur in the over-50s and grows rapidly, see case on pg 122). I would like to examine him.'

🖊 WHAT YOU SHOULD KNOW

[176] Although adenomas can arise anywhere in the gland, this is the most common site for **pleomorphic** adenomas.

[177] They can vary in size from just palpable to 20 cm in diameter but often will be 1–3 cm.

[178] **Adenomas** account for 90% of salivary gland neoplasms, and of these two-thirds are pleomorphic. Neoplasms in other salivary glands are rarer than in the parotid and are more frequently malignant.
On the other hand, **calculi** and **sialadenitis** (infection) are less common in the parotid than in the other salivary glands, probably because it is chiefly a serous-secreting gland (more watery), not mucus-secreting.

Monomorphic adenomas account for the remaining third of salivary gland adenomas. The commonest of these is **Warthin's tumour** (adenolymphoma), which is similar to pleomorphic adenoma except for the following features:

- Histologically there is no sign of stroma.
- It tends to arise in the lower part of the parotid gland, lower than the common site of a pleomorphic adenoma.
- They are soft and often fluctuate.
- They are more commonly bilateral.

Pleomorphic adenomas of the palate: the hard palate contains many small glands identical in structure and function to the salivary glands. Pleomorphic salivary adenomas can therefore arise on the palate. If it is not treated this non-tender lump can slowly enlarge and make speech and eating difficult.

CONTINUED on pg 120

PLEOMORPHIC ADENOMA OF PAROTID/ADENOLYMPHOMA/ WARTHIN'S TUMOUR

Examine this neck lump

(see pg 52)

'There is (in this middle-aged man) a non-tender lump just anterior and superior to the angle of the jaw[176] on the right. It is 2 cm in diameter, hemispherical[177] with a smooth surface and distinct edge. It is hard and rubbery, dull to percussion and not fluctuant, compressible, reducible or transilluminable. It arises from the subcutaneous tissues and the skin moves freely over it. It can be moved over the deep structures. The overlying and surrounding skin is normal, and the regional lymph nodes are not enlarged. The rest of the parotid gland and the contralateral gland are normal, and the facial nerve is not affected. There is no evidence of stones or inflammation of the gland. The most likely diagnosis is a pleomorphic adenoma of the parotid gland.'[178]

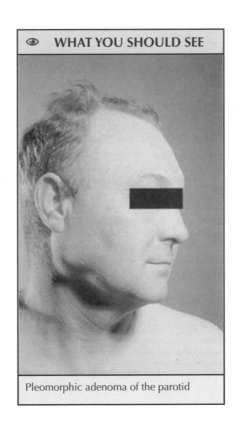

◉ WHAT YOU SHOULD SEE

Pleomorphic adenoma of the parotid

PLEOMORPHIC ADENOMA OF PAROTID/ADENOLYMPHOMA/ WARTHIN'S TUMOUR

✑ WHAT YOU SHOULD KNOW (CONT)

Anatomy of the parotid gland
Largest of the salivary glands, mostly serous (not mucous). Situated below the external auditory meatus behind the ramus of the mandible and in front of the sternocleidomastoid muscle. The facial nerve runs through the gland and divides it into superficial and deep lobes. The structures within the parotid gland are (lateral to medial): the facial nerve and its five terminal branches supplying the muscles of facial expression (the temporal, zygomatic, buccal, mandibular and cervical branches), the retromandibular vein, the external carotid artery (and its branches, the superficial temporal artery and the maxillary artery) and lymph nodes.

The parotid duct emerges from the facial process of the gland and runs forwards over the lateral surface of the masseter muscle, piercing the buccinator muscle and opening in the mouth opposite the upper second molar tooth. It can be palpated 1 cm below the zygomatic arch if the teeth are clenched.

The nerve supply is via parasympathetic secretomotor fibres from the inferior salivary nucleus of the ninth cranial nerve, which 'hitchhike' on the tympanic branch of the ninth cranial nerve, the lesser petrosal nerve, the otic ganglion and the auriculotemporal nerve. Disruption of these fibres leads to post-operative gustatory sweating (see below).

Management of a parotid lump
Investigations are controversial. Ultrasound and FNA are advocated by some but it can be difficult to distinguish between malignant and benign tumour. **Golden rule: do not cut into a parotid lump** (increases risk of implantation and recurrence). So no wedge biopsies, no Trucut.

If clinically benign: wide local excision or superficial parotidectomy. Low incidence of recurrence.
If clinically malignant: radical en bloc surgery plus radiotherapy. Very poor prognosis (<20% 5-year survival)

Parotidectomy
Definitions:
Conservative parotidectomy – all named branches of facial nerve preserved.
Radical parotidectomy – facial nerve sacrificed.
Superficial parotidectomy – removal of superficial part of parotid gland.
Total parotidectomy – removal of whole gland (conservative or radical).

Incision: S-shaped incision starting from tragus, curving under pinna to mastoid process then forward in the upper skin crease of the neck. Deepen incision, looking for the facial nerve just below and in front of the auditory meatus deep to the stylomastoid artery.

Procedure: follow facial nerve forwards, following the superior branch each time. When the anterior border is reached, reflect the superficial lobe forward and dissect it from the skin flap. Divide the parotid duct as far forward as possible and ligate it with catgut skin closure over a drain.

Beware: facial nerve, jugular vein, tumour in the deep lobe (requiring external carotid artery sacrifice).

Post-operative complications of parotidectomy:
- Haemorrhage
- Sloughing of skin flap
- Parotid duct fistula
- Facial nerve palsy (temporary or permanent)
- **Frey syndrome:** sweating on the cheek during a meal (gustatory sweating) due to inappropriate cross-regeneration of sympathetic and parasympathetic nerve fibres divided during the operation

PLEOMORPHIC ADENOMA OF PAROTID/ADENOLYMPHOMA/ WARTHIN'S TUMOUR

👁 WHAT YOU SHOULD SEE

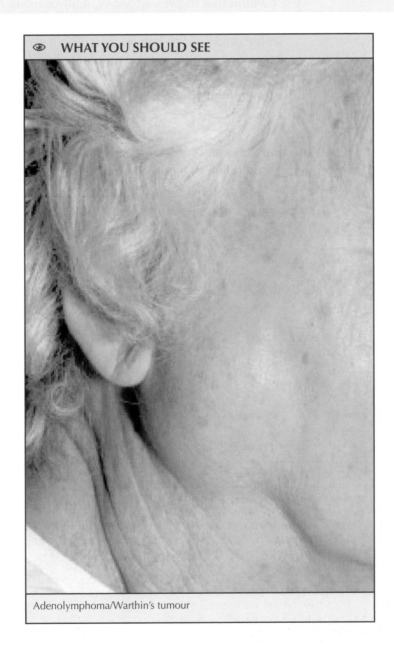

Adenolymphoma/Warthin's tumour

Take a history from this patient with a neck lump

(see pg 33)

CARCINOMA OF THE PAROTID GLAND

'I would like to present Mr W, a 60-year-old man. He presents with a 3- month history of swelling at the angle of the jaw on the right. It has rapidly increased in size and is painful. He has developed right-sided facial weakness. He has no previous medical history, takes no regular medication and has no known allergies. He lives with his wife and works in an office.

I am concerned that this man has carcinoma of the right parotid gland with facial nerve involvement. I would like to examine him.'

✎ WHAT YOU SHOULD KNOW

[179] The mass may infiltrate and become tethered to the skin.

[180] **Facial nerve palsy** (results in a Bell's palsy): absence of tone of the facial muscles on the affected side, asymmetry and less noticeable nasolabial fold, drooping of the corner of the mouth and drooping of the lower eyelid. On closing the eyes, the eyelids fail to close on the affected side (see figure on page 123). **Testing the facial nerve** (seventh cranial nerve): 'Raise your eyebrows, screw your eyes up tight, puff your cheeks out, whistle, show me your teeth.' Note that the facial nerve supplies the muscles of facial expression only and not facial sensation (supplied by the trigeminal nerve – the fifth cranial nerve).

[181] **Management of malignant parotid lump**: radical en bloc surgery plus radiotherapy. Very poor prognosis (<20% 5-year survival). If a lump thought to be benign is removed by superficial parotidectomy and then found to be malignant, the options are:
- Wait and see (if completely excised, acinic or mucoepidermoid tumour)
- Post-op radiotherapy (if adenoid cystic carcinoma or frank carcinoma), or
- Further more radical surgery (if completely excised)

If doubt exists clinically, wide excision biopsy is appropriate.

Examine this neck lump

(see pg 52)

CARCINOMA OF THE PAROTID GLAND

'There is (in this older patient) a painful, warm, but non-tender swelling over the angle of the jaw on the right. It is hemispherical, measuring 3 cm in diameter, with an irregular surface and indistinct edges. It is firm/hard, dull to percussion, not pulsatile, reducible, compressible or transilluminable. It arises from the deep structures and is fixed to them, but the skin moves over the lump with no sign of tethering.[179] The overlying skin is hyperaemic and hot. The surrounding skin is normal but there are enlarged lymph nodes (say where). The facial nerve is intact.[180] This is a hard, warm, fixed parotid mass with associated lymph nodes and I would be concerned to exclude a malignant lesion.'[181]

👁 **WHAT YOU SHOULD SEE**

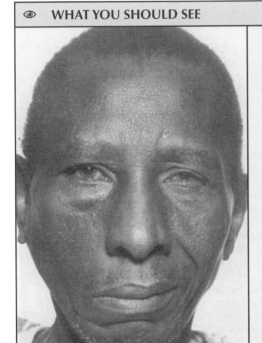

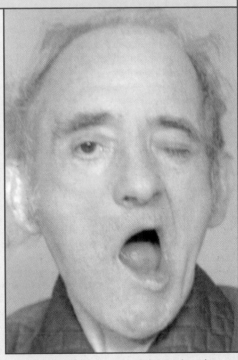

Facial nerve palsy from carcinoma of the parotid gland on the right – note drooping of right side of mouth, loss of nasolabial fold on the right

Facial nerve palsy – note inability to close the right eye

123

Take a history from this patient with a neck lump

(see pg 33)

CHRONIC PAROTITIS

'I would like to present Mr W, a 40-year-old man. He presents with a 3-month history of swelling at the angle of the jaw on the right. The swelling is intermittent and painful. It is worse before eating. He has no facial weakness. He has no previous medical history, takes no regular medication and has no known allergies. He lives with his wife and works in an office.

The intermittent swelling associated with eating suggests chronic parotitis due to a parotid gland calculus. I would like to examine him to confirm this.'

✐ WHAT YOU SHOULD KNOW

Chronic inflammation of the parotid gland is usually caused by a small calculus (rarer in the parotid – a serous-secreting gland – than in the other salivary glands which secrete a more mucous solution) or a fibrous stenosis blocking the mouth of the parotid duct.

History: recurrent swelling and aching pain of the parotid gland, worse before eating. Occasionally bilateral. The gland can eventually become permanently swollen.

Investigations: plain film (65% of submandibular gland stones are radio-opaque whereas 65% of parotid stones are radiolucent). Sialography outlines the ducts demonstrating calculi, duct stenosis and sialectasis.

Treatment: stones can be removed transorally. Gland resection may be required.

Acute parotitis, in contrast to chronic parotitis, is acutely tender, with generalised swelling of the whole parotid gland to up to three or four times larger than normal. The gland is red and hot, firm but indentable, not mobile and often associated with enlarged lymph nodes. A purulent discharge may be expressed from the duct. **Mumps** is the commonest cause of parotitis, (typically occurring in children during viral epidemics), but **acute bacterial parotitis** (usually staphylococcal) can occur in the elderly or debilitated, usually due to poor oral hygiene, dehydration and obstruction of the parotid duct by a stone or scarring. The symptoms are of an acute onset of continuous throbbing pain and swelling over the parotid gland worse on speaking and eating. There are also systemic signs of infection such as fever, rigors and malaise.

Other causes of enlargement of the salivary glands (sialomegaly) include the following:

Mikulicz syndrome: an autoimmune disorder involving enlargement of one or all of the parotid and submandibular glands, combined with a visible enlargement of the lachrymal glands and a dry mouth.

Sjögren syndrome: also an autoimmune disease, presents with the features of Mikulicz syndrome plus dry eyes and generalised arthritis.

Drugs: the contraceptive pill, thiouracil, co-proxamol, isoprenaline, phenylbutazone.

Sialectasis: a disease of unknown origin recognised by progressive destruction of the alveoli and parenchyma of the gland, with duct stenosis and cyst formation. Calculi may be found in the main ducts. The priority of management is excluding malignancy.

Sialadenosis.

Examine this neck lump

(see pg 52)

CHRONIC PAROTITIS

'The right parotid gland is generally enlarged and firm with distinct edges. It is tender and rubbery-hard. A stone can/cannot be felt in the duct. The other salivary glands are normal. This patient has the signs of chronic parotitis secondary to calculi.'

🗒 WHAT YOU SHOULD KNOW

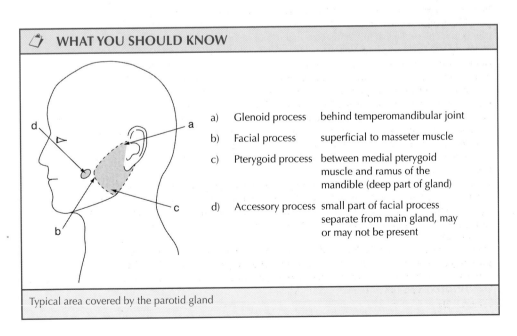

a)	Glenoid process	behind temperomandibular joint
b)	Facial process	superficial to masseter muscle
c)	Pterygoid process	between medial pterygoid muscle and ramus of the mandible (deep part of gland)
d)	Accessory process	small part of facial process separate from main gland, may or may not be present

Typical area covered by the parotid gland

Take a history from this patient with a neck lump

(see pg 33)

SUBMANDIBULAR CALCULI

'I would like to present Mr W, a 30-year-old man. He presents with a 3-month history of swelling beneath the jaw on the right. The swelling is intermittent and painful. It is worse before and during eating. He has no previous medical history, takes no regular medication and has no known allergies. He lives with his wife and works in an office.

The intermittent swelling associated with eating suggests a submandibular gland calculi. I would like to examine him to confirm this.'

📋 WHAT YOU SHOULD KNOW

Submandibular calculi are common because:
1. The gland lies below opening of duct (impedes drainage, encourages stasis).
2. Submandibular gland is a mucus-secreting rather than a serous gland.
A salivary gland calculus is composed of a similar mixture to the 'tartar' dentists scrape off your teeth: cellular debris, bacteria, mucus and calcium and magnesium phosphates.
History: young to middle-aged adults who complain of recurrent pain and swelling beneath the jaw, worse before and during eating. Gland may become persistently enlarged.
Anatomy: the **submandibular gland** is divided into deep and superficial parts by the posterior border of the mylohyoid. It is a mixed salivary gland, secreting mucus and serous saliva as opposed to the parotid, which is mainly a serous gland, and the sublingual gland, which is mainly mucus-secreting. The submandibular duct emerges from the superficial part of the gland, runs between mylohyoid and hyoglossus and enters the floor of the mouth next to the frenulum. Nerves at risk in excision of submandibular gland are the mandibular branch of the facial nerve, hypoglossal and lingual nerves.
The **sublingual gland** lies in front of the anterior border of the hyoglossus and medial to genioglossus. The glands form the sublingual fold of mucosa in the floor of the mouth and meet each other anteriorly.
Submandibular salivary gland tumours: pleomorphic adenomas, monomorphic adenomas and carcinomas of the submandibular gland are rare compared with the parotid gland but present in a similar way. Numbness of the anterior two-thirds of the tongue suggests infiltration of the lingual nerve.
Submandibular sialadenitis: infection of a submandibular gland is secondary to the presence of a stone in its duct or stenosis caused by previous stones passing through. The pain is more severe, throbbing and continuous than in the presence of stones without infection. The gland is more swollen and is red, hot and tender on examination.
[182] Unless infected.
[183] When the muscles of the floor of the mouth are tested, by asking the patient to push his tongue against the roof of the mouth, the gland becomes less mobile.
[184] **Bimanual palpation**: feel the lump between the gloved index finger of one hand inside the mouth and the fingers of the other hand on the outer surface of the lump.
[185] If the patient opens his mouth and lifts his tongue the orifices of the submandibular ducts are evident as small papillae on either side of the frenulum of the tongue. A stone may be visible impacted at the orifice of the duct. The presence of a stone in the duct may appear as a pink swelling along the floor of the mouth. The duct should be gently palpated to see if any swellings or stones can be appreciated and if any discharge can be expressed.
[186] To exclude systemic disease such as Sjögren syndrome (see pg 124).
CONTINUED on pg 128

Examine this neck lump

(see pg 45)

SUBMANDIBULAR CALCULI

'There is (in this young or middle-aged adult) a non-tender[182] but apparently intermittently painful lump beneath the horizontal ramus of the mandible on the mylohyoid muscle about 3 cm in front of the anterior border of the sternocleidomastoid muscle. It is a 4 cm wide, flattened ovoid, smooth with distinct anterior, posterior and inferior edges. It is rubbery hard, does not fluctuate or transilluminate, and is non-compressible, non-reducible and non-pulsatile. It is dull to percussion. The skin is freely movable over the lump, which is tethered to the deep structures.[183] On examining and palpating the floor of the mouth, there is no lump or ulcer evident from inside the mouth. Bimanual palpation of the lump shows it to lie beneath the floor of the mouth.[184] There is no visible or palpable stone in the submandibular duct, and I cannot express any pus from the orifice of the duct.[185] The overlying and surrounding skin is normal, and the regional lymph nodes are not enlarged. This is an enlarged submandibular gland. The history suggests a submandibular calculus. To complete my examination, I would like to examine the opposite submandibular gland and the parotid glands.'[186]

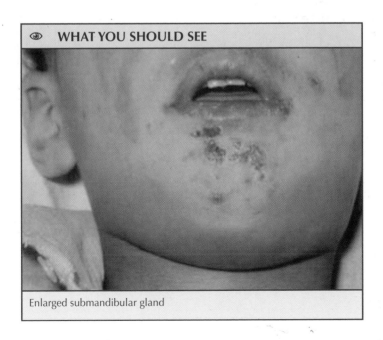

WHAT YOU SHOULD SEE

Enlarged submandibular gland

127

🖎 WHAT YOU SHOULD KNOW (CONT)

Other causes of a swelling on the floor of the mouth

Ranula: a large mucus-containing cyst, probably from acini of the sublingual gland secondary to obstruction. It is a tense, grey, translucent, spherical swelling just below the mucosa of the floor of the mouth and presents in the neck.

Sublingual dermoid cyst: this is a non-tender swelling above or below the mylohyoid muscle in the midline which is caused by entrapment of a portion of epidermis during embryological fusion of the facial processes. It usually presents between the ages of 10 and 25 years as a swelling under the tongue or just below the point of the chin, looking like a double chin. It is spherical, non-tender, smooth and well-defined and, although firm, it fluctuates. Bimanual palpation combined with asking the patient to contract the muscles of the floor of the mouth should make it clear whether the dermoid cyst is supra-mylohyoid or infra-mylohyoid.

👁 WHAT YOU SHOULD SEE

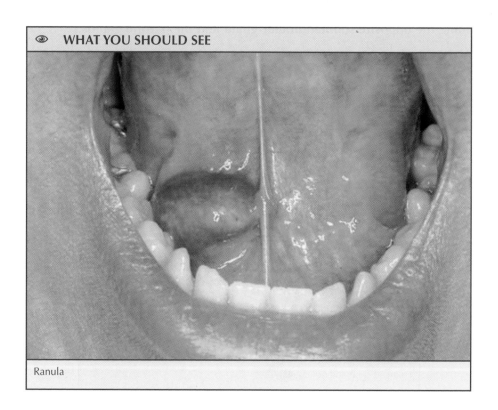

Ranula

SUBMANDIBULAR CALCULI

👁 WHAT YOU SHOULD SEE

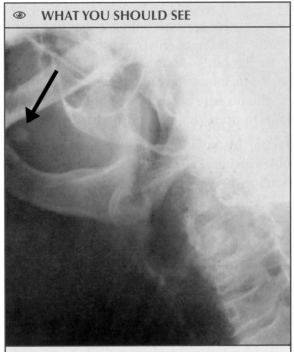

Radiograph of stone in submandibular duct (this case is due to adenoma, not calculi)

Take a history
from this
patient with a
lesion on his
face

(see pg 33)

BASAL CELL CARCINOMA

'I would like to present Mr W, a 60-year-old man. He presents with a 2-year history of a lesion on his right cheek. It is gradually increasing in size but is non-tender. He has not noticed any lesions or lumps elsewhere.[187] He has hypertension for which he takes an antihypertensive and has no known allergies. He lives with his wife and is retired but used to work as a sun-bed salesman and admits to using sun-beds regularly.

Given the length of the history I think this is a basal cell carcinoma. Other differential diagnoses include squamous cell carcinoma or keratoacanthoma. I would like to examine the patient to confirm my diagnosis.'

✎ WHAT YOU SHOULD KNOW

Definition: common slow-growing malignant epidermal tumour that rarely metastasises.
Epidemiology: most common skin cancer. Seen on the face of middle-aged or elderly fair people. Twice as likely in males than females.
Aetiology: sunlight, X-rays, arsenic, immunosuppressed patients, basal cell naevus syndrome (dominantly inherited, associated with multiple BCCs), people with inherited defects such as xeroderma pigmentosum.
Pathology:
Macroscopically: raised rolled (not everted) edges. Pearly nodules with visible fine blood vessels. Slow growing over years with central ulceration and scabbing.
Several variations:
Multifocal: emerge from epidermis and spread over several cm.
Nodular lesions: grow deep into dermis as cords and islands.
Flesh-coloured: commonest.
Scarring: cystic or pigmented (less common).
Microscopically, solid sheets of uniform, darkly staining cells arising from the basal layers of the skin. Histologically similar to basal cell layer of epidermis. NO prickle cells, NO epithelial pearls (seen in squamous cell carcinoma).
Spread: slow but steady local infiltration and destruction of surrounding tissues including skull, face, nose and eye. Hence the term 'rodent ulcer'. Lymphatic and haematological spread are extremely rare.
Treatment: excision has low recurrence rate if adequate. If advanced, extensive or invading nearby structures, radiotherapy gives good results. The prognosis is good.
[187] May arise on any part of the skin, including the anal margin, but 90% occur on the face above a line joining the angle of the mouth to the external auditory meatus. They are especially common around the eye, nasolabial folds and hairline of the scalp.
[188] Most patients present while the lesion is small but, if neglected, lesions can become bigger and erode large areas of the face (see pg 133).
[189] Of dried serum and epithelial cells, which bleeds slightly if picked off.
[190] **Differential diagnosis**: squamous cell carcinoma (shorter history, everted edge, see pg 134); keratoacanthoma (short history, deep, scabby slough, see pg 72).

Examine this lesion

(see pg 43)

BASAL CELL CARCINOMA

There is (in this fair-skinned, middle-aged or elderly man) a small, non-tender nodule just under the lateral aspect of the right eye.[187] The lesion is 1 cm in diameter[188], round with a rolled, pearly edge that is not everted, and a necrotic, ulcerated centre. The base (or centre) of the ulcer is covered with a shallow sloughy coat.[189] The lesion is confined to the skin and is freely moveable over the deep structures and the surrounding skin is normal/shows signs of sun damage. The regional lymph nodes are not enlarged. This is a basal cell carcinoma.'[190]

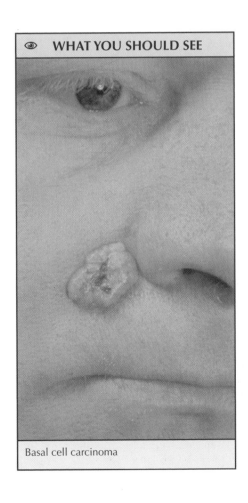

WHAT YOU SHOULD SEE

Basal cell carcinoma

BASAL CELL CARCINOMA

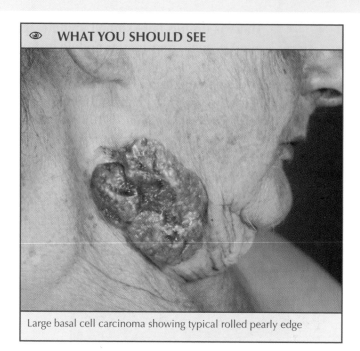

👁 **WHAT YOU SHOULD SEE**

Large basal cell carcinoma showing typical rolled pearly edge

BASAL CELL CARCINOMA

👁 WHAT YOU SHOULD SEE

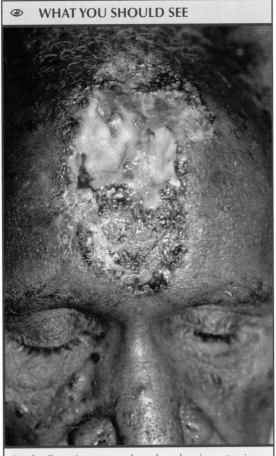

Basal cell carcinoma or rodent ulcer showing extensive tissue destruction

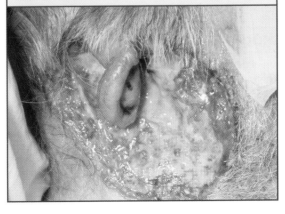

Take a history from this patient with a lesion on his face

(see pg 33)

SQUAMOUS CELL CARCINOMA

'I would like to present Mr W, an 80-year-old man. He presents with a 6-month history of a lesion on his right cheek. It is gradually increasing in size but is non-tender. He has also noticed non-tender neck lumps.[194] He has no other associated symptoms. He has hypertension, for which he takes an antihypertensive and has no known allergies. He lives with his wife and is retired but used to work as a sun-bed salesman and admits to using sun beds regularly.

Given the length of the history I think this is a squamous cell carcinoma. Other differential diagnoses include (see [195]). I would like to examine the patient to confirm my diagnosis.'

⤴ WHAT YOU SHOULD KNOW

[191] It can occur on any part of the skin but is more common in sun-exposed areas.

[192] Tendons, muscle and bone can be exposed in advanced, deep lesions.

[193] Advanced tumours may be fixed to underlying structures and immobile.

[194] Although it should be assumed that these are metastatic until proved otherwise, in one third of patients with palpable lymph nodes they are reactive, due to secondary infection of the ulcer.

[195] **Differential diagnoses** include: basal cell carcinoma (see pg 130: raised, pearly but not everted edge, slow growing, lymph nodes hardly ever involved), keratoacanthoma (see pg 72: no bleeding, history of spontaneous regression), malignant melanoma (see pg 138), solar keratosis (see pg 72), pyogenic granuloma (see pg 69: short history, soft red nodule covered with epithelium) and infected seborrhoeic wart (see pg 69).

CONTINUED on pg 136

Examine this
lesion

(see pg 43)

SQUAMOUS CELL
CARCINOMA

'There is (in this middle-aged or elderly, fair-skinned patient) an ulcer on the right cheek.[191] It is 2 cm in diameter and irregularly round in shape. It is a few millimetres deep, penetrating the skin to the subcutaneous fat, and has an everted edge. The base is covered in necrotic slough, dried serum and blood and there is pale, unhealthy granulation tissue. No underlying structures are evident beneath the subcutaneous fat.[192] The ulcer is confined to the skin and moves freely with it over the underlying muscles and bones.[193] The local lymph nodes (say which ones) are enlarged.[194] The surrounding tissues look normal apart from some adjacent inflammation. This is a squamous cell carcinoma.'[195]

◉ WHAT YOU SHOULD SEE

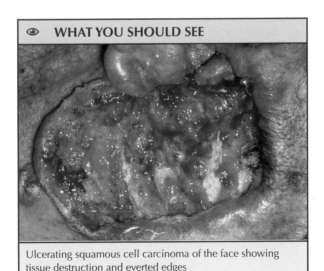

Ulcerating squamous cell carcinoma of the face showing tissue destruction and everted edges

☝ WHAT YOU SHOULD KNOW (CONT)

Definition: common invasive malignant epidermal tumour with a low but significant potential for metastasis.

Epidemiology: very common. Usually in elderly males, especially in sun-exposed areas, i.e. face and back of hands. More common in men than women.

Aetiology: predisposing factors include:

- Exposure to sunshine or irradiation
- Carcinogens (pitch, tar, soot, betel nuts, papillomavirus)
- Lupus vulgaris
- Immunosuppressive drugs
- Chronic ulceration, e.g. Marjolin's ulcer, which is malignant change in a long-standing scar, ulcer or sinus (typically chronic varicose ulcer, unhealed burn, sinus of chronic osteomyelitis). Marjolin's ulcer tends to be slow growing, painless and tends to spread to the lymphatics later than classic SCCs. The edge is not always raised and everted. Other features may be masked by the pre-existing ulcer/scar. Unusual nodules or changes in a chronic non-healing ulcer or scar should be viewed with suspicion and biopsied early. Despite being less invasive and slower growing than a spontaneous squamous cell carcinoma it should be treated as vigorously.
- Premalignant conditions, e.g. (1) Bowen's disease 'carcinoma in situ' – a premalignant intraepidermal carcinoma. Appears as a slow-growing thickened, brown or pink well-defined plaque. Flat papular clusters covered with crusts, it can look like eczema, and can occur on any part of the body, especially the trunk. It is not usually associated with sun damage. A small proportion progress to squamous cell carcinoma. Microscopically it is full-thickness dysplasia of the epidermis. Erythroplasia of Queyrat is Bowen's disease of the glans penis. Treatment is excision with a minimum 0.5 cm margin.
- Premalignant conditions, e.g. (2) Solar keratosis 'squamous cell carcinoma in situ' resulting from solar damage to the skin and hyperkeratosis of the skin. Usually found in old weather-beaten men (e.g. farmers) on the backs of fingers and hands, face and helix of the ears. The skin is usually yellow, grey or brown crusty patches from which arises a protruding plaque of horny skin; 25% progress to squamous cell carcinoma if untreated. Histologically there is hyperkeratosis and epidermal dysplasia. Unlike Bowen's disease there is dermal collagen damage. The treatment is excision, shaving, cryotherapy or topical application of 5FU chemotherapy. Developing tethering, fixity or regional enlarged lymph nodes are worrying features.

Pathology of squamous cell carcinoma: macroscopically a typical carcinomatous ulcer with raised everted edges and a central scab. 'In situ' squamous cell carcinoma is where the lesion has not invaded through the basement membrane of the dermo-epidermal junction. Microscopically solid columns of epithelial cells growing into dermis with epithelial pearls of central keratin surrounded by prickle cells. Spread: local infiltration and lymphatics; rarely haematological.

Clinical: hyperkeratotic and crusty on sun-damaged skin, e.g. pinna. Ulcerating if on lips or genitals. Friable or papilliferous varieties may occur.

Treatment: surgical excision as for basal cell carcinoma with a wider margin required in less well-differentiated lesion. Surgical block dissection or radiotherapy or both to treat regional node spread.

Prognosis: the local recurrence rate is twice that of basal cell carcinoma. Metastasis to local lymph nodes occurs in 5–10% of SCCs if left untreated – less in those arising in sun-damaged skin (0.5%) and more in tumours arising in mucosal surfaces, irradiated areas or Marjolin's ulcers (see above).

SQUAMOUS CELL CARCINOMA

👁 WHAT YOU SHOULD SEE

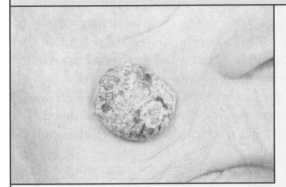

Raised squamous cell carcinoma on the face

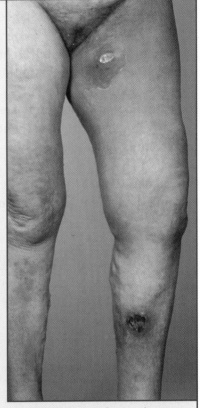

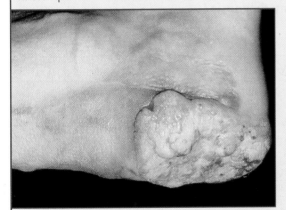

Marjolin's ulcer – a squamous cell carcinoma arising in a long-standing ulcer of the heel

Marjolin's ulcer – malignant change in a long-standing ulcer, showing involvement of the draining lymph nodes

137

Take a history from this patient with a lesion on his face

(see pg 33)

MALIGNANT MELANOMA

'I would like to present Mrs W, a 40-year-old woman. She presents with a 3-month history of a change in a pre-existing mole on her right cheek. It is gradually increasing in size and she thinks the pigmentation has altered. It itches and has bled when she has scratched it. She has not noticed any other lesions or lumps. She is otherwise fit and well. She takes no regular medication and has no known allergies. She lives with her husband and daughter. She works as a hairdresser. She uses sun beds regularly and has a holiday home in Spain which she visits frequently and she enjoys sunbathing.

The concern is that this could be a malignant melanoma. I would like to examine the patient to confirm my diagnosis.'

✏ WHAT YOU SHOULD KNOW

True malignant melanomas are usually treated so quickly and associated with such anxiety that they are not common examination cases, but it is so important that almost any suspicious skin lesion is likely to lead to a discussion about melanoma, and it is important to know the principles of pathology and management.

[196] The majority of malignant melanomas are found on the limbs, head, neck and trunk. Trunk melanomas are found more often in men, and lower limb melanomas in women.

[197] They may be any colour from pale pinkish brown (amelanotic melanoma) to black.

[198] Nowadays patients are quite aware of risks and usually present while their enlarging moles are quite small.

[199] This is the commonest presentation of malignant melanoma, but there are four common clinical types that differ significantly in appearance (see pictures on pg 142).

1. **Superficial spreading melanoma**: the most common type. It may occur on any part of the body, is usually palpable but thin with an irregular edge and a variegated colour.

2. **Nodular melanoma**: thick, protruding, with a smooth surface and regular outline. May become ulcerated and bleed.

3. **Lentigo maligna melanoma**: a malignant melanoma arising in a Hutchinson's lentigo. The malignant areas are thicker than the surrounding pigmented skin, usually darker in colour, but seldom ulcerate.

4. **Acral lentiginous melanoma** (including subungual melanoma): a rare type, but can present as a chronic paronychia or subungual haematoma. It is an irregular expanding area of brown or black pigmentation on the palm, sole or beneath a nail. This is the commonest type in black patients.

[200] **Management of regional lymph nodes**: If no clinical lymph nodes are detectable only certain subgroups are thought suitable for elective lymph node dissection (see Specialist referral, pg 140). If node involvement is suspected clinically, surgical clearance after FNA confirmation is indicated. Chemotherapy is generally used only for metastatic disease and radiotherapy only for certain types of melanoma (e.g. desmoplastic tumours). Regular follow-up is advisable, especially for thicker melanomas (at least 5 years) and recurrent disease.

[201] For metastatic spread. Lungs, liver and brain are the commonest blood-borne sites.

CONTINUED on pg 140

Examine this lesion

(see pg 43)

MALIGNANT MELANOMA

'There is (in this fair-skinned adult) a non-tender lump on the right cheek.[196] It is purple-black in colour[197] about 2 cm in diameter[198], roughly hemispherical, with an ulcerated, friable surface and irregular edges with surrounding satellite nodules. The primary tumour has a firm, solid consistency. Small satellite nodules feel hard.[199] The lump is not fluctuant, compressible, pulsatile or reducible. It arises from the skin and is not fixed to the deeper structures. The surrounding skin shows satellite nodules but is otherwise normal. The regional lymph nodes are/are not enlarged.[200] I would be concerned to exclude a malignant melanoma in this patient, and a complete examination would include listening to the chest and examining the liver.'[201]

👁 WHAT YOU SHOULD SEE

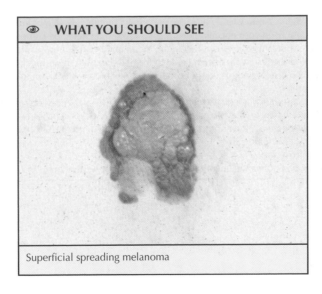

Superficial spreading melanoma

139

✐ WHAT YOU SHOULD KNOW (CONT)

Malignant melanoma continued

Definition: malignant melanoma is an increasingly common invasive malignant epidermal tumour of melanocytes with significant metastatic potential.

Epidemiology: 10/100 000 in UK, 42/100 000 in Australia. Mostly cutaneous but also occur in mucous membrane of nose, mouth, anus, conjunctiva, choroid and pigmented layer of retina. Rare in coloured races, increasingly common in white people. Black people tend to get them on the non-pigmented sole of the feet.

Aetiology: sunlight (both UVA and UVB implicated). Childhood exposure is linked with future development of melanoma. Sun beds and tanning lamps carry a potential risk.

Inheritance of multiple primary melanomas accounts for a small number of cases; 2% of all melanomas have a significant family history, and mutations on chromosomes 1, 6, 9, 10 and 11 have been implicated. Overall, however, familial melanoma is rare.

Congenital giant naevi (>20 cm maximum diameter at term) have an increased risk of malignant change, which may occur in the first ten years of life. Risks and benefits of excision versus observation are a difficult clinical decision. See figure on pg 143.

Pathology: half of malignant melanoma cases arise de novo in previously clear skin. Half arise in pre-existent junctional naevi from the melanoblasts in the basal layer of the epidermis (originating from neural crest cells embryologically). Some melanoblasts contain no pigment but all have a positive DOPA reaction (converting dihydroxyphenylalanine – DOPA – into melanin). Horizontal melanoma grows radially. Vertical melanoma grows into the dermis and is associated with metastasis. May cease to grow or regress naturally due to immune response. Antibodies may be seen early in disease but not in metastatic disease.

Signs of malignant change in a naevus:
1. Increase or irregularity in size or pigmentation
2. Bleeding or ulceration
3. Itching, pain or altered sensation
4. Spread of pigment from the edge of the tumour
5. Formation of daughter nodules
6. Lymph nodes/distant metastases.

Diagnosis of a suspicious skin lesion: any changing or new lesion not diagnosed clinically should be referred for a specialist opinion, or an **excision biopsy** should be performed for histopathological examination. The excision biopsy should always involve complete excision of the lesion, including full thickness of the skin with a **2-mm** lateral clearance margin. Incomplete, wedge or **incision biopsies** may be tempting in large lesions in cosmetically difficult areas but should **never** be carried out by a non-specialist because they may miss malignant foci in the lesion and because important diagnostic features involving the margins of the lesion are not available to the pathologist in these specimens.

Specialist referral: if the histology turns out to be malignant melanoma, specialist opinion should be sought for several reasons:
1. The scar must be excised with adequate margins (see below) and might need reconstructive surgery.
2. Lymph node dissection may be necessary (e.g. in clinically node-positive patients and in some clinically node-negative patients such as men with intermediate-thickness lesions of the trunk, or young patients with 1–2-mm-thick tumours).
3. Radiotherapy may be required (e.g. in desmoplastic melanomas).
4. Appropriate follow-up and management of any recurrence must be arranged.

MALIGNANT MELANOMA

☝ WHAT YOU SHOULD KNOW (CONT)

Histopathology reporting of malignant melanoma:
The four essential components of the report (apart from patient details and site) are:
1. Diagnosis of melanoma
2. Maximum tumour thickness according to Breslow's method to the nearest 0.1 mm
3. Completeness of excision
4. Microscopic margins of excision.
Other useful information includes histological classification, level of invasion (Clark), vascular invasion, lymphocytic infiltration, horizontal or vertical growth, predominant cell type.

Classification:
A modified version of the American Joint Committee on Cancer/Union Internationale Contre le Cancer (AJCC/UICC) staging system is the most widely used.

	AJCC staging	
	pT_x	Primary tumour cannot be assessed
	pT_0	No evidence of primary tumour
Clark level I	pT_{is}	Melanoma in situ (intraepidermal)
Clark level II	pT_1	<0.75 mm and invades the papillary dermis
Clark level III	pT_2	0.75–1.5-mm thick and/or invades to papillary/reticular dermis interface
Clark level IV	pT_3	1.5–4-mm thick and/or invades reticular dermis
	pT_{3a}	1.5–3-mm thick
	pT_{3b}	3–4 mm
	pT_4	>4 mm

Staging by the TNM system:

Stage I	pT_1/T_2	N_0	M_0
Stage II	pT_3/T_4	N_0	M_0
Stage III	Any p_T	N_{1-2}	M_0
Stage IV	Any p_T	any N	M_1

Treatment:
Excision margins depends on the maximum tumour thickness according to Breslow's method (available from the histology report). Remember an excision biopsy is inadequate for melanoma, as its margins are 2 mm, so the scar must be excised.

Melanoma in situ	5-mm margin
0.1–1.5-mm thick (pT_{1-2})	10-mm margin
1.6–4-mm thick (pT_3)	10–20-mm margin
>4-mm thick (pT_4)	20–30-mm margin

Historically very wide margins (up to 5 cm) were recommended, and the evidence is still controversial. This protocol is considered acceptable by John Keenly, Chairman of the Regional Cancer Organisation Expert Tumour Panel on Skin Cancer, Consultant plastic surgeon at Frenchay Hospital, Bristol (Ref: *Surgery* March 1999 Vol 17: 3 pg 62–66).

Prognosis: this relates most closely with Breslow thickness, nodal involvement and metastasis. Few patients with three or more nodes or disseminated disease survive 5 years.

Tumour thickness (mm)	approx. 10-year survival
<0.76	>95%
1.5–2.5	70%
4–7.99	50%
>8	30%

Other prognostic factors include anatomical site (trunk and scalp = worse prognosis than peripheral lesion) and type of growth (superficial spreading better than penetrating, ulcerating lesion).

MALIGNANT MELANOMA

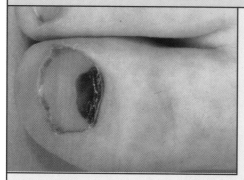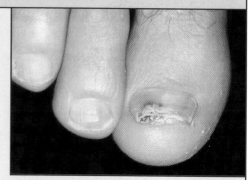

Subungual melanomas. These do not grow out with the nail. This characteristic is useful to elicit in the history, but diagnosis by biopsy should not be delayed in order to observe

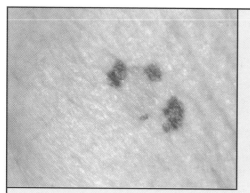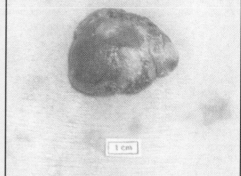

Lentigo maligna

Nodular malignant melanoma

BENIGN NAEVUS

👁 WHAT YOU SHOULD SEE

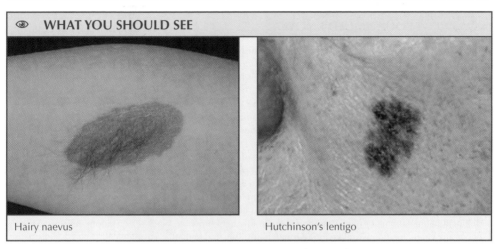

Hairy naevus

Hutchinson's lentigo

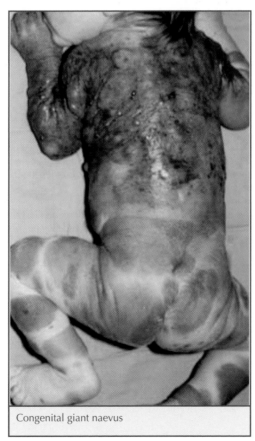

Congenital giant naevus

143

BENIGN NAEVUS

✏ WHAT YOU SHOULD KNOW

There are several pathologies causing a **brown blemish** on the skin.

1. **Freckle**: normal number of melanocytes in their normal position, each producing excess melanin.
2. **Lentigo**: increased number of melanocytes in their normal position, each producing normal quantities of melanin.
3. **Mole/pigmented naevus**: increased number of melanocytes in abnormal clusters at the dermo-epidermal junction producing normal or excess quantities of melanin.

There are four microscopic **types of pigmented naevus**:

a) Intradermal melanoma or naevus: common mole. Light or dark, flat or warty. Hairy mole is nearly always intradermal. Found everywhere except palm of hand, sole of foot or scrotal skin.

b) Compound melanoma or naevus: clinically indistinguishable from intradermal naevus but histologically it has junctional elements which make it potentially malignant.

c) Juvenile melanoma: melanomas before puberty are relatively unusual. Microscopically they may be indistinguishable from malignant melanoma but usually pursue a benign course.

d) Junctional melanoma or naevus: pigmented variably light brown to black. Flat, smooth, hairless. May occur anywhere, including (unlike intradermal) palm, sole and genitalia. Histologically, naevus cells seen in basal layers of epidermis as well as in dermis. Only a small percentage of junctional naevi undergo malignant change, but it is from this group that the vast majority of malignant melanomas arise.

4. **Dysplastic naevus**: as above with nuclear abnormalities but no invasion.
5. **Malignant melanoma**: a mole with signs of abnormal and excessive multiplication or invasion of adjacent tissues (see pg 139).
6. **Café au lait patches**
7. **Circumoral moles** of Peutz–Jeghers syndrome (see pg 297).

There are several **clinical varieties of mole**:

1. **Hairy mole**: always intradermal naevi. Contains sebaceous glands which may become infected. (See figure on pg 143.)
2. **Non-hairy mole**: may be intradermal, junctional or compound naevi.
3. **Blue naevus**: uncommon mole deep in the dermis with smooth overlying skin. Seen in children.
4. **Hutchinson lentigo**: a large area of pigmentation. Commonly appears in over-60s on the face and neck and slowly growing. Mainly smooth, but may develop rough areas of junctional activity which are at increased risk of malignant change.
5. **Congenital giant naevus** (see pg 143).

Treatment: most whites have 15–20 moles. They do not need excision unless they are disfiguring, a nuisance in some way (e.g. catching on clothes), premalignant (e.g. Hutchinson lentigo, congenital giant naevus) or develop any suspicious changes (see malignant melanoma, pg 138).

[202] Signs of malignant change in a mole.

BENIGN NAEVUS

Examine this lesion

(see pg 43)

'There is (in this patient of any age) a small, well-demarcated brown pigmented lump on the right cheek. It is hemispherical, 3 mm in diameter, with a slightly wrinkled surface and well-defined edges. It is soft, arises from the skin and is not deeply fixed. There is no evidence of excoriation, ulceration, variation of pigmentation, satellite nodules or extension of pigmentation beyond the edge of the lesion.[202]

The surrounding skin and draining lymph nodes are normal. This looks like a benign naevus but I would like to know if the patient has experienced enlargement or change in sensation of this lesion in recent weeks or months.'

👁 **WHAT YOU SHOULD SEE**

Benign naevi on the forearm

145

TEMPORAL ARTERITIS

📋 WHAT YOU SHOULD KNOW

Also known as giant cell arteritis, this is a vasculitis closely related to polymyalgia rheumatica.

Diagnosis: 2-cm biopsy of superficial temporal artery under local anaesthetic through an incision directly over the vessel (always palpate and mark the course of the vessel before infiltration of the lidocaine and adrenaline).

60% of biopsies show the characteristic histological features:

- Florid intimal thickening
- A round-cell infiltration through all layers of the arterial wall
- Destruction of the internal elastic lamina
- Giant cells

Treatment: is high-dose systemic steroids, gradually reducing as symptoms abate. Since steroids reduce the incidence of blindness and only 60% of biopsies are diagnostic, treatment should be started on grounds of clinical suspicion only. Some say this negates the need for a biopsy.

[203] Twice as common in women as in men.

[204] Including blurred vision, amaurosis fugax, diplopia, visual hallucinations. Visual loss occurs in between one third and one half of patients and becomes permanent if left untreated. It is caused by ischaemic changes in the ciliary arteries causing optic neuritis or infarction. Initially fundoscopy is normal but ischaemic papillopathy and thrombosis of the central retinal artery may occur. Ophthalmoplegia may also be a feature.

[205] This is variable – pulsation is often still felt.

[206] If you are confident at doing these – if not, don't volunteer! You could say 'send them for full visual acuity testing, fundoscopy and visual field mapping' and leave it to the ophthalmologist! Testing visual fields is simple if practised – get the patient to cover one eye with their hand and look straight ahead, preferably at a fixed point. You then steady their forehead with one hand and ask them to tell you when they can see your other hand. With index finger wiggling, bring your hand into the patient's line of vision from behind her head at 2, 4, 7 and 11 o'clock. Repeat on the other side. Visual acuity can be tested using a Snellen chart with the patient covering one eye at a time.

Take a history from and examine this patient with a lump on their forehead

(see pg 43)

TEMPORAL ARTERITIS

'There is (in this woman[203] over 60) a history of malaise, fever, myalgia, frontoparietal headache and visual disturbance.[204] The left temporal artery is thickened and prominent, tender to touch, with absent pulsation[205] and reddened overlying skin. This patient has temporal arteritis. I would like to examine/arrange for assessment of the visual acuity, visual fields and retina.'[206]

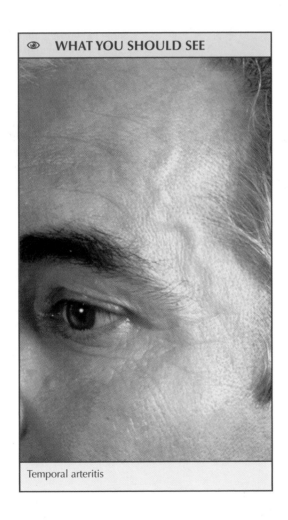

👁 WHAT YOU SHOULD SEE

Temporal arteritis

D SURVEY RESULTS

HEAD AND NECK

These results include cases seen in the new OSCE and the old style MRCS exam.

TOP 5 CASES

Type of case	Number seen in survey	Breakdown and details of cases
Lipoma	23	18 Lipoma 5 Dercum's disease Questions included differential diagnosis, management, incision lines, malignant potential.
Skin cancer	22	15 Basal cell carcinomas on face or scalp 1 Superficial spreading malignant melanoma 2 Same lady post malignant melanoma excision with skin graft behind knee and radiotherapy tattoo 2 Squamous cell carcinoma 1 Bowen's disease 1 Marjolin's ulcer under nail Questions included describe, examine, differential diagnoses, treatment (surgery vs radiotherapy), complications, skin closure, where else would you examine in malignant melanoma?
Thyroid	17	10 Goitre 5 Lump 2 Graves Questions included 'describe full examination', differential diagnosis, effects of retrosternal extension, causes of thyroid lump, anatomy of thyroid, embryology and blood and nerve supply.

Type of case	Number seen in survey	Breakdown and details of cases
Salivary glands	11	4 Parotid Lump ?cause 1 Pleomorphic adenoma, parotid 1 sebaceous cyst over parotid gland 1 post total parotidectomy 1 Warthins with bilateral parotid swelling 2 swollen submandibular gland, one with calculus 1 pleomorphic adenoma of salivary gland in palate Questions included differential diagnoses, bimanual palpation, management of calculi, principles of parotid surgery, risks of surgery, course of facial nerve, follow up.
Sebaceous cyst	8	All on head and neck

OTHER CASES

Type of case	Number seen in survey	Breakdown and details of cases
Thyroglossal cyst	7	Questions included movement on swallowing/sticking out tongue
Neck lumps	7	3 lymph node cases, two with tracheostomies 4 neck lump ?cause
Neurofibromata	6	All neurofibromatosis. One lower limb amputation due to neurofibromatosis. Questions included von Recklinghausen's syndrome, acoustic neuroma, MEN II, cafe au lait spots, genetics, associated disorders.
Tracheostomy	4	Also a feature in two 'lymph nodes in the neck' cases. Questions included long term requirements, indications, types, complications, side vs end tracheostomies and sudden airway obstruction.
Histiocytoma	2	
Dermoid cyst	2	1 congenital 1 implantation
Haemangioma	2	both periorbital
Benign papilloma	1	

Type of case	Number seen in survey	Breakdown and details of cases
Hypertrophic scar	1	
Keratoacanthoma	1	
Branchial cyst	1	
Seborrhoic keratosis	1	
Pharyngeal pouch	1	
Laryngectomy	1	With oesophageal speech
Submandibular gland	1	

CHAPTER 4
TRUNK AND THORAX

A The Histories 153

B The Examinations 183

C The OSCE Cases 205

A THE HISTORIES

CHEST PAIN

If you are asked to take a history from a patient with chest pain you need to initially ask questions to whittle down the potential differential diagnoses. It is a good start to try and differentiate between pleuritic and cardiac chest pain. Remember this is a surgical examination and therefore you are likely to see causes of chest pain that may present to surgeons or are post-operative complications e.g. IHD, oesophagitis, pneumonia/empyema, recurrent pneumothoraces, PE, mesothelioma.

You should then ask about relevant associated symptoms or risk factors that fit in with your differential. If you run into problems in the OSCE remember the essentials in the 'Combined Assessment Box' to get you back on track.

Introductions

'Hello, my name is Dr Parchment Smith. Can I please check your details? Would you mind if I asked you some questions about your chest pain?'

Ask about demographics.

'May I ask how old you are?'[1]

'What do/did you do for a living?'[2]

Presenting complaint (open question!)

'Can you tell me about what has caused you to come and see me today?'

---

[1] An older patient is more likely to have IHD/mesothelioma, whereas young thin men can get recurrent spontaneous pneumothoraces due to an apical bleb.

[2] Occupations which could be relevant include those where passive smoking occurs (prior to the smoking ban in the UK), e.g. bar worker, or those with asbestos exposure, e.g. shipyard worker, which is a risk factor for mesothelioma.

History of presenting complaint *(the patient may volunteer the following information but remember a systematic approach to taking a pain history is SIROD CASP)*

SITE: **'Where is the pain?'**[3]

INTENSITY: **'Can you rate the pain on a scale from 1 to 10, 1 being no pain and 10 the worst pain ever?'** *(this is subjective and it is more important to know how it affects their life, i.e.)* **'Does it limit your daily activities?'**[4], **'Does it wake you at night?'**

RADIATION: **'Does the pain move anywhere else?'**[5]

ONSET: **'Does the pain come on suddenly or gradually?'**

DURATION: **'How long does the pain last?'**[6]

CHARACTER: **'What is the pain like?'**[7] *(if they require prompting ask is it sharp, heavy or dull?)*

ALLEVIATING AND EXACERBATING FACTORS: **'Does anything make the pain better, or worse?'**[8]

SYMPTOMS ASSOCIATED WITH THE PAIN: **'Do you notice anything else when you get the pain?'** (e.g. nausea, sweating, shortness of breath, palpitations)

---

[3] Central chest pain is typically associated with angina (although obviously there are other causes). Interscapular pain is associated with aortic dissection. Pleuritic pain tends to be well localised to the area of inflammation.

[4] Prior to any surgical intervention for cardiac disease it is important to assess predicted peri-operative risk. It is vital that if you think that the pain is cardiac, you work out the degree to which your patient's daily activities are limited by their chest pain. One way is using the New York Heart Association Score (NYHA):
- NYHA 1 – patients with cardiac disease but without limitation of physical activity
- NYHA 2 – patients with cardiac disease resulting in a slight limitation of physical activity (fatigue/SOB/ palpitations) but comfortable at rest
- NYHA 3 – patients with cardiac disease resulting in marked limitation of physical activity but comfortable at rest
- NYHA 4 – patients with cardiac disease resulting in an inability to conduct any physical activity without discomfort. Symptoms of failure may be present at rest.

[5] IHD typically radiates to the jaw and left arm, although not exclusively.

[6] **Onset/duration**: angina will typically start suddenly, last several minutes and then settle. If it does not settle consider MI. Pleuritic pain will last while the inflammation continues.

[7] **Character**:   Cardiac pain: dull, heavy, aching
Pleuritic pain: sharp
Oesphagitis: burning

[8] **Exacerbating/alleviating factors**:

Angina:	Improved with GTN/rest
	Exacerbated by exercise
Unstable angina:	Improved/or not by GTN/rest
	Decreasing exercise tolerance
Pericarditis:	Improved with sitting forward
Pleuritic chest pain:	Worse on inspiration
Musculoskeletal pain:	Worse on pressing on the area/movement and inspiration
Oesophagitis:	Improved with antacids
	Worse on lying/with hot drinks/eating

PREVIOUS EPISODES: **'Have you had a pain like this before?'**[9] (if yes…) **'What did you do then?'**

You also need to ask about associated symptoms. The relevance of these questions will depend on what you think is going on.

1. **Do you get palpitations (a sensation of feeling your heart beat)?** *If yes,* **'When do these occur?', 'Can you beat out the rate and regularity of these palpitations for me?'**[10]
2. **'Have you ever lost consciousness during these episodes?'**[11]
3. **'Do you have a cough?'** *If yes,* **'Does this make the pain worse?', 'What do you cough up?'**[12]
4. **'Do ever get a fever with the pain?'**[12]

---

[9] **Previous episodes**: the management of these episodes can point towards a diagnosis. Are they getting more frequent and therefore require intervention?

[10] Palpitations associated with chest pain, SOB and syncope suggest cardiac disease. It can be useful for the patient to beat out the palpitations
- Regular tachycardia – anxiety, hyperthyroidism
- Irregular tachycardia – AF
- Investigate with TFTs/24-hour tape

[11] Syncope suggests haemodynamic compromise. The triad of symptoms of aortic stenosis are given by the acronym SAD: syncope, angina, dyspnoea.

[12] The presence of a purulent cough/pyrexia would suggest empyema or pneumonia.

Past medical and surgical history

In particular, what investigations have they had for the chest pain? Have they other diseases which are cardiovascular risk factors, such as diabetes, hypertension, hyperlipidaemia? Or do they have any other diseases associated with arteriopathy, e.g. IHD, TIA/CVA, PVD? Have they any risk factors for PE (e.g. post-operation, malignancy, OCP, thrombophilia)?

'Have you had any tests to investigate the chest pain?'[13], 'Have you had any treatment for the chest pain?'[14]

Medication and allergies

'Do you take any regular medication?', 'What medication if any do you take for your chest pain?', 'Do you have any allergies?'

Family history

'Do any diseases run in the family? In particular heart disease, stroke, diabetes, high cholesterol?'

---

[13] Investigations of the cause of the pain can give a useful clue to likely diagnoses:
- Cardiac chest pain: ECG, coronary angiography, echocardiogram
- Pleuritic chest pain: CXR (PA/lateral), CT chest, pulmonary function tests
- Oseophagitis: OGD (first investigation of choice), pH monitoring (gold standard to diagnose reflux)

[14] Treatment of the pain can also give a clue to diagnosis:

IHD: Initially medical management. When this fails – revascularisation: percutaneous coronary intervention (PCI) and coronary artery bypass grafting (CABG). Usually patients receive PCI first and therefore patients undergoing CABG are older with more severe disease.

Risk factors for cardiac surgery (these depend on the individual's risk factors):
- Death (can be calculated by various scoring systems, e.g. Parsonnet score and Euroscore)
- CVA (about 1%)
- MI (1%)
- Prolonged ventilation (1%)
- Wound infection (1–10%)

For more detail on cardiac surgery see Cardiothoracaic surgery section of *Essential Revision Notes for Intercollegiate MRCS: Book 2*.

Oesophagitis – initially medical management:
- Conservative treatment (lose weight, sleep in a more upright position, reduce alcohol)
- Antacids, H_2 blockers, proton-pump inhibitors
- If this fails consider anti-reflux surgery (see *Essential Revision Notes for Intercollegiate MRCS: Book 2* for details)

Empyema:
- Antibiotics
- Drain pus and obliterate empyema cavity by either:
  - Decortication of empyema (thoracotomy, empyema cavity broken down, rind picked off visceral pleura to allow re-expansion, apical/basal chest drains) or
  - Rib resection (aim to cut out a 1-cm section of rib to allow placement of a big chest drain to cause a drainage tract)

Mesothelioma: usually palliative

Pneumothorax:
- One-off: if <20% lung volume – observe with serial CXRs, >20% lung volume – chest drain (see pg 212)
- Recurrent: bullectomy and pleurodesis

Social history (smoking and drinking)

It is essential to take a careful smoking history. **'Are you a current or ex-smoker?'** *If yes, ask about smoking habits*. **'What do you smoke?', 'How many do you smoke a day', 'How long have you smoked for?'**
'Do you, or have you ever, drunk alcohol?' *If yes,* **'What type of alcohol do you drink?'** *(e.g. spirits, wine, beer)* **'How much do you drink per week?'** *(convert this to units per week)* **'How long have you drunk for?'**

Combined Assessment Box – CHEST PAIN

Ask:
- What is the pain like – heavy central chest pain or sharp and worse when breathing in?
- Are there any relieving or exacerbating factors?
- Ask about risk factors: smoking, occupation, diabetes, hypertension, hyperlipidaemia, family history etc.

Examine:
- Combine an examination of the heart with that of the chest (like you would do in a pre-assessment clinic)
- Inspect (SOB at rest/cyanosed/scars)
- Hands/arms (clubbing/splinter haemorrhages/cigarette stains/pulse/BP)
- Face/neck (eyes (pallor/xanthelasma/corneal arcus), mouth, JVP, central pulse, trachea)
- Chest (heart – palpate apex beat/auscultate), (lungs – chest expansion/percussion/tactile fremitus/auscultate/vocal fremitus)

SHORTNESS OF BREATH (SOB)

If you are asked to take a history from a patient with shortness of breath you need to initially ask questions to whittle down the potential differential diagnoses. Remember this is a surgical examination and therefore you are likely to see causes of shortness of breath (SOB) which present to surgeons or are post-operative complications, e.g. valvular heart disease, IHD, bronchogenic carcinoma, methothelioma, PE, pneumonia. You should then ask about relevant associated symptoms or risk factors that fit in with your differential. If you run into problems in the OSCE remember the essentials in the 'Combined Assessment Box' to get you back on track.

Introductions

'Hello, my name is Dr Parchment Smith. Can I please check your details? Would you mind if I asked you some questions about your breathing?'
Ask about demographics.
'May I ask how old you are?'[15]
'What do/did you do for a living?'[16]

Presenting complaint (open question!)

'What has caused you to come and see me today?'

History of presenting complaint *(the patient may volunteer the following information but questions you need to cover include)*
'How long have you been short of breath?'[17]
'Is it continuous or intermittent?'
'Is it getting worse, better or about the same?'[18]

---

[15] Increasing age is a risk factor for bronchogenic carcinoma and IHD, whereas young thin men are at risk of spontaneous pneumothorax. Patients must be <55 to be considered for lung transplantation.

[16] Occupations which could be relevant include those where passive smoking occurs (prior to the smoking ban in the UK), e.g. bar worker, or those with asbestos exposure, e.g. shipyard worker, which is a risk factor for mesothelioma.

[17] Duration of presenting complaint can help with diagnosis. A sudden onset of SOB post-operatively might suggest PE/pneumothorax, acute pulmunoary oedema (e.g. secondary to MI). A more gradual onset could be expected in cardiac failure or anaemia.

[18] If things are getting better, is this due to a new treatment of a chronic disease, e.g. onset of diuretic in heart failure, or due to resolution of the illness, e.g. in PE/pneumonia?

'Does anything in particular cause the breathlessness or make it worse?' *(In particular)* **'Does lying flat make your SOB worse?', 'How many pillows do you sleep on?'**[19]**, 'Do you wake up at night breathless?'**[20]

Try to clarify how limited they are by the SOB, e.g. **'How far can you walk before you get SOB? Can you climb a flight of stairs without stopping?'**[21]

CHAPTER 4
TRUNK AND THORAX

---

[19] This is orthopnoea – SOB worse on lying due to left ventricular failure. This can be quantified by the number of pillows the patient sleeps on.

[20] This is paroxysmal nocturnal dyspnoea (PND) – SOB on waking up due to left ventricular failure. Patients may typically rush to the open window gasping for breath. It resolves after approximately 10 minutes.

Cardiac diseases which can cause SOB include:

Aortic regurgitation: usually asymptomatic but can present with pulmonary hypertension, e.g. dyspnoea, orthopnoea, PND (angina and syncope are less common).

Aortic stenosis: the triad of symptoms of aortic stenosis are given by the acronym SAD: syncope, angina, dyspnoea. Risk factors include age, rheumatic fever, hypercalcaemia. Once symptomatic, the average survival without operation is 2–3 years. Severe aortic stenosis occurs when the valve area is $<1.0\,cm^2$ (normally it is 3–4 cm^2).

Mitral regirgitation: left atrial dilatation causing AF and pulmonary oedema.

Mitral stenosis: usually asymptomatic but can lead to pulmonary oedema and SOBOE.

ASD: usually asymptomatic until later life but can lead to pulmonary hypertension, e.g. dyspnoea, orthopnoea, PND, AF and paradoxical embolus leading to TIAs/CVAs.

VSD: usually presents in childhood with tachypnoea and poor feeding but small lesions may be undetected into adulthood and are often asymptomatic.

PDA: (patent ductus arteriosus, the abnormal persistence of a lumen in the ductus arteriosus, which should close after birth). Infants present with tachycardia, tachypnoea, poor feeding, irritability.

Fallot's tetralogy: (congenital malformation with VSD, pulmonary stenosis, over-riding aorta, right ventricular hypertrophy) cynanosed.

[21] Quantifying exercise tolerance is useful to get a general idea of the severity of the disease, make an assessment of fitness for surgery, get an idea of how their breathlessness affects the patient's life and provide a measurement against which to assess any intervention. Ways to quantify this include: How far can they walk on the flat before being limited by SOB? Can they climb a flight of stairs without stopping? Can they dress themselves without getting SOB?

159

You need to ask about associated symptoms that may either help you reach a diagnosis or be distressing to the patient and need treatment. The relevance of these questions depends on what you think is going on.

1. **'Do you have a cough?'** *If yes* **'Do you cough up any sputum?'**[22] *If yes,* **'What colour is it?'**, **'Have you noticed any blood in it?'**[23]
2. **'Do you get any chest pain?'**[24] *If yes,* **'How would you describe the pain? 'What brings it on?', 'What relieves it?'**
3. **'Do you ever get wheezy (noisy breathing)?'**[25]
4. **'Do you get a fever with the SOB?'**[26]
5. **'Have you noticed any leg swelling?'**[27]
6. **'Have you noticed any change in your voice (hoarseness)?'**[28]
7. **'Have you lost any weight recently?'**[29]

Past medical and surgical history

In particular, what investigations have they had for the shortness of breath? Have they had any procedures or operations? Have they required admission to hospital for treatment of their breathlessness?

'Have you had any tests to investigate the shortness of breath?'[30]
'Have you had any treatment for it?'[31]
'Have you been admitted to hospital with the breathlessness?' *If yes,* **'Did you require admission to HDU or ICU for ventilation?'**

---

[22] Cough-dry (e.g. ACEI or, if nocturnal, asthma) or are they coughing up sputum? If so, what colour is it? Yellowish sputum of the chronic smoker or if green think pneumonia.

[23] Causes of haemoptysis that might be seen by a surgeon include:
- Infective: pneumonia, TB, bronchiectasis
- Malignant: primary or secondary
- Traumatic: e.g. post-intubation
- Cardiovascular: pulmonary oedema (pink, frothy sputum)

[24] Chest pain may be pleuritic (sharp pain, worse on inspiration) or anginal (see Chest pain history pg 153). Mesothelioma is typified by severe and continuous chest pain.

[25] Patients presenting to thoracic surgery with other complaints often also have COPD due to smoking and therefore get wheeze. It is important to identify this as impaired lung function can increase the risk of surgery.

[26] Empyema can occur following any thoracic surgery or following pneumonia. Patients present with persistent fever, SOB and pleuritic chest pain.

[27] Think DVT/PE if unilateral leg swelling. Think heart failure if bilateral leg swelling.

[28] See Hoarseness history pg 41.

[29] Weight loss, loss of appetite and lethargy are symptoms of bronchogenic carcinoma, together with cough, haemoptysis, SOB, recurrent chest infections and, rarely, pneumothorax.

[30] Investigations can give you a good clue towards a diagnosis. A patient who has had coronary angiography and cardiac echocardiography or transoesophageal echo (TOE) might be more expected to have SOB due to cardiac disease. Investigations for bronchogenic carcinoma on the other hand include CT chest, bronchoscopy (flexible or, less commonly, rigid) and mediastinoscopy.

[31] Only about 10% of bronchogenic carcinomas are operated on in the UK. The main pathological division for surgeons is between small-cell carcinoma (poor prognosis, rarely operated on) and non-small-cell carcinoma (adenocarcinomas, SCC, carcinoid tumours).
Successful surgery depends on complete resection. Therefore to be considered for surgery there must be no metastases, no dissemination within the thorax, and no evidence of $N_{2/3}$ lymph nodes.

Medication and allergies

'Do you take any regular medication, including any inhalers?'
'Do you have any allergies?'

Family history

'Has anyone in the family had any problems with SOB?'[32]

Social history (smoking and drinking)

It is essential to take a careful smoking history. **'Are you a current or ex-smoker?'** *If yes, ask about smoking habits* **'What do you smoke?'**, **'How many do you smoke a day'**, **'How long have you smoked for?'**
'Do you, or have you ever, drunk alcohol?' *If yes,* **'What type of alcohol do you drink?'** *(e.g. spirits, wine, beer)* **'How much do you drink per week?'** *(convert this to units per week)* **'How long have you drunk for?'**

CHAPTER 4
TRUNK AND THORAX

Combined Assessment Box – SHORTNESS OF BREATH

Ask:
- Does anything make the breathlessness worse? (e.g. walking – if so, how far can they walk/lying flat)
- Do you get any associated problems? (e.g. cough/sputum or blood/chest pain/fever/wheeze/leg oedema)
- Have you lost any weight?
- Do you smoke, or have you ever smoked?

Examine:
- As with chest pain, you need to perform a combined respiratory and cardiac examination as you would do in a pre-assessment clinic (see the Chest pain history 'Combined Assessment Box')

Lung resections:
- Pneumonectomy (removal of a whole lung, for tumours which are centrally located or impinge on the proximal bronchial tree)
- Lobectomy (removal of a lobe, most common, increasingly using VATS or video-assisted thoracoscopic surgery); wedge resection (removal of a smaller piece of tissue – usually for benign disease)
- Bullectomy (e.g. apical bullectomy for removal of apical blebs in young patients with recurrent pneumothoraces)
- Lung biopsy (to provide tissue for diagnosis in diffuse lung disease)
- Pleurodesis (glueing the pleura together, e.g. in mesothelioma or pneumothorax)

Valvular surgery
Assess coronary artery disease pre-operatively to consider whether a combined CABG/valve procedure is necessary.
Pre-operatively minimise risk of endocarditis by dental/chest exam/urine dip/temperature.

Choice of valves
- Mechanical (long life, need warfarin, noisy, often used in young patients)
- Bioprothesis (shorter life, no warfarin, silent, often used in older patients or in those in whom warfarin would be inconvenient)
- For mitral regurgitation there is the less commonly used option to repair the valve
- Mitral stenosis is usually treated by percutaneous valvotomy

Risk factors
Early: Bleeding, arrhythmias, MI, CVA, pneumonia.
Late: endocarditis, paravalvular leak, complications of warfarin.

[32] In a patient with infective lung disease, seek a history of TB in the family or close contacts. Hypertrophic obstructive cardiomyopathy (HOCM) is an autosomal dominant trait and can be treated by septal myomectomy.

ABDOMINAL PAIN

If you are asked to take a history from a patient with abdominal pain you can use the structure of the 'SIROD CASP' pain history. The site of the pain is likely to give you a good list of potential diagnoses. You should then ask about relevant associated symptoms or risk factors that fit in with your differential. If you run into problems in the OSCE remember essentials in the 'Combined Assessment Box' to get you back on track.

A THE HISTORIES

Introductions

'Hello, my name is Dr Parchment Smith. Can I please check your details? Your GP has mentioned that you have had some abdominal pain, is this correct?'
Ask about demographics.
'May I ask how old you are?'[33]
'What do/did you do for a living?'[34]

Presenting complaint (open question!)

'Can you tell me a little about the pain you have been getting?'

History of presenting complaint *(the patient may volunteer the following information but questions you need to cover include)*
SITE: **'Where is the pain?'**[35]

---

[33] Think gallstones in 'fat, fair, fertile females in their forties'. You will need to exclude pregnancy in women of childbearing age. Keep testicular torsion in mind in young men with lower abdominal pain.
[34] It is important to ask about occupation, not only as a risk factor for diseases, e.g. smoking at work and colorectal cancer, but also to ascertain the patient's medical knowledge – there is little worse than patronising another healthcare professional accidentally.
[35] **Site** – think embryologically:

Upper abdominal pain	– foregut structures (gallbladder, liver, 1st and 2nd part of duodenum, stomach, superior portion of pancreas)
	– also heart/aorta/pneumonia
Central abdominal pain	– midgut structures (small bowel, Meckel's diverticulum, appendix, right colon)
Lower abdominal pain	– hindgut structures (bladder, uterus/ovaries/fallopian tubes – must exclude ectopic pregnancy in women of childbearing age, left colon)
	– also testicular pain
Flank pain	– kidney, aorta
Diffuse severe abdominal pain	– peritonitis

INTENSITY: **'Can you rate the pain on a scale from 1 to 10, 1 being no pain and 10 the worst pain ever?'**[36] *(This is subjective and it is more important to know how it affects their life, i.e.)* **'Does it keep you off work?'**, **'Does it wake you at night?'**

RADIATION: **'Does the pain move anywhere else?'**[37]

ONSET: **'Does the pain come on suddenly or gradually?'**

DURATION: **'How long does the pain last?'**[38]

CHARACTER: **'What is the pain like?'** *(If they require prompting, ask 'Is it sharp, dull, burning, colicky?')*[39]

ALLEVIATING AND EXACERBATING FACTORS: **'Does anything make the pain better, or worse?'**[40]

SYMPTOMS ASSOCIATED WITH THE PAIN: **'Do you notice anything else when you get the pain?'** *(e.g. jaundice, vomiting, change in bowel habit)*

PREVIOUS EPISODES: **'Have you had a pain like this before?'** *(if yes...)* **'What did you do then?'**

---

[36] **Severity** – very subjective. Remember ischaemic gut (although you are unlikely to see this in the OSCE), which can produce severe symptoms with minimal signs.

[37] **Radiation**
Upper abdominal pain:
- RUQ pain to back (biliary colic/cholecystitis)
- RUQ pain to shoulder tip (diaphragmatic irritation – cholecystits/perforated DU/subphrenic abscess)
Central abdominal pain:
- Central pain to back (pancreatitis/pancreatic cancer/aorta)
- Central/epigastric to RIF (appendix/perforated DU)
Flank pain radiating to groin/genitalia – renal colic/aorta

[38] **Length of time pain lasts:** colic is a pain which comes and goes caused by muscular spasm in a hollow viscus (gut, gallbladder, ureter)

[39] **Character** – fairly subjective:
- Burning pain – pancreatitis/PUD
- Colicky pain – see above

[40] **Precipitating/ relieving factors**
Relieving factors:
The peritonic patient will want to lie completely still, in contrast to the patient with colic, who will move about.
Precipitating factors:
Food – think PUD/biliary colic/mesenteric ischaemia.
Alcohol – think alcohol-related pancreatitis or gastritis in heavy drinkers.
Movement – worse in peritonitic patients.

You need to ask about associated symptoms that may either help you reach a diagnosis or be distressing to the patient and need treatment. The relevance of these questions will depend on the site of the pain and what you think is going on, based on the earlier questions.

1. **Any site**
    a. **Nausea/vomiting**
    b. **Weight loss**
    c. **Change in bowel habit**
    d. **PR bleeding**
    e. **Fever**
2. **Upper abdominal pain**[41]
    a. **Dysphagia**
    b. **Indigestion**
    c. **Jaundice**
3. **Lower abdominal pain**[42]
    a. **Urinary symptoms**
    b. **PV discharge** *(if female)*
    c. **LMP** *(if female)*
    d. **Ask if they could be pregnant** *(if female and of childbearing age)*

---

[41] **Associated symptoms of upper abdominal pain**
Dysphagia: see history pg 38 (reflux oesophagitis/oesophageal/gastric cancer)
Indigestion: PUD
Jaundice:
Nagging severe back pain of gradual onset – think pancreatic cancer.
Nagging RUQ pain of gradual onset with associated weight loss – think liver mets/cholangiocarcinoma/hepatitis.
Sudden onset colicky RUQ pain – think gallstones obstructing CBD.
[42] **Associated symptoms of lower abdominal pain**
Lower urinary tract symptoms: e.g. lower abdominal pain, frequency, dysuria, haematuria, incontinence.
NB Remember an inflamed appendix can irritate the bladder, mimicking some of the symptoms of UTI.
PV discharge: think of pelvic inflammatory disease. Usually primary due to organisms such as *Chlamydia trachomatis* or *Neisseria gonorrhoeae* (although it can occur secondary to GI infection, e.g. appendicitis or systemic infection, e.g. TB). Causes lower abdominal pain, fever and PV discharge. Ask about presence of an IUCD, which should be removed.
Last menstrual period:
a) If > 4 weeks ago, could they be pregnant? (To exclude an ectopic pregnancy you must obtain a negative pregnancy test in all women of childbearing age – you can still get an ectopic pregnancy in supposedly sterilised women.)
b) Mittelschmerz is typically mid-cycle (i.e. 2 weeks post-LMP) lower abdominal pain caused by a ruptured ovarian follicle.
c) If they are currently menstruating consider retrograde menstruation.
d) If they are 1 week prior to or during menstruation consider endometriosis – functioning endometrial tissue found outside the uterine cavity which can cause low abdominal pain starting 1 week prior to period.

Past medical and surgical history

In particular, what investigations have they had for the abdominal pain? Have they had any procedures or operations?
'Have you had any tests to investigate the pain?'[43]
'Have you had any treatment for it?'[44]

Medication and allergies

'Do you take any regular medication?'
'Do you have any allergies?'

Family history

'Do any diseases run in the family?'
'Has anyone in the family had any problems with similar symptoms?'

Social history (smoking and drinking)

It is essential to take a careful smoking history. **'Are you a current or ex-smoker?'** *If yes, ask about smoking habits.* **'What do you smoke?'**, **'How many do you smoke a day'**, **'How long have you smoked for?'**
'Do you, or have you ever, drunk alcohol?' *If yes,* **'What type of alcohol do you drink?'** *(e.g. spirits, wine, beer)* **'How much do you drink per week?'** *(convert this to units per week)* **'How long have you drunk for?'**

Combined Assessment Box – ABDOMINAL PAIN

Ask:
- Where do you feel the pain?
- Do you have any other problems associated with the pain? (e.g. jaundice, vomiting, loss of appetite, change in bowel habit, fever, urine, LMP)
- Have you lost any weight?

Examine:
- Observe (scars/masses/cachexia etc.)
- Hands
- Face (eyes for jaundice/mouth for ulcers etc.)
- Abdo (inspect/palpate for tenderness or masses/auscultate)
- Extras (say you would like to examine groins/genitalia/DRE)

---

[43] Previous investigations can be helpful in working out what is going on. If they have abdominal pain, have they had an OGD, USS, CT?
[44] Any treatment they have undergone can also be helpful. Are they post-op or post-procedure? If so, do they know the findings?

JAUNDICE

There are many different causes of jaundice.[45] *Start with an open question and then ask about relevant associated symptoms or risk factors. If you run into problems in the OSCE remember the essentials in the 'Combined Assessment Box' to get you back on track.*

Introductions

'Hello, my name is Dr Parchment Smith. Can I please check your details? Your GP has written that you have noticed a change in your skin colour – is that correct?'
Ask about demographics.
'May I ask how old you are?'[46]
'What do/did you do for a living?'[47]

Presenting complaint (open question!)

'Can you tell me a little about what has been going on?'

---

[45] Causes of jaundice – see 'What you should know' in OSCE case on pg 246.
[46] Think gallstones in 'fat, fair, fertile females in their forties'. Think malignancy in older patients.
[47] Occupation: think of risk factors for hepatitis, e.g. Needlestick in healthcare worker.

History of presenting complaint *(the patient may volunteer the following information but questions you need to cover include)*
'How long have you noticed the jaundice?'[48]
'Have you ever been jaundiced before?'[49]
'Have you noticed any change in you stools?'– 'or urine?'[50]
'Have you developed itchy skin?'[50]

You need to ask about associated symptoms that may either help you reach a diagnosis or be distressing to the patient and need treatment.
'Have you noticed any abdominal pain?'[51] *(If yes – expand on this using the abdominal pain history above. In particular: site, radiation, precipitating factors.)*
'How has your appetite been?', 'Have you lost any weight recently?' *(If yes:)*
'Do you know how much weight you have lost?'[52]
'Have you noticed any new pain in your joints?'[53]
'Have you noticed that you bruise more easily?'[53]
'Have you recently travelled abroad?' *(if yes)* **'Where did you go and what did you do there?'**[54]
If appropriate: **'Do you use intravenous drugs?', 'Have you got any tattoos?'**[54]

---

[48] Is this a long-standing illness, e.g. alcohol-related cirrhosis, or of short duration, e.g. a CBD stone?
[49] If they have had recurrent episodes of jaundice ask about how this was treated. Was any cause found?
[50] These symptoms suggest **obstructive jaundice**. There is no enterohepatic circulation, leading to pale stools (decreased stercobilinogen), dark urine (urobilinogen absent) and pruritus (bile acids in blood).
[51] Try to distinguish between fat intolerance (recurrent RUQ pain, worse with fatty food), which suggests gallstones, and constant epigastric boring pain associated with weight loss, which suggests malignancy.
[52] Malaise and anorexia can cause weight loss in hepatitis or malignancy.
[53] Joint pains can suggest **hepatitis**. An increased bruising tendency suggests **hepatocellular damage**.
[54] Risk factors for contracting hepatitis include recent travel, intravenous drug addiction, tattoos.

Past medical and surgical history

In particular, what investigations have they had for the jaundice? Have they had any procedures or operations?

'Have you had any tests to investigate the jaundice?'[55]

'Have you had any treatment for it?'

Medication and allergies

'Do you take any regular medication?'[56]

'Do you have any allergies?'

Family history

'Do any diseases run in the family?'[57]

---

[55] **Investigating jaundice**

This depends on what you think the cause of the jaundice is, but common initial investigations are

a) Blood tests

    (i) LFTs: **Bilirubin** (jaundice is defined as elevation of serum bilirubin – but it isn't clinically detectable until 35 mmol/l).

    Alkaline phosphatase (normal if pre-hepatic cause, mildly raised in hepatic causes, very high in post-hepatic causes).

    Aminotransferase (normal if pre-hepatic cause, very high in hepatic causes, normal or mildly raised in post-hepatic causes)

    (ii) PT usually prolonged in hepatic/post-hepatic causes of jaundice.

    (iii) Haemtological investigation if a haemolytic cause is suspected, e.g. Coombs' test.

    (iv) Hepatitis screen.

b) Imaging

    (i) Plain radiographs usually not helpful but may show: 10% of gallstones which are radio-opaque, calcification in chronic pancreatitis, air in the biliary tree (fistula between bowel and biliary tree, previous ERCP, gas-forming organisms in severe cholangitis), soft-tissue mass in the RUQ, which is an enlarged gallbladder.

    (ii) USS (essential baseline). It can show: gallstones in GB (but may miss duct stones), dilated bile or pancreatic ducts, level and cause of obstruction, mass in the pancreas, splenomegaly, ascites etc.

    (iii) MRCP – used to further investigate dilated ducts found on USS. Replacing ERCP (which is now regarded as a therapeutic procedure) as investigation of choice as it has none of the risks of ERCP. Also used to stage and assess tumour operability.

    (iv) EUS (endoscopic USS) – USS inserted into duodenum endoscopically. Especially useful in assessing the pancreatic head and bile duct and it is possible to perform a biopsy of a peri-ampullary mass. Also useful in picking up microlithiasis.

c) Invasive procedures

    (i) ERCP can be diagnostic or therapeutic (e.g. sphincterotomy/stone extraction/dilation of strictures/stenting of tumours). Complications include: pancreatitis, perforation, haemorrhage, contrast reactions, septicaemia.

[56] Medications which can cause jaundice include:

Hepatic jaundice: paracetamol, amiodarone, diclofenac, fluconazole, heparin, labetolol, diltiazem.

Obstructive 'cholestatic' jaundice: Augmentin, flucloxacillin, erythromycin, Septrin, captopril, phenothiazides.

[57] A family history of blood disorders suggests **haemolytic disorders**.

Social history (smoking and drinking)

'Are you a current or ex-smoker?' *If yes, ask about smoking habits.*
'What do you smoke?', 'How many do you smoke a day', 'How long have you smoked for?'
It is essential to take a careful alcohol history.[58]
'Do you, or have you ever, drunk alcohol?' *If yes,* **'What type of alcohol do you drink?'** *(e.g. spirits, wine, beer)* **'How much do you drink per week?'** *(convert this to units per week)* **'How long have you drunk for?'**

Combined Assessment Box – JAUNDICE

Ask:
- How long have you noticed the jaundice for?
- Do you get any abdominal pain? (If yes, is it RUQ and worse with fatty food, e.g. likely gallstones, or constant nagging pain, e.g. likely malignancy?)
- Have you lost any weight?
- Have you noticed a change in your stools/urine?
- Do you drink alcohol? (If so, quantify how much and for how long)
- Ask about other risk factors for hepatitis **if appropriate**, e.g. IV drugs, tattoos, travel

Examine:
- Essentially an abdominal examination:
- Inspect (general – jaundice/cachexia, chest – gynaecomastia/spider naevi, abdomen – scars/masses)
- Hands – clubbing/palmar erythema/leukonychia
- Abdomen – palpate for organomegaly, other masses, ascites

---

[58] Heavy alcohol use can suggest **cirrhosis**.

CHANGE IN BOWEL HABIT/ BLEEDING PER RECTUM

If you are asked to take a history from a patient with rectal bleeding or any other change in bowel habit, you can use the structure below. You should then ask about relevant associated symptoms or risk factors that fit in with your differential. If you run into problems in the OSCE remember the essentials in the 'Combined Assessment Box' to get you back on track.

Introductions

'Hello, my name is Dr Parchment Smith. Can I please check your details? I understand you've been passing some blood from your back passage. May I ask you a little about that?'
Ask about demographics.
'May I ask how old you are?'[59]
'What do/did you do for a living?'

Presenting complaint (open question!)

'What has been happening recently?'

History of presenting complaint *(the patient may volunteer the following information but questions you need to cover include)*

'How long have you noticed the bleeding?'[60]
'What colour is the blood? Is it bright-red like if you had cut your finger or dark?'[61]
'When does it occur?'
'Where do you notice the blood (on wiping/in the pan/mixed in/coating/or separate to the stool)?'[62]

---

[59] Young patients with bright-red rectal bleeding are less likely (although not definitely) to have a malignant cause for their symptoms. Fewer than 5% of cases of colorectal cancer occur in the under-40s.
[60] Differential diagnoses for rectal bleeding include: haemorrhoids, anal fissure, bowel cancer, polyps, inflammatory bowel disease, infective diarrhoea, angiodysplasia, diverticular disease. Length of symptoms can be useful in differentiating between a malignant process or benign. For instance, bright-red rectal bleeding which has been going on for years is more likely to be benign.
[61] Bright-red rectal bleeding suggests an anal canal bleeding source (e.g. haemorroids or fissure). Darker blood is likely to have come from further round the colon (e.g. IBD, carcinoma, angiodysplasia, diverticular disease). Melaena (tarry black stool which is foul-smelling) suggests an upper GI source (UGI bleeding if significant can cause fresh red PR bleeding but this only with a major PR bleed with associated haemodynamic instability, these patients should have an OGD first, prior to large-bowel investigations).
[62] Blood noticed on wiping, in the pan or coating the outside of the stool is likely to have an anal canal source. Blood mixed in with the stool is a more concerning symptom, suggestive of a colonic source.

'Do you pass any mucus or discharge from your back passage as well?'[63]
'Do you get any pain when you open your bowels?'[64]
'Do you have a sensation of incomplete emptying when you pass stools?'
'Have you noticed any other changes in your bowel habit?'[65] *(Try to establish what their 'normal' bowel habit was, how it differs now and how long this has gone on for.)*
'Do you suffer from diarrhoea or constipation?'[66]
'Have you noticed any weight loss?'[67]
'Is anyone at home suffering with the same problem?' *(Useful if you think it might be due to food poisoning.)*
'Have you been on any foreign travel recently?' *(Useful if you think an infective cause might be possible.)*
'Have you had any similar episodes previously?'

You need to ask about associated symptoms that may either help you reach a diagnosis or be distressing to the patient and need treatment. The relevance of these questions depend on what you think is going on.

1. 'Have you had any problems with nausea or vomiting?'
2. 'Have you had any difficulty swallowing?'
3. 'Have you had any indigestion-like symptoms?'
4. 'Have you had any abdominal pain or distension?' *(If yes, go into more details using your SIROD CASP structure from the abdominal pain history.)*
5. 'Have you noticed any jaundice?'
6. 'Have you noticed any fever?'

---

[63] Mucus with blood raises concern of rectal cancer or inflammatory bowel disease.

[64] Severe perianal pain on defecation suggests a fissure in ano. Patients describe it as though they are trying to pass glass. Fissures can also cause bright-red rectal bleeding. They are initially treated with topical creams such as GTN or diltiazem and, if these fail, with operative intervention such as botox injections or lateral sphincterotomy. Prolapsed haemorrhoids can also be painful.

[65] A change in bowel habit can be a change in defecation (e.g. frequency), stool (e.g. consistency, appearance of blood/mucus), or symptoms (pain, tenesmus, feeling of incomplete defecation).

[66] Diarrhoea can be defined as the passage of >3 loose stools per day. It is due to an increase in stool water content. Causes of bloody diarrhoea include: IBD, colonic carcinoma, food poisoning, diverticular disease. Constipation is infrequent or irregular defecation. Conditions in which constipation and PR bleeding can co-exist include: colonic carcinoma, Crohn's strictures, fissure in ano, haemorrhoids.

[67] Weight loss suggests IBD or carcinoma.

Past medical and surgical history

In particular, what investigations have they had for the abdominal pain? Have they had any procedures or operations? If you are taking a history from a woman with a change in bowel habit it is important to take an obstetric history (e.g. tears, prolonged labour, forceps deliveries).

'Have you had any tests to investigate the bleeding?'[68]
'Have you had any treatment for it?'[69]

Medication and allergies

'Do you take any regular medication?' *(In particular, ask about any anticoagulants such as clopidogrel, aspirin or warfarin, and iron tablets).*
'Do you have any allergies?'

---

[68] **Investigations**
The Department of Health criteria for patients more likely to have bowel cancer and therefore requiring more urgent investigation include:

- >40 years with a persistent change in bowel habit (>6 weeks) towards looser stools and rectal bleeding
- >60 years with a persistent change in bowel habit (>6 weeks) towards looser stools without rectal bleeding
- >60 years with rectal bleeding (dark or fresh) without any anal symptoms
- Iron deficiency anaemia (under 10g/dl in all men and post-menopausal women)
- Right-sided abdominal mass
- Palpable intraluminal rectal mass

Investigating PR bleeding depends on presentation. In a young person with bright-red rectal bleeding without other symptoms, proctoscopy, followed by flexible sigmoidoscopy could be appropriate. For patients with diarrhoea, rectal bleeding and weight loss it is necessary to examine the entire colon. There are several ways to do this and it depends on patient factors (mobility, anticoagulants) and local availability. Possibilities include: flexible/rigid sigmoidoscopy together with barium enema, colonoscopy, CT colonography.
[69] Depending on the pathology found: management of individual cases is covered in detail in the chapter on the Abdomen in *Essential Revision Notes for Intercollegiate MRCS: Book 2*.

Family history

'Do any diseases run in the family?'
'Do you have a family history of inflammatory bowel disease or bowel cancer?'[70]

Social history (drinking and smoking)

It is essential to take a careful smoking history.[71]
'Are you a current or ex-smoker?' *If yes, ask about smoking habits.*
'What do you smoke?', 'How many do you smoke a day', 'How long have you smoked for?'
'Do you, or have you ever, drunk alcohol?' *If yes,* **'What type of alcohol do you drink?'** *(e.g. spirits, wine, beer)* **'How much do you drink per week?'** *(convert this to units per week)* **'How long have you drunk for?'**

Combined Assessment Box – CHANGE IN BOWEL HABIT/BLEEDING PER RECTUM

Ask:
- What colour is the blood – bright red (anal canal type) or darker (higher)?
- Where do you notice the blood – on wiping/in the pan (anal canal bleeding) or mixed (higher)?
- Have you had any other change in bowel habit recently?
- Have you lost any weight?
- Ask about risk factors for IBD/colorectal cancer (e.g. smoking/family history)

Examine:
- Abdominal examination
- Inspect: scars, cachexia, jaundice
- Hands: clubbing
- Mouth: ulcers
- Abdomen: organomegaly, other masses, ascites, stomas
- Perianal: haemorrhoids, fistulae +/– setons

---

[70] 20–30% of patients with IBD have a family history.
[71] Smoking is a risk factor for Crohn's. Smoking is also a risk factor for colorectal cancer, together with family history, adenomatous colonic polyps, UC (and to a lesser degree Crohn's).

GROIN LUMP

If you are asked to take a history from a patient with a groin lump you can use the structure below. You should then ask about relevant associated symptoms or risk factors that fit in with your differential.[72] If you run into problems in the OSCE remember the essentials in the 'Combined Assessment Box' to get you back on track.

Introductions

'Hello, my name is Dr Parchment Smith. Can I please check your details? I understand you've noticed a lump in your right groin. May I ask you a little about that?'

Ask about demographics.

'May I ask how old you are?'
'What do/did you do for a living?'

Presenting complaint (open question!)

'What has been happening recently?'

History of presenting complaint *(the patient may volunteer the following information but questions you need to cover include)*

'How long have you noticed the lump?'
'Were you doing anything in particular when you first noticed the lump?' *(e.g. lifting)*
'Is it painful?'[73] *(use SIROD CASP to expand if necessary)*
'Has it increased in size since you first noticed it?'
'Does it disappear if you lie down/can you push it back inside?'[74]
'Have you had any previous lumps or swellings similar to this?'[75]
'Does it discharge?'[76]
If you think it could be a hernia ask about intermittent episodes of obstruction.
'Has the lump ever become red, painful or difficult to reduce? Did you have associated episodes of vomiting or your bowels not opening?'

---

[72] Differential diagnoses for a groin lump include: lipoma, sebaceous cyst, abscess, lymphadenopathy, femoral aneurysm (true/false), saphena varix, hernia (inguinal/femoral), ectopic testes, psoas abscess.

[73] A hernia may be uncomfortable but patients do not usually describe pain unless it incarcerates. An abscess may be painful.

[74] A groin lump which disappears on lying down could be a hernia or saphena varix (prominent varicosity near the SFJ)

[75] Is this a recurrent hernia?

[76] Discharge would suggest abscess or infected lymph node.

You need to ask about associated symptoms that may either help you reach a diagnosis or be distressing to the patient and need treatment. The relevance of these questions depends on what you think is going on.

'Do you have any urinary symptoms?'
'Do you suffer from constipation?'
'Do you suffer from a cough?'[77]
'Does your work/leisure time involve a lot of lifting?'
'Do you ever inject drugs in your groin?'[78] *(if appropriate)*
'Have you had any recent night sweats/weight loss?'[79]

Past medical and surgical history

In particular, what investigations have they had for the groin lump? Have they had any procedures or operations? If you think they might require operative intervention it is important to assess their current level of fitness for surgery.

'Have you had any tests to investigate the lump?'[80]
'Have you had any treatment for it?'[81]

---

[77] Risk factors for hernia: increased intra-abdominal pressure, e.g. urinary obstruction, constipation, cough, lifting.

[78] IVDU: increased chance of pseudoaneurysm. A presumed groin abscess in an IVDU should have an USS prior to incision and drainage to exclude a pseudoaneurysm.

[79] Lymphadenopathy due to lymphoma or TB could present in a groin. These patients may give a history of weight loss or night sweats.

[80] Investigations: in clinic perform full abdominal and groin examination, including peripheral vascular examination if appropriate. Most causes of groin lump can be diagnosed with clinical judgement. However, if diagnosis is unclear, an USS may be helpful.

[81] Management: see individual cases for management plan.

Medication and allergies

'Do you take any regular medication?'
'Do you have any allergies?'

Family history

'Do any diseases run in the family?'

Social history (smoking and drinking)

'Are you a current or ex-smoker?' *If yes, ask about smoking habits.* 'What do you smoke?', 'How many do you smoke a day', 'How long have you smoked for?'
'Do you, or have you ever, drunk alcohol?' *If yes,* 'What type of alcohol do you drink?' *(e.g. spirits, wine, beer)* 'How much do you drink per week?' *(Convert this to units per week)* 'How long have you drunk for?'

Combined Assessment Box – GROIN LUMP

Ask:
- Does the lump disappear on lying down (i.e. is it a hernia)?
- If you think it's a hernia check about episodes of incarceration/obstruction, which would make repair more urgent
- Ask about contributing factors e.g. cough/constipation/previous surgery/IV drug use.

Examine:
- Inspect relevant groin with patient standing (number of swellings/scars/overlying skin erythema or sinus)
- Palpate – initially scrotum for mass; if you think it's a hernia test for cough expansion, reducibility, control at external, internal rings
- Then abdominal or PVD examination if appropriate

HAEMATURIA

If you are asked to take a history from a patient with haematuria or other urinary tract symptoms you can use the structure below. You should then ask about relevant associated symptoms or risk factors that fit in with your differential. [82] *If you run into problems in the OSCE remember the essentials in the 'Combined Assessment Box' to get you back on track.*

Introductions
'Hello, my name is Dr Parchment Smith. Please can I check your details? I understand you've been passing some blood in your urine. May I ask you a little about that?'
Ask about demographics.
'May I ask how old you are?'
'What do/did you do for a living?'[83]

Presenting complaint (open question!)
'What has been happening recently?'

History of presenting complaint *(the patient may volunteer the following information but questions you need to cover include)*
'Have you seen the blood in your urine or did your doctor find it on a dipstick test?'[84] *(if macroscopic haematuria…)* **'How long have you noticed the blood in your urine?'**
'When in your stream do you notice the blood?'
'What colour is the blood?' *(i.e. bright-red/clots/pink)*

---

[82] Differential diagnoses for haematuria include: UTI, renal stones, bladder stones, carcinoma of the bladder, kidney or prostate.

[83] Occupation can be a risk factor in bladder cancer (rubber, dye, leather, textile industries). Other risk factors for bladder cancer include: smoking, chronic inflammation, e.g. bladder stone, recurrent infections, long-term catheters.

[84] **Haematuria**: if a patient presents with haematuria you need to exclude renal cell carcinoma and transitional cell carcinoma (bladder).
Causes: see above.
Presentation: can be macroscopic (of whom 20% will have an underlying malignancy) or microscopic (picked up on dipstick, of whom <5% will have an underlying malignancy).
Timing: Early in stream   suggests urethral/prostatic cause
            End of stream   suggests bladder neck
            Throughout stream   suggests higher renal tract
Colour: Dark blood   suggests higher renal tract
Need to exclude urinary discoloration which is not blood, e.g. caused by drugs such as rifampicin or food such as beetroot.

You need to ask about other urinary symptoms. It can be helpful to divide these into different categories (see below).

Ask about lower urinary tract symptoms. These can be storage symptoms e.g. frequency, nocturia, dysuria, urgency…[85]

'Are you passing urine more frequently than usual?'

'Do you get up at night to pass urine?' *(if yes)* **'How many times?'**

'Does it sting or burn when you pass urine?'

'Do you have to rush to get to the toilet to pass urine?

'Have you ever been incontinent of urine?'

…or voiding symptoms, e.g. hesitancy, straining, poor stream, terminal dribbling.[86]

'Does it take a while for you to start urinating?'

'Do you have to strain?'

'Is your stream less powerful than it was?'

'Do you find you dribble at the end of urination?'

'Have you ever had retention of urine – when you have been unable to pass urine and required a catheter?'[87]

Then ask about other associated symptoms.

'Have you ever passed air or faecal matter in your urine?'[88]

'Have you been getting any pain – where do you feel this?'[89] *(SIROD CASP)*

'Have you lost any weight?'

'Have you had a fever?'

---

[85] **Causes of lower urinary tract storage symptoms**: UTI, malignancy, reduced functional bladder capacity, distal ureter/bladder calculi.

[86] **Causes of lower urinary tract voiding symptoms**: in young men – urethral stricture; in older men – prostatic hypertrophy or malignancy.

[87] **Retention**: this can be acute – very painful and occurs on a background of chronic bladder outflow obstruction which is worsened by UTI/constipation/post-operation. Chronic retention is usually painless.

[88] **Pneumaturia**: due to fistulation of urinary tract with the bowel. Causes include: diverticulitis, IBD, malignancy of bowel/bladder.

[89] **Pain**:

	Site	Renal angle	kidney
		Flank	upper/mid-ureter
		Suprapubic	bladder (retention)
		Genitalia	lower ureter/testes
	Character	Dull	obstructive pain
		Colicky	calculus
	Radiation	Renal/ureteric colic can radiate from loin to groin and genitalia (due to common innervation from T11–12)	

Past medical and surgical history

In particular, what investigations have they had for the haematuria?[90] Have they had any procedures or operations?[91]
'Have you had any tests to investigate the blood in the urine?'
'Have you had any treatment for it?'

Medication and allergies

'Do you take any regular medication, including any anticoagulants such as warfarin?', 'Do you have any allergies?'

Family history

'Do any diseases run in the family?'[92]

Social history (drinking and smoking)

It is essential to take a careful smoking history. **'Are you a current or ex-smoker?'** *If yes, ask about smoking habits.* **'What do you smoke?', 'How many do you smoke a day', 'How long have you smoked for?'**
'Do you, or have you ever, drunk alcohol?' *If yes,* **'What type of alcohol do you drink?'** *(e.g. spirits, wine, beer)* **'How much do you drink per week?'** *(convert this to units per week)* **'How long have you drunk for?'**

Combined Assessment Box – HAEMATURIA

Ask:
- Have you seen blood in your urine or was it found on dipstick?
- Have you noticed any other changes when you pass urine?
- Have you had any associated pain?
- Have you lost weight/had a fever/lost your appetite?

Examine:
- Again, in the OSCE, essentially an abdominal examination
- Inspect: scars, cachexia, pallor
- Abdomen: organomegaly, other masses, site of tenderness
- Extras: explain you would want to perform a DRE of prostate (if male patient)

---

[90] **Investigation**:
Urgent investigation (i.e. 2 weeks) is required for patients with macroscopic haematuria or those >50 with microscopic haematuria. This is at a 'Haematuria clinic', where patients get:
- DRE prostate
- Urine cytology
- Urine culture
- KUB X-ray
- USS kidney/IVU
- Flexible cystoscopy

[91] **Management** as per cause *(see Essential Revision Notes for Intercollegiate MRCS: Book 1)*. If no cause found and concern persists in elderly – consider retrograde study of ureters / rigid cystoscopy +/- biopsy.
[92] 2% of renal cell carcinomas are familial (other risk factors include smoking, acquired renal cystic disease).

BREAST LUMP

If you are asked to take a history from a patient with a breast lump you can use the structure below. You should then ask about relevant associated symptoms or risk factors that fit in with your differential.[93] If you run into problems in the OSCE remember the essentials in the 'Combined Assessment Box' to get you back on track.

A THE HISTORIES

Introductions

'Hello, my name is Dr Parchment Smith. Please can I check your details? I understand you've noticed a lump in your left breast. May I ask you a little about that?'
Ask about demographics.
'May I ask how old you are?'[94]
'What do/did you do for a living?'

Presenting complaint (open question!)

'What has been happening recently?'

History of presenting complaint *(the patient may volunteer the following information but questions you need to cover include)*
'When and how did you first notice the lump?'
'Has it got bigger, smaller, stayed the same size since you first noticed it?'
'Is it painful?' (SIROD CASP)[95]

---

[93] Differential diagnoses for a breast lump include: abscess, sebaceous cyst, breast cyst, lipoma, fibroadenoma, carcinoma, fat necrosis.
[94] Breast cancer is more common with increasing age.
[95] Mastalgia: can be cyclical or non-cyclical (less common).
Cyclical mastalgia (younger women, either premenopausal or on HRT)
       Causes   No known cause
       Clinical features
                 Usually upper outer quadrant
                 Pain occurs 3–7 days prior to menstruation and improves at menstruation
       Treatment
                 Conservative i.e. supportive bra, NSAIDs, decrease caffeine intake
                 Medical management for 20% in whom above does not work – evening primrose oil (gamolenic acid), danazol, bromocriptine, tamoxifen.
Non-cyclical mastalgia (older women)
       Causes   Musculoskeletal (commonest)
                 Breast (hormonal/infection/tumour/benign change)
                 Lung disease
                 Gallstones
       Investigate with mammogram if > 35 and USS of tender area for all patients
       Treatment – exclude other causes. Conservative, i.e. supportive bra, NSAIDs, evening primrose oil, reduce caffeine intake

'Does it discharge? Have you had any discharge from your nipple?'[96] 'Have you noticed any skin/nipple changes?'

Then ask about associated symptoms or relevant risk factors.

'Have you noticed any lumps anywhere else for instance, in the other breast or your armpits?'

'Have you had any breast lumps previously – if so, were they biopsied or removed?'

'Have you had any previous breast imaging?'[97]

'Have you sustained any trauma to the breast?'[98]

(Ask about exposure to oestrogens – risk factor for breast cancer[99])

'Are you on the pill/HRT?' 'Have you had any children?' *If yes*, 'How old were you?', 'Did you breastfeed?', 'When did you start having periods/start the menopause?'

Past medical and surgical history

In particular, what investigations have they had for the breast lump. Have they had any procedures or operations?

'Have you had any tests to investigate the lump?', 'Do you have any other medical conditions?'[100]

---

[96] Discharge from the lump itself suggests an abscess. Abscesses are either lactating or non-lactating (these patients need triple assessment).

Nipple discharge
Colour

 Yellow: abscess/periductal mastitis
 Blood-stained: duct papilloma/carcinoma
 Clear: physiological/carcinoma
 Milky: lactating breast/drugs/prolactinoma/postpartum
 Green: duct ectasia

Unilateral or bilateral
Occurs spontaneously/when expressed
Arises from single (more concerning) or multiple ducts
Investigation – triple assessment and cytology of discharge if it is blood-stained or clear from a single duct.

[97] All women between the ages of 50 and 70 in England are invited for 3-yearly screening mammograms. Under-35s need investigating with an USS as the breast is too dense for mammography to be useful.

[98] Trauma to the breast can cause fat necrosis. It usually follows blunt injury or breast surgery, although there is no history of trauma in 50% of cases. Investigate with triple assessment. It may resolve but can be excised if there are concerns regarding diagnosis or symptoms.

[99] **Risk factors for breast cancer**:

Increased exposure to oestrogen

 Early menarche (<12)
 Late menopause (>55)
 Nulliparous
 First pregnancy > 30
 Never breastfed
 Currently using OCP/HRT
 > 5 years HRT use

Family history of breast cancer
Previous breast cancer, DCIS or LCIS

[100] Diabetes is a risk factor for breast abscesses.

Medication and allergies

'Do you take any regular medication?' 'Do you have any allergies?'

Family history

'Do any diseases run in the family? In particular, has anyone in the family had breast or ovarian cancer?'

Social history (drinking and smoking)

It is essential to take a careful smoking history.[101] **'Are you a current or ex-smoker?'** *If yes, ask about smoking habits.* **'What do you smoke?', 'How many do you smoke a day', 'How long have you smoked for?'**
'Do you, or have you ever, drunk alcohol?' *If yes,* **'What type of alcohol do you drink?'** *(e.g. spirits, wine, beer)* **'How much do you drink per week?'** *(convert this to units per week)* **'How long have you drunk for?'**

Combined Assessment Box – BREAST LUMP

Ask:
- Have you noticed any other lumps in your armpit/other breast?
- Have you noticed any nipple discharge?
- Ask about oestrogen exposure
- Have they any history of breast disease?
- Is there any family history of breast or ovarian cancer?

Examine:
- Inspect (with patient sitting – initially with hands on hip then with hands above head) for asymmetry, skin changes, nipple retraction, scars, radiotherapy tattoos
- Palpate – breast (four quadrants, centre and tail), axilla (four walls and apex), supraclavicular area

---

[101] Smoking is significant risk factor for breast abscesses.

B THE EXAMINATIONS

EXAMINATION OF THE HEART[102]

'Hello, my name is Dr Parchment Smith. May I please check your details? Do you mind if I examine you? Could you sit at 45° with your shirt off please?'

WASH/GEL YOUR HANDS BEFORE YOU TOUCH THE PATIENT

LOOK from the end of the bed, hands behind your back.

'I am just going to have a look at you first.'

On initial inspection look for breathlessness[103], cyanosis[104] or pallor[105]. Look for presence of malar flush[106], obvious scars[107] or ankle oedema[108].

'Can I look at your hands please?'

Look for clubbing[109] and splinter haemorrhages[110]. Check the radial pulse for rate and rhythm.[111]

Lift the hand above the patient's head and continue to feel the pulse to assess whether it is collapsing.[112]

Feel the other pulse at the same time to check for radio-radial delay.[113]

Feel the brachial pulses.

To the examiners: 'I would like to know the blood pressure?'

'Can I look in your eyes please?'

Look for pale sclera.[114]

'Can I look in your mouth please?'

Look for central cyanosis.[115]

---

[102] Of course, as a vital part of pre-operative assessment in the clinical setting, you will be familiar with the examination of the heart. Make sure you can do it slickly and know where to listen for murmurs and what they mean.

[103] Could indicate left heart failure.

[104] Can be central or peripheral.

[105] Indicating anaemia.

[106] Red cheeks associated with mitral stenosis.

[107] Midline sternal (valve replacement) or left thoracotomy (mitral stenosis).

[108] Right heart failure.

[109] Associated with cyanotic congenital heart defects and subacute bacterial endocarditis.

[110] Caused by infective endocarditis.

[111] Regularly irregular pulse suggests heart block; irregularly irregular is atrial fibrillation.

[112] Typical of aortic valve regurgitation or persistent ductus arteriosus.

[113] Suggests aortic dissection or coarctation.

[114] Anaemia.

[115] Congenital cyanotic heart disease.

'Turn your head away slightly please.'

Look for the JVP.[116]

'I'm just going to press gently on your tummy.'

Check the JVP rises on pressing the liver as expected.[117]

Feel the carotid pulse[118] *to assess for character*[119].

Look at the chest.

Look at the precordium for visible scars or pulsations.

'I'm just going to FEEL for your heart.'

Firstly feel the apex beat[120]*, then over the left sternal edge*[121]*, then over the manubrium*[122].

You are feeling for heaves or thrills.

'Now I'm going to LISTEN.'

Take out your stethoscope for auscultation.

'Could you roll over to your left please?'

You are just listening over the mitral area.[123]

'Can you sit up now please and breathe in, then out... now hold it?'

While you listen over the tricuspid area.[124]

---

[116] When the patient is sitting at 45° the JVP should be no more than 3 cm above the sternal angle (which is level with the base of the neck). The JVP is elevated in right heart failure, congestive cardiac failure, tricuspid incompetence, volume overload and pulmonary hypertension.

[117] If it doesn't there may be some obstruction of the vena cava.

[118] Palpated just lateral to the trachea (one at a time!).

[119] A 'water-hammer' carotid pulsation is due to a rigid aorta, high cardiac output, aortic regurgitation, patent ductus arteriosus.

[120] **The apex beat** is the most lateral and inferior point at which the fingers are raised with each systole. The normal apex beat is in the fifth left intercostal space 1 cm medial to the midclavicular line. Localise the apex beat as follows: feel for the first palpable intercostal space on the left 1 cm medial to the midclavicular line. This is the second intercostal space. Count down to the fifth space and feel around here for the most lateral inferior point at which you can feel the heart beating.

Strong/lifting apex beat suggests mitral or aortic incompetence.

Double apex beat suggests hypertrophic cardiomyopathy.

Tapping apex beat (palpable first heart sound) suggests mitral or tricuspid stenosis.

Forceful sustained apex beat suggests aortic stenosis or hypertension.

Deviated apex beat displaced laterally or inferiorly suggests enlarged heart.

[121] Thrills or tapping here indicates mitral valve disease.

Sternal heave indicates right ventricular hypertrophy (pulmonary hypertension).

[122] Palpable pulmonary second sound suggests pulmonary hypertension.

Precordial thrill suggests aortic stenosis.

[123] See figure opposite. **Mitral area:**

Site: left fourth intercostal space 1 cm medial to the midclavicular line.

Patient's position: Rolled over towards the left.

Murmurs you will hear: Pansystolic into axilla   = mitral regurgitation
                          Middiastolic   = mitral stenosis

[124] See figure opposite. **Tricuspid area:**

Site: fifth intercostal space on left border of sternum.

Patient's position: sat up, breathing out.

Murmurs you will hear: Early diastolic into apex   = aortic regurgitation

Less common right-sided murmurs and septal defect murmurs can best be heard here too (pansystolic = tricuspid regurgitation/VSD, ejection systolic = pulmonary stenosis/ASD, mid-diastolic = tricuspid stenosis).

184

'Breathe normally and rest back.'

Now you listen over the pulmonary area[125] *and aortic area*[126].

'Now let me listen to the arteries in the neck.'[127]

'Finally, could you lean forward so I can listen to your lung bases[128] **and check for sacral oedema**[129]**.'**

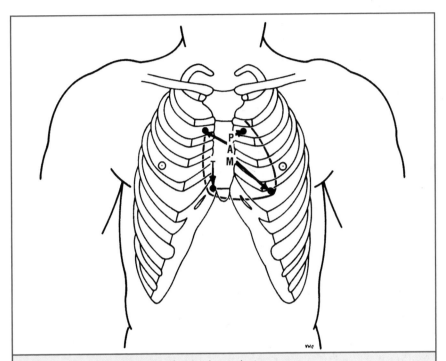

Position of heart valves and sites of optimal auscultation
P = pulmonary valve; A = aortic valve; M = mitral valve; T = tricuspid valve
Arrows indicate position where valves can be heard with the least interference

[125] See figure above. **Pulmonary area**:
<u>Site</u>: second intercostal space on left border of sternum.
<u>Patient's position</u>: sitting at 45°.
<u>You will hear</u>: increased splitting of second heart sound = right bundle branch block, pulmonary stenosis, ventricular septal defect, mitral regurgitation, atrial septal defect.

[126] See figure above. **Aortic area**:
<u>Site</u>: second intercostal space on right border of sternum.
<u>Patient's position</u>: sitting at 45°.
<u>Murmurs you will hear</u>:   Ejection systolic into carotid arteries = aortic stenosis
                                  Early diastolic = pulmonary regurgitation

[127] The ejection systolic murmur of aortic stenosis can be heard radiating into the carotids. Listen also for a carotid bruit.

[128] Crepitations suggest pulmonary oedema secondary to left heart failure.

[129] Secondary to right heart failure. Often more marked than ankle oedema in bedridden patients.

EXAMINATION OF THE RESPIRATORY SYSTEM

Introduce yourself and get the patient into position.[130]

'Hello, I'm Dr Parchment Smith. May I please check your details? Would you mind if I examined your chest? Can you sit up? Are you comfortable?'

WASH/GEL YOUR HANDS BEFORE YOU TOUCH THE PATIENT

Stand back, hands behind your back, and look at the patient and their surroundings.

On initial inspection do they look ill/thin[131], are they comfortable/breathless at rest, are they using their accessory muscles of respiration? Is their colour good/pale/cyanosed? What can you see around them, e.g. antibiotic drip/peak flow meter/oxygen/nebulisers?

Pick up both hands.

'Can I just have a look at your hands first?'

You are looking at the nails for clubbing[132], nicotine staining[133], cyanosis[134] or pallor. Also look for signs of rheumatoid disease[135] or long-term steroid use[136]. Look at the palms for pallor in the palmar creases or coal-dust tattoos[137].

To the patient:

'Could you hold both arms straight out please?'

Look for a tremor.[138]

'Could you cock your palms back like this please?'

Look for a CO_2 retention flap.[139]

---

[130] Sitting in bed at 45° to the horizontal.

[131] Weight loss not only occurs in carcinoma, but in emphysema and bronchiectasis.

[132] Thickening of the nailbed, loss of obtuse angle between the nail and nail-bed, increased curvature of the nail side to side and lengthways, increased fluctuation of the nail bed and drumstick appearance. Respiratory causes: carcinoma of the bronchus, suppurative lung diseases (empyema, bronchiectasis, lung abscess, cystic fibrosis), mesothelioma, fibrosing alveolitis.

[133] Smoking increases risk of carcinoma, bronchitis and emphysema.

[134] Peripheral cyanosis is not reliable – it may be significant or the patient may just be cold.

[135] Linked with fibrosing alveolitis.

[136] Thin skin, bruising.

[137] Coal workers are at greater risk of lung disease, including pneumoconiosis.

[138] Caused by beta-agonists (e.g. salbutamol) commonly used for asthma or COPD.

[139] This will never occur in an exam because it is a sign of severe CO_2 retention which would only be seen in a very ill patient whose respiratory function was severely compromised. If the examiner asks, tell him this, and say politely that you include it as part of a complete respiratory examination.

'Can I feel your pulse?'

While feeling the pulse count the respiratory rate and the pulse.
Check the pulse is neither bounding[140] nor racing[141].

'Can I just look into your eyes please? Look up please.'

Gently draw the skin below the eye down to look at the conjunctiva.
Look to see whether the conjunctiva is pale[142]/not pale/suffused[143].

'Can you stick your tongue out and lift it up please?'

Look for central cyanosis.

'Now I'm going to look at your neck. Turn to one side and relax the head.'

Check the JVP is not raised.[144]

'I'm just going to feel your windpipe, sorry if it's a bit uncomfortable.'

Check the trachea is central.[145]

Stand back again.

'I want to have a look at your chest now. Could you take off your top please? Put your hands on your hips.[146] Now take two deep breaths. Lovely.'

Look at the chest for obvious scars[147], radiation burns, abnormal shape or deformity. Check the chest moves normally[148] and symmetrically with respiration. Look for use of accessory muscles of respiration.[149] Listen for audible wheeze or stridor.[150]

Next, test for chest expansion. Spread your fingers and grasp the sides (not front) of the ribcage firmly under the nipples until the thumbs meet.

'Take the biggest breath you can and breathe out.'

CHAPTER 4 TRUNK AND THORAX

---

[140] In CO_2 retention.

[141] Tachycardia may occur if the patient is febrile, e.g. in pneumonia, or acutely breathless, e.g. in acute asthma.

[142] Pale conjunctiva is a clinical sign of anaemia (it does not prove that the patient is anaemic, only the haemoglobin measurement can do that).

[143] If there is superior vena caval obstruction, for example in bronchial carcinoma with enlarged lymph nodes, the venous drainage of the head will be congested and the sclera may look red and suffused.

[144] The JVP is raised in congestive cardiac failure, when the heart has failed. This is a common cause of breathlessness due to pulmonary oedema. The JVP can also be raised in SVC obstruction (see OSCE case on pg 116) but in this case it will be fixed and have no hepatojugular reflex.

[145] The trachea may be PUSHED away from the affected side (pleural effusion, tension pneumothorax, space-occupying mass) or PULLED towards it (collapse due to obstruction or infection, fibrosis, old TB). You may feel a tracheal tug if the chest is hyperinflated.

[146] Leave them with their hands on their hips throughout the examination for access and comfort.

[147] From thoracotomy, thoracoplasty, pneumonectomy.

[148] The movement becomes more up-and-down instead of in-and-out in conditions like emphysema.

[149] The patient braces his arms, uses his shoulder and neck muscles to help increase his chest volume. You may see the intercostal and supraclavicular spaces indrawing.

[150] Wheezy expiration is common in asthma, bronchitis, emphysema. Noisy inspiration (stridor) is due to obstruction e.g. by mediastinal masses or secretions in the upper airway.

Check whether expansion is normal/reduced on the right/left/both sides.[151]
Repeat this above the nipples.
'I'm just going to tap on your chest.'
Percuss[152] *from clavicles down, comparing sides. Don't forget the axillae.*
You need to check whether the percussion note is normal/dull/hyper-resonant/ stony-dull and in what area.
'Say '99' when I touch you.'
Assess tactile fremitus[153] *with the ulnar border of the hand from the clavicles down, comparing sides.*
You need to assess whether tactile fremitus is normal/increased/decreased and in what area.
'OK, now I'm going to have a listen. Breathe in and out through your mouth when I touch you with the stethoscope.'
Auscultate[154] *from clavicles down, comparing sides. Don't forget the axillae.*
'Now say '99' when I touch you with the stethoscope.'
Assess vocal fremitus from clavicles down, including axillae.
'Now can you lean forward so I can do all that again on your back? First let me feel your neck for any lumps or bumps.'
Repeat expansion, percussion, tactile fremitus, auscultation and vocal fremitus on the back of the chest.
'Let me press on your lower back.'
You are checking for presence of sacral oedma.[155]
Finally, if the examiners ask you what else you would like to do to complete you examination, say:
'To complete my examination I would like to examine for ankle oedema, see the peak flow reading, temperature and sputum pot for this patient. I would also like to see the X-rays.'

---

[151] This is a useful sign. Just remember that expansion is usually decreased on the diseased side.
[152] **Percussion**:
Hyper-resonant = pneumothorax or hyperinflation.
Dull = Collapse, consolidation or fibrosis.
Stony-dull = fluid, i.e. pleural effusion.
[153] **Tactile and vocal fremitus**:
Increased if it's solid or pus-filled (consolidation, collapse, fibrosis).
Decreased if it's air or water (pneumothorax, pleural effusion).
Normal in uncomplicated COPD or asthma.
[154] **Breath sounds**:
Vesicular is normal. Bronchial (just like if you listen over the trachea) in consolidation, collapse and fibrosis. Absent in collapse, pneumothorax, effusion. Added sounds: crackles/crepitations are early in inspiration in COPD and asthma, late in inspiration in fibrosing alveolitis and LVF, and change on coughing in bronchiectasis. A polyphonic wheeze is heard in asthma, but may be present in COPD also. Asthma and COPD have prolonged expiration.
[155] This may be a sign of congestive cardiac failure (like ankle oedema) in patients who have been sitting rather than standing.

EXAMINATION OF THE ABDOMEN

Introduce yourself and get the patient into position.[156]
'Hello, I'm Dr Parchment Smith. May I please check your details? Would you mind if I examined your tummy? Can you lie flat? Are you comfortable?'

WASH/GEL YOUR HANDS BEFORE YOU TOUCH THE PATIENT

Stand back, hands behind your back, and look at the patient and their surroundings.
Does the patient look well/ill/thin?[157] Are they comfortable/in pain, is their colour good/pale/jaundiced? What can you see around them, e.g. an intravenous drip/sick bowl?
Pick up both hands.
'Can I just have a look at your hands first?'
Look at the nails for clubbing[158], *leukonychia*[159], *koilonychia*[160]. *Look at the palm for Dupuytren's contractures*[161], *palmar erythema*[162], *pale palmar creases. On the skin of the hands look for jaundice, scratch marks*[163], *purpura*[164], *tattoos*[165].
'Could you hold both arms straight out please? And cock your palms back like this please?'
Look for a liver flap.[166]

---

[156] Lying flat with one pillow at the most, head and legs relaxed (legs not crossed) and arms relaxed by the side.
[157] Weight loss not only occurs in carcinoma, but in many other abdominal disorders such as inflammatory bowel disease, malabsorption and coeliac disease.
[158] The two gastrointestinal causes of clubbing are chronic liver disease and inflammatory bowel disease (i.e. Crohn's disease and ulcerative colitis).
[159] White nails caused by hypoalbuminaemia in chronic liver disease.
[160] Spoon-shaped nails caused by iron deficiency anaemia.
[161] Feel the palms. This thickening of the palmar fascia is better felt than seen. It is commonly associated with chronic liver disease but is also familial or idiopathic.
[162] Compare the patient's palm colour with your own. This redness of the palms sparing the centre is caused by increased levels of circulating oestrogen in liver failure; it is also seen in pregnancy and rheumatoid disease and may be idiopathic.
[163] Jaundiced patients are itchy.
[164] People with chronic liver failure bruise more easily due to loss of clotting factors.
[165] Hepatitis B can be contracted through tattoo needles.
[166] You will never see this sign of advanced liver disease and encephalopathy in an OSCE setting, but it might be seen on the wards.

'Can I just look into your eyes? Look up please.'

Gently draw the skin below the eye down to look at the conjunctiva. Assess whether the conjunctiva is pale[167]/not pale and the sclera is jaundiced[168]/not jaundiced.

'Could you open your mouth and stick out your tongue please?'

Look at the mouth for angular stomatitis[169] and telangiectasia[170]. Look for a smooth, red, beefy tongue[171], a pale tongue[172] or a blue tongue[173].

'I'm just going to shine a pen torch in your mouth.'

Look for ulcers[174], Peutz–Jeghers spots[175], telangiectasia and the general state of dentition.

'Now I'm going to feel your neck for any lumps or bumps.'

Feel in the left supraclavicular fossa for Virchow's node.[176]

'Could you take off your top/pull down your nightdress so I can see your chest and shoulders?'

Look for spider naevi[177], gynaecomastia[178], scratch marks and axillary hair loss. Next move on to the abdomen.

Initially inspect.

'Take a deep breath in and out please? Now cough.'[179]

---

[167] Pale conjunctiva is a clinical sign of anaemia (it does not prove that the patient is anaemic, only the haemoglobin measurement can do that).

[168] The sclera is the best place to see early or mild jaundice, or jaundice in Asian or black patients.

[169] Cracks at the corners of the mouth may indicate iron deficiency (but beware dribbly old ladies who also have cracked corners of their mouths!).

[170] A localised collection of non-contractile capillaries forms a red spot or telangiectasis. Telangiectasia may be found in and around the mouth and tongue, and may occur elsewhere in the gastrointestinal tract causing bleeding and anaemia. It may be part of a hereditary syndrome (Osler–Weber–Rendu hereditary haemorrhagic telangiectasia) or as part of the autoimmune CREST syndrome.

[171] Vitamin B12 deficiency.

[172] Clinical sign of anaemia.

[173] Cyanosis in liver disease.

[174] Seen in Crohn's disease.

[175] Small brownish-black macules on the lips and buccal mucosa (not tongue) may be associated with intestinal polyps in Peutz–Jeghers syndrome. The polyps can cause obstruction, intussusception or GI tract bleeding.

[176] The left supraclavicular node is classically one of the first palpable nodes to enlarge in gastric cancer.

[177] A bright-red spot on the skin with branching spider-like rays caused by dilation of superficial cutaneous arteries. Up to six may be normal, but more than that in the area drained by the superior vena cava (face, arms, upper trunk) can indicate liver disease.

[178] Abnormal breast tissue (in males only) may indicate an increase in circulating oestrogen in liver failure. Loss of axillary and chest hair and microgonadism can occur for the same reason.

[179] This should reveal any abdominal herniae. If you suspect any, ask the patient to lift both legs off the bed, keeping the knees straight. Divarication of the recti and incisional hernia (see OSCE case on pg 277) should be palpated to feel the extent and nature of the margins of the defect in the aponeurosis.

Look for obvious distension[180]*, swelling*[181]*, visible peristalsis or pulsation*[182] *of the abdomen. Look at the skin for scars (see diagram on pg 193), fistulae, or distended abdominal veins.*[183]

Next palpate the abdomen for masses and organomegaly (see diagram overleaf).

Kneel down. Ask the patient:

'Are you tender anywhere?'[184] **Just relax, arms by your sides.'**

Light palpation in the nine areas, then deeper in the four quadrants, resting over the epigastrium to feel for an aortic aneurysm. Then, starting in the right iliac fossa, palpate for the liver:

'Take deep breaths please in and out.'

Then, starting again in the right iliac fossa, palpate for the spleen:

'And again, deep breaths. I'm just going to pull you towards me.'

Deep palpation for spleen with patient rolled towards you. Then ballot for the kidneys.[185]

Next percuss the abdomen. Start from the right nipple down for the liver, left nipple down for the spleen, and pubic bone up for the bladder. Then tap from one flank to the other for flank dullness. If there is flank dullness, or there is a liver edge, or jaundice, you should demonstrate shifting dullness.[186]

'I'm going to listen to your tummy next.'

Listen for bowel sounds. Auscultate over all four quadrants[187]*, the epigastrium*[188]*, and over the liver*[189]*.*

Finally, if the examiners ask you what else you would like to do to complete you examination, say:

'To complete my examination I would like to examine the groins, external genitalia and do a DRE (digital rectal examination). I would also check for ankle oedema.'

---

[180] e.g. in ascites.

[181] Asymmetrical swelling may be seen due to constipation, organomegaly or a mass in the abdomen.

[182] e.g. aortic aneurysm.

[183] e.g. in portal hypertension. Abnormal veins should be stroked slowly in both directions to determine the direction of flow. In IVC obstruction the flow is upwards, in SVC obstruction it is downwards and in portal hypertension a caput medusae of veins flowing ray-like away from the umbilicus may be seen.

[184] If they are, touch that bit last.

[185] A common OSCE question is the differences between a kidney and a spleen: a spleen is not ballotable, moves diagonally with respiration not vertically, is dull to percussion, not resonant, and you can't get above it.

[186] For shifting dullness: tap from the resonant centre to the right side until you hear the note turn dull towards the flanks. LEAVE YOUR FINGER ON THE SPOT that was dull while the patient rolls away from you onto her left side. Wait for the fluid to settle, then tap on the same spot which now, being uppermost, should have gas beneath it and be resonant.

[187] There should always be bowel sounds. A silent abdomen may indicate peritonitis. Loud bowel sounds are called borborygmi. High-pitched 'tinkling' bowel sounds may indicate obstruction.

[188] You may hear an aortic bruit. If you do, renal artery bruits may be heard either side of the umbilicus and femoral bruits over the femoral arteries.

[189] A liver bruit may be heard in active hepatitis, tumour or arteriovenous malformation.

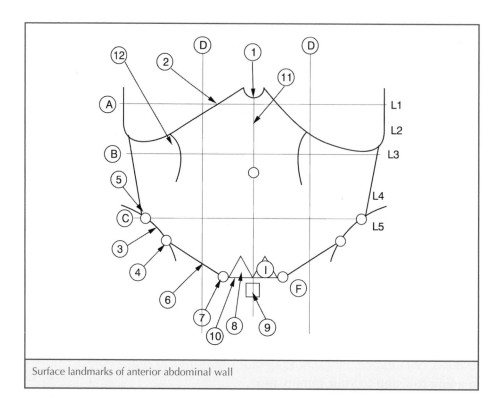

Surface landmarks of anterior abdominal wall

(A) **Transpyloric line**: halfway between jugular notch and pubic symphysis at L1 (pancreas lies here)

(B) **Subcostal line**: under lowest rib (rib 10 at L3)

(C) **Intertubercular line**: between the two tubercles of the iliac crest (L5)

(D) **Mid-clavicular line**: through midinguinal point, halfway between anterior superior iliac spine and symphysis pubis

(1) **Xiphoid process**: xiphisternal junction is at T9

(2) **Costal margins**: ribs 7–10 in front and 11 and 12 behind. Tenth costal cartilage is the lowest at L3

(3) **Iliac crest**: anterior superior iliac spine (ASIS) to posterior superior iliac spine (PSIS). Highest point is at L4

(4) **ASIS**

(5) **Tubercle of iliac crest**: 5 cm behind ASIS at L5

(6) **Inguinal ligament**: running from ASIS to pubic tubercle

(7) **Pubic tubercle**: tubercle on superior surface of pubis. Inguinal ligament attaches to it, as the lateral end of the superficial inguinal ring

(8) **Superficial inguinal ring**: inguinal hernia comes out above and medial to the pubic tubercle at point marked (I). Femoral hernia below and lateral to the pubic tubercle at point marked (F)

(9) **Symphysis pubis**: midline cartilaginous joint between pubic bones

(10) **Pubic crest**: ridge on superior surface of pubic bone medial to pubic tubercle

(11) **Linea alba**: symphysis pubis to xiphoid process midline

(12) **Linea semilunaris**: lateral edge of rectus. Crosses costal margin at ninth costal cartilage (tip of the gallbladder palpable here)

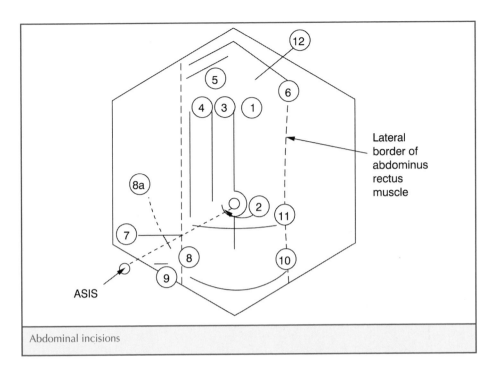

Lateral border of abdominus rectus muscle

ASIS

Abdominal incisions

(1) **Midline incision through the linea alba**: this provides good access, can be extended easily and is quick to make and close. It is relatively avascular. Is more painful than transverse incisions. Incision crosses Langer's lines. Poor cosmetic appearance. Narrow linea alba below umbilicus. Some vessels cross the midline. May cause bladder damage.

(2) **Subumbilical incision**: used for repair of paraumbilical hernia and laparoscopic port.

(3) **Paramedian incision**: 1.5 cm from midline through rectus abdominus. Was the only effective vertical incision in the days when the only available suture material was catgut. Takes longer to make than midline incision. Does not lend itself to closure by 'Jenkins rule' (use four times the length of the suture as the length of the wound). Poor cosmetic result. Can lead to infection in the rectus sheath. Other hazards include: the tendinous intersections must be dissected off; need to divide falciform ligament above umbilicus on the right; if rectus is split more than 1 cm from medial border, the intercostal nerves are disrupted, leading to denervation of the medial rectus (the rectus can be retracted without splitting to avoid this).

(4) **Pararectal**: now abandoned due to damage to nerves entering rectus sheath.

(5) **Kocher's incision**: 3 cm below and parallel to the costal margin from the midline to the rectus border. Good incision for cholecystectomy on the right and splenectomy on the left, **but** beware superior epigastric vessels. If wound is extended laterally, too many intercostal nerves are severed. Cannot be extended caudally.

(6) **Double Kocher's (rooftop) incision**: good access to liver and spleen. Useful for intrahepatic surgery. Used for radical pancreatic and gastric surgery and bilateral adrenalectomy.

(7) **Transverse muscle cutting incision**: can be across all muscles. Beware intercostal nerves.

(8) **McBurney's/gridiron**: classic approach to appendix 'through the junction of the outer and middle third of a line from the ASIS to the umbilicus at right angles to that line'. It can be modified into a skin-crease horizontal cut. The external oblique aponeurosis is cut in the line of the fibres and the internal oblique and transversus abdominus are split transversally in the line of the fibres. Beware – scarring if not horizontal – the iliohypogastric and ilioinguinal nerve – the deep circumflex artery.

(8a) **Rutherford Morrison incision**: the gridiron can be extended cephalad and laterally, obliquely splitting the external oblique to afford good access to the caecum, appendix and right colon.

CONTINUED OVERLEAF

193

(9) **Lanz**: this is a lower incision than the McBurney's and closer to the ASIS. It has a better cosmetic result (covered by bikini in ladies) but tends to divide the iliohypogastric and ilioinguinal nerves, leading to denervation of the inguinal canal mechanism, which can result in increased risk of inguinal hernia.

(10) **Pfannenstiel incision**: most frequently used transverse incision in adults. Excellent access to female genitalia for caesarian section and for bladder and prostate operations. Also used for bilateral hernia repair. The skin is incised in a downwardly convex arc into the suprapubic skin crease 2 cm above the pubis. The upper flap is raised and the rectus sheath incised 1 cm cephalic to the skin incision (not extending lateral to the rectus). The rectus is then divided longitudinally in the midline.

(11) **Transverse incision**: particularly useful in neonates and children who do not have the subdiaphragmatic and pelvic recesses of the adult. It heals securely and cosmetically well, with less pain and fewer respiratory problems than the longitudinal midline incision, but division of red muscle involves more blood loss and less secure closure than a longitudinal incision. It cannot be extended easily. It takes longer to make and to close. Limited access in adults to pelvic or subdiaphragmatic structures.

(12) **Thoraco-abdominal incision**: access to lower thorax and upper abdomen. Used for liver and biliary surgery on the right. Used for oesophageal, gastric and aortic surgery on the left.

NB **The ideal abdominal incision**: should allow easy and rapid access to the relevant structures; should allow easy extension, if necessary; should favour secure healing for the short term (dehiscence) and long term (herniation); should be relatively pain-free post-operatively; should have a satisfactory cosmetic appearance.

EXAMINATION OF AN ABDOMINAL AORTIC ANEURYSM

'Hello, my name is Dr Parchment Smith. Can I please check your details? Would you mind if I examined you? Would you lie down flat with just one pillow under your head?'

WASH/GEL YOUR HANDS BEFORE YOU TOUCH THE PATIENT

Stand back and look.

Does the patient look comfortable at rest? Is there an obvious pulsatile swelling in the upper abdomen? Do they look pale, in pain or breathless?

Start by looking at their hands[190] and feeling the pulse.

Check the pulse rate and rhythm and that it is equal in both wrists.[191] Check the palms are not cold or clammy[192] and that there is no pallor in the palmar creases[193] and no nicotine staining[194].

To the examiners: **'I would like to know the blood pressure in both arms.'[195]**

Look in the eyes.

You are looking for arcus senilis or xanthomata.[196]

In the neck check that the character of the carotid pulse is normal and that there are no bruits.[197]

---

[190] By doing this you give the examiners the chance to tell you that they just want you to feel the abdomen. Don't spend too long on the preliminaries, just indicate that you are looking for signs of the predisposing factors for aneurysm (hypertension, atherosclerosis due to smoking or hyperlipidaemia) and factors suggesting a leak (shock, tachycardia, anaemia, tenderness).

[191] In any patient with an aneurysm it is important to confirm that they are cardiovascularly stable with no tachycardia. Radio-radial delay (a discrepancy between the two radial pulses) is a well-known but rarely seen sign of aortic dissection.

[192] Signs of shock.

[193] Indicating anaemia, relevant because it may indicate:
1. Fitness for surgery.
2. Another, unrelated cause for an upper abdominal mass. (Stomach cancer lying across the aorta may present as a mass transmitting pulsations. It will not be expansile.)
3. A slow leak, e.g. in an inflammatory aneurysm.

[194] Smokers are more prone to arterial disease and have a poorer prognosis in major surgery.

[195] Hypertension is a risk factor for aortic aneurysms. Discrepancy in blood pressure in the two arms indicates large-vessel atherosclerosis or aortic dissection.

[196] Both signs of hyperlipidaemia.

[197] A patient undergoing aortic aneurysm repair who had significant carotid stenosis would be at high risk of intraoperative stroke.

Now look at the abdomen.

Look for an abnormal pulsating mass above the umbilicus Also check for any scars, especially sternotomy[198] or laparotomy[199] scars.

'Is your tummy tender?[200] Can I feel the lump please?'

Place your hand over the lump, gently trying to feel its extent and margins.

'Is this tender?'

Firstly, try to feel the character of the lump – is it firm, non-tender and pulsatile?[201]

Put your hands either side of the lump and allow them to be visibly pushed apart by the pulsations.

You are checking whether the lump is expansile.[202] Guess the transverse diameter.[203] Can you feel the upper limit? If so, this would suggest it is infrarenal.[204] Can you feel a bilobed structure below the umbilicus? If so, this would suggest it is extending into the iliacs. It might move slightly from side to side but not up and down.

'Can I feel in your groins please?'

Palpate the femoral pulses and check they are palpable. Does either side feel aneurysmal?[205]

'I'm just going to listen to the lump.'

Auscultate over the aneurysm, either side of it just under the ribcage (for renal artery bruits) and over the femoral pulses.

Finally, if the examiners ask you what else you would like to do to complete you examination, say:

'To complete my examination I would like to examine the heart and the legs for cardiac and peripheral vascular disease.'

---

[198] Previous cardiac surgery has implications for any major surgery planned.

[199] Previous surgery may make aortic aneurysm repair more difficult because of adhesions.

[200] A tender abdominal aortic aneurysm raises the suspicion of a leak or sudden expansion. If it is tender, the patient should not be sitting in an MRCS OSCE bay!

[201] Although an aneurysm is pulsatile, this is not a specific sign as any lump near an artery is likely to be pulsatile. Rest your hand on the lump and hold it still to appreciate the pulsation.

[202] Unlike the non-specific sign of pulsatility, an expansile mass is generally an aneurysm or (rarely) an extremely vascular tumour. An expansile mass will push the hands in opposite directions, whereas both hands will move in the same direction (usually up) when resting on a pulsatile mass.

[203] You can only estimate accurately if you have felt a few aneurysms, the diameter of which had been assessed by ultrasound – so start scouring the wards and clinics for these now! The transverse diameter of a normal (non-aneurysmal) aorta is 2–3 cm and it can be palpated in a slim patient. Patients with aneurysms around 5 cm are usually under surveillance and very stable so ideal for exams; it is unlikely that a patient whose aneurysm had suddenly expanded to 8 cm would be put into an OSCE for repeated palpation!

[204] Only 1–2% are suprarenal.

[205] There is an increased incidence of other aneurysms in a patient with an abdominal aortic aneurysm.

EXAMINATION OF A STOMA[206]

When asked to comment on a stoma, be methodical and state the obvious in an intelligent way. Even if you have no idea what type of stoma it is or what operation has occurred, there are ten things you should look for and comment on to get you through this case.

WASH/GEL YOUR HANDS BEFORE YOU TOUCH THE PATIENT

1. **Site**. Ileostomies are typically in the right iliac fossa, colostomies on the left. Midline loop colostomies are rarely done for relief of obstruction, usually in emergency cases. Sites may vary due to exceptional circumstances, so use it as a guide rather than relying on it absolutely.

2. **Calibre**. Colostomies are the largest, followed by ileostomies, then urostomies. Retraction or stenosis may make the lumen look smaller; prolapse may make a stoma look bigger.

3. **Number of lumens**. Is the stoma an end stoma or a loop or double-barrelled stoma? The non-productive lumen may look tiny and retracted and you have to look for it. There may be more than one stoma, for example a colostomy and mucous fistula after a modified Hartmann's, or a colostomy and urinary diversion after a pelvic clearance.

---

[206] **Types of stoma**

Gastrostomy	Caecostomy
Jejunostomy	Colostomy
Ileostomy	Urostomy

Indications for stoma

- **Feeding** e.g. gastrostomy following GI surgery, in CNS disease, in coma
- **Decompression** e.g. gastrostomy (usually temporary), caecostomy
- **Lavage** e.g. caecostomy on table before resecting distal colonic disease with primary anastomosis
- **Diversion** e.g. ileostomy to protect at-risk distal anastomosis, or to achieve bowel rest for Crohn's. Loop colostomies and double-barrelled colostomies facilitate closure later but are more difficult to manage
- **Exteriorisation** e.g. double-barrelled colostomy (not used for malignancy), resection with end colostomy and rectal stump (Hartmann's) when primary anastomosis is impossible (e.g. perforation, ischaemia, obstruction). Resection with end colostomy and mucous fistula (like Hartmann's but easier to rejoin). Permanent colostomy (e.g. after abdominoperineal resections in low rectal tumours). Permanent ileostomy (e.g. after panproctocolectomy for ulcerative colitis or familial polyposis coli)

Selecting a stoma site

Assess	Avoid	Problem patients
Before operation	Wound site	Wheelchair-bound
With clothes	Bony prominences	Amputees
Lying and standing	Existing scars	Obese
Good visibility	Umbilicus	Allergies
	Groin crease/skin fold	Psychological problems

4. **Spout**. Ileostomies have a spout to keep the irritating alkaline effluent away from the skin; colostomies do not unless they are prolapsing.

5. **Bag contents**. Often the most instantly informative. Green fluid ileal contents, faeces or urine? Even if the bag has been taken off, it will be lying somewhere around, and inspection of the contents (e.g. any mucus, blood) is a useful part of the examination.

6. **Scars**. What previous surgery has the patient had? Look particularly for evidence of previous closures of other stomas or mucus fistulae. The absence of a midline incision in the presence of a stoma indicates a trephine (usually defunctioning) colostomy or a laparoscopic procedure. The maturity of the scars also gives a clue as to how recently the surgery was performed.

7. **Complications of the stoma**. Mention the state of the stoma. Does it look healthy and well-constructed? Is it ischaemic, prolapsing, retracted, stenosed? Does it have a parastomal hernia (ask the patient to cough or raise his legs). Is the mucosa inflamed, are there polyps?

Complications of stoma

Technical problems

- **Ischaemia/gangrene**: abdominal wall defect too tight; injury to mesenteric vessels; re-siting is necessary
- **Prolapse or intussusception**: when bowel is not anchored to abdominal wall internally; reduction is easy but re-siting is needed if prolapse is recurrent
- **Parastomal herniae**: may cause difficulties with appliances; may contain bowel at risk of obstruction/ strangulation; re-siting may be needed
- **Stenosis**: poor initial siting; ischaemia; underlying disease process (carcinoma, inflammatory bowel disease); re-siting may be necessary if there is obstruction
- **Bowel contents spill over into efferent loop**: especially in loop colostomy; distal bowel is not adequately defunctioned if this occurs; split or double-barrelled stomas solve this; the efferent loop should always be sited cephalic to (above) the afferent loop
- **Reservoir ileostomies** have specific problems: valve failure; incontinence; obstruction; impaired blood supply

General problems

- **Stoma diarrhoea**: due to underlying disease; due to inappropriate diet; can lead to water and electrolyte imbalance, especially after ileostomy
- **Nutritional disorders**: vitamin B deficiency (megaloblastic anaemia); chronic microcytic normochromic anaemia
- **Kidney stones and gallstones**: caused by loss of terminal ileum; failure of bile salt absorption; excessive water loss
- **Short gut syndrome**: profuse fluid and electrolyte loss
- **Underlying disease**: may cause recurrent symptoms; Crohn's may cause peristomal fistulae or proximal obstruction
- **Psychological and sexual problems**

8. **Perineum**. Ask if the patient has a patent anal canal or a closed perineum to ascertain whether this is a temporary or permanent stoma. It will also give you a clue as to the operation: the commonest reasons for an abdominoperineal resection (APR) are a low rectal cancer, familial polyposis coli, or severe ulcerative
colitis.

9. **General condition of the patient**. Is this a terminally ill patient who has been given a palliative defunctioning colostomy? Or a very thin young woman whose Crohn's disease necessitated a temporary ileostomy? Or a healthy-looking middle-aged man long recovered from the low rectal tumour that needed an APR and end colostomy? Do they look malnourished or dehydrated (e.g. due to high-output stoma).

10. **Type of appliance**. A one-piece is where the whole appliance is connected to the skin by adhesive and the whole appliance has to be changed. A two-piece (more common for long-standing stomas) has a base-plate with a flange. The pouch only is changed regularly. Drainable, transparent pouches with a tap on the end are used in the post-operative period when the output is large and must be monitored. Closed, opaque bags are more common in the long term and may have charcoal filters to release flatus without odour.

Practical problems
- **Odour**: advice can be given on hygiene, diet and deodorant sprays
- **Flatus**: can be improved by diet and special filters
- **Skin problems**: usually due to an ill-fitting device. The problem is worsened as the stoma shrinks post-operatively. The problem can be counteracted by a barrier cream or two-piece appliance. Ileostomies with their irritant, copious output can be particularly troublesome. The patient may need a supporting belt if spout is not big enough.
- **Leakage**: transverse loop colostomies are especially prone to leakage. A poor site may be responsible. Methylcellulose bland paste around the appliance can help
- **Parastomal hernia**: a flexible pouch, supporting belt and filler paste can all help with this problem. Re-siting may be necessary.
- **Stoma prolapse**: may need surgical correction

Post-operative advice
- **Patient warned of problems**: oedematous stoma; copious offensive early output; transparent pouch to monitor stoma
- **Self-care programme**: patients observe, help them manage their own stoma
- **Counselling and support**: from stoma care nurse

EXAMINATION OF THE GROIN

Introduce yourself and get the patient into position.

'Hello, my name is Dr Parchment Smith. Can I please check your details? Would you mind if I examined your groin? Can you stand in front of me, on this step[207], trousers off please? I'm just going to have a look first of all.'

WASH/GEL YOUR HANDS BEFORE YOU TOUCH THE PATIENT

Look at the position of the lump.

Is there a swelling in one groin or both? Is the swelling large or small? Whereabouts is the swelling, e.g. scrotum[208]/groin crease[209]/groin[210].

If you can't see anything ask the patient:

'Is it aching or sore anywhere? Show me where.[211] OK, I'll be gentle. Does the lump ever pass into the sac (if male)? I'm going to gently feel your scrotum now (if male).'

Palpate the scrotum.

---

[207] There is usually a step by the bed. If there is, get the patient to stand on it. It looks more elegant to crouch in front of the patient looking up or straight ahead at the lump rather than being hunched over double, furtling in the low-down groin buried under the tum of a small, fat person! It will also be easier for the examiners to see the signs you are demonstrating. If there is not a step by the bed, don't bother – making an issue of it will just irritate the examiners.

[208] This could be an inguinal hernia, hydrocoele, testicular mass or epididymal cyst.

[209] An inguinal hernia usually lies above the groin crease. A lump filling the groin crease and extending down towards the upper thigh is more likely to be a femoral hernia.

[210] **Differential diagnosis of a lump in the groin**:
- Hernia   – direct inguinal
                – indirect inguinal
                – femoral
- Lymph nodes
- Saphena varix
- Ectopic testis
- Femoral aneurysm
- Hydrocoele of   – spermatic cord
                – canal of Nuck
- Lipoma of the cord
- Psoas bursa
- Psoas abscess

[211] On the one hand this might be construed as cheating, but on the other hand it is important to ascertain whether or not a lump is tender before you start, and if being so considerate has the added benefit of getting the patient to point out an otherwise invisible lump, so much the better!

If you can feel a mass in the scrotum[212] you need to determine three things:
- Firstly, can you get above it?[213] If not, it is probably a hernia.[214]
- Secondly, can you feel the testis separate from the mass?[215] If not, then the lump is either in the testis, such as a neoplasm or an orchitis, or around the testis, such as a haematocoele or a hydrocoele.[216]
- Thirdly, does it transilluminate?

'I'm just going to shine a light on the lump in your scrotum. Can I have the shades down please?'
Shading the front of the groin further with your hand, shine your pen torch from the back of the scrotum to see if the swelling lights up as a brilliantly illuminated pinky-red. If it does, it is fluid filled, either an epididymal cyst or a hydrocoele.
If you think the swelling is a hernia (i.e. you cannot get above it, it is separate from the testicle, and it does not transilluminate) then next palpate it from the side.
Stand next to the patient[217], one hand in the small of the patient's back and the palpating hand flat on the groin parallel to the inguinal ligament. Feel the temperature, tension and composition of the lump.
Next test for a cough impulse by compressing the lump gently but firmly, applying counter-pressure with your hand on the back.[218]

---

[212] Even if you can see an obvious lump in the groin, it is important to start with examination of the testicle because:
a) the hernia may extend into the scrotum;
b) you need to make sure there is one, as ectopic testis is a differential of a groin lump; and
c) people with dual pathology are commonly called upon to be OSCE cases.

The differential diagnosis of a lump in the scrotum

Can't get above it	Can't feel testicle separately	Transilluminable	Can get above it, can feel testicle separately and not transilluminable
Indirect inguinal hernia	Seminoma/teratoma	Hydrocoele	Epididymitis (incl. TB)
Infantile hydrocoele (rare)	Haematocoele	Epididymal cyst	Spermatocoele
Varicocoele	Hydrocoele		
	Syphilitic gumma		
	Orchitis		
	Torsion		

[213] Palpate the testicle. Above it should be only the narrow leash of cord structures and the thin scrotal skin. You should be able to feel the top of the testicle.
[214] If you can't get above the lump the swelling is an inguinoscrotal hernia, a varicocoele (which looks and feels characteristic see pg 288) or (rarely) an infantile hydrocoele.
[215] Trace the cord down until you feel the testicle. Work your fingers gently around it, trying to determine if the mass is separate from the testicle or not. The epididymis arises from the posterior aspect of the testicle. Is it the epididymis that is swollen? You might find it useful at this stage to feel the opposite testicle so you can feel what is normal for this patient (assuming he does not have dual pathology).
[216] If you can feel the testis separately it is probably an epididymal swelling such as an epididymal cyst or epididymitis.
[217] The reason for standing next to the patient is to be able to place your hand in exactly the same position as the patient's hand would be when supporting or reducing the hernia, i.e. putting a hand on the hernia and lifting it upwards and backwards.
[218] This stops you pushing the patient backwards.

'Can you cough please?

If it expands[219] on coughing, it has a positive cough impulse.

Now check for reducibility.

'Does the lump go back in sir? Can you get it back in yourself? Will you do that please, I don't want to hurt you.[220] That's great, thank you. Now I'll take it.'

Let the patient reduce it, then you take over and hold it reduced with gentle pressure.

Apply pressure over the external ring.[221] Ask the patient to **'cough please'.**

You are assessing whether the hernia is controlled at the external ring.[222]

Slide your hand back to rest over the internal ring, keeping a steady pressure so you are still controlling the hernia.[223] Ask the patient to **'cough again please'.**

You are assessing whether the hernia is controlled at the deep ring.[224]

Next, let go and watch the hernia reappear.[225] If it does not reappear spontaneously, ask the patient to cough again.

To the examiners: **'To complete my examination[226] I would like to examine the other groin with the patient standing and perform an abdominal and groin examination with the patient lying down.[227] My diagnosis is...'**

---

[219] It must expand, not just move, to be a positive cough impulse.

[220] Often the lump has not been reduced for years, or the patient has a special knack for getting the hernia back in. In any case, hurting the patient does not look good in the OSCE. The examiners, familiar with this scenario from clinic, will usually let you get away with this unless they are real sadists. If the patient refuses, or says that he's never tried to put it back, you have no option but to gently try to reduce it with your flat hand from underneath the lump (not poking it in with your fingers!), lifting it upwards and backwards. Press firmly to reduce the tension in the lump. Then gently squeeze the lower part of the swelling. As the lump gets softer, lift it up towards the external ring until the hernia has all passed in through this point.

[221] Remember that the inguinal hernia reduces into or through a point above and medial to the pubic tubercle (the external or superficial ring). A femoral hernia will (if reducible) reduce into or through a point below and lateral to the pubic tubercle. The upper crease of the mons (i.e. where the pot belly hangs over) indicates the crest of the pubis and the level of the pubic tubercle. These, you will remember, form the inferior and lateral margins respectively of the superficial inguinal ring, just lateral from the midline (see pg 192 and figure on pg 193). Once you have located this and feel the hernia is controlled by your hand, try to control it with a couple of fingers so the point at which the hernia is controlled is demonstrated more clearly. Having reduced the hernia and inspected the patient, you will have a reasonable idea whether the hernia is direct or indirect, so concentrate on demonstrating this.

[222] Both direct and indirect herniae are controlled at the external ring (but a femoral hernia will not be).

[223] The deep ring is situated 1.3 cm above the inguinal ligament, midway between the anterior superior iliac spine and the pubic tubercle. This is the 'midpoint of the inguinal ligament' just lateral to the femoral artery pulsation at the so-called 'midinguinal point'.

[224] If the hernia can only be held reduced at the external ring it is a direct inguinal hernia. If it can be controlled by pressure over the internal ring it is an indirect inguinal hernia. Bear in mind that some larger indirect inguinal herniae have an element of a direct hernia (posterior inguinal canal wall weakness) associated with them.

[225] An indirect hernia will seem to slide obliquely along the line of the canal whereas a direct hernia will project directly forwards.

[226] Percussing and auscultating the lump, if it is very large and you suspect it contains bowel, may be appropriate. Bowel sounds confirm the presence of loops of bowel within the sac, which increases the risk of obstruction or strangulation.

[227] Looking for things that might have increased the intra-abdominal pressure such as a large bladder, enlarged prostate, ascites, chronic intestinal obstruction and pregnancy.

EXAMINATION OF THE BREAST[228]

'Hello, my name is Dr Parchment Smith. Please can I check your details? Would you mind if I examined your breasts? Please sit at 45° with your shirt off, hands on your hips.'

WASH/GEL YOUR HANDS BEFORE YOU TOUCH THE PATIENT

Stand back, hands behind your back, and inspect.
- *Does the patient looks generally well, with no evidence of weight loss, jaundice, shortness of breath or pallor?*
- *Look at the breasts for asymmetry in size or shape, skin changes such as redness, puckering, peau d'orange, nodules or ulcers.*
- *Look at the nipple and areolae for retraction, destruction, asymmetry and discharge. Look at the axillae and arms for swelling, nodes, veins or wasting of muscles.*
- *Look for any signs of previous treatment such as mastectomy, scarring, radiation burns, telangiectasia, hair loss, lymphoedema or ink marks.*

'Could you raise your arms slowly over your head please?'
This enables you to look under the breasts[229] and at the axillae, in particular for any asymmetry or tethering.

'Thank you, put your hands behind your head and lean back. Now I would like to feel your breasts. Are they tender at all? Have you noticed any lumps yourself?'[230]

Start your examination on the side with no lump.
Palpate the breast with the flat of your fingers. Feel for abnormalities in all four quadrants, the centre, the nipple and the axillary tail.

Most lumps occur in the upper outer quadrant.
Next feel the axilla.

---

[228] **Causes of a breast lump**
Common cases in the OSCE will be:
- Carcinoma of the breast (see pg 218).
- Localised area of fibroadenosis – benign breast change (see pg 222).
- Cyst (see pg 222).
- Fibroadenoma (see pg 222).
Other OSCE cases you might see include fat necrosis, other cysts (cystadenoma, galactocoele, chronic abscess, retention cyst of glands of Montgomery), infections and inflammation, swelling arising from the chest wall (TB or tumour of a rib, lipoma, thrombosis of superficial veins, also known as Mondor's disease).
[229] You may have to lift a large or pendulous breast gently with the back of your hand to see the whole underside and inframammary fold.
[230] As anyone who has done a breast clinic can testify, finding a small breast lump is hard enough with the patient pointing it out, never mind when you don't even know which breast it is in. If the breast lump is large, ulcerating or obvious then you don't have to ask; otherwise, consider prompting the patient as above. Bear in mind that you run the risk of an examiner taking a dim view of this, or even considering it cheating. You could justify it as carrying out the examination as you would in a clinic, but it is a personal decision, and you must be happy in your own mind that you do not consider it cheating.

'Relax your arm, let me take your elbow.'

Holding the patient's forearm with your non-palpating hand, support the elbow and lift it to shoulder height. Ensuring the patient's arm is relaxed, systematically examine the four walls of the axilla (lateral, medial, anterior, posterior) and gently into the apex.

Next palpate the breast with the lump.[231]

Assess the lump.

To assess the fixity of the lump make sure the patient's hands are still on her hips and ask her to **'relax your arms'**. *Then, take the lump between your fingers and move it gently in the line of pectoralis major fibres, then at right angles to this plane.*

Ask the patient to **'press your fists into your hips, tensing your chest muscles'**. *Repeat the movement of the lump, noting if contraction of pectoralis major significantly restricts the movement of the lump.*

Next examine this axilla.

'Relax your arm and let me take your elbow.'

Repeat the axillary examination as above.

Feel the supraclavicular area on both sides.

Stand up and present to the examiners.

'There is a small, non-tender lump in the upper outer quadrant of the left breast. It is about 2 cm in diameter, round and irregular in shape, with a craggy surface and indistinct edges. It is stony-hard, not fluctuant, not pulsatile, compressible or reducible. It is tethered to the skin but does not appear to be fixed to the chest wall. It appears to arise from the subcutaneous breast tissue. The overlying skin is not warm or red and is intact. The surrounding skin is healthy.'

'To complete my examination I would like to CHECK FOR NIPPLE DISCHARGE[232], LISTEN TO THE CHEST and EXAMINE THE ABDOMEN for liver enlargement[233].'

---

[231] Examine it in the same way, identifying the lump and examining it as for the examination of a lump (see pg 43).

[232] In the clinical setting you would have asked about nipple discharge in the history. If it was a feature, you would try to express the discharge pressing on each quadrant in turn to determine which quadrant the discharge is from, also looking for whether the discharge is expressed from a single duct or multiple ducts, and assessing the nature of the discharge.

Causes of nipple discharge:
- Physiological (2/3rds of all discharge)
- Duct ectasia (watery, cheesy, often more than one duct, may be bloodstained)
- Duct papilloma (single duct, bloody)
- Epithelial hyperplasia (occasionally bloodstained, usually single duct)
- Galactorrhoea (?pregnant ?prolactin levels)
- Carcinoma (single duct discharge, watery, serous or bloody, usually associated with palpable mass)

[233] In order to look for signs of lung or liver metastases.

C THE OSCE CASES

HOW TO USE THIS SECTION

Common history or examination cases you might see in the exam appear in this section.

For each case, you will be given an example 'history question' and an example 'clinical examination question' which you could expect to find outside a station in the examination. Following each of these is an example of how to present a 'typical patient' with this complaint. You can then use these examples to practise with friends/colleagues. One of you should be the candidate and use the basic history and examination schemes to start you off. A second person should pretend to be the patient in the example given. A third person could be used as the examiner to check that all the questions or examination steps from the basic schemes are completed. The 'candidate' can then present their findings at the end and have a guess at a differential diagnosis. At the end of the 'station' the 'examiner' can then use the 'What you should know' section to ask the 'candidate' some questions about the case. Try and time yourselves so you get an idea of how long 9 minutes is.

In the actual exam you could be asked just to examine a patient, just to take a history, or to 'assess' the patient (i.e. do both). You therefore need to be flexible. Use the 'Combined Assessment Boxes' in the History and Examination sections if you get stuck.

Following this are photograph/s of the condition in the 'What you should see' section so that if you don't get a chance to see a particular case in all those outpatient clinics you will be attending before the exam at least you will have an idea of what it will look like!

Take a history from this patient with breathlessness

(see pg 158)

PLEURAL EFFUSION

'I would like to present Mr W, a 65-year-old retired publican. He has become increasingly short of breath for the last 4 months. It is worse when lying down and he is unable to get up his stairs at home without stopping. He has an associated cough, which is productive of yellow sputum and he has also noticed blood in it. He gets right-sided chest pain, which is severe and worse on inspiration. He had lost 2 stone in weight over this period. He has no other medical history. He takes no medication and has no known allergies. He is a smoker and has smoked for 50 pack years. He drinks 30 units of alcohol per week. He lives alone.

I am concerned this gentleman has a lung malignancy, although infection is another possibility. It sounds as though he may have a pleural effusion as his SOB is worse on lying down. I would like to examine his respiratory system to confirm my diagnosis.'

✎ WHAT YOU SHOULD KNOW

Causes:
Exudate (>30 g/l protein)
Neoplastic (primary or secondary)
Inflammatory: pneumonia/TB; PE; trauma; rheumatoid arthritis; SLE; subphrenic abscess; pancreatitis
Transudate (<30 mg/l protein)
Heart failure; liver cirrhosis; nephrotic syndrome
Meigs syndrome (ovarian fibroma)
Management of pleural effusion:
- Determine underlying cause and treat as appropriate
- Aspiration of pleural effusion
- Chest drain insertion (see pg 624)
- Pleurodesis (see pg 208)
Radiological signs of massive pleural effusion:
- Enlargement of ipsilateral hemithorax
- Displacement of mediastinum to contralateral side
- Severe depression/flattening/inversion of ipsilateral hemidiaphragm; visible air bronchogram

PLEURAL EFFUSION

Examine this patient's respiratory system

(see pg 186)

'The pulse is regular and the jugular venous pressure is not elevated. The trachea is central (or deviated away from the abnormal side) and the expansion is normal. The percussion note is stony-dull at the right base with diminished tactile fremitus and vocal resonance and diminished breath sounds. There is (may be) an area of bronchial breathing above the area of dullness. The diagnosis is a right pleural effusion.'

👁 WHAT YOU SHOULD SEE

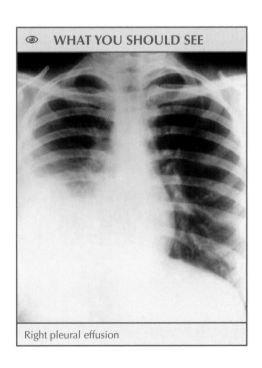

Right pleural effusion

PLEURAL EFFUSION

✍ MANAGEMENT OF PLEURAL EFFUSION

1. Aspiration of pleural effusion

Get AP and lateral X-rays, and percuss out the level of the effusion (see Chest x-ray signs of pleural effusion below).

Explain the procedure to the patient and obtain consent.

Sit the patient erect, leaning forward, with their arms folded on a table in front of them.

The site of aspiration is usually in the eighth intercostal space in the posterior axillary line.

Mark the site, and determine that it is below the level at which the percussion note changed from resonant to dull.

Using aseptic technique, set up a tray, prep the site and infiltrate with local anaesthetic.

A diagnostic tap can be performed using a 50-ml syringe with a green needle and distributing the fluid aspirated into three sterile specimen pots (like those used for MSUs) for cytology, biochemistry and microbiology. Try to get at least 20 ml into the cytology specimen pot to increase the yield of cells.

A therapeutic tap can be performed by inserting a grey venflon attached to a three-way tap, and using a 50-ml syringe to repeatedly aspirate and discharge the contents via the three-way tap into a sterile jug. As the fluid volume reduces, withdraw the needle and cover the puncture site with a sterile dressing.

2. Chest drain insertion

See Chapter 8, Chest drain insertion, pg 624.

3. Pleurodesis

In the case of recurrent or resistant pleural effusion, such as in untreatable malignancy, pleurodesis can be carried out in several different ways. Thoracoscopic pleurectomy, where the pleura is stripped from the lung, leaves an oozing, raw surface that sticks to the chest wall and heals fused to it, thus obliterating the pleural space. Chemical pleurodesis involves instilling (either down the chest drain or thoracoscopically) irritating chemicals (such as talc or tetracycline) that induce a fibrous reaction into the pleural space.

Chest X-ray signs of pleural effusion

- First 300 ml not visualised on PA view
- Lateral decubitus views may detect as little as 25 ml
- Hemidiaphragm and costophrenic sinuses obscured
- Meniscus-shaped semicircular upper surface with lowest point in midaxillary line.
- Associated collapse of ipsilateral lung

PLEURAL EFFUSION

👁 WHAT YOU SHOULD SEE

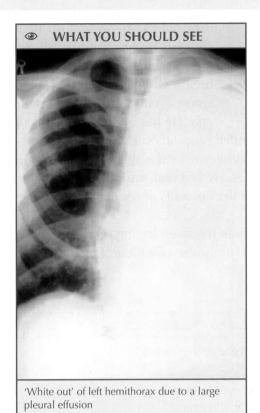

'White out' of left hemithorax due to a large pleural effusion

209

Take a history from this patient with breathlessness

(see pg 158)

PNEUMOTHORAX

'I would like to present Mr W, a 20-year-old student. He has had two episodes in the last 6 months when he has become acutely short of breath with associated severe left-sided chest pain, worse on inspiration. The last episode was 4 weeks ago. He has had no problems with his breathing prior to this. He attended hospital on each occasion and required chest drain insertion. He has no other medical history. He takes no medication and has no known allergies. He is a non-smoker. However, he drinks 30 units of alcohol per week. He lives in halls of residence at the local university.

I suspect this young man has been having recurrent spontaneous pneumothoraces due to rupture of a pleural bleb. I would like to examine his respiratory system.'

✏ WHAT YOU SHOULD KNOW

Definition: accumulation of air in the pleural space.
Pathophysiology: disruption of visceral pleura/trauma to parietal pleura.
Symptoms: dyspnoea in 80–90%; pleuritic back/shoulder pain.
Causes of pneumothorax: remember the mnemonic 'THE CHEST SET'
T rauma: Penetrating trauma
           Blunt trauma   a) rib fracture
                              b) increased intrathoracic pressure against closed glottis, lung
                                  contusion/laceration
                              c) bronchial rupture
H oneycomb lung (pulmonary fibrosis, cystic fibrosis, sarcoidosis, scleroderma, rheumatoid lung)
E mphysema, Esophageal rupture
C hronic obstructive pulmonary disease
H yaline membrane disease
E ndometriosis – catamenial pneumothorax = recurrent spontaneous pneumothorax during menstruation associated with endometriosis of the diaphragm (usually right-sided)
S pontaneous, Scleroderma
T uberous sclerosis
S arcoma (osteo), Sarcoidosis
E osinophilic granuloma
T uberculosis and fungus
X-ray signs of simple pneumothorax
White margin of visceral pleura separated from parietal pleura.
Absence of vascular markings beyond visceral pleural margin.
X-ray signs of tension pneumothorax
Displacement of mediastinum away from affected side.
Deep sulcus sign – on frontal view larger lateral costodiaphragmatic recess than on opposite side.
Diaphragmatic inversion.
Total/subtotal lung collapse.
Collapse of SVC/IVC/right heart border.
CONTINUED on pg 212

Examine this patient's respiratory system

(see pg 186)

PNEUMOTHORAX

'The right side of the chest (of this tall thin young adult male or old emphysematous man) expands poorly compared with the other side. The percussion note on the right side is hyper-resonant, the tactile fremitus, vocal resonance and breath sounds are all diminished. The trachea is central (deviation suggests a very large pneumothorax or a tension pneumothorax, not likely to be sitting untreated in the OSCE!). This is a right-sided pneumothorax.'

👁 WHAT YOU SHOULD SEE

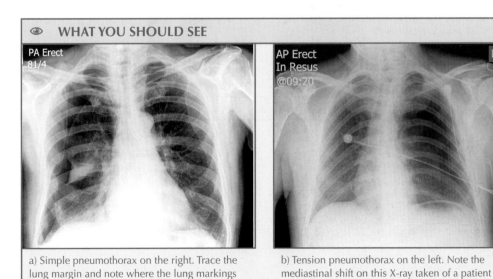

a) Simple pneumothorax on the right. Trace the lung margin and note where the lung markings stop. There is no mediastinal shift.

b) Tension pneumothorax on the left. Note the mediastinal shift on this X-ray taken of a patient in resus.

✐ WHAT YOU SHOULD KNOW (CONT)

Management of simple pneumothorax:
Treatment is not required in a healthy individual with a small pneumothorax.
Chest drain (see pg 624) indicated if:
- Larger pneumothorax associated with dyspnoea
- Increasing in size
- Not resolving after 1 week
- Pneumothorax complicating underlying severe chronic bronchitis with emphysema
- Pneumothorax exacerbating acute severe asthma
- Pneumonectomy (see pg 213) indicated in recurrent spontaneous pneumothorax.

Tension pneumothorax
<u>Definition</u>: a pneumothorax with a one-way valve air leak. Each breath tends to enlarge the pneumothorax, displacing the mediastinum. Tension pneumothorax is a medical emergency and should be diagnosed on clinical grounds and treated immediately, not delayed while an X-ray is arranged.
<u>Clinical signs</u>: SOB, shock, tracheal deviation, reduced breath sounds, neck vein distension, hyper-resonance.
<u>Treatment</u>: decompress urgently with cannula in second intercostal space in midclavicular line. This only buys time while a chest drain is inserted.
Chest drain in fifth intercostal space, anterior axillary line (see pg 624).
Oxygen, monitoring.

◉ WHAT YOU SHOULD SEE

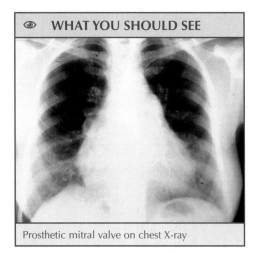

Prosthetic mitral valve on chest X-ray

PNEUMOTHORAX

👁 WHAT YOU SHOULD SEE

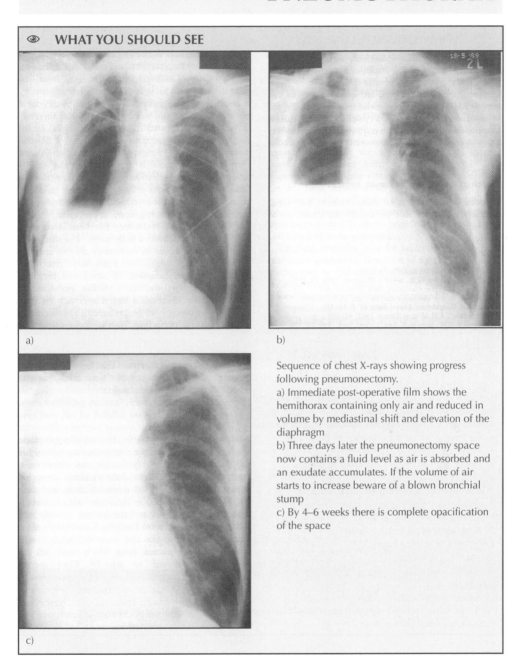

a)

b)

c)

Sequence of chest X-rays showing progress
following pneumonectomy.
a) Immediate post-operative film shows the
hemithorax containing only air and reduced in
volume by mediastinal shift and elevation of the
diaphragm
b) Three days later the pneumonectomy space
now contains a fluid level as air is absorbed and
an exudate accumulates. If the volume of air
starts to increase beware of a blown bronchial
stump
c) By 4–6 weeks there is complete opacification
of the space

✍ WHAT YOU SHOULD KNOW

Thoracotomy incisions

Posterolateral thoracotomy

Exposes lungs, oesophagus and thoracic aorta on the left.

Incision runs from a posterior point midway between the spinous processes of the vertebrae and the medial border of the scapula, and extending forwards in the line of the ribs two to three fingerbreadths below the tip of the scapula as far as the midaxillary line. The intercostal space that is opened is chosen according to the procedure: above the fifth rib for an upper lobectomy, above the sixth rib for a lower lobectomy, pneumonectomy, Ivor Lewis (two-phase) oesophagectomy or middle lobectomy on the right, above the seventh rib for access to the lower oesophagus. A thoracic incision can be extended across the cartilage of the costal margin and down into the diaphragm as a thoraco-abdominal incision.

Midline sternotomy

Exposes the anterior mediastinum and the pericardium.

Incision is from 1 cm below the suprasternal notch to approximately 6 cm below the xiphisternum. The sternum is divided with an air-driven vertical saw with a guarded tip (or an oscillating saw in a re-operation, to avoid the right ventricle firmly adherent to the sternum).

Right parasternal incision

Used for aortic and mitral valve procedures. Involves dislocation of the costosternal junction of two or more ribs.

Upper hemisternotomy (sternal incision T-cut)

This can be used for aortic and mitral valve procedures. The main advantage is in leaving half the sternum intact for stability; it also avoids an intercostal incision and the possibility of a chest wall hernia.

Anterior thoracotomy

Valuable for limited intrathoracic procedures, e.g. lung biopsy thoracoscopy, mediastinal node biopsy or pericardial fenestration.

Anterior mediastinostomy

Used for mediastinoscopy; can yield valuable information in the diagnosis of mediastinal tumours and the staging of thoracic disease.

Indications for an emergency thoracotomy in trauma

- 1.5 litres of blood drain immediately chest drain is inserted
- Blood loss continues at >200 ml/h
- Medial penetrating wound (front or back)
- EMD or cardiac arrest with hypovolaemia (for internal cardiac massage)

When not to do an emergency thoracotomy

- No qualified experienced surgeon present
- No electrical cardiac activity

[234] **X-ray signs of pneumonectomy**

Early signs (within 24 hours)

Partial filling of thorax.

Ipsilateral mediastinal shift and diaphragmatic elevation.

Late signs

Complete obliteration of space

NB Depression of diaphragm/shift of mediastinum to contralateral side indicates a bronchopleural fistula/empyema/haemorrhage.

Examine this patient's respiratory system

(see pg 186)

THORACOTOMY SCARS

'There is a midline sternotomy scar indicating previous cardiothoracic surgery. The commonest operations performed through this scar are coronary artery bypass surgery and aortic or mitral valve replacement. I would like to do a cardiovascular examination, look at the legs for vein harvest scars and see the chest X-rays.

There is a posterolateral thoracotomy scar indicating previous thoracic surgery. The commonest operations performed through this scar are partial or total pneumonectomy and oesophageal surgery. I would like to perform a respiratory examination and see the chest X-rays.'[234]

👁 **WHAT YOU SHOULD SEE**

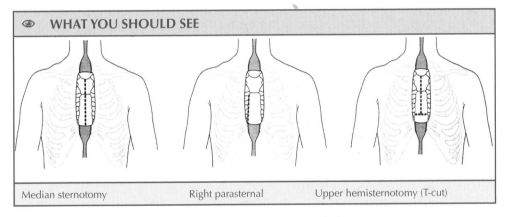

| Median sternotomy | Right parasternal | Upper hemisternotomy (T-cut) |

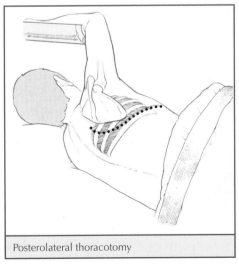

Posterolateral thoracotomy

Examine this patient's heart (see pg 183)

DEXTROCARDIA

'The pulse is regular, at 70 beats per minute and of good volume. The jugular venous pressure is not raised. The apex beat is not palpable on the left side, but can be felt in the fifth right intercostal space in the midclavicular line. The patient has dextrocardia. I would like to listen to the chest[235] and feel for a liver.'[236]

🗐 WHAT YOU SHOULD KNOW

Consider this diagnosis if you cannot feel an apex beat and then have difficulty hearing the heart sounds. As you move the stethoscope to the right, the heart sounds get louder. After auscultation, repeat the identification of the apex beat on the right side exactly as you would on the left (see Examination of the heart, pg 183).

[235] **Kartagener syndrome**: dextrocardia, bronchiectasis, situs inversus, infertility, dysplasia of frontal sinuses, sinusitis and otitis media. Patients have ciliary immotility.

[236] If **situs inversus** (lateral transposition of the viscera of the thorax and the abdomen) is present the patient is usually otherwise normal. Dextrocardia without situs inversus is usually associated with cardiac malformation. Dextrocardia can occur in Turner syndrome, a sex chromosome abnormality (usually XO), which results in short, infertile phenotypic girls who usually display characteristic features such as webbed neck or wide-spaced nipples, and are occasionally mildly learning-disabled.

DEXTROCARDIA

👁 WHAT YOU SHOULD SEE

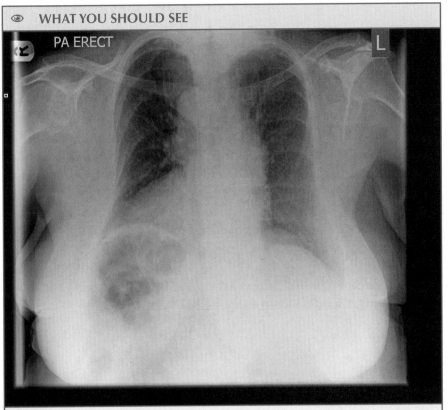

Dextrocardia
The heart shadow is on the right as well as the gastric bubble indicating situs inversus

CHAPTER 4
TRUNK AND THORAX

Take a history from this lady with a left breast lump

(see pg 180)

CARCINOMA OF THE BREAST

'I would like to present Mrs W, a 60-year-old retired teacher. She noticed a lump in her left breast 2 weeks ago. She is not sure how long it has been there, as she does not check her breasts regularly. It is non-tender. She has not noticed any other lumps in her breasts or axillae. She has not noticed any skin changes. She has had no nipple discharge. Her periods started aged 11 and finished aged 56. She is currently on HRT. She had no children and lives with her husband. She has no other medical history, takes no medications and has no allergies. She has not attended for screening mammograms as she was frightened because her mother had breast cancer aged 70. She does not smoke or drink.

I would be concerned to exclude breast cancer in this lady, who has several risk factors. Next, I would like to examine her.'

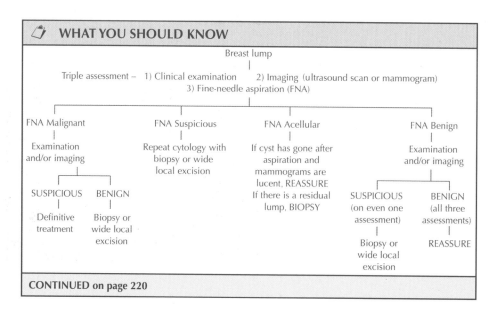

WHAT YOU SHOULD KNOW

Breast lump

Triple assessment – 1) Clinical examination   2) Imaging (ultrasound scan or mammogram)   3) Fine-needle aspiration (FNA)

FNA Malignant — Examination and/or imaging — SUSPICIOUS (Definitive treatment) / BENIGN (Biopsy or wide local excision)

FNA Suspicious — Repeat cytology with biopsy or wide local excision

FNA Acellular — If cyst has gone after aspiration and mammograms are lucent, REASSURE. If there is a residual lump, BIOPSY

FNA Benign — Examination and/or imaging — SUSPICIOUS (on even one assessment) Biopsy or wide local excision / BENIGN (all three assessments) REASSURE

CONTINUED on page 220

218

Examine this lady's breasts

(see pg 203)

CARCINOMA OF THE BREAST

'On initial inspection this (middle-aged or elderly) lady looks well with no signs of systemic disease. On inspection of the breasts there is fullness in the upper outer quadrant of the left breast. There are no obvious nipple changes, and the skin initially appears normal, but on raising the arms there is evidence of tethering and peau d'orange in the area. There are no signs of previous surgery or radiotherapy. On examination of the breast, there is a non-tender lump in the upper outer quadrant of the left breast. It is about 4 cm in diameter, hemispherical in shape, with an irregular surface and indistinct edges. It is stony-hard and craggy, and does not fluctuate or transilluminate and is not pulsatile, compressible or reducible. It arises deep to the skin, but the skin is tethered to it and can be seen to dimple when moved over the lump. The lump is also fixed to the underlying pectoralis muscle. There are enlarged axillary glands on the left, but the supraclavicular nodes, contralateral breast and axilla are free of palpable lumps. There is no evidence of lymphoedema in the left arm, and the patient denies alteration of power and sensation. If I saw this lady in clinic I would examine the chest and abdomen, and be concerned to investigate[237] the breast lump with urgent mammography and fine-needle aspiration cytology[238] or Trucut histology.'

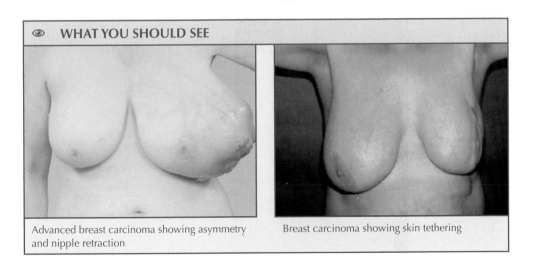

WHAT YOU SHOULD SEE

Advanced breast carcinoma showing asymmetry and nipple retraction

Breast carcinoma showing skin tethering

CARCINOMA OF THE BREAST

✐ WHAT YOU SHOULD KNOW

70% invasive ductal: firm hard scirrhous mass
10% lobular: bilateral in 20%, multicentric
10% tubular: picked up on screening, small stellate lesions
10% other: medullary (good prognosis, soft, fleshy); mucoid (good prognosis, rare); Paget's (poor prognosis, nipple excoriation and underlying intraductal tumour)

Staging of breast cancer (TNM):
T_{is} (Ca in situ); T_1 (<2 cm); T_2 (2–5 cm); T_3 (>5 cm)
T_{4a} (involves chest wall); T_{4b} (involves skin); T_{4c} (chest wall and skin); T_{4d} (inflammatory)
N_0 (no regional nodes); N_1 (mobile ipsilateral axillary); N_2 (fixed ipsilateral axillary); N_3 (internal thoracic ipsilateral)
M_0 (no mets); M_1 (distant mets including any contralateral axillary nodes and ANY supraclavicular nodes)

Prognostic indicators in breast cancer

Most important indicators – size of primary tumour, node status, tumour grade.
<u>Nottingham Prognostic Indicator (NPI)</u>
Tumour grade 1, 2 or 3.
LN status 1 (no nodes involved), 2 (1–3 nodes involved), 3 (>4 nodes involved)
NPI = (0.2 x tumour size in cm) + tumour grade + lymph node status
[237] Triple assessment is mandatory.
The important rule to remember is that if any one of the triple assessments suggests malignancy, a biopsy at the very least should be performed even if the other two tests suggest benign disease.
[238] It may be appropriate to say 'the diagnosis is carcinoma of the breast' if, for example, the examiners have said 'the lady is aware of her diagnosis' or 'tell us freely what you think this is' or ask you the diagnosis after you have moved away from the patient. If you are not sure, however, tact counts for a lot, so be clear about identifying the malignant features and then use a phrase such as 'concerned to exclude carcinoma'. Remember, however, that by the rules of triple assessment, a benign FNA and mammogram does not exclude carcinoma if clinical assessment is suspicious; that can only be excluded by an excision biopsy.

👁 WHAT YOU SHOULD SEE

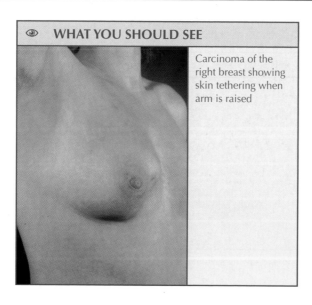

Carcinoma of the right breast showing skin tethering when arm is raised

CARCINOMA OF THE BREAST

👁 WHAT YOU SHOULD SEE

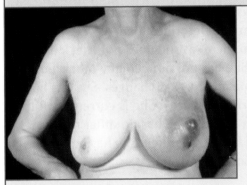

Carcinoma of the left breast showing erythema, asymmetry, enlargement of breast, ulceration and nipple retraction

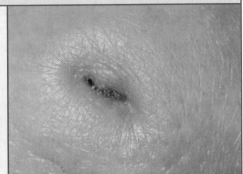

Carcinoma of the breast showing 'peau d'orange'

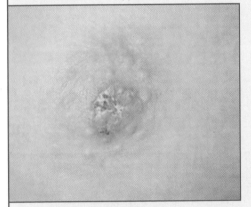

Paget's disease of the nipple

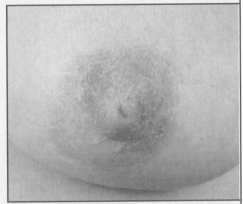

Eczema of the nipple

Differentiating this benign condition of eczema from the malignant Paget's disease is difficult but benign disease is suggested by
a) Areolar area rather than nipple affected
b) No underlying lesion on mammography
c) Benign imprint or scrape cytology after pressing or scraping the lesion onto a slide

NB An incisional biopsy of the affected skin is the only definitive investigation

221

Take a history from this lady with a left breast lump

(see pg 180)

FIBROADENOMA OF THE BREAST

'I would like to present Miss W, a 22-year-old student teacher. She noticed two lumps in her left breast 2 weeks ago. She estimates them both to be about 2 x 2 cm and describes them as very mobile. She is not sure how long they have been there, as she does not check her breasts regularly. They are non-tender. She has not noticed any other lumps in her breasts or axillae. She has not noticed any skin changes. She has had no nipple discharge. She started her periods aged 15. She is currently on the OCP. She has no children and lives with friends. She has no other medical history, takes no other medications and has no allergies. She has no family history of breast disease. She does not smoke or drink.

I suspect this lady has two fibroadenomas but to confirm this, I would like to examine her and she will require triple assessment.'

⌁ WHAT YOU SHOULD KNOW

Aberrations of normal development and involution. Common (90% of autopsies). Peaks in premenopausal years. Proliferation of epithelial cells. Often associated with cysts. Breasts often feel generally nodular. Cyclical changes typical. Surgery not needed if triple assessment negative.

Cysts
Part of the fibrocystic disease spectrum. Dilatation of acini and terminal ductules. Usually multiple. Can become very large. Typical appearance on imaging, especially ultrasound. Aspiration usually deflates cyst, producing greenish acellular aspirate. No treatment needed if clinical and imaging assessment negative **and** aspirate not bloodstained **and** no residual lump felt after aspiration. Often recur.

Fibroadenoma
Most common benign tumour of the breast. New growth of fibrous and glandular tissue. Common in premenopausal women. May change with cycle. Well circumscribed. Clinically feels like a mobile, smooth 'breast mouse'. Histologically, characteristic delicate cellular fibroblastic stroma enclosing glandular cystic spaces within an epithelial lining. Typical mammographic and ultrasonographic appearance. Does not require excision if definitively diagnosed on triple assessment but patient may be happier with lump excised.
Rare phylloides tumour: giant fibroadenomas 10–15 cm or bigger. These can cause pressure necrosis, gross deformity and can become malignant, so must be excised.

Examine this
lady's breasts

(see pg 203)

FIBROADENOMA
OF THE BREAST

'On general inspection this (young) lady looks well, with no signs of systemic disease. Inspection of the breasts reveals no asymmetry, skin changes or nipple changes and no evidence of previous surgery or radiotherapy. On examination of the breasts there is a small, non-tender lump in the upper outer quadrant of the left breast. It is 2 cm in diameter, round and smooth, with well-defined edges. It is firm and rubbery, not fluctuant, pulsatile reducible or compressible. It arises from the subcutaneous tissue and is very mobile, tethered neither to skin nor to underlying pectoralis major. There are no palpable lumps in either axilla, supraclavicular region or in the contralateral breast. My clinical diagnosis is a benign fibroadenoma.'

CHAPTER 4
TRUNK AND THORAX

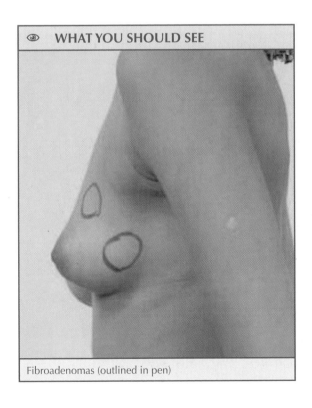

👁 **WHAT YOU SHOULD SEE**

Fibroadenomas (outlined in pen)

Examine this
lady's breast

(see pg 203)

POST-MASTECTOMY

'On general inspection this (middle-aged or elderly) lady looks thin, pale and short of breath at rest. Immediately evident is her previous left mastectomy, and the oedematous left arm. She also shows signs of chemotherapy, with hair loss and a cushingoid, flushed facial appearance. On inspection of the chest wall, there is a scar of previous mastectomy and axillary surgery on the left and ink markings and telangiectasia indicating radiotherapy. On examination there is no evidence of recurrence in the scar, but there are palpable nodes in the left axilla. The right axilla and breast and both supraclavicular areas are clear clinically. The left arm is markedly swollen with pitting oedema. The patient denies weakness and numbness. My diagnosis is previously surgically treated carcinoma of the breast with recurrent or residual disease being treated by adjuvant therapy. I would like to listen to the chest and examine the abdomen to complete my examination.'

◉ WHAT YOU SHOULD SEE

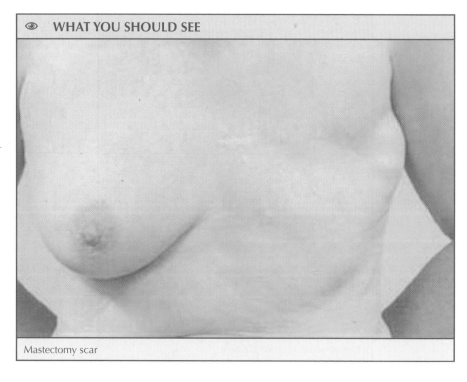

Mastectomy scar

✎ WHAT YOU SHOULD KNOW

Surgery for breast cancer

<u>Excision biopsy</u>: to diagnose, not to treat, e.g. in lesions suspicious on mammography but not palpable or borderline suspicious FNA but mammogram and clinical examination suggest benign disease. May need wire localisation under mammographic control pre-operatively if impalpable screen-detected lesion. Should remove no more than 20 g of tissue (not aiming for complete clearance as it is for diagnosis, not treatment). Will need definitive treatment if histology is positive and clearance is not complete.

<u>Wide local excision (breast conservation surgery)</u>: single, small (< 4 cm diameter in small breast) node-negative local disease. Aim is cure with good clearance. If margins not clear – mastectomy.

<u>Mastectomy</u>: large/central/multifocal disease or patient's preference. Also may be indicated in recurrence or inadequate clearance (affected margins) after wide local excision.

<u>Axillary node sampling</u>: used if the axilla is disease-free on pre-operative imaging. At least four palpable nodes are sampled from the axilla. If these contain metastatic disease the patient will require axillary clearance or radiotherapy to treat axilla.

<u>Sentinel node biopsy</u>: another technique used if the axilla is disease-free on pre-operative imaging. It aims to remove the sentinel nodes (1st lymph nodes to drain the breast). A radiolabelled colloid +/– blue dye is injected into the breast – a probe is used to find 'hot' and 'blue' nodes. If no histologically involved nodes, no further treatment needed. If involved node/s, need axillary clearance or radiotherapy to treat axilla.

<u>Axillary clearance</u>: removing level 1, 2 and 3 nodes (lateral, behind and medial to pectoralis minor). Even if nodes are positive, radiotherapy not needed after level 3 clearance unless recurrence detected later.

<u>Complications of mastectomy</u>: seroma, infection, flap necrosis.

<u>Complications of axillary surgery</u>: nerve damage (loss of sensation inner aspect upper arm due to intercostobrachial nerve injury), lymphoedema, wound infection, reduced range of shoulder movement.

Radiotherapy

<u>Breast</u>: all patients after breast conservation surgery. High-risk mastectomy patients (pectoralis major involvement or any two of the following: axillary lymph node involvement, lymphatic or vascular invasion, grade 3 cancer, tumour >4 cm diameter.

<u>Axilla</u>: if sentinel lymph node biopsy/axillary sampling shows positive nodes or in axillary recurrence if no previous radiotherapy (can only be given once).

<u>Complications of radiotherapy</u>: skin reactions, telangiectasia, cardiac damage, pneumonitis, osteoradionecrosis, lymphoedema in axillary radiotherapy (especially when combined with axillary surgery).

Adjuvant treatment

<u>Chemotherapy</u>: most effective in premenopausal patients. Considered if lymph node positive, ER –ve, grade 3, large tumour, lymphovascular invasion. Cyclophosphamide, methotrexate and fluorouracil are common agents used in UK. Side-effects include fatigue, alopecia and nausea.

<u>Oophorectomy</u> (or ovarian ablation by radiotherapy or gonadotropin-releasing hormone): only of benefit in premenopausal women.

<u>Tamoxifen</u>: (selective oestrogen receptor modulator). First-line treatment for pre/post menopausal ER+/PR+ patients with invasive breast cancer. History of thrombosis is relative contraindication. Side-effects include vaginal dryness, loss of libido and hot flushes.

<u>Aromatase inhibitors</u>: (block the peripheral conversion of androgens to oestrogen). Only in post-menopausal women. e.g. anastrozole, exemestane, letrozole.

Patients who are elderly and unsuitable for general anaesthetic with ER+ breast cancer can be treated by primary endocrine therapy to control disease progression.

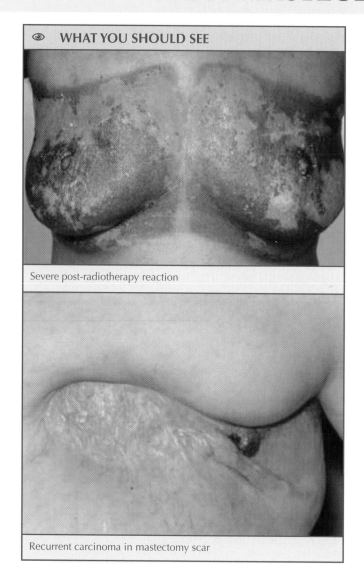

WHAT YOU SHOULD SEE

Severe post-radiotherapy reaction

Recurrent carcinoma in mastectomy scar

◉ WHAT YOU SHOULD SEE

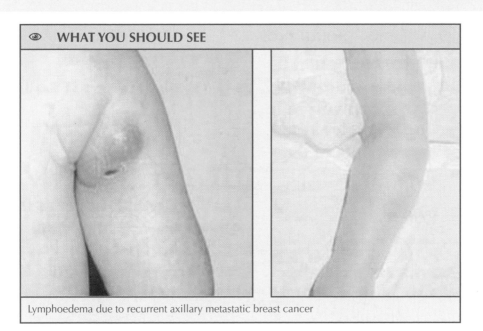

Lymphoedema due to recurrent axillary metastatic breast cancer

✍ WHAT YOU SHOULD KNOW

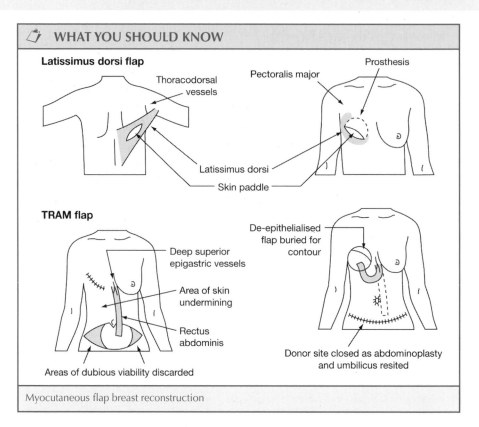

Latissimus dorsi flap

- Thoracodorsal vessels
- Latissimus dorsi
- Skin paddle
- Prosthesis
- Pectoralis major

TRAM flap

- Deep superior epigastric vessels
- Area of skin undermining
- Rectus abdominis
- Areas of dubious viability discarded
- De-epithelialised flap buried for contour
- Donor site closed as abdominoplasty and umbilicus resited

Myocutaneous flap breast reconstruction

◉ WHAT YOU SHOULD SEE

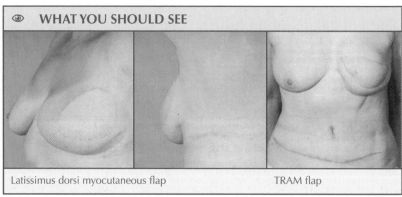

| Latissimus dorsi myocutaneous flap | TRAM flap |

Examine
this lady's
breast

(see pg
203)

BREAST RECONSTRUCTION

'On general inspection the patient looks well, with no signs of systemic disease. On inspection of the chest there has been previous surgery on the right breast. There is an ovoid scar over the breast and there is no nipple on the right. There is a transverse scar across the lower abdomen[239], indicating the donor site of what I presume to be a myocutaneous flap reconstruction. On examination of the breasts there is no evidence of recurrence in either breast, axilla or supraclavicular fossa. A full examination would include listening to the chest and examining the abdomen. My diagnosis is previous mastectomy, probably for carcinoma of the breast, with immediate or delayed reconstruction using a TRAM (transverse rectus abdominis myocutaneous) flap.'

✎ WHAT YOU SHOULD KNOW

Options for breast reconstruction

Immediate

Reduces the psychological trauma of the change in body image experienced after mastectomy.

No evidence that it increases rate of local or systemic relapse.

Radiotherapy can be carried out while prosthesis or expander is in situ.

Should be more widely available to patients.

Delayed

More widely available.

Needs well-healed scar and (except in the case of myocutaneous flaps) gives poor results after radiotherapy

Prosthesis

Suitable in small breasts with adequate skin flaps.

Mostly silicone or saline.

Problems include: fibrous capsules and contracture (reduced by textured prostheses), infection (5% of cases need removal), implant rupture (1%) resulting in silicone leakage which, contrary to media stories, has not been shown to increase the incidence of carcinogenesis, problems with other organs or connective tissue disorders.

Tissue expansion: suitable if there are adequate skin flaps and good skin closure in small- to medium-sized breasts. Silicone bag with filler port is initially inserted, and the expander has saline injected weekly. It should be overexpanded to produce ptosis. It is then replaced with a permanent prosthesis.

Myocutaneous flaps: suitable in large skin incisions, doubtful skin closure and large breasts. Can be used in delayed reconstruction if there has been previous radiotherapy (see figure opposite). Complications include flap necrosis, infection and abdominal herniae (in TRAM flaps).

Nipple reconstruction: best done after 6 months. Areola is reproduced using upper inner thigh skin, contralateral areola or tattooing. The nipple can be reconstructed using local tissue, the contralateral nipple or artificial adhesive nipples worn for a month at a time.

Other techniques: reduction mammoplasty or mastopexy of remaining breast may be indicated.

[239] Or the right side of the back in the case of a latissimus dorsi myocutaneous flap.

Take a history from this gentleman who had an abnormal abdominal ultrasound

(see pg 162)

ABDOMINAL AORTIC ANEURYSM

'I would like to present Mr P, a 75-year-old retired builder. He recently had an ultrasound scan organised by his GP to investigate recurrent UTIs. No abnormality of his urinary tract was seen, but the GP referral letter explains that a 6-cm aortic aneurysm was found incidentally. He has had no abdominal or back pain. His medical history includes hypertension, hypercholesterolaemia and IHD. He had an MI 2 years ago, which was treated with an angioplasty and he no longer gets anginal pain. The urologists are still investigating his recurrent UTIs. He takes antihypertensives and aspirin. He is allergic to penicillin – he said he had facial swelling and difficulty breathing when he last had it. His brother had an aortic aneurysm repair last year and Mr P is concerned as he had an MI intraoperatively. He has smoked for 60 pack years. He does not drink and lives with his wife.

This gentleman has an asymptomatic 6-cm abdominal aortic aneurysm discovered incidentally on USS.'

✍ WHAT YOU SHOULD KNOW

Definition: localised region of abnormal dilatation of the abdominal aorta defined as >3 cm diameter or at least 50% greater than the normal artery above it.
Epidemiology: rupture is the 13th leading cause of death in the western world. Incidence increases with age. More common in men, smokers, hypertensives and whites.
Presentation: 75% present as an incidental finding on clinical or radiological examination. Pain is usually a sign of expansion or potential rupture.
Complications:
Aneurysmal rupture:
The major complication of AAA. Thrombosis and embolisation are rare in comparison. Caused by increasing wall tension and decreasing wall thickness as the aneurysm enlarges in line with Laplace's law: wall stress = blood pressure x radius/wall thickness.
Thrombosis:
Usually accompanied by acute bilateral lower limb ischaemia, AAA thrombosis is associated with a poor outcome.
Embolisation
CONTINUED on pg 232

Examine this
gentleman's
abdomen

(see pg 195)

ABDOMINAL AORTIC ANEURYSM

'There is an expansile abdominal mass consistent with an abdominal aortic aneurysm of about 5 cm in diameter apparently extending from below the renal arteries to just above the bifurcation. It is non-tender and the patient is cardiovascularly stable.'

👁 **WHAT YOU SHOULD SEE**

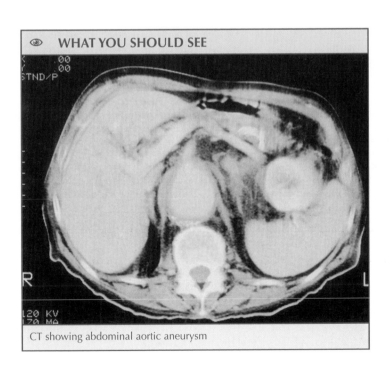

CT showing abdominal aortic aneurysm

ABDOMINAL AORTIC ANEURYSM

⚷ WHAT YOU SHOULD KNOW (CONT)

Investigations:

Clinical examination is only 50% diagnostic due to obesity, uncooperative patient, lumbar lordosis, adjacent tumour, aortic tortuosity. An aneurysm under 4 cm can rarely be felt except in thin individuals.

Plain X-ray: in < 50% of patients calcium in the aneurysm wall allows visualisation on plain abdominal (preferably lateral) X-ray.

Ultrasonography: good for initial diagnosis and screening, relationship with renal arteries but not good for imaging suprarenal aorta, iliacs, retroperitoneal leak, obese patients.

CT: e.g. CT angiogram. Useful to plan elective surgery and in stable patients with suspected leak but time consuming, high doses of irradiation, contrast material given.

MRI: more accurate evaluation of other vessels, MRA very useful but expensive, not widely available and can't be used in patients with pacemakers.

Causes of AAA:

Atherosclerosis.

Ehlers–Danlos syndrome types I and IV (abnormal collagen production).

Marfan syndrome (autosomal dominant condition often affecting the aortic root).

Tuberous sclerosis (rare autosomal dominant syndrome).

Takayasu's disease (inflammatory aortitis of children and young adults).

Syphilitic aneurysm (thoracic aortic endarteritis obliterans of the vaso vasorum in untreated tertiary syphilis).

Mycotic aneurysm (due to bacterial infection, commonly in drug users or the immunocompromised).

Polyarteritis nodosa (a vasculitis affecting the vasa vasorum).

Intima-media mucoid degenerative aneurysms (in middle-aged hypertensive Africans and Indians – aetiology unknown).

Symptoms:

75% asymptomatic.

Leaking aneurysms present with the characteristic triad of diffuse mid-abdominal pain, shock and a pulsatile abdominal mass.

Other presentations include back pain, flank pain, thrombosis or embolism.

Indications for surgery:

It is important to operate on an aneurysm before it ruptures. Elective AAA repair caries a mortality of 3.5–5%, whereas for the small proportion of patients with ruptured AAA who live long enough to make it to surgery, the mortality is 30–80%. The most important predictive factor of aneurysm rupture is size. In aneurysms >6 cm the 3-year survival is <50% if untreated, so these clearly need treatment if possible. Small aneurysms (less than 4 cm) tend not to rupture and enlarge very slowly, so these clearly are best left alone. Controversy surrounds intermediate-sized aneurysms (4–6 cm). The rate of rupture of aneurysms 4–6 cm in size is 6% per year over 3 years. The UK Small Aneurysm Trial confirms a low rate of rupture of aortic aneurysms less than 5.5 cm in diameter. The risk of surgery also varies depending on the age and fitness of the patient. Many surgeons would agree that, where the risk of surgery is less than 5% mortality, elective repair should be considered for patients with aneurysms over 5.5 cm. Smaller aneurysms should be scanned regularly.

✏ WHAT YOU SHOULD KNOW (CONT)

Surgery of AAA:

The transperitoneal endoaneurysmorrhaphy is the most common, where a synthetic graft is sewn into the opened aneurysm sac via an abdominal incision. Variations of this include a retroperitoneal approach (used for inflammatory aneurysms, battle-scarred abdomens, horseshoe kidney or suprarenal aneurysm), exclusion bypass technique and endoluminal stenting (for infrarenal aneurysms).

EVAR (endovascular AAA repair)

A prosthesis consisting of a vascular graft and metallic stent is introduced via a catheter through the femoral artery. Under fluoroscopic guidance it is inserted into the aneurysm.

Only 35-40% of AAAs are suitable.

Advantages: avoids abdominal incision, no aortic cross-clamping and physiological insult

Disadvantages: endoleak – type 1 – leak at proximal or distal attachment. Type 2 – failure to adequately exclude vessels feeding into the aneurysm sac, distal embolism, stent-graft migration.

Complications of surgery:

Intraoperative

Bleeding (especially with ruptured aneurysms).

Limb ischaemia due to a large dislodged embolus needing embolectomy, or microemboli causing 'trash foot', or thrombosis secondary to prolonged clamping.

Early post-operative

Cardiac: over 50% of post-operative deaths including MI, arrhythmias, CCF.

Pulmonary: including atelectasis, pneumonia.

Renal failure: especially in those with pre-existing renal impairment or peri-operative hypotension.

Gastrointestinal: infarction of the GI tract is surprisingly rare considering how often the inferior mesenteric artery is sacrificed. Acute gastritis is common.

Cerebrovascular: stroke can be avoided by pre-operative carotid endarterectomy in patients at risk.

Late post-operative

Graft infection (1%) may occur years after the surgery and is increased in the presence of malnutrition, immunosuppression, chronic disease, skin infections, groin incisions, ischaemic feet.

Aorto-enteric fistulae are rare but catastrophic. Enclosing the graft in the old aneurysm sac reduces this risk.

Anastomotic aneurysms most commonly occur in aortic bifemoral grafts.

Lymph leaks can cause seromas.

Sexual dysfunction is a result of damage to the autonomic plexus.

Recurrence of aneurysm proximal to the graft occurs in 3–8% of patients.

Graft thrombosis: rates are 3% at 10 years.

⟋ WHAT YOU SHOULD KNOW

- **Temporary**: to protect an ileorectal anastomosis; persistent low intestinal fistula; right-sided colonic trauma; preliminary to construction of ileo-anal reservoir
- **Permanent**: panproctocolectomy for: ulcerative colitis; severe Crohn's disease; familial polyposis coli; multiple colonic cancer

Forming an ileostomy

Usually in the right iliac fossa. A circular skin defect 2–3 cm in diameter is excised. A cruciate (trephine) incision is made in the underlying rectus. The peritoneum is incised. The stapled ileum, held in Babcock forceps, is passed through the incision in the peritoneum. The main abdominal wound is closed and dressed. The ileum is opened along the staple line. A 4–5-cm spout is formed by everting the stump and suturing the mucosa to the skin with interrupted absorbable sutures. A bite of the serosa is taken a few cm proximal to the stump with each stitch to evert the stoma. (*NB* 500ml/day of high-enzyme-content fluid is lost from a low-output ileostomy; one litre per day in a high-output ileostomy.)

- There may have been previous operations leaving stomas which have now been closed

Case 1: a colitic might have a subtotal colectomy leaving a mucous fistula and an end ileostomy. Problems with the rectal stump may lead to a completion proctectomy, leaving an end ileostomy and a scar in the left iliac fossa where the mucous fistula was.

Case 2: a patient with a low rectal cancer might have an abdominoperineal resection, leaving a colostomy. Subsequently if he developed another tumour in the right colon he might proceed to a completion colectomy, leaving an end ileostomy with a scar in the left iliac fossa at the site of the previous colostomy.

- Surgeons often leave a loop ileostomy to protect delayed reconstructive procedures

Case 1: a patient with rectal cancer has a defunctioning colostomy while having neoadjuvant chemo-radiotherapy before surgery. Later, he has a low anterior resection. At this operation the surgeon elects to defunction the bowel with a loop ileostomy, planning to close it after the anastomosis has healed. In the meantime the patient would have a right-sided loop ileostomy with a scar where the old colostomy used to be.

Case 2: a perforated left-sided diverticulitis is treated with an emergency Hartmann's procedure, leaving a colostomy. At a later date the Hartmann's procedure is reversed (the colon is rejoined to the rectal stump). At this operation the surgeon elects to defunction the bowel with a loop ileostomy, planning to close it after the anastomosis has healed. In the meantime the patient would have a right-sided loop ileostomy with a scar in the left iliac fossa where the old colostomy used to be.

Examine this gentleman's abdomen/stoma

(see pg 189/197)

Case 1
'There is a stoma in the right iliac fossa. There is one lumen which is small in calibre. There is a 2–3-cm spout and the contents of the bag are green and fluid. There is a midline scar and there are/and there are no scars of other, previous stomas in the left iliac fossa. This is an end ileostomy, most commonly performed after panproctocolectomy for ulcerative colitis, familial polyposis coli or multiple colonic cancer. I would like to know if this patient has an anal orifice and rectal stump (in which case reconstruction may be planned) or a perineal scar (in which case this is a permanent end ileostomy).'

Case 2
'There is a stoma in the right iliac fossa. There are two lumens, both of small calibre, the lower of which has a spout. The contents of the bag are green and fluid. There is a midline scar and there are/are no scars of other, previous stomas in the left iliac fossa. This is a loop ileostomy, most commonly formed to achieve temporary diversion to protect a distal anastomosis, a low intestinal fistula, achieve bowel rest in severe inflammatory disease or preliminary to construction of an ileo-anal reservoir.'

◉ WHAT YOU SHOULD SEE

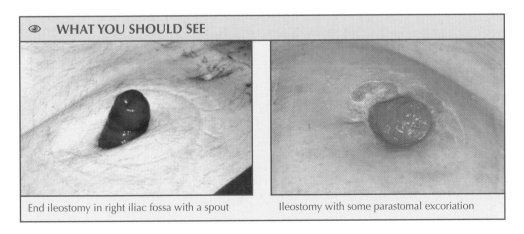

End ileostomy in right iliac fossa with a spout | Ileostomy with some parastomal excoriation

WHAT YOU SHOULD KNOW

Indications

- **Temporary**: to protect distal anastomosis; to achieve bowel rest (e.g. for perineal Crohn's); if primary anastomosis is not possible after resection (e.g. in the presence of perforation, sepsis, ischaemia or obstruction).
- **Permanent**: after abdominoperineal resection for low rectal tumours.

Types of colostomy

- **Loop colostomy**: this is used for diversion, usually in the sigmoid or right transverse colon. A loop of bowel is brought out through the abdominal wall incision, a small avascular window is made in the mesocolon, a colostomy bridge is passed through it and it is secured. The laparotomy wound (if present) is closed and then the stoma is opened and formed.
- **End colostomy and rectal stump (Hartmann's procedure)**: performed if a primary anastomosis is contraindicated. After resection, a colostomy is brought out using the proximal end of colon; the distal end (usually a rectal stump) is oversewn and left in the abdomen. This may be difficult to rejoin later, as the rectal stump may be hard to find unless it is traced to the peritoneum lining the anterior abdominal wall.
- **End colostomy and mucous fistula**: used in similar circumstances to a Hartmann's but instead of dropping the rectal stump back into the abdomen, it is brought out as a separate stoma which, being an efferent limb, only produces mucus. This makes the distal limb more accessible when the bowel is rejoined later. Alternatively, a mucous fistula can be brought out of the lower end of the laparotomy wound or in the left iliac fossa.
- **Double-barrelled colostomy**: used after resection when both limbs of the stoma can be brought to the skin surface adjacent to each other (e.g. mid-sigmoid perforation or volvulus). After resection, the proximal and distal limbs of the colon are sutured together along the antimesenteric border. This is as easy to close as a loop colostomy at a later date.

Closure of colostomies: best left for 6 weeks until inflammation and oedema have settled, so minimising the risk of a leak. After 10–12 weeks, mobilisation of the bowel may become more difficult because of fibrous adhesion formation.

Output of colostomies: mid-transverse colon – 200–300 ml/day, significant enzyme content; low colostomy – 100 ml/day, virtually no enzyme.

Alternative methods of colostomy management

Irrigation: flushing fluid into colon via stoma (no appliance needed); patient needs suitable bathroom facilities; not satisfactory for Crohn's.

COLOSTOMY

Case 1
'There is a stoma in the left iliac fossa. There is
one lumen which is large in calibre. There is no
spout and the contents of the bag are brown
and semi-solid. There is a midline scar and there
are/are no scars of other, previous stomas in the
right iliac fossa. This is a colostomy, which may be permanent (typically
after abdominoperineal resection of a low rectal tumour) or temporary
(typically after a Hartmann's procedure where primary anastomosis was
contraindicated due to sepsis or peritonitis). I would like to know if this
patient has an anal orifice and rectal stump (in which case reconstruction
may be planned) or a perineal scar (in which case this is a permanent end
colostomy).'

👁 **WHAT YOU SHOULD SEE**

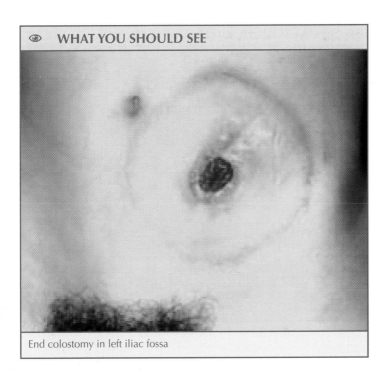

End colostomy in left iliac fossa

Case 2

'There are two stomas in the left iliac fossa. One has the typical appearance of a colostomy (large lumen, no spout, brown semi-solid bag contents) and the other has the typical appearance of a mucous fistula (large lumen, no spout, no bag, dry and recessed). There is a midline scar. This patient has had a large bowel resection during which primary anastomosis was contraindicated, and a mucous fistula was formed from the rectal stump to facilitate future reconstruction.'

Case 3

'There is a stoma in the left or right iliac fossa or in the epigastrium of the abdomen. There are two adjacent large-calibre lumens and no spout, and there are brown semi-solid products in the bag. This is a loop colostomy, which is usually used for diversion rather than resection. It is often sited in the right transverse colon, proximal to the middle colic artery, but can also be formed from the sigmoid colon. Indications include decompression of an emergency obstruction, prophylactic decompression before radiotherapy of a stenosing rectal tumour, or alleviation of obstructive symptoms in a patient not fit for major surgery.'

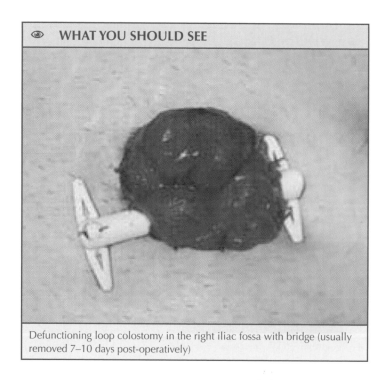

👁 **WHAT YOU SHOULD SEE**

Defunctioning loop colostomy in the right iliac fossa with bridge (usually removed 7–10 days post-operatively)

COMPLICATIONS OF STOMAS

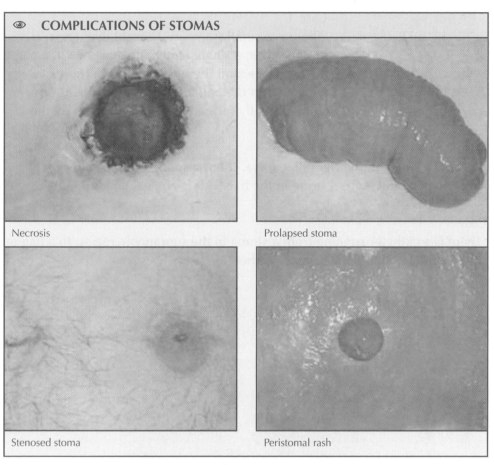

Necrosis

Prolapsed stoma

Stenosed stoma

Peristomal rash

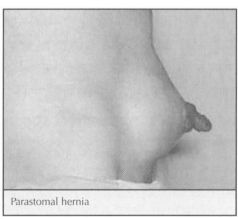

Parastomal hernia

Examine this gentleman's abdomen/stoma

(see pgs 189/197)

UROSTOMY

Case 1
'There is a small stoma in the right iliac fossa. It has no spout, a single lumen, no evidence of a bag, no discharge, and there is a catheterisation kit lying next to the patient. This is a continent urinary stoma, usually formed by the Mitrofanoff method.'

Case 2
'There is a stoma in the right iliac fossa. It has a spout, a small calibre, a single lumen, and there is urine in the bag. This is an ileal conduit.'

Case 3
'There is a catheter running from a stoma in the suprapubic region to a bag of urine. This is a suprapubic urinary catheter.'

✐ WHAT YOU SHOULD KNOW

Principle of urinary diversion:
Ureters are attached to the ileum and a conduit is created to the outside.
Techniques available include:
Urethral closure with a Mitrofanoff. The Mitrofanoff is the commonest procedure for creating a continent pouch, where the appendix is used to create a continent valve. The ileum and sigmoid colon have also been used. Intermittent self-catheterisation is required to empty the pouch, and the stoma is placed in a position that allows comfortable self-catheterisation.
Neobladder formed from ileum with Mitrofanoff diversion or indwelling suprapubic catheter. Formation of a neourethra using a segment of bladder to provide a catheterisable conduit just above the pubic symphysis.
Ileal conduit, which is an incontinent pouch that requires a bag to collect the urine. Early pouches were incontinent, attaching the ileum, ureters or bladder to the abdominal surface with closure or excision of the bladder.

UROSTOMY

👁 WHAT YOU SHOULD SEE

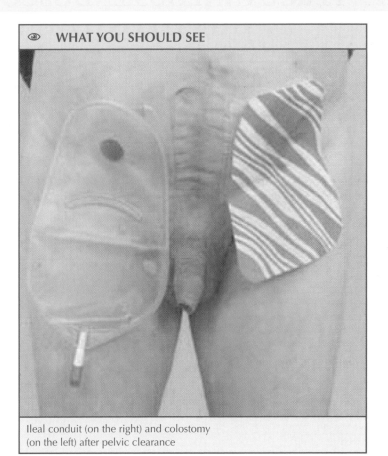

Ileal conduit (on the right) and colostomy
(on the left) after pelvic clearance

PERCUTANEOUS ENDOSCOPIC GASTROSTOMY (PEG)

✍ WHAT YOU SHOULD KNOW

Can be used for either gastric decompression or feeding.

Percutaneous endoscopic gastrostomy (PEG)

<u>Indications</u>

Feeding in patients with neurological impairment, oropharyngeal tumours or facial trauma.

Gastric decompression in patients with carcinomatosis, radiation enteritis or diabetic gastropathy obstruction.

To supplement nutrition in inflammatory bowel disease.

To establish a route for recycling bile in those with malignant biliary obstruction.

<u>Procedure</u> (see opposite)

After passing the endoscope, the anterior abdominal wall is transilluminated.

The abdominal wall is indented with the finger and the indentation observed from inside to select the insertion site.

After infiltration with local anaesthetic, a needle is passed through the abdominal wall into the lumen of the stomach.

A wire is passed through the needle and grabbed by a snare passed through the endoscope.

The endoscope is withdrawn with the snare and the wire until the wire comes out of the mouth.

The wire is then attached to the gastrostomy tube and pulled in a retrograde manner down the oesophagus, into the stomach and out of the abdominal wall where it is secured.

The position is checked by endoscopy.

Radiologically inserted gastrostomy (RIG)

<u>Indications</u>

As for PEG.

<u>Procedure</u>

Similar to PEG but under X-ray guidance.

NG tube placed.

Stomach filled with air.

Local anaesthetic to anterior abdominal wall.

Gastrostomy tube inserted under X-ray guidance.

Open gastrostomy

If the passage of an endoscope is prevented by tumour or stricture, an open procedure such as the Stamm gastrostomy is performed. This involves an upper midline laparotomy incision and insertion through a gastrostomy of a Malecot or mushroom catheter. The catheter is brought out of a stab incision in the left hypochondrium. The stomach is then sutured to the inside of the anterior abdominal wall.

Jejunostomy

This is often used after major upper gastrointestinal surgery as it enables nutrition to be infused at the jejunal level, and avoids gastric stasis. Many techniques are available, the commonest being the Witzel jejunostomy. In this (open) method, the jejunostomy is sited 30 cm distal to the ligament of Treitz on the antimesenteric border.

The catheter is fastened at the point of entry through the mucosa and then tunnelled in a seromuscular groove.

The tunnel is closed and the jejunostomy sutured to the anterior abdominal wall.

PERCUTANEOUS ENDOSCOPIC GASTROSTOMY (PEG)

Examine this
gentleman's
abdomen

(see pg 189)

'There is a feeding tube attached to a bag of
enteral nutrition entering the epigastrium. This
is a feeding gastrostomy, probably performed
percutaneously with endoscopic assistance (PEG).'

CHAPTER 4
TRUNK AND THORAX

📋 WHAT YOU SHOULD KNOW

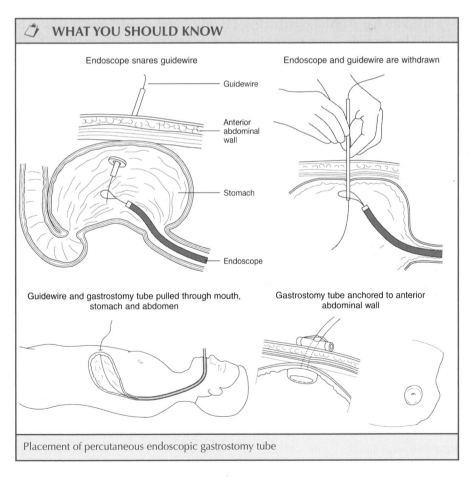

Endoscope snares guidewire

- Guidewire
- Anterior abdominal wall
- Stomach
- Endoscope

Endoscope and guidewire are withdrawn

Guidewire and gastrostomy tube pulled through mouth, stomach and abdomen

Gastrostomy tube anchored to anterior abdominal wall

Placement of percutaneous endoscopic gastrostomy tube

JAUNDICE

Take a history from this gentleman with jaundice

(see pg 166)

'I would like to present Mr P, a 55-year-old engineer. He noticed that his skin had turned yellow 1 week ago. During this week he has also noticed that his stools have been paler and more difficult to flush and his urine darker. Prior to this, he gives a 3-month history of general malaise with associated anorexia and he has lost 1 stone in weight.[240] He has been troubled with central abdominal pain radiating to his back. He describes it as a gnawing pain which often wakes him at night. Nothing makes it better, including the analgesia prescribed by his GP. His medical history includes type 2 diabetes[241] which is diet-controlled. He is only taking the analgesia which his GP prescribed for his abdominal pain – he cannot recall the name. He has smoked for 60 pack years. He drinks 4 units of alcohol a week. He lives with his wife and two young children.

This gentleman has painful obstructive jaundice and weight loss. I would be concerned to exclude a malignant cause such as a pancreatic malignancy.[242] I would next like to examine him in particular to feel for any abdominal mass which may be present.'

📄 WHAT YOU SHOULD KNOW

[240] **History of a jaundiced patient**
- Recent travel; drug addiction; joint pains; anorexia; malaise. **Suggests hepatitis**
- Alcohol addiction. **Suggests cirrhosis**
- Fat intolerance; recurrent right upper quadrant pain. **Suggests gallstones**
- Weight loss; constant epigastric boring pain. **Suggests malignancy**
- Family history of blood disorders. **Suggests haemolytic disorders**
- Bruising tendency. **Suggests hepatocellular damage**
- Pale stool, dark urine; pruritus. **Suggests obstructive jaundice**

[241] Risk factors for pancreatic carcinoma include diabetes and smoking.

[242] Clinical features of pancreatic cancer include weight loss (91% of cases), jaundice (71%), pain (83%), malaise (34%).

CONTINUED on pg 246

Examine this jaundiced gentleman's abdomen

(see pg 189)

JAUNDICE

'This patient looks frail and unwell and is obviously jaundiced. His skin and especially his conjunctivae, have a deep yellow-orange hue. He has finger clubbing, palmar erythema and leukonychia. There are more than six spider naevi on the chest, and he has gynaecomastia. There is ascites, hepatosplenomegaly and distended superficial abdominal veins. This patient has stigmata of chronic liver disease.'

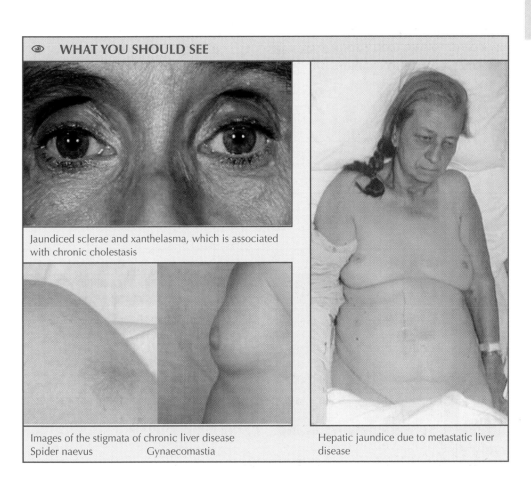

☞ WHAT YOU SHOULD SEE

Jaundiced sclerae and xanthelasma, which is associated with chronic cholestasis

Images of the stigmata of chronic liver disease
Spider naevus   Gynaecomastia

Hepatic jaundice due to metastatic liver disease

245

📋 CLASSIFICATION OF JAUNDICE

	Pre-hepatic	Hepatic jaundice	Post-hepatic (obstructive) jaundice

Causes	Spherocytosis
	Haemolytic anaemia
	Pernicious anaemia
	Incompatible blood
	  transfusion
		Hepatitis
		Cirrhosis
		Drugs
		Toxins (e.g.
		  phosphorus,
		  chloroform)
		Liver tumours
		  (primary or
		  secondary)
			Obstruction in the lumen - gallstones
			Obstruction in the wall - atresia, traumatic
			  stricture, tumour of bile duct, chronic
			  cholangitis, sclerosing cholangitis
			External compression - pancreatitis, tumour of
			  pancreas

Jaundice	Mild jaundice
	Bilirubin rarely
	  >100 µmol/l
	  unconjugated
		Variable jaundice
		May be conjugated
		  or unconjugated
			Variable jaundice
			Bilirubin may exceed 1000 µmol/l conjugated

Urine	Normal colour Bilirubin not present Urobilinogen raised	Dark Bilirubin may be present	Dark Bilirubin present
Stool	Normal colour Increased urobilinogen	Normal colour	Pale stools Stercobilinogen down
Alkaline Phosphatase	Normal	Mildly raised Very high in 1⁰ biliary cirrhosis	Very high

Amino Transferases	Normal	Typically very high
		  especially in acute
		  viral hepatitis or
		  cirrhosis
			Normal or moderately raised

Prothrombin time	Normal	Prolonged and not
		  correctable with
		  vitamin K
			Prolonged but correctable with vitamin K

👁 WHAT YOU SHOULD SEE

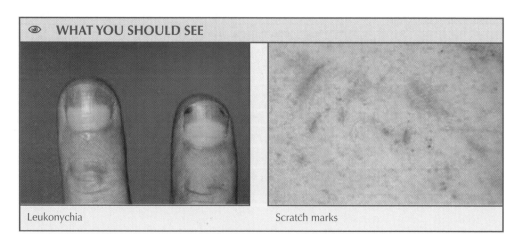

Leukonychia

Scratch marks

WHAT YOU SHOULD KNOW

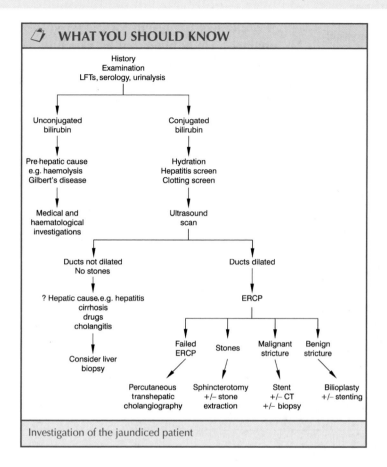

Investigation of the jaundiced patient

Take a history from this gentleman with jaundice and abdominal distension

(see pg 166/162)

ASCITES

'I would like to present Mr P, a 65-year-old retired engineer. He noticed that his skin had turned yellow 1 week ago. Prior to this, he gives a 6-month history of general malaise with associated anorexia. He thinks he has lost weight although he is unsure how much. He has also noticed his abdomen has gradually got distended. However, his bowels are opening normally and he has not been vomiting. He has had some intermittent right upper quadrant pain but this has not troubled him too much. His medical history includes an emergency right hemicolectomy 1 year ago for what sounds like a perforated caecal tumour. He does not think there was any spread at the time and he received chemotherapy post-operatively. He also has hypertension and takes an antihypertensive medication but he is unsure what. He has smoked for 60 pack years. He drinks 4 units of alcohol a week. He lives with his partner.

This gentleman has jaundice, weight loss and possibly ascites. I would be concerned to exclude metastatic caecal cancer as a cause for his symptoms. I would next like to examine him, in particular to feel for any ascites or abdominal mass which may be present.'

🗒 WHAT YOU SHOULD KNOW

Causes of ascites
- **Increased portal venous pressure**:
Pre-hepatic	Portal venous thrombosis; compression of portal vein by lymph nodes
Hepatic	Cirrhosis of the liver; multiple hepatic metastases
Post-hepatic	Budd–Chiari syndrome (thrombosis of hepatic vein)
Cardiac	Constrictive pericarditis; right heart failure
Pulmonary	Pulmonary hypertension; right heart failure
- **Hypoproteinaemia**
  Kidney disease associated with albuminuria
  Cirrhosis of the liver
  Cachexia of wasting diseases, malignancy and starvation
  Protein-losing enteropathies
- **Chronic peritonitis**
Physical	Post-irradiation; talc granuloma; tuberculous peritonitis
Infection	Tuberculous peritonitis
Neoplasms	Peritoneal metastases; mucus-forming tumours (pseudomyxoma peritonei)
- **Chylous ascites**
  Congenital abnormalities
  Trauma
  Primary or secondary lymph gland disease

[243] Due to floating, gas-filled bowel.

[244] In tense, large ascites.

CONTINUED on pg 251

Examine this
gentleman
with abdominal
distension

(see pg 189)

'There is a generalised swelling of the abdomen and the umbilicus is everted. The flanks are stony-dull to percussion but the centre is resonant.[243] The dullness is shifting and a fluid thrill can be demonstrated.[244] This is ascites.'

⊚ WHAT YOU SHOULD SEE

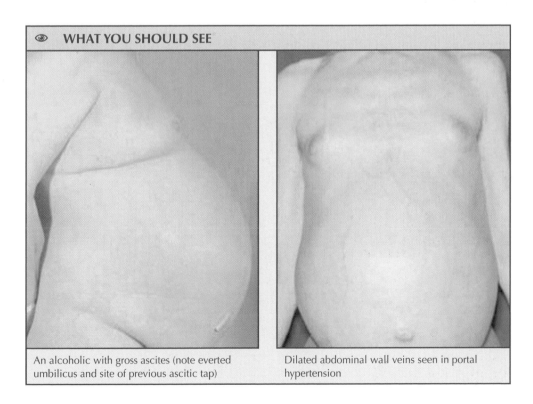

An alcoholic with gross ascites (note everted umbilicus and site of previous ascitic tap)

Dilated abdominal wall veins seen in portal hypertension

👁 **WHAT YOU SHOULD SEE**

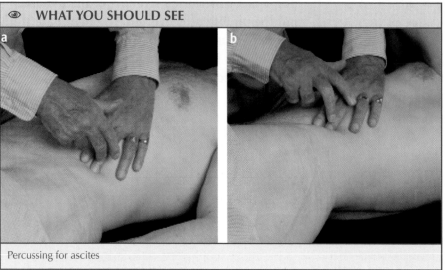

Percussing for ascites

WHAT YOU SHOULD KNOW (CONT)

Causes of portal hypertension

Worldwide, post-viral hepatitis is the commonest cause and in developed countries, alcoholic cirrhosis.

<u>Pre-sinusoidal</u>

- **Extrahepatic**: portal vein thrombosis; splenic vein thrombosis; arteriovenous fistula; tropical splenomegaly; immunological (lupoid); occlusion by tumour or pancreatitis
- **Intrahepatic**: schistosomiasis; chronic active hepatitis; early primary biliary cirrhosis; congenital hepatic fibrosis; sarcoidosis; toxins; idiopathic

<u>Sinusoidal</u>

- **Cirrhotic**: post-viral hepatitis; alcoholic; metabolic (e.g. Wilson's disease); drugs (e.g. methotraxate); cryptogenic
- **Non-cirrhotic**: acute alcoholic hepatitis; cytotoxic drugs; vitamin A intoxication

<u>Post-sinusoidal</u>

Budd–Chiari syndrome (tumour invasion of hepatic vein); veno-occlusive disease; caval abnormality; constrictive pericarditis.

Technique for aspiration of ascites

Explain what you are going to do to the patient, and obtain their consent.

The patient lies supine, with a pillow under the left hip to make them tilt slightly towards the right.

The right side of the abdomen is percussed, and the point at which the dull tone becomes resonant is noted and marked. Using aseptic technique, prep the area and infiltrate the skin with local anaesthetic. The site is two fingerbreadths superior to and medial to the anterior superior iliac spine.

Check that this is below the point marked earlier where the percussion note became resonant.

A diagnostic tap can be performed using a 50-ml syringe with a green needle and distributing the fluid aspirated into three sterile specimen pots (like those used for MSUs) for cytology, biochemistry and microbiology. Try to get at least 20 ml into the cytology specimen pot to increase the cell yield.

A therapeutic tap can be performed by inserting a grey venflon attached to a three-way tap, and using a 50-ml syringe to repeatedly aspirate and discharge the contents via the three way tap into a sterile jug. As the fluid volume reduces, withdraw the needle and cover the puncture site with a sterile dressing.

Beware withdrawing large amounts of fluid from frail patients: hypovolaemia can result from the ascites reaccumulating at the expense of the circulating volume. Intravenous salt-poor albumin infusion (20% human albumin solution) has been used to counteract this, but this has provoked controversy in recent years and is frowned upon by some units.

AN ABDOMINAL MASS

✍ WHAT YOU SHOULD KNOW

[245] **Solid tumours which can cause generalised abdominal distension**

Hepatomegaly	Fibroids
Splenomegaly	Large colon cancers
Pancreatic carcinoma	Polycystic kidneys
Retroperitoneal lymphadenopathy	Carcinoma of kidney
Retroperitoneal sarcoma	Carcinoma of liver
Nephroblastoma (in children)	Perinephric abscess
Ganglioneuroma (in children)	

✍ WHAT YOU SHOULD KNOW

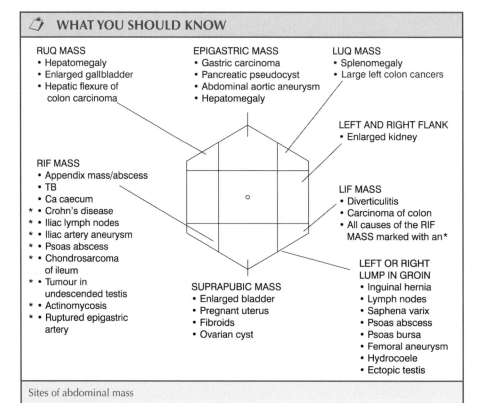

RUQ MASS
- Hepatomegaly
- Enlarged gallbladder
- Hepatic flexure of colon carcinoma

EPIGASTRIC MASS
- Gastric carcinoma
- Pancreatic pseudocyst
- Abdominal aortic aneurysm
- Hepatomegaly

LUQ MASS
- Splenomegaly
- Large left colon cancers

LEFT AND RIGHT FLANK
- Enlarged kidney

RIF MASS
- Appendix mass/abscess
- TB
- Ca caecum
* - Crohn's disease
* - Iliac lymph nodes
* - Iliac artery aneurysm
* - Psoas abscess
* - Chondrosarcoma of ileum
* - Tumour in undescended testis
* - Actinomycosis
* - Ruptured epigastric artery

LIF MASS
- Diverticulitis
- Carcinoma of colon
- All causes of the RIF MASS marked with an *

SUPRAPUBIC MASS
- Enlarged bladder
- Pregnant uterus
- Fibroids
- Ovarian cyst

LEFT OR RIGHT LUMP IN GROIN
- Inguinal hernia
- Lymph nodes
- Saphena varix
- Psoas abscess
- Psoas bursa
- Femoral aneurysm
- Hydrocoele
- Ectopic testis

Sites of abdominal mass

252

AN ABDOMINAL MASS

Take a history from and perform an examination of this gentleman with an abdominal mass

The 'presenting complaint' of a patient with an abdominal mass can be myriad. Depending on the cause of the mass, they may have noticed pain, weight loss, jaundice, anorexia etc. It is **not** common for patients to notice an abdominal mass and present purely with this. We therefore recommend that you use the 'abdominal pain history' on pg 162, which includes the abdominal symptoms which you should cover and you can modify it to fit your patient.

You will next need to carry out an examination of the abdomen (see pg 189).

When examining an abdominal mass, note the following:
- Position
- Shape
- Surface
- Edge
- Composition (consistency, fluctuation, fluid thrill)
- Resonance
- Pulsatility
- Tenderness
- Association with enlargement of palpable organs

The traditional 'six Fs' is a useful list of common causes of generalised distension: **F**oetus, **F**latus, **F**aeces, **F**at, **F**luid (free or encysted), and **F**ibroids and other solid tumours.[245]

Common abdominal masses are summarised in the diagram opposite and dealt with in more detail in the next few cases.

⟁ WHAT YOU SHOULD KNOW

Causes of enlargement of the liver

<u>Smooth, generalised enlargement, without jaundice</u>
Congestive heart failure
Cirrhosis
Reticuloses (e.g. lymphoma)
Hepatic vein obstruction (Budd–Chiari syndrome)
Amyloid disease

<u>Smooth generalised enlargement, with jaundice</u>
Infective hepatitis
Biliary tract obstruction (gallstones, carcinoma of pancreas)
Cholangitis
Portal pyaemia

<u>Knobbly generalised enlargement, without jaundice</u>
Secondary carcinoma
Macronodular cirrhosis
Polycystic disease
Primary hepatic carcinoma (hepatoma)

<u>Knobbly generalised enlargement, with jaundice</u>
Extensive secondary carcinoma
Cirrhosis
Localised swellings
Riedel's lobe
Secondary carcinoma
Hydatid cyst
Liver abscess
Primary multicentric hepatic carcinoma

Causes of cirrhosis of the liver

Alcohol, hepatitis B and hepatitis C account for 50% of cases of cirrhosis in this country. These and other causes are listed below.

- **Portal**: alcoholic; nutritional (protein deficiency); post-hepatic; idiopathic
- **Congenital**: haemochromatosis; Wilson's disease; α-1-antitrypsin deficiency; galactosaemia; type IV glycogen storage disease
- **Drug-induced**
- **Idiopathic**
- **Biliary**: primary biliary cirrhosis; secondary biliary cirrhosis
- **Cardiac**: congestive cardiac failure
- **Other**: chronic active hepatitis; schistosomiasis; sarcoidosis; viral hepatitis

Examine this gentleman's abdomen

(see pg 189)

HEPATOMEGALY

'There is a mass palpable in the right hypochondrium and epigastrium. It descends from below the right costal margin and costal angle. It moves with respiration and I cannot get above it. It is dull to percussion up to the level of the 8th rib in the mid-axillary line. The surface is smooth/knobbly. This is an enlarged liver.'

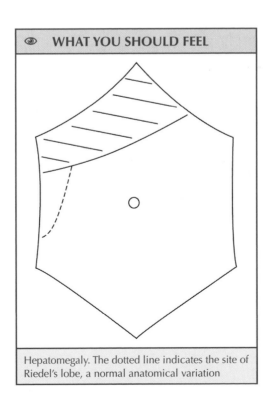

◉ **WHAT YOU SHOULD FEEL**

Hepatomegaly. The dotted line indicates the site of Riedel's lobe, a normal anatomical variation

SPLENOMEGALY

✍ WHAT YOU SHOULD KNOW

Causes of splenomegaly

<u>Cellular proliferation</u>
Myeloid and lymphatic leukaemia
Pernicious anaemia
Polycythaemia rubra vera
Spherocytosis
Thrombocytopenic purpura
Myelosclerosis
Mediterranean anaemia
<u>Infection</u>
Viral (glandular fever)
Bacterial (typhoid, typhus, TB, septicaemia)
Protozoal (malaria, kala-azar)
Spirochaetal (syphilis, leptospirosis)
<u>Congestion</u>
Portal hypertension (cirrhosis, portal vein thrombosis)
Hepatic vein obstruction
Congestive heart failure (cor pulmonale, constrictive pericarditis)
<u>Infarction</u>
Embolic (bacterial endocarditis, left atrium, left ventricle)
Thrombotic (splenic artery or vein thrombosis in polycythaemia and retroperitoneal malignancy)
<u>Cellular infiltration</u>
Amyloidosis
Gaucher's disease
<u>Collagen diseases</u>
Felty syndrome
Still's disease
<u>Space-occupying lesions</u>
Lymphoma
True solitary cysts
Polycystic disease
Hydatid cysts
Angioma
Lymphosarcoma

If you have trouble remembering long lists, try to just remember the seven headings and the first example of each.

SPLENOMEGALY

Examine this gentleman's abdomen

(see pg 189)

'There is a mass in the left hypochondrium. It appears from below the top of the left tenth rib and extends along the line of the rib towards the umbilicus. It is firm and smooth and has a notch on its upper edge (superomedial aspect). It moves with respiration, is dull to percussion and I cannot get above it. It is not ballotable. This is splenomegaly.'

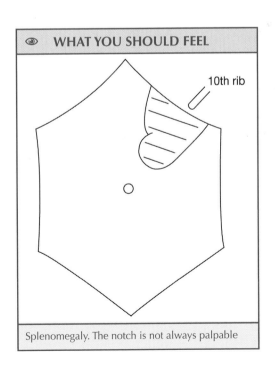

👁 **WHAT YOU SHOULD FEEL**

10th rib

Splenomegaly. The notch is not always palpable

✐ WHAT YOU SHOULD KNOW

Causes of an enlarged kidney
Hydronephrosis (may be bilateral)
Pyonephrosis
Perinephric abscess
Carcinoma or nephroblastoma (occasionally bilateral)
Solitary cysts
Polycystic disease (usually bilateral)
Hypertrophy
NB A mobile or low lying kidney may be easily palpable and so seem to be enlarged.
Differences between a spleen and a kidney on examination
A kidney is ballotable and reduces into the loin
The kidney moves vertically, not diagonally with respiration
The kidney is dull to percussion
The spleen has a notch
Clinical signs of chronic renal failure
Uraemia (yellow tint to skin)
Brown line on fingernails
Anaemia (decreased erythropoietin)
Hypertension
Fluid overload (high JVP, oedema)
Signs of renal support (AV fistula/shunt, peritoneal dialysis catheter)
Nephrectomy scar
Causes of chronic renal failure
Glomerulonephritis
Pyelonephritis
Diabetes mellitus
Hypertension
Clinical signs of polycystic kidneys
Bilaterally enlarged kidneys
Signs of chronic renal failure
AV fistula shunt on arm
Hypertension
Urine containing blood, protein, casts
Cysts will occur in other organs, e.g. berry aneurysms, liver cysts
Other affected family members (childhood variant is autosomal recessive, adult variant is autosomal dominant)
Complications of polycystic kidneys
Hypertension
UTIs
Haemorrhage into a cyst
Subarachnoid haemorrhage (association)

[246] This means it can be bounced between your hands, one on the anterior abdominal wall and the other behind the renal angle, rather like a ball being patted between the hands. This sign is diagnostic of a renal mass and depends on the mass reducing into the loin.

[247] Look for other signs of kidney transplantation following a long stint of renal failure, e.g. AV fistula.

Examine this gentleman's abdomen

(see pg 189)

ENLARGED KIDNEY

'There is a mass in the right/left flank. It is smooth and hemi-ovoid, moves with respiration and is not dull to percussion. It can be felt bimanually and is ballotable.[246] I can reduce it into the loin. This is an enlarged kidney.'

Examine this gentleman's abdomen

(see pg 189)

TRANSPLANTED KIDNEY

'There is a mass in the left iliac fossa with an overlying scar. It is smooth, ovoid, non-tender, and dull to percussion. There is a/is no nephrectomy scar on the same side. This is a transplanted kidney.'[247]

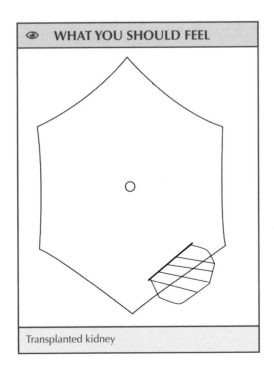

◉ WHAT YOU SHOULD FEEL

Transplanted kidney

ABDOMINAL CYSTS

Take a history from this gentleman with jaundice and abdominal distension

(see pgs 162/166)

'I would like to present Mr P, a 40-year-old unemployed gentleman. He noticed that his skin had turned yellow a week ago. He has also noticed that his stools are paler and urine darker. Over the last few weeks he has felt nauseated and has begun to vomit after eating. He thinks he has lost weight although he is unsure how much. He currently has no abdominal pain. His medical history includes an admission to hospital 3 months ago for pancreatitis. This was managed conservatively. He had an ultrasound of the abdomen at this time and does not think it showed any gallstones. He was told the pancreatitis was due to alcohol intake and advised to stop. He is currently trying to stop drinking and is taking disulfiram. He has smoked for 20 pack years. He denies drinking currently but prior to the pancreatitis was drinking 60 units of alcohol a week. He lives with his partner.

This gentleman has jaundice and vomiting after eating following a recent episode of pancreatitis. I would be concerned to exclude a pancreatic pseudocyst as a cause for his symptoms. I would next like to examine him, in particular to feel for any abdominal mass which may be present.'

Examine this gentleman's abdomen

(see pg 189)

ABDOMINAL CYSTS

Case 1

'There is (in this thin[248], middle-aged patient) a firm tender/non-tender, non-pulsatile mass in the epigastrium with an indistinct lower edge. The upper limit is not palpable. It is resonant to percussion and moves slightly with respiration. It is not possible to elicit fluctuation or a fluid thrill. The patient is/is not jaundiced and is/is not on total parenteral nutrition. This is a pancreatic pseudocyst.'[249]

Case 2

'There is a smooth, mobile, spherical swelling in the centre of the abdomen. It moves freely diagonally from the right hypochondrium to the left iliac fossa (at right angles to the root of the mesentery), but only slightly from the left hypochondrium to the right iliac fossa (parallel to the root of the mesentery). It is dull to percussion and is fluctuant, with a fluid thrill (if fixed). This is a mesenteric cyst.'[250]

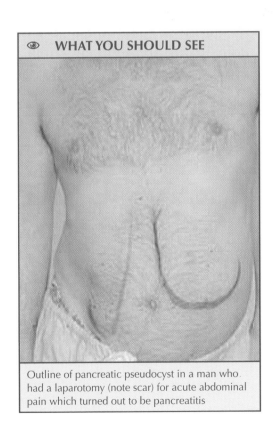

👁 WHAT YOU SHOULD SEE

Outline of pancreatic pseudocyst in a man who had a laparotomy (note scar) for acute abdominal pain which turned out to be pancreatitis

261

🗐 WHAT YOU SHOULD KNOW

Cystic swellings which can cause abdominal distension

Ovarian cysts	Hydronephrosis	Polycystic kidney	Urinary bladder
Pancreatic cysts	Mesenteric cysts	Hydatid cysts	

[248] Pseudocysts are most commonly a complication/sequela of severe pancreatitis, a debilitating and prolonged disease which tends to leave patients exhausted and malnourished.

[249] **Pancreatic pseudocyst**

Definition: a collection of serous fluid in relation to the pancreas following acute pancreatitis.

Site: the most common site is the lesser sac as a result of blockage of the gastroepiploic foramen by inflammatory adhesions. Pseudocysts can occur anywhere adjacent to, or sometimes within, the pancreas.

Incidence: routine ultrasound or CT will detect pseudocysts in up to 30% of patients with acute pancreatitis, and all but 5% resolve spontaneously.

Management: due to the natural history described above, conservative management is the treatment of choice.

Indications for drainage include:

Persisting pancreatic inflammation with hyperamylasaemia

Palpable abdominal swelling which may compress the stomach or duodenum and cause vomiting.

Infection or haemorrhage of the cyst

Methods of drainage:

Percutaneous under CT or USS control – often reaccumulate

Endoscopic drainage through the posterior wall of the stomach

Open pseudocysto-gastrostomy where an incision from the posterior wall of the stomach to the cyst is formed then the sac is sutured to the gastric wall

Open pseudocysto-jejenostomy for inferior cysts involves formation of a Roux loop

[250] **Mesenteric cysts**

These are cysts of clear fluid found in the mesentery arising from vestigial remnants of reduplicated bowel. They may be found by chance, being symptomless, or cause abdominal distension or recurrent colicky pain. Like all cysts they can rupture, twist, and have intraluminal bleeding. Twisting is rare because they are fixed within the small-bowel mesentery.

Examine this gentleman's abdomen

(see pg 189)

ENLARGED GALLBLADDER

'There is a mass in the right upper quadrant below the tip of the right ninth rib. It is smooth, hemi-ovoid, dull to percussion and moves with respiration. I cannot feel a space between the lump and the edge of the liver. This is an enlarged gallbladder.'

✐ WHAT YOU SHOULD KNOW

Causes of a large gallbladder
With jaundice
Carcinoma of head of pancreas
Carcinoma of ampulla of Vater
Gallstone formed in situ in common bile duct
Mucocoele due to stone in Hartmann's pouch and stone in common bile duct
Common bile duct cholangiocarcinoma
Without jaundice
Mucocoele
Empyema
Carcinoma of gallbladder
Acute cholecystitis
An enlarged gallbladder is usually due to obstruction of the cystic duct or common bile duct.
Obstruction of the cystic duct is usually by a gallstone and rarely by an intrinsic or extrinsic carcinoma. The patient is not jaundiced and the gallbladder will contain bile, mucus (a mucocoele) or pus (an empyema).
Obstruction of the common bile duct is usually by a stone or a carcinoma of the head of the pancreas. The patient will be jaundiced. Courvoisier's law states:
'In the presence of jaundice, the palpable gallbladder is unlikely to be due to stones.'
This is because previous inflammation will have made the gallbladder thick and non-distensible. The exceptions are:
Stones which form in the bile duct
Stones in the cystic duct as well as a stone or carcinoma in the bile duct

◉ WHAT YOU SHOULD SEE

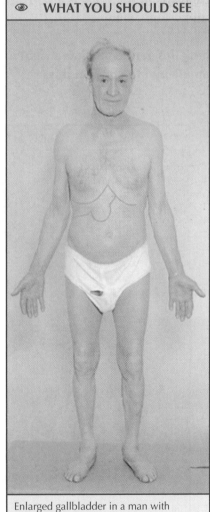

Enlarged gallbladder in a man with painless jaundice

Take a history from this gentleman with a right groin lump

(see pg 174)

INDIRECT INGUINAL HERNIA

'I would like to present Mr P, a 35-year-old personal trainer. He noticed a lump in his right groin 4 weeks ago. It appears on standing, coughing and when he lifts weights at work. It aches a bit towards the end of the day but is not painful. It has never got stuck out nor been irreducible and he has had no episodes of vomiting or abdominal pain which might suggest obstruction. He has no recent history of constipation, cough or urinary problems. He is otherwise fit and well and takes no medication with no known allergies. He is a non-smoker and does not drink alcohol. He lives alone.

I think this gentleman has a right inguinal hernia. I would next like to examine him to confirm this.'

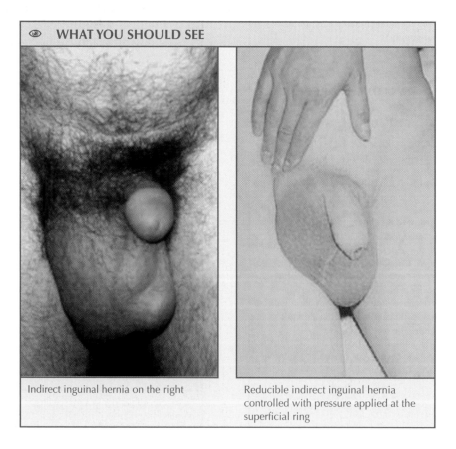

👁 WHAT YOU SHOULD SEE

Indirect inguinal hernia on the right

Reducible indirect inguinal hernia controlled with pressure applied at the superficial ring

Examine this patient's groin

(see pg 200)

INDIRECT INGUINAL HERNIA

Case 1

'There is (in this young/middle-aged patient) a visible lump in the right groin extending towards the scrotum. On examination the lump has an expansile cough impulse, is not tender and the overlying skin is normal. It is reducible through a point above and medial to the pubic tubercle, and is controlled both at the superficial and deep inguinal rings. This is a reducible indirect inguinal hernia and could be repaired electively if the patient is fit.[251] I would like to examine the other side, and would normally do a cardiorespiratory assessment and examine the abdomen.'

Case 2

'There is a large swelling in the right groin and scrotum. On examination the lump has an expansile cough impulse, is not tender, and the overlying skin is normal. It is not reducible but appears to emerge from a point above and medial to the pubic tubercle. The contents of the lump have liquid and gaseous components and there is evidence of bowel sounds indicating bowel loops within it. This is an irreducible or incarcerated inguinal hernia, and should be repaired promptly if the patient is fit. I would like to examine the other side, and would normally do a cardiorespiratory assessment and examine the abdomen.'

◉ WHAT YOU SHOULD SEE

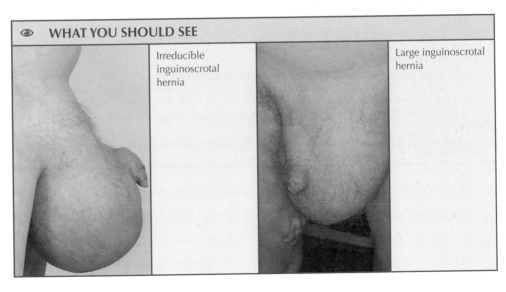

Irreducible inguinoscrotal hernia

Large inguinoscrotal hernia

265

WHAT YOU SHOULD KNOW

The indirect inguinal hernia is the most common type of groin hernia in children. It is thought to be caused by a congenital failure of the processus vaginalis to close (saccular theory of Russell). The indirect inguinal hernia sac is the remains of the processus vaginalis. The sac extends through the deep ring, canal and superficial ring. The inferior epigastric artery lies medial to the neck. In a complete sac the testis is found in the fundus. In an incomplete sac, the sac is limited to the canal or is inguinoscrotal or inguinolabial. The indirect hernia commonly descends into the scrotum.

Predisposing factors for indirect inguinal herniae
Male (bigger processus vaginalis)
Premature twins/low birth weight (processus vaginalis not closed)
Young (compared with direct herniae which become more common with age)
Africans (lower arch in more oblique African pelvis)
On the right (right testis descends later than left)
Testicular feminisation syndrome (genotypic male but androgen-insensitive so phenotypic female)
Increased intraperitoneal fluid (e.g. cardiac, cirrhotic, carcinomatosis, dialysis opens up processus vaginalis)

[251] Advantages of groin hernia repair under local anaesthetic (LA)
Early mobilisation
Decreased urinary retention, DVT/PE
Safer in high-risk patients
Decreased cost, increased patient turnover
No reduction in complications or increase in recurrence
If not fit for general anaesthetic

Anatomy of the inguinal canal
The inguinal ligament is the rolled-under inferior margin of the aponeurosis of the external oblique muscle and runs between the anterior superior iliac spine (ASIS) and the pubic tubercle.
The inguinal canal lies above the medial half of the inguinal ligament between the deep and superficial rings.
The deep inguinal ring is an opening in the transversalis fascia 1.3 cm above the inguinal ligament, midway between the ASIS and the pubic tubercle (the midpoint of the inguinal ligament). It lies lateral to the inferior epigastric vessels.
The superficial inguinal ring is a triangular opening in the external oblique aponeurosis. The lateral crus attaches to the pubic tubercle. The medial crus attaches to the pubic crest near the symphysis. The base of the superficial ring is the pubic crest.
The floor of the inguinal canal is formed by the inguinal canal and the lacunar ligament medially.
The ceiling of the inguinal canal is formed by, lateral to medial, the transverse abdominis, internal oblique and the conjoint tendon.
The anterior wall of the inguinal ligament is formed by the external oblique strengthened laterally by the internal oblique.
The posterior wall of the inguinal canal is formed by the transversalis fascia strengthened medially by the conjoint tendon.

✎ WHAT YOU SHOULD KNOW

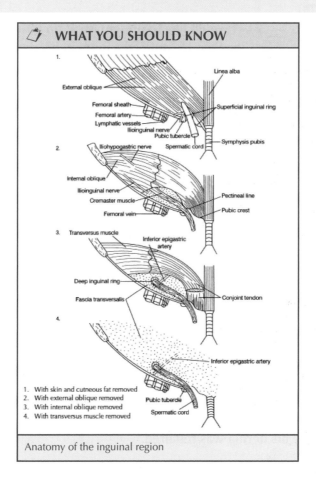

1. External oblique
   Linea alba
   Femoral sheath
   Superficial inguinal ring
   Femoral artery
   Lymphatic vessels
   Ilioinguinal nerve
   Pubic tubercle
   Iliohypogastric nerve
   Spermatic cord
   Symphysis pubis

2. Internal oblique
   Ilioinguinal nerve
   Pectineal line
   Cremaster muscle
   Pubic crest
   Femoral vein

3. Transversus muscle
   Inferior epigastric artery
   Deep inguinal ring
   Fascia transversalis
   Conjoint tendon

4. Inferior epigastric artery
   Pubic tubercle
   Spermatic cord

1. With skin and cutaneous fat removed
2. With external oblique removed
3. With internal oblique removed
4. With transversus muscle removed

Anatomy of the inguinal region

✎ WHAT YOU SHOULD KNOW (CONT)

Contents of the inguinal canal in the male

<u>Vas</u>

<u>Arteries</u>: testicular, artery to vas, cremasteric

<u>Veins</u>: the pampiniform plexus

<u>Lymphatic</u> vessels: the testis drains to the para-aortic lymph nodes; the coverings of the testis drain to the external iliac nodes

<u>Nerves</u>: Genital branch of the genitofemoral (supplies cremaster muscle)
Sympathetic nerves accompanying arteries
Ilioinguinal nerve (enters via the anterior wall of the canal) supplying the skin of the inguinal region, upper part of thigh and anterior third of scrotum or labia

<u>Processus vaginalis</u>: the obliterated remains of the peritoneal connection to the tunica vaginalis

All of the above are in the spermatic cord except the ilioinguinal nerve.

Take a history from this gentleman with a right groin lump

(see pg 174)

DIRECT INGUINAL HERNIA

'I would like to present Mr P, an 80-year-old retired banker. He noticed a lump in his right groin 1 year ago. He became more concerned about it over the last month because previously the lump would only appear on standing and coughing, but it has recently got stuck out on two occasions. He was just able to reduce it himself but it was very painful. He did not get any abdominal pain or vomiting during these episodes. He has a chronic cough and has become increasingly constipated recently. This has been associated with some dark-red rectal bleeding. He had a TURP 3 years ago and no longer has any problems urinating. His medical history includes the TURP, COPD and a DVT diagnosed 2 months ago. He is on regular inhalers but not home nebulisers or oxygen and can walk for 500 yards on the flat before he has to stop due to SOB. He is also taking warfarin for his recent DVT. He has no known allergies. He has smoked for 60 pack years but is a life-long teetotaller. He lives with his wife for whom he is the main carer.

I think this gentleman has a right inguinal hernia. I would next like to examine him to confirm this. It appears to have become incarcerated on two occasions and I would want to repair it promptly. However, he is on warfarin, which would need to be stopped pre-operatively. I am also concerned about his worsening constipation and PR bleeding and with his recent DVT I would want to exclude a colonic malignancy. Provision would also need to be made for his wife while his hernia was repaired.'

✎ WHAT YOU SHOULD KNOW

This is an acquired weakness in the abdominal wall so tends to develop in adulthood as compared with indirect herniae which are common in children. Around 35% of adult male inguinal herniae are direct; 5% are a combination of direct and indirect. The direct inguinal hernia sac lies behind the cord. The inferior epigastric artery lies lateral to the neck. The hernia passes directly forwards through the defect in the posterior wall (fascia transversalis) of the inguinal canal. The hernia does not typically run down alongside the cord to the scrotum but can do so.

Predisposing factors for direct inguinal herniae
- Males
- Old age
- Increased intra-abdominal pressure (e.g. chronic cough, obesity, constipation, prostatism)
- Smoking
- Aortic aneurysm (associated with collagen defect)
- Anatomical variant of the conjoint tendon (in 10% of adult white males)

CONTINUED on pg 270

Examine this patient's groin

(see pg 200)

DIRECT INGUINAL HERNIA

'There is a small swelling in the right groin. On examination the lump has an expansile cough impulse, is not tender and the overlying skin is normal. It is easily reducible and emerges from a point above and medial to the pubic tubercle. It is controlled by pressure over the superficial ring but not by pressure over the deep ring. This is a direct inguinal hernia and could be repaired electively, preferably under local anaesthetic if the patient is fit. Alternatively, if the lump is small, asymptomatic and the patient is elderly, an easily reducible direct inguinal hernia can safely be managed expectantly. I would like to examine the other side, and would normally do a cardiorespiratory assessment and examine the abdomen.'

◉ WHAT YOU SHOULD SEE

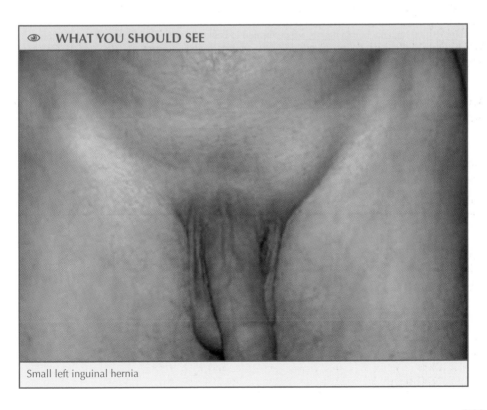

Small left inguinal hernia

⟁ WHAT YOU SHOULD KNOW (CONT)

Complications of herniae
- Incarceration, obstruction, strangulation
- Reduction en masse
- Richter's hernia (only antimesenteric margin of gut is strangulated in the sac)
- Maydl's hernia (a W-shaped loop of small gut lies in the hernia sac and the intervening loop is strangulated within the main abdominal cavity)
- Littre's hernia (hernia sac containing strangulated Meckel's diverticulum)
- Spontaneous or traumatic rupture of hernia sac
- Involvement in peritoneal disease process (e.g. metastatic disease, mesothelial hyperplasia, peritonitis, endometriosis)

Indications for groin hernia repair

Non-mandatory	Small, easily reducible, direct	Follow-up in 1 year (same for recurrent herniae)
Elective to be prioritised by job	Indirect, symptomatic direct	Because rate of strangulation of inguinal hernia is 0.3–2.9% per year – risk if irreducible or indirect
Prompt	Irreducible inguinal hernia History of <4 weeks	More risk of strangulation in first 3 months after appearing
Urgent	All femoral herniae	Within a month 50% strangulate
Emergency	Painful irreducible herniae	

2007 NICE Guidelines of Management of Groin Herniae state:
Around 70 000 inguinal hernia repairs are performed in England each year. In 2001/02, 95.9% mesh repairs were performed by open surgery, and 4.1% by laparoscopic surgery.

Techniques for **open repair** include:
- Open flat mesh (e.g. the Lichtenstein method). This is thought to be the principal surgical method of hernia repair in the UK.
- Open plug and mesh repair

Recent guidance from NICE has advised that: **laparoscopic repair** is the preferred technique for:
- Recurrent herniae (thus avoiding scar tissue from previous open repairs)
- Bilateral herniae (which can be repaired simultaneously)
- An option for primary repair of unilateral herniae (due to reduced incidence of long-term pain and numbness and potential for earlier return to normal activities)

Techniques for laparoscopic surgical repair include the transabdominal preperitoneal (TAPP) or the totally extraperitoneal (TEP) procedure.

📑 WHAT YOU SHOULD KNOW (CONT)

Post-operative complications of groin hernia repair

<u>Wound</u>: haematoma, sepsis, sinus

<u>Scrotal</u>: ischaemic orchitis, testicular atrophy, hydrocoele, genital oedema, damage to vas and vessels

<u>Special complications</u>: nerve injuries, persistent post-operative pain, compression of femoral vessels, urinary retention, impotence, mesh infection

<u>General complications</u>: chest infection, DVT, PE, cardiovascular problems, visceral injury

<u>Operation failure</u>: recurrence, missed hernia, dehiscence

<u>Mortality</u>

👁 WHAT YOU SHOULD SEE

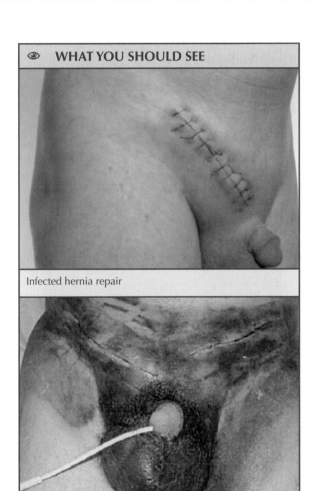

Infected hernia repair

Haematoma and urinary retention, two complications of hernia repair

Take a history
from this elderly
lady with a groin
lump

(see pg 174)

FEMORAL HERNIA

'I would like to present Mrs P, an 80-year-old woman. She has noticed a lump in her right groin today. She has had associated vomiting and colicky abdominal pain during the day. She opened her bowels yesterday but cannot recall passing stool or flatus today. Her medical history includes ischaemic heart disease and she has also lost weight recently (but is unsure why). She takes medication for her IHD and uses her GTN spray once a week, on average. She does not smoke or drink and lives in sheltered accommodation with carers visiting three times a day.

I suspect that this lady has an obstructed right groin hernia. Given her age, sex and weight loss this is likely to be a right femoral hernia which requires <u>urgent</u> exploration and fixation.'

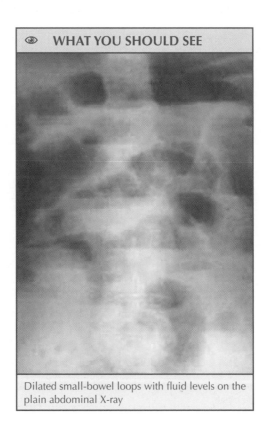

👁 **WHAT YOU SHOULD SEE**

Dilated small-bowel loops with fluid levels on the plain abdominal X-ray

Examine this patient's groin

(see pg 200)

FEMORAL HERNIA

'There is (in this elderly woman) a small non-tender lump bulging into the right groin crease. On examination the lump has an expansile cough impulse[252], is not tender and the overlying skin is normal. It is reducible[253] through a point below and lateral to the pubic tubercle. This is a femoral hernia and requires repair within 4 weeks. I would like to examine the other side, and would normally do a cardiorespiratory assessment and examine the abdomen.'

🖑 WHAT YOU SHOULD KNOW

[252] A narrow neck and adherence of the contents to the peritoneal sac mean that many femoral herniae do not have a cough impulse.
[253] The size of most femoral herniae can be reduced by firm pressure, but they often cannot be completely reduced because the contents are often adherent to the peritoneal sac.

👁 WHAT YOU SHOULD SEE

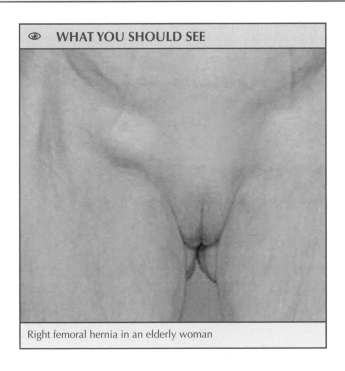

Right femoral hernia in an elderly woman

✍ WHAT YOU SHOULD KNOW (CONT)

Epidemiology

In females, femoral herniae are as common as indirect inguinal herniae. They are found 2.5 times more commonly in females because:

- Inguinal ligament makes a wider angle with the pubis in the female.
- Enlargement of the fat in the femoral canal in fat middle-aged ladies stretches the femoral canal; this fat then disappears in old age, leaving a bigger canal.
- Pregnancy increases intra-abdominal pressure and stretches the fascia transversalis.

Mechanics of femoral hernia

Femoral hernia enters the femoral canal through the femoral ring. The hernia arrives in the thigh next to the saphenous opening of the femoral sheath. The cribriform fascia over the saphenous opening becomes stretched over the hernia. The hernia enlarges upwards and medially into the superficial fascia of the inguinal ligament. Typically it lies between the superficial external pudendal and superficial epigastric veins, compressing the saphenous vein as it emerges through the saphenous opening.

Anatomy of the femoral sheath

The femoral sheath is a downward protrusion into the thigh of the fascial envelope lining the abdominal wall. It surrounds the femoral vessels and lymphatics for about 1 inch below the inguinal ligament. The sheath ends by fusing with the tunica adventitia of the femoral vessels. This occurs close to the saphenous opening in the deep fascia of the thigh. The anterior wall is continuous above with the fascia transversalis, the posterior wall is continuous above with the fascia iliacus/psoas fascia. It does not protrude below the inguinal ligament in the fetal position. The femoral sheath exists to provide freedom for vessel movement beneath the inguinal ligament during movement of the hip.

Contents of the femoral sheath

- Femoral artery in lateral compartment
- Femoral veins in intermediate compartment
- Lymphatics in medial compartment or femoral canal
- The femoral branch (L1) of the genitofemoral nerve pierces the anterior wall of the femoral sheath, running on the anterior surface of the external iliac artery

NB The femoral nerve lies in the iliac fossa between psoas and iliacus behind the fascia. Therefore it enters the thigh outside the femoral sheath.

Anatomy of the femoral canal

The femoral canal is the medial compartment of the femoral sheath, containing lymphatics. It is about 1.3 cm long, with an upper opening called the femoral ring. The femoral canal allows lymph vessels to be transmitted from the lower limbs to the abdomen and is also a dead space into which the femoral vein can expand when venous return increases. The femoral canal is the path taken by femoral herniae.

Contents of the femoral canal

- Fatty connective tissue
- Efferent lymph vessels from deep inguinal nodes
- The deep inguinal node of Cloquet, draining the penis/clitoris

Relations of the femoral ring

- Anteriorly the inguinal ligament
- Posteriorly the superior ramus of the pubis and the pectineal ligament
- Medially the lacunar ligament or ileopubic tract
- Laterally the femoral vein

These are also the margins of the neck of a femoral hernia. Note that three of the four are rigid, making the femoral hernia prone to strangulation.

☑ WHAT YOU SHOULD KNOW (CONT)

Characteristics of a typical femoral hernia
- Small (hard to find in an obese patient)
- Not reducible
- No cough impulse
- Often contains only omentum
- May contain a knuckle of bowel (most common site for a Richter's hernia)
- More common on the right
- 35–50% of all strangulated groin herniae in adults are femoral herniae

Differential diagnosis of femoral hernia

Inguinal hernia	Femoral artery aneurysm
Enlarged lymph gland	Sarcoma
Saphena varix	Ectopic testis
Ectopic testis	Obturator hernia
Psoas abscess	Psoas bursa
Lipoma	

Repair of femoral hernia
The main aims are to remove the peritoneal sac and repair the defects. Methods include:
- The crural/low/Lockwood approach is the simplest – used for elective repair but not recommended for strangulated hernia
- High/inguinal/Lothiessen approach reveals the femoral canal through the inguinal canal
- High/extraperitoneal/McEvedy approach – safest for strangulated hernia

Royal College of Surgeons Guidelines on Repair of Femoral Herniae
The Royal College of Surgeons recommends the high inguinal approach, except in thin females, when a low crural approach is acceptable. In complex, recurrent or obstructed herniae the high extraperitoneal approach is advised.

◉ WHAT YOU SHOULD SEE

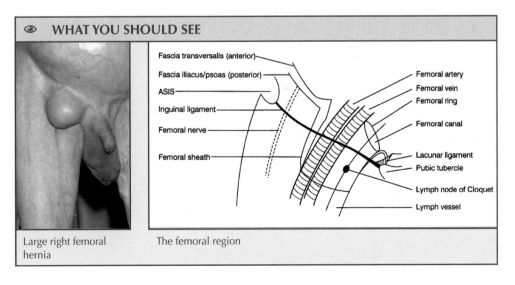

Large right femoral hernia

The femoral region

🗒 WHAT YOU SHOULD KNOW

Definition: Diffuse extension of peritoneum and abdominal contents through a weak scar.

Incidence: 6% of abdominal wounds at 5 years, 12% at 10 years. More common in caesarean section and gynaecological wounds.

Causes of incisional hernia:
- Technical failure by surgeon: haematoma, necrosis, sepsis, inept closure, poor incision, drains or stomas
- Tissue factors: age, immunosuppression, obesity, malignancy, malnutrition, infection
- High-risk incisions: lower/upper midline, lateral muscle splitting, subcostal, parastomal, transverse
- Pre-operative conditions: cardiopulmonary disease, obesity, diabetes, local skin/tissue sepsis

Surgical repair of incisional hernia
- Layer to layer anatomical repair (if there is no tissue loss)
- Mesh repair
- Composite mesh repair
- Laparoscopic incisional hernia repair
- Recurrence rates vary from 1% to 46% – lower (10%) with mesh repairs

Divarication of the recti can be mistaken for an incisional hernia, as it can occur after multiple midline incisions. Other causes include multiple pregnancies and prolonged abdominal distension. The linea alba stretches and fails to hold together the two longitudinal rectus abdominus muscles. The resulting gap may be as much as several inches, and allows a diffuse bulge to appear between the recti, more pronounced superiorly where the origin of the rectus muscles is further apart (on the lower ribs) than at their insertion at the pubis. Surgery is unnecessary unless there is a local defect within the divarication as they rarely strangulate.

Examine this gentleman's abdomen

(see pg 189)

INCISIONAL HERNIA

'There is a non-tender reducible lump with an expansile cough impulse under an old scar. The lump is about 10 cm by 6 cm and a defect in the abdominal wall can be felt which is about 4 cm by 2 cm. The extent of the hernia can be seen more clearly when the patient, lying flat, raises both straight legs just off the bed.

This is an incisional hernia. The wide neck and easy reducibility points to a low risk of strangulation.'

👁 WHAT YOU SHOULD SEE

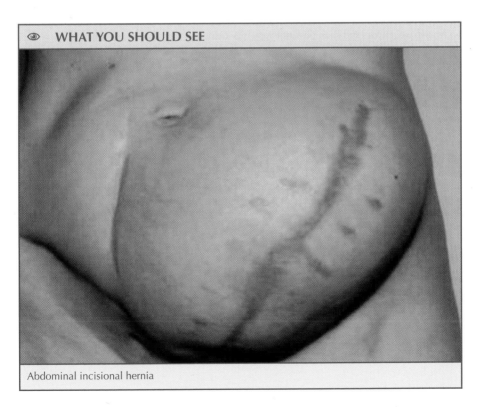

Abdominal incisional hernia

👁 WHAT YOU SHOULD KNOW

More common with increasing age, M = F.

Causes

Increased intra-abdominal pressure, e.g. ascites, multiple pregnancy, malignancy, chronic obstructive pulmonary disease or obesity.

Anatomy

The sac protrudes through a defect in the linea alba near the umbilical cicatrix but, unlike the true umbilical hernia, not through the cicatrix itself. Progressively increases in size. Usually contains just omentum but can contain transverse colon and sometimes small intestine. The neck of the sac is often very narrow compared with the sac contents, and very fibrous. Contents adhere to one another, the coverings and the omentum.

Coverings

Skin, superficial fascia, rectus sheath, transversalis fascia and sac. These stretch and fuse into a thin membrane, through which peristalsis may be seen.

Complications

Redness, excoriation, ulceration, gangrene, becoming pendulous, infection, faecal fistula, strangulation, incarceration and obstruction.

Clinical features

Usually irreducible. May present with pain due to incarceration and subacute obstruction. Strangulation is common due to narrow neck.

Difficulties with surgical repair

This may have significant mortality in old patients with large herniae. Problems include:

• Patients tend to be old with co-morbidity
• High risk of strangulation
• Difficult anatomy and reduction
• May have increased intra-abdominal pressure after reduction, which exacerbates respiratory problems
Pre-operative weight loss and chest physiotherapy may help.

Techniques of surgical repair

Mayo's operation 'vest over pants' – lower edge of rectus (pants) is brought up and fixed by non-absorbable sutures to behind the upper flap.

Mesh repair – especially useful if there is tissue loss.

Umbilical herniae

Incidence

• 3% neonates have umbilical herniae, most resolve spontaneously
• 3:1000 live births need further surgery
• More common in black children

Anatomy

Peritoneal sac penetrates through linea alba at umbilical cicatrix to lie in subcutaneous tissues between skin cicatrix. There is a narrow rigid neck at the aponeurosis.

Prognosis

• All decrease in size as child grows
• Few persist after puberty
• Some cause disfigurement or incarcerate
• Only a minority need an operation
• Must preserve the umbilicus to avoid stigmatising child
• Similar Mayo 'vest over pants' repair to adult repair (see above); absorbable polymer used

PARAUMBILICAL HERNIA

'There is (in this obese, middle-aged woman) a non-tender reducible lump with an expansile cough impulse adjacent to the umbilicus. The umbilicus is pushed to one side and is stretched into a characteristic crescent shape. The lump is about 3 cm in diameter and there is a fingertip-sized defect felt in the linea alba after it is reduced. This is a paraumbilical hernia. As strangulation is relatively common in these small-necked herniae, I would suggest surgical repair if the patient is fit. If the hernia is symptomatic, irreducible or has appeared recently, repair should be prompt.'

WHAT YOU SHOULD SEE

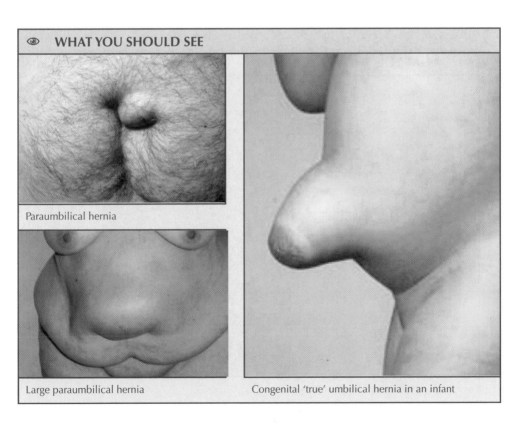

Paraumbilical hernia

Large paraumbilical hernia

Congenital 'true' umbilical hernia in an infant

279

Examine this patient's abdomen or Examine this patient's lump

(see pgs 43/ 189)

EPIGASTRIC HERNIA

'There is (in this young male patient) a small, firm, non-tender lump in the epigastrium.[254] It is irreducible, with no cough impulse. This is a likely epigastric hernia but the differential diagnosis is a lipoma.'

✎ WHAT YOU SHOULD KNOW

This is a protrusion of extraperitoneal fat or peritoneum through one of the lozenge-shaped fissures commonly found between the latticed fibres of the linea alba. Epigastric herniae can occur in children or adults and may cause disproportionate epigastric pain and upper gastrointestinal symptoms. They are cured by excision of sac and repair of linea alba. Around 30% have co-existing intra-abdominal disease causing symptoms and so should be fully investigated. It is often impossible to differentiate an epigastric hernia from a lipoma, as they are often irreducible and have no cough impulse due to their small neck. An ultrasound scan would differentiate the two.

[254] Or in the line of the linea alba anywhere from umbilicus to xiphisternum.

◉ WHAT YOU SHOULD SEE

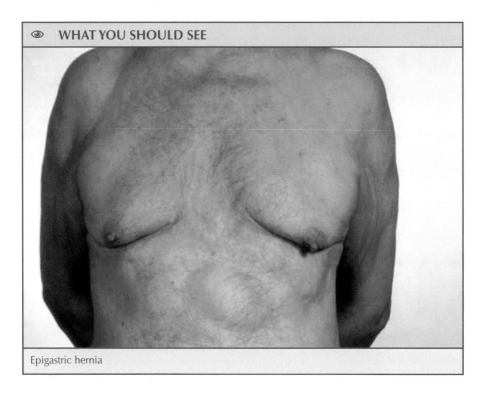

Epigastric hernia

SPIGELIAN HERNIA

'There is a diffuse swelling at the lateral border of the left rectus muscle. Although not acutely tender, the patient reports it as an aching lump. It is/is not reducible, arises from the deep tissues and the skin moves over it freely. There is no superficial bruising overlying the lump. This is likely to be a Spigelian hernia, but the differential diagnosis is a rectus sheath haematoma.'

✍ WHAT YOU SHOULD KNOW

These are also known as **semilunar line herniae** and account for 1% of abdominal herniae. The hernia protrudes through bands of internal oblique muscle as it enters the semilunar line. Most occur below the umbilicus adjacent to line of Douglas. It is usually deflected laterally by the external oblique and can be found near the iliac crest. The sac may enter rectus sheath and be confused with rectus muscle haematoma. They are more common in women than in men. They present as an aching lump and are diagnosed by ultrasound scan. They can strangulate. Repair is by excision of peritoneal sac and closure of the aponeurotic defect.

Other rare herniae
Lumbar hernia
These tend to occur after renal operations, lumbar abscesses or paralysis of lateral lumbar muscles by poliomyelitis or spina bifida. Spontaneous lumbar herniae occur through the lumbar triangle of Petit (formed by the iliac crest, posterior external oblique and anterior latissimus dorsi) or the quadrilateral lumbar space (formed by the 12th rib, lower border of serratus posterior inferior, anterior border of erector spinae and internal oblique).
Gluteal hernia emerges through the greater sciatic notch.
Obturator hernia emerges through the obturator foramen.
Sciatic hernia emerges through the lesser sciatic notch.

✍ WHAT YOU SHOULD KNOW

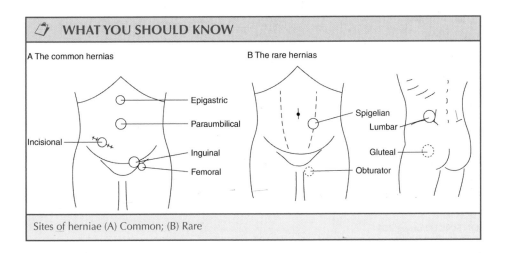

Sites of herniae (A) Common; (B) Rare

Take a history from this gentleman with a right testicular lump

(see pg 33)

HYDROCOELE

'I would like to present Mr P, a 60-year-old teacher. He noticed a lump in his right scrotum 2 months ago. It is non-tender. He has had no trauma or surgery to his scrotum previously. He has asthma, for which he only uses a salbutamol inhaler as required. He does not smoke or drink. He lives with his wife and young children.

The differential diagnosis includes a hydrocoele, epididymal cyst and inguinoscrotal hernia and I would like to examine him. If it is a scrotal lump I would need to exclude a testicular tumour with an ultrasound scan.'

🗎 WHAT YOU SHOULD KNOW

Definition
A **hydrocoele** is an abnormal quantity of serous fluid within the tunica vaginalis.

Causes
Primary hydrocoele (appears gradually and becomes large and tense; occur in children or elderly):
• Idiopathic
Secondary hydrocoele (appears rapidly in the presence of other symptoms, are not tense and often contain some altered blood. Occur most commonly between age 20 and 40):
• Trauma
• Epididymo-orchitis
• Tumour
• Lymphatic obstruction

Management
Exclude tumour: testicular tumours can present as hydrocoeles, so initially investigations are geared towards excluding tumour as an underlying cause. In the past aspirating the hydrocoele in order to palpate the testicle was considered reasonable; now this is absolutely contraindicated as it may seed the tumour to the scrotal skin.
Ultrasound imaging is the minimum investigation. Hydrocoeles which arise suddenly in young men are particularly suspicious.
Jaboulay's procedure: sac incised longitudinally, everted and approximated behind the cord.
Lord's operation: small incision through the scrotum and tunica allowing the testicle to be lifted from the sac and the scrotum. The sac is then plicated to the junction of the testis and epididymis.

Post-operative complications
• Recurrence
• Haematoma
• Infection
CONTINUED on pg 284

Examine this patient's groin

(see pg 200)

HYDROCOELE

'There is (in this middle-aged/elderly man) a large non-tender swelling filling the left scrotum. I can feel the cord above the swelling, but I cannot feel the testicle separate from the lump. It is brilliantly transilluminable, fluctuant and dull to percussion. The surface is smooth and well-defined and the consistency is tense/lax. The skin of the scrotum is freely mobile over the swelling. This is a vaginal hydrocoele. An abdominal examination and scrotal ultrasound are important to exclude an underlying cause.'

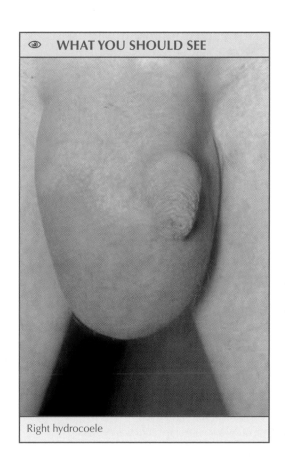

👁 **WHAT YOU SHOULD SEE**

Right hydrocoele

✎ WHAT YOU SHOULD KNOW (CONT)

The most common type is the **vaginal hydrocoele**, where the processus vaginalis is obliterated and the fluid collects only around the testicle. Thus the cord structures can be felt above the swelling, and the testicle cannot be felt separately.

Also common (but not seen so often in exams) is the **congenital hydrocoele**, seen in infants, where the hydrocoele communicates with the peritoneal cavity due to a patent processus vaginalis. They usually resolve within the first 6–12 months of life, but need surgery if they persist after a year.

An **infantile hydrocoele** is rare and involves the processus vaginalis being obliterated at or near the deep inguinal ring, but remaining patent in the cord and the scrotum. Thus fluid collects around the cord as well as around the testicle. In an infantile hydrocoele the cord cannot be palpated above the testicle, and it may therefore be confused with an inguinoscrotal hernia.

A **hydrocoele of the cord** is also rare and is a type of infantile hydrocoele where the fluid collection is restricted to the cord. Thus, unlike all the other types of hydrocoele, the testicle can be felt separately (hydrocoele of the cord is known as the 'third testis' as is an epididimal cyst). This can also be mistaken for a hernia.

◉ WHAT YOU SHOULD KNOW

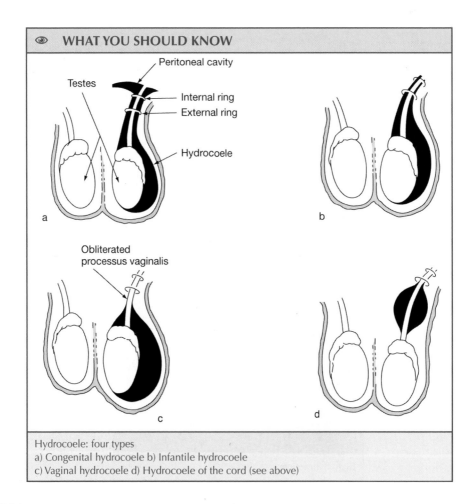

Hydrocoele: four types
a) Congenital hydrocoele b) Infantile hydrocoele
c) Vaginal hydrocoele d) Hydrocoele of the cord (see above)

✏ WHAT YOU SHOULD KNOW (CONT)

Other causes of intrascrotal swelling:

Acute epididymitis

Chlamydia is the commonest cause, followed by gonorrhoea, presenting between 18 and 35 years of age. Adults over 35 are most commonly affected by *Escherichia coli* secondary to urinary outflow obstruction. Other causes include smallpox, chickenpox, *E. coli* in children.

In the early stages a swollen tender epididymis lies behind a normal testis. Later, generalised tenderness, oedema, congestion and reactive hydrocoele can make it impossible to differentiate from torsion. Treatment is by antibiotics.

Chronic epididymitis

Usually due to tuberculosis, but can be caused by sarcoidosis, coccidioidomycosis and unresolved acute epididymitis (see above). Tuberculous epididymitis usually presents as a painless hard nodule separate from the testicle, but if it caseates it can envelop the testicle and cause a secondary hydrocoele. Ulceration through the scrotum can occur. Anti-tuberculous medical therapy may resolve this; if not, an epididectomy may be necessary.

Torsion of the testicle

Unlikely to feature in an exam. Acutely tender, high-riding testicle with thickened cord +/− a secondary hydrocoele.

Haematocoele

Collection of blood within the tunica vaginalis, usually caused by trauma or underlying malignant disease. The swelling has the same clinical features as a hydrocoele, except it is not transilluminable and may be tender.

Chronic haematocoeles become hard and non-tender and can be mistaken for a testicular tumour (see pg 292)

Gumma of the testis

This is due to syphilis, is rare and causes a hard, insensate, enlarged 'billiard ball' testis.

Orchitis

Acute orchitis in the absence of epididymitis is invariably due to a viral infection, usually mumps.

◉ WHAT YOU SHOULD SEE

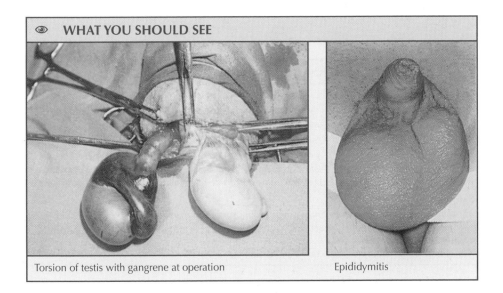

| Torsion of testis with gangrene at operation | Epididymitis |

Take a history from this gentleman with a right testicular lump

(see pg 33)

EPIDIDYMAL CYST

'I would like to present Mr P, a 60-year-old teacher. He has noticed multiple lumps in his right scrotum over the last 2 years. They are non-tender. He has had no trauma or surgery to his scrotum previously. He has atrial fibrillation, for which he takes warfarin. He is a non-smoker and non-drinker. He lives with his wife.

As he has multiple lumps it would suggest epididymal cysts. I would like to examine him to confirm this. As the lumps are non-tender and he is on warfarin for AF I would discuss the risks and benefits of conservative treatment.'

✐ WHAT YOU SHOULD KNOW

Definition
Fluid-filled swellings connected with the epididymis. May be a true epididymal cyst containing clear fluid or a spermatocoele containing grey, opaque fluid with spermatozoa. Because these are difficult to distinguish, they both tend to be called epididymal cysts.

Symptoms
Commonly occur in men over 40. Usually an asymptomatic swelling which appears like a 'third testicle'. They enlarge slowly, over years, are often multiple and can be bilateral. May develop pain or discomfort.

Treatment
Conservative, especially in young men, as surgery can disrupt sperm transport and reduce fertility. Cyst enucleation can be done in older patients, and epididymectomy is necessary occasionally to avoid operating on frequent recurrences.
[255] Varies from a few millimetres to over 10 cm in diameter.

Examine this patient's groin

(see pg 200)

EPIDIDYMAL CYST

'There is a non-tender swelling in the right scrotum. It is 4 cm in diameter[255], ovoid in shape with a well-defined, smooth but bosselated surface. It is firm, fluctuant, dull to percussion and brilliantly transilluminable. It is separate from the testicle and lies above it and behind the cord structures. The cord structures can be felt above the mass, and it is not reducible. This is an epididymal cyst. I would like to examine the other side.'

👁 WHAT YOU SHOULD SEE

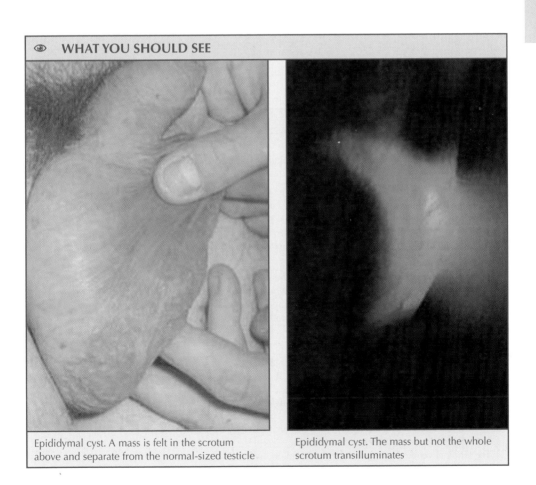

Epididymal cyst. A mass is felt in the scrotum above and separate from the normal-sized testicle

Epididymal cyst. The mass but not the whole scrotum transilluminates

287

Take a history from this gentleman with a left testicular lump

(see pg 33)

VARICOCOELE

'I would like to present Mr P, a 60-year-old teacher. He noticed a mass in his left scrotum 2 months ago. It aches at the end of the day. He has had no trauma or surgery to his scrotum previously. He has been feeling generally unwell lately, with a fever, and on direct questioning he describes haematuria. He has had no abdominal pain. He is otherwise fit and well. He is a non-smoker and non-drinker. He lives with his wife.

My differential includes a varicocoele, inguinoscrotal hernia, hydrocoele and epididymal cyst. I would like to examine him to whittle down this differential. I would also want to investigate his haematuria and fever to exclude a renal tract malignancy.'

✎ WHAT YOU SHOULD KNOW

Definition
A bunch of dilated and tortuous veins in the pampiniform plexus (i.e. varicose veins of the spermatic cord)

Symptoms
Occur in 25% of normal young men, usually unnoticed. Can, if large, cause a vague dragging sensation and aching pain in the scrotum or groin, and will cause that scrotum to hang lower than the other side. The testis below a large varicocoele may be a little smaller and softer than the testis on the other side, and bilateral varicocoeles may be associated with subfertility. The sudden appearance of a varicocoele in a middle-aged or old man raises the suspicion of retroperitoneal disease, e.g. renal carcinoma.

Varicocoele repair
Scrotal approach: rarely used because you can't be sure you've ligated all the veins.
Retroperitoneal approach: incision above the anterior superior iliac spine; testicular artery and veins identified, veins divided and ligated. Inguinal approach: more difficult to identify testicular artery.
Embolisation: by sclerosing solutions or balloon catheter (risk of PE).

Post-operative complications
Recurrence (via obturator collaterals).
Harder, more prominent varices until thrombus organises.
Hydrocoele formation.
[256] 98% of varicocoeles occur on the left because:
1. The left spermatic vein forms a more vertical angle with the left renal vein than the right does when it enters the vena cava.
2. The left renal vein is crossed by and may be compressed by the pelvic colon.
3. The left testicular vein is longer than the right.
4. The terminal venous valve is frequently absent on the left side.

Examine this patient's groin

(see pg 200)

VARICOCOELE

'There is (in this young man) a mass in the left scrotum.[256] It is a soft, irregularly shaped mass, above the testicle which can be felt separately. The cord structures can be felt around and through the swellings, which have the texture of the characteristic 'bag of worms'. The mass is compressible, enlarges and becomes firmer when the patient leans forwards, and disappears when the patient lies down. It does not transilluminate. This is a varicocoele, common and usually asymptomatic in young men, but needing investigation if it appears suddenly in middle or old age.'

👁 **WHAT YOU SHOULD SEE**

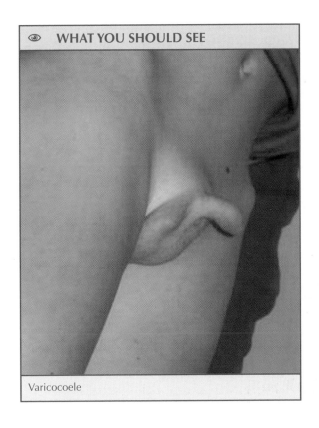

Varicocoele

Take a history from this gentleman with a left testicular lump

(see pg 33)

TESTICULAR TUMOUR

'I would like to present Mr P, a 30-year-old plumber. He noticed a mass in his left scrotum 2 months ago. It aches at the end of the day. He has had no trauma or surgery to his scrotum previously. He has had no abdominal or bone pain and no respiratory symptoms. He is otherwise fit and well. He is a non-smoker and non-drinker. He lives with his wife.

I would be concerned to exclude a testicular carcinoma, although my differential includes a varicocoele, inguinoscrotal hernia, hydrocoele and epididymal cyst. I would like to examine him to whittle down this differential.'

✎ WHAT YOU SHOULD KNOW

Epidemiology
Commonest solid tumour in young males, peaking at 25–35 years with a later peak over 60 years. Commoner in whites.

Aetiology/Predisposing factors
Family history
Cryptorchidism (undescended or maldescent)
Cryptorchidism in the opposite testicle (10%)
Trauma
Mumps
Higher socioeconomic group

Types of testicular cancer
Germ cell tumours
• Seminoma (about 50% germ cell tumour; tend to occur in men in their 30s)

Non-seminomatous germ cell tumours (NSGCTs)
• Embryonal cell carcinoma
• Teratoma
• Yolk sac tumour
• Choriocarcinoma (<1% of testicular tumours)
• Mixed (60% of NSGCTs have a mixed pattern of these histological subtypes)
Stomal tumours (rare)
All except choriocarcinoma show slow regional lymphatic spread to the para-aortic nodes, usually to the same side, although right testicular cancers can occasionally spread to the left para-aortic nodes. Choriocarcinoma shows early haematological spread.
CONTINUED on pg 291–292

Examine this patient's groin

(see pg 200)

TESTICULAR TUMOUR

'There is a firm, non-tender mass in the left scrotum. The testicle cannot be felt separately, but the epididymis can. The mass is not transilluminable (although there may be an associated hydrocoele). The diagnosis is of a testicular mass.[257] I would like to examine the opposite scrotum and the abdomen and supraclavicular area for lymphadenopathy.'[258]

🖹 WHAT YOU SHOULD KNOW (CONT)

[257] To prevent distress or misunderstanding, beware saying 'tumour', 'carcinoma' or 'cancer' in front of the patient. If pressed, say you would be concerned to exclude a malignancy or a neoplastic process, unless you are out of earshot of the patient.

[258] Abdominal nodes, being retroperitoneal, are rarely palpable. Gynaecomastia may occur. Haemoptysis is a sign of pulmonary metastases.

👁 WHAT YOU SHOULD SEE

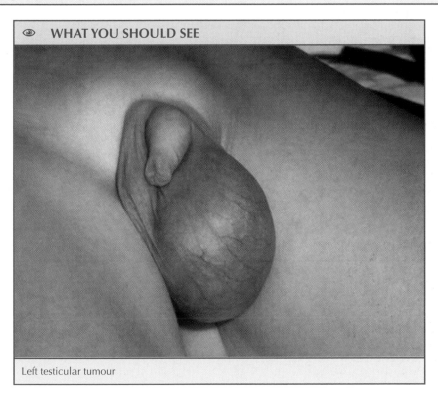

Left testicular tumour

TESTICULAR TUMOUR

C THE OSCE CASES

WHAT YOU SHOULD KNOW (CONT)

Staging

TNM (in the US) or Royal Marsden Hospital system (in the UK)

Royal Marsden Staging System	5-yr Survival rate (%)	
	Seminoma	NSGCTs
I – tumour confined to the testis	100	100
II – abdominal lymph node involvement (<2cm, 2–5cm, >5cm diameter)	93	95
III – lymph nodes above the diaphragm involved	90	}65
IV – extralymphatic or visceral metastases		

Symptoms

Painless mass in scrotum with dragging sensation, gynaecomastia, haemoptysis (if pulmonary involvement).

Tumour markers

Serum alpha-fetoprotein (AFP) – increased with NSGCTs but never with seminomas.

Human chorionic gonadotropin (HCG) – increased with NSGCTs but only in 7% of seminomas.

Other tumour markers include lactate dehydrogenase, placental alkaline phosphatase and gamma glutamyl transpeptidase.

Investigation

Scrotal USS to confirm diagnosis and assess other testis.

(NEVER ASPIRATE OR TRUCUT the mass as this risks scrotal skin seeding.)

Chest X-ray: shows 90% of pulmonary metastases.

Testicular tumour markers (see above).

CT abdomen: reveals retroperitoneal lymphadenopathy.

Management

Radical inguinal orchidectomy (cures about 80% of patients).

Principles of surgery include:

- Testicular prosthesis should be offered
- Early cross-clamping of the cord to avoid proximal haematological and lymphatic spread on handling the testicle
- Avoidance of scrotal incision to prevent seeding of tumour cells into scrotal skin

Post-operative management

Seminoma

Confined to testes: radiotherapy to para-aortic nodes reduces recurrence rate to 2%.

With lymph node metastases: radiotherapy. If large lymph node metastases or other metastatic disease – combination chemotherapy.

NSGCTs

Confined to testis: treatment varies in UK/USA. UK – close surveillance. USA – retroperitoneal lymph node dissection.

Metastatic NSGCTs: combination chemotherapy (e.g. bleomycin, etoposide and cisplatin, BEP).

Retroperitoneal lymph node dissection is controversial:

Advantages: allows accurate staging of patients.

Disadvantages: high morbidity and complications, e.g. retrograde ejaculation and infertility.

Up to 1/3 of resected masses are fibrotic with no signs of residual or recurrent tumour.

ABSENT TESTICLE

👁 WHAT YOU SHOULD SEE

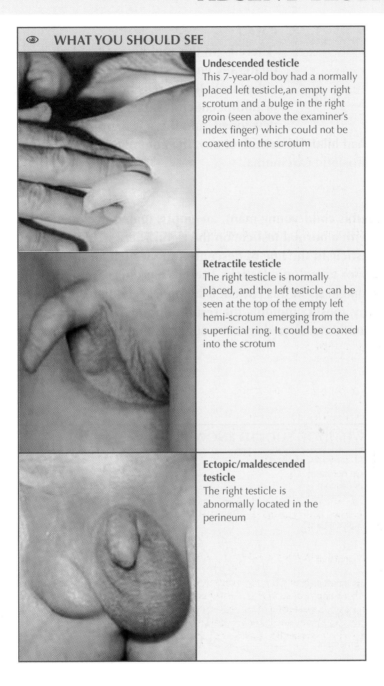

Undescended testicle
This 7-year-old boy had a normally placed left testicle, an empty right scrotum and a bulge in the right groin (seen above the examiner's index finger) which could not be coaxed into the scrotum

Retractile testicle
The right testicle is normally placed, and the left testicle can be seen at the top of the empty left hemi-scrotum emerging from the superficial ring. It could be coaxed into the scrotum

Ectopic/maldescended testicle
The right testicle is abnormally located in the perineum

293

ABSENT TESTICLE

Case 1

'There is (in this middle-aged/elderly man), a bilaterally empty scrotum with no evidence of either testicle. There is no evidence of an ectopic or undescended testicle, the scrotum is normally developed, and there is a groin/scrotal scar. This patient has had bilateral orchidectomy, the commonest indication being metastatic prostatic carcinoma.'

Case 2

'There is (in this child/young man), an empty, underdeveloped scrotum on the left with a normal testicle on the right. There is/is no evidence of the left testicle in the line of descent of the testicle or in any of the normal sites for an ectopic testicle. There is a groin scar on the left.[259] The differential diagnosis in this patient is an undescended testicle or a unilateral orchidectomy, most commonly the result of trauma, torsion or testicular cancer. The underdeveloped scrotum suggests that this is an undescended testicle.'[260]

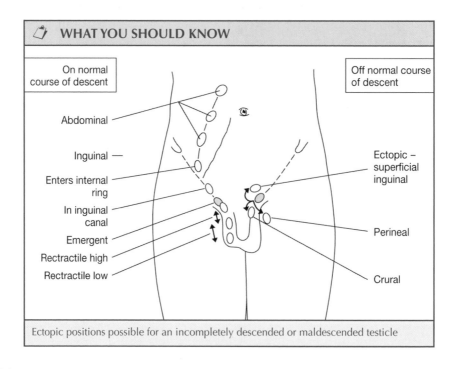

☞ **WHAT YOU SHOULD KNOW**

| On normal course of descent | | Off normal course of descent |

Abdominal
Inguinal
Enters internal ring
In inguinal canal
Emergent
Rectractile high
Rectractile low

Ectopic – superficial inguinal
Perineal
Crural

Ectopic positions possible for an incompletely descended or maldescended testicle

ABSENT TESTICLE

WHAT YOU SHOULD KNOW

[259] This could be due to previous exploration or attempted (and failed) orchidopexy in an undescended testicle.

Alternatively it could be the scar of the orchidectomy after trauma, tumour or torsion.

[260] **Management of the apparently missing testicle in a child**

1. Is it retractile rather than truly missing?

Parents report seeing it during bath-time.

Scrotum normally developed.

Testicle can be felt in the inguinal canal and coaxed into the scrotum on examination.

No further intervention is needed – testicle likely to descend normally by puberty. Follow up to check.

2. Is it undescended in the normal line of descent? (86%)

These carry increased risk of torsion, malignancy, decreased sperm production and concern to the child. Therefore these should be replaced in the scrotum (orchidopexy) in early childhood ('2 in the bag by the age of 2'). Eighty per cent of undescended testicles are palpable and for these the treatment is orchidopexy. Twenty per cent of undescended testicles are impalpable and of these a third are absent, a third are in the canal and a third are intra-abdominal.

Since surgery is always indicated, investigations such as ultrasound (unreliable), MRI and CT (Need anaesthetic) and laparoscopy (two-thirds are unnecessary and leads to open surgery) are not indicated. Alternatively, open exploration is via a high inguinal incision, allowing first the inguinal canal, then the abdominal cavity to be explored.

If a testis is located and is dysplastic it must be removed. If normal it must be replaced in the scrotum. Testicular biopsy is not indicated. Cord length is a limitation in orchidopexy, and a two-stage approach may be needed.

Alternatively, the Fowler–Stephens procedure is ligation of the testicular vessels, leaving the testicle dependent on collateral supply to the vas deferens. The orchidopexy is carried out later; success rates are about 50%.

Free transfer with microvascular anastomosis is also possible.

3. Is it maldescended or ectopic? (not in the normal line of descent – see figure on page 293 (2%)

Management is as for undescended testicle.

PEUTZ–JEGHERS SYNDROME

'There are small, brownish-black pigmented macules on the lips, around the mouth, and sometimes on the eyes, nose and buccal mucosa (but not on the tongue). There are also (maybe) similar lesions on the hands and fingers. If this pigmentation is associated with intestinal polyposis the diagnosis is Peutz–Jeghers syndrome.'

✐ WHAT YOU SHOULD KNOW

This is an autosomal dominant inherited syndrome consisting of the characteristic pigmentation around the lips associated with characteristic intestinal polyps. The polyps are most common in the small intestine but can occasionally occur in the colon. These are hamartomas: polyps with a very low malignant potential. Complications include intestinal obstruction or intussusception (causing recurrent colicky abdominal pain), bleeding (resulting in iron deficiency anaemia or frank gastrointestinal haemorrhage). Malignant transformation is rare. See Osler–Weber–Rendu syndrome for comparison (pg 496).

PEUTZ–JEGHERS SYNDROME

👁 WHAT YOU SHOULD SEE

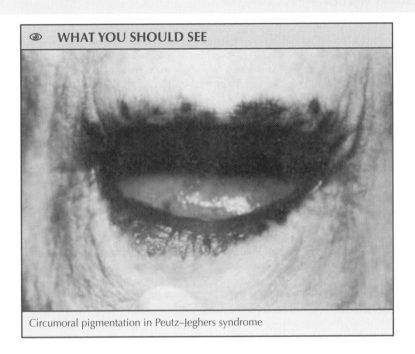

Circumoral pigmentation in Peutz–Jeghers syndrome

✎ WHAT YOU SHOULD KNOW

A pilonidal sinus is a subcutaneous sinus which contains hair, most commonly found in the natal cleft and associated with chronic inflammation and acute abscess formation. The condition is common and affects young adults. There are rare variants of the pilonidal sinus in other sites e.g. the webs of barbers' fingers, the axilla, the lumbar region in children. The latter are congenital and extend to the neural canal and dura.

Pathology

Perianal pilonidal sinuses are thought to be an acquired condition, starting at the onset of puberty when the hair follicles become distended and inflamed. The sinus usually consists of a midline opening or openings in the natal cleft about 5 cm from the anus. The primary track (lined with squamous cell epithelium) leads to a subcutaneous cavity containing granulation tissue and usually a nest of hairs. Secondary openings can be seen, often 2.5 cm lateral from the midline pits.

Clinical features

Patients are usually between the age of puberty and 40 years (75% male). Patients are often dark and hairy and may be obese. Fifty per cent present as emergencies with an acute pilonidal abscess. The rest have intermittent discomfort and discharge. Examination reveals the characteristic midline pit or pits, which may have hair protruding. Lateral pits may be present.

Treatment

Incision and drainage

An acute pilonidal abscess needs incision or excision and drainage under general anaesthetic with follow-up. Later treatment of the pilonidal sinus may be required when the abscess cavity has healed if there are residual problems (one third of patients require further treatment).

Excision of pits and laying open of sinus

This is usually done under GA. The midline pits and lateral openings are excised with a small area of surrounding skin. The cavity is curetted and packed loosely with a gauze ribbon. Frequent changes of dressing and close supervision are needed post-operatively. Regular rubbing with a finger avoids premature closure. Meticulous hygiene and shaving are important. Shaving may be stopped once the wound has healed.

Excision with primary suture

Some surgeons recommend excision of sinus with primary suturing of the defect. The advantages and disadvantages are given below. The proportions of wounds healed at 2 months are similar for both forms of treatment.

Advantages and disadvantages of laying open (versus primary closure) of pilonidal sinus

- Advantages: effective in most hands; shorter period in hospital; healing by secondary intention leaves broad, hairless scar which reduces recurrence
- Disadvantages: slower healing; open wound delays return to work; active wound care with frequent wound dressing

Recurrence

Occurs in up to 50%. Causes include:
- Neglect of wound care (e.g. shaving, finger treatment)
- Persisting poorly drained tracks
- Recurrent infection of hair follicle
- Midline scars

PILONIDAL SINUS

'There is, in this hirsute young man, a small, tender swelling in the midline, just above the natal cleft. In the line of this swelling are three tiny pits, one with hair protruding from it and at least two producing discharge on gentle palpation. There is also a pit 1 cm lateral to the midline on the right. This is an inflamed pilonidal sinus.'

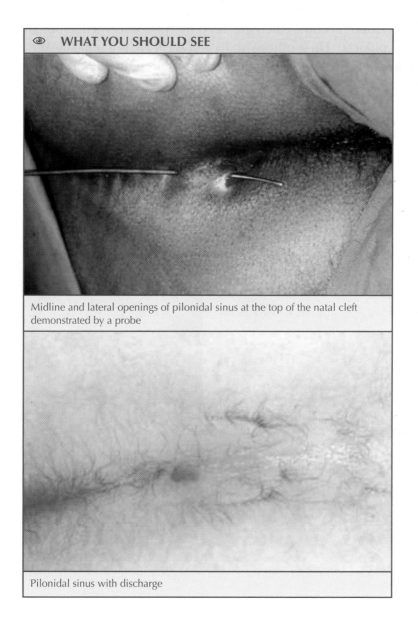

👁 WHAT YOU SHOULD SEE

Midline and lateral openings of pilonidal sinus at the top of the natal cleft demonstrated by a probe

Pilonidal sinus with discharge

Take a history of this patient with a change in bowel habit

(see pg 170)

CROHN'S DISEASE AND ULCERATIVE COLITIS

'I would like to present Mr P, a 31-year-old electrician. For the last 1 month he has had a change in bowel habit. He had gone from opening his bowel once a day to 12 times a day. The stool is loose with dark-red blood and mucus mixed in. He feels generally run down and has lost 1 stone in weight. He has occasional lower abdominal pain. He has not travelled recently, eaten any food he was concerned about and he has no ill contacts. He is otherwise fit and well. He is a non-smoker and non-drinker. He lives with his wife. He thinks his grandfather had ulcerative colitis.

I suspect this gentleman has a new diagnosis of inflammatory bowel disease[261]. I would like to examine him but I would consider admitting him for investigation and treatment.'

✎ WHAT YOU SHOULD SEE

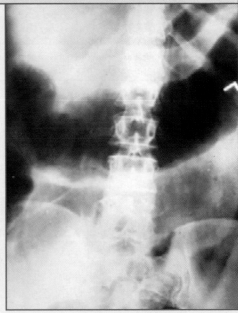

Barium enema showing 'hosepipe' colon in ulcerative colitis

Plain abdominal X-ray showing toxic megacolon

Examine this patient's abdomen

(see pg 189)

CROHN'S DISEASE AND ULCERATIVE COLITIS

'There is (in this thin young woman) multiple laparotomy scars, suggesting a chronic, relapsing abdominal condition which has led to crises requiring surgical intervention on several occasions. The scars are suggestive of poor healing complicated by infection, as they are irregular, wide and puckered. There is an enterocutaneous fistula discharging from a scar in the right iliac fossa. There are swollen lips and multiple mouth ulcers, and the patient gives a history of chronic diarrhoea. The perineum has a characteristic dusky blue discoloration, and there are multiple oedematous anal tags, fissures and ulceration around the anus. There is evidence of surgery on previous fistulae/there is a seton suture in situ. The diagnosis is Crohn's disease.'

👁 WHAT YOU SHOULD SEE

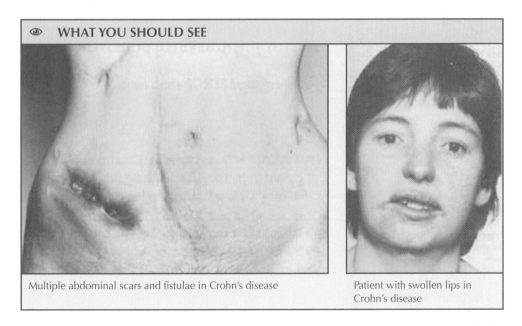

Multiple abdominal scars and fistulae in Crohn's disease

Patient with swollen lips in Crohn's disease

CROHN'S DISEASE AND ULCERATIVE COLITIS

✍ WHAT YOU SHOULD KNOW

[261]Inflammatory bowel disease is a chronic gastrointestinal inflammation without identifiable cause.

Crohn's disease

Although most commonly found in the terminal ileum, Crohn's disease can occur anywhere in the alimentary canal, from mouth to anus. It may be confined to the large bowel, or there may be involvement of both the small and large intestine. Perianal involvement is seen in 75% of patients.

Ulcerative colitis (UC)

This is a mucosal disease that almost invariably involves the rectum and then spreads more proximally in a continuous manner. Only 15% of cases extend more proximally than the splenic flexure. (This group has a greater risk of complications, including cancer.) In a few cases, the ileum is also affected (backwash ileitis).

Epidemiology

Both Crohn's disease and UC are more common in developing countries and in younger adults.

Aetiology

Unknown. Family history in 20–30%. ?post-infective ?autoimmune ?environmental ?dietary factors

Pathology

Crohn's disease: can affect the GI tract from mouth to anus, 70% involving small bowel. Perianal involvement in 50–70%. Skip lesions of abnormal areas with intervening normal mucosa. Whole thickness of bowel affected. Cobblestone appearance of mucosa, fatty encroachment on serosa. Fistulation to adjacent organs common. Non-caseating epithelioid granulomas in 60–70% of patients.
Ulcerative colitis: occurs in the rectum and extends continuously proximally. Can affect entire colon with 'backwash ileitis' but no other area of GI tract affected. Inflammation limited to mucosa, not transmural. Serosa not affected. Inflammatory pseudopolyps and small shallow ulcers. Granulomas not typical.

Clinical features

Typical features of Crohn's disease:
- Stricture formation leading to chronic intestinal obstruction
- Local perforation
- Abscess
- Fistula to exterior or other organs
- Colitis leading to diarrhoea, mucus and bleeding
- Anal fissures, ulcers, infections and skin tags
- Extraintestinal manifestations (see below)
- Anorexia, weight loss, malnutrition, anaemia, nausea

Typical features of UC:
- Bloody diarrhoea with mucus, urgency and incontinence
- Constipation in cases of limited proctitis
- Cramping abdominal pain
- Anorexia, weight loss, malnutrition, anaemia, nausea
- Extraintestinal manifestations (see below)
- It is important to recognise patients with severe acute colitis: severe local symptoms; frequency more than 10 stools/24 hours with blood; wasting, pallor, tachycardia, pyrexia; tender, distended abdomen; these patients may progress to acute toxic dilatation of the colon and perforation

CROHN'S DISEASE AND ULCERATIVE COLITIS

🗇 WHAT YOU SHOULD KNOW (CONT)

Extraintestinal manifestations of inflammatory bowel disease
<u>Related to disease activity</u>
- **Skin**: pyoderma gangrenosum; erythema nodosum
- **Mucous membranes**: aphthous ulcers of the mouth and vagina
- **Eyes**: iritis
- **Joints**: activity-related arthritis of large joints
<u>Unrelated to disease activity</u>
- **Joints/liver**: sacroiliitis; ankylosing spondylitis
- **Biliary tree**: chronic active hepatitis; cirrhosis; primary sclerosing cholangitis; bile duct carcinoma
- **Integument**: amyloidosis in Crohn's disease; fingernail clubbing
CONTINUED on pg 304

👁 WHAT YOU SHOULD SEE

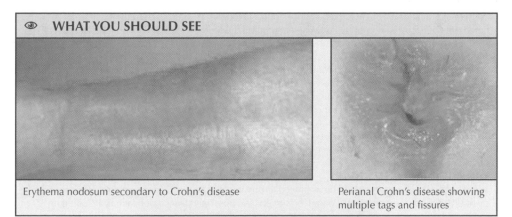

Erythema nodosum secondary to Crohn's disease

Perianal Crohn's disease showing multiple tags and fissures

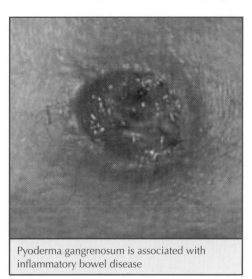

Pyoderma gangrenosum is associated with inflammatory bowel disease

CROHN'S DISEASE AND ULCERATIVE COLITIS

✐ WHAT YOU SHOULD KNOW (CONT)

Investigations

Sigmoidoscopy, colonoscopy, barium enema, small-bowel enema/barium meal, MRI, FBC, ESR, CRP, serum albumin, stool microscopy and culture.

Barium enema findings

Crohn's disease

Discontinuous distribution ('skip lesions'); rectal sparing common; 'cobblestone' appearance of mucosa; 'rose-thorn' spiculation ulcers; fistulae; strictures.

Ulcerative colitis

Featureless 'hosepipe' colon; decreased haustrae; affects rectum and spreads proximally; mucosal distortion; small ulcers and pseudopolyps; shortened colon.

Medical management

This is a complex topic but try to remember the basic principle: that anti-inflammatories are prescribed in a ladder of treatment for progressively severe or resistant inflammatory bowel disease. That ladder consists of 5-aminosalicylic acid preparations (for basic long-term control), steroids (for short-term control of flare-ups), azathioprine (for long-term control if becoming steriod-dependent) and anti-TNF biological agents such as Infliximab (indicated in certain complex cases).

Indications for surgery

To restore health in patients with chronic disease (e.g. in nutritional failure).

To eliminate the risks of side-effects of steroids in patients requiring long-term high doses of steroids. Premalignant change on colonoscopic surveillance.

Patients at high risk of developing cancer (ulcerative colitis with early onset, extensive colonic involvement and continuous symptoms).

To treat complications (usually emergency surgery) e.g. perforation, severe haemorrhage, toxic dilatation (>6 cm megacolon), stricture causing obstruction, fistulation or abscess formation, sepsis. Acute severe attack, need to defunction diseased bowel with an ileostomy.

Principles of surgery

In Crohn's disease, surgery should be as limited as possible and be reserved for patients with a specific operable problem, as it cannot be 'cured' by surgery and post-operative complications are common.

In UC, radical surgery is often employed, because removal of the diseased segment often cures the patient. Furthermore, patients are at risk of lethal toxic megacolon and have a tenfold increased risk of developing carcinoma in long-standing disease. The most common operations performed for UC are proctocolectomy with ileostomy, sphincter-preserving proctocolectomy with ileal pouch, colectomy with ileorectal anastomosis and subtotal colectomy with ileostomy and mucous fistula.

CROHN'S DISEASE AND ULCERATIVE COLITIS

WHAT YOU SHOULD SEE

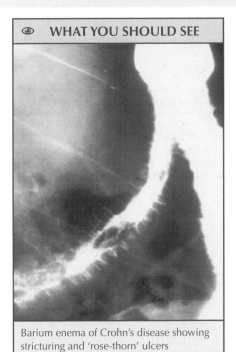

Barium enema of Crohn's disease showing stricturing and 'rose-thorn' ulcers

D SURVEY RESULTS

TRUNK AND THORAX

These results include cases seen in the new OSCE and the old style MRCS exam.

TOP 5 CASES

Type of case	Number seen in survey	Breakdown and details of cases
Groin herniae	26	22 Inguinal 1 Femoral 3 Unspecified (assumed groin) Questions included differential diagnoses, different types of hernia, different types of repair.
Scrotum	17	13 Hydrocoele 1 Testicular tumour 1 Bilateral orchidectomy for prostate cancer 1 Epididymal cyst 1 Tuberculosis of testicle and epididymis Questions included management of hydrocoele, tumour markers.
Stomas	16	5 General (site not specified) 4 Ileostomy 3 Colostomy 1 Urostomy 2 Ileal conduits 1 PEG post strike Questions included types of stoma, sites, indications, complications, 'work out what the operation was' TPN indications, problems with resecting terminal ilium, and discussion about other features in the patients such as Hickman line for chemotherapy, radiotherapy skin changes, supraclavicular lymph nodes.
Herniae (other than groin)	16	8 Incisional 5 Paraumbilical 2 Spegalian 1 Epigastric

Type of case	Number seen in survey	Breakdown and details of cases
Breast	14	8 post-operative 3 breast lump 3 post reconstruction Questions included sentinel nodes, tram flap, radiation side-effects, tamoxifen side-effects.

OTHER CASES

Type of case	Number seen in survey	Breakdown and details of cases
Liver disease	11	6 Jaundice (plus 3 hepatomegaly cases had jaundice) 4 Hepatomegaly (3 with jaundice, 1 with enlarged spleen) 1 T-tube after bile duct exploration 1 post total parotidectomy Questions included investigation of obstructive jaundice, features and complications of liver failure, anatomy of liver.
Splenomegaly	10	1 with enlarged liver Questions included causes of splenomegaly, differentiating kidney from spleen, 'what are these marks?' (radiotherapy ink marks).
Palpable kidney	9	3 Polycystic 2 Transplanted 2 Enlarged ?cause 1 Pelvic kidney 1 Hydronephrotic kidney
Abdominal mass (not liver, kidney or spleen)	7	1 Pancreatic pseudocyst 2 Palpable gall bladder 1 Left iliac fossa mass and gastric cancer on OGD 1 Psoas abscess 1 Left iliac fossa mass ?cause
Thoracic cases	5	1 Chest drain for pneumothorax 1 Thoracotomy scar 2 Dextrocardia 1 Malignant pleural effusion after mastectomy Questions included principles of chest drain, site of needle decompression of pneumothorax, indication for thoracotomy, why send a patient with dextrocardia to see an ENT surgeon?

Type of case	Number seen in survey	Breakdown and details of cases
Fistulae	3	2 Enterocutaneous fistula (at least one Crohn's). 1 Crohn's anus
Abdominal scars	3	Describe
Anatomy	2	Anatomy of large bowel and anal canal/rectum Anatomy of oesophagus and varices
Bladder	2	1 Ectopic bladder (no other details given) 1 Bladder cancer – pelvic mass, differential diagnosis and imaging
Peutz -Jeghers syndrome	2	
Abominal sepsis	1	With sigmoid diverticular abscess Questions included What is the condition? How would you treat? Why does the patient have hyperglycaemia?
Aortic stenosis	1	Questions included Why are these patients high anaesthetic risk? Mechanism of action of Doxazosin. Blood gas analysis.
Aortic regurgitation	1	
Colorectal tumours	1	Duke's classification
Heart chambers	1	Identification
Lungs	1	Surface anatomy of lungs and pleura. Lung fissures
Pancreatitis	1	
Pilonidal sinus	1	
Peyronie's disease	1	With Dupuytren's contracture
Pulmonary embolism	1	Identification from pathological specimen of lung hilum Basic pathology
Subclavian artery	1	

CHAPTER 5 LIMBS (INCLUDING SPINE)

A The Histories　　　　　　　　311

B The Examinations　　　　　325

CONTENTS

A THE HISTORIES

JOINT PAIN

If you are asked to take a history from a patient with joint pain you need to initially ask questions to whittle down the potential differential diagnoses. This will depend on the joint in question. Management depends on the stage of disease and the disability it causes so it is important to explore this thoroughly with your patient. You should then ask about relevant associated symptoms or risk factors that fit in with your differential diagnosis. If you run into problems in the OSCE remember the essential points in the 'Combined Assessment Box' to get you back on track.

Introductions

'Hello, my name is Dr Parchment Smith. Can I please check your details? Would you mind if I asked you some questions about your (whichever joint/s) pain?'

Ask about demographics.

'May I ask how old you are?'[1]

'What do/did you do for a living/hobby?'[2]

Presenting complaint (open question!)

'Can you tell me about what has caused you to come and see me today?'

---

[1] The frequency of OA increases with age. RA most commonly affects women in their 40s/50s.

[2] Occupations/hobbies can be relevant because they have caused the joint damage leading to OA through use (e.g. dancer). Eighty per cent of osteoarthritis is 'secondary osetoarthritis', i.e. caused by a previously damaged or congenitally abnormal joint. This can also be relevant as some types of professions may be more affected by the joint pain or treatment of it – a self employed gardener might be expected to have more to lose than an office worker who sits at a desk all day!

History of presenting complaint *(the patient may volunteer the following information but remember a systematic approach to taking a pain history is SIROD CASP)*

SITE: **'Where do you feel the pain?'**[3] *(If this is an upper limb problem it is appropriate to establish which is their dominant hand.)*

INTENSITY: **'Can you rate the pain on a scale from 1 to 10, 1 being no pain and 10 the worst pain ever?'** *(This is subjective and it is more important to know how it affects their life, e.g)* **'Does the pain limit your daily activities?'**[4] (if yes…) **'How does it restrict you?'**

e.g. (lower limb) **'How far can you walk?/Do you require a walking aid?'**
e.g. (upper limb) **'Can you dress yourself/do up buttons/reach the top shelves in your kitchen?'**

RADIATION: **'Does the pain move anywhere else?'**[5]

ONSET: **'Does the pain come on suddenly or gradually?'**[6]

DURATION: **'How long does the pain last?'**

CHARACTER: **'What is the pain like?'** *(e.g. sharp, dull, stabbing)*

ALLEVIATING AND EXACERBATING FACTORS: **'Does anything make the pain better, or worse?'**[7] In particular ask, **'Is the pain better or worse with exercise?'** **'Is the pain worse at any particular time of day?'**

SYMPTOMS ASSOCIATED WITH THE PAIN: **'Do you notice anything else when you get the pain?'**[8] *(e.g. instability, locking, weakness, stiffness)*

PREVIOUS EPISODES: **'Have you had a pain like this before?'**[9] *(if yes…)* **'What did you do then?'**

---

[3] **Site:** RA initially affects the proximal small joints of the hands and feet (the commonest initial presentation is the foot). It then spreads progressively to wrists, elbows, ankles and knees.
Primary OA: polyarthropathy mainly affecting the hands, hips, knees and spine.
Osteoporosis: commonly leads to fractures of thoracic and lumbar vertebrae, neck of femur, Colles' fracture at wrist.
Osteomalacia: bone pain often felt in pelvis, scapula and ribs. Fractures can occur most commonly in vertebral bodies and neck of femur.
Paget's commonly occurs in pelvis, thoracic and lumbar spine, femur, sacrum, skull, tibia and humerus.

[4] The limitation of daily activity is important; it can affect management decisions and can be used as a marker of progression of disease over time.

[5] **Radiation:** e.g. hip pain can radiate into the back and groin, and descend down the thigh.

[6] **Onset:** sudden would suggest fracture or infection or an acute flare of RA versus the gradual onset of osteoarthritis.

[7] **Exacerbating/alleviating factors:**

RA	– Worse on waking/rest
	– Relieved with exercise/NSAIDs
OA	– Worse at end of day/with exercise
	– Relieved with rest/simple analgesics

[8] **Associated symptoms** will depend on the joint in question.

[9] **Previous episodes:** in RA 80% patients will have recurrent flares, 5% have relentless progression, 15% have a low-grade clinical course.

You need to ask about associated symptoms. The relevance of these questions depends on what you think is going on.

1. **'Do you get joint stiffness?** *(if yes…)* **'When does it occur?/ How long does it last?'**[10/11]

2. **'Have you ever damaged that joint?/ Was there a problem with that joint when you were born?'**[12]

3. **'Do you get a fever associated with the pain?'**[13]

4. **'Do you have any weakness?'**

5. **'Do you have any loss of, or alteration in, sensation?'**

---

[10] Joint stiffness in the morning:
>   RA – Early morning joint stiffness > 30 mins (usually 1 hour until maximal improvement)
>   OA – Limited early-morning joint stiffness < 30mins

[11] Joint stiffness with rest:
>   RA – Stiffness after rest > 5 minutes
>   OA – Limited stiffness after rest < 5 minutes

[12] Secondary OA can be caused by previous damage to the joint, e.g. intra-articular fracture/congenital abnormality.

[13] Fever, e.g. septic arthritis, usually causes a rapid onset of spiking temperature (*Staphylococcus Aureus* most common organism; others include *Neisseria gonorrhoeae*, Group B streptococci, *Pneumococcus*). It most commonly affects the knee.

Past medical and surgical history

In particular, what investigations have they had for the pain? Do they have any other diseases which are risk factors for arthritis?[14] Or do they have any other diseases associated with rheumatoid arthritis?[15] Or any diseases that might affect surgical treatment?[16]

'Have you had any tests to investigate the pain?'[17] 'Have you had any treatment for it?' 'Do you have any other medical problems?'

Medication and allergies

'Do you take any regular medications?' 'What medication if any do you take for your joint pain?' 'Do you have any allergies?'

---

[14] Diseases which are **risk factors for secondary OA**:
- Hypermobility
- Diabetes and syringomyelia can lead to neuropathic joints
- Endocrine/metabolic diseases (acromegaly, Cushing's, gout, Wilson's disease, haemochromatosis)
- Haematological diseases (haemophilia, sickle cell disease)

[15] **Extra-articular manifestations of rheumatoid arthritis** from the top down:

Eye signs: episcleritis, cataracts due to chloroquine or steroids, scleromalacia perforans, Sjögren syndrome.

Chest signs: pleural effusion, fibrosing alveolitis, rheumatoid nodules, Caplan syndrome (rheumatoid nodules in lung fields associated with massive fibrotic reaction), obliterative bronchiolitis (due to penicillamine therapy).

Cardiac signs: pericarditis (40% at autopsy but rarely apparent clinically), granulomatous infiltration (rarely causing myocarditis, conduction defects and valvular incompetence).

Abdominal signs: splenomegaly in Felty syndrome; hepatosplenomegaly in secondary amyloidosis.

Neurological signs: peripheral neuropathy, mononeuritis multiplex, carpal tunnel syndrome.

Skin signs: leg ulceration, vasculitis, pyoderma gangrenosum.

Other autoimmune disorders: vitiligo, myasthenia gravis, hypothyroidism, primary biliary sclerosis.

[16] Diseases which could negatively affect joint replacement surgery are important to ask about; these include PVD, history of steroid use and diabetes, which can predispose to poorly healing wounds and hence prosthetic infections.

[17] **Investigation of arthritis**

X-ray appearance:	OA	(i) Loss of joint space
		(ii) Osteophyte formation
		(iii) Juxta-articular sclerosis
		(iv) Subarticular bone cysts
	RA	(i) Loss of joint space
		(ii) Periarticular erosions
		(iii) Joint-line thickening
		(iv) Juxta-articular osteoporosis
		(v) No osteophytes

RA: raised CRP/ESR in acute phase; rheumatoid factor (an autoantibody, it occurs in 70–80% of cases).

Family history

'Do any diseases run in the family?'[18]

Social history (smoking and drinking)

'Are you a current or ex-smoker?'[19] *If yes, ask about smoking habits.* 'What do you smoke?', 'How many do you smoke a day?', 'How long have you smoked for?'

'Do you, or have you ever, drunk alcohol?' *If yes,* 'What type of alcohol do you drink?' *(e.g. spirits, wine, beer)* 'How much do you drink per week?' *(convert this to units per week)* 'How long have you drunk for?'

Combined Assessment Box – JOINT PAIN

Ask:
- What makes the pain worse? (e.g. worse on waking and relieved on exercise, think RA; worse at end of day and worse with exercise, think OA)
- What associated symptoms do you get with the pain?
- How does the pain limit your daily activities?
- What treatments have you tried so far?
- Ask about risk factors, e.g. previous trauma/congenital abnormality with that joint or predisposing diseases

Examine:
- Look for – deformity, muscle wasting, scars, sinuses etc.
- Feel for – tenderness, temperature, nodules, fluid, crepitations etc.
- Movements – active, passive (note limitations) and functional (e.g. doing up buttons or walking)
- Special tests – depends on joint. See Examinations in section B

---

[18] Family history: RA has a likely genetic susceptibility (HLA-DR4), present in up to 90%.
[19] Smoking increases the risk of osteoporosis.

BACK PAIN

If you are asked to take a history from a patient with back pain you need to clearly be seen to ask about red flag symptoms of diseases such as malignant disease, spinal infections, osteoporosis/spinal fractures. You must also assess for symptoms of focal neurology. The urgency of investigation and management will depend on this. If the history is chronic, management will partly depend on the disability caused, so it is important to explore this thoroughly with your patient. This history is relevant for conditions seen in the Limbs (including Spine) specialty and the Neuroscience specialty sections of the OSCE.

You should then ask about relevant associated symptoms or risk factors that fit in with your differential. If you run into problems in the OSCE remember the essentials in the 'Combined Assessment Box' to get you back on track.

Introductions

'Hello, my name is Dr Parchment Smith. Can I please check your details? Would you mind if I asked you some questions about your back pain?'
Ask about demographics.
'May I ask how old you are?'[20]
'What do/did you do for a living/hobby?'[21]

Presenting complaint (open question!)

'Can you tell me about what has caused you to come and see me today?'

History of presenting complaint *(the patient may volunteer the following information but remember a systematic approach to taking a pain history is SIROD CASP)*

SITE: **'Where do you feel the pain?'**[22] (localised or diffuse?)
INTENSITY: **'Can you rate the pain on a scale from 1 to 10. 1 being no pain and 10 the worst pain ever?'** *(This is subjective and it is more important to know how it affects their life e.g.)* **'Does the pain limit your daily activities?'**[23]

---

[20] **Age:** red flag symptom if <20 or >55 (risk of tumour/infection).
[21] Does their occupation or hobby involve heavy lifting, putting them at greater risk of back injury? e.g. nurses, gym enthusiasts.
[22] **Site:** thoracic pain is a red flag symptom for potential fracture, tumour or infection.
[23] **Limiting daily activity:** this is a marker of severity, and the degree of limitation can also be used to monitor progression or resolution of symptoms.

(if yes) **'How does it restrict you?'** *e.g.* **'How far can you walk?/Do you require a walking aid?'**

RADIATION: **'Does the pain move anywhere else?'**[24] *(if into the legs)* **'How far down the leg?'**

ONSET: **'Did the pain come on suddenly or gradually?'**[25]

DURATION: **'How long does the pain last?'** (constant or related to position/ use?)[26]

CHARACTER: **'What is the pain like?'** *(dull, aching, sharp, knife-like)*

ALLEVIATING AND EXACERBATING FACTORS: **'Does anything make the pain better, or worse?'**[26] *In particular ask,* **'Is the pain better or worse with exercise?' 'Is the pain worse at any particular time of day?'**

SYMPTOMS ASSOCIATED WITH THE PAIN: **'Do you notice anything else when you get the pain?'**[26] *(e.g. weakness, wasting, fibrillation, gait problems, foot drop, ankle giving way)*

PREVIOUS EPISODES: **'Have you had a pain like this before?'**[27] *(if yes…)* **'What did you do then?'**

---

[24] **Radiation**: nerve root pain will typically radiate down one leg and into the foot. Paraesthesia/numbness in the same distribution may be present.

[25] **Onset**: Sudden: e.g. fracture or disc prolapse
        Gradual: e.g. anylosing spondylitis has an insidious onset

[26] **Mechanical back pain** tends to vary with physical activity and time – it is worse with exercise and at the end of the day. There are no neurological symptoms. It is usually due to degenerative changes and is managed conservatively. It is the commonest cause of lower back pain. Constant progressive pain (especially night or rest pain) is concerning and can point towards metatstatic deposits /infection in the spine.
Ankylosing spondylitis usually presents between ages 15–25 and is commoner in males. Symptoms include low back pain which differs from mechanical pain in that it is worse in the morning and eases with exercise. See case on pg 428.
Neurogenic claudication usually presents with backache, morning stiffness and aching in the legs on walking, usually after a variable distance, and it is relieved on flexion (these clues can be used to differentiate it from vascular claudication with which it can be confused). It is due to spinal stenosis.

[27] Previous episodes: management of lower back pain is covered in detail in The Elective Neurosurgery and Spinal Surgery section in *Essential Revision Notes for Intercollegiate MRCS: Book 2.*

You must ask about associated symptoms which are other red flag symptoms.

1. **'Have you had any problems with passing urine lately?'**[28]
2. **'Have you had any problems with your bowels lately?'**[28]
3. **'Have you developed any weakness?** *(if yes)* **'Where do you feel this?', 'Is it getting any better or worse?'**[29]
4. **'Do have any loss of sensation?** *(if yes)* **'Where do you feel this?', 'Is it getting better or worse?'**[29]
5. **'Do you have a fever associated with the pain?'**[30]
6. **'Have you lost any weight recently?'**[31]

Past medical and surgical history

In particular, what investigations/treatment have they had for the pain?
Have they other diseases which are risk factors for back disease?[32] *(e.g. red flag medical history would include carcinoma, immunosuppression, e.g. HIV or diabetes, osteoporosis)*
Have they a history of injury?

---

[28] **Cauda equina/cord compression:** signs/symptoms which point towards this surgical emergency include: alteration in micturition (either incontinence or retention), faecal incontinence, saddle anaesthesia, bilateral progressive lower limb weakness.

[29] **Sensory loss/weakness**
Symptoms of nerve root lesions in the lower limb (causes include compression by degenerative bone or disc disease, fracture, tumour or infection):

Level	Sensory loss	Motor weakness
L4	Medial knee and shin	Quadriceps
L5	Lateral calf and dorsum of foot	Extensor hallucis longus and ankle dorsiflexion
S1	Posterior calf and lateral border of foot	Flexor hallucis longus and ankle plantar-flexion

Prolapsed intervertebral disc is commonly caused by an annular tear allowing the nucleus pulposus to herniate through. This is most commonly posterolateral (anatomical weakness). It impinges on the nerve root, causing unilateral, localised symptoms as described above. L5/S1 is the most common site; 85% of these patients will settle with conservative management. If the disc prolapses posteriorly, it can cause spinal cord compression if above the level of L2 or cauda equina compression if below the level of L2. This requires urgent surgical decompression.

[30] Fever or night sweats can point towards spinal tumour or infection.
Spinal infections are either pyogenic or due to TB. Pyogenic infections are usually caused by blood-borne spread from a septic source, e.g. abscess. The commonest causative organism is *S. aureus*. Risk factors include: alcohol excess, IVDU, immunocompromise, rheumatoid arthritis, diabetes mellitus. Symptoms include severe constant pain, fever and weight loss. Management involves 6–12 weeks of antibiotics. Spinal TB is usually blood-borne from the lungs.

[31] Weight loss is a red flag for tumour/infection.
Spinal tumours can be primary or secondary. Common cancers which metastasise to bone are given below. The spread is most commonly haematogenous. Lesions either appear lytic (most) or sclerotic (e.g. prostate). Primary spinal tumours can arise from the bone, covering layers or the spinal cord itself.

[32] **Relevant PMHs:**   Cancer: primary tumours that commonly metastasise to bone can be recalled by the memory trick: **Br**east, **Br**ostate (prostate), **Br**idney (kidney), **Br**onchus, **By**roid (thyroid) and **Bl**adder
                  Osteoporosis: causes pathological wedge fractures. Treatment is of the underlying osteoporosis
                  Trauma
                  TB

'Have you had any tests to investigate the pain?'[33], 'Have you had any treatment for it?', 'Do you have any other medical problems?', 'Have you injured your spine?'[34]

Medication and allergies

'Do you take any regular medication?'[35] 'What medication, if any, do you take for your back pain?', 'Do you have any allergies?'

Family history

'Do any diseases run in the family?'[36]

Social history (smoking and drinking)[37]

'Are you a current or ex-smoker?'
If yes, ask about smoking habits 'What do you smoke?', 'How many do you smoke a day?', 'How long have you smoked for?'
'Do you, or have you ever, drunk alcohol?' *If yes,* 'What type of alcohol do you drink?' *(e.g. spirits, wine, beer)* 'How much do you drink per week?' *(convert this to units per week)* 'How long have you drunk for?'

Combined Assessment Box – BACK PAIN

Ask:
- What is the pain like? (constant, severe = suspicious; worst with exercise and at end of day = likely mechanical)
- Do you have any weakness, loss of sensation or pain radiating into the leg? (i.e. neurological symptoms)
- Do you have any bladder or bowel dysfunction (red flags for cauda equina syndrome)
- How does the pain limit your daily activities?

Examine:
- Look: from back for scoliosis/scars/swellings; from side for kyphosis/gibbus
- Palpate: vertebral column/erector spinae
- Movement: forward flexion, extension, lateral flexion, rotation
- Special tests: screen for prolapsed intervertebral disk; exclude hip disease as a cause for symptoms

---

[33] **Imaging of the spine**:
Plain X-rays (AP/lateral/oblique views, standing of thoracolumbar and lumbar spine, lateral bending and flexion/extension views).
CT – for bone.
MRI – for soft tissues such as disc, cord, nerves and ligaments.
Non-radiological investigations:
Blood tests – FBC, CRP, ESR, HLA-B27, blood cultures
Bone biochemistry
Protein electrophoresis
Needle biopsy
[34] Major or minor trauma raises suspicion of spinal fracture.
[35] Steroids are a risk factor for osteoporotic spinal fractures.
[36] Family history, e.g. ankylosing spondylitis, TB.
[37] Heavy smoking and alcohol intake are risk factors for chronicity of mechanical back pain. Alcohol excess is a risk factor for pyogenic spinal infections.

CLAUDICATION

If you are asked to take a history from a patient with possible claudication pain you need to initially ask questions to whittle down the potential differential diagnoses.[38] *Management depends on the degree of ischaemia, the disability caused and also on the fitness of these patients (who often have multiple co-morbidities) so it is important to explore this thoroughly with your patient.*

You should then ask about relevant associated symptoms or risk factors that fit in with your differential. If you run into problems in the OSCE remember the essentials in the 'Combined Assessment Box' to get you back on track.

Introductions
'Hello, my name is Dr Parchment Smith. Can I please check your details? Would you mind if I asked you some questions about your (whichever limb it is) pain?'
Ask about demographics.
'May I ask how old you are?'[39]
'What do/did you do for a living/hobby?'

Presenting complaint (open question!)
'Can you tell me about what has caused you to come and see me today?'

---

[38] **Differential diagnosis of limb pain:**
Spinal stenosis
       Pain relieved by bending over
       Variable claudication distance
Musculoskeletal
       Pain not instantly relieved by rest
       Associated with back pain
       Shooting sciatic pain
Cramp
       Occurs at night
       Not relieved by rest
[39] Age is a risk factor for atherosclerosis. In the UK 30% of those aged between 50 and 75 have detectable occlusive disease, of which 15% are symptomatic.
If you are presented with a much younger patient with claudication symptoms think about Buerger's disease (thromboangiitis obliterans) recurrent inflammation and thrombosis of distal arteries and veins which leads to ischaemia. This presents between the ages of 20 and 40, usually in male smokers (although it is becoming more common in women).

History of presenting complaint *(the patient may volunteer the following information but listed below are the important points which you need to make sure you cover)*

To confirm the pain is claudication:

'How far can you walk before you get the pain?'[40]

'Is it worse going uphill or in the cold weather?'[41]

'Is it just in the calf or in the buttock and thigh as well?'[42]

'How long does it take for the pain to go when you stop and rest? (e.g. in seconds or several minutes)?'[43]

To assess severity and progression:

'How long have you been suffering from this pain on walking?'

'Do you get pain that wakes you in the night? Do you swing your leg out of bed to help it go away?'[44]

'Do you get pain at rest?'[45]

'Have you ever had ulcers or sores on your leg?'[46]

'Do you get symptoms in your other leg?'[47]

---

[40] The pain from intermittent claudication will usually occur after the same distance each time the patient walks, the 'claudication distance'. This gets shorter as the disease progresses. Once the patient has rested they can usually walk the same distance again before the pain starts. This differentiates it from neurogenic claudication caused by spinal stenosis, when the walking distance before pain starts is variable.

[41] In intermittent claudication, the pain is caused by occlusion or stenosis of the proximal arteries; the pain will therefore get worse in situations where more blood is demanded by the muscle, such as walking uphill.

[42] The site of pain indicates which of the proximal arteries is most likely to be involved. Calf pain is usually due to SFA disease and thigh or buttock pain to distal aortic or iliac stenosis or occlusion. Leriche syndrome of buttock and thigh claudication with erectile dysfunction is due to bilateral distal aortic or proximal iliac stenosis or occlusion.

[43] The pain of intermittent claudication will be relieved by a short period of rest. It differs from neurogenic claudication, which is relieved by flexion of the back and therefore requires a change in position such as sitting rather than just rest.

[44] Night pain is usually felt at the extremities due to critical ischaemia. It is typically relieved by swinging the affected limb over the edge of the bed as gravity increases the blood supply.
Critical ischaemia refers to rest/night pain and tissue loss. It implies limb loss could be imminent without intervention. The ABPI is usually <0.4.

[45] Rest pain indicates critical ischaemia.

[46] Tissue loss or ulceration is due to critical ischaemia. See arterial ulcer case on pg 466. Gangrene is tissue necrosis resulting from critical ischaemia. It can be wet (if there is infection) or dry. Gas gangrene is due to *Clostridium* infection.

[47] Bilateral symptoms suggests bilateral disease.

Past medical and surgical history

In particular, what investigations or treatment have they had for the pain?

'Have you ever had any angiograms or ballooning to stretch your arteries?'[48]

Have they other diseases which are risk factors for peripheral vascular disease?[49]

Or do they have any other diseases associated with peripheral vascular disease?[50]

'Do you have any other medical problems?'

---

[48] **Investigations**:

These aim to assess severity, risk factors and co-morbidity

To assess severity:

- Ankle–brachial pressure index (ABPI) (see pg 376)
- Contrast angiography
- Magnetic resonance angiography (MRA) or CTA

To assess risk factors:

- Fasting lipids (hyperlipidaemia)
- ESR (vasculitis)
- Fasting blood glucose (diabetes)
- HbA1c (if known diabetic, to check control)
- Blood pressure (hypertension)
- Cholesterol (hypercholesterolaemia)

To assess comorbidity:

- U & Es
- Chest X-ray
- Lung function tests

Management:

Claudication is managed conservatively if possible:

- Smoking cessation
- Treat hypertension, diabetes, hypercholesterolaemia
- Lose weight
- Antiplatelet agents (aspirin, clopidogrel)
- Follow a graded exercise programme to increase collateral circulation

Eighty per cent of claudicants remain stable or improve when treated as above over 1 year; 50% over 5 years.

Ten per cent develop indications for intervention and 5% die of cardiovascular disease each year.

Indications for intervention

- Worsening life-limiting claudication despite the above measures
- Critical ischaemia, e.g. rest/night pain, tissue loss
- Sudden deterioration (e.g. acutely ischaemic limb)

Non-surgical options

- Balloon angioplasty (good for short, proximal occlusions)
- Stenting (can be combined with angioplasty)
- Lumbar sympathectomy (if arterial reconstruction not possible; chemical or surgical blockade of the lumbar sympathetic chain increases blood supply to the skin)
- Drugs (vasodilators which can increase blood supply to the skin, e.g. Iloprost™)

Surgery

- Endarterectomy
- Patch angioplasty
- Bypass: anatomical (e.g. femoral-popliteal, femoral-distal) or extra-anatomical (e.g. axillo-bifemoral). The graft can be autologous, e.g. long saphenous vein, or prosthetic, e.g. Dacron or PTFE grafts.

[49] Diseases which are risk factors for atherosclerosis include: hypertension, diabetes, hypercholesterolaemia.

[50] Other diseases associated with PVD include: ischaemic heart disease, TIA/CVA.

Medication and allergies

'Do you take any regular medication?', 'What medication if any do you take for your pain?', 'Do you have any allergies?'

Family history

'Do any diseases run in the family?'[51]

Social history (smoking and drinking)

'Are you a current or ex-smoker?'[52]
If yes, ask about smoking habits 'What do you smoke?', 'How many do you smoke a day?', 'How long have you smoked for?'
'Do you, or have you ever, drunk alcohol?' *If yes,* 'What type of alcohol do you drink?' *(e.g. spirits, wine, beer)* 'How much do you drink per week?' *(convert this to units per week)* 'How long have you drunk for?'

Combined Assessment Box – CLAUDICATION

Ask:
- How far can you walk?
- Where do you feel the pain? (calf/thigh/buttock)
- Do you get night pain?
- Do you get rest pain?
- Have you noticed any tissue loss?
- Ask about risk factors and other associated diseases (diabetes, smoking, hypercholesterolaemia etc.)

Examine:
- Look: general inspection for signs of cardiovascular disease, smoking; legs for pallor, venous guttering, discoloration, ulceration
- Palpation: temperature, capillary refill, pulses
- Auscultate for bruits
- Special tests: Buerger's test, ABPI

---

[51] A positive family history is a risk factor for PVD.
[52] Smoking is an important risk factor for PVD.

B THE EXAMINATIONS

EXAMINATION OF THE HIP

'Hello, I'm Dr Parchment Smith. Would you mind if I examine your hips? Can you stand in front of me please?'

WASH/GEL YOUR HANDS BEFORE YOU TOUCH THE PATIENT

Stand back, hands behind the back and LOOK.
From the front you are looking for pelvic tilting[53], muscle wasting[54] or rotational deformity[55].
From the side you are looking for scars[56] and an increase in lumbar lordosis[57].
From behind you are looking for scoliosis[58], gluteal muscle wasting and sinus scars.
'Now will you lie on the bed? Let me get your hips straight.'
Assess for SHORTENING.
Look for obvious shortening.[59] Ideally you should measure the true length and the apparent length.[60] If there is any discrepancy you should flex the knees and see if the shortening is of the femur or the tibia.[61] You can further assess femoral shortening by palpating the greater trochanters.[62]

---

[53] For example, from adduction or abduction deformity of the hip, short leg, scoliosis.
[54] Due to infection, disuse or polio.
[55] Common in osteoarthritis.
[56] Previous surgery, old TB sinuses.
[57] Suggests fixed flexion deformity of the hip.
[58] May be secondary to pelvic tilting, adduction deformity and/or shortening of a leg.
[59] **Causes of shortening of the leg**
1. True shortening: affected limb physically shorter than the other
a) Causes distal to the trochanters: old femoral or tibial fractures, growth disturbance (polio, bone or joint infection, epiphysial trauma)
b) Causes above the trochanters: coxa vara (from neck fractures, slipped epiphysis, Perthes' disease, congenital coxa vara), loss of articular cartilage (infection, arthritis) or dislocation
c) Lengthening of other limb (rare): stimulation of bone growth by increased vascularity (after tumour or fracture in children), coxa valga (following polio)
2. Apparent shortening: limb not altered in length but appears short as a result of an adduction contracture of the hip which has to be compensated for by tilting of the pelvis
[60] Lie patient square on couch. Adjust anterior superior iliac spines (ASIS) to be parallel. Heels should now be level. Measure ASIS to medial malleolus for true length, xiphisternum to medial malleolus for apparent length.
[61] Put heels together and flex knees to 90°. If the knee of the short leg is sitting proximal to the normal knee, the femur is short. If it sits distally, the tibia is shortened. This can be confirmed by measuring from the tibial tubercle to the medial malleolus.
[62] Put thumbs on ASIS and feel for greater trochanters with the fingers. If the distance is shorter on one side this suggests the pathology lies above the trochanters. It is not very reliable to measure the femoral shaft but in thin people the tip of the trochanter to the lateral joint line are the landmarks. NELATON'S LINE runs from the ASIS to the greater tuberosity and should pass the tip of the trochanter.

Next PALPATE the joint.

'I am going to feel around the hip joint, please let me know if it is tender.'

Palpate the head of the femur which should lie below the inguinal ligament just lateral to the femoral artery.

'Does it hurt when I rotate it like this?'

While you are doing this listen for crepitations.

Abduct the bent leg.

Next palpate adductor longus (which can be tender[63]) and, just below it, the lesser trochanter. In a young patient with hip pain you should palpate the ischial tuberosity if you suspect hamstring strain is the source of the hip pain. Next examine the MOVEMENTS at the hip.[64]

'I am going to move your hip joint, please let me know if it is tender.'

Place your hand behind the lumbar spine to assess its position. Now flex the good hip fully, observing with the hand that the lumbar curvature is fully flattened.

This is Thomas' test for a fixed flexion deformity.[65] If you felt the lumbar spine flatten and the opposite hip has remained on the bed, then this test is negative, indicating no gross loss of EXTENSION.

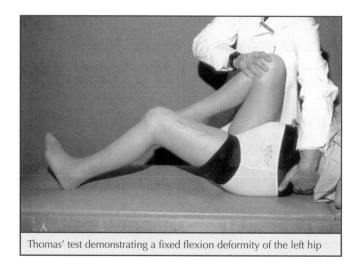

Thomas' test demonstrating a fixed flexion deformity of the left hip

---

[63] Especially in sports injuries (strain of adductor longus).

[64] For time-saving purposes most examiners would only expect you to examine the bad hip. 'Examine this patient's left hip', although technically you should examine both sides and compare the range of movements. Be prepared to do either as required.

[65] **Thomas' test** is a test of hip extension. If the hip being examined (the 'bad' hip) rises from the couch when the other hip is being flexed in the presence of a normal lumbar spine there is a fixed flexion deformity/loss of extension of the 'bad' hip.

Ask the patient to hold the good hip in the position which obliterates lumbar lordosis.

'Just hold your good leg there while I assess the FLEXION of your bad hip – how far can you bend your bad leg?'[66]

Next test ABDUCTION and ADDUCTION.

'Can you put both legs out straight, please.'

You need to make sure the pelvis does not contribute, so place your hand over the ASIS, fingers on one, thumb on the other.

'How far can you bring your leg out[67] and how far can it swing in over the other leg?'[68]

Next test INTERNAL AND EXTERNAL ROTATION.[69]

'Can you bend your knee up for me?'

With the knee and hip flexed to 90°, steady the knee over the hip and pull the foot out laterally (this is internal rotation of the hip[70]). Now move the foot medially (this is external rotation of the hip[71]).

Thomas' test earlier has shown you that there is no gross loss of extension, but a more subtle way to test this if you are concerned would be to turn the patient prone and check for extension in that way.[72]

---

[66] Flexion is tested using one hand under the pelvis to check no further movement occurs, and with the opposite hip held by the patient in enough flexion to obliterate the lumbar lordosis. Normal range 120°. The thigh should touch the abdomen.

[67] Normal range of abduction is 40°.

[68] Normal range of adduction is 25°. The legs should cross around mid-thigh.

[69] These tests are for hip rotation **in 90° of flexion**, the commonest way of testing rotation. Internal and external rotation of the hip **in extension** can be assessed by making the patient lie with legs extended and simply rolling the straight leg laterally and medially, observing any play at the knee. Alternatively, the patient can lie prone with his knees bent, feet in the air. (The hips will be extended although the knees are flexed.) The normal range of external and internal rotation in extension is 45° and 35° respectively.

[70] Normal range is 45° from the midline. Loss of internal rotation is common in most hip pathology.

[71] Normal range is 45° from the midline. Loss of external rotation is common in most hip pathology.

[72] To test for extension, turn the patient face down, put your hand on the small of his back to steady his pelvis and lift each straight leg up out behind him. This test is not usually necessary if you have done Thomas' test and is awkward in older, obese or immobile patients.

Next perform TRENDELENBURG'S TEST.

'Could you stand up please?'

Check that the anterior superior iliac spines are level.

'Now turn your back to me with your feet together. Now, keeping your knees together, just lift the foot of your good leg back off the floor and hold it there, standing on your bad leg.'

The pelvis on the opposite side to the supporting leg should rise. If it falls, the Trendelenburg's test is positive.[73]

Finally, if the examiners ask you what else you would like to do to complete your examination, say:

'To complete my examination I would like to see the patient WALK[74], do a NEUROLOGICAL examination and see the X-RAYS.'

---

[73] **Trendelenburg's test**: standing on one leg tests the abductors of the supporting leg (gluteus medius and minimus) which would normally pull on the pelvis, causing it to tilt (and the opposite side of the pelvis to rise) to bring the centre of gravity over the supporting foot (see Osteoarthritis of hip pg 386).

Reasons for a positive Trendelenburg's test include:

1. Gluteal paralysis or weakness (e.g. from polio or a muscle-wasting disease)
2. Gluteal inhibition from pain arising in the hip joint (most common cause in OSCE)
3. Coxa vara which shortens the distance between the origin and insertion of the gluteal muscles, causing gluteal insufficiency
4. Congenital dislocation of the hip (see Osteoarthritis of hip pg 386)

[74] Assess stride, dwell time on each side, pain, stiffness, shortening, Trendelenburg's gait. In cases of unilateral Trendelenburg's, there is a dipping movement on the affected side. In bilateral cases there is a waddling gait.

EXAMINATION OF THE KNEE

'Hello, I'm Dr Parchment Smith. Would you mind if I examined your knee? Could you lie flat?'

WASH/GEL YOUR HANDS BEFORE YOU TOUCH THE PATIENT

Stand back, hands behind the back, and LOOK.

Do the knees look symmetrical? Look for generalised[75] or localised[76] swelling, bruising[77], scars[78], signs of inflammation or a rash[79]. Also look for obvious deformity and quadriceps wasting.[80]

To the patient:

'Which is the bad knee? Is it tender?'

Begin to FEEL, starting with the back of the hand, comparing both sides and the feet for temperature to assess whether the knee is hot or not.[81]

Now start by examining the EXTENSOR APPARATUS.

Place a hand behind the knee and feel the quadriceps with the other hand.

To the patient:

'Can you press your leg down against my hand? Now do it again with your foot turned in, toes pointing up to the ceiling.'[82]

If quadriceps function appears abnormal you can compare the circumference of the legs 18 cm above the joint line.

Next feel for the position of the patella to ensure the upper borders of the patella are equal[83] and there is no tenderness or loss of soft tissue above the upper border[84], across the patella[85], across the lower border[86] or over the tibial tubercle[87].

---

[75] Swelling confined to the limits of the synovial cavity and suprapatellar pouch suggests effusion, haemarthrosis, pyarthrosis or a space-occupying lesion within the joint. Swelling beyond the limits of the joint suggests infection, tumour or major injury.

[76] Bursitis presents as localised swelling most commonly in the prepatellar or infrapatellar bursa. Meniscal cysts are localised swellings in the joint line. Exostoses occur on the bone.

[77] Suggests trauma to superficial tissues or ligaments (not usually seen in meniscal injuries).

[78] Of previous injury, arthroscopy or surgery.

[79] Psoriasis is associated with arthritis.

[80] Wasting of the quadriceps occurs because of disuse, generally from a painful or unstable lesion of the knee, or from infection or RA.

[81] A hot joint suggests active rheumatoid arthritis or infection.

[82] Extending the hip with the foot dorsiflexed and inverted emphasises the vastus medialis, which is involved in recurrent dislocation of the patella.

[83] If not, suspect patellar fracture, rupture of the patellar ligament, avulsion of the tibial tubercle.

[84] This suggests rupture of quadriceps tendon.

[85] This suggests fracture of patella.

[86] This suggests rupture of patellar ligament.

[87] This suggests avulsion of tibial tubercle.

The extensor apparatus may appear intact but ideally to confirm this you should assess the straight leg raise. Ask the patient to sit with legs dangling off the couch, support the ankle with your hand and ask them to straighten the knee while feeling the muscle.

Now examine for an EFFUSION:

The patellar tap test[88]:

Slide your hand firmly from 15 cm above the knee to the level of the upper border of the patella. Tap the patella firmly with three fingers and the thumb. Listen and feel for a click.

The fluid displacement test[89]:

Stroke the medial side of the joint to empty it. Then watch the medial side as you stroke the lateral side. Excess fluid will distend it.

If the examiners ask what you would do if you suspected a haemarthrosis[90] or pyoarthrosis[91] at this point tell them:

'I would aspirate the joint before proceeding with the examination.'

Pick up the skin and the relaxed quadriceps tendon above the patella[92] to assess whether the synovium feels grossly thickened.[93]

Now assess for TENDERNESS.

To the patient:

'Can you bend your knee please? Let me know if this feels sore.'

---

[88] If the effusion is too slight or too tense the test will be negative.

[89] If the effusion is too tense the test will be negative.

[90] A haemarthrosis usually occurs within half an hour of injury and gives a doughy feel to the suprapatellar region. It should always be aspirated before examination of the joint because of pain and ability to examine structures.

[91] The tenderness in pyoarthrosis usually impedes examination. It is also vital to get early exclusion of the diagnosis by microscopy.

[92] To assess the thickness of the synovial membrane in the suprapatellar pouch.

[93] It is thickened in rheumatoid arthritis and other inflammatory conditions such as villo-nodular synovitis.

Palpate the joint line for meniscus and fat-pad injury[94], the collateral ligaments and their attachments[95], the tibial tubercle for avulsion injuries or Osgood–Schlatter's disease[96], and the femoral condyles, especially medially, for osteochondritis dissecans[97].

Next assess MOVEMENT of the joint.

To the patient:

'Can I just lift your foot? You relax with the leg straight.'

Lift leg by ankle and check for full EXTENSION.[98] Then try active extension.[99]

'I'm just going to press on the knee to try to straighten your leg.'

Compare with the other side.

Assess whether the knee lacks full extension and, if so, by how many degrees. Assess whether there is any hyperextension.[100]

To the patient:

'Can you bend the knee? Pull your heel into your bottom as far as it will go. Now the other side.'

Check whether the patient has full FLEXION of 135°. If asked, ideally you would measure the angle or do serial heel to buttock distance (1 cm = 1.5° approximately).

---

[94] The fat pad may become tender and swollen and give pain on extension of the knee, especially when nipped between femur and tibia. Seen in osteoarthritis or young women with premenstrual fluid retention. Cured by excision of fat pad.

[95] Lateral ligament from lateral femoral epicondyle to head of fibula. Medial ligament consists of superficial and deep parts attached above to medial epicondyle and below to medial tibia either side of the semimembranosus groove.

[96] Occurring in the 10–16-year age group. Recurrent pain over tibial tuberosity that becomes tender and prominent. May be caused by partial avulsion of the tuberosity by the patellar ligament. Pain usually ceases with closure of the epiphysis. Management conservative so long as not completely avulsed.

[97] In teenage males as a result of the impingement of the femoral condyle against the tibial spines or cruciate ligaments. A segment of bone undergoes avascular necrosis. May separate and cause a loose body. Aching pain and recurrent effusion +/– locking. Conservative treatment includes quadriceps exercises. Fragment may be pinned or excised. Cavity may be drilled to encourage vascularisation.

[98] Full extension is 0°.

[99] A springy block to full extension is suggestive of bucket-handle meniscus tear. A rigid block to full extension is common in arthritic conditions (fixed flexion deformity).

[100] If hyperextended (X° of hyperextension) check the other leg and the elbow. Hyperextension (genu recurvatum) is seen in girls and is associated with a high patella, chondromalacia patellae, recurrent patellar dislocation and sometimes tears of the anterior cruciate, medial meniscus or medial ligament. It can be associated with ballet or high heels that retard upper tibial epiphysial growth. Polio and Charcot's disease are rare causes.

Next examine the stability of the knee[101] starting with the COLLATERAL LIGAMENTS.

Extend the knee fully. Grasp knee with one hand, heel of hand against the lateral knee, fingers under knee. Grasp the lower tibia with the other hand and push them in opposite directions, stressing the knee in valgus. Look for the knee opening up.[102] Compare the two sides. Repeat with knee flexed 30° and foot internally rotated.[103] (This is the valgus stress instability test, which tests for gross instability of the medial ligaments.)

Repeat, heel of hand medially, stressing the lateral side looking for varus stress instability.[104] If there were gross instability of the lateral ligaments, you should check the distribution of the common peroneal nerve[105] to ensure it has escaped injury.

Now examine the stability of the CRUCIATES.

Flex both knees to 90°; look from the side for tibial subluxation.

---

[101] **Summary of instability in the knee**
1. Valgus stress test +ve if medial ligament torn
2. Varus stress test +ve if lateral ligament torn
3. Anterior drawer test +ve if anterior cruciate torn
4. Posterior drawer test +ve if posterior cruciate torn
Rotatory instabilities:
5. Anteromedial instability with 1+3
   Medial tibial condyle subluxates anteriorly on anterior drawer test
6. Anterolateral instability with 2+3
   Lateral tibial condyle subluxates anteriorly on anterior drawer test test with MacIntosh test, Losee test or pivot shift test
7. Posterolateral instability with 2+4
   Lateral tibial condyle subluxates posteriorly on post-drawer test

[102] Moderate valgus is a sign of major medial and posterior ligament rupture. Severe valgus indicates additional cruciate (esp. posterior cruciate) rupture. The medial ligament may be slightly torn (sprain), calcified after haematoma (Pellegrini–Stieda disease) or ruptured. Partial tears are treated by immobilisation in plaster. Complete acute tears are repaired surgically.

[103] Abnormal amount of valgus in slight flexion suggests less extensive involvement of the medial structures.

[104] Instability in extension suggests lateral ligament complex and maybe posterior cruciate damage. The lateral ligament often tears at the fibular attachment close to the common peroneal nerve. Complete tears are treated surgically.

[105] Sensory loss over the dorsum and lateral side of the lower leg and loss of ability to dorsiflex the foot.

Sit on the foot. Grasping the tibia with both hands, pull tibia forward (see figure on pg 334). This is the anterior drawer test.[106] If there were any sign of rotational instability during the anterior drawer test this can be confirmed by the MacIntosh test[107], Losee test[108] or pivot shift test[109].

(The Lachman test[110] is an alternative to the anterior drawer test but more difficult with small hands!)

Now jerk tibia backwards. This is the posterior drawer test[111], see figure on pg 334.

Next examine the MENISCI.[112]

(You have already inspected for cysts[113] and palpated the joint line for tenderness earlier.)

Put your fingers and thumb along the joint line, palm on the patella. With knee flexed, sweep the foot around in a U shape. Extend the leg while listening for crepitus and feeling for clicks.

Now perform the McMurray test.

In the McMurray test for the medial meniscus (see figure on pg 334), the leg is flexed (1), the foot externally rotated (2) and the hip is abducted (3). Feel for clicks and grating while the leg is smoothly extended (4).

---

[106] If anterior displacement is >1.5 cm then anterior cruciate is almost certainly torn +/– medial ligament and capsule damage. If one condyle moves forward more than the other there may be anterolateral or antero-medial instability (anterior cruciate plus lateral or medial ligament injury respectively). Anterior cruciate tears often occur after tears of medial meniscus that block full extension. Isolated anterior cruciate tears do not often need surgery. If acute or associated with instability, surgery may involve:
a) adductor gracilis as dynamic replacement,
b) tube pedicle from iliotibial tract or
c) carbon fibre implants.

[107] **MacIntosh test (see figure overleaf):** fully extend knee. Hold foot in internal rotation (1). Apply valgus stress (2+3). Gradually flex knee (4), it will jerk at 30° as the tibial condyle reduces. It confirms rotatory instability.

[108] **Losee test:** as above but starting with leg flexed, pushing on fibular head, gradually extend it and hear clunk as tibial condyle subluxates.

[109] **Pivot shift test (see figure overleaf):** with foot tucked in under arm tilted in valgus (1) and internally rotated (2), hold lower leg firmly with both hands and flex knee (3). The femoral condyle should appear to jerk forward as tibial condyle reduces since the tibia is fixed, and jerk backwards as tibia subluxates when leg is extended.

[110] **Active Lachman test (see figure overleaf):** relax knee in 10° flexion. Hold femur with one hand and pull tibia forward with the other.
Passive Lachman test: knee rests on bolster flexed at 30°. Patient asked to extend leg that leads to anterior subluxation of tibia with posterior subluxation on relaxation. Indicates complete anterior cruciate tear.

[111] If displaces >1 cm, rupture of the posterior cruciate ligament is likely. If one condyle moves more than the other there may be posterolateral rotatory insufficiency (posterior cruciate + lateral ligaments).

[112] **Lesions of the menisci**
1. Congenital discoid meniscus in childhood – D-shaped meniscus extends towards tibial spines and blocks extension and causes clicking. Treatment is excision.
2. Meniscus tears in the young adult are usually a sporting injury when a flexed leg is twisted. Longitudinal split (bucket-handle tear) goes towards centre of joint and causes locking and rupture of anterior cruciate eventually in the case of the medial meniscus. Treated by excisions in whole or in part, rarely repair of peripheral lesions.
3. Degenerative meniscus lesions in middle age – usually horizontal. May resolve, may need excision.

[113] **Meniscal cysts** lie in the joint line, feel firm on palpation and are tender on deep pressure. They may be associated with tears and are usually on the lateral side. Be suspicious of cysts on the medial side; they may be ganglions arising from the insertion of sartorius, gracilis and semitendinosus.

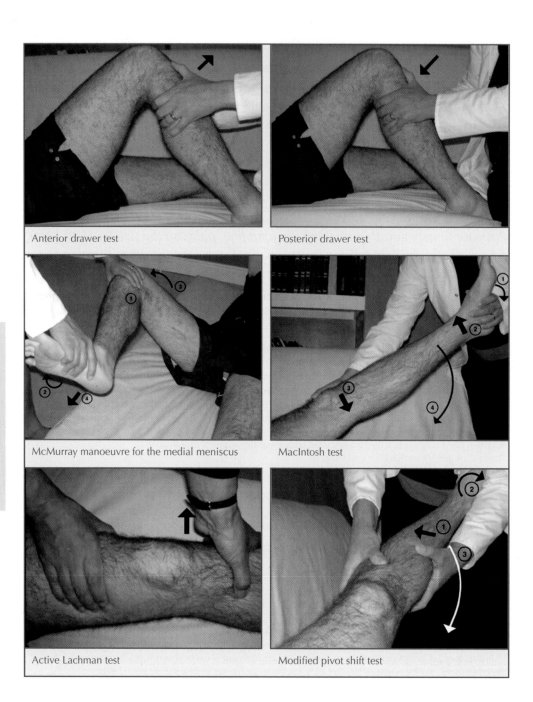

Anterior drawer test

Posterior drawer test

McMurray manoeuvre for the medial meniscus

MacIntosh test

Active Lachman test

Modified pivot shift test

Next have a closer look at the PATELLA.

You examined the extensor apparatus earlier. *You can palpate 2/3rds of the articular surface, which may be diseased in chondromalacia patellae[114] and check its mobility, which may be restricted in retropatellar arthritis.*

Displace the patella medially and laterally to palpate the under-surface. Move the patella from side to side and up and down. Then do it pressing down on the patella against the femur.

'Is this sore?'

Pain is suggestive of chondromalacia patellae or retropatellar arthritis. You could perform the apprehension test. *Try to push the patella laterally while flexing the extended knee.* Positive if patient gets jumpy and tries to stop you. A positive apprehension test indicates a tendency to recurrent dislocation.[115]

Next examine the knee from BEHIND.

Turn patient over, hold knee flexed. Palpate the popliteal region with the knee flexed, and then look for bursae[116] with the knee extended.

Finally, if the examiners ask you what else you would like to do to complete your examination, say:

'I would like to examine this patient's GAIT and look for GENU VARUM[117] or VALGUS[118] by observing her standing and then by requesting standing X-RAYS of the knee with all the weight on each leg in turn. In a child I would measure the INTER-MALLEOLAR GAP[119].'

---

[114] **Chondromalacia patellae** is common in girls. The articular surface of the patella becomes soft and spongy, giving rise to aching pain in front of the knee. It may follow recurrent dislocation of the patella and may lead to retropatellar osteoarthrosis. Treatment: immobilise in plaster; may need surgical paring or even patellectomy. Chronic anterior knee pain without changes of chondromalacia is common and just needs physiotherapy.

[115] **Recurrent dislocation of the patella** often follows a traumatic episode initially, often in a teenage girl. It may spontaneously reduce or need manipulation, and thereafter may recurrently dislocate or be permanently displaced laterally. Associated with knock-knees, hyperextension (genu recurvatum), a high patella, underdeveloped lateral femoral condyle or abnormal attachment to quadriceps. Galeazzi repair is used before epiphyseal closure using distal semitendinosus tendon. Hauser operation is used after epiphyseal closure. The tibial tuberosity is transposed medially and distally to alter the line of pull of the patellar tendon.

[116] See pg 434. Cystic swelling in popliteal region. Can cause pain, worse on flexion. Commonly semi-membranosus bursa but can be other bursae. Treatment is excision. Prepatellar and infrapatellar bursitis also occurs and can be aspirated or excised if recurrent.

[117] **Bow-leg** is common in childhood and often resolves. May be caused by tibia vara or rarely by rickets; treated by osteotomy. In adults osteoarthritis, rheumatoid arthritis or Paget's can be the cause.

[118] **Knock-knee** is seen in children, often with flat feet, and usually resolves by age 6. May contribute to recurrent dislocation. In adults often occurs with rheumatoid arthritis, uncorrected tibial plateau fractures or neurological disorders. Treatment is corrective osteotomy.

[119] In a child simply grasp the ankles while child is sitting or lying straight-legged. Rotate legs until patellae are vertical then bring legs together until the knees just touch and measure the gap between the malleoli. Serial measurements every 6 months.

335

EXAMINATION OF RHEUMATIC HANDS

'Hello, my name is Dr Parchment Smith. May I examine your hands please? Could you roll up your sleeves above the elbow? Put both your hands on your lap/on this table.'

WASH/GEL YOUR HANDS BEFORE TOUCHING THE PATIENT

LOOK at the hands.
You are looking for a symmetrical deforming polyarthropathy of the small joints of the hand. There may be spindling of the fingers due to soft-tissue swelling at the proximal interphalangeal joints and metacarpophalangeal joints but the distal interphalangeal joints are spared. Look for wasting of the small muscles of the hands.[120] The skin may look thin with some bruising.[121]

Pick the hands up and look at the fingers individually.
On closer inspection look for an ulnar deviation of the fingers,[122] radial deviation at the wrist, and swan neck[123]/boutonnière[124]/Z thumb deformities of the fingers/thumb. Look for scars of previous surgery over the wrist[125]/thumb[126]/interphalangeal joints[127]. Look to see whether the nail beds are pale, that there are/are no vasculitic lesions[128] in the nail folds or fingers and whether there is nail pitting or scaly rash.[129]

To the patient:
'Could you turn the hands over and show me your palms?'
On the palms you are looking for pallor in the palmar creases indicating anaemia[130], and palmar erythema[131].

---

[120] Disuse atrophy. Pain and deformity limit use.
[121] Due to steroid use.
[122] Due to subluxation and dislocation at the MCP joints.
[123] Swan neck – hyperextension of PIP joints with fixed flexion of MCP and DIP joints due to tendon prolapse (see OSCE case pg 400).
[124] Boutonnière (English translation – 'button hook') flexion deformity of PIP with extension contracture of DIP and MCP joints (see OSCE case pg 400).
[125] Usually arthrodesis for strength and stability.
[126] Usually arthrodesis in the MCP joint, again for strength and stability.
[127] Usually arthroplasty with silastic spacers for flexibility and pain relief.
[128] Nail-fold infarcts caused by an associated vasculitis that can also cause chronic leg ulceration, purpuric rash and Raynaud's phenomenon. The vasculitis is immune complex-induced and can affect small, medium or large vessels.
[129] **Psoriatic arthropathy** is an asymmetric arthropathy involving mainly the DIP joints with pitting of the fingernails, onycholysis and hyperkeratosis. There is a red and silvery scaly rash over the extensor surfaces and behind the ears (see OSCE case pg 406).
[130] There are five causes of anaemia in rheumatoid arthritis (see OSCE case pg 400).
[131] Redness around palm sparing the central area, associated with pregnancy, RA, liver disease.

Next PALPATE the joints.

FEEL each joint gently and quickly.

You are feeling for evidence of bony destruction of the PIP and MCP joints with sparing of the DIP joints. You should feel for any rheumatoid nodules[132] or Heberden's nodes[133] in the hands. Feel whether any joints are tender or warm at present.[134]

Feel the wrist.

Next carry out a basic assessment of MOVEMENT and FUNCTION.

Grip the arm.

To the patient:

'Can you move your wrist up and down? Now circle it. Can you grip my fingers? Harder! OK, can you touch each finger with your thumb like this? Now can you undo and do up the button on the front of your shirt?'

While they are doing this observe whether both power grip and pincer grip are complete/incomplete, and whether wrist function is normal/impaired.

Next test for sensory deficit.

First touch the little finger[135], then the index finger[136], then the anatomical snuffbox[137].

To the patient:

'Can you feel me touching you here? and here? and here?'

You are looking for SENSORY DEFICIT in the distribution of the median, ulnar and radial nerves.

'Finally, can I look at your ELBOW?'

Look/feel for any firm subcutaneous nodules.

Finally, if the examiners ask you what else you would like to do to complete your examination, say:

'To complete my examination I would like to see if any of the OTHER JOINTS are affected[138] and look for EXTRA-ARTICULAR MANIFESTATIONS of rheumatoid arthritis[139]. I would also like to see the X-rays of these hands[140].'

---

[132] Firm subcutaneous nodules caused by immune-complex deposition.

[133] Bony osteophytes which occur in osteoarthritis secondary to rheumatoid arthritis. Primary osteoarthritis of the hands tends to affect the thumb and distal interphalangeal joints of the fingers. In general it is not as mutilating or deforming as rheumatoid disease.

[134] Indicating 'active' arthritis.

[135] Ulnar nerve: typically affected by rheumatoid nodules on the elbows. Usually better to assess nerves by sensation rather than power because the hand may be too weak to assess motor supply.

[136] Median nerve: affected in carpal tunnel syndrome, associated with RA.

[137] Radial nerve: no specific associations, but bear in mind that sensation in any distribution can be affected by cervical spine disease.

[138] Typically knees, neck, elbows, shoulders.

[139] Extra-articular manifestations of rheumatoid arthritis, see Joint pain history pg 311.

[140] X-ray signs of rheumatoid **arthritis**, see Joint pain history pg 311.

EXAMINATION OF THE SHOULDER

'Hello, my name is Dr Parchment Smith. Would you mind if I examined your shoulder? Will you take a seat in the centre of the room please?'

WASH/GEL YOUR HANDS BEFORE TOUCHING THE PATIENT

LOOK from the front, crouching down.

Inspect for asymmetry and obvious deformity. From the centre out, look in particular for a prominent sternoclavicular joint[141], deformity of the clavicle[142], prominent acromioclavicular joint[143] and deltoid wasting[144].

Move to the side.

From the side look for swelling of the joint.[145]

Look from above.

From above look for swelling, asymmetry of the supraclavicular fossae or deformity of the clavicle.

Move behind.

From behind inspect the scapulae and the back, again for asymmetry, wasting, abnormally high or small scapula.[146]

To the patient:

'Can you stand up and push your hands against the wall?'

Look for winging of the scapula.[147]

---

[141] Indicates subluxation. **Dislocation of the sternoclavicular joint** is comparatively uncommon. There is always a history of trauma and joint asymmetry is obvious. Hard to see on X-ray, only rarely needs surgery.

[142] Indicates an old fracture.

[143] Indicates subluxation or osteoarthritis. **Acromioclavicular dislocation** can occur as a result of a fall on the outstretched hand. In major injuries the conoid and trapezoid ligaments are torn and the clavicle is very unstable. Surgical fixation of the clavicle to coronoid may be needed. Normally only a sling is needed. Hard to see on X-ray.

[144] Disuse or axillary nerve palsy.

[145] Infection or inflammatory reaction, e.g. from calcifying supraspinatus tendinitis or from trauma. **Calcifying supraspinatus tendinitis** often accompanies degenerative changes in the shoulder cuff. The mechanism is local deposition of calcium salts; can be asymptomatic or can give rise to sudden incapacitating subdeltoid bursitis. Tender, swollen, warm acute joint relieved by aspiration, hydrocortisone injections or curettage.

[146] Occurs in Sprengel shoulder and in the Klippel–Feil syndrome. There are several related congenital malformations affecting the neck and shoulder girdle. In the most minor cases one of the scapulae may be slightly smaller or higher than the other.
Sprengel shoulder: congenital malformation with one or both shoulders high, scapulae small, +/– webs of skin running from the shoulder to neck.
Klippel–Feil syndrome: high scapulae, short neck, multiple anomalies of cervical vertebrae including vertebral body fusions, spina bifida. Also associated with diastomatomyelia, cord tethering, lumbosacral lipomata and renal abnormalities.

[147] Due to weakness of serratus anterior (see OSCE case pg 417).

Now FEEL.

'I am now going to feel the joint. Tell me if this is tender?'[148]

Feel the anterior and lateral aspects of the glenohumeral joint.[149]

'Lift your arm for me please.'

Feel the humeral shaft and head via the axilla.[150] *Next palpate the acromio-clavicular joint for tenderness or lipping*[151]*, and move the arm while palpating it, listening for crepitations*[152] *and for tenderness during movement*[153]*. Next feel for local tenderness along the clavicle*[154] *and finally the sternoclavicular joint. Now go on to MOVE the joint – do the movements yourself to encourage the patient!*

'Can you raise both arms slowly out to the side like this? Carry on right over your head. Can your shoulders touch your ears? Is it painful at all? Hold your arms there. Now release them slowly back down to your side, telling me if it's sore, thank you.'

---

[148] **Infections around the shoulder**
Staphylococcal osteitis of the proximal humerus is the commonest infection in UK but still pretty rare.
TB of the shoulder is now rare. Moist form: commonest in first two decades of life, shoulder swollen, abundant pus production, rapid destruction. Dry form: caries sicca in older patients, slow progress, little destruction or pus formation.
Gonococcal arthritis of the shoulder is uncommon; there is moderate swelling of the joint and great pain that often seems out of keeping with the physical signs.

[149] Diffuse tenderness is suggestive of infection or calcifying supraspinatus tendinitis.

[150] Exostoses of the proximal humeral shaft are palpable via this route.

[151] Tenderness is found after recent dislocations and in osteoarthritis. Lipping is usually palpable in osteoarthritis.
Osteoarthritis of the glenohumeral joint is rare and most frequently occurs secondary to aseptic necrosis of the humeral head, which can be idiopathic, follow high fractures or occur in deep-sea divers. Rheumatoid is more common. Osteoarthritis in the acromioclavicular joint gives rise to prolonged pain associated with shoulder movements. Usually obvious prominence of the joint with arthritic lipping and well-localised tenderness. Conservative treatment with local heat and exercises may be helpful but occasionally acromionectomy may be needed.

[152] In osteoarthritis.

[153] Sudden tenderness during a portion of the arc of movement is found in tears or inflammatory lesions involving the shoulder cuff and/or subdeltoid bursa. **Shoulder cuff tears** can result from sudden traction. They occur most readily in the middle-aged where degenerative changes in the shoulder cuff have become established. Most commonly the supraspinatus tendon is involved, thereby causing difficulty initiating abduction of the arm. In other cases a torn or inflamed supraspinatus tendon impinges upon the acromion during abduction, giving rise to a painful arc of movement. The range of passive movements is not initially disturbed but limitation of rotation may supervene, leading to a 'frozen shoulder'.

[154] Tender in sternoclavicular dislocations, infections (especially TB), tumours (rare) and radionecrosis (e.g. after treatment for breast cancer, which may be mistaken for mets). X-ray if local tenderness is seen.

When observing active ABDUCTION look for initiation of abduction[155], painful arc during abduction[156], and ability to hold the arm fully abducted[157]. If the patient has restricted active abduction[158], test the passive abduction, rotating the arm externally first.[159]

Next test abduction with a fixed scapula.[160] Then test adduction[161] which should be around 50°. Now look from the side.

'Can you swing your arms forward and right above your head?'
You are checking active FORWARD FLEXION, which is normally 165°.

'Now swing them back.' Backward extension should be 60°.

'Could you put your arms behind your back as high up as you can, reaching for your shoulder blade?' This is a screening test of internal rotation.[162]

'Can you put your hands behind your head?' This is a screening test of external rotation.[163]

'Keep your hands behind your head. I am just going to gently pull your elbows back to check for any difference. Now tuck your elbows into your sides, elbows bent, hands stretched out in front. Swing your hands out like a door.' (see figure opposite). This is EXTERNAL ROTATION in extension exclusively at the glenohumeral joint.[164]

---

[155] Difficulty in initiating abduction is suggestive of a shoulder cuff or supraspinatus tendon tear. These patients may use a trick movement to initiate abduction, i.e. leaning over or 'flicking' the arm out. After initiation the deltoid takes over.

[156] A painful arc from 70° to 100° is suggestive of a shoulder cuff lesion (e.g. tear, degenerative changes). A higher painful arc from 100 to 150° is suggestive of osteoarthritis of the acromioclavicular joint.

[157] If the patient can hold the arm up in a vertical position, deltoid and the axillary nerve are likely to be intact.

[158] Restricted abduction will occur in **frozen shoulder**. This is a clinical syndrome caused by various pathologies that can seldom be differentiated. Affects the middle-aged whose shoulder cuffs are degenerative. Severe limitation of glenohumeral joint movement, especially internal rotation, and pain which disturbs sleep are characteristic. Frequently a history of minor trauma, immobility or myocardial infarct initiating symptoms. X-rays usually normal. Treatment includes graduated shoulder exercises, hydrocortisone injections or MUA.

[159] This delays the impingement of the greater tuberosity on the glenoid rim, thus increasing the gleno-humeral range of abduction to slightly over 90°.

[160] Fix the angle of the scapula with one hand; abduct the arm with the other. You should get 90° glenohumeral abduction unless this joint is restricted.

[161] Patient puts his hand on the opposite shoulder; you swing his elbow across his chest.

[162] Hand should reach top of scapula on opposite side. Screens internal rotation in extension. This movement is commonly affected in frozen shoulder.

[163] Should be able to get hands behind the neck. Screens external rotation at 90° abduction. This movement is compromised in frozen shoulder.

[164] The normal range is 70° external rotation (from forearms sticking straight out forwards).

'Now swing your arms in across your stomach, keeping the elbows in to the side.' This is INTERNAL ROTATION exclusively at the glenohumeral joint (see figure below).

'Lift your elbows out to the side to the level of the shoulders, forearms hanging down like a puppet. Now swing the arms up till you're standing like a weight lifter.' This is a check of internal and external rotation in abduction (see figure below).

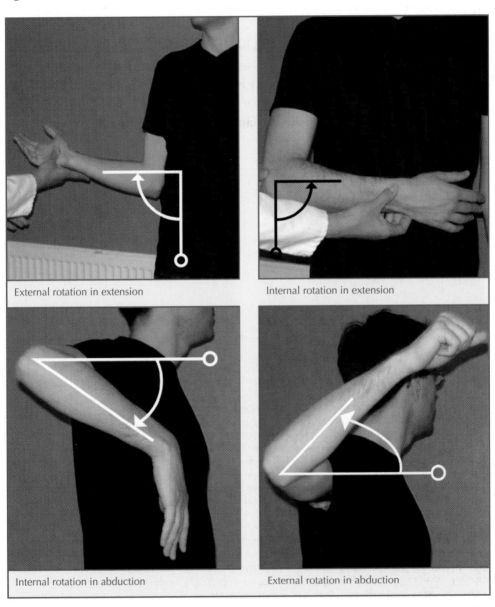

External rotation in extension

Internal rotation in extension

Internal rotation in abduction

External rotation in abduction

341

Next feel for CREPITATIONS.

Place one hand over the shoulder, the middle finger lying along the acromioclavicular joint. Abduct the arm, feeling and listening for crepitations.[165]

Next check for DELTOID POWER.[166]

'Lift your elbow out to the side. I'm going to feel this muscle. Keep your elbow there. Don't let me push it down. Can you feel me touching you here on the shoulder?'

Finally, if the examiners ask you what else you would like to do to complete your examination, say:

To complete my examination, I would like to examine the CERVICAL SPINE[167] **and check SENSATION and REFLEXES in the arm. Depending on the history there are certain special tests that may be appropriate, such as the DRAWER TESTS (of Gerber and Ganz)**[168]**, tests for recurrent dislocation**[169] **or the test for RUPTURED LONG TENDON OF BICEPS.**[170] **Finally, I would like to see the X-rays.'**

---

[165] This may indicate osteoarthritis of the acromioclavicular joint (common) or glenohumeral joint (less common).

[166] Traction injuries of the axillary nerve resulting in deltoid involvement and numb 'regimental badge' area are seen after dislocations of the shoulder.

[167] Shoulder pain or arm weakness can be due to problems with the cervical spine.

[168] **Drawer tests of Gerber and Ganz**

For anterior dislocation (patient lying supine): hold upper arm relaxed in one hand, in 90° abduction, slightly flexed and in slight external rotation. Hold scapula in other hand with thumb on coracoid and fingers behind. Try to pull the humeral head anteriorly. Observe movements, clicks and patient apprehension (can use axial radiographs).

For posterior dislocation (patient supine): hold forearm in one hand. Elbow flexed, shoulder in slight flexion and 90° abduction. With other hand put thumb lateral to coracoid, pressing humeral head backwards with thumb while you internally rotate the shoulder and flex it to 80°. Feel for backward displacement with the thumb. Can use X-rays.

[169] **Recurrent dislocation of the shoulder** is seen in the 20–40 age group. History of previous frank dislocations of the shoulder with less trauma each time. Repair advised if four or more dislocations. Beware **habitual dislocation of the shoulder** in a psychotic patient or one with joint laxity syndrome in which the patient painlessly voluntarily dislocates and reduces shoulder. X-ray changes may be absent.

[170] Support elbow, hold wrist with other hand and get patient to flex elbow against resistance. If the long tendon of biceps is ruptured, belly of biceps will appear globular in shape. Compare sides. **Rupture of the long head of biceps** can occur spontaneously or as the result of a sudden muscular effort, usually in a middle aged or elderly patient in whom degenerative tendon changes are present. No treatment is usually required (see OSCE case pg 453).

342

EXAMINATION OF THE NECK

'Hello, my name is Dr Parchment Smith. May I examine your neck? Could you sit on a chair facing me? I would like the neck and shoulders exposed if possible.'

WASH/GEL YOUR HANDS BEFORE TOUCHING THE PATIENT

Stand back and LOOK from the front, then move to inspect from behind.
You are looking for asymmetry or obvious deformity, torticollis,
scars, sinuses or muscle wasting. Check the head is held in a normal position.
Next FEEL the neck.[171]
'Is it tender anywhere?'
From behind feel gently in the midline from the occiput downwards for localised tenderness, increased temperature and any obvious step or deformity.[172]
Now feel the lateral aspects of the vertebrae for masses and tenderness laterally.
Now feel the supraclavicular fossae from behind for a prominent cervical rib[173]*, tumour masses, or enlarged lymph nodes. Quickly feel for obvious abnormalities in the anterior triangle of the neck such as the thyroid gland. Next move on to assess neck MOVEMENTS.*[174]
Look from the side.

---

[171] **Cervical spondylosis** (osteoarthritis of the cervical spine) is the most common condition affecting the neck. It can start in the third decade and usually affects the disc between C5 and C6. It is difficult to detect a restriction of movement clinically because of the compensating mobility of the other cervical vertebrae. Sharply localised pain centrally or to the side of the neck is felt, often radiating to the occiput or to the lower scapula. Nerve root involvement leads to pain or neurological signs in the arm in a dermatomal distribution. Infections such as TB causing **osteitis of the cervical spine** are rare in the UK but can produce localised pain or a 'step' due to vertebral collapse.
[172] Note the most prominent spinous process is that of T1, not the so called 'vertebra prominens' C7.
[173] See pg 498.
[174] A **goniometer** is an instrument for measuring these angles accurately. Don't try to use one but know the principle (look through it and read off the angle using a spatula clenched in the patient's teeth as a marker).

'Could you put your chin to your chest please?'
This allows you to assess FORWARD FLEXION.[175]
'Now tip your head as far back as it can go.'
This assesses EXTENSION.[176]
Touch your ear to your shoulder like this; good, now the other side.'
This is LATERAL FLEXION[177].
'Now can you look backwards over your right shoulder? and your left?'
This is testing for ROTATION.[178]
Next feel for crepitations.[179]
'Can you bend your head forward and back as if you are slowly nodding?'
Spread your hands on each side of the neck and feel as the patient flexes and extends his neck.
Step away from the patient.
Finally, if the examiners ask you what else you would like to do to complete your examination, say:
'To complete my examination I would like to check for the signs of a CERVICAL RIB[180], do a NEUROLOGICAL EXAMINATION of the arms[181] and view the lateral, AP and peg view[182] X-RAYS.

---

[175] Normally the chin can touch the chest.
[176] The plane of the nose and the forehead should be nearly horizontal. Watch out for the lumbar spine and thoracic spine bending back to contribute.
[177] The ear should touch the shoulder with only slight shoulder shrugging (45°). If lateral flexion cannot be carried out without forward flexion this is indicative of atlanto-axial and atlanto-occipital joint disease. These two joints are responsible for about a fifth of the total range of lateral flexion. Loss is common in osteoarthritis.
[178] Normally the chin falls just short of the plane of the shoulder (80° to either side). About a third of this movement occurs in the first two cervical joints. Rotation is usually restricted and painful in osteoarthritis of the spine.
[179] Facet joint crepitations are normally detected in this way and are a common finding in cervical osteoarthritis.
[180] See pg 498.
[181] See pg 356.
[182] Anterior-posterior through the mouth views of C1–C3 showing the odontoid process.

344

EXAMINATION OF A CERVICAL SPINE X-RAY

Is it complete? Can you see all seven cervical vertebrae and the top of the first thoracic vertebra?

Lateral view

1. Cervical curve: normally convex anteriorly, can be:
- Reduced (positional error or spasm)
- Kinked (subluxation or intense local spasm)

2. General shape of the vertebrae, noting:
- Vertebral fusion (congenital)
- Vertebral collapse (fracture, tumour, TB)

3. Position of each vertebra compared with those above and below it.
Displacement occurs in dislocation, which may be unilateral (25% displacement) or bilateral facet dislocation (50% displacement).

4. Disc spaces and margins, looking for:
- Disc-space narrowing (osteoarthritis)
- Anterior and posterior lipping (osteoarthritis)
- Fusion (ankylosing spondylitis)

5. Fractures: unstable fractures of C3–7 show one or more of the following signs:
- Disruption of the anterior and all of the posterior elements
- A fracture with the upper vertebra over-riding the vertebra beneath it by more than 3 mm
- A fracture with angulation between two adjoining vertebra of more than 11°

6. The position of the odontoid peg
- The anterior arch of the atlas should not lie more than 4 mm in front of the axis (rupture/laxity of transverse ligament)
- Upward migration of the odontoid peg is seen in rheumatoid arthritis

7. The pharyngeal shadow
If this is not lying close to the vertebral bodies there may be a space-occupying haematoma, tumour or retropharyngeal abscess.

8. Flexion and extension views: to detect instability.

AP view

Shape of vertebral bodies: lateral wedging may result from fracture, tumour or infection. A cervical rib may be seen.

C1–3 through the mouth (peg) views

1. Symmetry in alignment of the odontoid process with the atlas.
2. Fracture through odontoid peg (beware congenital failure of fusion of ossification centres, which looks like a fracture.

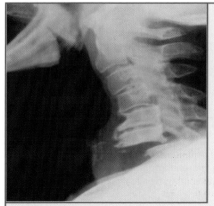

Lateral C spine X-ray showing anterior dislocation of C6 on C7

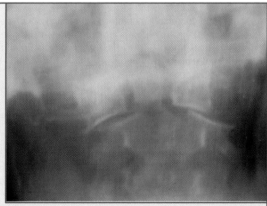

'Peg view' showing fracture of odontoid process

EXAMINATION OF THE BACK

'Hello, my name is Dr Parchment Smith. May I examine your back? Can you stand with your back to me with your trousers down?'

WASH/GEL YOUR HANDS BEFORE TOUCHING THE PATIENT

Stand back and LOOK.

From the back you are looking for any obvious scoliosis.[183] Also look for any obvious swellings[184], scars[185], abnormal pigmentation[186], hair[187], or café au lait spots[188].

If there is a scoliosis, ask the patient to sit to exclude a compensatory scoliosis[189] and bend forward to exclude a postural scoliosis[190] before diagnosing a structural scoliosis.[191]

Now look from the side.

From the side you are looking for a kyphosis[192] or a gibbus[193] of the thoracic frame. Also look at the lumbar curvature.[194]

Next PALPATE the spine.

FEEL from the prominent T1 vertebral spine down, palpating between the spines of the vertebrae, the muscles either side of the lumbar spine, and along the sacroiliac joint.

---

[183] Scoliosis is a lateral curvature of the spine. The commonest cause for a scoliosis is a protective scoliosis secondary to a prolapsed intervertebral disc.

[184] A fat pad may indicate spina bifida.

[185] Previous thoracotomy or spinal surgery.

[186] May indicate spina bifida.

[187] May indicate spina bifida.

[188] May indicate neurofibromatosis.

[189] For example in a shortened leg.

[190] Occurs most commonly in adolescent girls and usually resolves spontaneously.

[191] In structural scoliosis there is alteration of vertebral shape and mobility, and the deformity cannot be corrected by alteration of posture, and on sitting forward a rib hump may be seen.

True structural scoliosis may be

- Idiopathic (the commonest)
- Congenital (e.g. hemivertebra, fused vertebra, fused ribs)
- Paralytic (e.g. polio)
- Neuropathic (e.g. neurofibromatosis, cerebral palsy, spina bifida, syringomyelia, Friedreich's ataxia)
- Myopathic (e.g. muscular dystrophy, arthrogryphosis)
- Metabolic (e.g. Marfan syndrome, rickets)

[192] **Kyphosis** is an increased forward curvature of the spine. The commonest causes are senile kyphosis (worsened by osteoporosis, osteomalacia and pathological fracture) and ankylosing spondylitis. Scheuermann's disease (spinal osteochondrosis) is idiopathic vertebral wedging that often leads to osteoarthritis.

[193] **A gibbus** is an undue prominence of a spinous process often associated with an abrupt angular kyphosis. The commonest causes are fracture (traumatic or pathological), tuberculosis or a congenital vertebral abnormality.

[194] Flattened in prolapsed intervertebral disc, osteoarthritis of the spine, infected vertebral bodies and ankylosing spondylitis. Increased curvature is seen as a normal variant (especially in women), in spondylolisthesis or secondary to increased thoracic kyphosis or to a flexion deformity of the hip.

'Tell me if it's tender here… here… here.'

You are looking for tenderness over the lumbar spine[195], over the lumbar muscles[196] and along the sacroiliac joints[197].

Slide your fingers down the spine feeling for a step in the lumbar spine.[198]

'Bend forwards please.'

Lightly tap the spine with your fist from the neck to the sacroiliac joint, looking for marked localised pain on percussion.[199]

Next test MOVEMENTS.

'Can you try to lean forwards as far as you can?'

This estimates FORWARD FLEXION. *Can the patient flex to within 7 cm of the floor?*[200] *If his flexion is limited you can mark the spine to determine whether the limitation is in the thoracic or in the lumbar spine.*[201]

'Now can you stand with your hands on your buttocks and lean back slowly, letting your hands slide down the back of your leg?'

This is EXTENSION, which is normally about 30° in total.[202]

'Now can you stand up straight with your hands resting against your thighs? Lean to the left, not leaning forwards or back, and slide your hand down your left leg. Now to the right.'

This checks LATERAL FLEXION, which should be around 30°.[203]

'Now can you sit down, cross your arms and, without moving your bottom on the seat, twist your shoulders as far round as you can … to the left … now the right.'

This is checking ROTATION, which is normally up to 40°.[204]

Next screen for a PROLAPSED INTERVERTEBRAL DISC.

'Could you lie down flat on your back please?'

---

[195] Common in prolapsed intervertebral discs.

[196] Common in prolapsed intervertebral discs or mechanical back pain.

[197] Seen in mechanical back pain and sacroiliac joint infections.

[198] Due to spondylolisthesis, where the vertebra (usually L5) slips forward on S1 due to a fracture or fatigue of the part of L5 anterior to the downward-projecting inferior articular process (spondylolysis). Incidence increases with age. It causes low back pain radiating into the buttock and may need local spinal fusion, especially if associated with disc protrusion or stretching of the cauda equina or lumbosacral plexus.

[199] TB or other joint infections.

[200] This is the normal range. It is an indication of overall thoracic and lumbar movement but be aware that the hips play an important role in this action and may mask limitations in the spine or limit flexion in the presence of a normal spine. Actual normal range of flexion is 45° thoracic and 60° lumbar.

[201] To mark the spine use **Schrober's method**: mark a point midline between the dimples of Venus and another point 10 cm above it. This approximates to the lumbar spine. Measure the distance between the two points when the patient is standing and when the spine is maximally flexed forwards. The increase should be 8–10 cm (<3 cm suggests severe restriction). Do the same for the thoracic spine, marking the prominent T1 spinous process and a point 20 cm distal to that. The increase should be about 8 cm. Gross restriction of flexion is an outstanding feature of ankylosing spondylitis.

[202] Theoretically 25° thoracic, 35° lumbar but usually only 30° total. Pain on extension is common in prolapsed intervertebral disc.

[203] The contributions of the thoracic and lumbar spine are about equal.

[204] This is almost entirely thoracic, with <5° contributed by the lumbar spine.

To the patient:

'Bend your knee with your foot in the air[205] **and let me move your foot out… and in.'**

This is a quick test to eliminate gross osteoarthritis of the hips, which can be confused with lower back pain (see figure opposite).

Next do a straight leg raise test.[206]

'Can you straighten the leg and let me lift it? Stop me when you feel pain.'

Lift the leg by the heel keeping the knee straight.

'Now? Is that pain along the back of your leg or in your back? What about if I move your foot like this?'

Passively dorsiflex the foot.

If you suspect a high prolapse you could perform the reverse Lasègue test.[207]

If you suspect functional overlay you could also test for this.[208]

Next test the sacroiliac joint (see figure opposite).

'Can you bend the knee? I'm just going to press it across your body.[209] **Does that make the pain worse? Now I'm going to grasp your hip bones**[210] **– does this make the pain worse?'**

---

[205] The hip and knee should be flexed to 90°. You are doing a quick check for external and internal rotation at the hip.

[206] The **straight leg raise** (see figure opposite) test for nerve root irritation (usually by lateral disc prolapse).
If paraesthesia or radiating root pains (sciatica) down the leg (must be distinguished from hamstring tightness).
Raising the good leg can produce signs in the relaxed bad leg.
Passive dorsiflexion increases tension in the nerve roots.
Central disc prolapsed if pain is in the back.

[207] The **reverse Lasègue test** for high lumbar disc lesions (see figure opposite)
(rare compared with L5/S1 and L4/L5 lesions)
Lay the patient prone.
Flex each knee in turn.
This stretches the femoral nerve roots and gives rise to pain in high lumbar lesions.
Lifting the knee off the bed thus extending the hip will aggravate it.

[208] **Tests for functional overlay** (e.g. malingerers, Munchausen's)
1. Sit them up after the straight leg raise and pretend to examine their back. If they can sit up with their legs straight they should have been able to straight leg raise to 90°.
2. Make the patient stand with his arms straight, firmly held by the sides, and tell him to turn from side to side. Most of the rotation occurs in the legs so should not be restricted by back pathology.

[209] Flex the hip and knee and forcibly adduct the hip. Pain is very non-specific but may suggest early ankylosing spondylitis, tuberculosis and other infections, Reiter syndrome or sacroiliitis.

[210] Hook the thumbs round the anterior superior iliac spines and try to 'open out' the pelvis. Pain suggests sacroiliac involvement.

Finally, if the examiners ask you what else you would like to do to complete your examination, say:

'To complete my examination I would do a neurological examination of the legs[211], check the femoral pulses[212] and do an abdominal examination[213]. I would also check the ESR[214] and the AP and lateral thoracic and lumbar spine X-rays.'

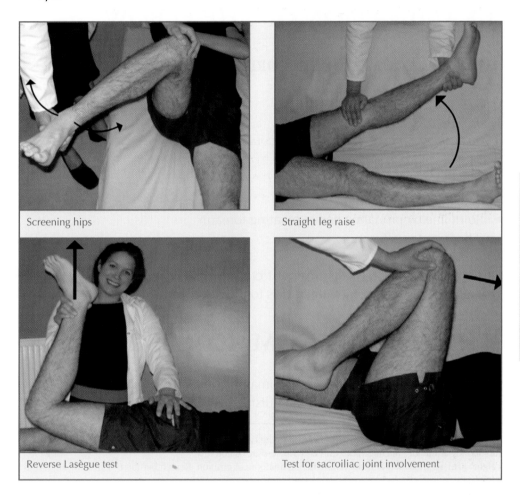

Screening hips

Straight leg raise

Reverse Lasègue test

Test for sacroiliac joint involvement

---

[211] See pg 365. Especially important are the ankle jerk (S1,2) or knee jerk (L3,4), power on dorsiflexion (L4,5) and plantar-flexion (S1,2) and sensation at the lateral border of the foot (S1).

[212] Back, buttock and leg pain can be claudication due to iliac artery stenosis, especially if exercise-related.

[213] Ensure no gross abdominal malignancy is causing the back pain by radiation (e.g. pancreatic), metastasis (e.g. prostate) or nerve involvement (e.g. colonic).

[214] Normal in prolapsed disc, mechanical back pain and Scheuermann's disease, but almost invariably elevated in ankylosing spondylitis, infections and neoplasms. False positives are common.

EXAMINATION OF THE OTHER JOINTS

If required to examine any joints other than those described in detail on previous pages, follow the principle of LOOK, FEEL then MOVE.

EXAMINATION OF THE ELBOW

WASH/GEL YOUR HANDS BEFORE TOUCHING THE PATIENT

LOOK
Valgus, varus, wasting, lumps, scars.
FEEL
Back and sides.
Warmth, nodules, synovium, fluid.
Palpate:
- Either side of olecranon
- Joint line by pronating and supinating forearm
- Ulnar nerve

MOVE
Flexion and extension (with arms outstretched, level with shoulders).
Pronation and supination (with elbows to the sides, flexed at 90°).

THE ELBOW – COMMON OSCE CASES

Cubitus varus or cubitus valgus[215], rheumatoid arthritis[216], osteoarthritis[217], tennis elbow[218], ulnar neuritis[219], olecranon bursitis (see pg 432), myositis ossificans[220].

---

[215] **Cubitus varus or valgus**: decrease or increase in the carrying angle of the elbow, commonly after supracondylar fracture in childhood. Can be corrected by osteotomy.
Valgus = **L**ateral deviation of distal limb when in anatomical position. Remember there is an **L** in va**l**gus and **l**ateral.

[216] **Rheumatoid arthritis**: may be unilateral or bilateral. Characteristic RA of hands is often present. Look for rheumatoid nodules. Arthroplasty may be considered if functional disablement is severe.

[217] **Osteoarthritis**: primary in manual labourers, commonly secondary to old fractures. May have loose bodies causing locking of the joint.

[218] **Tendonitis of the common extensor origin**: the commonest cause of elbow pain. Usually aged 35–50 years. Pain on lateral side of elbow, difficulty holding objects at arm's length. Ask about repetitive movements, e.g. sweeping, painting and decorating. Relieved by injections of steroid and local anaesthetic. **Common flexor origin tendonitis** on the medial side of the elbow (golfer's elbow) is less common.

[219] **Ulnar neuritis**: irritation of the ulnar nerve after trauma or due to excess mobility as the nerve slips repeatedly over the medial epicondyle. Can be anchored or transposed.

[220] **Myositis ossificans**: most commonly occurs after supracondylar fractures or dislocated elbow. Due to calcification in the haematoma of the brachialis muscle. Can also occur after inadequate immobilisation or aggressive passive physiotherapy. Leads to mechanical block to flexion. Treatment is prevention and delayed excision if necessary.

350

EXAMINATION OF THE ANKLE AND FOOT

WASH/GEL YOUR HANDS BEFORE TOUCHING THE PATIENT

LOOK

Standing

Legs, ankles, feet, arches, toes, obvious deformity.
Plantigrade foot (both heel and forefoot squarely on the floor), intoeing, genu valgum, flat foot, eversion, inversion, splaying, proportion.

Sitting

Heel: exostosis, bursitis, talipes, old fracture.
Dorsum: exostoses from 5th metacarpal head or base, cuneiform exostosis, dorsal ganglion – check dorsalis pedis pulse.
Big toe: hallux valgus, bunion, gout, hallux rigidus, hallux flexus. Callous underneath?
Toenails: onychogryphosis, subungual exostosis, fungal infection, psoriasis.
Toes: length, clawing, hammer-toe, mallet toe, quinti varus, corns.
Sole: hyperhidrosis, athlete's foot, ulcers, callus, verruca, plantar fasciitis.

FEEL

Tenderness: heel (Sever's disease, exostosis, fasciitis, bursitis, pes cavus), forefoot, medial malleolus (tarsal tunnel syndrome), big toe.
Joint crepitations.
Temperature.

MOVE

Ankle joint: *hold the shin still and grip the whole heel. Move the foot – there should be plantar-flexion (55° from right angle), dorsiflexion (15° from right angle).*
Subtalar joint: *hold the ankle still and grip the lower heel. Move the heel – there should be inversion (10°), eversion (20°).*
Forefoot (midtarsal and tarsometatarsal): *hold the heel still and grip the forefoot – there should be inversion (15°), eversion (10°).*
Now check plantar and dorsal flexion of the first, fifth and third metatarsophalangeal joints.
Finally get the patient to curl their toes then extend them.

LIGAMENTS OF THE ANKLE AND FOOT

There are three main ligaments round the ankle:
1. Lateral ligament from fibula to talus and calcaneus. *Feel for it below the lateral malleolus. Test for it by forcibly inverting the foot – if lax it will open up.*
2. Medial (deltoid) ligament from the tibia to the talus, navicular, calcaneus and spring ligament. Very strong, rarely torn without a fracture.
3. The inferior tibiofibular ligament. *Feel for it just above the joint line on the dorsal surface of the ankle between the fibula and tibia. Test for it by dorsiflexing the foot (will produce pain) and trying to move the talus laterally (will displace laterally if ligament is disrupted).*

THE ACHILLES TENDON

Palpate for a defect, then palpate while the patient plantar-flexes against resistance (or stands on tiptoes).

ANKLE AND FOOT – COMMON CASES

Ankle

Diastasis/unstable ankle[221], ruptured Achilles[222], shortened Achilles[223], tenosynovitis[224], pseudogout (see pg 411).

Forefoot

Pes cavus (see pg 446), gout (see pg 411), verrucas (see pg 69), march fracture[225], Freiberg's disease[226], anterior metatarsalgia[227], Morton's neuroma[228], rheumatoid arthritis[229], tarsal tunnel syndrome[230], hammer-toe[231], mallet toe[232].

---

[221] **Diastasis**: usually a result of fractures or ligamentous injury. The function of the ankle is reliant on the restoration of the mortice joint. If the lateral ligament is ruptured the talus can tilt in the mortice, leading to chronic instability. If the inferior ligament is damaged, lateral displacement of the fibula and lateral drift of the talus (diastasis) may result.

[222] **Ruptured Achilles' tendon**: this is disrupted as a result of sudden plantar-flexion and is commoner in a tendon weakened by degeneration in the middle-aged. Surgical repair or conservative management in plaster are often successful.

[223] **Shortened Achilles' tendon**: this results in plantar-flexion of the foot and clumsiness of gait as the heel fails to reach the ground. Usually associated with congenital or neurological deformities such as polio or club-foot, but can be secondary to ischaemic contracture or be idiopathic.

[224] **Tenosynovitis**: associated with unusual activities (e.g. dancing), flat foot, rheumatoid arthritis or degenerative changes, this inflammation causes pain and puffiness behind either malleolus. Tibialis posterior and peroneus longus are most commonly affected and may rupture. Treatment is rest in plaster.

[225] **March fracture**: this fracture of the second metatarsal occurs in young adults after unaccustomed activity. It can also affect the third and fourth metatarsals. It usually settles within 6 weeks of union of the fracture.

[226] **Freiberg's disease** is osteochondritis of the second metatarsal head. Palpable deformity and pain may eventually necessitate excision.

[227] **Anterior metatarsalgia**: this is pain under the metatarsal heads, often associated with splay foot (a widening of the foot at that level). It is the commonest cause of forefoot pain, although other causes should be excluded. It typically occurs in middle-aged women and is associated with obesity, prolonged standing, flattened medial longitudinal arches, weak intrinsic muscles, claw toes and callosities on the sole. Shoe inserts and chiropody are the first lines of treatment.

[228] **Morton's neuroma**: this is a plantar or digital neuroma commonly affecting the plantar nerve running between the third and fourth metatarsal heads to the third web space. Any of the other digital nerves can be affected, usually just before the bifurcation at the toe clefts. It causes piercing pain in the foot. It typically occurs in women aged 25–45 years and is treated by excision.

[229] Deformities seen in the **rheumatoid foot** include pes planus, splay foot, hallux valgus, claw toes, anterior metatarsalgia and hammer-toes. Surgical shoes with moulded insoles can alleviate symptoms. Fowler's arthroplasty of all the metatarsophalangeal joints and reconstruction of the metatarsal weight-bearing pad is a surgical option for severe cases.

[230] **Tarsal tunnel syndrome**: caused when the posterior tibial nerve is compressed beneath the flexor retinaculum, causing dysaesthesia in the sole of the foot and the toes. Flexor retinaculum division relieves tarsal tunnel syndrome.

[231] **Hammer-toe**: flexion deformity of the proximal interphalangeal joint causing dorsal callus. Chiropody or joint fusion remedies the situation. Can accompany hallux valgus in which case this should also be corrected.

[232] **Mallet toe**: flexion deformity of the distal interphalangeal joint. Can cause nail problems or callosities. Treatment is chiropody, joint fusion or amputation of distal phalanx.

Big toe

Ingrowing toenail (see pg 414), hallux valgus (see pg 408), hallux rigidus, bunion, gout (see pg 411).

Dorsal and medial side of the foot

Flat-foot[233], cuneiform exostoses (see pg 444)[234], Köhler's disease[235], osteoarthritis, rheumatoid arthritis.

Heel

Calcaneal exostosis (see pg 444), bursitis, plantar fasciitis[236].

In children

Club-foot[237], Sever's disease[238], intoeing[239].

---

[233] **Flat-foot** (pes planus) or the absence of the arches of the foot is normal in young children. It can persist in cases of knock-knees and deformities of the heel and tibia. Well-fitting shoes, supportive insoles and occasionally physiotherapy are normally all that are required. Peroneal (spastic) flat-foot is a painful condition typically seen in adolescent boys due to spasm of peroneal muscles. The foot is everted and fixed and gait is disturbed. It may be related to ossification of a congenital cartilaginous bar that can be excised. Incipient flat-foot in adults is a gradual flattening of the arches due to obesity, prolonged standing and degenerative changes. Secondary arthritis may occur. Weight loss, physiotherapy and arch supports are the mainstays of treatment.

[234] **Cuneiform exostoses**: these can all cause blisters, callosities and difficulty with shoe fitting and can be treated by local excision.

[235] **Köhler's disease**: osteochondritis of the navicular occurring in children aged 3–10 years. It is self-limiting.

[236] **Plantar fasciitis** is tearing of the calcaneal attachment of the plantar fascia. Usually occurs in the middle-aged due to degenerative changes. Treatment is heel supports, physiotherapy or steroid injections.

[237] **Talipes equinovarus (club-foot)** is the commonest major congenital foot deformity involving:
- Varus deformity of heel
- Adduction of forefoot
- Plantar-flexion
- Inversion

Treatment in order of severity of deformity may involve:
- Corrective stretching
- Splintage
- Corrective plasters
- Surgery to soft tissues (e.g. Achilles' tendon and plantar fascia)
- Wedge excision of bone and fusion of the midtarsal and subtalar joints.

Talipes calcaneus is a much rarer condition in which the dorsum of the foot lies against the shin.

[238] **Sever's disease** is chronic heel pain in children aged 6–12 years arising from the calcaneal epiphysis. Thought to be osteochondritis due to the pull of the Achilles' tendon. Settles spontaneously.

[239] **Intoeing** is internal rotation of feet in toddlers causing tripping and falling; usually corrects itself by the age of 6. Deformity of the tibia is a rare cause in persistent cases.

EXAMINATION OF THE WRIST

WASH/GEL YOUR HANDS BEFORE TOUCHING THE PATIENT

LOOK

Scars, deformity.

Swelling: diffuse, localised.

FEEL

Warmth, tenderness, bony landmarks.

MOVE

'Prayer' position (palms together) – dorsiflexion.

Backs of hands together – palmar-flexion.

Radial deviation.

Ulnar deviation.

Pronation.

Supination.

THE WRIST – SPECIAL TESTS

For de Quervain's tenosynovitis[240], Tinel's sign for carpal tunnel syndrome (see OSCE case pg 418), neurological examination of hand (see OSCE case pg 356).

THE WRIST – COMMON CASES

Ganglions (see OSCE case pg 428), carpal tunnel syndrome (see OSCE case pg 418), de Quervain's tenosynovitis[241], rheumatoid arthritis[242], carpometacarpal osteoarthritis of the thumb, complications of Colles' fracture (see OSCE case pg 436).

---

[240] **Finkelstein's test**: ask the patient to make a fist with the thumb tucked in under the fingers. Now steady the wrist and move the hand into ulnar deviation. This is very painful in de Quervain's tenosynovitis.
[241] **De Quervain's**: this is tenosynovitis involving abductor pollicis longus and extensor pollicis brevis. Occurs in the middle-aged and leads to localised tenderness and swelling on the lateral aspect of the radius (just proximal to the anatomical snuffbox). There is weakness of grip. Treatment is rest or splitting lateral wall of the fibrous tendon sheaths.
[242] **Rheumatoid arthritis**: common. Gross swelling, local heat, pain and stiffness. Hands usually have typical rheumatoid features (see OSCE case pg 400).

NEUROLOGICAL EXAMINATION OF THE UPPER LIMB

It is likely if you are asked to perform a neurological examination of the hand or arm in the limbs (including spine) station that the abnormality will either be an ulnar nerve palsy (see pg 422), a radial nerve palsy (see pg 424) or a median nerve palsy, with or without carpal tunnel syndrome (see pg 418). If it is immediately obvious which one it is, you should proceed with the appropriate examination. If it is not, you may need to do a more general neurological examination of the upper limb (see below); alternatively the instructions may ask you directly to 'examine this patient's ulnar/median/ radial nerve.'

Vague instructions such as 'Examine this patient's arms' test your flexibility – rise to the challenge! If nothing springs out at you and you have no idea which nerve or joint to examine, start off with a logical, general upper limb examination and if pathology becomes evident, move to a more specific examination as appropriate.

'Hello, I'm Dr Parchment Smith. Would you mind if I had a look at your arms? Could you take your shirt off please?'

WASH/GEL YOUR HANDS BEFORE YOU TOUCH THE PATIENT
Take a step back.
On general inspection look for obvious abnormalities regarding the patient himself, or his face[243] or neck[244].
To the patient:
'Put your arms out in front of you please? Lean forward so I can look at your back.'
Look to see whether the patient moves his arms easily and check there are no obvious deformities[245], scars, tremor, muscle wasting or swollen joints.
Let him sit back again.

---

[243] Look for asymmetry (hemiplegia), nystagmus (cerebellar problems), wasting (muscular dystrophy), ptosis, small pupil (Horner syndrome, syringomyelia).
[244] Enlarged lymph nodes or Pancoast's tumour (can invade brachial plexus), cervical spondylosis (common cause of arm neurology via cervical cord or nerve root compression).
[245] Look at:

Shoulders	Scars, winging of scapula, stiffness
Elbows	Psoriasis, rheumatoid nodules, scars over ulnar nerve
Hands	Tremor, swollen joints, pitting nails, clubbing, vasculitic lesions, claw hand
Muscles	Wasting, fasciculation, asymmetry

To the patient:

'I am now going to examine your arms. Are they painful or stiff anywhere sir?[246] **Relax your arm, sir, and let me move your hand.'**

You are testing for TONE.[247]

Next test for POWER.

To the patient:

'Put your elbows out to the side; don't let me push them down (deltoid, C5). Bend your elbows; don't let me pull them straight (biceps, C5, C6). Push against me; don't let me bend your elbows (triceps, C7). Squeeze my fingers (C8, T1, gross, functional test). Hold your fingers out straight; don't let me bend them down (radial nerve, C7 – finger extension). Make a fist and cock your wrists back. Don't let me pull your wrists forward or back (wrist extension, radial nerve C7). Spread your fingers; don't let me push them together (dorsal interossei – ulnar). Hold this piece of paper between your fingers, don't let me pull it out (palmar interossei, ulnar). Point your thumb to the ceiling; stop me pushing it down (abductor pollicis brevis- median nerve).'

Next test COORDINATION.

To the patient:

'Can you do this?'

Slowly pat the back of one hand with the palm of the other.

'Now flip your hand each time like this' (continue in the same rhythm, pat with the palm then the dorsum of the active hand in turn).[248] **'Now go faster. Try it with the other hand now. Touch my finger, then your nose. Do it faster. Now keep going as I move my finger… keep going. Now with the other hand.'**

To the examiners:

'I need a tendon hammer to check REFLEXES.'[249]

To the patient:

'Relax your hands on your lap, palms upward.'

Check biceps, triceps and supinator.[250]

---

[246] This is a gamble, but if you can't see anything obvious by now you need to go fishing without cheating. It is acceptable to check for pain before you touch the patient, and if you phrase it carefully you will seem considerate and may prompt the patient to say 'It's my arthritis in this left elbow', which will help you move on to a more targeted and appropriate examination.

[247] Take his hand as if you are going to shake it, and hold his elbow lightly in your other hand. Shake hand slowly and exaggeratedly, up and down and in gentle circles, moving whole arm forward and back at elbow simultaneously. Repeat with other hand to compare sides. Look for cogwheel rigidity (Parkinson's), increased tone/spasticity (upper motor lesion like CVA) reduced tone/flaccidity (lower motor lesion like plexus or nerve injury). Beware stiff joints or contractures in long-standing paralysis of any cause that may mimic increased tone.

[248] Inability to do this is dysdiadochokinesis – try to chant it as you pat your hand when demonstrating the test in practice to help you remember – dys-dia-do-cho-ki-ne-sis! The test highlights defects in cerebellar dysfunction.

[249] They should have a tendon hammer if it is appropriate for this examination. If not, don't insist – take the hint, it's probably meant to be a joint examination!

[250] Biceps – strike your own finger resting on patient's antecubital fossa (C5, C6).
Triceps – strike just above the back of the elbow (C7).
Supinator – strike your own finger resting on the base of the patient's thumb (C5, C6). These take practice to do impressively!

Next test SENSATION.[251]

To the patient:

'Close your eyes and tell me if you can feel me touch you here. Does it feel the same on the other side? Say yes when you feel me touch you.'

Stand up and say to the examiners:

'A full neurological examination includes JOINT POSITION[252] and VIBRATION SENSE[253]. To complete the examination of the arm I would like to check the range of movement of the neck, shoulder, elbow and wrist and check the pulses.'[254]

---

[251] Light touch and pinprick. Know your dermatomes or, alternatively, remember this list: neck (C3), collarbone (C4), shoulder (C5), at elbow laterally (C6), either side of the index finger (C6 radial side, C7 ulnar side), hypothenar eminence (C8), at elbow medially (T1), inner arm (T2), armpit (T3).

[252] It is unlikely that the examiners will want you to go this far, but it is part of a full neurological examination, so you should know how to do it. Hold the base of the thumb steady with one hand and, with the other, hold the sides of the terminal phalanx of the thumb. Moving it up, tell the patient 'this is up' and moving it down 'this is down'. Get the patient to close his eyes and tell you whether you are moving the thumb up or down.

[253] Similarly, vibration sense is rarely formally tested in a surgical exam, but in glove and stocking paraesthesia and peripheral neuropathies it is the first to go. Using a tuning fork, which they will have if needed, strike the tuning fork firmly to set it buzzing and place it on the patient's sternum or forehead. 'Can you feel that buzzing? Tell me if it feels the same here on your wrist.' If yes, vibration sense is intact. If not, move up to elbow then clavicle to determine a level.

[254] If still completely stuck at least you will have gone through a sensible examination of the limb as requested. If the neurology, joints and circulation are all normal, say so. If you have done a thorough examination the examiners will have to agree. Maybe the case is not a particularly suitable one for the OSCE, or the arms are normal. In any case you will have taken a sensible, professional approach as you would in clinic to exclude any significant pathology. So long as you can show off your examination skills do not despair! Few candidates would have been as impressive if the case really is that obscure. See examinations for individual joints (shoulder pg 338, elbow pg 350, neck pg 343) and for vascular examination of the upper limb (pg 377).

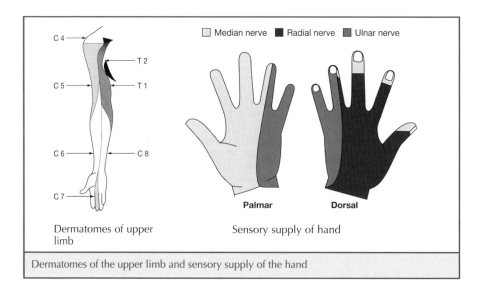

Dermatomes of the upper limb and sensory supply of the hand

EXAMINATION OF THE MEDIAN NERVE[255]

'Hello, my name is Dr Parchment Smith. Would you mind if I examined your hands? Would you roll up your sleeves and place your hands palm up on your lap/this table please?'

WASH/GEL YOUR HANDS BEFORE YOU TOUCH THE PATIENT

On INSPECTION look for thenar wasting and a simian thumb[256], decreased pulp of the index finger[257], cigarette burns or local trauma between the index and middle finger[258], wasting of the lateral aspect of the forearm[259], and the benediction sign[260].

To the patient:

'Can you stretch both arms out please?'

Look for cubitus valgus or varus indicating an old supracondylar fracture, and scars around the elbow, forearm and wrist.[261]

Next you should PALPATE the nerve where it is superficial.

To the patient:

'Can you bend your wrist pushing against me with your fist?[262] Is it tender? Do you feel any numbness or tingling in your hand when I feel it?[263]'

Next move on to test SENSATION.

To the patient:

'Can you feel me touch you here?[264] Here? Here? Does it feel the same as here on the other hand?'

---

[255] **For roots, course and branches see pg 420.**

[256] Due to wasting of the thenar eminence – Simian means 'like a monkey.' The thumb lies in the plane of the hand instead of at right angles to it.

[257] Due to denervation of the lateral two and a half fingers.

[258] Due to denervation.

[259] In high lesions.

[260] The benediction sign is the extended index finger (like that of a Benedictine monk giving a blessing) caused in high lesions of the median nerve. This is due to the paralysis of flexor digitorum profundus, which normally holds the index finger partially flexed at rest.

[261] Causes of damage to the median nerve see pg 420.

[262] The nerve lies superficially between the prominent tendons of flexor carpi radialis and palmaris longus (sometimes absent) which are easily seen on the palmar side of the wrist when the fist is flexed against resistance.

[263] Note: this is not the fixed flexion test for carpal tunnel syndrome (see later); they are only flexing the wrist to demonstrate the position of the tendons you need for landmarks.

[264] Use a pin if one is provided (gently!), otherwise touch lightly with your finger. Do not stroke over a large area, and do not poke too hard. Compare with the other hand if sensation is present but altered. The deficit is present on the radial side of the palm and thumb and the radial two and a half fingers on the palmar side and the radial two and a half fingers and the tip of the thumb on the dorsal side.

Then move on to test POWER.

To the patient:

'Lie your hand on the table, palm up please. I'm going to hold your wrist so you don't move your hand. Now lift your thumb up off the table to touch my finger.[265] **Push against it! Keep the rest of your hand still! Now, can I hold your thumb and ask you just to wiggle the tip of it?**[266] **Finally I'm going to hold your hand like a handshake. Now can you twist against my hand while I feel your forearm?'**[267]

Turn to the examiners:

'The patient shows signs of a high/low median nerve palsy. There is no evidence of the cause/it appears to be caused by…. (If a low lesion) I would like to carry out some of the tests for carpal tunnel syndrome if time allows.'[268]

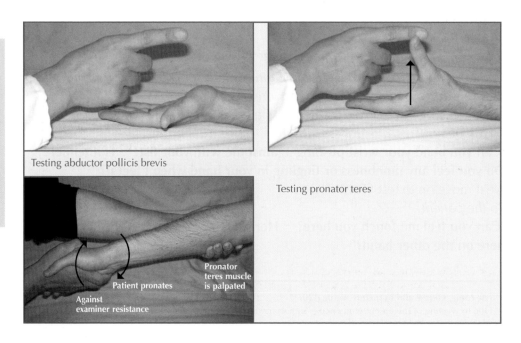

Testing abductor pollicis brevis

Testing pronator teres

Patient pronates

Pronator teres muscle is palpated

Against examiner resistance

---

[265] This tests abductor pollicis brevis, which is invariably and exclusively supplied by the median nerve. If you have time to do only one test for the median nerve, this is it. As the patient resists, feel for the muscle in the thenar eminence and compare it with the other side.

[266] To test for **flexor pollicis longus** (affected in lesions proximal to the wrist or in injuries to the anterior interosseous branch) immobilise the proximal phalangeal joint of the thumb and ask the patient to flex the distal interphalangeal joint.

[267] This tests for **pronator teres**. The patient extends the elbow, hand supine. You hold his hand and resist as he tries to pronate. Feel for contraction medially and just distal to the elbow (try it on a friend and identify pronator teres). Pain and tenderness over pronator teres is found in the pronator teres entrapment syndrome.

[268] **Diagnostic tests for carpal tunnel syndrome** (see pg 418) include:
- Fixed flexion
- Tourniquet test
- Nerve conduction tests (not a bedside test)

EXAMINATION OF THE ULNAR NERVE[269]

'Hello, my name is Dr Parchment Smith. Would you mind if I examined your hands? Would you roll up your sleeves and place your hands palm up on your lap/this table please?'

WASH/GEL YOUR HANDS BEFORE YOU TOUCH THE PATIENT

On INSPECTION look for a claw hand[270], ulceration of the skin[271], brittle nails[272], trophic changes. Also look for wasting of the hypothenar eminence[273], the dorsal first web space[274] and the medial forearm[275].
To the patient:
'Can you stretch both arms out please?'
Next look for cubitus valgus or varus indicating an old supracondylar fracture, and scars around the elbow, forearm and wrist.
Then move on to PALPATE the nerve, first at the elbow.
To the patient:
'Can you straighten and bend your elbow please?[276] Then at the wrist.[277] Is it tender? Do you feel any numbness or tingling in your hand when I feel it?'
Next test SENSATION.
To the patient:
'Can you feel me touch you here?[278] Here? Here? Does it feel the same as here on the other hand?'

---

[269] **For roots, course and branches see pg 421.**
[270] Due to flexed proximal interphalangeal (PIP) joints. If the distal interphalangeal (DIP) joints are also affected, it paradoxically suggests a more DISTAL lesion – the deformity is more marked when the flexor digitorum profundus is intact (the ulnar paradox).
[271] Due to unnoticed trauma on the desensitised medial skin of the dorsum and palm and the medial (ulnar) one and a half digits.
[272] Due to denervation.
[273] Due to denervation of the hypothenar muscles.
[274] Between thumb and index finger (see figure on pg 403) due to wasting of the interossei muscles.
[275] Lesions proximal to the wrist only, due to denervation of the flexor carpi ulnaris and the flexor digitorum profundus.
[276] The nerve is palpable in the groove of the medial epicondyle (test this on yourself). If it snaps over the medial epicondyle while the joint is moved this may indicate a traumatic ulnar neuritis caused by a deficiency in the tissues which normally anchor it.
[277] Just lateral to the flexor carpi ulnaris, which is visible on the medial palmar side of the wrist when the fist is flexed against resistance.
[278] Use a pin if one is provided (gently!); otherwise touch lightly with your finger. Do not stroke over a large area, and do not poke too hard. Compare with the other hand if sensation is present but altered. The deficit is most reliable on the ulnar side of the palm over the hypothenar eminence. There should also be loss of sensation over the ulnar one and a half fingers. Loss of sensation on the ulnar side of the dorsum of the hand indicates a lesion proximal to the wrist.

Next move on to test POWER.

To the patient:

'Hold your hand out. Palm down, fingers together please. I'm just going to slide this card between your index and middle fingers. Keep your fingers straight! Can you grip the card between those fingers and stop me pulling it out? Now between your middle and ring fingers... and finally between your ring and little fingers.'

This tests the interossei muscles. (See figure opposite.)

To the patient:

'Now put your hand, palm down, on the table. Can you push your index finger against my finger?'

You are testing abduction of the index finger, which relies on the first dorsal interosseus.

'Now push your little finger out against my finger.'

You are testing abduction of the little finger, which relies on the abductor digiti minimi.

Finally perform FROMENT'S TEST for adductor pollicis.

'Could you grab hold of this sheet of paper with your thumb on top of it, holding it against the side of your index finger? Now stop me pulling the paper away.'

If the adductor pollicis is denervated the thumb will flex at the interphalangeal joint using the thumb flexors to compensate (see figure opposite).

Turn to the examiners:

'The patient shows signs of an ulnar nerve palsy. There is no evidence of the cause/It appears to be caused by...[279] I could also test for flexor carpi ulnaris[280] and flexor digitorum profundus[281] which are both affected in a proximal lesion[282].'

---

[279] **For common causes of ulnar nerve palsy (distal to proximal) see pg 421.**

[280] **Test for FCU:** patient palmar-flexes fist against resistance and the tendon is palpated on the medial palmar side of the wrist. It also helps abduction of the straight little finger.

[281] **Test for FDP:** hold little finger PIP joint still and ask patient to flex DIP joint. Loss of power indicates lesion at or above the elbow.

[282] **Signs of a distal ulnar nerve lesion** (e.g. at wrist):
- Flexor carpi ulnaris intact
- Ulnar half of flexor digitorum profundus is intact (paradoxically worse claw hand)
- No muscle wasting of forearm
- Sensation of ulnar side of dorsum of hand intact

Signs of a proximal ulnar nerve lesion (e.g. at elbow):
- FCU affected (decreased abduction of little finger)
- Ulnar half of FDP affected (decreased flexion of DIP joint of little finger)
- Muscle wasting of medial forearm
- Sensation of ulnar side of dorsum of hand affected

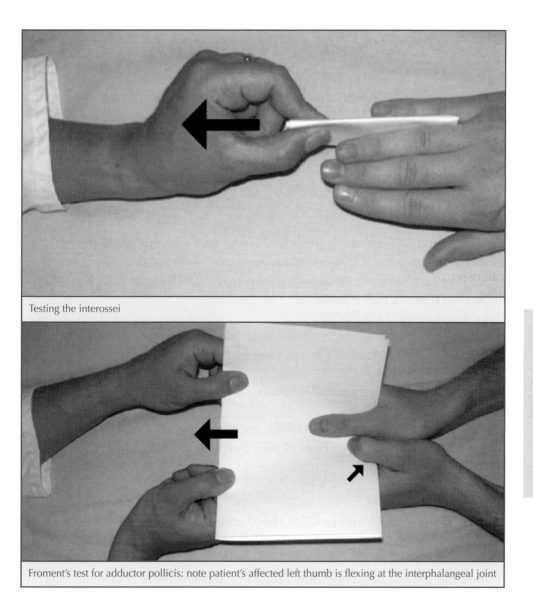

Testing the interossei

Froment's test for adductor pollicis: note patient's affected left thumb is flexing at the interphalangeal joint

'Hello, my name is Dr Parchment Smith. Would you mind if I examined your hands? Would you roll up your sleeves and stretch your arms out in front of you please?'

WASH/GEL YOUR HANDS BEFORE YOU TOUCH THE PATIENT

On INSPECTION look for wrist drop[284], forearm wasting[285] and triceps wasting[286]. Next test POWER.

To the patient:

'Can you bend your elbow in to your side and give me your hand, palm down? I will support your wrist. Can you extend your fingers? Straighten them. Don't let me push them down. Now make a fist. Try to cock the fist back. Don't let me pull it down.'

You are testing the EXTENSORS.[287]

'Now straighten your elbow. Can you turn your hand over? I'm going to hold your hand. Do it again, don't let me stop you.'

You are testing SUPINATOR.[288]

'Now with your fist in a neutral position, can you bend your elbow? Don't let me stop you.'

You are testing BRACHIORADIALIS.[289]

'Now try and straighten that bent elbow. Don't let me stop you.'

You are feeling for TRICEPS.[290]

Next move on to test SENSATION.

To the patient:

Can you feel me touch you here?[291] Here? Here? Does it feel the same as here on the other hand?'

To the examiners:

'I think this patient has a high/low radial nerve palsy. There is evidence that this may have been caused by....'[292]

---

[283] **For roots, course and branches see pg 424.**

[284] Due to loss of extensors.

[285] Due to loss of extensors, the muscle bulk of which is in the forearm.

[286] In high lesions.

[287] Extensors of wrist and fingers are weakened in radial nerve palsy.

[288] Testing **supinator**. Straighten the elbow to exclude biceps that also supinates. Loss of supinator suggests a lesion proximal to the exit of the supinator tunnel.

[289] Look at and feel **brachioradialis**. Loss of power suggests a lesion above the supinator tunnel.

[290] **Triceps** weakness suggests a lesion at mid-humeral level. Loss of all triceps activity suggests a high (plexus) lesion.

[291] Use a pin if one is provided (gently!); otherwise touch lightly with your finger. Do not stroke over a large area, and do not poke too hard. Compare with the other hand if sensation is present but altered. The deficit is present just over the anatomical snuffbox (the dorsum of the wrist on the radial side) in lesions distal to the elbow. Loss of sensation along the back of the forearm suggests a higher lesion.

[292] **Causes of damage of radial nerve see pg 424.**

NEUROLOGICAL EXAMINATION OF THE LOWER LIMB

'Hello, my name is Dr Parchment Smith. Do you mind if I examine your legs? Could you take your trousers off and sit with your legs stretched out straight ahead of you on the couch please?'

WASH/GEL YOUR HANDS BEFORE YOU TOUCH THE PATIENT

On general INSPECTION of the patient look for asymmetry[293], nystagmus[294], muscle wasting[295], fasciculation[296] and pes cavus[297].

Next examine the muscle TONE.

To the patient:

'Relax the legs please if you can.'

Roll each thigh gently from side to side (hip) and lift the knee a couple of inches and let it drop (knee). Note resistance, jerkiness, spasm or lack of tone.

Next move on to examine POWER.

To the patient:

'Lift the whole, straight leg up. Don't let me push it down (hip flexors, L2, L3). Now push your straight leg into the bed against my hand (hip extensors L4, L5). Bend your knee. Push it straight against resistance (knee extensors, L3, L4). Pull your heel in to your buttocks against my hand (knee flexors, L5, S1). Flex your foot, don't let me pull it down (tibialis anterior and long extensors of the toes, L4, L5). Now point your toe against my hand (calf muscles, S1, S2).'

---

[293] Typical of CVA (very common).

[294] Suggests cerebellar dysfunction.

[295] Typical of lower motor neurone lesions, but disuse atrophy will be evident even in upper motor lesions.
Typical patterns (old polio or infantile hemiplegia: unilateral muscle loss, one small leg):
Charcot–Marie–Tooth disease: muscle wasting stopping partway up leg (champagne bottle leg)
Diabetic amyotrophy: isolated anterior thigh
Polymyositis: generalised proximal wasting
Wasted hands indicate motor neurone disease, Charcot–Marie–Tooth disease and syringomyelia.

[296] Lower motor neurone problem, almost always motor neurone disease.

[297] High arched foot with clawed toes (Friedreich's ataxia, Charcot–Marie–Tooth disease).

Next examine COORDINATION.[298]

To the patient:

'Could you run your heel up and down your shin? Now the other side.'

To the examiners:

'Now to examine REFLEXES, could I have a tendon hammer please?'

To the patient:

'Relax as I do these if you can.'

First support the knee and tap just above tibial tuberosity (L3, L4). Then, bend the knee and let it fall to the side, gently dorsiflex the foot and tap the Achilles' tendon (L5, S1). Firmly dorsiflex foot in a sudden movement to try and elicit CLONUS (typical of an upper motor lesion). Scrape the lateral sole of the foot (gently, warn the patient: **'bit of a scratch'***) in an arc to elicit BABINSKI'S SIGN.*[299]

Move on to examine SENSATION.[300]

To the patient:

'Can you feel this pin as sharp on your foot? Does it feel different on the other side? Please say 'Now' when you feel the pin as I work my way up the leg. Next I'll repeat that with cotton wool.'

A complete examination should include vibration and proprioception.[301] *To examine VIBRATION use a tuning fork.*[302] *To examine PROPRIOCEPTION*[303] *ask the patient:*

'Please close your eyes. I'm going to hold your big toe still with one hand and just move the tip up or down with my other hand. Tell me if it's moving up or down… now… now… now.'

---

[298] Affected in cerebellar lesions.

[299] Normally the first movement of the great toe is plantar-flexion (the toe points down). If the toes go UP (dorsiflex) this is a positive test, indicating an upper motor neurone lesion, most commonly CVA.

[300] **Deficits in sensation and what they mean**:

Outer thigh (L2) Inner thigh (L3) Inner calf (L4) Outer calf (L5) Medial foot (L5) Lateral foot (S1).

Stocking distribution: peripheral neuropathy. Most common sensory defect (causes: idiopathic, diabetes, B12 deficiency in alcoholics, drug toxicity, Charcot–Marie–Tooth).

Front of thigh, medial calf and foot: femoral nerve (and saphenous nerve, its terminal branch). Also look for reduced knee jerk, wasted quadriceps, reduced hip flexion. Causes of injury usually indirect, e.g. iliacus muscle haematoma in haemophiliacs.

First web space, dorsum of foot and lower leg: common peroneal nerve. Also look for foot drop, abnormal gait. Causes of injury: trauma or pressure at fibular neck, compartment syndrome, ganglion.

Sole of foot: posterior tibial nerve or sciatic nerve. If posterior tibial nerve, look for clawing of toes, loss of toe flexion. Injuries caused by tibial fractures, compartment syndrome, trauma behind medial malleolus, tarsal tunnel syndrome. If sciatic nerve, look for extensive wasting and loss of power of hamstrings and all compartments of lower leg, drop foot and loss of sensation on the sole, dorsum and entire lateral aspect of the lower leg. Injuries caused by hip dislocation, hip surgery, pelvic fractures.

[301] The examiners may stop you there! However, you should know how to do these tests just in case!

[302] They will have a tuning fork if it is needed. Strike the tuning fork firmly to set it buzzing and place it on the patient's sternum or forehead. 'Can you feel that buzzing? Tell me if it feels the same here on your ankle.' If yes, vibration sense is intact. If not, move up to knee then iliac crest to determine a level. In most peripheral neuropathies vibration sense is the first to go.

[303] Explain to the patient what you mean by 'up' and 'down' before he closes his eyes. Hold the toe by the lateral aspects.

Finally I would like to see the patient WALK[304] and perform ROMBERG'S TEST[305].'

[304] If the examiners indicate or hint that you should examine the gait ask if the patient can walk without help. Then:

'Walk normally to that wall please and then back to us'

Wide-based gait – cerebellar ataxia.

Stiff 'walking through mud' gait – spastic paraplegia.

Stamping gait – sensory ataxia (should have positive Romberg's test also).

Stooped, hesitant shuffling gait with no arm swing – Parkinson's.

High-stepping gait – foot drop (e.g after peroneal nerve injury).

One leg stiff with semicircular swing and ipsilateral arm flexed – hemiplegia.

Lumbar lordosis, swaying trunk and waddling gait – Duchenne muscular dystrophy and proximal myopathy.

Broad-based 'walking on ice' gait – apraxia, senile degenerative disease (especially of frontal lobe).

'Walk in a line putting your heel to your toe like this' – exacerbates ataxia, which side do they fall to?

'Walk on tiptoes (S1). Now walk on your heels (L5).' – cannot do it in foot drop.

[305] Romberg's test. **'Stand with your feet together and your hands outstretched. Good. Now close your eyes.'** Positive if patient is more unsteady with eyes closed. Suggests ataxia, e.g. subacute combined degeneration, tabes dorsalis.

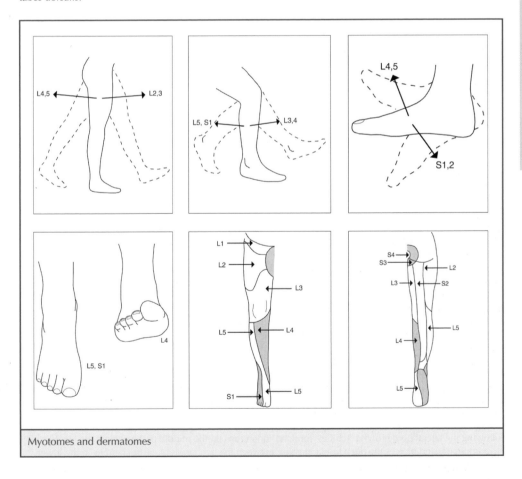

Myotomes and dermatomes

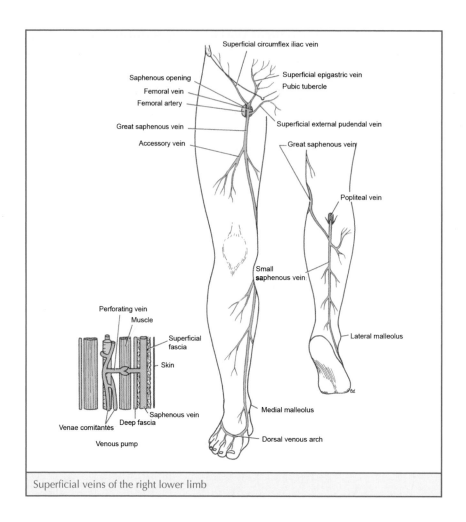

Superficial circumflex iliac vein

Saphenous opening

Femoral vein

Femoral artery

Great saphenous vein

Accessory vein

Superficial epigastric vein

Pubic tubercle

Superficial external pudendal vein

Great saphenous vein

Popliteal vein

Perforating vein

Muscle

Superficial fascia

Skin

Small saphenous vein

Lateral malleolus

Venae comitantes

Deep fascia

Saphenous vein

Venous pump

Medial malleolus

Dorsal venous arch

Superficial veins of the right lower limb

The course of the long (or great) saphenous vein is as follows: draining the medial end of the dorsal venous arch of the foot, the long saphenous vein passes directly in front of the medial malleolus (the best place for a cut-down or to start a vein harvest for cardiac surgery) and ascends with the saphenous nerve (of which you have to beware in vein harvest) in the superficial fascia over the medial side of the leg. It then passes behind the knee and curves forward around the medial side of the thigh. It passes through the lower part of the saphenous opening in the deep fascia and joins the femoral vein 4 cm below and lateral to the pubic tubercle. The tributaries of the long saphenous vein are shown above. The common sites where the superficial long saphenous vein communicates with the deep venous system via perforators are shown in the figure on pg 371.

The course of the short (or small) saphenous vein is as follows: draining the lateral part of the dorsal venous arch of the foot, the short saphenous vein ascends behind the lateral malleolus and runs with the sural nerve following the lateral border of the Achilles' tendon. It then runs up the middle of the back of the leg (like a stocking seam) and pierces the deep fascia, passing between the two heads of gastrocnemius in the lower part of the popliteal fossa. It drains into the popliteal vein, but an anatomical variant is seen where it (or a branch of it) joins the long saphenous vein. The tributaries of the short saphenous vein are shown above.

EXAMINATION OF VARICOSE VEINS

'Hello, my name is Dr Parchment Smith. Would you mind if I examined your legs? Could you stand up with your trousers off please?'[306]

WASH/GEL YOUR HANDS BEFORE TOUCHING THE PATIENT

Crouch down and LOOK at the legs systematically but briskly.[307]
On inspection you are looking for visible dilated or tortuous subcutaneous veins.[308] *Also look for venous stars*[309] *and any sign of venous insufficiency in the gaiter area*[310] *such as oedema*[311]*, haemosiderin deposition*[312]*, lipodermatosclerosis*[313]*, eczema*[314] *and ulceration*[315]*.*
'Turn around please.'
Have a look at the back of the legs.
'I'm just going to feel your veins and then press for a second on your ankle.'
Palpate any obvious varicose veins, then check for pitting oedema. Turn the patient back around to face you and palpate behind the medial border of the tibia for tender defects in the deep fascia.[316]

---

[306] On a platform or step if provided.

[307] Look from the feet up to the groin on both legs, concentrating on the gaiter area and the medial aspect of the leg, then turn the patient around and repeat the inspection from behind. The veins are often easier to feel than to see, and take a while to fill up, so if there are no obviously distended veins, start by pointing out the skin changes and then look for varicosities by gently feeling along the course of the long and short saphenous veins (see opposite).

[308] **See figures and footnote opposite.**

[309] These are tiny intradermal blue patches consisting of minute veins radiating from a single feeding vein.

[310] **Gaiter** *(n)* old fashioned leather covering for lower leg or ankle – the term 'gaiter area' refers to the lower medial one third of the leg and is the area typically first affected with visible skin changes in chronic venous insufficiency.

[311] Typically pitting, especially in the earlier stages.

[312] This is caused by the loss of red blood cells into the tissues, a consequence of raised venous pressure. ·

[313] A term given to the skin and subcutaneous tissue changes of chronic venous hypertension; a progressive sclerosis of the skin and subcutaneous fat by fibrin deposition, tissue death and scarring.

[314] Which can lead to ulceration.

[315] See pgs 457–459 for typical features of a venous ulcer.

[316] See figures on pg 371.

'Is it tender anywhere?'

You are looking for evidence of perforator incompetence.[317]

To the patient:

'Do you mind if I feel in the groins?'

Palpate the saphenofemoral junction just medial to the femoral pulse. Feel for the presence of a varix here.[318]

'Cough please.'

Can you feel a strong cough impulse suggesting an incompetent saphenofemoral junction?

To the patient:

'I'm just going to tap over this area and feel lower down.'

Rest a hand on the medial calf just below the knee and tap the saphena varix. Can you feel the tap impulse[319] distally, indicating incompetent valves below the saphenofemoral junction?

Next perform the TOURNIQUET TEST.[320]

To the patient:

'Could you lie down please? I'm going to lift your ankle gently and rest it on my shoulder.[321] Keep your leg straight if you can, please.'

Lift the leg, put the ankle on your shoulder and stroke the leg firmly.

---

[317] The sites of communication between the deep and superficial venous systems (see figure opposite) are often the areas where varicose veins start. With exercise, the pressure exerted upon the deep venous system by the calf pump can result in blood being forced out into the superficial system at these sites if the valves are incompetent, thus reducing the efficiency of venous drainage of the leg, increasing intravenous pressure (venous hypertension) and dilating the superficial system (varicose veins). Disconnecting the two systems at the site of these incompetent perforators will restore the calf pump to correct functioning only if the deep system is patent and has functioning valves. If the deep system is also incompetent, operating on the superficial veins will make the matter worse.

[318] A swelling over the saphenofemoral junction with a cough impulse indicates an incompetent valve at that junction between the deep and superficial system. When the intra-abdominal pressure is suddenly raised by a cough the pressure in the deep venous system increases as well, but normally functioning valves would protect the superficial venous system from expanding.

[319] Normally functioning valves prevent the backflow of blood down the vein, so a fluid wave would be interrupted at the first valve. This wave is transmitted down the leg if the valves are incompetent. This sign is in practice difficult to elicit and unreliable, and like many of the other tests in this traditional varicose vein examination, have been superseded in clinical practice by Doppler ultrasound testing (see pg 373).

[320] **Trendelenburg's test** is a version of the tourniquet test whereby the saphenofemoral junction is controlled by a finger placed firmly over it. It is notoriously unreliable as it is difficult to maintain complete occlusion of the junction with your finger while the patient struggles to her feet. Only the most sadistic of examiners would refuse to accept the tourniquet test as an alternative which works on the same principle. The principle is that if the superficial system does not fill then the varicosities are controlled at the level of the tourniquet (i.e. the saphenofemoral junction). Thus, disconnecting this junction would improve the varicosities. On the other hand, if the superficial system does fill, this indicates that the incompetence is occurring below the level of the tourniquet (usually one of the perforators), so disconnection of the saphenofemoral junction is not the whole answer.

[321] Although now replaced by Doppler in most modern clinics, examiners ask hapless candidates to perform this test time and time again. This is probably because, as you can imagine, it quickly sorts out the wheat from the chaff. It takes practice to do smoothly, professionally and elegantly. Try it on your flatmate today, and on three obese inpatients on your ward tomorrow. You will regret it in the exam if you don't!

'I'm just emptying your veins.'[322]

Put the tourniquet around the upper thigh.[323]

'Stand up please.'

Do the veins fill immediately?

If not, the varicosities are controlled at the level of the saphenofemoral junction.

If they do fill immediately the varicosities are not controlled at the level of the saphenofemoral junction, suggesting incompetence lower down.

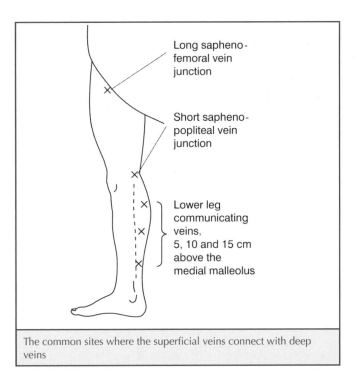

Long sapheno-
femoral vein
junction

Short sapheno-
popliteal vein
junction

Lower leg
communicating
veins,
5, 10 and 15 cm
above the
medial malleolus

The common sites where the superficial veins connect with deep veins

---

[322] The varicosities should collapse when the patient lies down and the veins are at the level of the heart. If they remain engorged, you should suspect an arteriovenous fistula or a physical obstruction to the venous drainage of the leg instead of varicose veins. Are the veins pulsatile? Is there a thrill or a bruit? Is there a pelvic or abdominal mass?

[323] This does not have to be up in the groin; two-thirds of the way between the knee and groin is fine as there are rarely important perforators below the saphenofemoral junction above the knee (see figure above).

Next perform PERTHES' TEST.[324]

'While I leave the tourniquet on, could you go up and down on tiptoes please?'

If the veins get better, the deep venous system appears to be functioning.

If the veins get worse and the patient develops severe discomfort there may be problems with the deep venous system.

---

[324] **Principles of Perthes' test**: you have controlled the varicose veins by blocking off the superficial venous system with the tourniquet. The venous drainage of the leg is now carried out exclusively by the deep venous system as it would if the patient had surgical disconnection of the saphenofemoral junction. By getting the patient to go up and down on her toes you are increasing arterial blood supply and activating the calf pump – the calf muscles are squeezing the blood out of the deep veins and encouraging venous return. If the deep veins are patent this will reduce venous engorgement of the limb. If the deep system is not patent or the valves are incompetent, the effect will be the opposite. With the deep system incapable of draining the leg and the superficial system temporarily disconnected, the increased blood supply into the exercising leg has nowhere to drain, and the patient will experience a bursting pain of venous engorgement. This test illustrates why it is so important to check the patency of the deep venous system before carrying out varicose vein surgery. If the presenting complaint of venous insufficiency and engorgement of superficial veins is secondary to a non-functioning deep venous system (for example, after a deep vein thrombosis) then stripping the superficial system on which the patient is relying will only make it worse. To avoid this:
1. Ask about a history of DVT.
2. Be suspicious of unilateral varicose veins or those in an unusual distribution.
3. Confirm by ultrasound the patency and competence of the deep venous system in any patients in whom doubt exists.

Stand and say to the examiners:

'The tourniquet test can be performed at different levels. A complete examination would include an abdominal and rectal examination[325] as well as Doppler ultrasound assessment[326].'

---

[325] Especially if the varicose veins have appeared suddenly. This may be a sign of venous obstruction in the abdomen or pelvis by a space-occupying lesion (e.g. ovarian or rectal carcinoma).

[326] This has now superseded the tourniquet test and Perthes' test in clinical practice and it is likely that over the next few years the examiners will increasingly ask for hand-held Doppler ultrasound examination to be performed. You must practice this before the exam – go to any vascular clinic and ask the consultant or registrar to watch you do it.

Doppler ultrasound test:

<u>Indications</u>: to detect venous reflux in long saphenous, short saphenous and calf communicating veins. Valuable in detecting saphenous and deep venous reflux.

<u>Procedure</u>: put some ultrasound jelly on the groin and on the hand-held Doppler probe. Locate the femoral artery with the probe (it will be audible) and move the probe a centimetre medially to it, over the saphenofemoral junction (this will not normally be audible). Still listening over that spot with the Doppler, squeeze the calf muscle of the same leg firmly with your other hand and let go immediately. This will squeeze some blood up the femoral vein, past the saphenofemoral junction into the common femoral vein. You will hear it WHOOSH past the junction as you listen. This will be followed by a short WOP sound as you let go the calf and the blood column falls back as far as the valve just beneath it, which stops it falling any further. If the saphenofemoral junction is incompetent, blood will not stop falling with a sharp WOP sound but will continue to leak through the incompetent valve back down into the leg, giving a long WHOOOP second sound. So WHOOSH-WOP = competent SFJ, WHOOSH-WHOOOP = incompetent SFJ. This can be repeated at any of the perforators.

In a second part to the test, you can ensure that the prolonged second sound is not due to leakage of blood back down the deep system. This would happen in the case of incompetent deep vein valves in a leg with, for example, previous DVT. Place a tourniquet round the upper thigh and repeat the test. If the long second sound WHOOOP is now shortened, it is the superficial system which has an incompetent valve, probably at the saphenofemoral junction, so surgical disconnection of the saphenofemoral junction would probably improve the situation. If the long second sound WHOOOP is still long, the blood must be leaking back through valves in the deep system, as you have occluded the superficial system with the tourniquet. In that case, operating on the superficial veins would worsen the situation.

Other venous investigations:

<u>Invasive ambulatory venous pressure measurement</u>

<u>Bipedal ascending phlebography</u>

Injecting non-ionic contrast media into foot veins with ankle tourniquets to direct ionic contrast into the deep system – a useful method of detecting post-thrombotic damage and also confirms the presence of incompetent calf communicating veins.

<u>Varicography</u>

Injection of surface veins with contrast (e.g. in previous surgery).

EXAMINATION OF THE ISCHAEMIC OR DIABETIC LEG

'Hello, my name is Dr Parchment Smith. Would you mind if I examined your leg? Could you lie down with your trousers and socks off please?'

WASH/GEL YOU HANDS BEFORE TOUCHING THE PATIENT

Stand back and LOOK.

On general inspection you are looking for signs of cardiovascular disease[327], cigarette smoking[328] or diabetes[329]. Look at the legs for pallor, guttering of the veins[330], discoloration[331] and ulcers[332].

To the patient:

'Is the leg painful?[333] Which one is worse?'

To the examiners: **'I will perform Buerger's test at the end of the examination and proceed now to PALPATION'** *or* **'As part of the inspection I would like to perform Buerger's test[334].'**

To perform Buerger's test, say to the patient:

'I am going to support your heel. Could you raise your leg slowly to 90° keeping your leg straight please? The foot should remain pink until 90°.[335] The second part of Buerger's test is if you sit up, swinging the legs over the edge of the bed. If the legs go engorged and purple, Buerger's test is positive.'

Crouch down and have a good, quick look at the feet while waiting for the colour change.

---

[327] Such as shortness of breath, sternotomy scars, nearby GTN spray.

[328] Such as nicotine-stained teeth, hair or fingers. The huge majority of patients with peripheral vascular disease are either diabetics or smokers.

[329] Features of diabetes in the leg and elsewhere (see pg 472).

[330] In a severely ischaemic foot the veins are collapsed and look like pale blue gutters in the subcutaneous tissue. In a normal circulation the veins never have time to empty fully because the arteries keep refilling them, even if the leg is elevated. Venous guttering on raising the leg 10–15° above the horizontal is a sign of significant ischaemia.

[331] The ischaemic leg is typically pale but a severely ischaemic leg can be red ('sunset foot') due to acute inflammation and cellulitis secondary to tissue ischaemia. Individual toes may show the purpley-black hue of a gangrenous digit; this may be hard, well demarcated and painless ('dry gangrene') or infected, soft and moist with surrounding painful cellulitic tissue ('wet gangrene').

[332] See pg 458 and pg 471.

[333] Pain at rest is an indication of severe (pregangrenous) ischaemia. Painful ischaemic ulcers might be present. Absence of pain in an obviously ulcerated leg is highly suggestive of diabetes, in which ischaemia often co-exists with a peripheral neuropathy.

[334] This should traditionally be done as part of 'inspection' but I advise you to omit this, proceed directly to PALPATION and leave the now outdated Buerger's test till the end of the examination.

[335] If the foot goes pale at 50° this indicates severe ischaemia; 25° indicates critical ischaemia.

In the meantime look at the pressure areas to check that there are no ulcers.[336]

'Now would you lie back down again?'

Next proceed to PALPATION.

Feel the temperature of the foot with the back of your hand.[337] *Is either side cooler? Assess capillary refill time by pressing the big toe with your finger and see how long the colour takes to return.*[338]

Next palpate the PULSES.[339]

'I'm just going to feel the main artery in your groin, sir.'[340]

Palpate both femoral pulses[341], *popliteal pulses*[342], *dorsalis pedis pulses*[343] *and posterior tibial pulses*[344]. *Finally palpate for an aortic aneurysm.*

'Can I just feel the artery in your tummy, sir. Now I'm going to listen. Just breathe normally.'

Get your stethoscope out to AUSCULTATE. Listen[345] *over the aorta*[346], *renal arteries, femoral arteries, and superficial femoral artery as it emerges from the adductor canal about two-thirds of the way down the thigh on the antero-medial aspect.*[347]

---

[336] Heel, malleoli, head of fifth metatarsal, tips of toes, between the toes and the ball of the foot are typical sites for ischaemic ulceration. In the diabetic foot, neuropathic ulcers on the soles of the feet may also be seen.

[337] This is traditional because the physician's palm is warm and moist (especially in exams!) and therefore not as sensitive to temperature differences as the cool, dry back of the hand.

[338] Two seconds is normal.

[339] In a diabetic, the pulses can be normal in a patient with ischaemic toes due to small-vessel disease. Alternatively they may be reduced, as diabetics are also predisposed to large-vessel disease.

[340] Warn the patient you are going to feel his groin! Personally, I usually start with the foot pulses and work up, but this is not traditional, and was questioned by the examiners when I did the exam, so I think it is safer to start with the femoral pulses and work down. Whichever you choose, have a justification and be prepared to switch rather than argue if the examiners insist.

[341] Halfway between the pubic symphysis and the anterior superior iliac spine (the mid-inguinal point – the femoral nerve lies lateral and the vein lies medial to it).

[342] The most difficult to feel reliably – try to feel it NOW on your flatmate/brother/mum or you will wish you had in your exam. Letting the knee relax and flex slightly, hold it with both hands and feel in the popliteal fossa with your fingers, keeping both thumbs on the tibial tuberosity. The pulse is usually lower than you think, and best felt against the posterior surface of the tibia below the joint line.

[343] Feel across the dorsum of the foot. The artery runs from a point midway between the malleoli to the cleft between the first and second metatarsal bones.

[344] The posterior tibial artery lies one third of the way between the tip of the medial malleolus and the point of the heel but can be more easily felt 2.5 cm higher, where it runs just behind the medial malleolus.

[345] With the small bell of the stethoscope, not pressing too hard.

[346] The aorta bifurcates at the level of the umbilicus.

[347] This is a common place for stenosis and it is gratifying to hear a bruit here in a leg with palpable femoral pulses but no pulses palpable distally.

Turn to the examiners:

'To complete the examination I would examine the rest of the vascular tree, especially the carotid arteries.[348] I would look for heart murmurs, atrial fibrillation[349] and check the blood pressure in both arms.[350] I would also perform a neurological examination on the legs.[351] Finally I would like to assess the ankle–brachial pressure index.'[352]

---

[348] Listening for a carotid bruit.

[349] Both sources of emboli which can cause acute severe ischaemia. In addition, patients with arteriopathies often have a history of ischaemic heart disease which can result in murmurs or AF.

[350] To exclude subclavian or innominate artery disease.

[351] See pg 365 Neurological examination of lower limb. Especially important in a diabetic, where you would expect glove and stocking anaesthesia and mononeuropathies affecting single nerves or trunks. A complete cardiovascular examination should include a full neurological examination including fundoscopy, as cerebrovascular disease in any area of the brain can result from arteriopathy.

[352] To do this you need a Doppler probe and a sphygmomanometer with a large enough cuff to encircle the patient's thigh. The patient lies supine. The brachial systolic blood pressure (i.e. the pressure at which the brachial pulse becomes inaudible when the cuff is inflated around the upper arm) is compared with the pressure at which the foot pulse becomes inaudible when the cuff is inflated around the thigh. The ankle–brachial pressure index (ABPI) is the ankle pressure expressed as a percentage of the brachial pressure. If the ankle pressure is greater than the brachial pressure the ABPI is greater than 1 and ischaemia is unlikely. If the ankle pressure is 70% or less of the brachial pressure, ischaemia is more likely and further investigations may be indicated. Note that ABPIs may appear to be greater than 1 in the presence of ischaemia if the large arteries of the legs are so calcified that inflation of the cuff fails to compress them. This is typical in diabetic large-vessel arteriopathy, so diabetic patients often have misleadingly high ABPIs even if they have significant ischaemia.

EXAMINATION OF THE ISCHAEMIC ARM

'Hello, my name is Dr Parchment Smith. Would you mind if I examined your arms? Could you sit with your top off please?'

WASH/GEL YOU HANDS BEFORE TOUCHING THE PATIENT

Stand back and LOOK.

Look for obvious signs of cardiovascular disease. Is the patient short of breath, overweight or cyanosed and are there signs of previous cardiac surgery?[353]

Take the hands.

On inspection of the hands look for cyanosis, nicotine staining[354], clubbing[355], vasculitic lesions[356], wasting of the pulp of the finger[357], skin changes, pallor or discoloration.

FEEL the temperature of the hands with the back of your own hands.

Do the hands feel warm and well perfused?

Next check the CAPILLARY REFILL.[358]

It is normal at less than 2 seconds.

Feel the radial PULSE.

Determine the rate and rhythm.[359]

---

[353] Such as a sternotomy wound. Look also for tell-tale hints like sugar-free drinks or a GTN spray on the bedside table.

[354] Heavy smokers are more prone to arterial disease and cardiac disease, which can cause emboli.

[355] Causes of clubbing which relate to an apparently ischaemic arm:
- Carcinoma of the bronchus may cause thoracic outlet syndrome or hypercoagulability.
- Cyanotic congenital heart disease can be a source of emboli.
- Thyrotoxicosis is a common cause of atrial fibrillation, which can be a source of emboli.
- Bacterial endocarditis can cause emboli resulting in splinter haemorrhages.

[356] In embolic disease, small-vessel disease or spasm (e.g. Raynaud's phenomenon), small scars or painful ischaemic ulcers may be seen, most often in the fingertips and nail beds. Repeated paronychia (infections around the nail) can occur and be slow to heal. Unilateral changes suggest emboli from a cardiac or subclavian source (e.g. in thoracic outlet syndrome). Bilateral changes suggest Raynaud's phenomenon.

[357] Repeated episodes of digital artery spasm or temporary blockage by emboli causes the fingers to become wasted, thin and pointed. This is most marked at the pulps. The hand becomes cold and the joints stiff. This can occur in peripheral atherosclerosis or in long-standing Raynaud's phenomenon.

[358] Do this by pressing on the patient's fingertip to blanch it, then count how long it takes for the colour to return. Normal is less than 2 seconds.

[359] Atrial fibrillation can cause emboli.

Raise the patients arm so the wrist is above the heart and feel the character of the pulse with the flat of the palm.

Assess whether the pulse is collapsing or not.[360]

Lower the hand. Feel the other radial pulse simultaneously for radio-radial delay.[361]

Next test for weakening of the pulse while stretching the thoracic inlet.

'I'm just going to pull on your arm while I feel the pulse ... and the other side.'

While feeling the pulse, put gentle traction on the shoulder by pulling the upper arm out from the body.[362]

Next perform ALLEN'S TEST.

'Could you make a fist please?'

Occlude both the patient's radial and ulnar arteries by pressing down on both pulses at the wrist with your thumbs.[363]

'Now open the palm.'

It will be white. *Let go of the thumb over the ulnar artery (keeping the pressure on the radial artery) and watch the palm pink up – it should take just a couple of seconds to start going pink. If the palm goes pink the ulnar artery should be patent.*

'Can we do that again please? Make a fist.'

Press on both arteries again.

'Now open your palm.'

Release the thumb over the radial artery only and watch the palm pink up. This means the radial artery looks patent.

Feel the brachial pulse.

---

[360] Suggesting aortic valve incompetence.

[361] Classically suggests aortic dissection.

[362] The pulse is diminished in certain positions in thoracic outlet syndrome (see pg 498). This includes traction on the shoulder. This is not diagnostic but if the pulse is not similarly obliterated on the asymptomatic side it raises suspicions. Another test is to ask the patient to turn his head towards the affected side, take a deep breath in and hold it. In thoracic outlet syndrome the scalenus anterior is most likely to obstruct the subclavian in this position, obliterating the radial pulse. The structures that can cause **thoracic outlet syndrome** include abnormal first rib, scalenus anterior, clavicle, scalenus medius, heads of the median nerve, transverse processes of cervical vertebrae, or pathological features such as a previous fractured clavicle or first rib, tumour or lymphadenopathy.

[363] Press on the pulses AFTER the patient has made a fist.

Say to the examiners:

'I would like to know the blood pressure in both arms.'

To the patient:

'Can I just feel for the pulse in your armpit? And now in your neck.'

Feel for the axillary, the subclavian and the carotid pulse on each side. Do the pulses feel normal and symmetrical?

Next feel for a CERVICAL RIB.[364] Then listen for a bruit in the carotid and subclavian arteries.

Listen over each in turn. Finally, stand up and say to the examiners:

'A complete examination would include a cardiovascular survey of the heart[365], the lower limb[366], and a neurological examination of the arm[367].'

---

[364] Very rarely felt on examination. There may be a fullness at the root of the neck behind the clavicular head of the sternocleidomastoid or a prominent subclavian artery pulse but it is usually not enough to justify a diagnosis. It is diagnosed on X-ray (see pg 500).

[365] See pg 183 because ischaemic heart disease (which can cause murmurs and arrhythmias which you would detect on examination) is a source of emboli.

[366] See pg 369, a commoner site than the upper limb for peripheral vascular disease, one would expect the legs to be affected in a patient with generalised arteriopathy.

[367] See pg 356 because some seemingly ischaemic symptoms can be neurological in origin. Also the two disorders can co-exist (e.g. in diabetics).

EXAMINATION OF AN ULCER

'Hello, my name is Dr Parchment Smith. Can I have a look at this please? Is it painful at all?'[368]

WASH/GEL YOU HANDS BEFORE TOUCHING THE PATIENT

Site[369]*: assess size of the ulcer*[370] *and the site.*
Look at and describe the shape, depth[371] *and edges*[372]*.*
Is it irregularly/regularly round in shape? How deep is the ulcer? Are the edges sharp or sloping?

---

[368] Whether the ulcer is painful is very useful information, as neuropathic ulcers and ulcers in people with diabetic neuropathy are typically painless, whereas venous or arterial ulcers are typically painful.

[369] Different ulcers have typical sites. The commonest ulcers are a venous ulcer (pg 457, typically on the medial side of the gaiter area), a neuropathic ulcer (pg 474, typically in an area susceptible to trauma such as the sole of the foot or the heel) and an ischaemic ulcer (pg 470, typically at the periphery of the limb or pressure areas).

[370] An ulcer is a defect or excavation of the surface. It applies not only to skin and epithelium, but the surface of any tissue or organ.

[371] Note the depth in mm or describe it in relation to the structures (e.g. superficial, through full thickness of skin, down to bone, down to tendon).

[372] Types of edge:

Flat sloping edge: a healing ulcer. Usually shallow. Typical of venous ulcer.

Punched out/vertical edge: follows rapid death and sloughing of a full thickness of skin without successful attempts at self-repair. Typical of neuropathic or vascular ulcers. Historically typical of syphilitic ulcer (now rare).

Undermined edge: when infection affects subcutaneous tissues more than the skin, e.g. pressure sores. Historically typical of tuberculous ulcer (now rare).

Rolled edge: develops when there is slow growth of tissue in the edge of an ulcer. Almost diagnostic of a basal cell carcinoma (see pg 130).

Everted or heaped edge: develops when tissue at the edge of the ulcer is growing quickly and spilling over the normal skin. Typical of a carcinoma.

Look at the base.[373]

Is it covered in healthy granulation tissue? Are there any sloughy areas? Is there any obvious discharge or visible tendons or bone?'[374]

Feel the surrounding tissues, feeling for foot pulses, observing capillary refill, looking for any signs of venous disease (see pg 458–459), ischaemia (see pg 466),diabetes (see pg 472), neuropathy (see pg 472).[375]

Diagnosis.

'My diagnosis is...'[376]

---

[373] The base or floor of an ulcer may look:

Healthy with pink granulation tissue (usually associated with shallow sloping edges and evidence of a margin of previously involved surrounding skin which is now healing).

Sloughy with green or yellow infected areas stuck to it. This is usually associated with a discharge and should be swabbed and treated with topical antibiotics if needed (rarely) and with a dressing which dissolves and lifts off the slough. Venous ulcers and pressure sores are commonly sloughy.

Necrotic with black or grey dead tissue – these will have to slough off, be lifted off with a suitable dressing or debrided before the ulcer can begin to heal. Vascular or neuropathic ulcers can have this appearance. Pressure sores often start off as necrotic areas.

Avascular with a pale, clean shiny base. This is usually associated with deep, punched-out edges and peripheral vascular disease. These ulcers are usually slow to heal and may need the circulation improving by angioplasty or surgery. Tissue loss like this is one of the indications for a peripheral bypass if angioplasty is not suitable and bypass is possible.

[374] Apart from demonstrating the depth of the ulcer, the significance of bone or tendon at the base of an ulcer is that this is not a suitable surface to apply a split skin graft onto, as there is no underlying blood supply.

[375] The vascular and neurological status of the surrounding skin is crucial in determining the type of ulcer, especially in a foot ulcer. The exceptions are an obvious malignant ulcer in another site, e.g. trunk or face, in which case the draining lymph nodes are much more important. In a foot ulcer, the very least that should be done is to feel for the foot pulses (see Examination of ischaemic leg, pg 374), look for any evidence of venous insufficiency (see Examination of varicose veins, pg 369) and check sensation (see Neurological examination of lower limb, pg 365).

[376] Common ulcers you will see in your exam: venous (see pg 457), ischaemic (see pg 470), diabetic/ neuropathic (see pg 474) or a mixture of these. Neoplastic ulcers, e.g. basal cell carcinoma (see pg 130), squamous cell carcinoma (see pg 134), malignant melanoma (see pg 138) and Marjolin's ulcer (see pg 137) should also be recognised. Less common exam cases include vasculitic ulcers (due to rheumatoid arthritis or scleroderma), syphilitic or tuberculous ulcers. Pyoderma gangrenosum, necrobiosis lipoidica and lymphangiosarcoma can also present as ulcers.

C THE OSCE CASES

HOW TO USE THIS SECTION

Common history or examination cases you might see in the exam appear in this section.

For each case, there will be given an example 'OSCE question' which you could expect to find outside a station in the examination. Following this is an example of how to present a 'typical patient' with this complaint. You can then use these examples to practise with friends/colleagues. One of you should be the 'candidate' and use the basic history and examination schemes to start you off. A second person should be the 'patient' and pretend to be the patient in the example given. A third person could be used as the 'examiner' to check that all the questions or examination steps from the basic schemes are completed. The 'candidate' can then present their findings at the end and have a guess at a differential diagnosis. At the end of the 'station' the 'examiner' can then use the 'What you should know' section to ask the 'candidate' some questions about the case. Try and time yourselves so you get an idea of how long 9 minutes is.

Following this are photograph/s of the condition in the 'What you should see' section so that if you don't get a chance to see a particular case in all those outpatient clinics you will be attending before the exam at least you will have an idea what it will look like!

Take a history from this gentleman with a painful right hip

(see pg 311)

OSTEOARTHRITIS OF THE HIP

'I would like to present Mr W, a 60-year-old retired gardener. He has had pain in his right hip for 2 years. It is getting more frequent and for the last 3 months he has been getting pain at night. He feels the pain in his right groin and it radiates down his right thigh to the knee. It is worst at the end of the day and gets better if he rests. He has also been getting increased stiffness and has to rely on his wife to put on his shoes and socks. He tells me that she is getting rather fed up with this! His GP has been prescribing him painkillers and he has a stick. However, he can only walk 50 yards to the corner shop, limited by pain. He cannot recall having any previous problems with his hip. He has no other medical problems. He takes no other medication and has no known allergies. He is a non-smoker. He lives with his wife in a bungalow.

I think this gentleman has primary osteoarthritis of his right hip. I would like to examine his hip to confirm my diagnosis.'

✎ WHAT YOU SHOULD KNOW

OA hip can develop in a relatively young adult as a sequel to congenital subluxation, Perthes' disease, coxa vara, acetabular deformities or injury. In the older patient it can also be secondary to rheumatoid arthritis (see pg 387, Rheumatoid arthritis of the hip), avascular necrosis or Paget's disease (see pg 441). When no underlying cause is present it is referred to as 'primary osteoarthritis'.

[377] **Symptoms** are long-standing groin pain radiating to the knee after activity. It may become constant and disturb sleep. Stiffness is initially after rest but it increases until putting on socks and shoes is difficult. Ask about previous injury, illness or surgery (see above).

[378] **Radiological findings include**: decreased joint space, sub-articular sclerosis, cyst formation and osteophytes.

Treatment is conservative (walking aids, analgesia, physiotherapy) and surgery (most commonly arthroplasty).

Examine this gentleman's right hip

(see pg 325)

OSTEOARTHRITIS OF THE HIP

'The right leg lies in external rotation and adduction with apparent shortening. Thomas' test reveals fixed flexion. Mild muscle wasting is detectable. The greater trochanter is somewhat high and posterior and deep pressure elicits mild tenderness. There is marked restriction of all hip movements but movement is painless within this limited range. There is an obvious limp and positive Trendelenburg test. I would like to ask the patient a few questions[377] and see the X-rays[378], but my diagnosis is osteoarthritis of the hip.'

◉ WHAT YOU SHOULD SEE

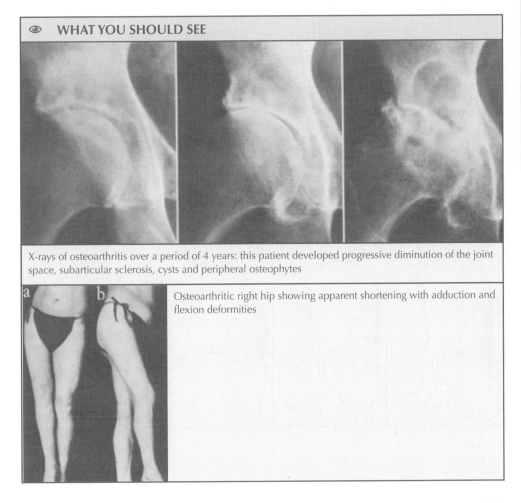

X-rays of osteoarthritis over a period of 4 years: this patient developed progressive diminution of the joint space, subarticular sclerosis, cysts and peripheral osteophytes

Osteoarthritic right hip showing apparent shortening with adduction and flexion deformities

👁 WHAT YOU SHOULD SEE

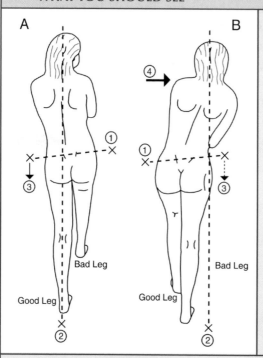

Trendelenburg test

A) **Normal (negative Trendelenburg test)** –
Hip is higher on the side of the lifted leg (1)
Centre of gravity is over supporting leg (2)
When standing on a healthy leg, the hip
abductors (gluteus medius and minimus) of
the supporting leg contract to pull the pelvis
down on that side (3). The pelvis is tilted so
the opposite hip is lifted (1) and the centre of
gravity is brought over the supporting leg (2) so
the patient can hold steady for 30 seconds.

B) **Abnormal (positive Trendelenburg test)** –
Hip is not higher on the side of the lifted leg
(1), or position cannot be held for 30 seconds.
When standing on the affected side, the hip
abductors of the supporting leg fail to pull the
pelvis down on that side (3). The opposite hip
cannot be lifted (1). Do not allow the patient's
upper body to tilt in compensation (4). The
centre of gravity will fall outside the supporting
leg if the opposite hip does not drop, so a
positive Trendelenburg's is either the opposite
hip falling below the horizontal (1) or the
patient is unable to hold the position.

Reasons for a positive Trendelenburg test:
1) Pain arising in the hip joint inhibiting the gluteal muscles
2) Gluteal paralysis or weakness from polio or a muscle wasting disease
3) Gluteal inefficiency from coxa vara
4) Gluteal inefficiency from congenital dislocation of the hip
5) False positive due to pain, generalised weakness, poor cooperation or bad balance (10% of patients)

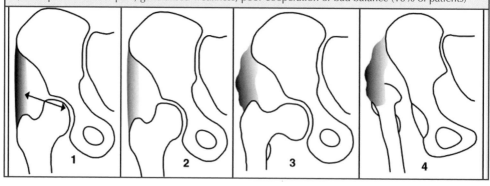

RHEUMATOID ARTHRITIS OF THE HIP

👁 WHAT YOU SHOULD SEE

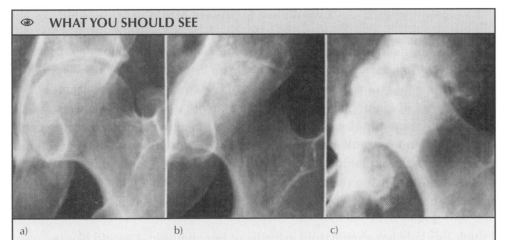

a)   b)   c)

Three stages in the development of rheumatoid arthritis:
a) Loss of joint space
b) Erosion of bone after cartilage has disappeared
c) Perforation of the acetabular floor – such marked destruction is more likely to occur if the patient is taking corticosteroids

Take a history from this lady with a painful right hip

(see pg 311)

RHEUMATOID ARTHRITIS OF THE HIP

'I would like to present Mrs W, a 60-year-old housewife. She has had rheumatoid arthritis for 15 years. Her main problem at present is her right hip. This has been gradually getting increasingly painful over the last 6 months. She feels the pain in her right groin, it does not radiate. It is worst on waking but does not wake her at night. She has begun to walk with a limp and uses a stick. She finds that her hip is particularly stiff at the beginning of the day. She can recall no previous problems with this hip. She has no other medical problems apart from the rheumatoid arthritis. She takes analgesia and a disease-modifying drug for the rheumatoid arthritis. She has no known allergies. She doesn't smoke or drink. She lives with her partner in a bungalow.

I think this lady has rheumatoid arthritis of her right hip. I would like to examine her hip to confirm my diagnosis.'

✎ WHAT YOU SHOULD KNOW

The hip joint is frequently affected by rheumatoid arthritis. The hallmark of the disease is progressive bone destruction on both sides of the joint without any reactive osteophyte formation. The patient complains of pain in the groin, which has come on insidiously, and a limp. When more severe, moving from sitting becomes difficult, and even movement in bed is painful.

[379]**X-rays**
Early RA: osteoporosis, loss of joint space.
Later RA: erosion of acetabulum and femoral head.
Severe: gross bone destruction. Perforation of acetabulum.

Treatment
Once cartilage and bone are eroded, no medical treatment will influence the progression to joint destruction.
Total hip replacement relieves pain and deformity and improves mobility. Even in young patients this tends to be undertaken as polyarthropathy limits activity so that the implants do not wear out rapidly.

Total hip replacement
Charnley low-friction arthroplasty: this or one of its variants is the most widely used replacement. This prosthesis comprises a socket of high-density polyethylene and a replacement femoral head of stainless steel. Both components are anchored with quick-setting acrylic cement. If a lateral approach is used, the greater trochanter is usually detached and replaced at the end of the operation with stainless steel wires.
Other replacements
NICE guidelines require surgeons to choose a design with 10-year follow-up and 90% survival.
Many variations: some need no cement, some are modular designs where there is a separate interchangeable head, stem, cup, which allows adjustment.
Hip re-surfacing – the patient's femoral head and acetabulum are resurfaced with metal caps.
Ceramic femoral heads – may last longer and are therefore often used in younger patients.
Hemiarthroplasty
Where functional requirements are not expected to be very high (e.g. after intracapsular hip fractures in the very elderly) the femoral head is replaced with a stemmed prosthesis and the acetabulum is not replaced.

Examine this
lady's right hip

(see pg 325)

RHEUMATOID ARTHRITIS OF THE HIP

'This lady (with extensive rheumatoid disease affecting many joints) has a painful right hip. The buttock and thigh are markedly wasted, with the limb held in external rotation and fixed flexion. All movements are restricted and painful. The diagnosis is rheumatoid arthritis of the hip. I would like to see the X-rays[379] of this patient.'

✍ WHAT YOU SHOULD KNOW (CONT)

Surgical approaches to the hip
The direct lateral and posterior approach are used most frequently.

Direct lateral approach
Lateral incision over the greater trochanter in line with the femur. Fascia lata is incised and split. The anterior tendon of gluteus medius and vastus lateralis is divided. The cut edge of gluteus medius and vastus lateralis is lifted anteriorly to reveal the anterior joint capsule.

Posterior approach
Lateral incision over the greater trochanter in line with the femur. Fascia lata is incised and split. This approach involves splitting of the middle of gluteus maximus in the line of its fibres. Piriformis, obturator internus and the gemelli are divided at their femoral attachments to expose the joint. The sciatic nerve is retracted medially and protected by turning the cut ends of obturator internus and gemelli backwards over the nerve.

Anterior approach
Through the interval between sartorius and tensor fascia lata, detaching the tensor fascia lata, rectus femoris, anterior parts of gluteus medius and iliacus from the hip so that upper and anterior parts of the joint capsule can be accessed. Structures to avoid: lateral femoral cutaneous nerve, femoral nerve, ascending branch of lateral femoral circumflex artery.

Anterolateral approach
Between tensor fascia lata and gluteus medius. It involves partial or complete detachment of some or all of the abductor mechanism so that the hip can be abducted during reaming of the femoral shaft and so that the acetabulum can be more fully exposed. Beware of the femoral nerve as it is the most laterally placed structure in the neurovascular bundle in the femoral triangle, mostly compression neuropraxia from misplaced retraction results. The femoral artery and vein are at risk from retractors that penetrate iliopsoas. Beware of the ascending branches of the lateral circumflex femoral vessels which are deep to the tensor and gluteus medius.

Post-operative complications
Dislocation: stability depends on 1) initial alignment, 2) time since surgery – gets progressively more stable, 3) degree of use/violence of trauma. Treatment is closed or open reduction, revision in severe cases.

Component failure: socket failure is rare, but the stem of the femoral prosthesis can fracture. Risk is increased in overweight patient or varus alignment. The wires around the greater trochanter may break, or the trochanter itself may fail to unite, causing local discomfort and a Trendelenburg gait.

Component loosening and infection: this usually occurs at the interface of cement and bone in the area of the femoral stem. The loosening is seen on X-ray and is usually due to infection, although often no causative organism is identified. Revision procedures are fraught and necessitate thorough debridement under antibiotic cover and reinsertion of a fresh prosthesis specially designed to accommodate migration or loss of bone stock. Antibiotic-loaded cement may also be used, but in some cases the prosthesis has to be removed altogether with disastrous results for the patient's mobility.

Take a history from this lady with a painful right hip

(see pg 311)

FRACTURED NECK OF FEMUR

'I would like to present Mrs W, an 80-year-old retired nurse. She was admitted to hospital 1 week ago following a trip and fall. She was unable to get up after the fall and had severe right hip pain. She was operated on the next day. Her previous history includes a fractured wrist 6 months ago which was treated conservatively. She was told following this that she has osteoporosis. She also has hypertension. She takes an antihypertensive drug, along with vitamin D and calcium supplements. She has no allergies to any medications. She is an ex-smoker of 20 pack years. She does not drink. She lived alone prior to admission but has decided to move into a residential home on discharge.

I think this lady with osteoporosis fractured her right neck of femur which has been fixed during her admission. I would like to see her X-rays to confirm my diagnosis.'

✎ WHAT YOU SHOULD KNOW

Two types of fracture:
1. Intracapsular fracture see figure (a) on pg 392.
Subcapital, cervical or basal.
Disrupt blood supply from diaphysis and risk retinacular blood supply so high risk of avascular necrosis.
Classified Garden's stage I – IV (see figure on pg 392)
<u>Management</u>:
Undisplaced (Garden I and II): internal fixation (2–3 screws).
Displaced (Garden III and IV): hemiarthroplasty (e.g. Austin Moore or Thompson), ORIF in younger patients.
2. Extracapsular fracture see figure (c) on pg 393.
Can be: intertrochanteric, basal or subtrochanteric.
Classification based on number of fragments provided by fracture (e.g. two-part, three-part, four-part).
<u>Management</u>:
Intertrochanteric and basal fractures: dynamic hip screw (DHS) – closed reduction using traction on fracture table. The screw is inserted into the neck and head and can slide in the barrel of the plate, which is attached to the femoral shaft. Intramedullary fixation device is an alternative.
Subtrochanteric fractures: ORIF.

Examine this
lady's hips

(see pg 325)

FRACTURED
NECK OF FEMUR

'There is (in this elderly lady) a scar over the right
hip. The right leg is shortened and externally rotated
with marked loss of range of movement at the hip. This patient has had a
fractured neck of femur and has secondary osteoarthritis. I would like to see
her X-rays.'

✐ WHAT YOU SHOULD KNOW (CONT)

Complications of fractured neck of femur surgery
Usually elderly and frail patients, so mortality is 14–36% at 1 year. Complications include infection,
dislocation, femoral screws loosening, acetabular erosion, non-union, osteoarthritis, avascular necrosis.
Avascular necrosis following fractured neck of femur
There is a high incidence of avascular necrosis of the femoral head in Garden III or IV fractures due to
the disruption of the nutrient artery in the shaft and the retinacular vessels in the capsule leaving only
the vessel in the ligamentum teres which might not be sufficient to prevent ischaemia of the femoral
head (see figure on pg 393). The bone dies and eventually collapses, with distortion of the femoral head
and irreversible damage to the joint. This causes pain and loss of function. The treatment is total joint
replacement. Other causes of avascular necrosis of the femoral head include Perthes' disease, dislocation
of the hip and slipped upper femoral epiphysis.
Other femoral injuries
Adolescents: slipped upper femoral epiphysis.
Adults: hip dislocation as opposed to fracture.
Elderly: fractured neck of femur.
These will reveal the operation she has had (see figure overleaf) and might reveal avascular necrosis
(see pg 393).

👁 WHAT YOU SHOULD SEE

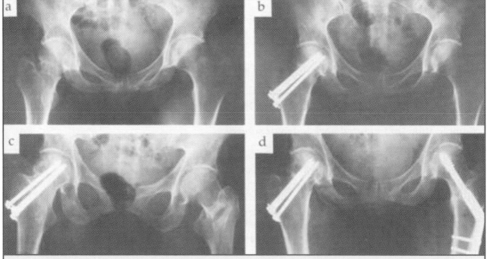

Garden's classification of femoral neck fractures (intracapsular)

a) Stage I: incomplete (so-called abducted or impacted)

b) Stage II: complete without displacement

c) Stage III: complete with partial displacement – fragments still connected by posterior retinacular attachment; the femoral trabeculae are malaligned

d) Stage IV: complete with full displacement – the proximal fragment is free and lies correctly in the acetabulum so that the trabeculae appear normally aligned

This elderly woman was osteoporotic but otherwise well, until she stumbled and fractured the right femoral neck (a). The fracture was fixed with three long screws (b) and united soundly. Then, a year later, she tripped and sustained an intertrochanteric fracture on the left side (c). This needed more extensive fixation – a large screw fitted to a plate attached to the femoral shaft (d).

FRACTURED NECK OF FEMUR

👁 WHAT YOU SHOULD SEE

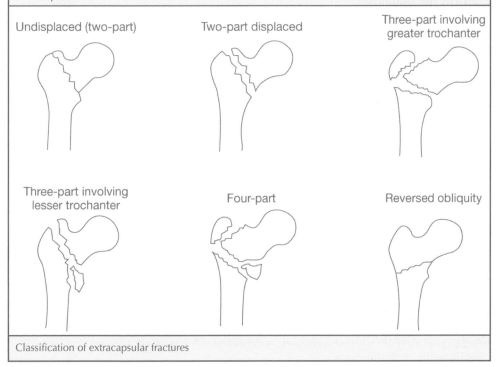

(a) The blood supply to the femoral head comes from (1) a vessel in the ligamentum teres, (2) the retinacular vessels and (3) the nutrient artery. Fracture of the femoral neck interrupts at least one source of supply and can seriously compromise the others. Even an impacted fracture (b), if it is displaced in marked valgus, can lead to avascular necrosis. Avascular necrosis as a result of femoral neck fracture (extracapsular) (c)

Undisplaced (two-part)

Two-part displaced

Three-part involving greater trochanter

Three-part involving lesser trochanter

Four-part

Reversed obliquity

Classification of extracapsular fractures

393

Take a history
from this man
with a painful
right knee

(see pg 311)

OSTEOARTHRITIS OF THE KNEE

'I would like to present Mr W, a 70-year-old retired accountant. He has had 6 months of worsening right knee pain. It is worse after use, especially after climbing stairs. He has no pain at night. He also complains of bilateral hip pain but this is not as severe. He finds his knee stiffens up if he rests it. It occasionally swells but has never given way or locked. He gives a history of a footballing injury affecting that knee 20 years ago but can't recall the details. His previous medical history includes asthma and a TURP 2 years ago; he had no problems with the general anaesthetic. He takes a salbutamol inhaler as required. He can't take NSAIDs as they have given him severe heartburn in the past. He is a non-smoker and teetotaller. He lives in a fourth floor flat with his wife.

I think this gentleman has osteoarthritis of the right knee, possibly secondary to his previous injury. I would like to examine him and see his X-rays to confirm the diagnosis.'

✎ WHAT YOU SHOULD KNOW

Symptoms: are pain after use (especially up stairs), stiffness after rest, swelling, giving way and locking. Hip and back can typically also be affected. There may be a history of past trauma and operations. [380] Soft-tissue calcification in the suprapatellar region or in the joint itself.
[381] **Treatment**:
Conservative: especially quadriceps exercises, analgesia and walking aids.
Joint injections: steroid injections.
Surgery: realignment osteotomy of tibia (in younger patients with only one compartment affected).
Arthroplasty: can be uni-compartmental, patella-femoral replacement or whole tibiofemoral articulation replacement. This is considered when conservative management has failed and the pain, stiffness and immobility affect the patient's quality of life.

Examine this patient's right knee

(see pg 329)

OSTEOARTHRITIS OF THE KNEE

'There is an obvious deformity/scar of a previous operation (secondary osteoarthritis). There is swelling and deformity of the knee joints with development of varus (or valgus) deformity. There is wasting and weakness of the quadriceps. The presence of osteophytes distinguishes this from rheumatoid arthritis. There is little effusion and no warmth (except during an exacerbation). The synovial membrane is not thickened. Range of movement is reduced and there is crepitus in the knee. Pressure on the patella elicits pain. On a weight-bearing X-ray I would expect to see diminished tibiofemoral joint space (often only in one compartment), subchondral sclerosis, osteophytes and chondrocalcinosis.[380] This patient has osteoarthritis of the right knee.'[381]

👁 WHAT YOU SHOULD SEE

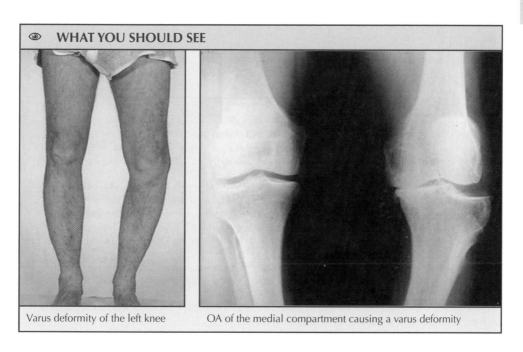

Varus deformity of the left knee | OA of the medial compartment causing a varus deformity

Take a history
from this lady
with a painful
right knee

(see pg 311)

RHEUMATOID ARTHRITIS OF THE KNEE

'I would like to present Mrs W, a 60-year-old housewife. She has had rheumatoid arthritis for 15 years. Her main problem at present is bilateral knee pain, the right being worse than the left. This has been gradually getting increasingly painful over the last 6 months. The pain is worst on waking and the pain in her right knee wakes her at night. She has begun to walk with a limp and uses a stick. She finds that her knees are particularly stiff at the beginning of the day. She can recall no previous problems with her knees. Her knees occasionally swell but have never given way or locked. Neither knee is currently red or hot she tells me.[382] She has no other medical problems apart from the rheumatoid arthritis. She takes analgesia and a disease-modifying drug for the rheumatoid arthritis. She has no known allergies. She doesn't smoke or drink. She lives with her partner in a bungalow.

I think this lady has rheumatoid arthritis of her knees, the right being more advanced than the left. I would like to examine her knees and see her X-rays to confirm my diagnosis.'

✏ WHAT YOU SHOULD KNOW

Occasionally, rheumatoid arthritis starts in the knee as a chronic monoarticular synovitis but is more often part of a polyarthropathy. An elderly patient with 'burnt out' chronic rheumatoid disease (case 1) is far more likely to be found for the OSCE examination than someone with an acute synovitis or flare-up of their monoarthritis (case 2). Treatment of the acute flare-up involves systemic medication (e.g. non-steroidal anti-inflammatory drugs, steroids, immunosuppressants), local splintage and steroid injections with synovectomy reserved for severe or resistant cases. Treatment of the chronic disability depends on the degree of deformity, disability and loss of cartilage and bone. If changes are detected early an arthroscopic synovectomy can be considered, but joint replacement is advised once the joint is unstable.

[382] These factors determine whether the patient has an acute flare-up (see case 2) or quiescent arthritis. The latter is more likely to come to the OSCE.

[383] Show periarticular osteoporosis, loss of joint space, marginal erosions and an absence of osteophytes, distinguishing it from the sclerotic picture of osteoarthritis, in which osteophytes are a characteristic feature.

[384] It is possible to develop OA of the knee secondary to joint disease of the hip or ankle or previous trauma or surgery that put abnormal stresses on the joint.

Examine this lady's right knee

(see pg 329)

RHEUMATOID ARTHRITIS OF THE KNEE

Case 1

'The patient has extensive rheumatoid disease affecting many joints, most obviously in her hands (and say where else). She has wasting of the quadriceps and painless restriction of the knee joint. There is no effusion or thickened synovium palpable, and the joint is not red or hot.[382] There is valgus/varus and fixed flexion deformities and instability of the joint. The diagnosis is chronic rheumatoid arthritis. I would like to see her weight-bearing X-rays,[383] which would exclude osteoarthritis secondary to rheumatoid disease elsewhere (e.g. the hip).'[384]

Case 2

Alternatively (but not as likely in the OSCE):
'The patient (who may or may not have signs of rheumatic disease in other joints) has a painful, warm, swollen knee with a large effusion and a thickened synovium easily palpable. Movement and mobility are restricted by pain. The diagnosis is acute rheumatoid arthritis of the knee but septic arthritis and gout (see pg 411) should be excluded by careful history and aspiration if necessary.'

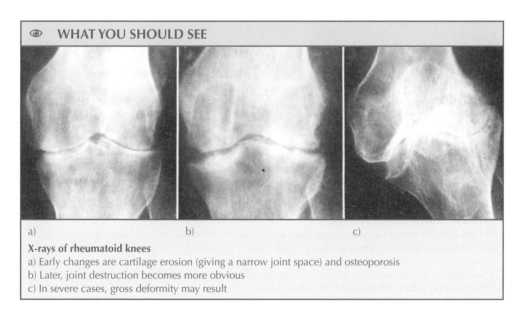

👁 **WHAT YOU SHOULD SEE**

a)   b)   c)

X-rays of rheumatoid knees
a) Early changes are cartilage erosion (giving a narrow joint space) and osteoporosis
b) Later, joint destruction becomes more obvious
c) In severe cases, gross deformity may result

Take a history from this man who has a problem with his hands

(see pg 311)

DUPUYTREN'S CONTRACTURE

'I would like to present Mr W, a 40-year-old farm labourer. He has gradually developed painless bilateral contractures of his ring fingers.[385] He is finding that it has begun to affect his ability to do his job. He tells me his father had the same problem and ended up requiring operative intervention.[386] He has no contractures of his feet or other areas.[387/388] He has no other medical problems, in particular he has had no significant trauma to his hands or diabetes which can be associated with this condition.[389] He takes no regular medications and has no known drug allergies. He doesn't smoke or drink. He lives alone.

I think this gentleman has familial Dupuytren's contracture. I would like to examine his hands to confirm my diagnosis.'

📄 WHAT YOU SHOULD KNOW

Definition: nodular hypertrophy and contracture of the palmar aponeurosis.

Causes:
- Idiopathic
- Familial (autosomal dominant)
- Alcoholic liver disease
- Trauma
- Manual labour
- Drugs (e.g. phenobarbital)
- Diabetes
- AIDS
- Peyronie's disease

Epidemiology: 5%, usually middle-aged men.

Differential diagnosis: skin contractures secondary to burns or scarring; tendon contracture (thickened cord moves on passive flexion of the finger).

Treatment (surgery): careful dissection and excision of the thickened part of the aponeurosis. 'Zed-plasty' is often needed to lengthen the wound and permit adequate skin closure. Post-operative splinting and physiotherapy are important. Recurrence can occur in progressive cases.

[385] Most commonly affects the ring finger.
[386] Familial trait is the main association.
[387] Can affect the plantar aponeurosis.
[388] Fibrosis of the corpus cavernosum causing curvature of the penis may be associated with Dupuytren's. The examiners are unlikely to expect you to confirm this so choose a tactful way of telling them you know about the association!
[389] Alcoholism is associated with Dupuytren's and can produce a large fatty liver.
[390] The knuckle pads of the hands are often thickened.

Examine this gentleman's hands

(see pg 336)

DUPUYTREN'S CONTRACTURE

'There is a painless, bilateral (or unilateral) nodular thickening of the palm, especially on the ulnar side, extending distally to involve the ring/little finger. It is causing a fixed flexion deformity of the little (+/– ring) finger(s) at the metacarpophalangeal (+/– proximal interphalangeal) joints. There is evidence of previous surgery over this area/on the other palm. This is Dupuytren's contracture.'

Common examiner's question: 'What else would you like to examine?'
Answer: **'The soles of the feet[387], the liver[389], the dorsal knuckle pads.[390] Dupuytren's is also associated with Peyronie's disease.'[388]**

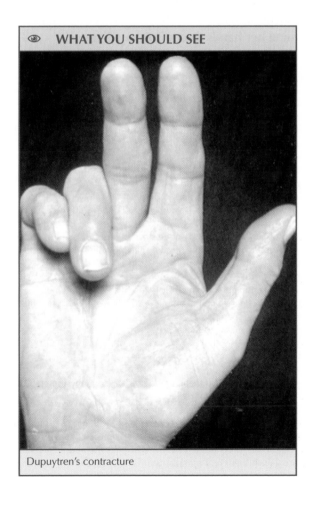

👁 **WHAT YOU SHOULD SEE**

Dupuytren's contracture

Take a history from this lady who has a problem with her hands

(see pg 311)

RHEUMATOID ARTHRITIS OF THE HANDS

'I would like to present Mrs W, a 60-year-old housewife. She has recently been diagnosed with rheumatoid arthritis. She initially noticed her hands were warm and moist.[391] She has subsequently developed swelling and pain bilaterally in some of the joints (she points to her MCP and PIP joints).[392] She has not noticed any deformity of her hands. She finds it difficult to perform some tasks such as writing or doing up buttons due to pain. She has no concerns about any of her other joints or history of trauma. She has no other medical problems. She is only taking simple analgesia currently and is awaiting an appointment with the physiotherapist. She has no known drug allergies. She doesn't smoke or drink. He lives with her husband and 30-year-old son with learning difficulties for whom she is the main carer. She has found this difficult lately. I think this lady has rheumatoid arthritis of her hands but has not yet developed deformities. I would like to examine her hands to confirm my diagnosis.'

✎ WHAT YOU SHOULD KNOW

A traditionally common case.

[391] Warmth and moistness are early changes in rheumatoid hands.

[392] Later changes include joint swelling and tenderness, muscle wasting and ultimately deformity.

[393] There are five causes of anaemia in rheumatoid arthritis.

1. **Anaemia of chronic disease**
2. **GI bleed** due to NSAIDs use
3. **Bone marrow suppression** by gold, phenylbutazone, indometacin, penicillamine
4. Associated **pernicious anaemia** leading to megaloblastic anaemia
5. **Felty syndrome** – rheumatoid arthritis, neutropenia and splenomegaly. Occurs in 5% of older patients with long-standing RA

[394] **X-ray signs of rheumatoid arthritis** depend on the stage of disease. Features include soft-tissue swelling, periarticular osteoporosis, narrowing of joint space, marginal bony erosions (especially around the wrist), articular destruction and joint deformity.

Treatment of rheumatoid arthritis

1. Stop the synovitis. Anti-inflammatories (symptomatic not disease modifying).
Disease-modifying drugs (gold, penicillamine, immunosuppressive drugs. Side-effects on liver, kidney, bone marrow so monitor and use sparingly).
Corticosteroids (during flare-ups, many side-effects).
Rest and splintage.
Intra-articular injections.
Synovectomy (last resort).
2. Prevent deformity. Surgery (joint replacement, tendon repair etc.); physiotherapy (passive and active)
3. Reconstruct. Arthrodesis, osteotomy, joint replacement.
4. Rehabilitate. Physiotherapy, keep active, treat co-morbidity.
Swan neck – hyperextension of PIP joints with fixed flexion of MCP and DIP joints due to tendon prolapse. The two lateral slips of the extensor tendon usually rupture or stretch, and so cannot extend the distal phalanx, while the pull of the central tendon hyperextends the middle phalanx. Can be corrected by check-rein procedure that shortens and reimplants the lateral slips of the extensor tendons.

Examine this lady's hands

(see pg 336)

RHEUMATOID ARTHRITIS OF THE HANDS

'There is symmetrical deforming polyarthropathy of the joints with spindling of the fingers, affecting the MCP and PIP joints but sparing the DIP joints. There is wasting of the small muscles of the hand. Typical features are seen, such as ulnar deviation at the MCP joints with radial deviation at the wrist, swan-neck/boutonnière/'Z' thumb deformities (say where). There is thin skin, bruising, pale nail beds[393] and vasculitic lesions. The palms show pale palmar creases and palmar erythema. I can feel joint destruction and rheumatoid nodules. This patient has rheumatoid arthritis. I would like to look at the elbows, assess function and neurology and see the X-rays.'[394]

👁 **WHAT YOU SHOULD SEE**

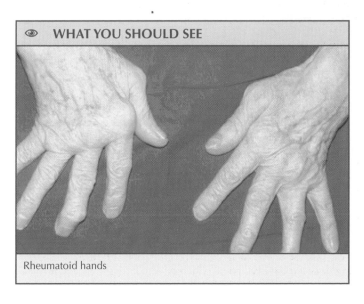

Rheumatoid hands

RHEUMATOID ARTHRITIS OF THE HANDS

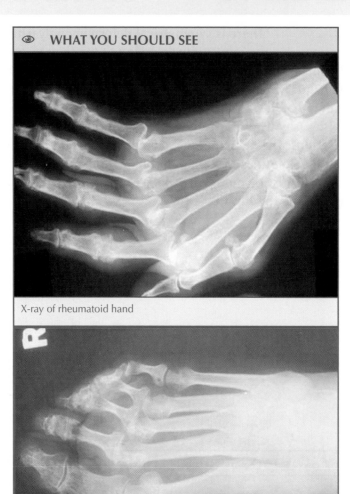

👁 WHAT YOU SHOULD SEE

X-ray of rheumatoid hand

X-ray of rheumatoid foot
Note soft-tissue swelling, periarticular osteoporosis, narrowing of joint space, marginal bony erosions, articular destruction and joint deformity

RHEUMATOID ARTHRITIS
OF THE HANDS

👁 WHAT YOU SHOULD SEE

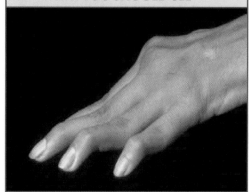

Swan-neck deformity

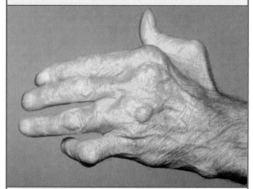

Rheumatoid hand showing deforming polyarthropathy affecting MCP and PIP joints, sparing DIP joints. Note the Z thumb, boutonnière deformity of the little finger, wasting of the small muscles of the hand and rheumatoid nodules

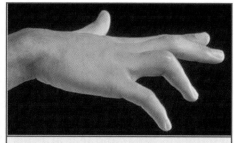

Rheumatoid hand showing boutonnière deformity, most marked in the ring finger

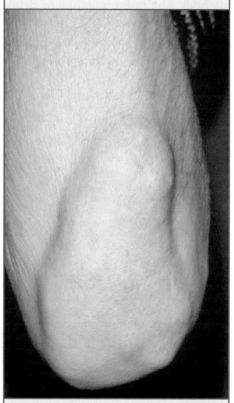

Rheumatoid nodules on elbow

OSTEOARTHRITIS OF THE HANDS

'I would like to present Mrs W, a 60-year-old retired tailor. She has noticed that over the last few years she has developed what she describes as prominent nodules on the joints at the end of her fingers and the base of her thumb. They become painful with use and her hands are slightly stiffer at the start of the day. She therefore cannot do the needlework she used to. She has had a right knee replacement 3 years ago for what she describes as 'wear and tear arthritis'. She can recall no trauma to her hands. She is only taking simple analgesia as she requires it. She has no known drug allergies. She doesn't smoke or drink. He lives with her husband.

I think this lady has osteoarthritis of the hands. I would like to examine her hands to confirm my diagnosis.'

📋 WHAT YOU SHOULD KNOW

Definition: a disease process of synovial joints characterised by focal areas of loss of hyaline articular cartilage associated with increased activity in marginal and subchondral bone.
Sites affected: DIP joints and base of the thumb.
Aetiology: secondary OA associated with a clear abnormality or primary/idiopathic. Risk factors include previous trauma, repetitive occupation and hypermobility.
Epidemiology of osteoarthritis: 1% overall, up to 10% of over-60s.
X-ray findings: joint-space narrowing, osteophyte formation, subchondral sclerosis, subchondral cysts.
Management:
Conservative: prevention, physiotherapy.
Analgesia: non-steroidal.
[395] Bony swellings in distal interphalangeal joints which form insidiously or from a hyaluronate-filled cyst that may be painful and warm. Nodal disease is more common in women and runs in families.

Examine this lady's hands

(see pg 336)

OSTEOARTHRITIS OF THE HANDS

'There are Heberden's nodes[395] present at the bases of the distal phalanges and Bouchard's nodes at the proximal interphalangeal joints. There is a 'square hand' deformity due to subluxation of the base of the first metacarpal. The patient has osteoarthritis of the hands.'

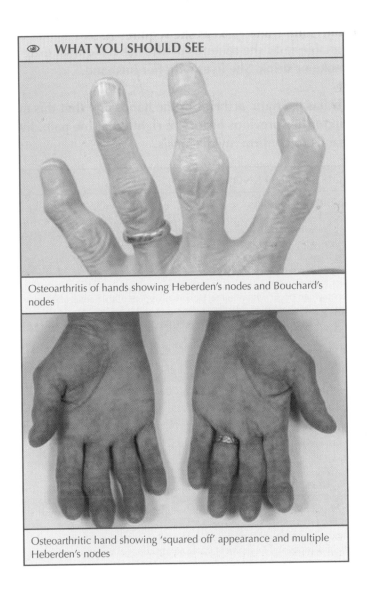

👁 **WHAT YOU SHOULD SEE**

Osteoarthritis of hands showing Heberden's nodes and Bouchard's nodes

Osteoarthritic hand showing 'squared off' appearance and multiple Heberden's nodes

Take a history from this lady who has a problem with her hands

(see pg 311)

PSORIATIC ARTHRITIS OF THE HANDS

'I would like to present Mrs W, a 35-year-old shop assistant. Her main complaint is of pain in some of the joints at the ends of her fingers in her right (dominant) hand. She had a similar problem in her right great toe 6 months ago which her GP treated as gout. She currently does not have any functional restriction but she is very upset at changes in her fingernails which are thickened and she considers them unsightly. She tells me she is spending a fortune on nail varnish! She has psoriasis mainly in her scalp which was diagnosed 5 years ago.[398] She can recall no trauma to her hands. She is only taking simple analgesia as she requires it. She has no known drug allergies. She doesn't smoke or drink. She lives with her husband.

I think this lady has psoriatic arthritis of the hands and that this might also be the explanation for her previous history of right great toe pain. I would like to examine her hands to confirm my diagnosis.'

✍ WHAT YOU SHOULD KNOW

Other forms of psoriatic arthropathy include:
- Arthritis mutilans
- Arthritis clinically indistinguishable from rheumatoid arthritis but consistently seronegative
- Asymmetrical oligo- or mono-arthropathy

Ankylosing spondylitis occurring alone or in conjunction with any of the other forms.

[396] Loosening or separation of nail from nail bed.

[397] Thick scale under nails.

[398] Psoriatic arthropathy can occur with minimal skin involvement. Other areas affected are typically the knees and other extensor aspects, the scalp, behind the ears and in the navel.

[399] **Incidence**: 1–5% of Caucasians in NW Europe and USA. Rare in Japanese, African Americans, American Indians.

Radiological findings
- Soft-tissue swelling (sausage digit)
- Asymmetrical destruction of distal interphalangeal joints
- 'Pencil in cup' deformity – erosions with adjacent bone proliferation
- Ankylosis
- Sclerosis of terminal phalanx (ivory phalanx)

Other joints affected
- Feet, especially first toe interphalangeal joint
- Lower cervical, thoracic, upper lumbar spine
- Sacroiliac joint

Treatments:
Sunlight, ultraviolet light, coal tar, dithranol, local steroids, PUVA (psoralen drugs and ultraviolet light). Disease modifying drugs. Newer anti-TNF treatments such as infliximab being used for severe cases.

Systemic steroids and antimetabolites rarely used, chloroquine contraindicated.

Analgesia, anti-inflammatories and intra-articular steroid injections alleviate symptoms.

Examine this lady's hands

(see pg 336)

PSORIATIC ARTHRITIS
OF THE HANDS

'There is an asymmetrical arthropathy involving the terminal interphalangeal joints of the hands.[396] The fingernails are pitted with onycholysis, thickened nail plates and hyperkeratosis.[397] There are patches of psoriasis at the elbows.[398] The plaques are red with a silvery, scaly surface and tend to be circular with well-defined edges. This patient has psoriatic arthritis.[399]

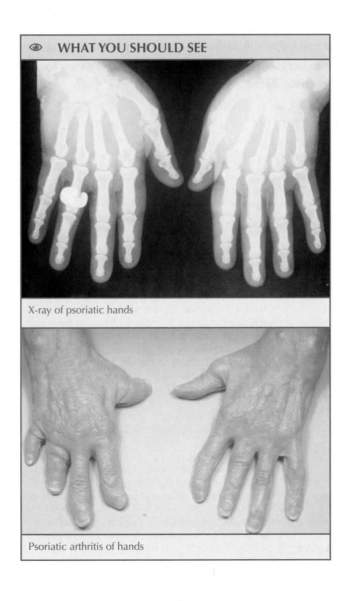

👁 **WHAT YOU SHOULD SEE**

X-ray of psoriatic hands

Psoriatic arthritis of hands

Take a history from this lady who has a problem with her feet

(see pg 311)

HALLUX VALGUS

'I would like to present Mrs W, a 60-year-old shop assistant. Her main complaint is of painful bunions on both her feet. She has always taken great pride in wearing stiletto-heeled shoes but these are now too painful. She also dislikes the way her feet look. She has had no injury to her feet and has no pain in her other joints. She has no other medical problems and no known drug allergies. She is only taking simple analgesia as she requires it. She has smoked for 20 pack years and drinks 6 units per week. She lives with her husband.

I think this lady has bilateral hallux valgus complicated by bunion formation which has been exacerbated by wearing narrow footwear. I would like to examine her feet to confirm my diagnosis.'

✍ WHAT YOU SHOULD KNOW

Definition: the commonest of the foot deformities, the underlying deformity is usually metatarsus primus varus (splaying of the forefoot) which predisposes to a lateral angulation of the big toe in cultures where people wear shoes.

Causes:	Congenital metatarsus varus (often hereditary)
	Loss of muscle tone in the forefoot in old people
	Rheumatoid arthritis
	Worsened by narrow or pointed shoes (especially in women). In people who have never worn shoes (e.g. developing countries) the big toe remains in line with the first metatarsal, retaining the fan-shaped appearance of the forefoot.
Epidemiology:	Usually bilateral
	Most common in the sixth decade
	Most common in females
	Familial variety presents in adolescence
Symptoms:	Deformity
	Pain, usually due to complications such as:
	Inflamed bunion (protective bursa over first metatarsal head)
	Hammer-toe
	Metatarsalgia
	Secondary osteoarthritis of the first metatarsophalangeal (MTP) joint
X-ray findings:	Should be weight bearing. Shows degree of metatarsal and hallux angulation and subluxation or osteoarthritic changes of the first MTP joint.
Conservative treatment:	Wide shoes with soft uppers; padding to protect bunion/hammer-toe; foot exercises; anterior platform support to relieve metatarsalgia.

CONTINUED ON pg 410

Examine this
lady's feet

(see pg 351)

HALLUX VALGUS

'There is marked hallux valgus bilaterally with prominence of the first metatarsal head, worse on the left/right. Typical associated features seen here include widening of the forefoot, bunions, crowding and deformity (?overlapping) of the second toe, medial rotation of the hallux, and hammer-toes (say which toes).'

◉ WHAT YOU SHOULD SEE

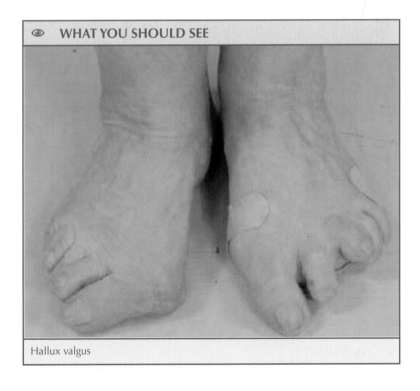

Hallux valgus

📋 WHAT YOU SHOULD KNOW (CONT)

Surgical treatment: (see diagram below):
a) <u>Distal soft-tissue realignment with distal osteotomy of first metatarsal</u> (e.g. Mitchell's osteotomy). For mild/moderate deformity.
b) <u>Shaft osteotomy or proximal osteotomy</u> is needed for more severe deformity.
c) <u>Keller's operation</u> was the simplest solution for elderly patients but is now less in favour.
Post-operative complications: redistribution of stresses on weight bearing can lead to aching forefoot or even stress fractures of the metatarsal bones, especially in osteoporotic patients.
Other conditions of the great toe:
<u>Hallux rigidus</u>: primary osteoarthritis of the first metatarsophalangeal joint results in stiffness and pain. There is thickening due to circumferential exostosis formation. This affects walking, which normally involves considerable dorsiflexion at this joint. The toe may be held flexed (hallux flexus). It is common in men and can be treated by MUA or fusion. A stiff-soled shoe relieves symptoms.
<u>Bunion</u>: a protective bursa formed at pressure areas, e.g. hallux valgus.
<u>Gout</u> (see pg 411).
<u>Ingrowing toenail</u> (see pg 414).

📋 WHAT YOU SHOULD KNOW

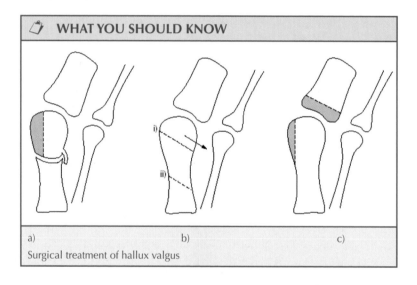

a)   b)   c)
Surgical treatment of hallux valgus

GOUT

✎ WHAT YOU SHOULD KNOW

Definition: hyperuricaemia associated with recurrent attacks of acute arthritis triggered by crystallisation of urates in joints, with asymptomatic intervals. In severe cases there is eventual development of tophaceous gout with aggregates of urates in and around joints and chronic (often crippling) gouty arthritis.

Aetiology: 90% primary (mostly idiopathic, due to increased uric acid production or decreased excretion); 10% secondary to diuretics (thiazides especially), myeloproliferative/lymphoproliferative disorders and chronic renal failure.

Distribution: 90% big toe, also instep, ankle, heel, knee, small joints of the hands.

Pathological features:

1. Acute arthritis: acute inflammatory synovitis stimulated by monosodium urate crystals (long, needle-shaped, birefringent on microscopy). Leucocytes and macrophages release cytokines.

2. Chronic arthritis: urate precipitates in the synovial membrane following acute attacks stimulating a pannus (inflammatory overgrowth) over the synovium and cartilage, degrading cartilage and bone.

3. Tophi: urate deposition in periarticular tissues surrounded by intense inflammatory reaction. Typical chalky exudative deposits can cause overlying skin necrosis and exude a paste of monosodium urate crystals (hence the unlikely story of the patient who kept the darts score on the pub blackboard with his gouty hands having no need of chalk!).

4. Kidney disease: acute uric acid nephropathy, nephrolithiasis, chronic uric acid nephropathy.

Associations: obesity, type IV hyperlipidaemia, hypertension, diabetes and ischaemic heart disease.

Treatment:

1. Treat acute attack: anti-inflammatories, e.g. NSAIDs (e.g. indometacin) or, rarely, colchicine.

2. Prophylaxis: reduce precipitating factors (alcohol, obesity, diuretics); decrease uric acid production (allopurinol); increase uric acid secretion (uricosurics e.g. probenecid). Beware: altering uric acid metabolism can precipitate an attack, so do not start allopurinol during an acute attack.

Tophi occur on the helix of the ear, some tendon sheaths, and can also occur in the patella bursa, kidneys, aorta and myocardium; typically occur on the the the ulnar surface of the forearm, olecranon bursa, the Achilles' tendon and other pressure points.

Septic arthritis is excluded by joint aspiration. Microscopy shows typical crystals. Blood uric acid may or may not be raised.

Radiological findings: typically seen late (>6 years after first attack)

1. Soft-tissue swelling

2. 'Punched-out' erosions. These start near joint margins and have a classic overhanging sclerotic margin. They are mostly set back from the articular surface.

3. Eccentric soft-tissue masses in a periarticular location in tophaceous gout (rarely do these calcify).

4. Cartilage destruction (and hence joint-space narrowing) is not typical except in very late cases and there is not typically osteoporosis (differentiating it from rheumatoid).

5. Chondrocalcinosis occurs in 5% of cases.

Pseudogout

Acute and chronic inflammatory joint disease caused by the deposition of either crystals of calcium pyrophosphate or basic calcium phosphates in the articular cartilage and menisci, usually involving knees, ankles, wrists, elbows, hips or spine.

Aetiology: hereditary (autosomal dominant); metabolic (hyperparathyroidism, haemochromatosis, hypothyroidism); idiopathic; post-surgical/trauma. Pathology is similar to gout but with short, rhomboid, water-soluble crystals.

X-rays show calcification in soft tissues and linear densities in articular cartilage parallel to subchondral bone.

Serum calcium is normal.

Treatment involves rest, aspiration and steroid injections. Not as easy to control as gout.

Take a history from this man who has a problem with his right great toe

'I would like to present Mr W, a 60-year-old school caretaker. He has a 2-week history of a severely painful right great toe. He has no pain in any other joints and cannot recall any history of injury to this toe. He has had two similar episodes, both of which settled spontaneously. He has multiple medical problems, including chronic renal failure, diabetes, hypertension. He is on multiple medications, including what he describes as a 'water tablet', although he cannot recall its name. He has no known drug allergies. He has smoked for 60 pack years and drinks 40 units of alcohol per week. He lives with his wife.

I think this gentleman has gout of the right great toe. I would like to examine his feet to confirm my diagnosis.'

👁 **WHAT YOU SHOULD SEE**

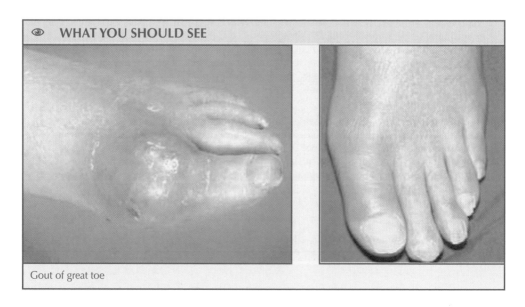

Gout of great toe

412

Examine this gentleman's feet/or hands
(see pgs 351/336)

GOUT

'There is an asymmetrical swelling affecting the small joints of the hands with tophi formation in the periarticular tissues. The joints are (in some cases) severely deformed. There are tophi on the helix of the ear and in some of the tendon sheaths. This is chronic tophaceous gout.'

Alternatively:

'There is swelling, redness and heat over the metatarsophalangeal joint of the big toe. It is exquisitely tender, but the patient shows no signs of systemic sepsis such as fever, sweating or rigors. This looks typical of acute gout, but if the patient had no previous history, septic arthritis would have to be excluded.

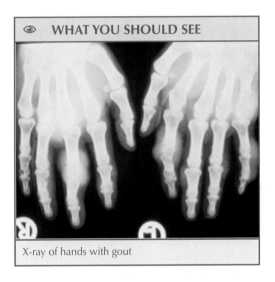

⊙ WHAT YOU SHOULD SEE

X-ray of hands with gout

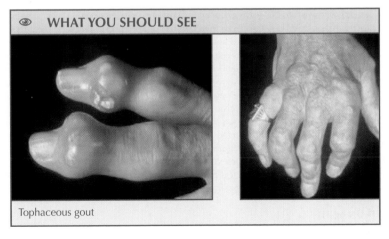

⊙ WHAT YOU SHOULD SEE

Tophaceous gout

413

Take a history from this man who has a problem with his right great toenail

INGROWING TOENAIL

'I would like to present Mr W, a 25-year-old accountant. His main complaint is of an ingrowing right great toe, which has developed over the last 4 months. He thinks it is currently infected as over the last 2 weeks it has been discharging a yellowish fluid and has become red and hot. He has no pain in any of his other joints and can recall no history of injury to this toe. He has asthma which sounds fairly brittle and he has been admitted to HDU twice this year with exacerbations. He has no known drug allergies. He does not smoke or drink.

I think this gentleman has an infected ingrowing right great toenail. I would like to examine his feet to confirm my diagnosis. Given his brittle asthma, an operation under local anaesthesia rather than general should be recommended once the infection settles.'

WHAT YOU SHOULD KNOW

[400] Encourage correctly fitting footwear and horizontal nail cutting.

[401] In the presence of gross sepsis or as a first line of treatment, **avulsion of the nail** may allow things to settle. However, recurrence should be expected and a definitive operation planned in case of this. Avulsion is easily carried out under local anaesthetic ring block, with the nail simply pulled out, leaving the entire nail bed to grow a new nail.

[402] In young patients who wish to conserve a toenail for cosmesis, **wedge excision** is the treatment of choice. The procedure is carried out after gross infection has settled, under general or ring-block local anaesthesia with a rubber tourniquet applied at the base of the toe. The toenail is divided longitudinally one third of the width of the nail from the affected margin with a scalpel, and the ingrowing portion is avulsed, leaving the central portion of the nail intact. The exposed strip of nail bed, granulation tissue and a margin of healthy skin are excised in a deep wedge extending proximally to the base of the distal phalanx. The wedge must be deep and wide enough to ensure complete removal of the lateral portion of the germinal matrix, because inadequate excision is followed by regrowth of a troublesome nail spike. If there is doubt about the removal of the corners, curette with a Volkmann spoon or phenol ablation. If phenol is used the surrounding skin is protected with petroleum jelly and the residual phenol is carefully rinsed with saline. The wedge is closed by suturing the skin margin to the cut edge of the nail with a non-absorbable suture. For both the wedge excision and Zadik's procedure the toe is dressed with paraffin gauze, bulky gauze and crepe. The tourniquet is removed. The foot is elevated for 24 hours and firm bandaging treats any post-operative bleeding. The patient should wear open-toed sandals until the wounds are healed.

CONTINUED ON pg 416

Examine this gentleman's feet

(see pg 351)

INGROWING TOENAIL

'The patient has ingrowing toenails on the lateral and medial sides of both great toes. There is evidence of recurrent infection, worse on the lateral side of the right great toe (for example), which is currently infected, with erythema, tenderness and a seropurulent discharge. The treatment options for ingrowing toenails include conservative measures[400], avulsion of the nail[401], wedge excision[402] and Zadik's procedure[403]. As this patient is young, foot pulses are good[404], the nail obviously symptomatic, and the current sepsis not severe, I would suggest wedge excisions on the medial and lateral sides of both great toes (or whichever margins are affected) to preserve the central nail for cosmesis. I would discuss the benefits of general and local anaesthetic,[405] explain the procedure and the possible complications,[406] and suggest a course of antibiotics and open footwear for 2 weeks pre-operatively to minimise the infection of that right toe.'

◉ WHAT YOU SHOULD SEE

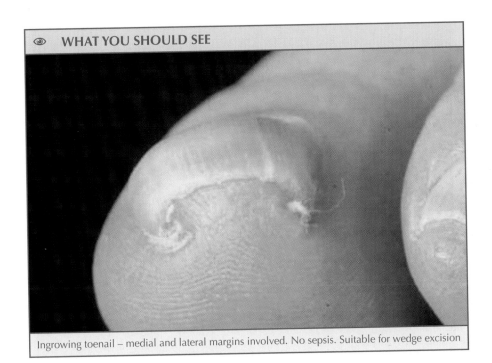

Ingrowing toenail – medial and lateral margins involved. No sepsis. Suitable for wedge excision

---

✐ WHAT YOU SHOULD KNOW (CONT)

[403] Zadik described **radical excision of the nail root**. This is more suitable in older patients with recurrent disease. The patient must be warned that the nail will never grow back after this procedure. Under GA or LA with a tourniquet applied, the entire nail is avulsed. Two oblique incisions are made from the corner of the nail bed to the crease of the distal interphalangeal joint. A skin flap is then raised with a scalpel from the proximal and lateral flaps thus formed. These are retracted to expose the underlying germinal matrix. A distal transverse incision in the nail bed is made and the entire germinal matrix is dissected proximally off the periosteum, taking care to include the lateral and medial corners of the matrix from which spikes of nail may grow if left behind. The whole 'nail bed' is removed. The skin flaps are sutured to the nail bed.

[404] It is important to exclude peripheral vascular disease as, if present, the implications of sepsis are more severe, wound healing is likely to be compromised, and the most minimal procedure likely to be useful should be selected (e.g. avulsion).

[405] Ingrowing toenail surgery is usually suitable for day case surgery if the patient is fit. **Ring block** using a local anaesthetic such as 1% lidocaine provides adequate regional anaesthesia but the procedure can be performed under GA if the patient prefers. To achieve a ring block, the needle is introduced through the dorsal skin at the base of the digit and is advanced just to one side of the phalanx until it can be seen tenting the thick plantar skin (the digital nerves run nearer the plantar than the dorsal surface). The procedure is repeated on the other side. Local anaesthetic with adrenaline should not be used because of the risk of digital ischaemia (the end-digital arteries run with the nerves).

[406] Intraoperative hazards: damage to extensor hallucis longus tendon; opening the distal interphalangeal joint; failure to excise the nail root.

Post-operative complications: infection of soft tissues (common) and osteomyelitis (rare); bleeding; recurrence or growth of nail spike.

👁 WHAT YOU SHOULD SEE

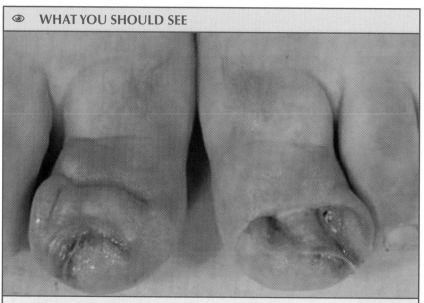

Bilateral ingrowing toenails with severe sepsis. It is important to check the peripheral circulation before undertaking surgery. Simple nail avulsions may be required to allow the sepsis to settle before the definitive operation is performed – probably bilateral Zadik's procedure if the patient is elderly and does not mind about the cosmetic result

Examine this gentleman's shoulder and ask him some questions about it

(see pg 338)

WINGING OF THE SCAPULA

'There is winging of the (left or right) scapula evident when the patient, viewed from behind, extends his arms, puts his palms against the wall and pushes. He gives/doesn't give a history of previous trauma or surgery. Winging of the scapula is a sign of weakness of serratus anterior, which can arise from damage to the long thoracic nerve, injury to the brachial plexus, injury or viral infections of the 5th, 6th and 7th cervical nerves and certain types of muscular dystrophy.'[407]

✍ WHAT YOU SHOULD KNOW

[407] Disability is usually slight and is best accepted. If function is markedly impaired the scapula can be stabilised by tendon transfer.

👁 WHAT YOU SHOULD SEE

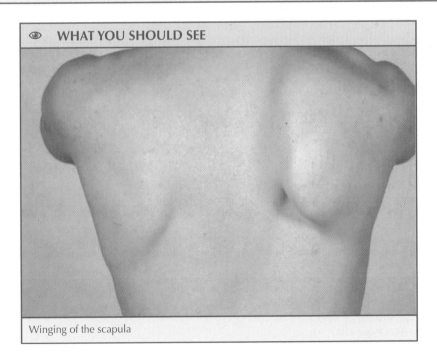

Winging of the scapula

Examine this lady with numbness of her right hand

(see pg 359)

MEDIAN NERVE PALSY AND CARPAL TUNNEL SYNDROME

'I would like to present Mrs W, a 55-year-old secretary. She presents with a 6-month history of tingling and numbness in her right (dominant) hand. She has noticed the first three and a half digits are affected and denies any spread into her forearm. Her symptoms are worst at night and she finds when she shakes her hand this improves them. She has not noticed any weakness in her hand, although she is finding that the numbness comes on while she is typing at work which concerns her. She denies any previous trauma to that wrist and her only medical history is of obesity.[407] She takes NSAIDs for the tingling but is on no other medication and has no allergies. She neither smokes nor drinks alcohol.

I suspect this lady has right-sided carpal tunnel syndrome but I would like to examine her to confirm this diagnosis.'

WHAT YOU SHOULD KNOW

Definition of carpal tunnel syndrome: compression and/or ischaemia of the median nerve due to swelling of the flexor retinaculum.

[407] The patient is typically obese, middle-aged and female. The story is characteristic – pain, numbness or paraesthesia worse at night. Patient hangs arm out of bed, shaking it. Knitting or holding a newspaper may bring the pain on in the day. The discomfort can be referred beyond the cutaneous distribution of the median nerve in the hand, up over the whole forearm, but the sensory signs are confined to the distribution of the median nerve.

[408] **Causes of carpal tunnel syndrome**:

Can occur in healthy people	Can be a sign of underlying disease
pregnancy	acromegaly
obesity	rheumatoid arthritis
occupational	diabetes
previous trauma	idiopathic myxoedema
contraceptive pill	
unaccustomed activity (e.g. housepainting)	

[409] **Diagnostic tests**: be prepared to carry out any of the first three.

Tinel's test: percussion over the carpal tunnel producing tingling in the distribution of the nerve (Tinel's sign).

Phalen's test: the patient flexes both wrists for 60 seconds and this reproduces symptoms. Symptoms relieved when wrists relaxed. Positive in 50%. Symptoms may be induced by hyperextension of the wrist in some patients.

Tourniquet test: apply sphygmomanometer just above systolic pressure for 1–2 minutes to reproduce symptoms.

Nerve conduction tests: not a bedside test but a diagnostic investigation. Differentiates from cervical spondylosis involving C6 and C7.

CONTINUED ON pg 420

Examine this lady with numbness of her right hand

(see pg 359)

MEDIAN NERVE PALSY AND CARPAL TUNNEL SYNDROME

'There is sensory loss over the palmar aspects of the first three and a half fingers and wasting of the thenar eminence. There is weakness of abduction, flexion and opposition of the thumb. The diagnosis is median nerve palsy. The flexor muscles of the forearm are not involved, suggesting carpal tunnel syndrome[408], I would like to perform some diagnostic tests[409] and look for an underlying cause.'

Alternatively:
'The symptoms you describe are suggestive of carpal tunnel syndrome. Tinel's test/Phalen's test (or the tourniquet test) are positive but the median nerve shows no deficit. The diagnosis is carpal tunnel syndrome.'

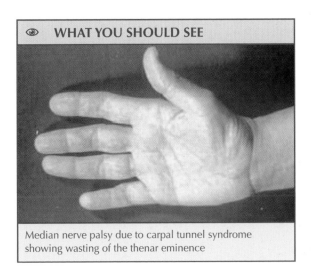

WHAT YOU SHOULD SEE

Median nerve palsy due to carpal tunnel syndrome showing wasting of the thenar eminence

419

WHAT YOU SHOULD KNOW

Facts about the median nerve:

Nerve roots: lateral and medial cords of brachial plexus, C (5), 6, 7, 8, T1.

Course: the medial root crosses in front of the third part of the axillary artery to join the lateral root. It runs downwards on the lateral side of the brachial artery, crossing to the medial side halfway down the upper arm. It is superficial but is crossed at the elbow by the bicipital aponeurosis. It passes between the two heads of pronator teres, separated from the ulnar artery by the ulnar head of pronator teres. It runs down behind flexor digitorum superficialis and is attached to its deep surface by connective tissue. It rests posteriorly on flexor digitorum profundus. At the wrist the median nerve emerges from the lateral border of the flexor digitorum superficialis muscle and lies behind the tendon of the palmaris longus. It enters the palm by passing behind the flexor retinaculum and immediately divides into lateral and medial branches, each of which gives muscular and cutaneous terminal branches.

Branches supply:

Near the elbow	In the forearm (via anterior interosseous branch)
Flexor digitorum superficialis	Flexor pollicis longus
Flexor carpi radialis	Half of flexor digitorum profundus
Palmaris longus	Pronator quadratus
Pronator teres	

In the hand

Motor – the 'LOAF' muscles of the thenar eminence:
  L ateral two lumbricals
  O pponens pollicis
  A bductor pollicis
  F lexor pollicis brevis

Sensation of the lateral palm and lateral two and a half fingers.

Causes of damage to the median nerve:

1. Carpal tunnel syndrome: can occur after wrist fractures
2. At the wrist: especially from lacerations here
3. In the forearm: (anterior interosseous nerve) from forearm bone fractures
4. Distal to the elbow: pronator teres nerve entrapment syndrome
5. At the elbow: e.g. after dislocation

FACTS ABOUT
THE ULNAR NERVE

📋 **WHAT YOU SHOULD KNOW**

Facts about the ulnar nerve:

Nerve roots: medial cord of brachial plexus, C8 T1.

Course: descends between axillary artery and vein and then runs down on the medial side of the brachial artery as far as the middle of the arm. Here, at the insertion of the coracobrachialis, the nerve pierces the medial fascial septum, accompanied by the superior ulnar collateral artery, and enters the posterior compartment of the arm. It descends behind the septum, covered posteriorly by the medial head of triceps. At the elbow it lies superficially behind the medial epicondyle of the humerus on the medial ligament of the elbow joint. It enters the forearm between the two heads of origin of the flexor carpi ulnaris (FCU). It runs down the forearm between FCU and flexor digitorum profundus (FDP) medial to the ulnar artery. At the wrist the ulnar nerve becomes superficial and lies between FCU and FDS tendons, entering the palm in front of flexor retinaculum, lateral to the pisiform base, and divides into a superficial branch which ends in muscular and cutaneus branches, and a deep branch which runs backwards between the abductor digiti minimi and the flexor digiti minimi, piercing the opponens digiti minimi and winding around the hook of the hamate. It passes laterally in the deep palmar arch, giving off muscular branches.

Branches in the forearm supply:

Muscles	Flexor carpi ulnaris
	50% of flexor digitorum profundus
Skin	Dorsal cutaneous branch
	Medial skin of dorsum of hand
	Medial 1½ digits
Joints	Elbow joint

Branches in the hand supply:

Muscles	Hypothenar muscles
	The interossei
	Two medial lumbricals
	Adductor pollicis
Skin	Superficial palmar branch
	Palmar 1½ digits
	Palmar cutaneous branch
	Medial skin of palm

Common causes of ulnar nerve palsy (distal to proximal):

1. Ulnar tunnel syndrome where the nerve passes between the pisiform and the hook of the hamate (e.g. due to a ganglion or fractured hook of the hamate). The most distal lesions affect the deep palmar branch and are entirely motor

2. At the wrist from lacerations, occupational trauma and ganglia

3. Distal to the elbow by compression as it passes between the two heads of flexor carpi ulnaris

4. At the level of the medial epicondyle where it is very superficial due to trauma,, local friction, pressure or stretching, e.g. in cubitus valgus or osteoarthritis

5. After supracondylar fractures or other fractures around the elbow

6. In the brachial plexus due to trauma

Take a history from this boy with numbness and weakness of his right hand and arm

ULNAR NERVE PALSY

'I would like to present Joe W, a 12-year-old boy. He presents with a 3-month history of weakness of his right (dominant) hand and tingling and numbness of the little finger of his right hand. Of significance, Joe fell out of a tree 3 months ago, sustaining a supracondylar fracture of his right arm which was treated with what sounds like a closed reduction and k-wire insertion according to Joe's description. He denies having any weakness or numbness following the fall but prior to the fixation. He has no other medical history and takes no medication, with no known allergies. He lives with his mother and sister.

I suspect this boy has sustained a right sided ulnar nerve injury, possibly iatrogenic due to the fixation of his supracondylar fracture. I would like to examine him to confirm this diagnosis.'

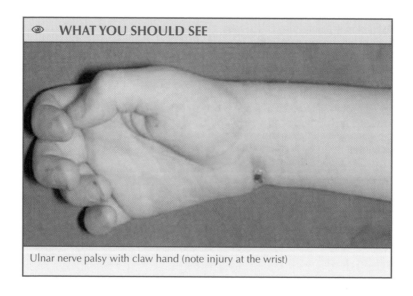

👁 **WHAT YOU SHOULD SEE**

Ulnar nerve palsy with claw hand (note injury at the wrist)

Examine this boy with numbness and weakness of his right hand and arm

(see pg 361)

ULNAR NERVE PALSY

'The hand shows generalised muscle wasting and weakness, sparing the thenar eminence, with features of a claw hand. There is loss of sensation over the fifth finger, the ulnar half of the fourth finger and the ulnar side of the hand on both dorsal and palmar surfaces. There is weakness of the interossei and abductor digiti minimi. Froment's test is positive, indicating weakness of adductor pollicis. The diagnosis is ulnar nerve palsy. I would like to look for scarring at the wrist/elbow.'

◉ WHAT YOU SHOULD SEE

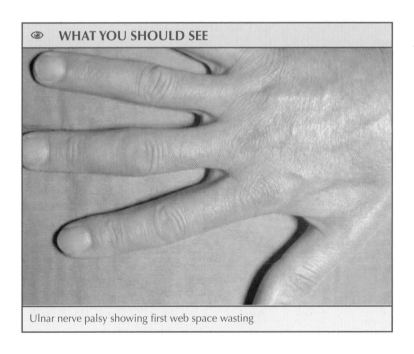

Ulnar nerve palsy showing first web space wasting

RADIAL NERVE PALSY

'I would like to present Mr W, a 40-year-old driving instructor. He presents with a 2-month history of wrist drop of his right (dominant) hand. He had a degree of numbness but this has improved, as has his weakness to some degree. Of significance, Mr W was involved in a motor vehicle accident 3 months ago when he sustained a fracture of the mid-shaft of his right humerus which was treated non-operatively. He noticed the weakness after he was placed in the cast. He has no other medical history and takes no medication with no known allergies. He is a non-smoker and drinks 4 units of alcohol per week.

I suspect this man has sustained a right-sided radial nerve injury following a fracture of the mid-shaft of the right humerus. It sounds as though it is improving slightly. I would like to examine him to confirm this diagnosis.'

✏ WHAT YOU SHOULD KNOW

Facts about the radial nerve:

Nerve roots: posterior cord of brachial plexus C5, 6, 7.

Course: arises posterior to the axillary artery. Runs with profunda brachii artery between long and medial heads of triceps. Runs in spiral groove of humerus between medial and lateral heads of triceps (where it is susceptible to injury in humerus fractures). Lies deep to brachioradialis.

Branches supply:

Above the elbow:

Muscles: triceps, brachialis (lateral part), brachioradialis, extensor carpi radialis longus.

Skin: posterior cutaneous branch, to back of arm and forearm

Joint: elbow

Below the elbow: enters lateral cubital fossa. Divides into:

1. Posterior interosseous branch (runs between two heads of supinator, passing into posterior compartment). Supplies supinator and all extensors

2. Superficial radial nerve (under brachioradialis and lateral to radial artery). Supplies skin of dorsum of radial side of hand and lateral three and a half digits

Causes of damage of radial nerve:

In axilla

- 'Saturday night' palsy – neuropraxia from sleeping with arm over back of the chair
- Ill-fitting crutches

Mid-humerus

- Fractures of humerus
- Tourniquet palsies

At and below elbow

- Elbow dislocations
- Monteggia fractures
- Ganglia
- Surgical trauma

Examine this man with numbness/ weakness of his right hand/arm

(see pg 364)

RADIAL NERVE PALSY

'There is wrist drop and sensory loss over the first dorsal interosseous. This is radial nerve palsy.' Weakness of the supinator and brachioadialis muscles suggests a lesion above the supinator tunnel.[410] Weakness of the triceps suggests a lesion at or above the mid-humerus.'

WHAT YOU SHOULD KNOW (CONT)

[410] **Supinator tunnel**: the fibres of the supinator muscle are arranged in two planes, between which the deep branch of the radial nerve lies. The supinator arises from the lateral epicondyle of the humerus, the elbow joint and superior radioulnar joint and the supinator crest and fossa of the ulna. It inserts into the posterior, lateral and anterior aspects of the neck and shaft of the radius as far as the oblique line.

WHAT YOU SHOULD SEE

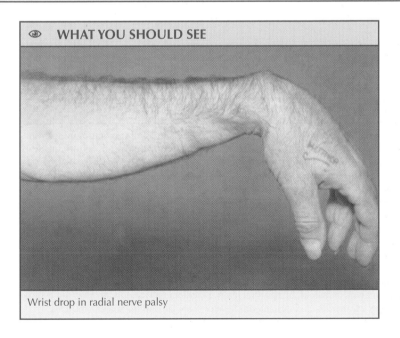

Wrist drop in radial nerve palsy

Take a history from this boy with numbness/weakness of his right hand/arm

'I would like to present Joe W, a 4-year-boy. His mother tells me that since birth he has had a weak right (dominant) hand. He is unable to lift his arm and it hangs at his side. She says he also seems to complain of a loss of sensation on the outer aspect of his arm. He has had a variety of different treatments. He has no other history of trauma to this arm. He has no other medical conditions and takes no medications. She is not aware that he has any allergies to medications. He is due to start school in 3 months' time.

I suspect this boy has Erb's palsy due to a brachial plexus injury at birth. I would like to examine him to confirm this diagnosis.'

✎ WHAT YOU SHOULD KNOW

Traumatic lesion of the **upper** portion of the brachial plexus (C5 and C6 roots or upper trunks).

Causes: traction injuries, e.g. birth trauma (classic Erb's palsy), shoulder hits an obstacle when the patient is thrown from a vehicle (typically a motorcycle).

Prognosis and management: in birth injury, full recovery occurs in a third of cases, with residual weakness of shoulder abduction and elbow flexion in two-thirds. Sensory loss seldom persists. Prevention of contractures is a priority. Prognosis is worse if more of the brachial plexus (i.e. lower portions too) is involved.

Klumpke's paralysis is a rarer birth injury than Erb's palsy and involves the cords of the **lower** brachial plexus (C8, T1) following traction with the arm extended. It results in paralysis of the intrinsic muscles of the hand with a claw-hand deformity, weakness of the medial fingers and wrist flexors and a sensory loss over the medial forearm, hand and medial two fingers. Cervical sympathetic paralysis, giving rise to Horner syndrome, is frequently associated.

[411] There is paralysis of deltoid, biceps, brachialis, brachioradialis and (if the roots are avulsed from the cords) rotator cuff muscles, serratus anterior, levator scapulae and the scalene muscles.

Examine this gentleman with numbness/ weakness of his left arm

(see pg 356)

ERB'S PALSY

'The arm hangs at the side, internally rotated at the shoulder, with the elbow extended and the forearm pronated in the 'waiter's tip' position.[411] There are/are not scars of trauma and surgery around the shoulder. Shoulder abduction and elbow flexion are not possible. The biceps and brachioradialis reflex jerks are absent. Sensory loss affects the lateral aspect of the shoulder and upper arm and the radial border of the forearm. The diagnosis is Erb's palsy.'

⊚ WHAT YOU SHOULD SEE

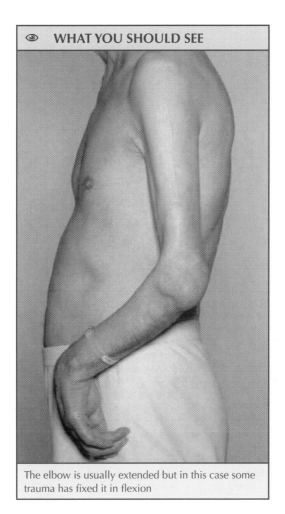

The elbow is usually extended but in this case some trauma has fixed it in flexion

Take a history from this lady with a lump on her right wrist

GANGLION

'I would like to present Miss W, a 25-year-old teaching assistant. She noticed a lump on the inner aspect of her right (dominant) wrist 6 months ago. It is non-tender and has not affected function or sensation. She has no other lumps and can recall no history of injury at this site. She dislikes it as she finds it unsightly. She has asthma for which she only requires a salbutamol inhaler as required. She has no known drug allergies. She does not smoke but drinks 20 units of alcohol per week. She lives with her fiancé.

I think this lady is most likely to have a ganglion. I would like to examine her to confirm my diagnosis.'

⟁ WHAT YOU SHOULD KNOW

Definition: a cystic degeneration in the joint capsule or tendon sheath resulting in a distended sheath containing fluid.

Clinical presentation: usually arises from the radiocarpal joint of young adults as described above. Tiny ganglia of this type can occur in the fingers. Fluctuations in size and rupture from trauma are common (the old fashioned home treatment of a ganglion was to hit it with the family bible!).

Treatment: patients may want it removed for cosmetic reasons or because it causes a persistent pain, ache or nuisance. It can be aspirated or excised, both carrying a risk of recurrence (especially the former). Excision may reveal a surprisingly deep root continuous with the underlying synovial joint, so is often done under general or regional, rather than local anaesthetic. Injection with steroids has been shown to reduce recurrence.

Compound palmar ganglion: a chronic inflammatory condition affecting the flexor tendon sheath. Large cystic mass is palpated proximal and distal to the flexor retinaculum and can be shown to be continuous, with cross-fluctuation.

Examine the lump on this patient's right wrist

(see pg 355)

GANGLION

'There is a smooth 2-cm subcutaneous lump on the extensor aspect (typically) of the wrist which is well-defined, cystic and (occasionally) seems to move with the extensor tendons. It is more obvious when the wrist is flexed. This is a ganglion.'

👁 WHAT YOU SHOULD SEE

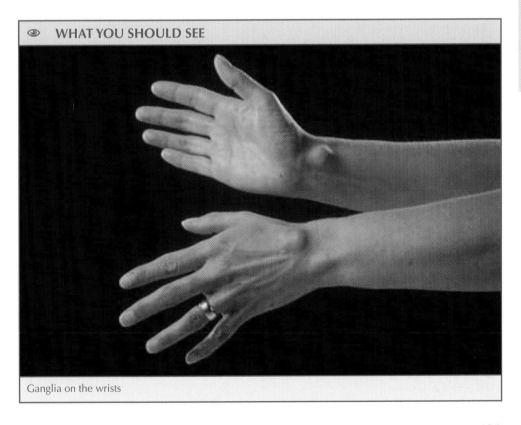

Ganglia on the wrists

✍ WHAT YOU SHOULD KNOW

Principle: a fracture is held by transfixing screws which pass through the bone above and below the fracture and are attached to an external frame.

Indications:
1. Fractures with severe soft-tissue damage – where the wound can be left open for inspection, dressing or skin grafting
2. Fractures associated with nerve and/or vessel damage
3. Severely comminuted and unstable fractures
4. Fractures of the pelvis – which often cannot be held by any other method
5. Infected fractures – internal fixation may lead to infected plates or nails

Complications of external fixation:
1. Pin track infection – especially if fixator is present for over 6 weeks
2. Delayed union due to
a) Healing ends being held apart by fixator
b) Reduced load transmission through the bone (stress shielding), which is avoided by special fixators allowing axial loading or by removing fixator at 6–8 weeks and replacing it with a splint, allowing bone loading

Ilizarov circular frame:
Allows good control of fragment position but requires specialist skill to apply and manage.

[358] **Gustilo and Anderson's classification of open fractures**:
Type 1: wound < 1 cm, little soft-tissue damage, simple fracture
Type 2: wound >1 cm long, not extensive soft-tissue damage, moderate contamination, moderate fracture comminution
Type 3: extensive soft-tissue damage. Contamination and comminution
Type A: soft-tissue coverage adequate
Type B: extensive soft-tissue injury requires a local/free flap for coverage
Type C: arterial injury needing repair

Examine this patient's leg and ask him about his injury

EXTERNAL FIXATORS

'There is an external fixator on the right leg of this patient. There is a healing open wound over the mid-shaft of the tibia on the anterior aspect of the leg. The quadriceps and calf muscles on the right look wasted/do not look wasted when compared with the left leg. The pin tracks look clean. He tells me he was a pedestrian involved in an RTA where his right leg was hit by a car bumper. This was his only injury. He describes sustaining an open fracture of the tibia.[358] This has been held externally due to the need for wound care and risk of infection. I would like to examine the distal neurology and circulation.'

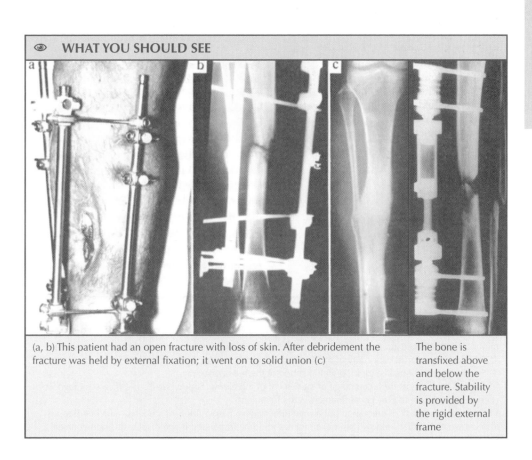

👁 WHAT YOU SHOULD SEE

(a, b) This patient had an open fracture with loss of skin. After debridement the fracture was held by external fixation; it went on to solid union (c)

The bone is transfixed above and below the fracture. Stability is provided by the rigid external frame

OLECRANON BURSITIS

'I would like to present Dr W, a 25-year-old Surgical CT1. She has noticed a lump on the outer aspect of her right (dominant) elbow for the last 4 months. It is generally non-tender unless she leans on it. It has not affected function or sensation. She has no other lumps. She has no recent fever. She has been writing quite a bit recently as she is studying for her MRCS part A exam! She cannot recall any acute trauma at this site. She dislikes it as she finds it unsightly. She has no other medical history. She takes no regular medications and has no known drug allergies. She does not smoke but drinks 20 units of alcohol per week. She lives with her fiancé.

I think this lady is most likely to have a olecranon bursitis bought on by microtrauma from the repetitive action of writing. I would like to examine her to confirm my diagnosis.'

✐ WHAT YOU SHOULD KNOW

The small subcutaneous bursa over the olecranon process of the ulna can become enlarged by repeated minor trauma. A more acute, painful bursitis can be caused by infection, gout or rheumatoid arthritis.
[412] Such as polyarthritis, especially of the joints of the hands (see pg 400).
[413] Such as bilateral bursitis, tophi, or calcification of the bursa on X-ray.
[414] Such as fever, rigors, reduced range of movement of the elbow. Septic bursitis is difficult to diagnose except by aspiration of pus. Local drainage is the treatment.
[415] Occupations at risk of olecranon bursitis include miners, carpet fitters or students – the condition is also known as 'scholar's elbow' (your examiners should be impressed if you display this sign yourself!)

OLECRANON BURSITIS

'There is (in this young, otherwise healthy patient) a red, hot, tender, fluctuant lump in the subcutaneous tissues over the extensor surface of the elbow. The range of movement of the joint is not affected. This is olecranon bursitis. I would like to look for signs of rheumatoid arthritis[412], gout[413] and infection,[414] and ask the patient her occupation[415].'

👁 WHAT YOU SHOULD SEE

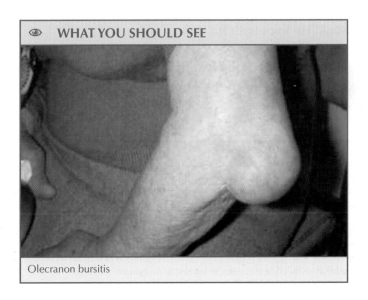

Olecranon bursitis

Take a history from this man who has a lump on his right knee

BURSAE OF THE KNEE AND BAKER'S CYST

Case 1

'I would like to present Mr W, a 40-year-old carpet fitter. He has noticed a lump over his right kneecap for the last 4 months. It is generally non-tender unless he kneels on it. It has not affected function or sensation. He has no other lumps. He kneels a lot as part of his work but cannot recall any acute trauma at this site. He has no other medical history. He takes no regular medications and has no known drug allergies. He has smoked for 15 pack years and drinks 20 units of alcohol per week. He lives with his wife and three young children.

I think this gentleman is most likely to have a prepatellar bursitis bought on by microtrauma from the repetitive action of kneeling. I would like to examine him to confirm my diagnosis.'

Case 2

'I would like to present Mr W, a 70-year-old retired carpet fitter. He has noticed a lump at the back of his knee for the last 4 months. It is more obvious on standing. The lump is non-tender. He has a long-standing history of right knee stiffness and pain and has been diagnosed by his GP with osteoarthritis of this knee. He cannot recall any acute trauma at this site. He has no other medical history. He takes no regular medications and has no known drug allergies. He has smoked for 35 pack years and drinks 20 units of alcohol per week. He lives with his wife.

I think this gentleman is most likely to have a Baker's cyst of the right knee with associated osteoarthritis of this knee. I would like to examine him to confirm my diagnosis.'

✎ WHAT YOU SHOULD KNOW

The two commonest sites for symptomatic bursae (other than over a hallux valgus) are prepatellar and infrapatellar. These bursae become inflamed by constant friction, leading to a tender and swollen bursitis.
A **prepatellar bursitis** (housemaid's knee) is common in miners and carpet layers lying directly over the patella.
An **infrapatellar bursitis** (clergyman's knee) is exacerbated in people who kneel more upright and lies superficial to the patellar ligament. Other sites for bursitis include the olecranon (scholar's elbow), Achilles' tendon, hallux and shoulder. Treatment is avoidance of the exacerbating activity, firm bandaging and occasional aspiration. In chronic cases the lump can be excised.

Examine the lump on this patient's right knee

(see pg 329)

BURSAE OF THE KNEE AND BAKER'S CYST

Case 1
'There is a fluctuant swelling lying directly over the patella (or distal to the patella overlying the patellar ligament) but the joint itself is normal. The lump is not red or hot but (may be) tender. This is prepatellar/infrapatellar bursitis.'

Case 2
'There is (in this patient with chronic arthritis) a fluctuant swelling in the popliteal fossa. It is non-tender, non-pulsatile[416] and is/is not associated with an effusion of the knee joint. This is either a Baker's cyst (popliteal cyst) or a semimembranosus bursa[417] (if medially placed with no associated arthritis).'

✎ WHAT YOU SHOULD KNOW (CONT)

A **Baker's cyst** or popliteal cyst usually develops in patients with chronic arthritis of the knee. It is a synovial sac bulging from the back of the joint. Occasionally it can leak or rupture into the calf, causing pain and swelling that is difficult to distinguish from a deep vein thrombosis. Joint aspiration and intra-articular injection of corticosteroid will reduce the effusion and relieve discomfort.

[416] It is important to differentiate these swellings from a popliteal aneurysm.

[417] The bursa between the semimembranosus muscle and the medial head of gastrocnemius can become enlarged. It presents as a painless lump in the medial part of the popliteal fossa. It is fluctuant but fluid and cannot be pushed between the muscles back into the joint. Unlike Baker's cyst, the knee is usually normal. If the lump aches it can be excised.

👁 WHAT YOU SHOULD SEE

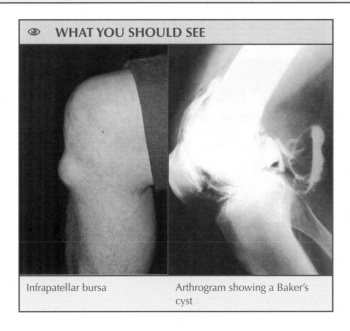

Infrapatellar bursa   Arthrogram showing a Baker's cyst

WHAT YOU SHOULD KNOW

Thickening of the fibrous tendon sheath (usually after local trauma or unaccustomed activity) leads to narrowing of the sheath. A flexor tendon may become trapped at the entrance to the sheath until in forced extension; it passes the constriction with a snap (triggering). Rheumatoid tenosynovitis can cause a similar activity. Treatment is to stop aggravating activity if possible, but injection with prednisolone into the tendon sheath (but not into the tendon itself) is usually successful. In refractory cases surgery is required in which the fibrous sheath is incised, allowing the tendon to move freely.

Related conditions

De Quervain's disease (stenosing tenovaginitis)

The sheath containing the extensor pollicis brevis and abductor pollicis longus becomes inflamed and thickened as a result of excessive or unaccustomed activity such as pruning roses or wringing out clothes. Typically women aged 30–50 years; complain of pain on radial side of wrist +/– swelling. The tenderness can be pinpointed to the tip of the radial styloid. **Finkelstein's test** confirms diagnosis: pain on passive adduction of thumb across palm and pain on active extension of thumb against resistance. Treatment as for trigger finger. Occasionally splintage of the wrist enforces rest.

Mallet finger/baseball finger

From injury to extensor tendon of terminal phalanx (e.g. by a cricket ball or baseball which forcibly ruptures the tendon). Patient cannot actively straighten terminal interphalangeal joint, so when all the fingers are extended the affected finger is bent at the TIP joint, although it can be passively straightened with ease. Treatment is by splintage for 6 weeks with the distal joint extended and the proximal interphalangeal joint flexed to allow tendon to reattach. K-wire fixation is another option.

Ruptured extensor pollicis longus

The long thumb extensor can rupture where it crosses the wrist (e.g. after a Colles' fracture or in rheumatoid arthritis). If the patient puts hands on a table, palm down, they cannot lift the thumb into the air (diagnostic test). Direct repair is unsatisfactory and a tendon transfer using the extensor indicis is needed.

Dropped finger

Sudden loss of finger extension at the metacarpophalangeal joint due to tendon rupture at the wrist (e.g. in rheumatoid arthritis). If direct repair is not possible, the distal portion can be attached to an adjacent finger extensor.

[418] Can be any digit, but typically the middle or ring fingers. The thumb may be affected in children.

TRIGGER FINGER

'This patient's middle (or ring[418]) finger on his right (dominant) hand remains flexed when he tries to open his hands from a fist. On further effort, or with help from the other hand, it suddenly straightens with a snap. The finger clicks when he bends it and a tender nodule is felt in front of the affected sheath. The diagnosis is stenosing tenovaginitis or trigger finger.'

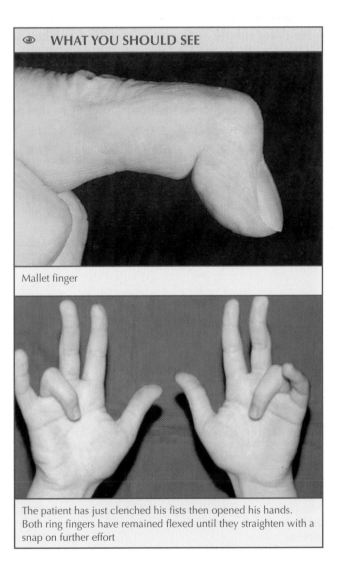

👁 **WHAT YOU SHOULD SEE**

Mallet finger

The patient has just clenched his fists then opened his hands. Both ring fingers have remained flexed until they straighten with a snap on further effort

Take a history from this young man with back pain

(see pg 316)

ANKYLOSING SPONDYLITIS

'I would like to present Mr W, a 20-year-old telesales operative. He has been getting increasing lower back pain over the last 6 months. It is worst in the morning and gets better after movement. He has no other joint pain. He finds his spine is stiffer than it used to be. He has no functional deficit and no changes to sensation or bowel/bladder function. He cannot recall any injury to his back. He is concerned as his father has ankylosing spondylitis and he thinks that he may be developing the same condition.[419] He has not noticed any deformity himself. He has no other medical history. He takes simple analgesia as required and has no known drug allergies. He does not smoke but drinks 20 units of alcohol per week. He lives with flatmates.

I would be concerned to exclude ankylosing spondylitis in this gentleman. Initially, I would like to examine him.'

✍ WHAT YOU SHOULD KNOW

[419] **Beware**, this condition may be completely undetected if the patient is propped up in a hospital bed. Get them to try and look at the ceiling.

[420] In an attempt to keep the visual axis horizontal (otherwise they are looking at their feet).

[421] Because the patient breathes by increased diaphragmatic excursion.

[422] **X-ray features**: typical loss of lumbar lordosis, increased thoracic kyphosis and compensatory c-spine extension seen on lateral views.

Fuzziness or erosion of sacroiliac joints is typical.

Ossification of the intervertebral discs – syndesmophytes bridge the intervertebral space, giving a typical bamboo spine appearance on AP/PA views.

CONTINUED ON pg 440

Examine this young man's back/or neck

(see pgs 346/343)

ANKYLOSING SPONDYLITIS

'This young man has loss of lumbar lordosis and a fixed kyphosis compensated for by extension of the cervical spine[420], producing a stooped 'question mark' posture. When I ask the patient to turn his head he turns his whole body. The range of movement of the spine is reduced in all directions, especially extension. Chest expansion is reduced and there is a prominent abdomen.[421] The diagnosis is ankylosing spondylitis. I would be interested in this patient's lumbar and thoracic spine X-rays.'[422]

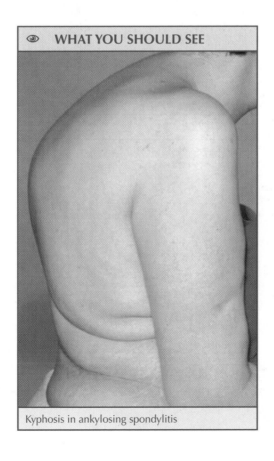

👁 **WHAT YOU SHOULD SEE**

Kyphosis in ankylosing spondylitis

WHAT YOU SHOULD KNOW (CONT)

Definition: idiopathic inflammatory disease mainly localised to the spine.

Epidemiology: young men (M:F/5:1), age of onset 15–25 years. More common in Western Europe.

Cause: unknown; 90–95% have HLA-B27; 1/4 of relatives affected.

Distribution: sacroiliac joints typically affected; vertebral joints often affected. Hips and shoulders sometimes involved. May present as an asymmetrical peripheral arthritis, usually of the large, weight-bearing joints. Small joints of hands and feet very rarely involved. May complain of painful heels at the site of insertion of the Achilles' tendon.

Pathological process: inflammation of ligamentous insertions → granulation tissue formation → erosion of articular cartilage and bone → replacement by fibrous tissue → ossification of fibrous tissue → ankylosis (fusion).

Clinical features: low back pain (differentiated from mechanical low back pain because it is typically worse in the morning and eases with exercise whereas mechanical back pain is brought on by exercise). Stiff spine (decreased movement in all directions, especially extension).

Deformity (as described in text on previous pages).

The wall test: if a healthy person stands with his back against the wall, the heels, buttocks, scapula and occiput should all be able to touch the wall simultaneously. If spine extension is diminished this is impossible.

Associated diseases (also associated with HLA-B27): inflammatory bowel disease, Reiter syndrome, *Yersinia* arthritis, acute anterior uveitis, psoriatic arthritis.

Extraskeletal manifestations: iritis (30%), aortitis (4%), apical pulmonary fibrosis, cardiac conduction defects (10%). Neurological complications (due to atlanto-axial dislocation or traumatic fracture of a rigid spine can result in tetra/paraplegia). Sciatica is also common and secondary amyloidosis.

Investigations: ESR is elevated, HLA-B27 +ve in 90%

Treatment: Analgesia (non-steroidal)

Exercise and intensive physiotherapy – this is the mainstay of preventing deterioration

Postural training

Joint replacement (e.g. hips) – may be necessary but have a very poor outcome

Vertebral osteotomy – severe flexion deformity of the spine can be partially corrected.

WHAT YOU SHOULD SEE

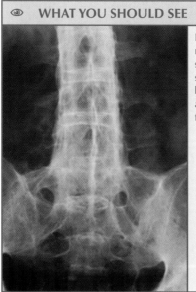

Lumbar spine X-ray of ankylosing spondylitis showing bamboo spine and sacroiliac fusion

PAGET'S DISEASE

✎ WHAT YOU SHOULD KNOW

Paget's disease is a non-inflammatory derangement of bone metabolism occurring in up to 10% of British people aged over 70 years, most of whom are asymptomatic. The bone is enlarged and thickened but because of the abnormal internal architecture, is unusually brittle. The cause is unknown but may be post-viral.

Pathology:
Initial osteolytic stage
Mixed osteolytic/osteoblastic stage
Final burnt-out quiescent osteosclerotic stage

Clinical presentation:
Incidental finding on X-ray
Pain, dull, constant, worse at night
Pathological fracture or non-union of a fracture
Deformity (e.g. bowing of tibia/femur, kyphosis)
Headaches, nerve root pain
Deafness (as a result of progressive closure of skull foramina and involvement of the ossicles)
Sarcoma in the elderly is rare and when it happens is often secondary to Paget's; it carries a poor prognosis
Rarer complications of Paget's – optic atrophy, brainstem signs, urolithiasis, high-output cardiac failure

X-rays:
General features: the bone is thick and dense with increased cortical thickening. The trabeculae are coarse and widely separated, giving a streaky or honeycomb appearance.
Skull X-rays: in the lytic stage osteoporosis circumscripta (sharply defined lytic areas) starts in the lower parts of the frontal and occipital regions and can cross suture lines to involve large areas of the skull vault. In the sclerotic stage the skull vault thickens and 'cotton wool' areas of sclerotic bone are seen. The facial bones are not commonly affected.

Diagnosis: raised plasma alkaline phosphatase and hydroxyproline. Raised urinary hydroxyproline.

Treatment: not indicated except in specific circumstances, when drugs such as calcitonin and bisphosphonates can be used.

Indications for treatment:
Persistent bone pain
Repeated fractures
Neurological complications (excluding deafness)
High-output cardiac failure
Hypercalcaemia due to immobilisation
Before and after bone surgery, where there is a risk of excessive haemorrhage
[423] Paget's disease is the only cause of true bowing of the tibia apart from rickets.

PAGET'S DISEASE

'I would like to present Mr W, a 60-year-old estate agent. He has a history over the last 2 years of dull pain in his left tibia. It has become constant and is worse at night. He has also noticed a change in the appearance of his leg, which looks bowed. He has no other painful areas and has no functional or neurological deficit. He cannot recall any injury to his leg. He has no other medical history. He takes simple analgesia as required and has no known drug allergies. He does not smoke but drinks 20 units of alcohol per week. He lives with his partner.

I would be concerned to exclude Paget's disease in this gentleman. Initially, I would like to examine him.'

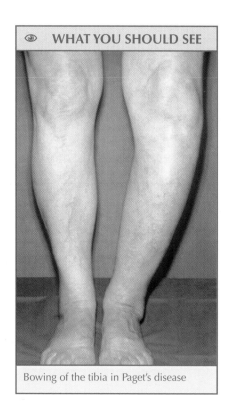

👁 **WHAT YOU SHOULD SEE**

Bowing of the tibia in Paget's disease

PAGET'S DISEASE

'There is (in this elderly patient) enlargement of the skull. There is also bowing of the tibia[423] (and more rarely the femur), which is warmer than the unaffected leg. The patient is kyphotic. I note the hearing aid. The diagnosis is Paget's disease. I would like to see the X-rays of the skull.

◉ WHAT YOU SHOULD SEE

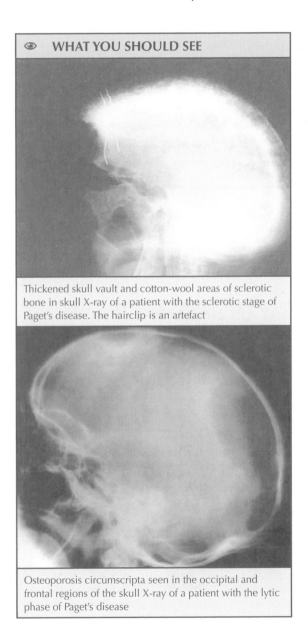

Thickened skull vault and cotton-wool areas of sclerotic bone in skull X-ray of a patient with the sclerotic stage of Paget's disease. The hairclip is an artefact

Osteoporosis circumscripta seen in the occipital and frontal regions of the skull X-ray of a patient with the lytic phase of Paget's disease

443

⌁ WHAT YOU SHOULD KNOW

This is the most common tumour of bone. It starts, usually in adolescence, as a cartilaginous overgrowth at the edge of the epiphysial plate and has usually ossified by the time it is palpable. On X-ray it is well-defined; often it looks smaller than it feels because the cartilage cap is invisible.

[424] **Calcaneal exostosis**: prominence of the calcaneus above and to the sides of the Achilles' tendon insertion causes blisters, calluses and difficulty in shoe fitting.

Cuneiform exostosis: formed by lipping of the first metatarsal and medial cuneiform.

Fifth metatarsal head: often associated with a varus deformity of the fifth toe (quinti varus).

Fifth metatarsal base: often unduly prominent in the narrow foot but seldom requires excision.

Subungual exostosis: commonest in the great toe and requires excision. May also occur under fingernails.

Tibial or femoral exostosis: seen at the diaphysis (around the knee).

Can also occur in other sites (e.g. humerus), typically arising from the epiphysial plate.

[425] Exostosis is a benign tumour that continues to grow as long as the parent bone grows: any further growth after that is suggestive of malignant change. If, as an adult, the lump becomes suddenly bigger or painful then excision is urgent – it may have become malignant. Otherwise, excision is only necessary if the lump is troublesome.

[426] Due to friction against footwear, in which case it may be tender.

[427] Exostoses may be multiple, especially in the familial form (hereditary multiple exostoses, or diaphyseal aclasis).

◉ WHAT YOU SHOULD SEE

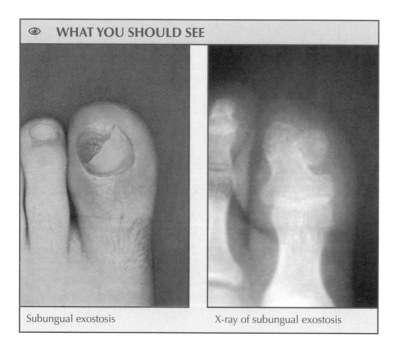

| Subungual exostosis | X-ray of subungual exostosis |

444

Take a history from and examine this young man with a lump on his foot

(see pgs 351–354)

EXOSTOSIS

'There is (in this young person) a (1–2-cm) bony-hard non-tender lump arising from the (say which typical site).[424] He says it is not painful but is troublesome as it can rub on footwear. It has been there for 3 years and has slowly increased in size over this time.[425]. It has (may have) a bursa overlying it.[426] There are no other similar lumps evident.[427]

This is typical of an osteochondroma, also known as a cartilage-capped exostosis.'

👁 WHAT YOU SHOULD SEE

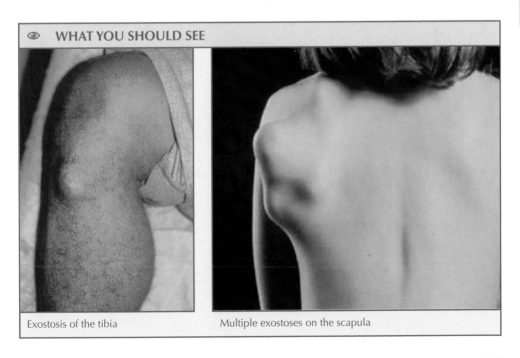

Exostosis of the tibia   Multiple exostoses on the scapula

🏷 WHAT YOU SHOULD KNOW

Abnormally high longitudinal arches produced by muscle imbalance. Usually associated with spastic diplegia, Friedreich's ataxia, Charcot–Marie–Tooth disease, polio or spina bifida. A neurological cause should always be sought if not obvious. In mild cases no treatment is required but special shoes may be required. Aims of surgery are to relieve symptoms and prevent skin breakdown in these areas. Options include correcting varus deformity of the heel, wedge osteotomy of the tarsus or metatarsal bases, fusion of PIP joints and flexor to extensor tendon transplants. Complex surgery should be deferred until the patient is over 16 years.

[428] **Friedreich's ataxia**: a progressive hereditary autosomal recessive ataxia with onset in childhood or adolescence. It is caused by spinocerebellar degeneration and is characterised by pes cavus, kyphoscoliosis, a clumsy, lurching, broad-based gait and intention tremor affecting the lower limbs, upper limbs, trunk and head. Knee and ankle jerks are absent and the plantar response is extensor. Position and vibration sense are diminished in the feet. Coordination tests such as rapid alternate motion, finger-nose and heel-shin tests are impaired (see neurological examination of the lower limb, pg 365 and upper limb, pg 356). There may be nystagmus and dysarthria. Corrective foot or spinal surgery may be needed but death usually occurs before the age of 50.

[429] **Charcot–Marie–Tooth disease** is a hereditary motor and sensory neuropathy that usually presents in childhood or adolescence with difficulty in walking and pes cavus. There is muscle wasting restricted to below the knee, giving rise to an 'inverted champagne bottle' appearance and a high-stepping gait due to foot drop. The tendon reflexes become depressed and there is a variable degree of sensory loss. Affected individuals may be helped by the use of orthotic appliances and sometimes by surgical correction of the foot deformity or tendon transfer.

[430] **Spastic paraparesis** has many causes, including multiple sclerosis, cord compression, trauma to the spinal cord, birth injury (cerebral palsy) and motor neurone disease. The patient is usually wheelchair-bound. The tone in the legs is increased and they are weak, with contractures and disuse atrophy. There is bilateral ankle clonus and the plantar responses are extensor.

[431] **Polio** may affect only one leg that will be short, wasted, weak, flaccid with absent reflexes and a normal plantar response. The affected leg may show true shortening due to growth impairment if the limb was affected in childhood.

Examine this young man with a deformity of his feet

(see pg 351)

PES CAVUS

'The feet are markedly deformed with a high arch and clawed toes. There is first metatarsal drop, varus deformity of the heel, decreased subtalar mobility, weakness of intrinsic muscles, and calloses under the metatarsal heads and heel. This is pes cavus. Although it can be an isolated, familial problem, neurological problems such as Friedreich's ataxia[428], Charcot–Marie–Tooth disease[429], spastic paraparesis[430], polio[431], and spina bifida should be excluded.'

CHAPTER 5
LIMBS AND SPINE

👁 **WHAT YOU SHOULD SEE**

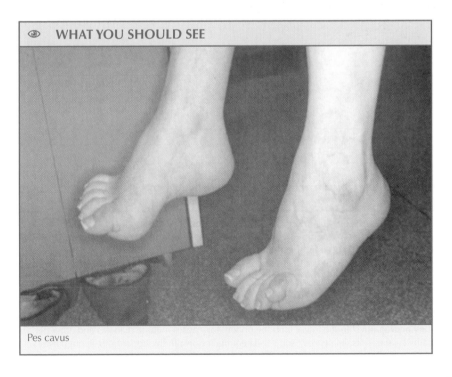

Pes cavus

Take a history
from this
gentleman
with severe
deformity of his
knees and ankles

CHARCOT'S JOINT

'I would like to present Mr W, an 80-year-old retired printer. He has developed severely deformed ankle and knee joints over the last 3 years. He explains that he gets no pain in these joints. He is currently unable to walk and confined to a wheelchair due to his deformity. He tells me that he cannot sense where his joints are in space; nor can he feel touch sensation over this area. He has no problems with his other joints. He has sustained a number of falls in which he has injured his knees and ankles over the last 3 years. Of note he is a type 2 diabetic, which was diagnosed 40 years ago. He is now on insulin. His other medical history includes hypertension. He is on multiple antihypertensives but has no known drug allergies. He does not smoke but drinks 40 units of alcohol per week.

I suspect this gentleman has Charcot's joints secondary to his diabetes. Initially, I would like to examine him to confirm this diagnosis.'

⌨ WHAT YOU SHOULD KNOW

Charcot's disease or neuropathic arthritis is a rapidly progressive degeneration in a joint that lacks position sense and protective pain sensation. There is marked destruction of articular cartilage and the underlying bone, and microscopic spicules of bone become embedded in the synovium. Ligaments and capsule are lax and at the joint periphery there is florid new bone formation. X-rays show obvious gross bone destruction. The joint may be subluxated or dislocated. There are irregular calcified masses in the capsule. Treatment is of the underlying cause, but the affected joint can only be stabilised (e.g. with a caliper). Surgery is not usually useful or successful.

[432] Ask **'Have you ever suffered from any of the following: diabetes, syphilis, leprosy, spinal cord injury, hereditary neuropathy?'** In the lower limb the underlying causes include diabetes and other peripheral neuropathies, tabes dorsalis, leprosy and cauda equina lesions. In the upper limb, syringomyelia.

Examine this gentleman's knee

(see pgs 329)

CHARCOT'S JOINT

'This knee is markedly deformed and swollen, with a large effusion, gross instability and an abnormally increased range of movement, accompanied by loud crepitus. Despite this, the joint is painless, which suggests a neuropathic arthritis or Charcot's joint. I would like to carry out a neurological examination of the leg (see pg 365) or ask the patient a couple of questions about his medical history.'[432]

👁 WHAT YOU SHOULD SEE

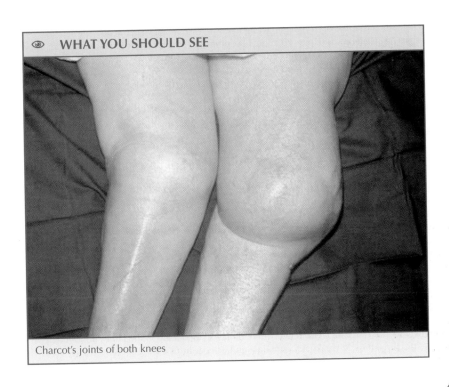

Charcot's joints of both knees

> Take a history from this gentleman with tingling in his hands

ACROMEGALY

'I would like to present Mr W, a 40-year-old newsagent. His main complaint today is of 6 months of tingling in the thumb, index and middle fingers of his hands bilaterally. This is worse at night. He has no associated weakness and no recent injuries. He also gives a history of a gradual onset of a variety of different symptoms over the past 12 years. These include increasing shoe and hat size and a change in his facial appearance. He has also found that he has been sweating excessively. He has a constant headache with associated change in his vision.[433] His other medical history includes hypertension. He is on an antihypertensive but has no known drug allergies. He does not smoke but drinks 40 units of alcohol per week. I suspect this gentleman has bilateral carpal tunnel syndrome, perhaps secondary to acromegaly. Initially, I would like to examine him to confirm this diagnosis.'

WHAT YOU SHOULD KNOW

This is a rare condition caused by excess of growth hormone, usually due to a hypersecreting pituitary adenoma. The mean age of onset is 27 years but the mean age of presentation is over 40 years due to the vague and insidious nature of the symptoms. These patients will not become giants unless the hormonal imbalance begins before epiphysial closure (i.e. adolescence). After this no further lengthening of the long bones is possible. The orthopaedic implications in this case are limited (a predisposition to osteoarthritis and carpal tunnel syndrome), but there are neurological signs too (visual field disturbance, median nerve palsy, third nerve palsy).

Symptoms: sweating, increased size of gloves, shoes, hats, dentures and rings. Paraesthesia of hands and feet. Digital pain and stiffness. Arthralgia, hypogonadism, headache, visual field disturbance.

Clinical signs: as listed opposite plus goitre, gynaecomastia, galactorrhoea, small gonads (all due to hypopituitarism due to space-occupying adenoma in pituitary), greasy skin, acne, prominent superficial veins of extremities, cardiomegaly, third nerve palsy.

Other features: diabetes mellitus, hypertension, hypercalciuria, hypercalcaemia, diabetes insipidus, osteoporosis.

MEN type I: acromegaly caused by a pituitary tumour may be sporadic or may be part of the multiple endocrine neoplasia syndrome type I (Werner syndrome) which involves two or more of:
- Pituitary tumour
- Islet cell tumour
- Primary hyperparathyroidism
- Adrenocortical adenoma

Investigations: comparative study of old photographs of the patient; skull X-ray; glucose tolerance test (normal growth hormone levels are nearly nil 60 minutes after 75 g oral glucose, but are elevated in acromegalics). CT/MRI of pituitary.

Treatment: trans-sphenoidal hypophysectomy, transfrontal hypophysectomy, external beam irradiation, radioactive implants, bromocriptine.

[433] Typically peripheral field defect due to enlargement of the pituitary mass pressing on the medial aspects of both optic tracts at the optic chiasma, causing bitemporal hemianopia. Get the patient to cover each eye in turn, looking straight ahead, and tell you when he can see your finger coming around from the periphery of his vision in each of the four quadrants. He should show marked delay in seeing the finger coming in from the lateral side (as if he were wearing blinkers).

[435] This gives him the appearance of a circus giant (many of whom were acromegalic). Don't say this in front of the patient in case it gives offence! Think of 'Jaws,' the villain in the James Bond movie.

[436] Due to proximal muscle weakness, arthralgia and osteoarthritis.

450

> Examine this gentleman's hands and general appearance and then review his X-rays[434]

'This patient's hands are large, doughy and spade-shaped and the skin over the back of them is thickened. There is (may be) loss of the thenar eminence bilaterally, which is evidence of carpal tunnel syndrome (offer to carry out the carpal tunnel syndrome/median nerve examination on pg 359 if so). The patient's face has some unusual characteristics, with a large lower jaw, full lips and prominent supraorbital ridges. There is poor occlusion of the teeth, the lower teeth overbiting in front of the upper. The nose, tongue and ears are enlarged.[435] He is kyphotic, with bowed legs and a rolling gait. He has difficulty standing from his seat.[436] He has a deep, husky voice and is hirsute. The diagnosis is acromegaly.'

👁 **WHAT YOU SHOULD SEE**

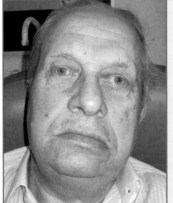
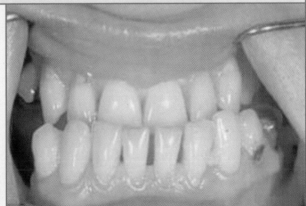

Acromegalic face

The teeth in acromegaly showing interdentate separation

WHAT YOU SHOULD KNOW (CONT)

[434] **Features of acromegalic X-rays** (see below)

Skull:
    Enlargement and erosion of the pituitary fossa
    Prognathism (increased angle of mandible)
    Enlarged paranasal air sinuses and mastoids
    Enlargement of the occipital protuberance

Vertebrae:
    An increase in AP and transverse dimensions
    Posterior scalloping
    Kyphosis

Hands:
    'Spade like' with broadening of the fingers
    Terminal tufts ('oak trees')
    Widening of metacarpophalangeal joints due to cartilage hypertrophy
    Joints: Premature osteoarthritis and chondrocalcinosis

Soft tissues:
    Increased heel pad thickness (>25 mm)

WHAT YOU SHOULD SEE

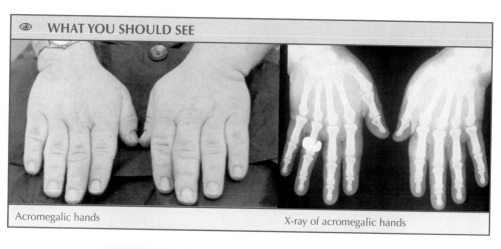

Acromegalic hands

X-ray of acromegalic hands

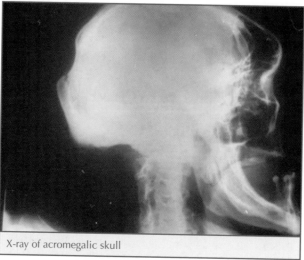

X-ray of acromegalic skull

RUPTURED BICEPS TENDON

'This (middle-aged or older) gentleman volunteers in his local charity shop. He was lifting a particularly heavy box 1 week ago when he felt a snap in his right (dominant) upper arm.[437] It aches a bit but otherwise he has no symptoms. On examination, he still has good function of his shoulder and elbow but, when the elbow is flexed actively against resistance, the belly of the biceps muscle contracts into a prominent lump which is abnormal compared with the other side.

The diagnosis is a tear of the long head of biceps.'

🖉 WHAT YOU SHOULD KNOW

Usually preceded by degeneration and fraying, tears of the long head of biceps normally require no surgical treatment.

Related conditions:

Bicipital tendonitis: usually occurring together with rotator cuff impingement or after unaccustomed shoulder activity. Sharp localised tenderness in the bicipital groove, worse on flexion against resistance. Rest or occasionally steroid injections usually settle it.

Tears of the distal biceps tendon: rare. Follow an acute flexion strain of the elbow rather than after degeneration. The tendon tears cleanly or is avulsed from the radial tuberosity. Difficult to diagnose; clues include suggestive history, pain in lower forearm, local bruising and loss of power in elbow flexion and supination. The tendon should be repaired to preserve full function.

[437] Usually while lifting, the patient feels something snap. The shoulder and upper arm ache for a while but then feel normal. Function usually returns to normal when the tenderness has settled.

👁 WHAT YOU SHOULD SEE

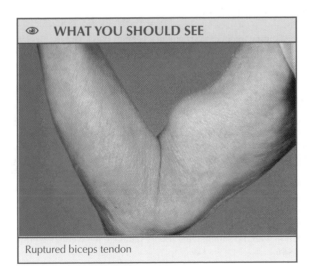

Ruptured biceps tendon

VARICOSE VEINS

'I would like to present Mrs W, a 40-year-old hairdresser. She has had bilateral varicose veins for the last 6 months. She finds that her legs ache at the end of the day, especially when she is working, as she is on her feet the majority of the time. She also dislikes the cosmetic appearance. She denies any skin changes, ulceration or bleeding. Her mother also had varicose veins, which required operation. She has no history of DVT. She has no other medical problems, takes no medication and has no known drug allergies. She has smoked for 20 pack years and drinks 21 units of alcohol per week.

This lady gives a history of varicose veins which are primary in aetiology. Initially, I would like to examine her to confirm this diagnosis.'

✏ WHAT YOU SHOULD KNOW

Aetiology of varicose veins:
Primary: Idiopathic
Secondary: Deep vein thrombosis, pregnancy, pelvic tumours, congenital disorders (see Klippel–Trenaunay syndrome, pg 508)
Commonest in long saphenous distribution but also occur in short saphenous distribution.
Factors predisposing to varicose veins:
Age, female, parity, occupation, family history, obesity.
Pathology:
Primary weakness of the wall of the vein causes dilation just below the valve, which causes valvular incompetence, leading to varicosity.
Symptoms:
Unsightliness, ache on standing, night cramps, ankle swelling, skin changes, ulceration.
Treatment:
Conservative:
Elastic support stockings
Sclerotherapy – injection of a sclerosant directly into the vein followed by compression bandaging. Works well for small varicosities
Surgery:
'High tie' (saphenofemoral disconnection and ligation) stripping and multiple avulsions.
The saphenous vein and all the tributaries which enter the saphenous vein near the saphenofemoral junction are ligated and divided. The saphenous vein itself must be ligated flush with the femoral vein but must not narrow it. A stripper is then passed into the saphenous vein, down the thigh and out of an incision just above the knee. The vein is thus stripped from the thigh, and previously marked varicosities below the knee are avulsed through individual stab incisions. Stripping the long saphenous vein below the knee is often discouraged because of its close association with the sural nerve, which supplies sensation to the medial side of the foot. The short saphenous vein can be similarly disconnected at the saphenopopliteal junction with the patient lying prone. Bandage the whole leg firmly.
CONTINUED ON pg 456

Examine this lady's varicose veins

(see pg 369)

VARICOSE VEINS

'On inspection there are visible dilated varicose veins on both legs, in the distribution of the long saphenous vein. There is evidence of venous insufficiency in the gaiter area, with oedema, pigmentation, lipodermatosclerosis and eczema. On the lower right leg there is a large venous ulcer (see case, pg 458). There is a palpable saphena varix in both groins with a cough impulse. There is a positive tap test. The tourniquet test reveals that the veins are controlled at the saphenofemoral junction. Doppler examination confirms an incompetent saphenofemoral junction and a competent deep system. The foot pulses and perfusion are good. This patient has varicose veins with signs of venous insufficiency. Indications are that a high tie and stripping would improve her symptoms.'

👁 WHAT YOU SHOULD SEE

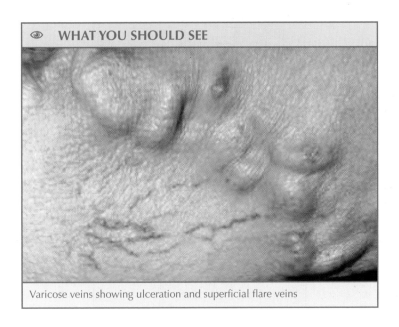

Varicose veins showing ulceration and superficial flare veins

✍ WHAT YOU SHOULD KNOW (CONT)

Tributaries entering near the saphenofemoral junction:
- Superficial inferior epigastric vein
- Deep external pudendal vein
- Superficial external pudendal vein
- Posteromedial vein of the thigh
- Anterolateral vein of the thigh
- Superficial circumflex iliac vein

These should be ligated, along with the saphenous vein, to prevent recurrence.

Post-operative complications:

Tie on the saphenofemoral/saphenopopliteal junction slips off – always do a transfixion stitch for this important tie. If it slips off immediate re-exploration is indicated

Wound infection (especially groin)

Haematoma or bleeding – minimised by firm bandaging

Recurrence – often because tributaries (above) have been missed. Later recurrences may reflect underlying valvular weakness in the superficial venous system

Other treatment options:

Laser, foam injection, radiofrequency ablation. These cause damage to endothelium which is then compressed by bandaging.

◉ WHAT YOU SHOULD SEE

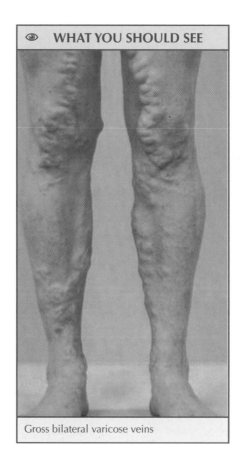

Gross bilateral varicose veins

VENOUS ULCER

✐ WHAT YOU SHOULD KNOW

[438] Healthy granulation tissue in a healing ulcer.
[439] If long-standing.
[440] If infected and enlarging.
[441] **Management of a venous ulcer**
Remember this eight-point plan:
1. Exclude co-existing ischaemia and treat if present
By measuring ankle–brachial pressure index (see pg 374, examination of the ischaemic limb) the degree of ischaemia, if present, can be defined. Mixed ulcers exist where arterial and venous factors prevent healing, and they are much more difficult to treat than simple venous ulcers. In such mixed ulcers any ischaemic component must be corrected first if possible (by angioplasty or surgery) before the venous element is treated. This is because (a) an ulcer will not heal in the absence of sufficient blood supply, and (b) the methods of treating a venous ulcer will further compromise the blood supply and lead to complications.
2. Elevation
This improves venous return but it is notoriously difficult to ensure compliance and some patients are admitted to hospital just to ensure their bed is on a slope and their feet are elevated above the hips while at rest.
3. Four-layer bandaging
These layers are
a) Non-adherent dressing to protect the ulcer
b) Wool to cushion the dressing and protect the vulnerable surrounding skin
c) Graduated compression bandage – the functional component of the dressing, which encourages venous return. It runs from foot to thigh
d) Tubular bandage – an elastic bandage which merely keeps the whole dressing in place and stops the compression bandage from unravelling
4. Weekly dressing and measuring
Preferably in a specialist clinic; 80–90% are healed within 12 months. Complications such as infection and Marjolin's ulcer are looked out for at these weekly assessments. Infected ulcers should be swabbed and treated with topical agents (e.g. Betadine dressing), not systemic antibiotics.
5. Plastic surgery
If healing is not progressing excision of ulcer base and skin grafting may be appropriate.
AFTER HEALING:
6. Investigate venous system
e.g. by duplex Doppler, venous pressure measurements or venography to assess the sites of valve incompetence and function of the deep venous system.
7. Saphenous surgery
Successful in preventing reulceration in patients with normal deep veins but contraindicated in post-thrombotic limbs.
8. Preventative measures
TED stockings, avoid minor trauma.

> Take a history from this lady with an ulcer on her leg

VENOUS ULCER

'I would like to present Mrs W, an 80-year-old retired cook. She has an ulcer on the inside of her left leg. It initially began as a dark-purple patch 3 months ago. Since then the skin has broken down and an ulcer has formed. It is non-tender. It discharges a clear fluid and is not red or hot. She also has long-term swollen ankles, although she has no symptoms of peripheral vascular disease. She has cardiac failure for which she is on diuretics. She has had two MIs over 10 years ago and had coronary stenting. She lives in a nursing home and mobilises with a zimmer frame. She has no drug allergies, is a lifelong non-smoker and teetotaller.

I think this lady has a venous ulcer. Initially, I would like to examine her to confirm this diagnosis.'

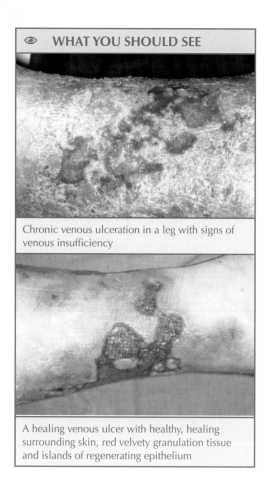

WHAT YOU SHOULD SEE

Chronic venous ulceration in a leg with signs of venous insufficiency

A healing venous ulcer with healthy, healing surrounding skin, red velvety granulation tissue and islands of regenerating epithelium

VENOUS ULCER

'There is a large, shallow, painful, ulcer on the medial side of the gaiter area in a well-perfused foot with good pulses. The edges are gently sloping or terraced and the base is red and velvety[438]/white and fibrous[439]/yellow, sloughy and offensive[440]. Surrounding tissues show signs of long-standing venous disease, including oedema, haemosiderin deposition, lipodermatosclerosis and varicose veins. This is a venous ulcer.'[441]

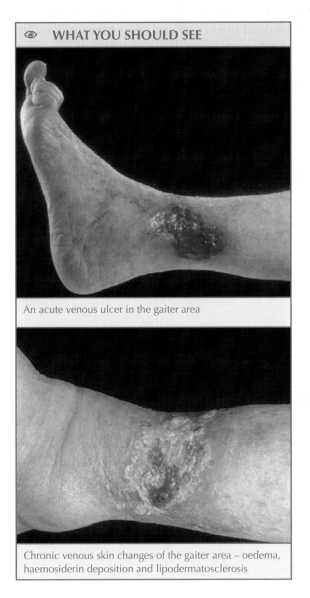

⊙ WHAT YOU SHOULD SEE

An acute venous ulcer in the gaiter area

Chronic venous skin changes of the gaiter area – oedema, haemosiderin deposition and lipodermatosclerosis

DEEP VEIN THROMBOSIS

'I would like to present Mrs W, a 64-year-old housewife. She is currently an inpatient following an elective left total hip replacement 5 days ago. She complains of a 1-day history of a tender, swollen left calf. She has had no similar problems before. She has no complaints of chest pain or SOB. She has been wearing TED stockings since the operation and having a daily injection of low-molecular-weight heparin. She has no other medical history of note. She takes no medication, has no drug allergies, is a lifelong non-smoker and teetotaller.

I think this lady has developed a left leg DVT following her THR despite DVT prevention measures. Initially, I would like to examine her to confirm this diagnosis.'

✏️ WHAT YOU SHOULD KNOW

Risk factors for DVT

Patient	Procedure	Underlying disease
Old	Type of operation (pelvic)	General injury
Female	Type of anaesthesia (GA)	Local injury
Winter	Long operation	Malignancy
Caucasian	Immobilisation	Cardiac failure
Sedentary occupation	Bedrest	Myocardial infarction
Obesity	Dehydration	Arterial ischaemia
Pregnancy		Protein C and S deficiency

Drugs	Venous disorders
Combined oral contraceptive pill	Previous DVT/PE
Intravenous saline	Varicose veins
Haemostatic treatment	Vasculitis (e.g. Buerger's, Behçet's)
Other drugs	Congenital venous abnormalities (e.g. Klippel–Trenaunay syndrome)

Incidence
98% arise in the deep veins of legs and pelvis, 2% at other sites. If no prophylaxis were used, 30% of all patients over 40 having major surgery would develop DVTs (60% after hip surgery).

Pathogenesis of DVT
Remember Virchow's triad, a common exam question. Stasis, wall damage and hypercoagulability make up the triad, and disruption of any one of these predisposes to thrombogenesis. Aschoff's theory of thrombosis is a four-stage hypothesis:
1. Corallin thrombus plug forms (platelets adhere to endothelial surface, fibrin and red cells are deposited on top)
2. Blood flow occluded
3. Rapidly propagating thrombus forms
4. Thrombus becomes organised

CONTINUED ON pg 462

Examine this lady's left leg

DEEP VEIN THROMBOSIS

'The left lower leg is swollen, red, hot and tender. There is pitting oedema to the knee. The calf muscle is hard and tender, and passive dorsiflexion of the foot causes pain in the calf (Homan's sign). There are bruises on the abdomen/thigh in keeping with subcutaneous injections of low-molecular-weight heparin. This is a deep vein thrombosis.'

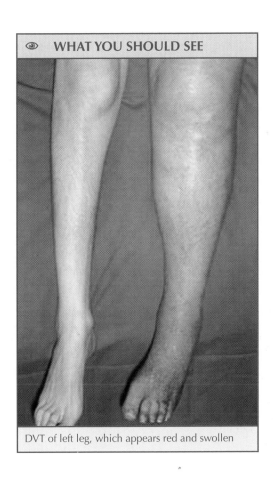

👁 WHAT YOU SHOULD SEE

DVT of left leg, which appears red and swollen

WHAT YOU SHOULD KNOW (CONT)

Swelling may be just around the ankle or extend to the groin depending on the extent of the thrombosis. Few conditions make the calf muscle stiff and hard, although many make it tender.

Homan's test

Although the classic bedside test for DVT, Homan's test, is unreliable. Some say that repeatedly performing the test can dislodge thrombus and cause a pulmonary embolus, but others say that most emboli come from the large veins, not the calf veins. Because of this controversy, you may find it wiser to offer to perform the test and proceed only if the examiners appear to approve of it.

Differential diagnosis for DVT

- Torn gastrocnemius muscle
- Ruptured Baker's cyst
- Calf haematoma
- Lymphoedema and cellulitis
- Acute arterial ischaemia
- Obstruction of veins and lymphatics
- Fractured femur
- Superficial thrombophlebitis
- Acute arteritis/haemarthrosis of the knee
- Achilles' tendonitis
- Peripheral oedema
- Sarcoma
- Myositis ossificans

Prophylaxis of DVT

Pre-operative:	Intra-operative	Post-operative:
Stop pill 6 weeks before	Care in positioning	Heparin
Keep mobile	Flowtron boots	Early mobilisation
Identify high-risk patients	Keep time on the table	Deep breathing to aid
Subcutaneous heparin	to a minimum	venous return
or IV dextran	Keep well hydrated	Clinical vigilance for signs of DVT
	Elevate foot of bed	TED stockings
	Feet up when sat out	
	Don't cross legs	

Complications of DVT

Pulmonary embolus: most originating from femoral, iliac and pelvic veins.

Venous gangrene: rare complication of massive ileofemoral thrombosis. Phlegmasia alba dolens (white leg) is followed by phlegmasia cerulea dolens (blue leg) and finally venous gangrene and toxaemia.

Pulmonary hypertension: develops after recurrent emboli.

Paradoxical embolus: in the presence of a patent foramen ovale or ductus arteriosus, emboli from venous thrombosis can produce an arterial occlusion in the limbs or brain.

Management of DVT

- Anticoagulation (LMW heparin, warfarin)
- Inferior vena cava filter
- Thrombolysis with streptokinase or TPA (not after major surgery!)

Superficial thrombophlebitis

Definition: venous thrombosis affecting the superficial veins.

Causes: varicose veins, sclerotherapy, trauma, chemical irritation, local sepsis. Associated with carcinoma and DVT.

Clinical: painful, hard, hot, reddened subcutaneous cord.

Treatment: analgesia and external elastic support. Condition is usually self-limiting. Surgical treatment is rarely indicated unless the upper end of the long saphenous vein is involved (superficial vein ligation described by John Hunter in 1784).

Complications: recurrence should suggest thrombophlebitis migrans associated with underlying carcinoma. Co-existent DVT is common; ultrasound or venography may be indicated.

DEEP VEIN THROMBOSIS

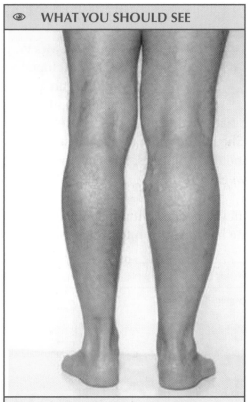

Deep vein thrombosis. Note dilated superficial veins on the right

CHAPTER 5
LIMBS AND SPINE

AXILLARY VEIN THROMBOSIS

'I would like to present Mrs W, a 44-year-old housewife. She has developed a painful, swollen, warm right arm. It began a day after she painted her living room. She has no other history of injury. She has never had anything like this before. She has no complaints of chest pain or SOB. She has no other medical history of note. She takes no medication and has no drug allergies. She has smoked for 20 pack years and drinks 14 units per week.

I think this lady has developed a right upper limb venous occlusion. Initially, I would like to examine her to confirm this diagnosis.'

🖐 WHAT YOU SHOULD KNOW

Accounts for 1–2% of all venous thromboses.
Causes:
Idiopathic; cervical rib; thoracic outlet obstruction (see pg 498).
History:
Affects right hand most commonly and develops after excessive or unusual exercise (nick-named 'effort thrombosis').
Patients are often young (35–45 years).
Presents with discomfort and weakness.
Investigations:
Chest X-ray and CT thorax to exclude Pancoast's tumour or lymphoma; cervical spine X-ray to exclude cervical rib. Brachial venography is required to confirm diagnosis and extent of thrombosis.
Management:
Conservative – especially if patient presents late. Most untreated patients develop good collateral pathways and become symptom-free after a few months.
Anticoagulants – usually given for 3 months to prevent propagation of thrombus or the faint possibility of pulmonary embolus.
Thrombolysis – streptokinase or TPA may reduce late sequelae of chronic venous insufficiency.
Surgical decompression – combined with thrombectomy.
Surgical bypass – utilising internal jugular vein.

Course of axillary vein
- Brachial artery venae comitantes join basilic vein at the lower border of teres major axillary vein
- Runs upwards on the medial side of the axillary artery
- Ends at the lateral border of the first rib by becoming the subclavian vein
- Tributaries include:
  - Cephalic vein
  - Highest thoracic vein
  - Thoraco-acromial vein
  - Lateral thoracic vein
  - Subscapular vein
  - Anterior circumflex humeral vein
  - Posterior circumflex humeral vein
The last six correspond with the branches of the axillary artery.

AXILLARY VEIN THROMBOSIS

'The right arm is painful and weak. The fingers, hand and forearm feel cool and are swollen and blue. There is pitting oedema on the dorsum of the hand and the subcutaneous veins appear distended, with enlarged collateral veins over the shoulder and chest. The upper limb pulses are present and undiminished. The finger movements are diminished, but sensation is intact and movement of the rest of the arm is limited only by pain and swelling. A tender cord can be felt along the course of the axillary vein (see opposite). There is no palpable cervical rib and no cervical lymphadenopathy. The diagnosis is axillary vein thrombosis.'

👁 WHAT YOU SHOULD SEE

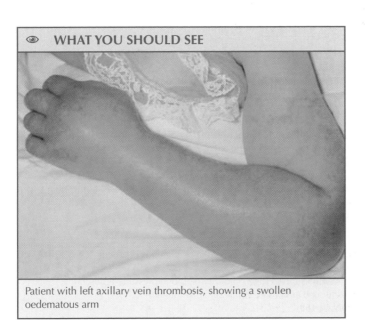

Patient with left axillary vein thrombosis, showing a swollen oedematous arm

465

Take a history from this man with a painful leg

(see pg 320)

ISCHAEMIC LEG

'I would like to present Mr W, a 72-year-old retired plumber. He complains of bilateral lower limb pain, right greater than left. He feels it in his calves. Initially it would only occur on walking but lately he has it at rest. He also gets the pain at night and will hang his right leg out of the bed to try to get some relief. He has no ulceration that he has noticed. His medical history includes diabetes, hypertension and hypercholesterolaemia and he had a stroke 2 years ago. He is on multiple medications and is allergic to penicillin. He lives with his daughter and her family, who are his carers. He has a 60 pack year smoking history and drinks 30 units of alcohol per week.

I think this gentleman has bilateral PVD with stenosis/occlusion in the SFA with symptoms of critical ischaemia. Initially, I would like to examine him to confirm this diagnosis.'

✏ WHAT YOU SHOULD KNOW

Peripheral vascular disease of lower limbs

Aetiology

The main cause of arterial disease in the lower limb is <u>atherosclerosis</u>, either thrombotic or embolic. Other causes include:

<u>Thromboembolism</u> from another source (cardiac, aortic or other aneurysms)

<u>Anatomical or developmental anomalies</u> (popliteal entrapment syndrome, persistent sciatic artery, adventitial cystic disease, fibromuscular dysplasia)

<u>Inflammatory conditions</u> (Buerger's disease, vasculitis, repetitive trauma)

<u>Vasospastic conditions</u> (Raynaud's phenomenon, ergotism, IV drug use)

<u>Hypercoagulable states</u> (anticoagulant deficiency, e.g. protein C or S, polycythaemia, malignancy, thrombocytosis)

Symptoms

Intermittent claudication involving the calf in SFA disease, the thigh and buttock in iliac disease

Rest pain and night pain indicates more severe insufficiency

Ulceration from small ulcers to major tissue loss

Investigations

Ankle–brachial pressure index (see pg 376).

Contrast angiography (generally only needed if intervention is planned)

Magnetic resonance angiography (MRA)

Assess risk factors such as blood sugar, cholesterol, blood pressure, lipids

Assess co-morbidity such as cardiac, renal and lung function

CONTINUED ON pg 468

Examine this gentleman's legs

(see pg 374)

ISCHAEMIC LEG

'This (male, middle-aged to elderly) patient has nicotine-stained fingers. His legs are pale, with venous guttering, cyanosis and rubor around the feet. The left foot is painful at rest with two painful ulcers, one on the heel and one on the middle toe. Buerger's test is positive with an angle of 50° on the right and 30° on the left, suggesting ischaemia. The feet are cool and capillary refill is delayed at 4 seconds. The femoral pulses are present, but on the left the popliteal pulses are diminished and the foot pulses are absent. On the right the pulses are present. There is a bruit over the left superficial femoral artery two-thirds of the way down the medial thigh. This patient has significant bilateral peripheral vascular disease, worse on the left with a likely atherosclerotic stricture at the left adductor hiatus, complicated by rest pain and tissue loss. I would like to have a hand-held Doppler and sphygmomanometer to check the ankle–brachial pressure indices.'

👁 **WHAT YOU SHOULD SEE**

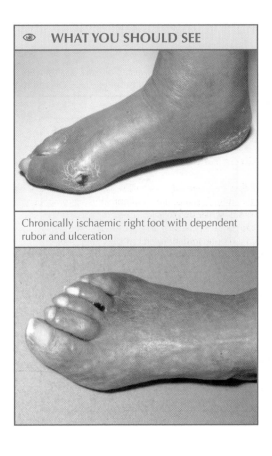

Chronically ischaemic right foot with dependent rubor and ulceration

☝ WHAT YOU SHOULD KNOW (CONT)

Management of peripheral vascular disease
Claudication is managed conservatively if possible:
Stop smoking
Treat hypertension, diabetes, hypercholesterolaemia
Lose weight
Take 75–325 mg aspirin daily
Avoid diuretics and beta-blockers
Follow a graded exercise programme to increase collateral circulation
Do not get an angiogram unless you are planning intervention
Eighty per cent of claudicants remain stable or improve when treated as above over 1 year, 50% over 5 years; 10% develop indications for intervention and 5% die of cardiovascular disease each year.

Indications for intervention
Worsening life-limiting claudication despite the above measures
Rest pain
Tissue loss (ulcers)
Sudden deterioration (e.g. acutely ischaemic limb)

Options for intervention
Percutaneous endovascular revascularisation
Balloon angioplasty
Stenting
Best in focal SFA stenosis or isolated iliac lesions.
Extensive disease may require surgery.
Surgery
Endarterectomy
Patch angioplasty
Bypass: anatomical (e.g. femoral-popliteal, femoral-distal) or extra-anatomical (e.g. axillo-bifemoral). The graft can be autologous (e.g. long saphenous vein) or prosthetic (e.g. Dacron or PTFE grafts).

◉ WHAT YOU SHOULD SEE

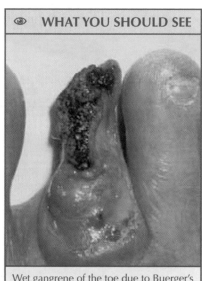

Wet gangrene of the toe due to Buerger's disease

ISCHAEMIC LEG

👁 WHAT YOU SHOULD SEE

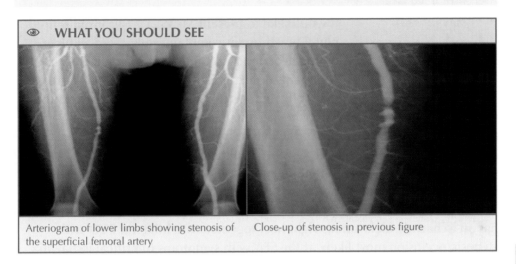

Arteriogram of lower limbs showing stenosis of the superficial femoral artery

Close-up of stenosis in previous figure

📋 WHAT YOU SHOULD KNOW

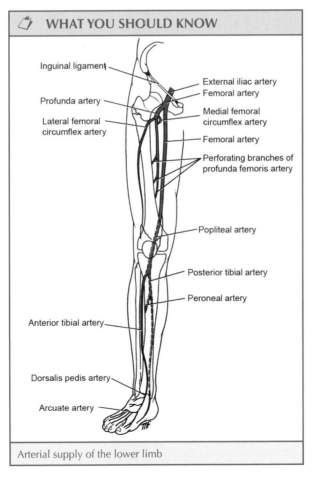

Inguinal ligament

Profunda artery

Lateral femoral circumflex artery

External iliac artery
Femoral artery
Medial femoral circumflex artery
Femoral artery
Perforating branches of profunda femoris artery

Popliteal artery

Posterior tibial artery

Peroneal artery

Anterior tibial artery

Dorsalis pedis artery

Arcuate artery

Arterial supply of the lower limb

Take a history
from this man
with a leg ulcer

(see pg 320)

ISCHAEMIC ULCER

'I would like to present Mr W, a 72-year-old retired plumber. His main complaint today is of an ulcer on the heel of his right foot. It is painful. He also complains of bilateral lower limb pain, right greater than left. He feels it in his calves. Initially it would only occur on walking but lately he has it at rest. He also gets the pain at night and will hang his right leg out of the bed to try to get some relief. His medical history includes diabetes, hypertension, hypercholesterolaemia and he had a stroke 2 years ago. He is on multiple medications and is allergic to penicillin. He lives with his daughter and her family who are his carers. He has a 60 pack year smoking history and drinks 30 units of alcohol per week. This gentleman has an ischaemic ulcer on his right heel together with bilateral PVD with stenosis/occlusion most likely at the SFA with symptoms of critical ischaemia. Initially, I would like to examine him to confirm this diagnosis.'

✏ WHAT YOU SHOULD KNOW

[442] Heel, malleoli, head of fifth metatarsal, tips of toes, between the toes and the ball of the foot are typical sites for ischaemic ulceration.
[443] See pg 374.
[444] Even if the ulcer is painful, examination of the ischaemic leg (especially in a diabetic) will often show loss of superficial and deep sensation, weakness of movement and loss of reflexes.

Management of an ischaemic ulcer
An ulcer will not heal in the absence of sufficient blood supply, so the main aim of management is to restore circulation to the affected limb.
1. Angioplasty: in more fortunate patients, an angioplastiable lesion will be detected and the situation can be improved by angioplasty.
2. Bypass: in those without an angioplastiable lesion, surgical reconstruction may be possible. Critical ischaemia (rest pain) and tissue loss (ulceration) are said by some vascular surgeons to be the only indications for bypass surgery (which is not now routinely offered to patients with simple claudication due to high rates of restenosis).
3. Amputation: in some unfortunate patients (e.g. those with extensive atherosclerosis or small-vessel disease) bypass is not possible and amputation is the only option to relieve pain and prevent progressive tissue loss, infection and gangrene.
4. Local care: in the meantime, nursing care includes avoiding ill-fitting footwear, applying non-adherent dressings, avoiding compression bandages, and prescribing topical antiseptics if necessary.
5. Conservative measures: the usual advice to improve circulation (see pg 468, ischaemic leg) – give up smoking, improve walking distances, take regular aspirin (or anticoagulants if indicated) and reduce cholesterol – should be given as appropriate.

Other causes of ischaemic ulceration
By far the most common causes of ischaemic ulceration is atherosclerosis (usually of the large arteries) and diabetic arteriopathy (affecting both large and small arteries). Other causes include:
Large artery: embolism
Small artery: Raynaud's disease (see pg 501), scleroderma (see pg 504), Buerger's disease (see pg 468), embolism
Physical agents: pressure, radiation, trauma, electric burns
'Trash foot' caused by multiple emboli

Examine this gentleman's leg ulcer

(see pg 380)

ISCHAEMIC ULCER

'There is a small, painful ulcer over the heel of the right foot.[442] It is punched-out in appearance, with steep edges and a pale, bloodless/sloughy infected base. The underlying tendon/joint/bone can/cannot be seen in the base. The leg itself is pale and cool with absent foot pulses and no obvious signs of venous disease. This is an ischaemic ulcer. I would like to formally examine the leg for ischaemia[443] and neuropathy[444].'

👁 WHAT YOU SHOULD SEE

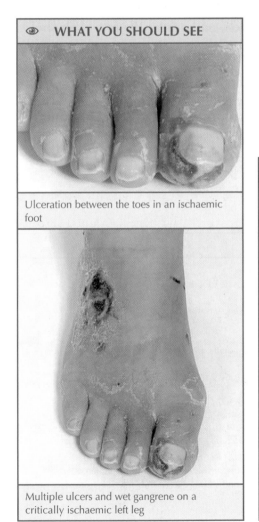

Ulceration between the toes in an ischaemic foot

Multiple ulcers and wet gangrene on a critically ischaemic left leg

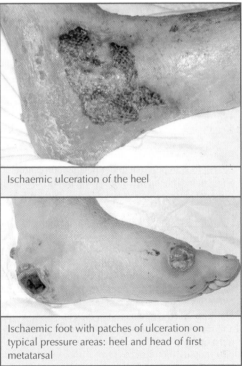

Ischaemic ulceration of the heel

Ischaemic foot with patches of ulceration on typical pressure areas: heel and head of first metatarsal

Take a history from this diabetic man who has had problems with his legs

(see pg 320)

'I would like to present Mr W, a 72-year-old retired roofer. He has been diabetic since his early twenties and says he has struggled with his glycaemic control. He has had problems with both his legs for 10 years. He has no sensation in his feet, which has predisposed him to injury, and 6 months ago he had to have his right great toe amputated for gangrene. He currently has an ulcer over the right heel. It is non-tender. Before he got this ulcer, he could only walk 50 yards with a stick before he was limited by pain in his right buttock. He does not get pain at rest. His medical history includes diabetes, hypertension and hypercholesterolaemia, and he had a MI 2 years ago. He is on multiple medications and is allergic to penicillin. He lives in a residential home. He has a 60 pack year smoking history and drinks 30 units of alcohol per week.

This gentleman has several features of diabetic leg, including ulceration, gangrene of a digit requiring amputation, peripheral neuropathy and PVD of the right iliac system. Initially, I would like to examine him to confirm this diagnosis.'

✎ WHAT YOU SHOULD KNOW

Features of diabetes in the leg and elsewhere

Neuropathic ulcers: or signs of trauma secondary to insensate foot (e.g. may stand on a tack and not notice it for days).

Charcot's joint: painless disorganised joint due to decreased sensation (see pg 448).

Loss of foot arches: due to peripheral neuropathy.

Shiny hairless leg: said to be typical but is non-specific.

Amputated toes: small-vessel disease often leads to loss of digits, either by surgery or autoamputation of a gangrenous digit.

Necrobiosis lipoidica diabeticorum: erythematous plaques over shins with a waxy appearance and brown pigmentation. Can scar, become scaly or ulcerate.

Infections: such as paronychia due to poor circulation and being immunocompromised.

Xanthomata: grey-yellow plaques of lipid in the skin, often in the skin of the eyelid.

Acanthosis nigricans: brown pigmentation of the skin, typically in skin folds such as the axilla.

Granuloma annulare: groups of flesh-coloured papules on extensor surfaces of hands and fingers.

NB ABPIs may appear to be greater than 1 in the presence of ischaemia if the large arteries of the legs are so calcified that inflation of the cuff fails to compress them. This is typical in diabetic large-vessel arteriopathy, so diabetic patients often have misleadingly high ABPIs even if they have significant ischaemia.

(See footnotes on pg 374–376)

Examine
this diabetic
gentleman's leg

(see pg 374)

DIABETIC LEG

'There is, in this patient, evidence of previous digital amputation of the right great toe. The sole of the left foot has a painless neuropathic ulcer (see pg 474) and there is a Charcot's joint (see pg 448) at the left ankle. There is loss of the foot arches, lipoatrophy and necrobiosis lipoidica diabeticorum. There is loss of sensation in a stocking distribution bilaterally. The femoral and popliteal pulses are present bilaterally, as are the foot pulses on the left; the ankle–brachial pressure index is more than 1, but the feet are cold, ulcerated and discoloured, with poor capillary refill. This patient is diabetic with significant neuropathy and small-vessel arteriopathy of both legs.'

⊙ WHAT YOU SHOULD SEE

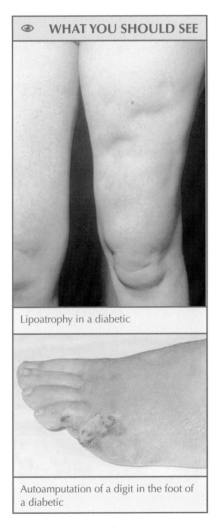

Lipoatrophy in a diabetic

Autoamputation of a digit in the foot of a diabetic

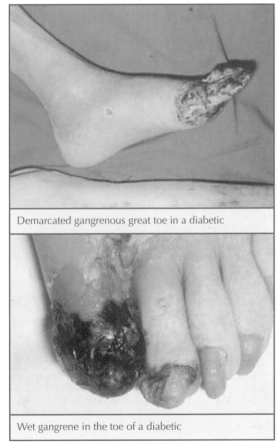

Demarcated gangrenous great toe in a diabetic

Wet gangrene in the toe of a diabetic

NEUROPATHIC ULCER

[445] It is common to have dual pathology, for example in diabetics with neuropathy where co-existing peripheral vascular disease produces a mixed ulcer, which delays healing. This may occur even in the presence of good foot pulses, as small-vessel disease is more common in diabetics. Checking the capillary refill around the ulcer gives a good indication of whether there is a reasonable blood supply, but beware infected ulcers, when superficial cellulitis can mask underlying ischaemia.

Causes of neuropathic ulcer

Peripheral neuropathy: diabetes mellitus, nerve injury, leprosy.
Spinal cord lesions: spina bifida, tabes dorsalis, syringomyelia.

Make a full
assessment of
this diabetic
man with an
ulcer

(see pgs 320
and 474)

NEUROPATHIC ULCER

'This diabetic gentleman has had a small, painless ulcer on the sole of his right foot for the last 3 months. Over the last 6 months he has gradually noticed that he is no longer able to feel sensation over his feet. He has not had any other problems with his feet to date. He has hypertension, ischaemic heart disease, atrial fibrillation and hyercholesterolaemia. He is on warfarin as well as a variety of other medications. He has no known allergies. He mobilises with a stick and lives with his wife. He is a 50 pack year smoker who drinks 6 units of alcohol per week. On examination, the ulcer is deep, with punched-out edges and pink granulation tissue in the base. The surrounding skin is insensate and has good capillary refill.[445] There are good foot pulses and no evidence of venous insufficiency.

This is a neuropathic ulcer. I would like to carry out a neurological examination of the lower limb.'

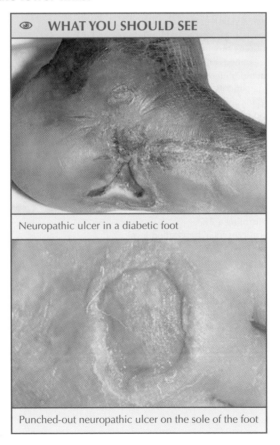

WHAT YOU SHOULD SEE

Neuropathic ulcer in a diabetic foot

Punched-out neuropathic ulcer on the sole of the foot

CHAPTER 5
LIMBS AND SPINE

WHAT YOU SHOULD KNOW

Amputations
Commonest cause in developed countries: end-stage peripheral vascular disease; diabetes
Commonest cause in developing countries: trauma; infection

Pre-operative care
Counselling.
Optimise nutrition, hydration and cardiac and respiratory status.
DVT prophylaxis.
Be sure vascular salvage bypass is inappropriate.

Selection of amputation levels
Should not rely solely on clinical assessment.
Digital or part-foot amputations only suitable for those with small-vessel disease and no large-vessel compromise (e.g. some diabetics, vasculitides) or in those undergoing revascularisation procedures (bypass or angioplasty).
Trans-tibial (below-knee amputation – BKA) should always be attempted if feasible.
Usually feasible if thigh systolic pressure is >70 mmHg or if angiography shows good inflow to the profunda artery.
Trans-femoral (above-knee amputations – AKA) cannot always be avoided but have many disadvantages.

Types of amputation
Digital.
Ray (includes most of metatarsal bone).
Part-foot trans-metatarsal (e.g. in revascularised limb or selected diabetics).
Lisfranc's (midfoot amputation – rare in vascular disease).
Chopart's (leaves behind calcaneus and talus – rarely used).
Syme's (distal 1cm of tibia and fibula excised and heel flap sutured under to form stump). Useful in trauma, especially of young patients, but limited use in peripheral vascular disease)
Below knee: gold standard for end-stage peripheral vascular disease (see below).
Above knee: most common for end-stage peripheral vascular disease (see below).

Advantages of BKA
Maximises chances of patient mobility.
Preserves limb length.
Reduced energy and oxygen requirements compared with AKA.
Much higher chance of rehabilitation than AKA.
Much less likely to be wheelchair-bound than AKA.
Live longer and have better quality of life than AKA.

Principles involved in performing a BKA
10 cm distal to tibial tuberosity is ideal transection level.
Burgess–Romano technique involves long posterior flap (see figure on pg 479).
Fascia overlying soleus and gastrocnemius must be preserved with posterior skin flap; muscles may be excised.
Posterior tibial nerve should be pulled down, then excised to allow it to retract.
Fibula must be divided proximal to the tibia.
Tibial transection should be bevelled and filed to leave no sharp points.
Deep fascia of posterior flap is sutured to deep fascia or periosteum anteriorly.
CONTINUED on pg 478

AMPUTEE

Make a full assessment of this man who has recently had an amputation

'I would like to present Mr W, a 60-year-old man who had a left below-knee amputation 3 months ago. Prior to the amputation he had pain and ulceration of the leg and was told there was no other option available. He is just managing to mobilise on his stump. He has had some problems with phantom pain in the stump. He has pain in his right leg too on walking distances greater than 30 yards but no rest or night pain. He is hypertensive and has ischaemic heart disease. He is not diabetic. He is a lifelong smoker for 50 pack years. On examination, the amputation appears to have been performed by a Burgess–Romano trans-tibial technique with a long posterior flap. It is well shaped, an appropriate length and well healed. There is/is no evidence of previous vascular surgery on that leg.[446] The opposite leg shows evidence of peripheral vascular disease.'

⊙ WHAT YOU SHOULD SEE

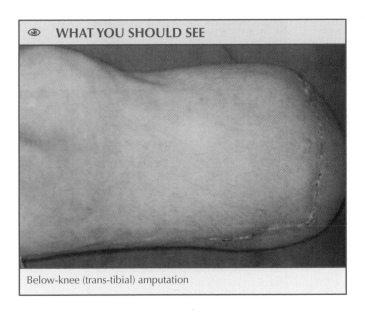

Below-knee (trans-tibial) amputation

📑 WHAT YOU SHOULD KNOW (CONT)

Principles involved in performing an AKA

Performed too often in this country for peripheral vascular disease.

Use anterior-posterior flaps as shown opposite.

Keep stump as long as possible without compromising healing.

Transect nerves 5 cm proximal to bone transection level.

Ideally residual adductor muscles should be fixed to the lateral femur to prevent it lying abducted.

Quadriceps should be fixed to the posterior femur to cover the stump and prevent it lying flexed.

These last two are rarely done, usually because the AKA is often left to junior team members.

Post-operative management

Pain control (spinal, epidural PCA, epidural catheter placed alongside sciatic nerve intraoperatively).

Wound care (antibiotics, reduce oedema, avoid trauma, e.g. plaster of Paris dressing).

Nutrition.

Treatment of concurrent medical illness (e.g. diabetes, cardiac disease).

Management of contralateral limb (may also have vascular disease).

Early mobilisation and fitting of prosthesis.

Attention to psychological problems.

Long-term prognosis

Limited life expectancy (far lower 5-year survival rate than Dukes' B colon cancer patients).

50% develop critical ischaemia in the other leg.

Many continue to smoke and so are at risk of cancer, respiratory and cardiovascular disease.

Diabetes, cardiac and cerebrovascular disease increase morbidity and mortality.

[446] Look for scars in the groin and medial thigh and knee.

👁 WHAT YOU SHOULD SEE

Syme's amputation

Chopart's amputation

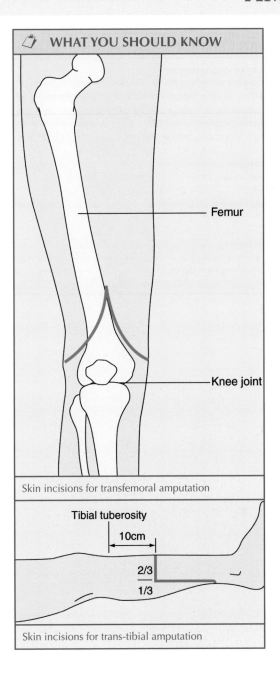

📋 **WHAT YOU SHOULD KNOW**

Femur

Knee joint

Skin incisions for transfemoral amputation

Tibial tuberosity

10cm

2/3

1/3

Skin incisions for trans-tibial amputation

SUBCLAVIAN STEAL SYNDROME

Pathogenesis of the subclavian steal syndrome:

Atherosclerosis rarely causes upper limb ischaemia because of good collaterals and the decreased frequency of atheroma in these vessels. When it does, it is usually subclavian artery stenosis. If the occlusion is in the proximal part of the subclavian artery, patients may experience vertebrobasilar symptoms when they exercise the affected limb. This is because the vertebral artery on the side of the stenosis acts as a collateral – blood flow actually reverses – 'stealing' blood from the circle of Willis and cerebral vessels.

Causes of subclavian obstruction:

Atherosclerosis, arteritis, embolism, thoracic outlet syndrome (see pg 498).

Diagnosis: Arteriography.

Treatment: reconstruction of subclavian artery by
- Angioplasty
- Stenting
- Carotid-to-subclavian bypass

If the axillary or brachial artery is occluded, a long vein bypass must be taken from a healthy artery above the occlusion to an unaffected segment beyond, tunnelling the bypass through the thoracic outlet. These bypasses are often difficult to perform and tend to occlude early.

Make a full assessment of this lady with a recent history of collapse

SUBCLAVIAN STEAL SYNDROME

'I would like to present Mrs W, a 50-year-old woman. She was admitted to hospital under the medics with a collapse last week. She describes washing her windows with her right (dominant) arm before losing consciousness. Previously, she has noticed episodes of dizziness while performing activities using her arm, such as stacking the shelves in the supermarket where she works, but has never lost consciousness before. She has no other associated symptoms. She is a 35 pack year smoker.

On examination, there are decreased pulses in the right arm and the blood pressure is reduced compared with the left. There is a supraclavicular bruit. The diagnosis is subclavian steal syndrome.'

◉ WHAT YOU SHOULD SEE

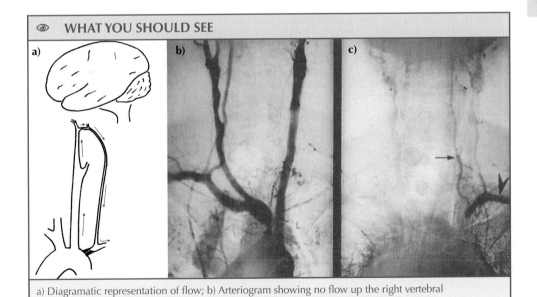

a) Diagramatic representation of flow; b) Arteriogram showing no flow up the right vertebral or subclavian arteries; c) Later film shows retrograde flow down the vertebral artery (arrow), filling the subclavian artery (arrowhead)

FEMORAL ARTERY ANEURYSM

🗐 WHAT YOU SHOULD KNOW

Aetiology:

True femoral artery aneurysms (rare)

<u>Atherosclerosis</u>: commonest cause of true femoral artery aneurysm. A third are asymptomatic. Risk of rupture is low (5–15%) due to the muscular fascial surrounding compartment but pressure of expansion can cause occlusion or acute thrombosis, resulting in an acutely ischaemic limb.

<u>Infection</u>: used to be a common cause of true femoral artery aneurysms due to septic emboli from endocarditis, but now that antibiotics are in use they are much less common.

False femoral artery aneurysms (common)

<u>Puncture aneurysms</u> following cannulation of or aspiration from the femoral artery.

<u>Para-anastomotic false aneurysm</u> should raise the suspicion of an infected graft. Other predisposing factors include synthetic graft, silk sutures, small arterial wall tissue bites, haematoma.

<u>Mycotic false aneurysms</u>: common in intravenous drug addicts.

Symptoms: 29% asymptomatic, 30% local symptoms (groin swelling, hyperaesthesia, local pain). Other presentations include: peripheral ischaemia from aneurysm thrombosis or emboli, groin pain radiating into leg, distal neuropathy, or, in mycotic false aneurysms, red hot tender swelling +/– necrosis of overlying skin.

Investigations:

<u>Angiography or MRA</u> visualises the aorta and iliacs as well as the distal circulation to identify other aneurysms in true aneurysms, and the run-off and other anastomotic sites in para-anastomotic aneurysms.

<u>Colour flow duplex scanning</u>: used to identify iatrogenic puncture aneurysms and show effectiveness of direct pressure on stopping the leak. Quick and effective way of confirming mycotic aneurysm which may need immediate surgery.

Management:

<u>True atherosclerotic femoral artery aneurysms over 3 cm</u>: elective interposition graft with Dacron or PTFE (veins are too small).

<u>Infected false aneurysms</u>: ligation of healthy arteries proximal and distal, wide debridement of infected tissues, and bypass (may be extra-anatomic). Alternatively, arterial ligation may be possible without reconstruction if there is good collateral circulation.

<u>Iatrogenic false aneurysm following percutaneous catheterisation</u>: ultrasound-guided compression treatment (10-minute sessions) or surgery if symptomatic, rupturing or thrombosed.

[447] Such as dusky toes or purpuric skin lesions.

[448] 85% of patients with true atherosclerotic femoral artery aneurysms have an aortic, iliac or popliteal aneurysm, and 70% are bilateral. Aortic and iliac aneurysms take precedence over femoral aneurysms as far as treatment goes, as they cause more complications.

FEMORAL ARTERY ANEURYSM

'I would like to present Mr W, a 58-year-old man. He has noticed a lump in his right groin for the last 5 months. It is asymptomatic. He is a 40 pack year smoker but has no other medical history. On examination, there is a 4-cm pulsatile swelling in the right groin, midway between the pubic tubercle and the anterior superior iliac spine. The mass is expansile, and there is an audible bruit. There are no overlying scars or bruises indicating previous surgery or intervention, and the swelling is not red, hot or tender, which would indicate infection. The distal circulation, sensation and power of the limb are normal, and there is no evidence of embolic disease.[447]

This is a femoral artery aneurysm, and the history of smoking and absence of evidence of iatrogenic injury or infection point to a true atherosclerotic aneurysm. I would like to examine the other groin and the abdomen and popliteal fossae.'[448]

👁 WHAT YOU SHOULD SEE

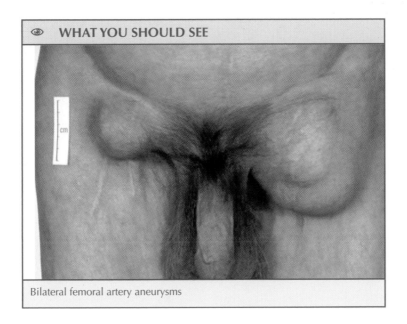

Bilateral femoral artery aneurysms

POPLITEAL ARTERY ANEURYSM

⟋ WHAT YOU SHOULD KNOW

Definition: external diameter >2 cm or more than one and a half times the normal proximal popliteal artery diameter.

Epidemiology: commonest over the age of 50. More common in men than women.

Aetiology: atherosclerosis is by far the most common. Also popliteal entrapment syndrome, collagen disorders (such as Behçet's disease), fibromuscular dysplasia, infection and blunt or penetrating trauma.

Symptoms: a third are asymptomatic. Distal embolisation may cause claudication, rest pain, gangrene or acute ischaemic event. Acute occlusion of the aneurysm causes acute lower limb ischaemia. Tibial nerve compression results in pain in the distribution of that nerve. Popliteal vein occlusion or thrombosis may occur, resulting in deep vein thrombosis. Acute ischaemic emergencies (due to aneurysmal thrombosis or embolisation) are the presenting complaint in 52–77% of cases, resulting in amputation in 16–20% of patients.

Investigations: aim to determine extent and shape of aneurysm, presence of intraluminal thrombus and the condition of inflow and outflow vessels. Methods include duplex scanning, angiography or MRA. Colour flow duplex examination is best for monitoring aneurysms which are not operated on.

Management:

Acute ischaemia with sensory and motor impairment: urgent bypass surgery +/– distal vessel thrombectomy or intra-arterial injection of thrombolytic agent.

Occluded aneurysm without critical ischaemia: thrombolysis retains more of the limb run-off vessels.

Asymptomatic: elective surgery – conservative management is associated with poor outcome.

Surgery: Interposition saphenous vein bypass graft with aneurysm exclusion, usually by medial approach (although posterior or supragenicular approaches can also be used). Vein grafts in patients with good run-off perform better than synthetic grafts and results are good with 75–100% 5-year patency.

[449] The tibial nerve supplies sensation to the sole of the foot and power to the great toe flexors. The peroneal nerve supplies sensation to the anterior and lateral surface of the lower leg and foot, and power to the ankle and foot extensors. Both may be compressed by a large popliteal aneurysm.

[450] 38–58% bilateral; 32% associated with more proximal aneurysms.

POPLITEAL ARTERY ANEURYSM

'I would like to present Mr W, a 76-year-old man with an expansile lump at the back of his right knee which he noticed 3 months ago. He has had no leg pain or skin changes. His medical history includes an AAA repair 2 years ago and he is 40 pack year smoker. On examination, there is a 3-cm pulsatile swelling in the popliteal fossa. The mass is expansile and has an audible bruit on auscultation. The distal limb shows no sign of ischaemia or embolic disease (see examination of ischaemic leg, pg 374), and sensation and power are intact.[449]

This is a popliteal artery aneurysm. I would like to examine the opposite popliteal fossa and the groins.'[450]

WHAT YOU SHOULD KNOW

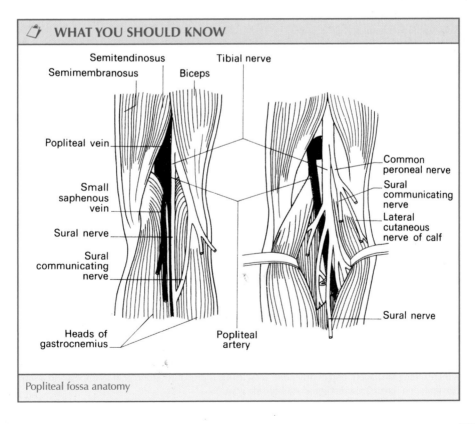

Semitendinosus
Semimembranosus
Biceps
Tibial nerve
Popliteal vein
Small saphenous vein
Sural nerve
Sural communicating nerve
Heads of gastrocnemius
Popliteal artery
Common peroneal nerve
Sural communicating nerve
Lateral cutaneous nerve of calf
Sural nerve

Popliteal fossa anatomy

SURGICAL ARTERIOVENOUS FISTULA

'I would like to present Mr W, a 45-year-old right-handed diabetic man. He had an arteriovenous fistula created under local anaesthetic in his left (non-dominant) forearm 2 years ago for haemodialysis. He has had no problems with it thus far, in particular no thrombosis, infection or symptoms of distal embolisation. He has diabetic nephropathy, which is the cause of his renal failure.

This sounds like a radiocephalic surgical arteriovenous fistula but I would like to examine him to confirm this.'

✍ WHAT YOU SHOULD KNOW

These cause grossly dilated veins and are created primarily for ease of vascular access in patients with renal failure who need regular haemodialysis. It avoids the need for long-term percutaneous central venous catheter which carries risks of infection, venous stenosis and thrombosis.

Types of arteriovenous fistula

Autogenous: direct joining of a vein with a neighbouring artery – usually end-vein to side artery using the Brescia–Cimino technique.

Autogenous bridge: a vein and artery are joined using a separate vein graft (e.g. saphenous vein).

Synthetic straight bridge grafts: PTFE or other synthetic graft material is used to bridge between an artery and a vein. Other graft materials include bovine carotid arteries, human umbilical vein or cryopreserved cadaveric vein grafts.

Loop grafts: usually synthetic. An artery and vein are joined by a loop of graft tunnelled subcutaneously.

Sites of arteriovenous fistulae

In order of preference: radiocephalic, brachiocephalic, forearm loop, upper arm straight. The non-dominant hand and more distal sites are usually considered first.

Pre-operative questions you should know to ask

Dominant hand?

Previous attempts at access and reasons for failure?

Examine forearm veins, if necessary using a proximal tourniquet (40 mmHg).

Aim for autogenous but warn of risks of synthetic bridges in case veins aren't good enough.

Perform Allen's test (see pg 378) to evaluate potential arterial inflow sites. Non-palpable pulses should not be used.

Exclude local or systemic infection.

Post-operative complications

Nerve injury: especially radial and median.

Thrombosis: usually due to poor flow, kinking or compression by haematoma.

Steal phenomenon: claudication symptoms due to inadequate perfusion – treated by ligating artery just distal to graft, except in proximal fistulae which require bypass.

Infection: especially in synthetic grafts.

False aneurysm.

[451] Palpate the fistula, trying to determine two things:

1. Is there any synthetic material present? This is probably a PTFE bridge graft.

2. Is there a long U-shaped loop of distended vessel? This is probably a loop graft as opposed to a straight bridge graft or a direct Brescia–Cimino end-to-side graft.

SURGICAL ARTERIOVENOUS FISTULA

'There is (in this young or middle-aged patient) a grossly dilated pulsatile vessel in the forearm of the non-dominant arm with an overlying scar. There is an audible bruit. The distal limb is well perfused with good pulses and no signs of venous insufficiency. There are/are no signs of previous, more distal surgery or surgery on the opposite arm. There is a scar on the neck compatible with a previous central venous line. The patient is not uraemic and looks well nourished and in good health. This is a surgical arteriovenous fistula[451] created for ease of venous access, probably for haemodialysis in a patient with renal failure.'

☞ WHAT YOU SHOULD SEE

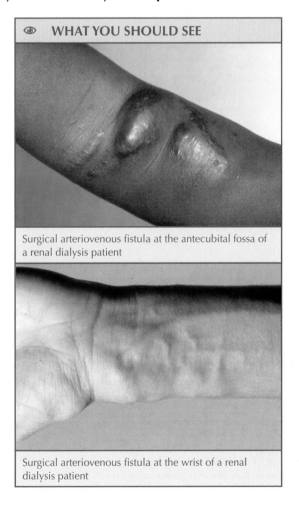

Surgical arteriovenous fistula at the antecubital fossa of a renal dialysis patient

Surgical arteriovenous fistula at the wrist of a renal dialysis patient

CONGENITAL ARTERIOVENOUS FISTULA: CIRSOID ANEURYSM

> Make a full assessment of this lady with a lump on her left arm

'I would like to present Mrs W, a 35-year-old 32 weeks pregnant woman. She has developed a pulsatile swelling on her left arm. It can ache but she is otherwise asymptomatic. She has no other similar lumps. She is fit and well. On examination, there is a soft, warm, pulsatile swelling on the left arm[452] covered by dilated cutaneous channels in the overlying skin.[453] It is hemispherical, about 4 cm in diameter, with a smooth edge. It is fluctuant, compressible and has a palpable thrill and audible bruit.

This is a localised arteriovenous fistula, or cirsoid aneurysm.'

 WHAT YOU SHOULD KNOW

Definition: a pathological connection between arteries and veins. May be localised, diffuse, large or small. May form aneurysms. Rare (<1 per million).

Localised fistula (cirsoid aneurysms)

Investigations: selective arteriography and CT scanning

Differential diagnoses:

Metastatic deposits of a typically vascular tumour such as thyroid carcinoma (important to exclude this)

Traumatic arteriovenous fistulae

Treatment:

Expectant if asymptomatic or develops during pregnancy

Therapeutic embolisation or occlusion of feeding vessel

Surgical excision. Simple ligation of feeding vessels and direct injection or sclerosants are ineffective.

[452] Common in the head, neck and limbs.

[453] It has been described as looking like a bag of pulsating worms.

CONGENITAL ARTERIOVENOUS FISTULA: CIRSOID ANEURYSM

WHAT YOU SHOULD SEE

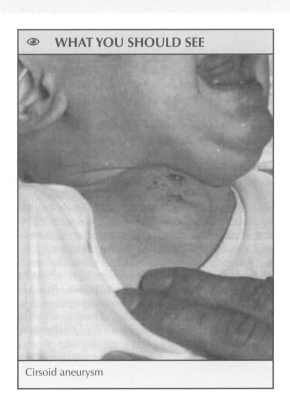

Cirsoid aneurysm

CONGENITAL ARTERIOVENOUS FISTULA: PARKES–WEBER SYNDROME

> Make a full assessment of this gentleman's left leg

'I would like to present Mr W, a 40-year-old gentleman. From birth he has had an abnormality with his left leg. It has become enlarged causing a limp and he tires easily when walking. He has multiple dilated pulsatile veins on his legs. Recently he has also developed breathlessness on lying and walking and tells me he has been diagnosed with cardiac failure. On examination, he has an enlarged left leg, which is covered in dilated veins and shows features of lipodermatosclerosis and ulceration. The leg is warm and pink and increased in both length and width. There is bony as well as soft tissue enlargement. The dilated veins are pulsatile with palpable thrills and audible bruits on auscultation. The veins do not collapse on elevation. These are multiple arteriovenous fistulae. The condition is called Parkes–Weber syndrome, also known as Robertson's giant limb, with associated high-output cardiac failure.'

✏ WHAT YOU SHOULD KNOW

Complications:
Lipodermatosclerosis and ulceration as a result of chronic venous insufficiency
High-output cardiac failure and cardiomegaly
Severe thrombocytopenia
Differential diagnoses:
Klippel–Trenaunay syndrome (see pg 508)
Lymphoedema (see pg 505)
Diagnosis:
Venography, arteriography
Treatment:
Expectant, embolisation, ligation of feeding vessels, microsphere injection, surgical 'skeletalisation' under tourniquet control
Amputation in exceptional circumstances
Complications of treatment:
Embolisation, infarction, recurrence
Branham's bradycardic response: occluding the circulation of the enlarged limb with a sphygmomanometer cuff causes a bradycardia because it increases the peripheral resistance

CONGENITAL ARTERIOVENOUS FISTULA: PARKES–WEBER SYNDROME

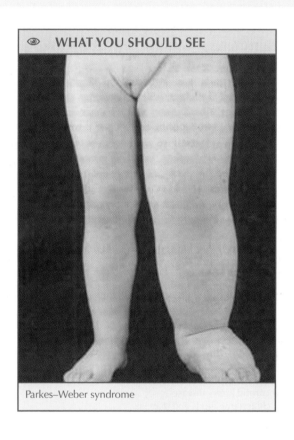

👁 **WHAT YOU SHOULD SEE**

Parkes–Weber syndrome

CAROTID ARTERY DISEASE

⌕ WHAT YOU SHOULD KNOW

Definitions:

Transient ischaemic attack (TIA) is a focal neurological deficit completely resolving within 24 hours.

Amaurosis fugax or transient monocular blindness (TMB) is a monocular visual disturbance or loss, commonly described as a descending curtain or mist completely resolving within 24 hours.

Reversible ischaemic neurological deficit (RIND) lasts longer than 24 hours but resolves completely within 30 days. Despite this recovery, CT scans may show residual lesions in up to 30% of TIAs and up to 60% of RINDs.

Stroke leaves a permanent neurological deficit ranging from a mild weakness to a coma with permanent paralysis.

Epidemiology:

A third of ischaemic strokes originate from atherosclerosis of the great vessels supplying the brain, a third from the heart and a quarter from small-vessel occlusions (lacunar strokes), now also known to be due to great vessel atherosclerosis.

Risk factors for atherosclerosis of the carotid artery

Smoking, obesity, family history, male, hypertension, diabetes, hypercholesterolaemia, hyperlipidaemia.

Investigations:

Carotid artery duplex scan determines vessel diameters and flow velocities with accuracy in good hands of up to 95%.

Carotid angiograms are used where duplex accuracy is uncertain, or if disease is suspected outside the cervical region. Aortic arch injections allow visualisation of the aortic arch branches and the vertebral arteries, but overlapping vessels and insensitivity for ulcerated carotid lesions are drawbacks. Selective carotid artery catheterisation shows the carotid bifurcation and intracranial vessels more clearly and identifies areas of irregularity or ulceration.

Complications of angiography include haematoma, pseudoaneurysm, adverse dye reactions and neurological events caused by emboli, hypotension or vascular spasm. TIAs occur in 0.8–4% and permanent deficits in 0.1–1.3% of carotid angiograms.

MRA (magnetic resonance angiography) is replacing invasive angiography.

Medical management of carotid artery disease

Control of hypertension, cholesterol, lipids and diabetes

Stop smoking

Aspirin (dose controversial)

Antiplatelet drugs

Warfarin is used to prevent stroke from cardiac or hypercoagulable cause, but not for carotid atherosclerosis.

Indications for carotid endarterectomy

Symptomatic stenoses >70%.

Some asymptomatic stenoses (see pg 494)

Crescendo TIAs with severe stenosis

Fluctuating neurological defect post-CVA with severe stenosis

Acute stroke with severe stenosis (after patient is neurologically stable)

[454] Although neck bruits are neither sensitive nor specific for carotid bifurcation stenosis, their presence in association with neurological symptoms is an important clinical finding.

[455] He will be eligible only if he has >70% stenosis in the artery supplying the affected area.

CONTINUED on pg 494

CAROTID ARTERY DISEASE

Make a full assessment of this gentleman who has recently had a TIA

'I would like to present Mr W, a 66-year-old man with a history of a TIA affecting his right side 6 weeks ago. He has no residual neurology. The patient denies previous strokes or TIAs and has never had amaurosis fugax of the left eye. His medical history includes hypercholesterolaemia and hypertension. He is a 35 pack year smoker. His father had a stroke at a similar age. On examination he has a bruit over the left carotid artery.[454]

The diagnosis is symptomatic left carotid artery disease, and evaluation of the extent of his carotid artery stenosis would be needed before offering him a carotid endarterectomy.'[455]

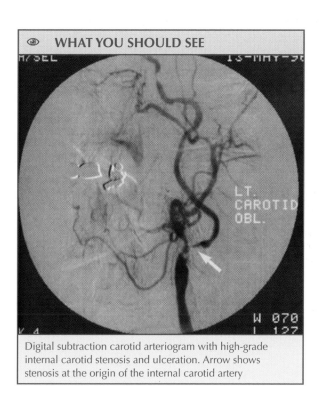

👁 **WHAT YOU SHOULD SEE**

Digital subtraction carotid arteriogram with high-grade internal carotid stenosis and ulceration. Arrow shows stenosis at the origin of the internal carotid artery

CAROTID ARTERY DISEASE

How important trials have determined treatment regimes

Patients with neurological symptoms in the previous 4 months in the territory of a carotid artery with 70–99% stenosis (European Carotid Surgery Trial 1998 and North American Symptomatic Carotid Endarterectomy Trial (NASCENT) 1991 showed benefit in these patients when compared with optimal medical treatment alone).

Management of asymptomatic patients is more controversial. Asymptomatic patients with a carotid artery stenosis of more than 60% were shown to benefit from carotid endarterectomy in the Asymptomatic Carotid Atherosclerosis Study (ACAS) in 1987, so much so that the trial was stopped by the National Institute of Health in 1994. However, statistically significant differences were not seen for 3 years, so generally surgery in asymptomatic patients tends to be reserved for:

- Patients with low operative risk and good life expectancy
- High-grade stenosis (e.g. over 70%)
- Progressive or ulcerated lesions

The GALA trial 2008 found that there was no definite difference in outcome following carotid surgery under local versus general anaesthetic and concluded that choice of anaesthetic should be made on an individual basis.

Carotid artery surgery

Internal carotid endarterectomy involves removing the plaque of atheroma and the media, leaving the adventitia of the artery. Incision along the anterior border of sternocleidomastoid. Some surgeons routinely use a shunt, some do so selectively. Some use intra-operative transcranial Doppler to monitor the flow, some do not. Some surgeons routinely use a vein or prosthetic patch to enlarge the diameter, some do so selectively.

Complications of carotid endarterectomy

Perioperative stroke due to:

- Cerebral ischaemia during clamping
- Embolisation of debris during or after the operation
- Thrombosis at the endarterectomy site

Cervical haematoma

Cranial nerve neuropraxia, especially:

- Recurrent laryngeal
- Hypoglossal
- Marginal mandibular
- Glossopharyngeal
- Superior laryngeal

Recurrent stenosis (5–15% of patients) due to hyperplasia or recurrent atherosclerosis. If symptomatic, reoperation is indicated.

Carotid artery angioplasty and stenting

New treatment modality which may become more popular.

HYPERHIDROSIS

'I would like to present Mr W, a 20-year-old project manager. He complains of profuse sweating of the hands, axilla and feet since puberty. He finds this socially disabling. He has no other medical problems and takes no regular medications.

On examination, his hands are moist and warm. This patient has hyperhidrosis.'

⚙ WHAT YOU SHOULD KNOW

Hyperhidrosis is not an infection but an increase in sweat production from sweat glands (usually of the hands, axilla or feet). The majority are idiopathic, but secondary hyperhidrosis includes:

Hyperhidrosis erythematosus traumatica: a rare occupational form of the condition in which sweating occurs in skin in contact with a vibrating tool.

Syringomyelia can cause facial hyperhidrosis.

Frey syndrome post-parotidectomy (see pg 120) where 'gustatory sweating' is caused by disturbance of sympathetic and parasympathetic nerve fibres.

Treatment of hyperhidrosis:
1. Topical aluminium hexachloride
2. Botulinum toxin (decreases sympathetic activity, best for axilla)
3. Excision of hair-bearing axillary skin (again best for axilla)
4. Thoracoscopic sympathectomy for palms
5. Chemical lumbar sympathectomy for feet
6. Avoid total sympathectomy (leads to postural hypertension)

Thoracoscopic sympathectomy is replacing the old open approach. A laparoscope is inserted into the pleural space and the lung deflated. The second to fourth sympathetic ganglia are obliterated with diathermy. Complications include pneumothorax, Horner syndrome and compensatory hyperhidrosis.

◉ WHAT YOU SHOULD SEE

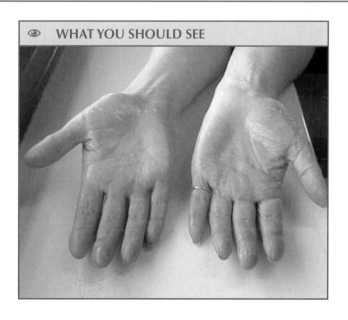

OSLER–WEBER–RENDU SYNDROME

'I would like to present Mrs W, a 55-year-old woman who presents with intermittent rectal bleeding for 5 years. It is dark blood. She has had no other change in bowel habit. She occasionally gets associated abdominal pain. She has had no weight loss. She has a previous medical history of daily nosebleeds which started when she was 20. A year after this she developed multiple telangiectasia on her face. She has never had haemoptysis. However, she is anaemic and takes iron supplements and has had to have transfusions previously. Her mother had similar symptoms.

I think this woman has Osler–Weber–Rendu syndrome with rectal bleeding secondary to telangectasia of her GI tract, although it would be important to exclude a colonic malignancy.'

✍ WHAT YOU SHOULD KNOW

Also known as **hereditary haemorrhagic telangiectasia**, this is a rare autosomal dominant genetic condition.

The telangiectasia are found throughout the gastrointestinal and genitourinary systems. The main clinical implications are repeated bleeding from these sites which increase in frequency with age and can result in anaemia. Coagulation screening tests are normal.

Treatment:
- Cautery of bleeding points (e.g. endoscopically)
- Oral oestrogen: converts columnar to stratified squamous epithelium and can reduce bleeding
- Long-term iron therapy if necessary

[456] Small groups of dilated venules that blanch on pressure and bleed easily after minor trauma.
[457] Look in the mouth and under the tongue.

OSLER–WEBER–RENDU SYNDROME

'This patient has multiple telangiectasia[456] on the face and on the mucosa of the mouth[457] and nose. She has pale sclerae and looks anaemic. There are also telangiectasia on the hands. The skin is not tight, shiny and smooth as in patients with scleroderma, and although there are telangiectasia on the hands there are none of the features of scleroderma (see pg 501). This patient has Osler–Weber–Rendu syndrome.'

👁 WHAT YOU SHOULD SEE

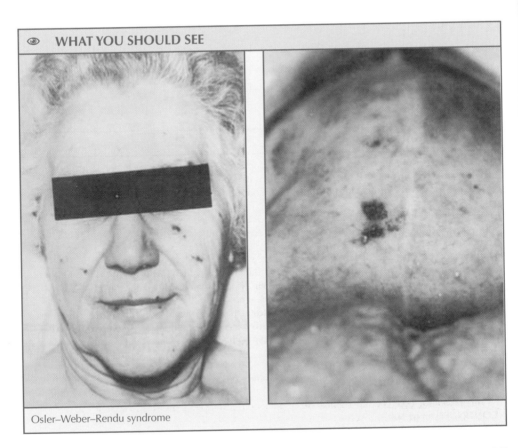

Osler–Weber–Rendu syndrome

> Take a history from this lady with a swollen left arm

CERVICAL RIB/ THORACIC OUTLET SYNDROME

'I would like to present Ms W, a 37-year-old museum guide. She presents with a number of symptoms related to her left (non-dominant) arm. She complains of left neck and shoulder pain with tingling in her fingers; latterly she has also noticed weakness of the grip of her left hand. Her left arm has gradually become swollen and aches. She has also noticed discoloration of her fingers. She cannot recall a history of trauma to this arm. She has no medical history and takes no regular medication with no known drug allergies. She lives with her husband and they have twin toddlers. She has no family history of note.

I think this lady has left thoracic outlet obstruction with compression of the subclavian vessels and branches of the brachial plexus.'

🖉 WHAT YOU SHOULD KNOW

Thoracic outlet syndrome is compression, occlusion or damage of the subclavian artery in the neck, most often by a cervical rib. It may be associated with signs of compression of the somatic and sympathetic nerves and the main veins draining the upper limb. Compression by other structures at the thoracic inlet has been reported and includes:
- A congenital fibrous band where a cervical rib would be found
- Muscular hypertrophy (e.g. in swimmers, of the scalenus muscles)
- Previous fractures of the first rib or clavicle
- Tumours or lymphadenopathy in the neck

458 Cervical rib is rarely visible or palpable unless it is large or the patient is very thin.

459 Seventy per cent of cervical ribs are bilateral but the symptoms are usually unilateral.

460 Often the only clinical clue to an underlying cervical rib.

461 Ipsilateral contracted pupil, enophthalamos (eyeball not as protruberant as the other side), slight ptosis (eyelid drooping) due to damage to the sympathetic nervous system, in this case by compression as the nerves run out of the spinal cord at C8/T1/T2 to the sympathetic chain, stellate ganglion and carotid sympathetic plexus.

462 See axillary vein thrombosis, pg 464.

463 If axillary vein thrombosis occurs, collateral veins develop on skin over shoulder and scapula.

464 Like a soldier standing to attention.

465 This nerve root loops over the cervical rib.

CONTINUED on pg 500

CERVICAL RIB/ THORACIC OUTLET SYNDROME

'There is a bony swelling[458] in the left side[459] of the root of the neck. The subclavian artery pulsation is more prominent[460] on this side and has a bruit. There is no sign of Horner syndrome.[461] There are signs of venous obstruction of the left upper limb,[462] including distended arm veins[463] which do not collapse even on elevating the arm, cyanosis of the hand and arm and pitting oedema. There are signs of arterial spasm or ischaemia affecting the fingers and the hands. The radial pulse is decreased on the left on traction of the shoulder and when the shoulders are braced back[464] and the patient turns his head away. Roo's test (abduction and external rotation of the arm) precipitates symptoms. There are also signs of T1 root compression[465] in the wasted small muscles of the hands and loss of sensation on the medial side of the arm. The diagnosis is thoracic outlet syndrome secondary to a cervical rib. I would like to know the blood pressure bilaterally.'

👁 WHAT YOU SHOULD SEE

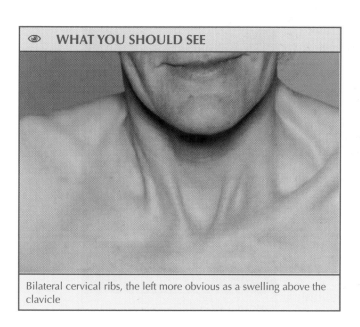

Bilateral cervical ribs, the left more obvious as a swelling above the clavicle

---

✐ WHAT YOU SHOULD KNOW (CONT)

Cervical rib occurs in 0.4% of the population, usually C7; 60% are symptomatic.
Clinical signs as outlined are almost always unilateral; can progress to areas of necrosis or patchy gangrene. Acute thrombosis may cause massive ischaemia of the upper limb but this is unusual due to a good collateral circulation.

Mechanism: the rib can compress the artery against any of the following:

Scalenus anterior	Clavicle (previous fracture increases risk)
Two heads of scalenus medius	Congenital band between rib and clavicle
Heads of the median nerve	Transverse processes of cervical vertebrae
Hypertrophied neck muscles (e.g. in swimmers)	Abnormal first rib (e.g. fracture, tumour)

Differential diagnosis:

Thoracic outlet syndrome is over-diagnosed. You must exclude:

Cervical spondylosis	Cervical disc protrusions	Carpal tunnel syndrome
Spinal cord tumours	Syringomyelia	Axillary vein thrombosis
Pancoast's tumour	Osteoarthritis of shoulder	Atherosclerosis
Supraspinatus tendonitis	Ulnar neuritis	Takayasu's disease
Buerger's disease		

Investigations:

X-ray of cervical spine, shoulder and thoracic inlet
MRA

Treatment:

<u>Conservative</u>: posture, physiotherapy
<u>Surgical decompression</u>: most commonly excision of cervical rib or first rib

---

👁 WHAT YOU SHOULD SEE

A plain X-ray showing cervical rib

RAYNAUD'S DISEASE/ PHENOMENON

✎ WHAT YOU SHOULD KNOW

[466] You may be asked to 'make a full assessment of this girl whose hands are painful in the cold.' It is immediately obvious what the diagnosis is, but what you get marks for are the questions you ask and the way in which you examine what is, essentially, a normal upper limb. The scheme on the following pages shows how to get maximum mileage out of eliciting important and relevant negative findings.

Raynaud's phenomenon: episodic extreme digital vasospasm. A series of colour changes in the skin of the hands or feet following exposure to the cold in the order 'WBC' (white, blue, crimson).

Raynaud's disease: primary idiopathic, i.e. Raynaud's phenomenon which cannot be ascribed to a known cause. Case 1 is typical of primary idiopathic Raynaud's disease. Case 2 is typical of Raynaud's phenomenon, secondary to sclerodema or CREST.

[467] The severity of the signs and the calcinosis should alert you to the fact that systemic sclerosis (also known as scleroderma) is the cause of the symptoms rather than Raynaud's disease. This should point you towards looking for the other signs of scleroderma or CREST syndrome (oesophageal involvement, telangiectasia).

Pathology:

White phase: severe arterial spasm.

Blue phase: a very slow trickle of deoxygenated blood through dilated capillaries and venous congestion caused by persistent venous spasm.

Red phase: reactive hyperaemia following relaxation of arteriolar spasm, making the skin red, hot and painful.

Causes of Raynaud's phenomenon:

Idiopathic: primary idiopathic is called Raynaud's disease. Usually in young girls. May be hereditary.

Arterial diseases: emboli from: subclavian artery aneurysm, stenotic subclavian artery, damaged subclavian artery crossing cervical rib, thoracic outlet syndrome, atherosclerosis, Buerger's disease.

Connective tissue diseases e.g. scleroderma: as part of the CREST syndrome of Calcinosis, Raynaud's, oEsophageal (American spelling) dysmotility, Sclerodactyly and Telangiectasia, rheumatoid, SLE, PAN.

Trauma: vibrating tools, refrigeration units, repeated cold water.

Drugs: combined oral contraceptive pill, beta-blockers.

Blood abnormalities: cold agglutinins, cryoglobulins, polycythaemia.

Investigations:

Aim to exclude the above causes.

Full blood count, ESR, rheumatoid and autoantibodies screen.

CXR for cervical rib.

If suspicious of subclavian artery or large-vessel disease, duplex, CT/MRI may be indicated.

If suspicious of CREST syndrome, barium swallow.

Treatment:

If Raynaud's phenomenon, treat underlying cause (see above).

For primary Raynaud's disease:

Conservative: reduce exposure to the cold (warm or even heated gloves, avoid cold water), stop smoking.

Medical: nifedipine and prostacyclins have been used.

Surgical: cervical sympathectomy (cervical or transaxillary approach, or laparoscopic).

Acrocyanosis – persistently blue, cold hands and feet. Susceptible to chilblains.

Erythrocyanosis frigida/Bazin's disease

This is a form of cold sensitivity on a part of the leg frequently exposed to the wind, rain and cold. It affects healthy girls aged 15–25 years of stout build with fat, often hairless legs. The lower posterior and medial aspect of the lower leg becomes red-blue and swollen. The swollen area is tender, susceptible to chilblains and superficial ulceration. Often the swelling is more noticeable than the discoloration and can be mistaken for lymphoedema. For those of you old enough to remember the popular 'Viz' magazine, it is highly likely that the blotchy-legged characters in the 'Fat Slags' comic strip suffered from this condition!

RAYNAUD'S DISEASE/ PHENOMENON

Case 1[466]

'I would like to present Miss W, a 22-year-old charity worker. She gives a history of hands which become extremely painful in the cold and show characteristic colour changes of turning white, blue and crimson in turn. She has no family history of this, and has no history of working with vibrating tools, refrigeration units or cold water. She denies diabetes or scleroderma, and is not on the contraceptive pill or beta-blockers. On examination of the upper limb, the hands show no discoloration at present, there are no splinter haemorrhages, wasting of the pulps of the fingers or ulcers. The peripheral pulses and capillary refill are normal, there is no diminution of the radial pulse with traction, and there is no audible subclavian bruit. Palpation of the neck reveals no signs of cervical rib or previous clavicle fractures. There is no obvious focal neurology, although I would like to perform a full neurological examination of the upper limb (see pg 356).

My diagnosis is primary idiopathic Raynaud's disease.'

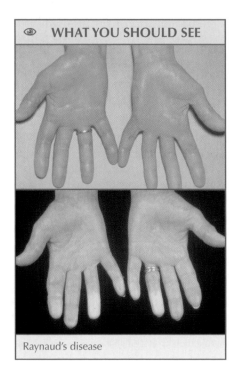

WHAT YOU SHOULD SEE

Raynaud's disease

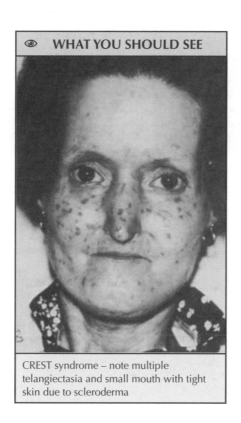

Make a full assessment of this woman with painful hands

RAYNAUD'S DISEASE/ PHENOMENON

Case 2

'I would like to present Mrs W, a 47-year-old barrister. She gives a history of hands which become extremely painful in the cold and show characteristic colour changes of turning white, blue and crimson in turn. On examination of the hands, they are reddish-blue in colour with dry, smooth, shiny, tight skin and brittle nails. Several trophic changes can be seen which include vasculitic lesions, tiny scars and ulceration of the fingertips, finger pulp atrophy and paronychia. There are nodules of calcinosis palpable in some of the fingers. The wrist pulses are normal, as are the other pulses in the upper limb. On inspection of the patient's face the skin is smooth, shiny and tight, especially around the mouth, which looks small and pinched, and there is telangiectasia of the face and pigmentation.

The diagnosis is Raynaud's phenomenon secondary to scleroderma/CREST[467] syndrome.'

👁 WHAT YOU SHOULD SEE

CREST syndrome – note multiple telangiectasia and small mouth with tight skin due to scleroderma

RAYNAUD'S DISEASE/ PHENOMENON

👁 WHAT YOU SHOULD SEE

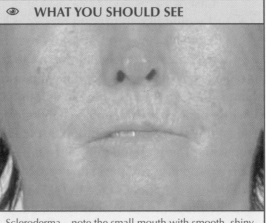

Scleroderma – note the small mouth with smooth, shiny, tight skin

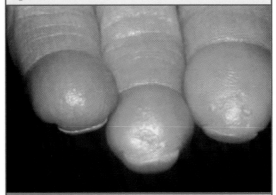

Scleroderma – note fingertip atrophy and ulceration due to vasculitic lesions

CLASSIFICATION OF LYMPHOEDEMA

👁 WHAT YOU SHOULD SEE

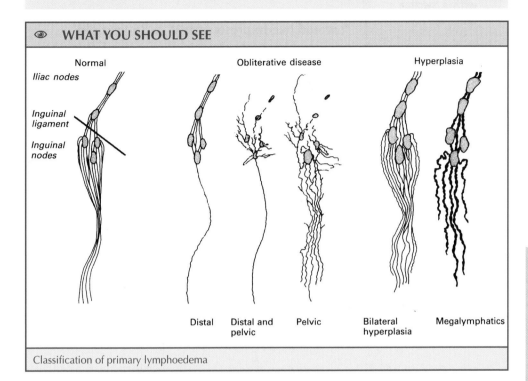

Normal

Iliac nodes

Inguinal ligament

Inguinal nodes

Obliterative disease

Hyperplasia

Distal   Distal and   Pelvic   Bilateral   Megalymphatics
          pelvic   hyperplasia

Classification of primary lymphoedema

🗒 WHAT YOU SHOULD KNOW

Classification:
There are three main categories into which the oedematous lower limb can be classified: oedema which is not real lymphoedema, secondary lymphoedema and primary lymphoedema.

1. Oedema which is not real lymphoedema (i.e. not a result of a fault in the lymphatic system)

Systemic	Venous	Others
Cardiac failure	Post-thrombotic syndrome	AV malformations
Renal failure	Iliac venous obstruction	Lipoedema
Hepatic failure	Klippel–Trenaunay syndrome	Lipodystrophy
Hypoproteinaemia	Extrinsic pressure – tumour	Disuse (e.g. if wheelchair-bound)
Allergic disorders	– retroperitoneal	Fat
Hereditary angioedema	fibrosis	Factitious
Idiopathic cyclical oedema	– pregnancy	Gigantism

2. Secondary lymphoedema (i.e. known cause of lymphatic system failure)
Surgical excision: after block dissection. Occurs in <10% of cases. Worse after radiotherapy.
Radiotherapy: produces block of fibrous tissue which cannot be transgressed by new lymphatic pathway.
Filariasis: infestation by *Wuchereria bancrofti* leading to tropical disease elephantiasis. Also TB and other chronic infections.
Silica: this ore in soil can enter the lymphatic system through bare feet and blocks the inguinal nodes.
Cancer: e.g. breast.
3. Primary lymphoedema (lymphatic system failure of unknown cause)
Usually unilateral. Initially pitting then progresses to non-pitting.
Milroy's disease is congenital hereditary primary lymphoedema due to aplasia of lymph trunks. It is rare (accounts for 3% of primary lymphoedema). Most other cases of primary lymphoedema are due to abnormal or occluded vessels. Twenty per cent have a family history of swollen legs.

505

> Take a history from this man with a swollen left leg

'I would like to present Mr W, a 26-year-old engineer. He has a chronically swollen left leg. He has had no previous surgery or radiotherapy on this limb. He has had troublesome episodes of cellulitis in this leg which have settled with elevation and antibiotics. He is otherwise fit and well.

I would like to examine him to confirm my provisional diagnosis of idiopathic lymphoedema.'

✏ WHAT YOU SHOULD KNOW (CONT)

Definition:
Lymphoedema is an accumulation of tissue fluid resulting from a fault in the lymphatic system, primarily affecting the legs (80%). In contrast, oedema is an accumulation of tissue fluid in patients in whom a lymphatic abnormality has not been confirmed.

Investigations:
Lymphoscintigraphy (a radioactive tracer is injected into the foot and progress monitored as it progresses into proximal lymphatics. Delayed transit confirms diagnosis).

Treatment:
NOT diuretics
Exclude other causes of oedema
Elevation
Compression stockings
Compression device, e.g. serial pneumatic compression device
Occasionally debulking surgery or bypass surgery (indicated in <10% of patients)
Surgical methods include enteromesenteric bridge (pelvic plexus joined to iliac nodes to bypass blocked pelvic nodes)
Must be done before distal lymphatics obliterate; poor outcome
[468] Due to shoes.

LYMPHOEDEMA

Examine this man with a swollen left leg

'There is a grossly enlarged left leg with non-pitting swelling extending from the foot to the groin. The skin of the lower leg is thick and pigmented, with warty skin excrescences. The toes are squared off[468] and there is a moist ulcer secreting clear, watery fluid. In the groin there are grossly enlarged inguinal lymph nodes but no sign of previous surgery or radiotherapy. This is chronic lymphoedema.'

👁 WHAT YOU SHOULD SEE

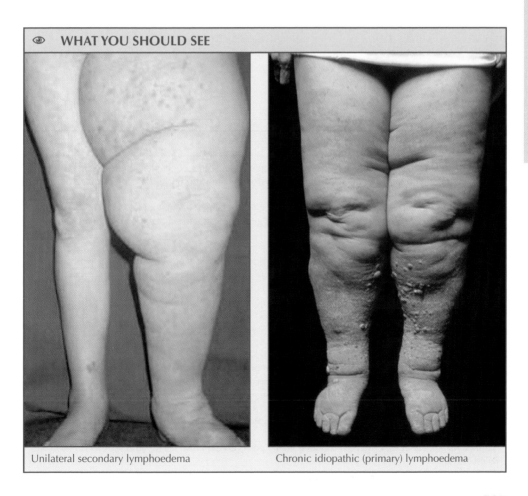

Unilateral secondary lymphoedema

Chronic idiopathic (primary) lymphoedema

Take a history from this man with a swollen left leg

KLIPPEL–TRENAUNAY SYNDROME

'I would like to present Mr W, a 24-year-old office worker. He has had problems with his left leg since birth. It is swollen and larger than his right leg, which causes him to limp. He has had varicose veins and 'port wine stains' on this leg as long as he can remember. He denies rectal bleeding or haematuria. He is otherwise fit and well, takes no medications and has no known allergies. He lives alone and is a non-smoker and does not drink alcohol.

From the history it sounds as though this gentleman has Klippel–Trenaunay syndrome but I would like to examine his leg to confirm my diagnosis.'

✎ WHAT YOU SHOULD KNOW

Diffuse mesodermal abnormality associated with lymphatic and other congenital abnormalities. Usually detected soon after birth when the naevus, limb hypertrophy and varicose veins become apparent.

Complications and associations:

Pelvic venous anomalies in 25% which may cause rectal bleeding or haematuria.

Lymphoedema, spina bifida, syndactyly, coxa vara, digital agenesis, atresia of ear canal, clinodactyly, increased incidence of DVT.

Investigations:

Duplex venography (to confirm deep vein function). Arteriography excludes Parkes–Weber syndrome where multiple AV fistulae are present, which results in limb hypertrophy (see pg 490).

Treatment:

Conservative:

Elastic stockings

Camouflage creams

Cover with DVT prophylaxis during surgery

Surgery:

Only if deep veins are normal, no history of DVT, symptoms not relieved by conservative measures

Ligation of deep to superficial communication. Varices stripped out or avulsed. Recurrence common

Limb debulking (result usually unsightly)

Amputation of giant digit/s

[469] There may also be bone hypertrophy and limb lengthening, leading to abnormal gait, joint problems and lumbar backache.

[470] The aberrant lateral varicose vein connects with a persistent primitive lateral limb vein which has failed to regress.

KLIPPEL–TRENAUNAY SYNDROME

'There is an enlarged left leg with soft-tissue hypertrophy.[469] There are extensive varicose veins unusually situated on the lateral side of the limb[470] with none of the normal signs of venous insufficiency. These veins are not pulsatile, and there does not appear to be an arteriovenous shunt. There is an extensive pale-purple naevus on the same limb. The combination of a cutaneous naevus, varicose veins, bone and soft-tissue abnormalities suggest the Klippel–Trenaunay syndrome.'

👁 WHAT YOU SHOULD SEE

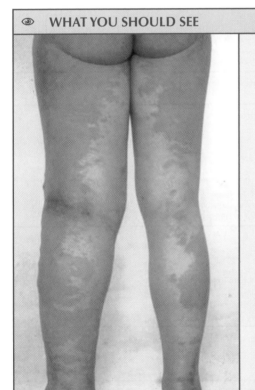

Klippel–Trenaunay syndrome. The extensive pale-purple naevus is obvious, as is the soft-tissue hypertrophy. The dilated lateral varicose veins are just visible

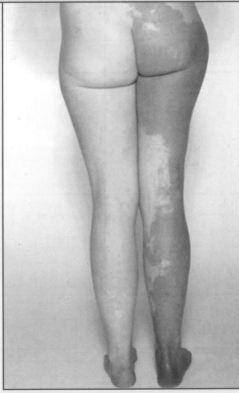

Klippel–Trenaunay syndrome. The bony and soft-tissue overgrowth can be seen by the fact that the affected right leg is longer than the left, causing pelvic tilting when standing

509

D SURVEY RESULTS

LIMBS (INCLUDING SPINE)

These results include cases seen in the new OSCE and the old style MRCS exam.

TOP 5 CASES

Type of case	Number seen in survey	Breakdown and details of cases
Venous disease of legs	33	18 Varicose veins (3 with saphena varix) 9 Chronic venous skin changes (5 lipodermatosclerosis) 6 Venous ulcer Questions included examine, do Trendelenburg's test, use Doppler probe, aetiology, treatment, anatomy.
Ischaemic leg (excluding diabetic leg)	29	13 Examine leg with peripheral vascular disease (PVD) 7 Examine leg post bypass surgery or stenting 3 Look at this angiogram 6 Amputations due to PVD Questions included history, examination, measuring of ankle-brachial pressure indices, anatomy of pulses, treatment of PVD, Beurger's test, sources of emboli, how is angiography performed, complications of amputation.
Dupuytren's contracture	26	Questions included causes, treatment options, anatomy, skin grafts, related features.
Knee	22	12 Osteoarthritis, one with total knee replacement 2 Rheumatoid arthritis 2 Effusion 2 Anterior cruciate injury 1 Patient post-op with PE and DVT 1 Paget's disease 1 Seronegative arthritis (+ inflammatory bowel disease?) 1 Apparently normal knee Questions included history, examination, anterior drawer test, arthroscopy scars, X-ray changes of osteoarthritis, problems associated with rheumatoid disease.
Hip	21	3 Examine hip ?diagnosis 7 Osteoarthritis 4 Avascular necrosis 6 Postoperative 1 Bilateral congenital 'problems' (not specified) Questions included preoperative assessment, Garden classification, features of Paget's disease, surgical approaches to the hip, screws and complications. Three candidates were shown hip X-rays.

OTHER CASES

Type of case	Number seen in survey	Breakdown and details of cases
Rheumatoid hand	17	Standard questions on features of rheumatoid hand

Type of case	Number seen in survey	Breakdown and details of cases
Aneurysm	15	7 Abdominal aortic 4 Popliteal 1 Femoral 2 False (1 groin post femoral-distal vein graft, 1 radial) 1 Brachial artery post surgical AV fistula formation Questions included risk factors, management, indications for surgery, angiograms, other sites for aneurysms, look at CT scan.
Great toe	14	9 Hallux valgus 2 Rheumatoid arthritis 2 Hallux rigidus 1 Claw toes Questions included causes and treatment options of hallux valgus, features of rheumatoid arthritis..
Arteriovenous fistula	12	9 on forearm for renal transplant patients 1 In groin for renal transplant 1 Multiple Cimino fistulae and false aneurysm 1 Congenital AV malformation Questions included indications, complications, what is a Brescia fistula, what is a Cimino fistula.
Osler-Weber-Rendu syndrome	12	
Diabetic feet	9	3 Ischaemic toe 2 Ulcer 2 Amputation 2 Peripheral vascular disease Questions included examine feet, examine legs, why are the pedal pulses present?
Upper limb neurology	9	4 Ulnar nerve palsy (1 with cervical rib, 1 with elbow trauma 2 radial nerve palsy (1 causing hyperaesthesia, 1 at the level of the brachial plexus) 2 posterior brachial plexus cord injury 1 examination of median nerve (also see carpal tunnel)
Carpal tunnel	7	3 cases with thenar muscle wasting. Questions included treatment and operative details.
Wrist	7	2 Colles'fracture 2 Rheumatoid arthritis 1 Avascular necrosis of scaphoid 1 Carpometacarpal osteoarthritis 1 Examine extensor tendons pathology not specified Questions included how to manipulate Colles' fracture, anaesthetic methods used, complications, wrist arthrodesis in rheumatoid disease for volar subluxation.
External fixators	6	2 Wrist, 1 with carpal tunnel decompression 3 Tibia 1 Femur Questions included complications of external fixation, surgical anatomy of the hip, median nerve supply, X-rays of radius and ulnar fracture.
Ganglion	6	3 Wrist 1 Thumb 2 Not specified
Venous disease of upper body	5	2 IVC obstruction 2 Axillary vein thrombosis 1 ?cervical varicose veins (examiners did not know either!) Questions included examine, investigations, management, anticoagulation.

Type of case	Number seen in survey	Breakdown and details of cases
Upper limb ischaemia	4	1 Subclavian artery thrombosis 1 Axillary artery thrombosis 1 Critical ischaemia 1 Thoracic outlet syndrome Questions included Allen's test.
Carotid disease	3	1 Bruit and history of transient ischaemic attack 1 Carotid artery stenosis – signs not specified 1 Carotid aneurysm
Deep vein thrombosis	3	Questions included history, examination, aetiology, diagnosis, investigations, management, use a Doppler, interpret venogram
Elbow	3	All olecranon bursa. 2 in Superficial Lesions bay
Hyperhidrosis	3	Questions included anatomy of sympathetic chain, typical history
Lymphoedema	3	Including congenital and gross bilateral lymphoedema
Raynaud's	3	Examine hands and take history
Shoulder	3	1 Rheumatoid arthritis 1 Decreased range of movement ?cause 1 Old scar and atrophy of muscles ?radical dissection Questions included examine movements, take short history.
Ankylosing spondylitis	2	Questions included cervical spine examination, hip and knee examination, X-ray features.
Exostosis	2	
Paget's disease	2	Both tibia. Questions included complications and X-ray features.
Trigger finger	2	Asked about treatment options
Winged scapula	2	
Anatomy	1	Major skeletal landmarks, which muscles attach or which nerves and vessels run by these points
Ankle	1	Arthritis after tibial fracture (with X-ray)
Back pain	1	
Bone graft	1	
Cervical rib	1	
Hand	1	Anatomy
Gout	1	Tophi on finger, asked differential diagnosis.
Ingrowing toenail	1	
Lower limb neurology	1	
Osteochondro-sarcoma of chest wall	1	

CHAPTER 6
NEUROSCIENCES

A The Histories   515

B The Examinations   525

C The OSCE cases   531

D Survey Results   554

A THE HISTORIES

HEADACHE

Headaches are very common; an extremely small percentage of patients presenting with this symptom will have a serious underlying surgical condition. The key to a good history is identifying 'red flag' signs that may warrant further investigation, with the ultimate aim of ruling out (or in) a space-occupying lesion. It is also worth noting that many brain tumours will not present with headache as the primary complaint.

Introductions

'Hello, my name is Ryan Mathew. Please can I check your details? Would you mind if I asked you some questions about your symptoms?'
Ask about demographics.
'May I ask how old you are?'
'Are you right- or left-handed?'[1]
'What do/did you do for a living?'[1]

Presenting complaint (open question!)

'What has caused you to come and see me today?'

History of presenting complaint

'How long have you had headaches for?' *(days or weeks)*
'Is there anything that might have brought it on?'[2]
'Can you point on your head where the pain is worst? Does the pain go anywhere?'[3]
'Have you ever had a headache that was sudden and very severe?'[4]
'Are the headaches worse at any time of the day? Do they get worse with sneezing, straining or coughing?'[5]

---

[1] Even the majority of people who are left-handed have a dominant left cerebral hemisphere (approximately 75%). Hemisphere dominance and occupation may be relevant for future surgical decisions and risk calculation.

[2] Post-traumatic headaches can occur following head injury.

[3] Space-occupying lesions are not usually well localised on the surface of the head but sinusitis as a cause may be well localised. Cervical spondylosis can cause occipital headaches.

[4] A missed subarachnoid haemorrhage can present with persisting headaches and/or symptoms related to an underlying aneurysm.

[5] In normal people, intracranial pressure is highest in the morning after lying down all night and is transiently raised by these actions.

'Do you know when the headaches are going to come on?'[6]
'Do you notice anything else when the headaches come on, such as changes to your vision?'[6]
'When did you last visit an optician? Do you notice if your headaches come on when straining your eyes, such as watching TV or using the computer for a long time?'[7]
'Have you ever had a seizure or blacked out? Have you noticed any weakness or numbness in your arms or legs?'[8]

Past medical and surgical history

'Have you ever had headaches in the past?'[9]
'Have you ever had any brain operations? Have you ever had chemo/radiotherapy?'[10]

Medication and allergies

'Do you take any regular medication?[11] Do you have any allergies?'

Family history

'Has anyone in your family ever suffered from headaches? Has anyone in your family ever had an operation on their brain?'[12]

Social history (smoking and drinking)

'Do you smoke? Do you take any recreational drugs?'[13] *(if relevant)*

---

[6] Aura and visual symptoms with headaches may point to migraines. Raised ICP may cause papilloedema and visual blurring.

[7] If no recent eye test in the last year.

[8] Hydrocephalus, tumours and chronic subdural haematomas can cause focal neurological signs. Temporal tumours predominantly present with seizures. Meningiomas may present with seizures alone or associated with headache.

[9] Recurring, chronic.

[10] Asking about previous brain tumours or cerebral aneurysms is difficult as there may not be any obvious clues. Direct questions about these pathologies may alert the patient to your line of thought and provoke alarm.

[11] The combined oral contraceptive pill can cause headaches as a side-effect. A number of other prescribed medications can cause headaches, including: vasodilators (sympathomimetics, calcium-channel blockers, antihistamines, bronchodilators, ergotamine), dopamine agonists, non-steroidal anti-inflammatories and even codeine.

[12] Migraines, aneurysms and brain tumours can be familial. Any known family history may point to the relevant pathology.

[13] Smokers are at increased risk of cerebral aneurysm formation and dilation. Cocaine use is associated with chronic headaches.

SPECIFIC TYPES OF HEADACHE

Tension headache – the commonest form of headache experienced, diffuse, dull, aching with a 'tight band', may have concomitant depression or stressors.

Migraine – can exist with or without aura, characterised by unilateral throbbing headache, more common in females, often familial, various subtypes, managed by neurologists.

Cluster headache – severe unilateral pain around one eye, more common in males, onset in middle age, can be associated with conjunctival injection, lacrimation, rhinorrhoea and, occasionally, a transient Horner syndrome.

Giant cell (temporal) arteritis – idiopathic, autoimmune disease, affects the elderly, most commonly affects the superficial temporal artery.

Post-traumatic headache – headaches similar in character to migraine or tension-type headache following head injury, can be associated with poor concentration, irritability and emotional lability.

Low-pressure headache – post lumbar puncture, occult CSF leak following epidural anaesthesia, over-drainage of CSF in shunted patients, worse when erect, eased by lying flat.

Idiopathic intracranial hypertension – most common in overweight young females, characterised by diffuse aching pain, associated with deterioration in visual acuity, papilloedema on fundoscopy.

LIMB WEAKNESS

Limb weakness can be secondary to central (brain or spine) or peripheral causes. Space-occupying lesions such as brain tumours and subdural collections most commonly cause contralateral weakness, although indentation of the cerebral peduncle on the side opposite to the pathology by the tentorium cerebelli can cause ipsilateral weakness. Limb weakness alone therefore plays a limited role in localising the side of the pathology in the brain. Motor deficits are not often detected with root lesions between T2 and L1 and above C5. Mononeuropathies or plexus damage can cause whole-limb or specific muscle group weakness.

Introductions

'Hello, my name is Ryan Mathew. Please can I check your details? Would you mind if I asked you some questions about your symptoms?'
Ask about demographics.
'May I ask how old you are?'
'Are you right- or left-handed?'[14]
'What do/did you do for a living?'[14]

Presenting complaint (open question!)

'What has caused you to come and see me today?'

History of presenting complaint

'How long have you noticed that you are not as strong on one side/in one arm/leg?'[15] *(hours, days or weeks)*
Is there anything that might have brought it on?[16]

---

[14] Even the majority of people who are left-handed have a dominant left cerebral hemisphere (approximately 75%). Hemisphere dominance and occupation may be relevant for future surgical decisions and risk calculation. Degenerative spinal conditions may result from labour-intensive jobs.
[15] Spinal infarcts can present with limb weakness suddenly. Spinal tumours (depending on their location) and epidural collections such as abscesses and haematomas can present with rapidly progressive symptoms.
[16] Trauma can damage individual nerves or plexuses. Strenuous exercise can cause a neuritis. Violent coughing or sneezing can cause acute cervical disc protrusion. Heavy lifting can cause lumbar disc protrusion.

'Does the strength come and go, or is it weak all the time? Is it getting worse, or has it stayed the same?'
'Is there anything that brings it on or makes it worse?'

'Are there any head positions that make the symptoms worse?'[17]
'Do you suffer from neck and/or back pain?'[18]
'Is there anything that makes it better?'[19]

'Do you have any pain or numbness in the parts that are not as strong?'
'Do you find yourself unsteady on your feet? Have you been falling?'[20]
'Have you have had any problems with your waterworks or bowels? Have you had any problems getting or maintaining an erection?'[21]

'Have you noticed any other symptoms associated with your weakness, such as headaches, seizures, blackouts or visual problems?'[22]

---

[17] Being able to recreate the symptoms when turning the neck to the same side with axial compression may point to a cervical radiculopathy (Spurling's manoeuvre).

[18] Neck/back pain may reveal an underlying degenerate spine.

[19] Neurogenic claudication caused by lumbar canal stenosis can result in weakness, paraesthesia and root pain on standing or walking. It is classically relieved by bending or sitting.

[20] Lack of coordination can present as weakness and vice versa. Gait or sphincteric disturbance may be a sign of a progressive cervical myelopathy.

[21] A central lumbar disc protrusion causing foot drop may be associated with leg pain, paraesthesia, sensory loss and sphincter disturbance.

[22] Hydrocephalus, tumours and chronic subdural haematomas can cause focal neurological signs such as weakness. Associated symptoms may help localise a central lesion. Seizures can cause focal weakness in the postictal period (Todd's paresis).

Past medical and surgical history

'Have you ever had any operations? Have you ever had chemo/radiotherapy?'[23]
'Do you have arthritis?'[24]

Family history

'Has anyone in your family ever suffered from headaches? Has anyone in your family ever had an operation on their brain?'[25]

Social history (smoking and drinking)

'How much alcohol do you drink?'[26]

Combined Assessment Box – LIMB WEAKNESS

Ask:
- Insidious or sudden onset? Length of history?
- Affects one side or just one limb?
- Associated symptoms, e.g. seizures, visual symptoms, pain/sensory disturbance, LOC, headaches

Examine:
- Full cranial nerve examination
- Fundoscopy
- Neck movements, full midline spinal tenderness
- Digital rectal examination and perianal sensation
- Peripheral neurological examination including cerebellar function

---

[23] Recurrence of brain or spinal tumours can present with limb weakness. Recurrence of lung tumours can present as Pancoast's. Previous limb reconstruction surgery may have caused a mononeuropathy.
[24] Arthritis elsewhere may be related to arthritis affecting the spine resulting in a degenerative picture.
[25] Migraines, aneurysms and brain tumours can be familial. Any known family history may point to the relevant pathology. Migraines can cause transient focal weakness.
[26] Alcohol can reduce seizure threshold and a Todd's paresis may result.

SPINAL CORD SYNDROMES

Anterior cord syndrome (anterior spinal artery syndrome) – compression of the anterior spinal artery, usually results in complete motor deficit and loss of pain and temperature sensation below the level of the lesion, vibration and joint position sense preserved, worst prognosis of all cord syndromes.

Central cord syndrome – incomplete injury, arms affected more than legs, result of trauma, motor deficit (especially loss of fine motor control) below the site of the lesion, sensory loss and bladder dysfunction may also occur, variable prognosis.

Brown–Séquard syndrome – rare, ipsilateral pyramidal weakness and upper motor signs, ipsilateral joint position sense and two-point discrimination impaired, contralateral pain and temperature sensation loss causing dysaesthesia, bladder symptoms infrequent, variable prognosis.

Mononeuropathies and plexus lesions
Brachial plexus gives off important motor branches:
- Nerve to rhomboids
- Long thoracic nerve to serratus anterior
- Pectoral nerves to pectoralis major
- Suprascapular nerve to supraspinatus and infraspinatus
- Nerve to latissimus dorsi
- Axillary nerve
- Radial nerve
- Median nerve
- Ulnar nerve

Brachial plexus lesions:
- Erb–Duchenne paralysis
- Posterior cord lesion
- Klumpke's paralysis
- Thoracic outlet syndrome
- Pancoast's tumour
- Brachial neuritis

Lumbosacral plexus lesions:
- Upper lumbosacral plexus lesion
- Lower lumbosacral plexus lesion

Mononeuropathies:
- Long thoracic nerve
- Suprascapular nerve
- Axillary nerve
- Musculocutaneous nerve
- Radial nerve
- Median nerve and carpal tunnel syndrome
- Ulnar nerve
- Femoral nerve
- Obturator nerve
- Sciatic nerve
- Common peroneal nerve
- Posterior tibial nerve and tarsal tunnel syndrome

DYSPHASIA/DYSARTHRIA

Dysarthria is a disturbance of the articulation of speech. Language, the content of the speech, is not affected in a purely dysarthric patient. Dysphasia is an inability to produce (expressive) or comprehend (receptive) spoken and/or written language. This is an acquired deficit, secondary to damage to the relevant areas of the brain. This is a very difficult history to take and, if there is a severe deficit, potentially a very short one.

Introductions

'Hello, my name is Ryan Mathew. Please can I check your details? Would you mind if I asked you some questions about your symptoms?'
Ask about demographics.
'May I ask how old you are?'
'Are you right- or left-handed?'[27]
'What do/did you do for a living?'[27]

Presenting complaint (open question!)

'What has caused you to come and see me today?'

History of presenting complaint

'How long have you noticed difficulty with your speech?' *(hours, days or weeks)* **'Is there anything that might have brought it on?'**[28]
'Do you understand the things I say? If so, is it difficult to find the right words?'[29]
'Has your memory been affected?'
'Is your reading and writing affected?'
'Are you able to chew and swallow food normally?'[29]

---

[27] Even the majority of people who are left-handed have a dominant left cerebral hemisphere (approximately 75%). Hemisphere dominance and occupation may be relevant for future surgical decisions and risk calculation.
The patient may not be able to answer any of these questions and the history may have to stop. It may be worth asking if they can write down their answers – this may reveal that comprehension is intact, and assesses handwriting.
[28] Head injury can cause disorder of speech and language. Confusion as a result of a chronic subdural haematoma secondary to trauma may be differentiated by disorientation to time, place and person.
[29] Lesions of the brainstem can affect other cranial nerves apart from those related to production of speech (X and XII).

'Have you noticed any other symptoms associated with your speech problems, such as headaches, seizures, blackouts or visual problems?'[30]
'Have you noticed any weakness in your face or arm?'[31]

Past medical and surgical history

'Have you ever had any operations? Have you ever had chemo/radiotherapy?'[32]

Family history

'Has anyone in your family ever suffered from headaches? Has anyone in your family ever had an operation on their brain?'[33]

Combined Assessment Box – DYSPHASIA/DYSARTHRIA

Ask:
- Awareness of speech or language problem?
- Problems with memory or word finding?
- Associated symptoms, e.g. weakness or numbness of limbs, swallowing or mastication problems

Examine:
- Full cranial nerve examination
- Fundoscopy
- Content and fluency of speech
- Test simple and complex commands
- Assess object naming, reading, writing, repetition

---

[30] Hydrocephalus, tumours and chronic subdural haematomas can cause focal neurological signs. Associated symptoms may help localise a central lesion. Global dysphasia is associated with visual field defects.
[31] Broca's (motor) area is adjacent to the motor strip serving the arm and face on the contralateral side. Lesions may cause associated weakness. Lesions affecting the facial nerve can cause weakness of the muscles of expression, resulting in dysarthria.
[32] Recurrence of brain tumours can present with speech and language deficits.
[33] Migraines, aneurysms and brain tumours can be familial. Any known family history may point to the relevant pathology.

TYPES OF DYSPHASIA

Broca's dysphasia – frustrated, hesitant speech, non-fluent, may be restricted to few words, comprehension good, handwriting poor, may have co-existing contralateral (usually right) arm or face weakness (Broca's area dominant – usually left – inferior frontal lobe).
Wernicke's dysphasia – speech nonsensical but fluent, comprehension impaired, patient has poor insight of problem, handwriting poor.
Global dysphasia – non-fluent speech, comprehension impaired, usually occurs as a result of a large area of dominant (usually left) hemisphere being damaged, resulting in associated weakness/sensory deficit (usually right-sided).
Conduction dysphasia – lesion of the arcuate fasciculus, causing loss of integration between Wernicke's and Broca's areas, fluent but nonsensical speech, comprehension normal, poor repetition.

STROKE

Stroke (ischaemic or haemorrhagic) may present with speech disturbance, facial and/or limb weakness. It may also present with reduced conscious level secondary to raised intracranial pressure. This in turn may be due to hydrocephalus (as a result of intraventricular blood), mass effect from the haematoma or oedema associated with the infarct. Stroke is managed by neurologists. Neurosurgeons may be involved in placing an external ventricular device to manage acute hydrocephalus or performing a decompressive craniectomy for middle cerebral artery territory infarcts that have caused life-threatening oedema.

B THE EXAMINATIONS

There is a degree of crossover in the examination techniques you will need to be familiar with in the 'Limbs (including spine)' and the 'Neurosciences' sections. For convenience, these are covered in the Limbs (including spine) chapter and the page references are below:

- Spine examination pg 346
- Upper limb neurological examination pg 356
- Lower limb neurological examination pg 365

CRANIAL NERVE EXAMINATION

'Hello, my name is Ryan Mathew. Would you mind if I examined the function of the nerves in your head and neck? Could you sit on a chair, away from the wall please?'

WASH/GEL YOUR HANDS BEFORE YOU TOUCH THE PATIENT

Stand with your hands behind your back and look from the front.
Look for any obvious facial droop, ptosis, ocular palsy, hearing aids, signs of previous surgery, or muscle wasting in the neck.

'Have you noticed any change in your sense of smell?'[34]
State that you would objectively examine olfactory nerve function using pungent odours (e.g. coffee, cinnamon, soap), blocking each nostril in turn, if the patient answered 'yes'.

'Please close one eye with your hand and look at the chart ahead. Read out the smallest row that you can see clearly. Now do the same with your other eye. And now do it with both eyes open.'
Hold a Snellen chart at 6 m/20 feet from the patient.[35]

'I'm now going to make the room dark and shine a bright light into each eye so that I can look at the back of your eyes.[36] **Please pick a point on the wall ahead and concentrate on it.'**

---

[34] Head injury, including blunt trauma, can cause damage to the olfactory nerve, as can frontal lobe tumours and meningitis. Iatrogenic injury can be caused by trans-sphenoidal procedures (e.g. resection of pituitary tumours), maxillofacial or ENT surgery. Avoid testing with noxious odours as pain sensation to the nasal epithelium is carried by the trigeminal nerve and can result in false positives.

[35] Most rooms do not have 6 m available so a half-sized chart is used and held at 3 m/10 feet. If vision is less than 20/200, one can use finger counting at 1 foot and at 6 inches, hand movements or light perception.

[36] Fundoscopy is a difficult skill and takes a lot of practice to master. Furthermore, it is uncomfortable for the patient and compliance is variable. Check for the red reflex initially. Look into a patient's right eye while holding the ophthalmoscope in your right hand. Examine the left eye by walking around to the other side of the patient and hold the ophthalmoscope in your left hand. Identify a major vessel, adjust the lens till it is in focus and follow it to the optic disc. Assess for increased intracranial pressure by examining for papilloedema and absent venous pulsations. Blood in the centre of the disc may suggest subarachnoid haemorrhage.

'I'm now going to check your peripheral vision. Please cover one eye with your hand. Look directly at me with your open eye throughout the examination.'[37]

Let the patient choose which eye to start with and mirror them with your own hand. *With your free hand, start your index finger in a position where both you and your patient should not be able to see it – this may involve you sitting quite close to your patient. Now bring your finger in from the periphery towards the midline, wiggling it as you do so. Now switch the hand covering your eye and test the nasal field (if you have mirrored your patient, you will have invariably tested the temporal field first). Do this in three positions (upper, middle and lower) for each nasal and temporal field per eye.*[38]

'I'm just going to shine this light into each eye. Sorry if it's a little uncomfortable.'

Shine the light of the ophthalmoscope into each eye twice, firstly looking for the direct and then for the consensual pupillary reflex. Keep the base of your palm on the bridge of the patient's nose to avoid light crossover.

'Now, please follow the tip of my pen with your eyes, keeping your head still.'

Fix the patient's head by gently holding the chin or forehead and trace an imaginary 'H' in the air, watching for any palsies in eye movement. Check for any nystagmus (physiological nystagmus can occur at the extremes of gaze). Finally bring the tip in towards the nose and watch for symmetrical convergence.

'Now please look to one corner of the room and then quickly back to the tip of my pen.'

This tests the accommodation reflex.

'I'm now going to touch both sides of your face. Tell me if it feels weaker on one side compared with the other.'

Test sensation[39] *of the face in the ophthalmic, maxillary and mandibular divisions.*

---

[37] The physiological blind spot should be identifiable in the temporal portion of the visual field.

[38] This is gross visual field testing by confrontation. Formal testing is done with Goldmann perimeter fields.

[39] Formal testing involves light touch, pinprick and temperature sensation. Assess for a divisional/root pattern or a concentric brainstem pattern.

'I'm now going to blow gently into each eye to test your blink reflex.'
Keeping the base of your palm on the bridge of the patient's nose, blow gently into each eye in turn and watch for a reflex blink.

'Please close your jaw tight and keep your teeth clenched.'
Inspect for muscle wasting and thinning in the temporalis fossa. Feel the temporalis and masseter muscles. Attempt to open the patient's jaw.
'Now please open your jaw.'
Watch for deviation of the jaw to one side. Weakness or paralysis of the pterygoid muscles will cause deviation to the affected side.
'I'm now going to place a finger on your chin and tap gently.'
With the jaw slightly open, place a finger on the chin and tap on your own finger with the tendon hammer. A slight jerk is normal. Bilateral upper motor neurone lesions will result in an increased jerk.

'I'm now going to ask you to make some funny expressions to test the muscles of your face. Please show me your teeth. Now smile. Now please raise your eyebrows. Now please screw your eyes tight shut and don't let me open them. Now puff out your cheeks and don't let me push them in.'
Examine for any asymmetry or weakness when performing tests. Taste may be tested by placing small amounts of sugar and salt on the anterior aspect of each side of the tongue.

'I'm now going to whisper some numbers into your ear while blocking the other ear. Please tell me if you can't hear them clearly.'
Occlude hearing to one ear by blocking and rubbing the external acoustic meatus while whispering into the ear to be tested – this tests the cochlear component of the auditory nerve.
'Tell me which ear you hear this buzzing in loudest.'[40]
Using your fingers to initiate the tuning fork, place the base of it on the vertex.
'I'll now place the fork at the back of your ear. Tell me if you can hear it. When it stops, I'll move it round to your ear. Tell me which one is louder.'[41]
Place the base of an initiated tuning fork onto the mastoid bone. Assuming the patient can hear it at this point, move it round to the external acoustic meatus when the patient informs you that the sound has disappeared. The patient should be able to hear the sound again.

---

[40] In conductive deafness, sound is heard loudest in the affected ear. In sensorineural deafness, sound is heard loudest in the normal ear.
[41] Air conduction should be better than bone conduction. In conductive deafness, bone conduction is superior. Both air and bone conduction are reduced in sensorineural deafness.

'Please open your mouth and say 'ah'.
Note any asymmetry of the uvula, which should rise to phonation and will deviate away from the side of any paralysis.[42a]

'I'm now going to test a reflex at the back of your throat by pressing this wooden spatula onto the back of your mouth. It may feel uncomfortable for a brief moment.'
Touch the soft palate, pharynx or tonsil on each side with a disposable tongue depressor. Examine sensitivity on each side and the symmetry of the resultant palatal contraction.[42b]

'Please now push my hand away when I place it against your chin. Also try and shrug your shoulders against my hands.'
Place the palm of one hand against one side of the chin and ask the patient to push it away. Repeat on the other side and compare the sides[43]. Go behind the patient and ask the patient to shrug the shoulders. Attempt to depress the shoulders while they resist.

'Now please open your mouth and stick your tongue out. Move it from side to side.'[44]
Inspect for normal protrusion and any deviation (towards the side of weakness).

Stand back and present your findings in a succinct and logical order to your examiners.

[42a] If there is unilateral vocal cord paralysis, the voice may be high pitched and/or hoarse. Bilateral vocal cord paralysis may result in dyspnoea or stridor.
[42b] It is most safely tested formally by a speech and language therapist. Swallowing difficulties and regurgitation should have been picked up in the history.
[43] Note that head turning to each side is mediated by the contralateral sternomastoid muscle.
[44] Beware that facial weakness can create an apparent deviation – check tongue with respect to the teeth if this is present. Remember the tongue is a muscle and therefore observe for wasting (increased folds).

C THE OSCE CASES

HOW TO USE THIS SECTION

Common history or examination cases you might see in the exam appear below.

For each case, there will be given an example 'OSCE question' which you could expect to find outside a station in the examination. Following this is an example of how to present a 'typical patient' with this complaint. You can then use these examples to practise with friends/colleagues. One of you should be the 'candidate' and use the basic history and examination schemes to start you off. A second person should be the 'patient' and pretend to be the patient in the example given. A third person could be used as the 'examiner' to check that all the questions or examination steps from the basic schemes are completed. The 'candidate' can then present their findings at the end and have a guess at a differential diagnosis. At the end of the 'station' the 'examiner' can then use the 'What you should know' section to ask the 'candidate' some questions about the case. Try and time yourselves so you get an idea of how long 9 minutes is.

Following this are images of the condition so that if you don't get a chance to see a particular case in all those outpatient clinics you will be attending before the exam at least you will have an idea what it will look like!

Take a history from this patient. His family feel that he has become more confused recently and is unsteady on his feet

(see pg 518)

CHRONIC SUBDURAL HAEMATOMA

'I would like to present Mr R, an 80-year-old right-hand-dominant retired printer. He has become increasingly confused and somnolent over the past 2–3 days. He is normally active and cognitively intact. He is also usually independently mobile but has been reluctant to be so during this time. When attempting to stand him, he leans to one side. His daughter recalls that he fell about 10 days ago and banged his head.[45] There was no loss of consciousness at the time and he was seemingly OK. His past medical history includes atrial fibrillation, high cholesterol and benign prostatic hypertrophy. He takes warfarin, a statin and a proton pump inhibitor. He has no known drug allergies. He does not smoke or drink alcohol. He is a retired printer and lives alone in a bungalow. He does not receive any home help and is independent in terms of all ADLs.

My diagnosis is chronic subdural haematoma. I would like to examine him to confirm the diagnosis.'

C THE OSCE CASES

⟁ WHAT YOU SHOULD KNOW

This is a traumatic brain injury but 50% present without a history of trauma. It usually occurs in the context of pre-existing brain atrophy, when cerebral veins are tented across the subdural space.

[45] A minor head injury can result in shearing of the veins, causing blood to leak into the subdural space. As this is a low-volume leak and the atrophied brain creates space in the cranial vault, it may take time to accumulate sufficient haematoma to cause symptoms. Risk factors include age, alcohol excess, dementia, low CSF pressure (overdrainage of shunt), anticoagulation and a coagulopathy.

[46] It presents with confusion, deterioration in conscious level (may be fluctuating) and, occasionally, a gradual onset of focal neurological signs such as limb weakness. It can present acutely if there is a re-bleed into a pre-existing collection.

Surgical management involves burr-hole drainage of the subdural space. The risks specific to this pathology are of re-collection and a need for further surgery. It can be performed under local or general anaesthetic. Usually frontal and parietal burr holes are drilled in order to create a connection in the subdural space. The haematoma is then washed out with warmed normal saline until clear. A drain is left in situ if the brain has failed to re-expand, in order to minimise the risk of re-collection.

CHRONIC SUBDURAL HAEMATOMA

'On examination, Mr R opens his eyes to speech and is able to follow commands. He is disorientated to time, place and person.[46] His Glasgow coma score is therefore 13/15 (E3 V4 M6). Cranial nerves are grossly intact. Peripheral neurological examination reveals a mild right-sided weakness, power grade 4/5 throughout.[46] There is a right-sided pronator drift. He is unable to stand unaided. I would like to check this man's INR and arrange for a CT scan of his head to investigate further.'

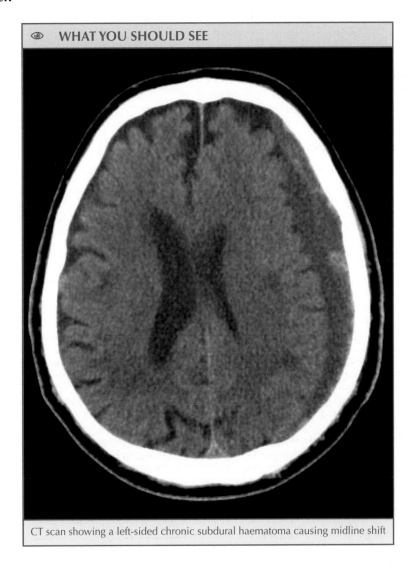

👁 **WHAT YOU SHOULD SEE**

CT scan showing a left-sided chronic subdural haematoma causing midline shift

Take a history from this patient who presents with a headache

(see pg 515)

SUBARACHNOID HAEMORRHAGE

'I would like to present Mrs H, a 46-year-old left-hand-dominant secretary. She had a sudden-onset occipital headache at work today while at the computer. She described it as the worst headache of her life. The headache has persisted and now she finds the light uncomfortable. There was no loss of consciousness and she has not had a seizure. She is normally fit and well. She takes no medications and has no known drug allergies. She lives with her husband and two children. She smokes 25 cigarettes a day and consumes approximately 20 units of alcohol a week. There is no relevant family history.

My diagnosis is subarachnoid haemorrhage. I would like to examine her to confirm the diagnosis.'

WHAT YOU SHOULD KNOW

Subarachnoid haemorrhage (SAH) occurs in approximately 10–15 per 100 000 per year. It is predominantly diagnosed from the history, with confirmation by imaging.

Risk factors include female gender, smoking, hypertension, positive family history, atherosclerotic disease and polycystic kidney disease.

Presenting features are sudden-onset headache, vomiting, meningism, loss of consciousness, coma, focal neurological signs and seizures. A low-grade pyrexia may be present.

[47] In CT-negative patients, a diagnostic lumbar puncture should be performed 6–12 hours post-ictus. If this is normal, then no further investigation is required. The presence of Hb breakdown products in the CSF is highly suspicious of SAH. All patients with proven SAH (CT or LP) should be transferred to a neurosurgical unit.

Cerebral aneurysms account for the vast majority, with other causes including AV malformations, bleeding diatheses, anticoagulants, tumours and vasculitis. There is a small group of patients in which no underlying cause is found.

CT angiography with 3D reconstruction will pick up approximately 95% of underlying aneurysms but those less than 2–3 mm may still be missed. Formal catheter angiography may be indicated for further investigation.

Extracranial complications include cardiac arrhythmias, myocardial infarction, neurogenic pulmonary oedema and stress ulcers. Re-bleeding (prior to securing of the aneurysm) and hydrocephalus are the predominant **intracranial complications**. Any deterioration in the patient's conscious level warrants immediate repeat CT scan.

Treatment of aneurysmal SAH is predominantly by endovascular coil embolisation or vascular stenting. For those with aneurysms not amenable to endovascular options, craniotomy and clipping remain the treatment. Aneurysmal SAHs that present with life-threatening sylvian fissure haematomas are usually clipped following evacuation of the clot.

SUBARACHNOID HAEMORRHAGE

'On examination, Mrs H opens her eyes to speech, is fully orientated to time, place and person and is able to follow commands. Her Glasgow coma score is therefore 14/15 (E3 V5 M6). Cranial nerves are grossly intact. Fundoscopy reveals normal findings. Peripheral neurological examination is entirely normal. There is mild photophobia and neck stiffness. Her temperature is 37.5°C.

I would like to arrange for a CT scan[47] of her head to investigate the possibility of a subarachnoid haemorrhage.'

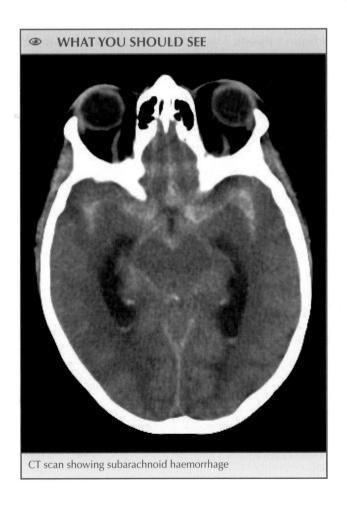

👁 **WHAT YOU SHOULD SEE**

CT scan showing subarachnoid haemorrhage

Take a history from this patient who presents with odd behaviour

BRAIN TUMOURS –
CEREBRAL METASTASES

'I would like to present Mrs T, a 77-year-old right-hand-dominant retired seamstress. Her family have noticed that she has been behaving increasingly oddly for the past few weeks. Her daughter found her in the bath, confused and disorientated. The patient became combative and aggressive when her daughter tried to help her to her bed. She has insulin-dependent diabetes, COPD, chronic renal failure, osteoarthritis, bilateral knee replacements and had a malignant melanoma excised from her back 10 years ago. She takes insulin, inhalers, NSAIDs and paracetamol. She is not on any anticoagulation or antiplatelet agents. She has no known drug allergies. She lives alone in a bungalow and has home help twice a day. She is an ex-smoker with a 60 pack year history and consumes alcohol occasionally. There is no family history of note.

My diagnosis is brain tumour. I would like to examine her to elicit any focal neurological deficits.'

✎ WHAT YOU SHOULD KNOW

[48] In metastases, tissue diagnosis is key to the management, and therefore lesions which are radiographically suspicious are further investigated with breast and testicular examination, along with a chest/abdominal/pelvis CT. The aim of this is to find a more accessible lesion from which to obtain tissue.
[49] Cerebral metastases may be multiple and therefore MRI is the imaging modality of choice as it is more sensitive to smaller lesions.
In the absence of primary pathology being discovered, a biopsy or excision of a single superficial metastasis may be offered.
Patients with treated primary disease and a superficial single metastasis may be offered surgery plus adjuvant radiotherapy.

BRAIN TUMOURS –
CEREBRAL METASTASES

'On examination, Mrs T opens her eyes to speech, utters inappropriate words and is able to follow commands. Her Glasgow coma score is therefore 12/15 (E3 V3 M6). Cranial nerves are grossly intact. Fundoscopy reveals normal findings. Peripheral neurological examination reveals a mild global weakness.

I would like to arrange for a pre- and post-contrast CT scan of her head to investigate the possibility of a tumour. If this was to reveal a cerebral lesion, I would then like to perform a CT chest/abdomen/pelvis[48] to investigate for primary tumours, and a pre- and post-contrast MRI[49] of the head to investigate for multiple cerebral metastases.'

👁 WHAT YOU SHOULD SEE

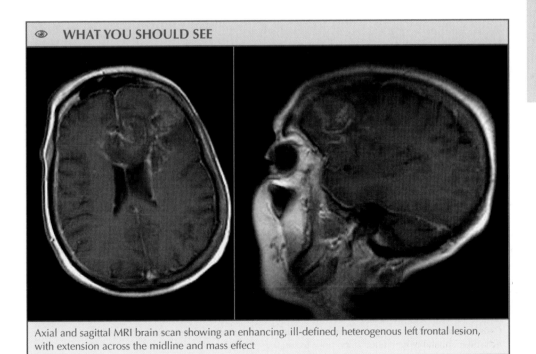

Axial and sagittal MRI brain scan showing an enhancing, ill-defined, heterogenous left frontal lesion, with extension across the midline and mass effect

537

BRAIN TUMOURS – PRIMARY BRAIN TUMOURS

'I would like to present Miss B, a 34-year-old right-hand-dominant shop owner. She was at the gym when she had a generalised tonic-clonic seizure lasting 1 minute that self-terminated. She complains of headaches, worse in the mornings for the past 6 weeks. She is normally fit, well and very active. She takes no medications and has no known drug allergies. She lives with her partner, smokes occasionally and consumes approximately 30 units of alcohol a week, mostly at the weekends. There is no family history of note.

My diagnosis is a primary brain tumour. I would like to examine her to elicit any focal neurological deficits.'

✎ WHAT YOU SHOULD KNOW

There are many different types of primary brain tumour. The type is determined by the location and the cell of origin.

Meningiomas are extra-axial tumours which arise from the arachnoid cells in the dura mater. They are predominantly benign. They can be further subclassified into typical or atypical. They are characterised by their dural attachment and cause symptoms due to their mass effect. The extent of resection, along with the fate of the dural attachment, determines recurrence.

Intraventricular or posterior fossa tumours may initially present in a similar way to acute hydrocephalus due to blockage of the CSF channels by the lesion.

An MDT approach to the management of tumours is essential, especially in cases such as pituitary lesions (endocrinology) and acoustic schwannomas (ENT).

Certain tumours (such as meningiomas) can be very vascular and angiography may be useful to determine suitability for embolisation prior to surgery.

BRAIN TUMOURS – PRIMARY BRAIN TUMOURS

'On examination, Miss B has her eyes open spontaneously, is fully orientated to time, place and person and is able to follow commands. Her Glasgow coma score is therefore 15/15. Cranial nerves are grossly intact. Fundoscopy reveals mild bilateral papilloedema. Peripheral neurological examination is normal.

I would like to arrange for a CT scan of her head pre- and post-contrast to investigate the possibility of a brain tumour.'

👁 WHAT YOU SHOULD SEE

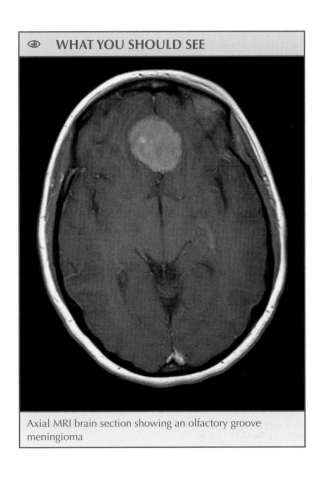

Axial MRI brain section showing an olfactory groove meningioma

HYDROCEPHALUS

'I would like to present Miss F, a 19-year-old right-hand-dominant woman. Her parents have noticed that she has become increasingly drowsy over the day, wanting to sleep and not willing to interact. She had meningitis as a baby and had a shunt inserted for resulting hydrocephalus. She has had three revisions in total, the last being 6 years ago. She has not had any seizures or lost consciousness. She has no other past medical history, takes no medications and has no known drug allergies. She lives with her parents. She is a non-smoker and does not drink alcohol. There is no family history of note.

My diagnosis is hydrocephalus secondary to shunt malfunction. I would like to examine her to elicit any focal neurological deficits.'

⟁ WHAT YOU SHOULD KNOW

Hydrocephalus can be communicating (failure of resorption or over-production of CSF) or non-communicating (intraventricular tumours, aqueduct stenosis or external compressive lesions).
Treatment includes removal of the obstructive lesion, external ventricular drainage (EVD), shunting (e.g. ventriculo-peritoneal, ventriculo-atrial) and endoscopic third ventriculostomy.
Normal-pressure hydrocephalus
This is a condition affecting the elderly that is characterised by ventriculomegaly on a background of brain atrophy. The classic triad of symptoms is gait ataxia, dementia and urinary incontinence.
Idiopathic intracranial hypertension (formerly benign intracranial hypertension)
This is a condition seen in young, overweight females. Symptoms include headaches and visual disturbance. Fundoscopy reveals papilloedema. An LP with high opening pressure on manometry and an improvement in symptoms with CSF drainage is usually diagnostic. Management is with a lumbo-peritoneal shunt, although it has variable success.
[50] Shunts may fail due to loss of continuity (e.g. tubing fracture), infection or blockage. Infected shunts should be removed and EVDs placed as a temporising measure for CSF diversion. Intrathecal antibiotics can also be administered via the EVD.

HYDROCEPHALUS

'On examination, Miss F has her eyes closed, appears drowsy and is only verbalising to pain. She localises to painful stimulus. Her Glasgow coma score is 8/15 (E1 V2 M5). Examination was difficult due to the patient's obtunded state. Fundoscopy revealed bilateral papilloedema. The remainder of the cranial nerves and peripheral neurological examination were grossly normal.

I would like to arrange for an anaesthetic review and investigate the possibility of a shunt malfunction[50] by arranging for a CT scan of her head, X-rays of her skull, chest and abdomen.'

◉ WHAT YOU SHOULD SEE

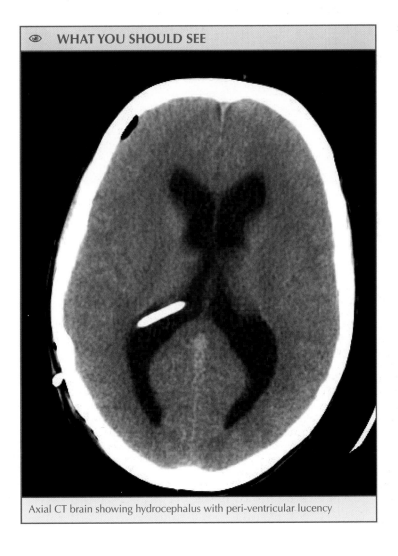

Axial CT brain showing hydrocephalus with peri-ventricular lucency

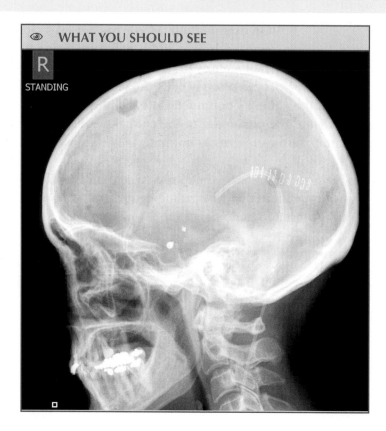

WHAT YOU SHOULD SEE

R

STANDING

WHAT YOU SHOULD SEE

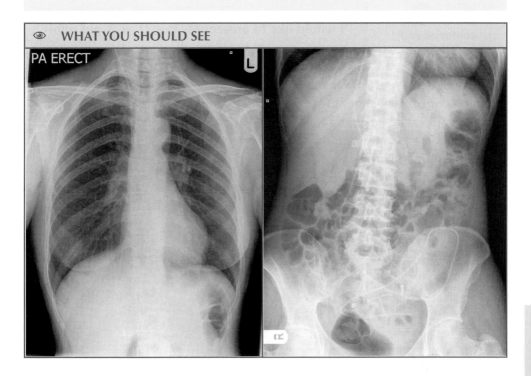

PA ERECT

L

CEREBRAL ABSCESS

'I would like to present Mr V, a 37-year-old right-hand-dominant company director. His wife reports that he has been complaining of right earache for the past 2 weeks. He went to see his GP who prescribed steroid ear drops. He has also been complaining of frontal headaches over the past 2 days, which are worse on bending and coughing. Today, he had a generalised tonic-clonic seizure, lasting 30 seconds, that was self-terminating. He has diet-controlled diabetes, takes no medications and has no known drug allergies. He lives with his wife. He is a non-smoker and consumes approximately 10 units of alcohol a week. There is no relevant family history.

My diagnosis is cerebral abscess. I would like to examine him to elicit any focal neurological deficits.'

🗒 WHAT YOU SHOULD KNOW

Abscesses can form in the extradural or subdural space, or within the brain parenchyma. Routes of infection include haematogenous spread (e.g. endocarditis) or local spread from sinus infections or skull fractures.

Identifying the responsible pathogen is essential in directing focused antibiotic therapy.

Symptoms may be those of raised intracranial pressure, sepsis and focal neurological deficits. Abscess rupture can present as an acute deterioration.

Peripheral blood cultures may be negative and serum inflammatory markers might only be marginally elevated.

Specialised MRI sequences may be used to differentiate between high-grade tumours (such as cerebral metastases) and abscesses.

Management consists of treating the source and administering a prolonged course of IV antibiotics. Burr-hole drainage or surgical excision may be required.

CEREBRAL ABSCESS

'On examination, Mr V has his eyes open, is orientated to place but not to time or person, and is able to follow commands. His Glasgow coma score is therefore 14/15 (E4 V4 M6). Cranial nerves are grossly intact. Fundoscopy reveals normal findings. Peripheral neurological examination is entirely normal. There is mild photophobia and neck stiffness. His temperature is 38.5°C. Otoscopy reveals a discharging right ear and a normal left ear.

I would like to arrange for a pre- and post-contrast CT scan of his head to investigate the possibility of a cerebral abscess.'

WHAT YOU SHOULD SEE

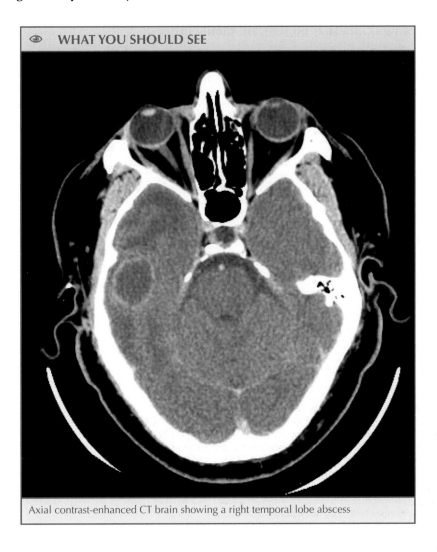

Axial contrast-enhanced CT brain showing a right temporal lobe abscess

Take a history from this patient who presents with low back pain and difficulty voiding

(see pg 316)

CAUDA EQUINA SYNDROME

'I would like to present Miss G, a 32-year-old right-hand-dominant florist. She has a 10-year history of low back pain. Over the past day, she has noticed increased pain in the sciatic distribution, radiating from her buttocks to her calves. There is also numbness of the lateral aspect of both her feet. She has been incontinent of urine twice and is unable to feel a full bladder. She also complains of numbness around her back passage. There is no disturbance of bowel function. She is otherwise normally fit and well. She takes paracetamol when required and has no known drug allergies. She lives alone, is a non-smoker and consumes approximately 25 units of alcohol a week. There is no relevant family history.

My diagnosis is cauda equina syndrome. I would like to examine her to elicit any focal neurological deficits.'

⌇ WHAT YOU SHOULD KNOW

Cauda equina syndrome (CES) is characterised by lower limb radicular symptoms in addition to sphincter disturbance, diminished perianal, perineal, rectal and bladder sensation. Saddle anaesthesia can be the initial presenting complaint.

CES is an acute neurosurgical condition. Surgical management of the compression is required within 24 hours of the onset of symptoms in order to salvage sphincter function.

[51] CES is a clinical diagnosis. History and examination (including PR) findings are key to determining the need for an urgent MRI of the lumbosacral spine.

Examine this patient's neurological system
(see pg 365)

CAUDA EQUINA SYNDROME

'On examination, Miss G is in obvious discomfort and has an antalgic gait. There is no midline thoracic or lumbar tenderness on palpation. Peripheral neurological examination reveals bilateral lower limb weakness 3⁺/5 globally. Sensation to pinprick and light touch is reduced in the lateral aspect of both feet. Ankle jerks are absent bilaterally. Knee jerks are present normally. Plantars are equivocal and there is no clonus. Straight leg raise is diminished bilaterally to 35° with a positive sciatic stretch. Tone and coordination is normal throughout. Digital rectal examination with a chaperone revealed normal anal tone and reduced perianal sensation.

I would like to arrange for an MRI scan[51] of her lumbosacral spine to investigate the possibility of an acute disc protrusion causing cauda equina syndrome.'

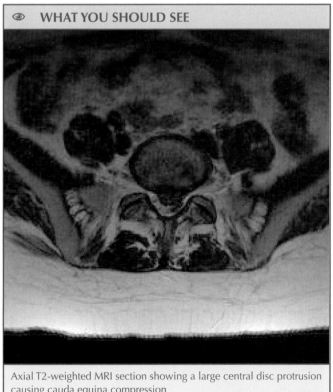

👁 WHAT YOU SHOULD SEE

Axial T2-weighted MRI section showing a large central disc protrusion causing cauda equina compression

👁 WHAT YOU SHOULD SEE

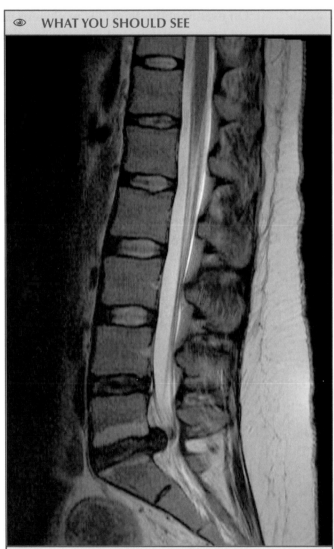

Sagittal T2-weighted MRI section showing a large L5/S1 disc protrusion causing cauda equina compression

SPINAL NERVE ROOT COMPRESSION

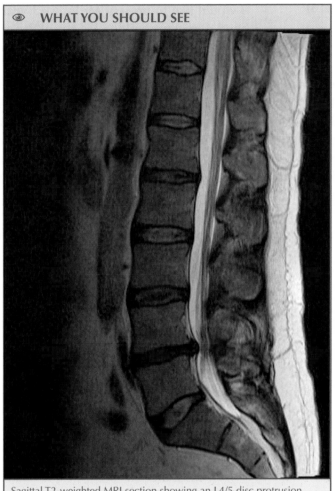

👁 **WHAT YOU SHOULD SEE**

Sagittal T2-weighted MRI section showing an L4/5 disc protrusion

Take a history
from this
patient who
presents with
pain radiating
down one leg

(see pg 518)

SPINAL NERVE ROOT COMPRESSION

'I would like to present Mr W, a 43-year-old right-hand-dominant builder. He has a 20-year history of low back pain, initially brought on by sudden heavy lifting. He has an 8-month history of pain radiating from his left buttock down to the lateral aspect of his calf. He also gets intermittent pins and needles in the sole of his left foot. His right leg is unaffected. He has some difficulty mobilising due to the pain. Bowel and bladder function is normal. He reports no erectile dysfunction. He has high cholesterol and hypertension. He takes aspirin, a statin and a beta-blocker. He lives with his wife. He is a non-smoker and consumes approximately 35 units of alcohol a week. There is no relevant family history.

My diagnosis is left L5 nerve root compression. I would like to examine him to elicit any focal neurological deficits.'

✏ WHAT YOU SHOULD KNOW

Different nerve roots are affected by central disc versus lateral disc protrusion
Damage to the tough outer layer of the disc (annulus fibrosis), usually due to degeneration, allows the soft central nucleus pulposus to herniate. Disc prolapse is usually either central or lateral.
A lateral disc prolapse is most likely to affect the exiting nerve root of the level above, while a central disc prolapse is most likely to affect the exiting nerve root of the level below.
Nerve root compression can lead to pain, numbness, muscle wasting, weakness and paraesthesiae.
In a degenerate spine, there may be multi-level disease and so a good knowledge and understanding of dermatomes and myotomes (see pg 367) is essential for correlating clinical and radiological findings.

Examine this patient's neurological system (see pg 365)

SPINAL NERVE ROOT COMPRESSION

'On examination, Mr W is uncomfortable lying down. There is no midline lumbar tenderness on palpation. He has a mild antalgic gait but is able to tiptoe and heel walk. Tone, power and coordination are normal in both lower limbs. Sensation is diminished to light touch and pinprick on the lateral aspect of his left calf and sole. Sensation is normal in the right leg. Straight leg raise in the right leg is 70° but diminished in the left leg to 35°, with a positive sciatic stretch sign. Reflexes are equal and normal bilaterally. There is no clonus, and plantars are downgoing bilaterally.

I would like to arrange for an MRI of his lumbosacral spine to investigate the possibility of spinal nerve root compression.'

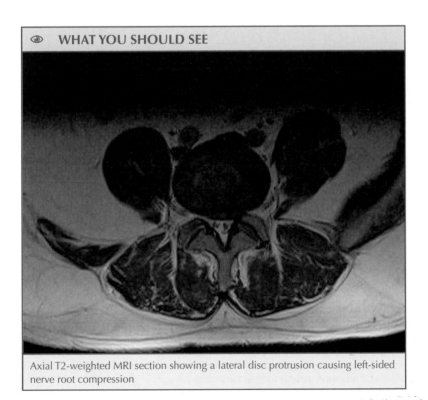

👁 WHAT YOU SHOULD SEE

Axial T2-weighted MRI section showing a lateral disc protrusion causing left-sided nerve root compression

TRIGEMINAL NEURALGIA

'I would like to present Mrs L, a 46-year-old, right-hand-dominant housewife. She has been experiencing sharp, shooting pains in the right side[52] of her face, predominantly in the forehead and cheek. She experiences up to 50 attacks a day, each lasting a few seconds. Triggers include brushing her teeth, brushing her hair and cold foods. The pain is not controlled with simple analgesia. She is hypertensive. She takes an ACE-inhibitor and aspirin. She has no known drug allergies. She lives with her husband and two children. She is a non-smoker and does not drink alcohol. There is no relevant family history.

My diagnosis is trigeminal neuralgia. I would like to examine her to confirm my diagnosis.'

✑ WHAT YOU SHOULD KNOW

Trigeminal neuralgia is characterised by severe attacks of stabbing pain in the distribution of one or more of the divisions served by the trigeminal nerve.

[52] The maxillary and mandibular divisions are more affected than the ophthalmic, and it seldom occurs bilaterally.

[53] Trigeminal neuralgia can be caused by compression of the root entry zone by a vascular loop of a nearby artery or by tumours in the cerebellopontine angle.

Demyelination secondary to multiple sclerosis is associated with trigeminal neuralgia.

A mix of strong analgesic agents may be required to control the pain and these can cause significant side-effects such as drowsiness. Surgical treatment options include percutaneous thermocoagulation, microvascular decompression and stereotactic radiosurgery.

TRIGEMINAL NEURALGIA

'On examination, Mrs L has her eyes open, is fully orientated to time, place and person, and is able to follow commands. Her Glasgow coma score is therefore 15/15. Cranial nerves I–IV and VI–XII are normal. Corneal reflexes are present bilaterally. Facial sensation is intact but the pain is reproducible in the ophthalmic and maxillary divisions of the trigeminal nerve.[52] Fundoscopy reveals normal findings. Peripheral neurological examination is entirely normal.

I would like to arrange for an MRI scan of her head to investigate the possibility of a compressive vascular loop[53] on the trigeminal nerve.'

◉ WHAT YOU SHOULD SEE

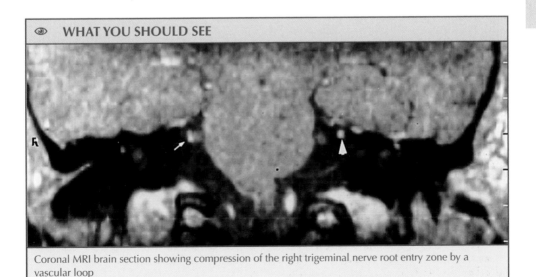

Coronal MRI brain section showing compression of the right trigeminal nerve root entry zone by a vascular loop

D SURVEY RESULTS

NEUROSCIENCES

Neuroscience is a recent addition to the new MRCS Part B OSCE. As such, there is limited data about cases that have appeared in the examination.

The table opposite gives information about the types of case that appeared in the old-format examination before the new changes were introduced.

Please note that there is also crossover with the Limbs (including spine) specialty area.

These results include cases seen in the new OSCE and the old style MRCS exam.

Type of case	Number seen in survey	Breakdown and details of cases
Upper limb neurology	9	4 Ulnar nerve palsy (1 with cervical rib, 1 with elbow trauma 2 radial nerve palsy (1 causing hyperaesthesia, 1 at the level of the brachial plexus) 2 posterior brachial plexus cord injury 1 examination of median nerve (also see carpal tunnel)
Carpal tunnel	7	3 cases with thenar muscle wasting. Questions included treatment and operative details.
Lower limb neurology	1	

SECTION 2:
COMMUNICATION
SKILLS

CHAPTER 7
COMMUNICATION
SKILLS

A Structure of the station 561

B Verbal communication skills with patients/relatives 563

C Verbal communication skills with your colleagues 571

D Written communication skills 577

E Special cases 579

CONTENTS

A STRUCTURE OF THE STATION

There is an emphasis on communication skills in the OSCE. These are primarily assessed in the communication skills stations. However, you should also expect to be assessed on your ability to communicate in other stations.

The domain which covers communication skills requires you to demonstrate: 'the ability to assimilate information, identify what is important and convey it to others clearly, using a variety of methods; the capacity to adjust behaviour and language (written/spoken) as appropriate to the needs of differing situations; the ability actively and clearly to engage the patient/carer/ colleague(s) in open dialogue'.

At the time of publication, all of the dedicated communication skills stations are manned by one or two examiners who will observe the candidate's behaviour during a role-play in a variety of clinical scenarios. These clinical scenarios will be based on the MRCS syllabus but candidates may need to indicate if/when the limits of their knowledge or authority are reached.

The marking scheme requires that for a 'pass' mark the candidate:

- Adapts language/behaviour as needed and adjusts style of questioning/ response as appropriate
- Confirms that there is common understanding
- Demonstrates clarity and focus in communication (written/spoken)
- Is able to express ideas clearly to others (written/spoken)
- Uses technical language appropriately and correctly
- Demonstrates active listening towards others
- Establishes relationship of respect with others

You should expect to be assessed on a variety of methods of communication in a range of different clinical scenarios and, to some extent, you will need to rely on your ability to be an adaptable and natural professional communicator.

This section acts as a guide that covers the areas of communicating with patients and carers, communicating with other healthcare professionals and written communication. We will then look at some specific cases.

B VERBAL COMMUNICATION SKILLS WITH PATIENTS/ CARERS

Quite often you will have an angry or upset patient/carer to deal with in these stations; this allows the examiners to observe your ability to communicate in difficult situations. To be honest, these are also scenarios in which you will not uncommonly find yourself during the course of your day-to-day work. You are no doubt already an excellent communicator and no book can teach you this anyway! We will therefore concentrate on giving some tips on dealing with the difficult scenarios and a general structure to follow in the OSCE.

POSSIBLE SCENARIOS

When revising for any communication skills station you first need to consider which common scenarios you might come across. Within the context of communication with patients/carers we have broadly divided these up into **information giving** scenarios and **discussing bad news/situations** scenarios:

Information giving
- Obtaining informed consent for a straightforward operation or procedure
- Explaining the relevance, process and/or the risks and benefits of investigations
- Explaining a diagnosis or differential diagnosis

Discussing bad news/situations
- Discussing resuscitation status
- Discussing a poor prognosis with a patient/carer
- Discussing unsatisfactory care
- Discussing an unfavourable outcome of surgery
- Discussing lack of facilities, e.g. no ICU/HDU beds, causing cancellation of an elective operation

FOUR-POINT OVERVIEW FOR ANY COMMUNICATION SKILLS SCENARIO WITH A PATIENT/CARER

1. Firstly, introductions.

2. Next:
   - During an **'information giving scenario'** assess the simulated patient's/carer's understanding first.
   - Or, in a **'discussing bad news/situation scenario'** ask for the patient's/carer's point of view of what has been going on first.
   - Give them plenty of time.

3. Next, say what you're going to say, say it and then, having checked for any questions, repeat what you have said.

4. Finally, confirm what the patient/carer can expect to happen next and make sure that the lines of communication remain open.

TOP TIPS WHEN COMMUNICATING WITH PATIENTS/CARERS

Information giving:

- Avoid jargon and explain any medical terms
- Explain any uncertainties in diagnosis/outcome/prognosis
- Check understanding before moving on
- Give time for them to ask questions
- Recognise the limits of your own competence and refer them to a senior colleague if necessary
- Ensure follow-up arrangements are made
- Give information for other points of contact (for example specialist nurses)

Discussing bad news/situations (including with the Angry or Upset):

- Use body language
  - o Maintain good (but non-threatening) eye contact and an open posture
- Be polite and friendly
  - o No matter what! e.g. to Mr Angry who starts off standing up shouting at you – **'Please take a seat, sir.'** Often the simulated patients will have instructions to calm down once such a suggestion is made by the candidate
- Ask for patient's/carer's **i**deas, **c**oncerns or **e**xpectations ('ICE')
- Use initially 'open' questions and then 'closed' questions to clarify the details
- Demonstrate empathy
  - o This is different from sympathy. For instance, do say **'I can understand why that would upset you'** rather than **'Oh dear poor you, I had a similar situation myself...'**
- Recognise anger/upset
  - o e.g. to Mrs Upset: **'Here, please take a tissue Mrs Upset'**
- Respond to complaints/concerns and demonstrate a willingness to learn from these
- Apologise if appropriate
- Give information on how to proceed with a complaint (for example PALS in the UK – see notes on dealing with a complaint, pg 579)

TEN-POINT GENERAL STRUCTURE OF A DISCUSSION WITH A PATIENT/ CARER

1. Starting the discussion

Greeting:
Say Good morning etc.
Shake hands.
Smile and look friendly, with open body language (even in the face of obvious hostility).

Introductions:
Say who you are.
Confirm who they are and their relationship to the patient if appropriate.
Say what you had to do with the case and what you are here for.

Make the patient/relative comfortable:
Invite them to sit.
Make sure you are at the same level – if they are sitting do not stand over them!
If you are sitting at a desk, sit yourself and the patient/carer on two chairs at a corner so the desk does not come between you.

2. Give the patient/carer time to tell their side first

If 'information giving scenario':
- What is their impression of what has happened so far?
- What do they understand?
- Do they have any concerns?
- What information do they want from you and what do they want you to do?

If 'discussing bad news/situations scenario':
- What is their impression of what has happened so far?
- What do they understand?
- Do they have any concerns?
- What information do they want from you and what do they want you to do?

* Why are they angry/upset?

In this section you must **listen** to the patient/carer without interrupting them. Let them talk until they run out of steam, gently asking questions to fill in gaps to coax their worries out.

You can tell when the patient/carer has said all they want to say when:
* They stop or say 'That's everything.'
* In the case of 'ranters', they start to repeat themselves.

During this part of the scenario you can demonstrate your skills in:
a) Use of **open questions** at the beginning of the section, e.g. **'Tell me what happened'** and **closed questions** to clarify points, e.g. **'How long had that been going on for?'**
b) **Facilitation** by nodding your head and **repeating** statements made by your patient/carer, e.g. **'So you went to the ward to find her – what happened then?'**
c) **Empathising with the patient/carer**

It is important to put yourself in the position of the patient/carer. Nod, listen with interest, and look sad and shocked at appropriate intervals. Say things like: **'That must have been awful for you and your family.'** If you give the impression that you are listening to what they have to say with respect and interest you will calm the actor down, even in the face of hostility.

Beware not to go too far and never directly criticise the actions of a colleague. It seems like an easy way to get on the patient's/carer's side, but it is unprofessional and its consequences can be disastrous, both in the OSCE and in real life! Phases such as: **'I can't really comment on the actions of that doctor, but I can see how frustrated you must have been'** can be helpful.

3. Summarise the patient's/carer's input and confirm you are dealing with the correct issues

It is important to listen to your patient's/carer's report and to organise the key factors in your own mind. This enables you to **summarise** and **present** them back to confirm you have all the information.

For example, in a complaint case, it is important to try to identify the key issues while listening to the patient/carer venting their anger/complaint/frustrations. There are usually only **two or three key issues** that have upset someone, and by presenting these back to your patient/carer the examiner will be given the impression that you have been listening carefully, have taken note of worries and have treated them seriously. It also enables you to deal with each point systematically. At the end of the list, check with your patient/carer that you haven't missed out any points.

4. Outline your plan for the consultation

You now need to tell the patient/carer the information they need to know. Tell them this so that they know it is now your turn to speak and are prepared for what they are going to hear. Phrases such as: **'I understand what you are saying. Let me take your points one by one and we'll go through what has happened.'** or **'I'm going to give you your results and then we can discuss them.'** are useful.

5. Present the information in a structured way

The information should be given in a methodical manner, whether taking consent, giving out test results or dealing with a complaint. It may help to number points and deal with them methodically. Use clear statements, avoiding jargon.

This section usually takes the longest, and you may have to be creative and repeat your points to get the actor to accept/understand them. Be gentle, not confrontational. When you have got through all the points, go on to the next section.

6. Express your sorrow/apologise

It is essential that you say how sorry you are for the pain suffered by the reason for the complaint, or the bad news you have broken. Saying sorry is not equal to accepting responsibility for negligence, and may be all the simulated patient/carer wants to hear.

7. Summarise the key facts

Once you have finished the discussion, summarise what you have said and check that your patient/carer:
• Is satisfied with the explanations in the complaint situation
• Understands the implications of the bad news, and
• Understands the procedure and its complications – if consenting

Repetition may be required when explaining a complicated subject.

8. Ensure any new worries/enquiries are dealt with systematically

Although this is usually towards the end of the consultation, it may be the moment at which the majority of fears and worries are shown. Asking questions such as **'Is that all clear? Is there anything that worries you in particular that you would like to discuss?'** should help the patient/carer to express any concerns. Don't forget to elicit their view: **'Has this conversation helped you?'**

This section gives you the chance to demonstrate skills in:
a) Listening empathetically (see above).
b) Showing that you can list all concerns in a summarised form, so that they can be dealt with one at a time.
c) Dealing with something which appears irresolvable, or if you don't have the information you need. You should consider referral to the appropriate service. **'I can arrange for you to discuss that further with the stoma care nurse/bereavement counsellor/the consultant performing the operation if you wish.'**

9. Summarise key facts again and outline action plan

10. Ending the discussion

Offer a future contact:
- This may be yourself or an appropriate colleague such as a breast care nurse or a colorectal nurse specialist.
- Ensure the patient is clear as to how they can contact that person **'Remember, if there are any problems just ring the hospital and ask for Mr Black's secretary. She will be able to contact one of our team.'**

Polite departure, stating next point of contact:
- Shake hands.
- Say when you will see them next/when the next planned procedure will be.

SUMMARY: GENERAL STRUCTURE OF A DISCUSSION WITH A PATIENT/CARER

1. Start the discussion
2. Give the patient/carer time to tell their side first
3. Summarise the patient's/carer's input and confirm you are dealing with the correct issues
4. Outline your plan for the consultation
5. Present the information in a structured way
6. Express your sorrow/apologise
7. Summarise the key facts
8. Deal systematically with any new concerns
9. Re-summarise key facts and outline immediate action
10. End the discussion

C VERBAL COMMUNICATION WITH YOUR COLLEAGUES

This is a very different skill from that of communicating with a patient or carer. For instance, it is obviously acceptable to use more technical language in this interview. The intention will usually be to succinctly present the relevant details of a patient or situation and request the advice or assistance of a colleague. You must take into account who your audience is and tailor your presentation appropriately.

We have all been on the other end of a poor referral from another healthcare professional at some time. Now is the time to reflect on this – what left you feeling so dissatisfied? Often it is due to poor structure, a lack of knowledge of the patient or a lack of clarity of the aim of the referral. Therefore, it is important to think about what facts you would need to know, and in what order, so that you could make a decision if you were the person on the other end of the conversation.

It is essential to remain scrupulously polite and friendly as even the grumpiest actor will find it difficult to continue shouting in the face of unrelenting pleasantness. It is all too easy to get into an argument if you find you are not getting the response you hoped for. This is a mistake as examiners will be looking for a mature attitude and eventually you will have to come to some kind of resolution at the end of the station, even if it is to discuss the problem with a more senior colleague.

POSSIBLE SCENARIOS

It is important to consider what common scenarios might be expected in the exam so you can practise these with a friend/colleague beforehand. For the OSCE it is likely that in those scenarios which involve communicating with your colleagues you will be in the position of presenting a problem and seeking advice or assistance.

For instance:

- Presenting case information to the consultant on call on the acute ward round
- Discussing a management plan with the on-call consultant on the telephone
- Telephone referral to another specialty, e.g. anaesthetics/radiology
- Handing over a patient to a colleague at shift change

FOUR-POINT OVERVIEW OF A DISCUSSION WITH ANOTHER HEALTHCARE PROFESSIONAL

This should follow that age-old general structure of: **'say what you're going to say, say it and then say what you've said'**.

1. Introductions.
2. Usually you will give information first. Be succinct.
3. Next, listen 'actively' to your colleague's advice (whether helpful or not), before beginning negotiations, if necessary!
4. Confirm what you have agreed at the end of the conversation to make sure you are both certain of the plan. Keep the lines of communication open.

TOP TIPS WHEN COMMUNICATING WITH OTHER HEALTHCARE PROFESSIONALS
• Be polite and friendly
• Body language – eye contact and open posture
• Be precise about what you want from the conversation
• Present your facts in a logical manner
• Give only relevant information
• Listen to your colleague's response actively
• Refer to a senior colleague if you are not reaching a conclusion

SEVEN-POINT GENERAL STRUCTURE OF A DISCUSSION WITH ANOTHER HEALTHCARE PROFESSIONAL

1.   Starting the discussion

Greeting:

Say Good morning etc.

Introductions:

Say who you are: **'I'm Dr ....'**

State your level and specialty: **'The general surgery CT2 on-call'**.

State where you are calling from (if appropriate): **'I'm calling from resus.'**

Confirm who you are speaking to (name/grade/specialty) **'Can I confirm who you are?'**

2.   Getting their attention

After the introductions you need to explain briefly why you have contacted them and what you want from them. They can then consider this while you give them a more detailed history. For instance, when discussing a case with the on-call anaesthetist, **'I'm calling about a young boy with an open fracture who will need to be operated on tonight.'**

3.   Presenting the case/situation

This is the time to demonstrate you can give relevant information in a logical sequence so that it is easy for the other person to follow. For example, when presenting a patient's case start with the demographics: **'ED is a 45-year-old man on the elective surgical ward. I think he needs to move to HDU and may require non-invasive ventilation.'**

Next, give the salient details about the current problem: **'He is 4 days post anterior resection and has become increasingly short of breath today with a cough productive of green sputum. He denies chest pain.'**

In the case of a critically unwell patient present your clinical findings in an 'ABCD' structure: **'He is maintaining his own airway but is tachypnoeic with a respiratory rate of 30. His saturations are 88% on 60% high-flow. On auscultation of his chest he has crepitations at the right base and diffuse wheeze. His pulse is 100 and BP 110/60 with a good urine output of 50 ml per hour. His abdomen is soft and non-tender. His temperature is 38.5.'**

Give any pertinent background history: **'He has COPD and is on inhalers at home.'**

Cover any important positive and negative investigations you have: **'His arterial blood gas on 60% shows a pH of 7.32, pO$_2$ of 8.0, pCO$_2$ of 6.7, bicarbonate of 31 and base excess of –3. His chest X-ray shows some right basal consolidation, his ECG is normal.'**

Then briefly summarise any management you have initiated and response to it: **'He has had salbutamol and Atrovent nebulisers and I have started him on intravenous antibiotics for a hospital-acquired pneumonia. These do not seem to have made a difference yet.'**

Finally, reiterate what advice or assistance you want from them: **'I think he is tiring and might need admission to HDU for non-invasive ventilation, which they won't do on the ward. I am concerned and would like you to come and see him shortly please.'**

4. Listening to their response 'actively'

You have contacted your colleague for their advice, so no matter whether you disagree with their response it is important that you allow them to reply. Give them a chance to do this without interrupting. You will need to be listening carefully anyway in order to respond to their points.

This also gives you the opportunity to demonstrate:
a) Your active listening skills, such as nodding and giving what are described as 'minimal encouragers' such as **'ah'**, **'yes'** or **'I see'**.
b) Your use of eye contact and open body language.

You will know when they are finished as they will:
a) Stop talking, or
b) Ask you a clarifying question.

5. Summarising what you think they have said and acknowledging any issues

If they have agreed with you and are going to do what you have asked then thank your lucky stars (and them) and confirm point by point what they have agreed to do and when and how you can contact them if you require further assistance.

If they disagree with your plan summarise what you think they have been saying in order, point by point, to be sure that you are not at cross purposes. Then politely acknowledge their concerns and go through them in turn to see if there is any way you can clarify things and reach an agreement. Ultimately, if you cannot see a way to resolve things then it is appropriate to refer the issue to your senior (this can be a useful way to get out of a difficult situation that seems to be going round in circles but try not to use this too obviously as a threat; for instance **'If you won't do what I want then I will get my consultant to call your consultant,'** which sounds like the kind of thing that should only be heard in the playground). Instead, acknowledge the level of your competency, for example: **'I agree this is a difficult situation and we seem to be deadlocked. I think it would be best if I were to ask my consultant for their advice and get back to you.'**

It is always sensible from a medicolegal point of view to record the outcome of the conversation in the notes and this may also encourage a more generous response. For instance: **'I will just record our conversation in the notes. Please could I take your name again?'**

6. Summarising the outcome, agreeing a plan and keeping the lines of communication open!

Summarise the plan for how you will proceed and within what timescale. For instance: **'So I will have a chat with my consultant and get back to you in about 5 minutes. What number can I get you on?'**

7. Ending the discussion

End things politely. Thank them for their help (or if they have been very unhelpful then you could thank them for their time!).

SUMMARY
1. Start the discussion
2. Get their attention
3. Present the case/situation
4. Listen to their response 'actively'
5. Summarise what you think they have said and acknowledge any issues
6. Summarise the outcome, agree a plan and keep the lines of communication open!
7. End the discussion

D WRITTEN COMMUNICATION SKILLS

There are some key skills in good written communication, whether you are writing a letter or filling in a request form.

- Clear and legible writing. Traditionally doctors are notoriously bad at this! Writing in capitals may make your writing more legible but bear in mind that it takes much longer. Your pen should be black.
- Avoid using abbreviations; what they mean to you may not be the same as what they mean to the person who reads it.
- Provide all necessary 'demographic' data. For instance, with a letter, clearly address it to the intended recipient. Make sure you date your correspondence. Provide details of the patient, including name, address, date of birth and hospital or NHS number. At the end provide details of who you are, your position, the name of the consultant responsible for the patient's care and how and where you can be contacted for clarification.
- The substance of your letter or request should provide all relevant clinical information in an accurate and organised manner. For instance, in a discharge summary make it clear what was done, when and why, and record any complications and their outcomes, accurately list any medication changes and give advice about follow-up arrangements or suture removal if appropriate. In the instance of a request card make it clear what you are looking for with the investigation and any factors about the patient that may affect the test; for instance, record a creatinine level on a contrast CT, or an INR result on a liver biopsy request card.

POSSIBLE SCENARIOS

- Clinical letter to a colleague in primary care, following an outpatient appointment or discharge from hospital
- Patient transfer letters
- Referral letters
- Investigation request forms
- Operation notes for straightforward cases

577

EXAMPLE OSCES TO PRACTISE

- Writing to a GP regarding management of anticoagulation in a patient on warfarin for a heart valve replacement prior to an elective hernia repair
- Counselling a relative of a patient with liver metastases and issues around resuscitation orders
- Telephone conversation with an anaesthetic registrar, discussing a patient with renal failure and perforation who requires escalation of treatment

E SPECIAL CASES

DEALING WITH A COMPLAINT

1. Starting the discussion

Greeting:
'Good morning,' shake hands and smile.

Introductions and explain your role and why you are there:
Say who you are. **'I'm Dr Parchment Smith. I am one of the CT2 surgical doctors on Mr Black's team who helped look after your mother. I understand you have some concerns about her care and I'm here to find out what they are and to see if I can help.'**

Confirm who they are and their relationship to the patient if appropriate:
'Are you Mr Angry, son of Mrs Poorly?'

Make the patient/carer comfortable:
'Take a seat, sir.'

2. Give the patient/carer time to tell their side first

'Mr Angry, I understand you have some concerns about your mother's treatment. Would you tell me about these, please?'

Empathise with the patient/carer: **'I see what you mean. That must have been awful for you and your family.'**

3. **Summarise your patient's/carer's issues and confirm you are dealing with the same problems**

'As I understand it, Mr Angry, the problems are threefold. Firstly, your mother had to wait in A&E for over twelve hours, which must have been very distressing. Secondly, when you arrived on the ward you didn't get to see the consultant, which was the main reason your family had been waiting in the hospital and, lastly, you were not informed when your mother was taken to the operating theatre. Since she unfortunately died on the intensive care unit afterwards, you and your family didn't have the chance to say a proper goodbye.

Are those the main issues, or was there any other aspect of her care that you are unhappy with?'

4. **Outline your plan for the consultation**

'I understand what you're saying Mr Angry, but if you'll allow me I'd like to take these points one by one so that I can try to explain how I think these problems occurred.'

5. **Structured information giving**

'Taking the first point, I agree that twelve hours is a ridiculous amount of time for a seriously ill woman to spend in A&E *(empathy)*. I hope you understand that the bed crisis is a serious problem for the National Health Service and our team faces this problem each day *(reason for problem beyond our control)*. Our FY2 tried her best to find her a bed by discussing the problem with our bed manager and she even considered transferring your mother to the General Infirmary fifteen miles away. However, both your sister and our consultant did not believe this journey to be in her best interests *(measures taken at the time by the team to try to solve the problem)*. I'm sure you'll agree that the staff did everything in their power to make your mother as comfortable as possible in such bad circumstances. The A&E sister freed up a side room for her, and the FY2 was able to start all the necessary treatment, including a drip and analgesia *(emphasise the positive care given)*. I must say that your situation was intolerable and I'm deeply sorry for the distress it caused you and your family *(apologise unreservedly)*. I hope you feel that the staff tried everything they could to get your mother a suitable bed as soon as possible. *(Try to get resolution and agreement from the patient before moving onto the second point.)*

Secondly, the fact that your mother didn't see the consultant until two in the morning.........'

Continue until all the complaints have been addressed.

6. Express your sorrow/apologise

'I would like to say how sorry I am that you had such an awful experience. I'm sure I speak for all of the staff when I apologise for the distressing situation you and your family suffered.'

7. Summarise the key facts

'So in summary, Mr Angry, I think we agree that you and your family had a terrible experience that was made worse by some unfortunate problems here at the hospital. I apologise for this.

Firstly, the bed situation, I hope you understand, was out of our control. However, we did everything we could under the circumstances.

Secondly, Mr Black was mortified that you didn't realise he had seen your mother in A&E, and I am sorry that you were under the impression that he would be waiting for you on the ward.

Thirdly, it was a shame that your mobile phone had no signal. We did try to contact you to inform you of your mother's sudden deterioration, but our main priority was to get her to the operating theatre as quickly as possible. I can only apologise that we weren't able to tell you about it before the event.'

8. Deal systematically with any new concerns

'I can understand that you wanted to speak to Mr Black himself today but unfortunately he has had to go to theatre with an emergency case *(problem beyond our control)*. I hope that I have been a help in discussing the difficulties there were with your mother's care today. If you would like to see Mr Black I can help you arrange another time with his secretary *(taking positive steps to amend the problem)*.'

9. Summarise key facts again and outline immediate action

'Is there anything else that worries you in particular that you would like to discuss? So, Mr Angry, I'll leave it with you to contact Mr Black's secretary if you or your sister would like to take up the offer of a chat with him.'

Check there are no outstanding issues:
'Is that alright? Is there anything we haven't covered that you would like to discuss with me?'

10. Ending the discussion

Offer your services as a future contact:
'Is there anything else I can arrange for you? Remember if there are any problems, just ring the hospital and ask for Mr Black's secretary and she can ensure that one of us contacts you. I'm Dr Parchment Smith, Mr Black's CT2.'

Departure:
Shake hands. **'Goodbye Mr Angry, don't hesitate to contact us.'**

COMPLAINTS

Definition: An expression of dissatisfaction requiring a response.
Most complaints start as concerns. It is important to try and resolve them on the spot. By careful handling this may prove possible. If not, the complaint could become more 'formal'.

From April 2009 the Department of Health has advised a single approach to complaints for all its organisations, including the NHS.

PALS (Patient Advice and Liaison Services) handle a large amount of the complaints made to the NHS. There is also a designated complaints manager in your trust. They must record all written or e-mailed complaints and all verbal complaints which are not resolved to the complainant's satisfaction by the next working day. All complaints must be acknowledged and an offer made to discuss them within 3 working days.

All complaints must be made within 12 months of the incident or within 12 months of the complainant becoming aware of the matter about which they are complaining.

The Parliamentary and Health Service Ombudsman, who is responsible for dealing with NHS complaints which cannot be resolved locally, has devised the 'Six Principles of Good Complaint Handling':
1. Getting it right
2. Being customer focused
3. Being open and accountable
4. Acting fairly and proportionately
5. Putting things right
6. Seeking continuous improvement
Ref: (www.ombudsman.org.uk/pdfs/Principles_of_Good_Complaint_Handling.pdf)

OBTAINING INFORMED CONSENT

1. **Starting the discussion**

Greeting and explain how you are involved in the case and why you are there:
'Good morning.' Shake hands and smile/look friendly. **'I'm Dr Parchment Smith, one of the CT2 surgical doctors on Mr Black's team.'**

Introductions:
'Can I please check, are you Mr Pre-op?'

Make your patient/carer comfortable:
'Take a seat, sir.'

2. Give the patient/carer time to tell their side first

'Mr Pre-op, what information have you been given about your operation, and do you know why you're having it?'

Empathise with patient/carer:
Listen encouragingly, nodding and saying, **'That's right.'**

3. **Summarise your patient/carers input and confirm you are dealing with the correct issues**

'Yes, Mr Pre-op, we have found a blockage in the bowel that we need to operate on. The biopsy results show that it is a cancer causing this blockage. The CT scan shows that there is no evidence of spread.'

4. **Outline your plan for the consultation**

'Mr Pre-op, I would like to explain the operation we are planning to do, including when and how we are hoping to do it. I would also like to tell you about the recovery time and discuss the possible complications. Please feel free to stop me at any time if there is something you don't understand. This is also the time to ask me about anything that may be worrying or confusing you. When everything is clear, I will ask for signed consent.'

5. **Give the patient/carer information in a structured way**

You should now go through the consent procedure as outlined in the next section, getting the patient to sign the consent form only when it is clear that they understand everything.

The main areas that should be covered are listed in detail below:

- Indication for treatment
- Diagnosis, prognosis, what would happen if we didn't operate, what the aim of surgery is, and any available alternatives
- Details of the surgery
- Pre-operative preparation, the planned procedure, pain relief (e.g. patient-controlled analgesia, epidurals) and post-operative care (e.g. HDU)
- Complications – common ones, even if trivial; serious ones, even if rare
- Expected outcome and follow-up
- Chances of success, permanent changes such as stomas, plans for adjuvant therapy and post-operative scans or endoscopy
- The team involved – mention the consultant in overall care and explain that juniors will be helping in the operation/overall care. Emphasise the multidisciplinary team
- Unforeseen procedures – the patient should be warned that unexpected procedures would be carried out if anything happens which isn't expected. These would only be carried out if they could not be safely delayed and were in the patient's best interests
- Objections to the treatments to be noted, e.g. Jehovah's Witness wishing to decline blood transfusions
- Patient's rights – patient can withdraw consent and seek a second opinion

Once you are sure the patient has understood and does not need more information or more time to think about it, ask them to sign the consent form.

6. Express your sorrow/apologise

'I know this must be an anxious time for you, Mr Pre-op. I'm sorry to overwhelm you with all this information, but it's important that you understand what we are going to do. Don't worry, you are in good hands and we will be doing our very best for you.'

7. Check your patient/carer has understood the key facts

'So, Mr Pre-op, you understand that you will be starting a course of radiotherapy at Cookridge Hospital next Wednesday. When it is completed we will book you in for surgery. You will come into hospital on the Thursday for your operation on the Friday.'

'The operation involves removing the bit of bowel with the cancer in it, which includes the lowest part of your bowel. This means that we will have to seal up your back passage and leave you with a permanent bag on your tummy where your bowel motions will collect. The stoma nurse will be having a chat with you about the details of this on Monday.

After your operation you will go to the high dependency unit for a couple of days, but if all goes well we would hope to have you home within a fortnight.

After your surgery, when we have analysed the cancer, we will decide if you need chemotherapy, but if it is at an early stage we won't need to. You will be kept under regular follow-up.'

8. Ask for any other new worries and deal with them systematically
'Is that all clear? Is there anything that worries you in particular that you would like to discuss?'

9. Summarise key facts again and outline immediate action
'So, Mr Pre-op, you will see Dr Radio at Cookridge Hospital next Wednesday and we'll see you after your radiotherapy.'

Check the actor is happy with this and does not have any outstanding issues.

'Is that alright? Is there anything we haven't covered that you would like to discuss with me?'

11. Ending the discussion
Offer your services as a future contact:
'Is there anything else I can arrange for you? Remember, if there are any problems just contact the colorectal nurse specialist, who can usually help and, if not, she can make sure that one of us contacts you.'

Departure stating next point of contact:
'Goodbye, Mr Pre-op. I'll see you in a few weeks' time.'

OBTAINING CONSENT

The GMC gives useful guidelines in GMC's 2008 'Consent: Patients and doctors making decisions together'.

These guidelines are summarised below; the original booklet is available from the General Medical Council, or online at http://gmc-uk.org/static/documents/content/Consent_2008.pdf.

What kind of procedures do you need to seek consent for?
- You should get written consent if a treatment involves significant risks.

Who can obtain consent?
- To obtain consent you must have sufficient knowledge of the proposed investigation or treatment and know the risks involved.

Who can give consent?
- No one else can make a decision on behalf of a patient who has capacity.
- If a patient lacks capacity the doctor must work with those close to patient and other members of the team.
- At age 16 a young person can be treated as an adult and can be presumed to have capacity to decide.
- Patients under 16 may have the capacity to consent – 'Gillick competence' – i.e. they are competent to understand what is involved.
- Where a competent child refuses treatment, a person with parental responsibility or the court may authorise investigation or treatment that is in the child's best interests.
- Where a child is under 16 and is not competent, a person with parental responsibility may authorise treatments which are in the child's best interest.
- Those with parental responsibility may refuse intervention on behalf of an incompetent child under 16, but you are not bound by that refusal and may seek a ruling from the court.
- In an emergency, you may treat an incompetent child against the wishes of those with parental responsibility where you consider it is in the child's best interests, provided it is limited to that treatment which is reasonably required in that emergency (e.g. you can give a life-saving blood transfusion to the incompetent child of Jehovah's Witness parents who refuse to consent, but not to a competent Jehovah's Witness who refuses consent, whatever their age).
- Pregnant women and consent: the right to decide applies equally to pregnant women as it does to other patients, and includes the right to refuse treatment where the treatment is intended to benefit the unborn child.

Additional support you might need
- Check whether the patient requires any additional support to understand you, such as an interpreter.
- Check whether the patient would like a written/audio record of the discussion.
- Involve a patient's relative/advocate in the discussion if the patient wants this.

OBTAINING CONSENT

<u>When to seek consent</u>

- Give information at a time and place when the patient will be best able to understand it.
- Give the patient time to reflect before they make a decision.
- A signed consent is not sufficient evidence that a patient has given or still gives informed consent to the proposed treatment in all its aspects, and their decision must be reviewed close to the time of treatment.

<u>What you must cover</u>

- Explain the risks and benefits and side-effects of all options, including the option to have no treatment.
- You must tell patients if a treatment could result in a serious adverse outcome, even if the likelihood is very small, or of less serious side-effects if they occur frequently.
- You should tell the patient what to do if they experience a complication.
- You should recognise that individual patients may want more or less information in making their decisions.
- You must ensure your patient has understood.

<u>Consent in the emergency situation</u>

- In an emergency when you can't get written consent it is acceptable to get verbal consent but this must be recorded in the notes.
- If verbal consent is not possible you can treat the patient without consent providing it is immediately necessary to save their life.

BREAKING BAD NEWS

1. Starting the discussion

Greeting:
'Good morning.' Shake hands, smile.

Introduction and explain your involvement in the case and why you are there:
Say who you are: **'I'm Dr Parchment Smith. Are you Mrs Anxious? I am one of the CT2 surgical doctors on Mr Black's team and am here to discuss the results of your tests.'**

Make the patient/carer comfortable:
'Take a seat madam *(or 'sir', depending on case).* **Have you anyone here with you today? Would you like them to come in as well?'**

2. Give the patient/carer time to tell their side first

'Mrs Anxious, I'd like to start by asking you what you have been told so far about what has happened and why you are here today.'

Empathise with your patient/carer:
'Yes that's right, it is quite complicated.'

3. Summarise the patient's/carer's input and confirm you are dealing with the correct issues

'Yes, Mrs Anxious, we have got the results of the cells we took from your breast. As you know, we also did a mammogram, and I have the results here also.'

4. Outline your plan for the consultation

'Mrs Anxious, I am going to give you the results of the biopsies and scans and have a chat with you about where we need to go from now. Would you like me to give you the full details of the diagnosis, or is there someone else you would like to bring in with you first?' *(You might want to bring in one of the breast care nurses who can act as the patient's advocate too.)*

5. Give the information in a structured way

'I'm afraid that the results show the lump is a cancer.' *(Give the diagnosis and don't use misleading terms such as growth/shadow.)*

Allow a pause for a reaction. If there is none, ask her how she feels: **'Are you OK? It's a shock, I know. How do you feel?'**

Check how much information the patient wants to know.

'Would you like me to tell you the details, or would you like to know what happens now?'
Depending on the response, give a detailed outline or summarised outline of the facts. Avoid jargon and use aids such as repetition or diagrams. (See 'Educating' in the next section, *Notes on Breaking Bad News*.)

'The mammograms and the cells we looked at both show that this is cancer of the breast. It is quite a small lump, so the best course of action is to remove the lump and some of the glands in the armpit in an operation. This can be arranged for you urgently next week. You will be in hospital for up to a couple of days, and then will be reviewed in clinic where we will let you know whether the operation has been successful in removing the cancer. We may then refer you to the oncologist, who will decide whether you require any medical treatment after the surgery.'

Check that they have understood:
'It's a lot of information – am I making sense to you?'

Ask if you have covered all they want to know:
'Is there anything else you would like to know at this stage?'

6. Express your sorrow/apologise

'I can see you're upset. I'm sorry to have to give you this news.'

7. Check your patient has understood the key facts

This may mean repeating yourself.

'So, Mrs Anxious, you understand that the mammogram and the cells show that the lump is cancer of the breast. We plan to admit you to hospital on Thursday for an operation to remove the cancer, and some of the glands from under your arm. Tomorrow, you will meet with our breast care nurse to have a chance to discuss any further questions. You may be in hospital for up to one to two days after your operation, and then you will be seen back in clinic to discuss whether you need any further treatment.'

8. Ask for any other or new worries and deal with them systematically

'Is that all clear? Is there anything in particular you would like to discuss?'

9. Summarise key facts again and outline immediate action

'So Mrs Anxious, you have an appointment with the breast care nurse tomorrow, and we'll see you on Thursday morning on ward A2.'

Check the patient does not have any outstanding issues:
'Is that alright? Is there anything we haven't covered that you'd like to discuss with me?'

10. Ending the discussion

Offer your services as a future contact:
'If there are any problems and you need to contact us please ring the breast care nurse. She can usually help and can contact us if needed. My name is Dr Parchment Smith, if you want to speak to me.'

Departure, stating next point of contact:
Shake hands.

'Goodbye Mrs Anxious. I'll see you on Thursday.'

BREAKING BAD NEWS

1. Getting started

How?

In person, not by phone or letter.

Where?

In a private room/curtains drawn around bed/both sitting down.

Who?

Relatives, friend or nurse present, as the patient wishes.

What?

Normal courtesies (Say hello, use patient's name, introduce yourself).

Start with a general question to get the conversation going two ways, assess the patient's mental state and make the patient feel you care (**'How are you today. Are you up to having a chat for a few minutes?'**).

2. Finding out how much the patient knows

How much have they been told?

'What have the doctors told you so far about the illness?'

How much have they understood?

'Have you been thinking that the illness might be serious?'

What is their level of understanding?

This will guide you to the level that you have to pitch your information.

Are they talking in simple terms:

'Well, Doctor says I've a growth of some kind and thank goodness, I thought, it's not a tumour or even worse, a cancer.'

Or are they very well educated with a good medical knowledge and wide vocabulary:

'My family doctor thought it might be multiple sclerosis, and now Prof Brown tells me the visual-evoked potentials show optic neuritis.'

What are their feelings?

Distressed, anxious, brave but trembly, offhand and defensive, hostile, in denial?

3. Finding out how much the patient wants to know

'Would you like me to give you the full details of the diagnosis?'

'Are you the type of person who wants to know all the details of what's wrong, or would you prefer if I just tell you what's going to happen next?'

'If your condition is serious, how much would you like to know about it?'

'That's fine. If you change your mind or want any questions answered at future visits, just ask me at any time. I won't push information at you if you don't want it.'

CONTINUED overleaf

4. <u>Sharing information</u>

Decide on your agenda:

- Diagnosis
- Treatment plan
- Prognosis
- Support

Start from the patient's starting point (aligning)

Repeat to the patient what they have said to you and reinforce those things they have said which are correct (gives patient confidence that you are taking their point of view seriously and respect them).

Give the information you need to tell clearly (educating)

Give the information in small chunks with warning shots.

'Well, the situation does appear to be more serious than that.'

Do not use jargon.

Say tumour AND THEN cancer, not space-occupying lesion or malignancy.

Check reception and clarify.

'Am I making sense? Do you follow what I'm saying?'

Make sure you both mean the same thing.

'Do you understand what I mean when I say it's incurable?'

Repeat important points.

'So, as I said, the main facts are...'

'It's a lot of information, but basically...'

Use diagrams and written messages.

Use any printed or recorded information available.

Check your level – too complicated or too patronising?

Listen for the patient's agenda.

'Is there anything you particularly want to talk through/are worried about?'

Be prepared for the 'last minute' query – the hidden question.

5. <u>Responding to the patient's feelings</u>

Identify and acknowledge the patient's reaction.

Allow silence if needed.

Denial is perfectly natural and should be challenged only if causing serious problems for the patient.

Anger and blame need to be acknowledged; exploring the causes can follow later.

Despair and depression must be acknowledged. Allow the patient to express their feelings and offer support.

Awkward questions may be asked, such as 'How long have I got?' You may have no honest answer and you may have to reply as such.

Collusion, where relatives ask the doctor not to tell the patient, is a common request. It must be made clear that the duty of the doctor lies first to the patient, but reasons for collusion need to be explored.

6. Planning and follow-through

Organising and planning

Planning for the future is a good way to alleviate the bewildered, dispirited, disorganised thoughts of a patient who has just received bad news.

Demonstrate an understanding of the patient's problem list.

Identify the problems that are 'fixable' and those that are not.

Make a plan, putting the 'fixable' problems in order of priority and explain what you are going to do about each one.

Prepare the patient for the worst and give them some hope for the best.

Identify coping strategies of the patient and reinforce them.

'I think it's brilliant that you and your wife have started attending a support group and I would encourage this as long as you find it helpful.'

Identify other sources of support for the patient and incorporate them.

'Your daughter was asking if she could come up and help – perhaps you could let her do some of the shopping and housework once a week?'

Make a contract and follow it through

Summarise the plan you have formulated.

Check there are no outstanding issues.

Outline what will happen next and what the patient is expected to do.

Make sure you leave an avenue open for further communication.

'So the cancer care nurse will contact you on Monday and we'll see you on Friday to discuss the CT results.'

'So the oncologist will expect you at Cookridge Hospital a week on Thursday. I haven't made a formal arrangement to see you again, but you know to contact your GP or ring Mr Black's secretary if you have any problems in the meantime.'

WRITING AN OPERATION NOTE

A useful ten-point guide to structuring an operation note is given below to ensure you don't miss any essential point-scoring parts in a stressful situation such as the OSCE.

1.   Demographic details

Name, DOB, hospital number.
e.g. 'Joanne Smith, 01/01/1990, PAT0001.'

2.   Staff details

You, your assistant and the anaesthetist.
e.g. 'Dr CT Surgeon, Mrs AS Sistant, Dr AN Aesthetist.'

3.   Date/location

e.g. '01/01/2010, Theatre 3, General Theatres, District General Hospital.'

4.   Operation title

e.g. 'Laparoscopic Appendicetomy.'

5.   Indication

A short sentence summarising the reason for the operation.
e.g. 'Right iliac fossa pain for 2 days with raised WCC and CRP.'

6.   Incision

In the case of laparoscopic surgery describe your port sites, technique of gaining access, size of all ports inserted and degree of pneumoperitoneum.
e.g. 'Supraumbilical 10-mm port, open Hassan technique, 15 mmHg pneumoperitoneum. 5-mm ports in left iliac fossa and suprapubic region inserted under direct vision.'

7.   Findings

Again, a short list of abnormal and relevant normal findings.
e.g. 'Inflammed appendix with straw-coloured fluid in the pelvis. Normal right and left ovary and uterus, small bowel normal and no evidence of a Meckel's diverticulum.'

8. Procedure

A systematic list of the steps you went through during the main part of the procedure.

e.g. 'Findings as above. Photographs taken. Sample of fluid taken for culture and sensitivity. Mesoappendix dissected with hook diathermy. Appendix cleared to base (base looked healthy). 3 PDS endoloops applied to base. Washout 1 litre. Haemostasis. Appendix removed in specimen retrieval bag via supraumbilical port (sent to histology). All ports removed under direct vision.'

9. Closure

A list of what you used to close from deep to superficial.

e.g. 'J-PDS to sheath at supraumbilical port. 3/0 Monocryl subcutaneous to skin. No drain.'

10. Post-operative instructions

This is one of the most important steps and will inform other doctors/nurses what to do next. A clear set of instructions will often save lots of questions later.

e.g. 'Routine post-op observations, analgesia, no further doses of antibiotics (had cefuroxime and metronidazole during operation), eat and drink as able, home when safe (possibly tomorrow if well), routine outpatient appointment.'

SECTION 3: SURGICAL SKILLS AND PATIENT SAFETY

CHAPTER 8
SURGICAL SKILLS

A STRUCTURE OF THE STATION

Surgical skills and patient safety are assessed in the same context area. This area is covered in two stations, both of which are generic and will be manned. Although there may be some overlap in the OSCE, for convenience we will consider these two areas separately, in this chapter and in Chapter 9, Patient Safety.

POSSIBLE OSCE STATIONS

- Scrubbing up
- Prepping and draping
- Opening a midline abdominal incision
- Suturing a wound
- Debridement of a wound
- Benign skin or subcutaneous lesion excision biopsy (common scenario)
- Abscess drainage (although models not widely available)
- Central line insertion
- Arterial line insertion
- Chest drain insertion

LEVEL OF SURGICAL SKILLS REQUIRED IN THE OSCE

This domain is described as: 'the ability to perform manual tasks related to surgery which demand manual dexterity, hand/eye coordination and visual-spatial awareness'. The marking scheme for the domain requires that for a pass mark you need to show the examiners that:

- You achieve the task effectively
- You complete the task in a timely manner
- You demonstrate an organised approach
- You show dexterity, and
- You demonstrate good hand/eye coordination

TYPES OF SURGICAL SKILL YOU COULD BE ASKED TO DEMONSTRATE

The Intercollegiate Surgical Curriculum Programme (ISCP) syllabus states that for the initial stage of surgical training you should be able to demonstrate how to perform the following essential basic surgical skills:

- Incision of skin and subcutaneous tissue
- Closure of skin and subcutaneous tissue
- Knot tying
- Haemostasis of superficial vessels
- Retraction of tissue appropriately
- Handling of tissue appropriately
- Use of drains appropriately

The best way to gain these skills is by practice, either in a skills laboratory or in theatre. I ruined a sofa by practising knot tying on it for hours on end, leaving bits of thread everywhere! While this may seem a bit odd, it is these hours of practice that make these simple but essential skills second nature so that you can perform them well under stressful circumstances – be that suturing a piece of foam in the OSCE or ligating a bleeding vessel in theatre. We will cover the theory behind these skills and give some 'top tips' but this book cannot give you these skills – only practice, practice, practice can!

B SURGICAL SKILLS

INCISION OF SKIN AND SUBCUTANEOUS TISSUE

KEY POINTS
• Choice of instrument
• Accuracy
• Langer's lines
• Ability to use scalpel, diathermy and scissors

Choice of instrument

You can either use a scalpel or monopolar cutting diathermy to make a skin incision. It is unlikely in the OSCE that they will set up diathermy as it could burn the foam models! We will therefore concentrate on correct use of the scalpel.

Where to place your incision (accuracy and Langer's lines)

This will obviously depend on what you are doing. Planning can make all the difference as a poorly placed incision can make the rest of the operation more difficult. In 'real life' you can use anatomical landmarks to help. Langer's lines are handy guides (this is the direction in which the skin creases) and incisions made parallel to these can often heal and scar better. However, in the OSCE these will not be available. You need to consider what models might be available to the examiners in the OSCE. It is therefore realistic to expect that you might be required either to open a routine skin incision (such as a model of an anterior abdominal wall through which you are required to make a midline incision) or to perform an elliptical incision to remove a lesion.

If you have the option to use a skin marker to draw your intended site for incision this can increase your accuracy and allows you to readjust your marks if they do not look ideal at first (which obviously you can't do with a scalpel)!

Scalpel

Safety first – top tips!

- You may be provided with a disposable scalpel but, if not, you will need to attach the blade to a scalpel using a haemostat (clip). Never handle the blade with your hands.
- If passing the scalpel between people it should be placed in a kidney dish. If (for whatever reason) there is no kidney dish available then hand the scalpel handle first (never blade first).

Two techniques for using the scalpel

- For most routine incisions (such as most of a midline abdominal skin incision), hold the scalpel as you would hold a knife you use to eat with. This allows you to apply pressure along the whole length of the blade. Use your other hand (away from the direction you are cutting in!) to stretch the 'skin' to make the incision easier for you.
- For more tricky incisions (such as skirting around the umbilicus in a midline abdominal skin incision), hold the scalpel as a pen and use the tip of the blade to cut with.

Size/shape of blade

There are many different sizes of blade. We list the common sizes and shapes below to give you an idea of which to select in the OSCE for a particular task.

Size 10 has curved edge and flat back (the typical shape you think of for a scalpel). It is small and good for making skin incisions.
Size 11 has a triangular blade with a sharp point and flat cutting edge. It is also small and most useful for precision cutting.
Size 15 is a smaller version of the 10 and often used for excision biopsy.
Size 20 is a larger version of the 10 and used for instance for opening midline abdominal incisions.

Monopolar diathermy

Safety first

- The issue of diathermy safety is covered in Chapter 9, Patient Safety, see page 644.

Using the diathermy

Hold the monopolar diathermy stick like a pen and use the 'cutting' setting to make a skin incision. Once below skin use the 'coag' setting to deepen your incision through the subcutaneous fat as it causes less bleeding. However, it is unlikely that you will be asked to use diathermy in the exam as it would burn the foam models!

Scissors

Once you are through subcutaneous fat you can use scissors to open fascial layers. There are two types of scissors – heavier ones for cutting sutures and finer ones for cutting tissues. Make sure you pick the right ones in the exam!

Top tips for handling scissors

- Use the tips. They cut better and you avoid the risk of cutting something else which might have got caught in the blades.
- Place just the tips of your thumb and ring finger into the holes and use the index finger of your other hand to steady the scissors.

CLOSURE OF SKIN AND SUBCUTANEOUS TISSUE

KEY POINTS
• Options for closure
• Suture choice
• Needle choice
• Safe closure practice
• Accurate and tension-free apposition of wound edges

Options for closure

You would usually close a wound in layers. Firstly closing fascia, then subcutaneous fat and, finally, skin. There are many different options available to you when closing a wound and there are often several 'correct' options; which is used will depend on surgeon preference. You can use a variety of suturing techniques.

Interrupted sutures

- Can be used for closing fascia, subcutaneous fat or skin
- Space sutures evenly and keep the distance from the incision the same on each side
- Place sutures at 90° to the line of the incision
- Place your knots to one side of the incision
- Useful for closing an excision biopsy in the OSCE

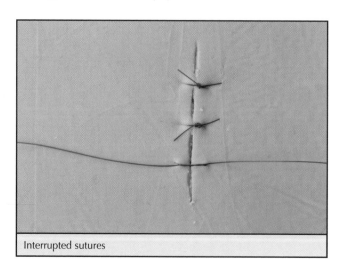

Interrupted sutures

Continuous sutures

- Used, for instance, for mass closure of an abdominal midline incision
- If you use a single suture you must place your first stitch and then secure this with a knot. If you are using a loop suture then you simply place your first stitch and then place the needle through the loop to secure it.
- You will need an assistant to 'follow' you by holding the suture at the same tension as that with which you hand it to them. It is your responsibility to ensure that the tension in the running suture is correct (too tight and you can distort the wound and tissues, too loose and you may end up with a gaping wound).

Subcuticular sutures

- A continuous stitch used to close skin. You can use either an absorbable or a non-absorbable suture.
- Absorbable suture: initially you need to place a stitch in the subcuticular layer and then tie a buried knot. Once the wound is closed many surgeons tie an Aberdeen knot and then bury this by coming through the wound and out of the skin at a distant site and cutting the suture close to the skin.
- Non-absorbable suture: you must obviously leave a means to remove it. This is often achieved by securing the ends with beads.
- Each stitch should include a small bite of tissue. Ensure that each bite is taken at the same depth. At the end it should look a little like a 'ladder' of stitches (see figure).

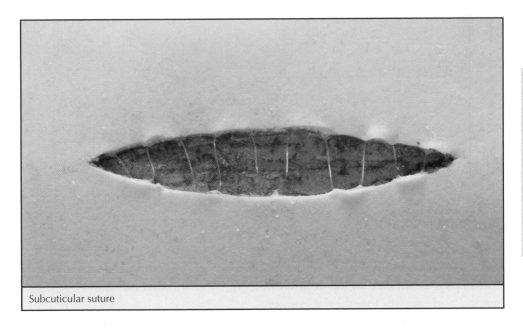

Subcuticular suture

Mattress sutures

- Useful if you want to evert or invert a wound edge. They are a strong suture and can be helpful if it is a large, gaping wound (although ideally you would not want to close any wound under tension).
- These can be either vertical or horizontal (see figure). For a vertical mattress take a bite about 1 cm from the edge of the wound, into the middle. Then take a bite of the other side of the wound, also about 1 cm from the edge. Reverse your needle and take a small bite (the closer to the edge the more accurately you can evert the tissue) into the middle and repeat for the other side before tying a knot. Leave the ends about 0.5 cm long so that whoever has to remove the suture in a few days' time has something to grab onto.

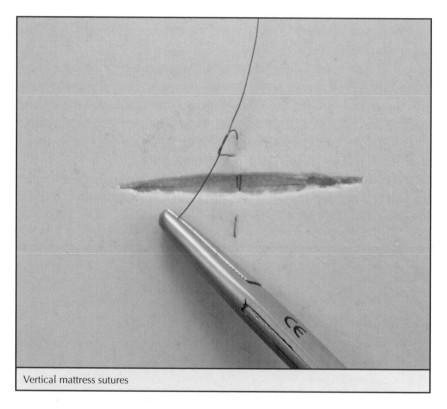

Vertical mattress sutures

Skin staples/clips

These can be used to close incisions where cosmetic results are not essential; they are often used in wounds that might be contaminated. It is essential that skin staples are placed in the centre of the incision and that the skin edges are everted and brought together accurately.

Suture choice

There are four important factors to consider before choosing your suture:

1. Is it absorbable or non-absorbable?

Absorbable sutures provide tensile strength to a wound for a variable amount of time. Vicryl rapide™ for instance provides 7–10 days of wound support and is therefore good for closing wounds inside the mouth where you would only want tensile strength for a short period. PDS II (polydioxanone suture) provides wound support for up to 6 weeks and so is commonly used in mass abdominal wall closures. These sutures will still be present for a period of time after they stop providing tensile strength, but before being fully absorbed. For instance, PDS II does not degrade completely for up to 6 months.

Non-absorbable sutures, as their name would suggest, do not absorb and hence are useful in situations when you need tensile strength long term, as in sutured hernia repairs.

2. Is it monofilament or multifilament?

Monofilament sutures are made of one strand, as opposed to multifilament, or braided sutures, which are made up of lots of strands. These two sutures have very different properties. A monofilament suture is preferable in some circumstances as it has fewer nooks and crannies for bacteria to hide in. A monofilament suture also passes smoothly through tissue. However, it is often hard to handle as it is more slippery and you often need more throws on your knot to ensure it is secure. It also exhibits 'memory' and can tangle back up into the shape it was in in the packet. Multifilament or braided sutures are much easier to knot and handle as they do not exhibit 'memory'.

3. What size is the suture?

Sutures come in different diameters, offering different tensile strengths. Common suture sizes you will use vary from 1 (thickest), 0, 2/0, 3/0, 4/0, 5/0 to 6/0 (finest). If you need to select a suture size in the exam think about what tissue you are being asked to close. Appropriate sizes for different situation are given below:

Skin: Face 6/0

Limbs 5/0, 4/0

Abdomen or trunk 4/0, 3/0

Subcutaneous fat 2/0, 3/0

Fascia: 1, 0

4. Is it dyed or undyed?

Most sutures come in dyed or undyed versions. While it can be easier to see a dyed suture against tissues you must remember to use an undyed suture for closing skin as a dyed suture might show through.

Examples of different suture materials and when to use them

This list is by no means exhaustive. It is just designed to give you a selection of options during the exam.

Absorbable monofilament sutures

PDS II (polydioxanone suture): provides wound support for up to 6 weeks and lasts in the tissue for up to 6 months. Common uses include mass closure of the abdominal wall, bowel anastomoses.

Poliglecaprone (e.g. Monocryl™): loses 20–30% of its tensile strength by 2 weeks and lasts in the tissues for up to 3–4 months. Common uses include subcuticular skin closure.

Absorbable multifilament

Polyglactin 910 (e.g. Vicryl™): provides 3–4 weeks of tensile strength and lasts in the tissues for just over 2 months. Also available as Vicryl rapide, which has been treated so that it absorbs more quickly and provides 7–10 days of wound support. Common uses include skin closure, ligating vessels.

Polyglycolic acid (e.g. Dexon): loses about 20% of its tensile strength at 2 weeks and lasts in tissue for 3 to 4 months. Common uses include ligating vessels.

Non-absorbable monofilament

Nylon (e.g. Ethilon™): commonly used for interrupted skin closure.

Prolene: retains its tensile strength indefinitely. Common uses include sutured hernia fixation techniques, vascular anastomoses.

Non-absorbable multifilament

Polyester (e.g. Ethibond™): retains its tensile strength indefinitely. Common uses include sutured hernia repair.

Silk: natural fibre. In theory, non-absorbable, but loses most of its tensile strength within a year. Common uses include suturing drains in position.

Needle choice/handling

Needle handling

One of the things the examiners may look at in the technical skills section of the exam is correct handling of the needle. Three top tips are:

1. Never handle the needle; always use your needle holder and forceps to pick it up.
2. It can be difficult in some sets of instruments to differentiate a haemostat (clip) from a needle holder. Look at the gripping surface – if it is cross-hatched it is a needle holder; if the indentations all run in the same direction it is a haemostat (clip).
3. Hold the needle about a third of the way from the swaged end (i.e. the end with the suture in it). In real life, sometimes you might find it easier to hold the needle about halfway round but particularly in tough tissue (do not do this in the exam as the foam models should be nice and soft).

Needle choice

As with sutures there are many different types of needle available to the surgeon. Below we will go through common needle types which you might come across. There are two main choices to make when selecting a needle:

1. The type of point:

- **Round-bodied needles**: these don't cut the tissue but, instead, separate it and therefore the tissue closes tightly over the suture once the needle has passed through. They are therefore used in softer tissues and those which require a nice tight closure of tissue over the suture line such as in anastomoses. These round-bodied needles come in blunt taperpoint versions which prevent sharps injuries and are also used for suturing friable tissue such as the liver.

- **Cutting needles**: as opposed to round-bodied needles, these cut through the tissues. They are commonly used for tougher tissues such as skin and fascia. There are three main types:
  o Tapercut™, with a cutting tip and then a round-bodied needle
  o 'Cutting needles', which have a triangular cross-section with the apex pointing up, as opposed to …
  o 'Reverse cutting needles', which have the apex on the outside and are therefore stronger and useful in tougher tissue

2. **The shape of the needle**:
- **Straight needle**: commonly used for subcuticular skin incisions (although many surgeons prefer a curved needle for this)
- **1/4 of a circle**: mostly used in ophthalmics
- **3/8 of a circle**: can be used for fascia
- **1/2 of a circle**: commonly used for skin closure
- **5/8 of a circle**: useful for when you are stitching in a deep hole where it is difficult to get room to turn your needle and grasp the point again, e.g. pelvis or oral
- **J-shaped needle**: also used to get into awkward small deep wounds such as port-site closure after laparoscopic surgery or closing the defect in femoral herniae

KNOT TYING

KEY POINTS

- Choice of material for tensile strength, handling characteristics and knotting
- Single-handed knots
- Instrument ties
- Superficial and deep knots

Choice of material for tensile strength, handling characteristics and knotting

Some of this has been covered above. However, a good way to select the correct suture is to think about what you would use to ligate a vessel. You need a suture material that is going to be easy to knot (as you don't want your knot to slip in this situation) so you might prefer a braided (or multifilament) suture. This is why Vicryl™ is often used; in this situation you only require three throws as your suture is unlikely to slip (whereas with monofilament sutures you often require up to six throws). Then you need to think about the tensile strength and therefore the diameter of suture you require: for smaller vessels you might use a 2/0 Vicryl™ but for tying large vessels, e.g. the IMA, you might use a 0 Vicryl™ tie.

Knotting techniques

Different situations require different knotting techniques and it is essential that you have the full gamut of knots in your arsenal:

- Single-handed
- Double-handed
- Instrument
- Superficial and deep

However, in the OSCE you are likely to have to tie either single-handed or instrument knots for superficial ties and these are also the basis for all other knot combinations. We will therefore cover these briefly below (although we would expect that you would be an expert knotter by now!).

Single-handed knots

This is essentially your standard hand tie. You would use this if you were ligating vessels or tying at depth (i.e. at times when an instrument tie is inappropriate). Ideally, you should be able to tie knots with either hand. We will describe a left-handed tie.

- Start with the short end of your suture in your left hand, stretched over your forefinger and held between middle finger and thumb. Hold the long end of the suture in your right hand.
- Bring the long end held in your right hand over your left index finger.
- Hook your left index finger under the suture held by your left hand and then pull this through the loop you've created.
- Pull your right hand away from you and left hand towards you to get a flat knot.
- Stay in this position and prepare for the second knot.
- Hold the short suture in your left hand between forefinger and thumb and loop the thread around your other three fingers.
- Bring the suture end in your right hand over the middle finger.
- Use the tip of your left middle finger to hook the suture in your left hand under that in your right.
- Pull the knot flat by stretching your left hand away from you and the right hand towards you.
- Repeat the first index-finger knot.

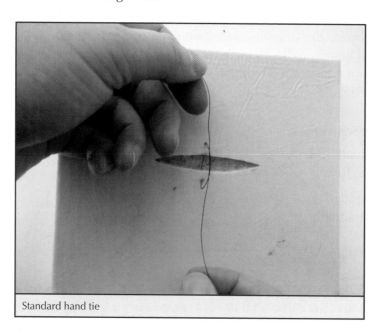

Standard hand tie

If you are tying at depth follow this procedure but tie your knot where you can see it at the end of the suture and then snug it down with your left index finger before tying the second knot (again where you can see it at the end of the suture), then snugging this down in a similar manner. You need to have 'soft hands' when tying knots and do not tug hard on the sutures or you may tug off the tissue!

If you are tying a knot with a monofilament designed to bring two pieces of tissue together it is often helpful to place two of the first index-finger throws on before snugging this first knot down as this is less likely to unravel before you have a chance to place your second knot.

Instrument ties

These are useful for tying skin sutures as you can use less suture material (because you don't have to get it round your fingers). It is tempting to give the knot a good tug with your instruments though, so be mindful to avoid this so your knots don't strangle the tissue!

- Take the long end of the suture in your left hand and the needle holder in your right hand.
- Place the instrument over the thread and loop round it.
- Grab the short end of the suture with the tips of your needle holder and push you left hand away from you and pull your right hand towards you to get a flat knot. (Sometimes, if the tissue is difficult to pull together and the suture slippery, it can be useful to put two loops of suture over your needle holder before you grab the end of the suture as this knot is less likely to unravel before you can tie the next one.)
- Next do the same again but instead of putting the needle holder over the suture place it under the suture.
- Push your right hand away from you and pull your left hand towards you to lay a flat knot.
- Repeat the first knot.

Instrument tie

HAEMOSTASIS OF SUPERFICIAL VESSELS

KEY POINTS
• Diathermy
• Clip application
• Tie ligation
• Suture ligation

Diathermy

Again, the key to this is to consider what is most likely to be available in the exam. While diathermy is a common means of providing haemostasis in real life (be it bipolar or monopolar) it is unlikely, for reasons already given, that you would be asked to demonstrate this in the OSCE.

Clip application

There are many different clipping devices and while it is important to apply these accurately to a vessel there is little scope for you to demonstrate your technical skills. Also, because clipping devices are variable and expensive they may not be used widely in the OSCE. However, if you are asked to use a clipping device the top tips are:

- **Placing the device**: ensure that the clip is completely around the vessel and does not contain any excess tissue.
- **Deploying the device**: do so with confidence and speed; if you take too long to gently squeeze the device the clip might not fully close.
- **Number of clips**: I usually put two clips on the end of the vessel which is staying in situ as clips are not infallible and can fall off.

Tie ligation

A possible scenario might be that you are provided with a model of a vessel and asked to tie ligate it. Dissect out the vessel from surrounding tissue using a haemostat – make sure to clear enough of the vessel to apply two haemostats and to cut between them. Apply the haemostats to the vessel so that the curves are facing each other, i.e. ( ). Cut in-between. Select your suture to ligate the vessel. A 2/0 Vicryl™ would be a reasonable choice for a small/medium vessel. This might come in lengths or on a reel, either will do. Ask an assistant to hold the haemostat while you hand-tie a knot around the vessel. Be sure to tie nice and close to the haemostat. Ask the assistant to remove the haemostat once you are in a position to snug the knot down. Complete your knot, cut the suture and repeat.

Suture ligation

Transfixing a vessel

If you have got a largish vessel in a haemostat with some surrounding tissue it can be useful to transfix this to ensure that your tie does not slip. Using a Vicryl™ (2/0) stitch, pass the needle under the haemostat and through the tissue beneath it. First tie a knot on one side and then take the suture around the clip and tie a knot on the other side while your assistant slowly removes the clip. Complete the knot.

Suturing a vessel

If, for instance, you are dealing with a troublesome vessel in a scalp laceration use a suture and place a stitch under the vessel at 90° to it. Pull your stitch through enough so that you can hold both ends up and see if this halts the bleeding – if not, place another stitch further along the vessel in the same manner.

TISSUE RETRACTION AND TISSUE HANDLING

KEY POINTS

- Appropriate application of instruments and respect for tissues
- Choice of instruments, e.g. forceps
- Placement of retractors

Appropriate application of instruments, respect for tissues and choice of instruments (e.g. forceps)

Being respectful to tissues is an essential skill and one unfortunately you cannot learn from a book. One important aspect is to ensure you use the correct tools to hold tissue; for instance, reserve the toothed forceps for tougher tissues such as fascia and skin and use the non-toothed ones for more delicate tissue such as bowel.

Placement of retractors

Use of retractors is another instance when respect for tissue should be upmost in your mind. If your assistant has to pull with all their might on the retractor this might well be damaging the tissue they are retracting – think whether increasing the size of your incision might make access easier. Similarly be mindful what your retractor is retracting – are you absent-mindedly pulling on the spleen or liver?

A self-retaining retractor can be useful to free up an assistant or if you don't have one! Be sure to be careful where these blades go as you open the retractor so you don't inadvertently damage anything.

USE OF DRAINS

KEY POINTS

- Indications
- Types
- Insertion/fixation
- Management/removal

Indications

The use of drains is a thorny subject as different surgeons have different and often completely opposing views on them. Therefore below we give you a 'rough guide to drains' although you may notice practice varies depending where and for whom you are working.

There are a variety of indications for using a drain listed below:

Treatment:

- Draining established collections such as blood, pus, other fluids or even air, e.g. chest or ascitic drains
- To establish controlled fistula formation, e.g. a T-tube in the CBD

Preventative:

- Draining potential post-operative collection or seroma which has the potential to become infected, e.g. post-mastectomy
- Draining an area where there is a risk of a leak or bleed in which the drain would allow prompt detection and treatment, e.g. post-thyroidectomy or a bowel anastomosis

Types

Drains can be classified in several ways:

Open versus closed

- Open drains, e.g. corrugated drain which is drained into a stoma bag. Often used to drain infected soft-tissue wounds.
- Closed drains, e.g. tube drains attached to a bag/bottle. These can be further subclassified into **active versus passive**
    - o Active (i.e. on suction) e.g. a Redivac drain. Often used in situations where there is nothing fragile nearby which might get sucked into a drain, e.g. post-mastectomy.

o Passive (i.e. not on suction – works via gravity and the difference in pressure between the body cavity the drain is in and the outside), e.g. a Robinson drain or T-tube. Used in situations when there are things about which you don't want to get sucked into a drain such as intra-abdominally.

Insertion/fixation

Insertion

Some drains come attached to a trocar, which can be used to pierce a way through tissue for the drain to go through. Only use these trocars if you can point them away from anything which could get inadvertently damaged. Other drains are just tubes and you will need to make a small skin incision with a knife and then use a haemostat (from inside pointing out!) to make a track for the drain to go through. Make sure you place the drain where you want it and fix it in place before you close.

Fixation

Drains can be fixed with dressings or sutured into place using a silk or similar suture. Place a suture beside (but not through!) the drain and tie a knot, then wrap the suture securely round the drain like a pair of Roman sandals or ballet shoes. Make sure you have tied it securely – give it a little tug as once a drain falls out on the ward it can't be simply replaced.

Management/removal

Your management of drains needs to be guided by knowledge of their risks:

Risks of drains

- Risk of infection, which increases with the length of time a drain is left in for.
- Suction drains can suck up vulnerable tissue around them and cause damage.
- Drains can be unwieldy things to have attached and can reduce your patient's mobility post-op.
- Drains can get blocked – if they do removal is often the only option.
- Pain.

Management

Monitor the <u>amount</u> of fluid drained over a given period and <u>what</u> is being drained (haemoserous, frank blood, pus, bile etc.). Ensure prompt removal of the drain once it is no longer required (this will vary depending on what the drain is being used for and on surgeon choice).

C OSCE STATION EXAMPLES

This section contains two example OCSEs to give you a flavour of what you can expect in the exam.

BENIGN SKIN OR SUBCUTANEOUS LESION EXCISION BIOPSY

Your consultant has consented a 45-year-old lady for excision of a skin lesion from her left arm under local anaesthetic. However, he has been called away to an emergency in the acute theatre and has asked you to perform the procedure.

This station offers you a good chance to demonstrate a range of different surgical skills. However, it is likely that you will also be assessed on areas such as 'patient safety' or 'communication skills' in this station too so be aware that it is not all about how well you tie your knots!

Introductions
- Introduce yourself and check the patient's details.
- Explain that your consultant has been called away and that you are a trainee and will be doing the procedure if they don't object.

Consenting and marking
- Check all the documentation that is available:
  - Check the referral/clinic letter – is it the correct lesion/side, does it mention any pre-existing conditions that might affect the procedure, e.g. are they on warfarin?
  - Check through the consent with the patient – again agree on the correct side, make sure that they still consent to the procedure.
- Mark the patient yourself (fill in a 'correct site of surgery form' if one is available).
- Take a brief history from the patient – check allergies (especially to local anaesthetic), ensure they have no bleeding disorders/aren't on any anticoagulants.

Getting ready

- Gather all the equipment you need (think through the stages of the procedure and you won't forget anything). Open the sterile equipment onto a clean, draped trolley.

Infiltrating the local anaesthetic

- You must calculate the available dose of local anaesthetic you can safely give, which is dependent on the patient's weight. I would choose 1% lidocaine with adrenaline for this operation, which is likely to be of fairly short duration (do not use local anaesthetic with adrenaline in an end organ (digit/penis etc.) as it can compromise the blood supply).
- Wash your hands. Put on gloves.
- Check the local anaesthetic and the expiry date.
- Draw up the local with a green needle into a 5- or 10-ml syringe.
- Dispose of the green needle and replace with an orange or blue one.
- Clean the skin.
- Warn the patient when you are about to infiltrate (**'a little sting coming up'**).
- Insert the needle to the hilt. You must draw back to ensure you are not in a vessel and then infiltrate local while withdrawing the needle. Repeat until the area is fully infiltrated. If you need to reinsert the needle it is kindest to go through an area you have already anaesthetised.
- Dispose of the orange needle.
- At this stage I would scrub, put on sterile gloves and fully prep and drape the area.
- Check your local has worked by pinching the skin with your forceps. You need to explain to the patient: **'You will feel me pushing and pulling a bit but you should not feel pain. Let me know if it is tender and I can insert more local anaesthetic.'**

Removing the lesion

- Make an elliptical incision around the lesion with your scalpel (mark the area you intend to incise with a marker pen first if one is available).
- Bear in mind that to close the wound in a tension-free manner the length of the wound should be about three times the width of the wound.
- Remove the lesion using either the knife or the scissors.
- This will need to be sent for histology so place it carefully to one side. You might want to mark it with a long lateral and short superior marking suture so that the histologists can orientate it but I would offer to do this rather than actually do it as it is likely to take up quite a lot of your precious time.
- In reality, you would now turn your attention to haemostasis but the model is unlikely to bleed!

Closing the wound

- It is easiest to close this type of wound on a model with an interrupted suture (although in real life you may choose to do a subcuticular closure). I would advise selecting a non-absorbable monofilament in 3/0 or 4/0, e.g. nylon (Ethilon™).
- If there is any tension in your wound, two tips are:
  - o Undermine the skin edges.
  - o Place your first stitch in the centre of the wound to halve it and then put the next two stitches in to quarter it and then fill in the gaps.
- Place a dressing on the wound if one is available.

Clearing up

- Dispose of all sharps in your sharps bin and the rest in a yellow/orange clinical waste bag.
- Put your specimen in an appropriate pot – label it and fill in the relevant form.
- Make sure the patient knows your follow-up plans. **'I hope you are feeling OK. I will arrange for you to have some painkillers to take home. We will organise the district nurse to remove your sutures in 5 days' time and we will see you back in outpatients in 3 weeks' time with the results of the specimen we have removed.'**

CHEST DRAIN INSERTION

Indications

Bear in mind these anatomical facts

- The left hemidiaphragm with the spleen beneath it rises to the fifth rib at rest.
- The right hemidiaphragm with the liver beneath it rises to the fourth space.
- Either hemidiaphragm can be raised due to collapse or phrenic nerve damage due to pathology of that lung.
- The intercostal bundle of nerves, arteries and vein, runs inferior to each rib, so placing the drain just superiorly to the rib avoids damage to these structures.
- The safest site is therefore the fifth intercostal space in the anterior axillary line.

Pre-procedure checks

- Select the size of drain (30 F for pus or blood, 20–24 F for fluid or air) and make sure the underwater seal bottle is ready.
- Check the chest X-ray and check the side is correct (beware mediastinal shift).
- Explain the procedure to the patient and obtain consent.
- Sit the patient up at 45° with the ipsilateral arm behind their head (they are often not comfortable lying flat).

Procedure

- Using an aseptic technique, set up a tray and prep and drape the site.
- Infiltrate just above the sixth rib with local anaesthetic. The syringe fills with fluid when aspirated as it enters the pleural space. (You should use local even if the patient is unconscious as it allows you to aspirate to ensure you are in the pleural space.)
- Make a generous stab incision in the line of the intercostal space with a scalpel after an appropriate pause for the local anaesthetic to take effect (this is a minithoracotomy).
- Deepen the incision with a combination of blunt dissection using a haemostat until the pleura is reached.
- Insert a finger into the thoracic cavity to confirm that the lung is not adherent to the parietal pleura at this site and there is a clear, safe path for your chest tube.
- Insert a purse-string or mattress suture across the incision (non-absorbable) and tie it loosely, to be used for closure after removal of the chest drain.

- Take the selected drain and REMOVE THE TROCAR. A trocar should never be used. Instead, insert a haemostat into one of the perforations in the chest drain to stiffen it and make it easier to guide into the hole, making sure it does not protrude from the end (see figure a, below). This should be withdrawn as soon as the drain is through the chest wall (see figure b, below).
- Slide the chest drain in through the tract made by your finger, directing it apically for a pneumothorax or basally for a pleural effusion. Connect the drain to the underwater seal and make sure the water level 'swings' with each breath.
- With another stitch, tie the tube in place and place a sterile gauze dressing around the exit site of the drain (see figure c).
- Make sure you check the chest X-ray to confirm correct positioning of the drain.

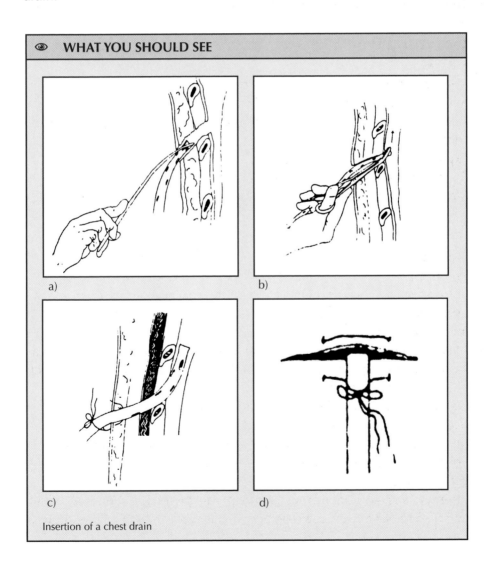

👁 **WHAT YOU SHOULD SEE**

a)

b)

c)

d)

Insertion of a chest drain

CHAPTER 9
PATIENT SAFETY

A Structure of the station   629

B Scenarios   630

A STRUCTURE OF THE STATION

'Patient safety' is currently linked to the 'technical skills' domain of the exam. However, as explained in the previous chapter, for the purposes of this book we are dealing with these topics separately. Because the OSCE is a new exam there are very few examples of previous stations in this context area and therefore the following gives you a flavour of potential questions based on topics concerning patient safety from the MRCS/ISCP syllabus.

B SCENARIOS

PRE-OPERATIVE ASSESSMENT AND PRE-OPERATIVE MANAGEMENT OF CO-EXISTING CONDITIONS

What is the purpose of pre-operative assessment?

'The purpose of pre-operative assessment is to prepare the patient as fully as possible before considering surgical intervention. The aims are to improve patient safety and minimise cancellations. The pre-assessment clinic allows you to do this as it gives you an opportunity to:

- Anticipate difficulties
- Make advanced preparation and organise facilities, equipment and expertise
- Minimise the chance of errors
- Alleviate any relevant fear/anxiety perceived by the patient'

What are the common factors resulting in cancellation of elective surgery and how can the pre-assessment clinic reduce the risk of cancellation?

Common factors which result in the cancellation of surgery include:

- An inadequately controlled pre-existing medical condition
- Inadequate investigation of a pre-existing medical condition
- A new acute medical condition

The pre-assessment clinic allows the identification of pre-existing medical conditions and an opportunity to thoroughly investigate these and optimise them prior to elective surgery. Liaising with an anaesthetist or other specialists at this early stage is useful. As new acute medical conditions (e.g. chest infection) can occur between pre-assessment and elective admission, it is still important to carry out a review of the patient on admission.'

What does the extent of the pre-operative preparation required for a particular patient depend on?

'The extent of pre-operative preparation for an individual patient depends on several factors...

Firstly, how urgently is the surgery needed? This would affect the amount of time available for preparation and what my priorities would be. If it was an elective or expedited operation, I would carry out a thorough preparation. However, if it was an urgent or immediate case my priorities would be active resuscitation, as well as obtaining quick, vital tests such as FBC, U&Es, group and save, an ECG and CXR.

Secondly, the nature of the surgery would determine the extent of pre-operative preparation required: for instance, a minor or intermediate-grade case is likely to need less pre-operative preparation than a major or major plus case.

Other co-morbidities which the patient has would also affect what pre-operative assessment would be appropriate.'

Thank you. We will come back to that later. You mentioned classifying surgery into elective, expedited, urgent and immediate – can you explain these terms?

'The classification of surgery according to the National Confidential Enquiry into Patient Outcomes and Deaths (NCEPOD) has sought to improve patient safety. It groups operations into four areas according to clinical need:

- <u>Elective</u>: or mutually convenient timing
- <u>Expedited</u>: (or semi-elective) early surgery under time limits (e.g. 3 weeks for malignancy)
- <u>Urgent</u>: as soon as possible after adequate resuscitation and within 24 hours
- <u>Immediate</u>: life-saving procedure with resuscitation simultaneous with surgery

What tasks might you perform at a pre-assessment clinic in order to maximise patient safety before elective admission?

'Pre-operative preparation of a patient before admission might include:

- **History**
- **Physical examination**
- **Investigations as indicated, such as:**
  - ○ **Blood tests**
  - ○ **Urinalysis**
  - ○ **ECG**
  - ○ **Radiological investigations**
  - ○ **Microbiological investigations**
  - ○ **Special tests**
- **Counselling and consent**
- **Prescription of medication such as prophylactic antibiotics or venous thromboembolism prophylaxis'**

You mentioned earlier that the extent of pre-operative preparation would depend on the patient's co-morbidities. It is imperative that a patient is adequately investigated pre-operatively, but unnecessary investigations can put a patient at unnecessary risk. Can you expand on when the pre-operative tests you have just mentioned would be appropriate?

'In general terms when considering appropriate investigations for a patient I consider:

- **Simple investigations first**
- **Safety (non-invasive before invasive investigation if possible)**
- **Cost versus benefit**
- **The likelihood of an investigation providing an answer (sensitivity and specificity of the investigation)**

There are NICE (National Institute for Health and Clinical Excellence) guidelines regarding which elective patients should have which pre-operative tests. They consider each test in turn and look at different patient variables, including: age, ASA grade (and what co-morbidity causes a raised ASA grade) and grade of surgery (minor, intermediate, major or major plus).'

PRE-OPERATIVE TESTS

1. Full blood count (FBC)

Almost all surgical patients have an FBC measured. However, it is particularly important in:
- All emergency pre-op cases
- All elective pre-op cases of any ASA, aged >40 undergoing >intermediate surgery
- All elective cases if ASA >II
- All elective cardiovascular surgery

2. U&Es
- Most emergency pre-op cases, especially patients on an intravenous infusion for >24 hours
- All elective pre-op cases >60 undergoing any grade of surgery
- Or any elective pre-op, any age, undergoing major or major plus
- Or any patient ASA >II

3. Amylase
- Perform in all adult emergency admissions with abdominal pain before considering surgery to exclude pancreatitis as the cause

4. Random blood glucose
- Emergency admissions with pancreatitis, especially if suspecting pancreatitis
- Pre-op elective cases, any age, undergoing major or major plus surgery
- Or if ASA III due to renal disease

5. Clotting tests
- Any age undergoing major plus surgery
- ASA III (cardiovascular) or ASA II/III (renal), any age, major or major plus
- If on any anticoagulation

6. LFTs (liver function tests)
- If pre-op for liver/biliary surgery

7. Sickle cell test
- Different hospitals have different protocols but it would be wise to perform a sickle cell test in all patients of African or Caribbean origin in whom surgery is planned and anyone with sickle cell disease in the family
- Informed consent should be obtained

8. Pregnancy test
- Ask all pre-op female patients of childbearing age if they could be pregnant
- If yes, test for pregnancy
- Informed consent should be obtained

9. Urine dipstick
- All pre-op elective

10. ECG
- All emergency admissions with upper abdominal pain or tachycardia
- All patients >40 years and any grade of surgery
- All pre-op cardiovascular surgery
- All ASA II/III (due to cardiovascular disease)

11. ABGs
- Acute patients with suspected pancreatitis, perforation or ischaemic gut
- All ASA II/III (due to respiratory disease) or ASA III (due to cardiovascular disease or renal disease)
- ASA II (respiratory or renal) any age undergoing major or major plus surgery

12. Lung function tests
- ASA II (respiratory), >40, major/major plus
- ASA III (respiratory), any age, intermediate and above.'

Would you use the same guidelines for investigating children pre-operatively?
**'Usually no pre-op tests are required for children undergoing elective
minor or intermediate surgery unless they have specific co-morbidities, e.g.
diabetes. An exception is cardiac surgery, when all patients should have FBC,
U&Es, ECG and CXR. If a child is undergoing a major or major plus procedure
I would consider FBC, U&Es and urine tests but I would liaise closely with the
anaesthetist.'**

*At what stage prior to surgery does the pre-assessment clinic take place and
why?*
**'The pre-assessment clinic aims to assess surgical patients 2–4 weeks prior to
admission for elective surgery. Pre-assessment is timed so that:**

- **The gap between assessment and surgery is long enough so that a suitable
  response can be made to any problem highlighted**
- **The gap between assessment and surgery is short enough so that many new
  problems are unlikely to arise in the interim**
- **It is close enough to surgery to enable the surgical team to identify current
  pre-op problems**
- **High-risk patients can undergo early anaesthetic review**
- **Peri-operative problems can be anticipated and suitable arrangements
  made (e.g. book HDU/ICU bed for the high-risk patient)**
- **There is a chance for assessment by allied specialities (e.g. dietician, stoma
  nurse, occupational therapist, social worker)**
- **The patient can be admitted to hospital closer to the time of surgery,
  therefore reducing hospital stay'**

*Pre-assessment is often run by following a set protocol for the pre-operative
management of each patient group. What advantages and disadvantages does
a protocol-led system have?*
**'The advantages of a protocol are that it acts as an aide-mémoire in clinic and
reduces variability between clerking by juniors. It also allows gaps in pre-
op work to be easily visible. However, I am wary of pre-ordered situations
as they can be dangerous and every instruction must be reviewed on an
individual patient basis. For example, the patient may be allergic to the
antibiotic prescribed as part of the pre-assessment work-up and alternatives
should be given.'**

What safety precautions should be taken when marking a patient pre-operatively?

'Pre-operative marking is necessary to minimise error. It is especially important when the patient is having a unilateral procedure (e.g. on a limb or the groin), the patient is having a lesion excised, a symptomatic or tender area is being operated on (e.g. an epigastric hernia), or a stoma is being created.

Marking should take place after consent on the morning of surgery, but before any premedication is given. It is important that I explain to the patient that I am marking the site for surgery. I would confirm the procedure and the site with the notes, the patient and the consent form. I would position the patient appropriately, e.g. standing for marking varicose veins or supine for abdominal surgery. It is important to use a surgical marker that will not come off during skin preparation. I usually mark the area clearly with an arrow; there are occasions when it is appropriate to write the name of the procedure on the patient as well, for instance in breast surgery.'

What concerns would you have if a patient you saw in the pre-assessment clinic had been on high-dose steroids for inflammatory bowel disease for the last 5 weeks?

'It would be important to prescribe intravenous steroid cover for the period of surgery if the patient is not going to be weaned off steroids prior to the operation, especially if they are undergoing intra-abdominal surgery and might be nil by mouth or have poor absorption post-operatively. Glucocorticoid deficiency in the peri-operative period can present as increasing cardiac failure that is unresponsive to catecholamines, or as an addisonian crisis with vomiting and cardiovascular collapse. Depending on the length of use of steroids, the patient might need a higher dose of steroids during the peri-operative period to counteract the stress of surgery. They should also have a PPI prescribed to prevent peptic ulceration, which is a risk of both steroid use and the stress of surgery.

Steroid use can lead to problems with wound healing due to skin thinning and impaired glucose tolerance. These patients are also predisposed to infection.'

Bariatric surgery rates are increasing – what additional risks does the obese patient have who is undergoing surgery?

'Surgery in obese patients is often technically more challenging and therefore it takes longer; increased adipose tissue predisposes to haematoma formation and subsequent wound infection. Obese patients are also often diabetic and are therefore at even greater risk of infections and poor wound healing. The poor-quality abdominal musculature also predisposes to dehiscence.

Additionally, obese patients have a significantly increased risk of other post-operative complications. These include respiratory problems due to decreased chest wall compliance and inefficient respiratory muscles which lead to prolonged atelectasis and the risk of chest infections. Their oxygen consumption is increased due to the metabolic demands from excess fat and the increased work of breathing. Obstructive sleep apnoea is more common in the obese. Due to increased gastric volume and high intra-abdominal pressure these patients are also predisposed to gastric aspiration.'

DAY-CASE SURGERY

What details would you include on a printed instruction sheet for a patient attending for day-case surgery?

'Patients should be well informed and receive both full verbal and printed instructions in order to minimise adverse outcomes after day-case surgery. These should include:

- A brief description of the surgical problem
- An outline of the nature of the surgery to be undertaken
- Pre-operative instructions
- Requirements for day surgery, e.g. a relative/friend to pick them up and stay with them for 24 hours
- Post-operative instructions, including details about the nature of possible complications, what to do about them and when and who to contact for advice (e.g. the day-case unit, GP, A&E)
- Advice on when to return to work and other activities
- Instructions about any appropriate appointments for follow-up or suture removal'

What are the advantages and disadvantages of day-case surgery?

'Advantages of day-case surgery include:

- A firm date and time for operation with less risk of cancellation
- Minimum time away from home
- Greater efficiency of operating list scheduling
- Cost-effective

However, there are several disadvantages, including:

- Requirement of adequate aftercare at home
- Contingency requirements for inpatient admission or readmission in cases of unexpected complications or inadequate analgesia etc.'

Thank you, it seems that day-case surgery has many advantages. What do you think are the contraindications to day-case surgery?

'I think of the contraindications in terms of medical and social contraindications. Medical contraindications to day case surgery include:

- Unfit patients (ASA class > II)
- Obese patients (BMI > 35)
- Specific problems (e.g. bowel resections)
- Extent of pathology (e.g. large inguinoscrotal hernia)
- Operation longer than 1 hour
- Psychologically unsuitable
- Concept of day surgery unacceptable to patient

There are social contraindications to day-case surgery too, such as:

- Patient lives further than 1 hour away from the unit
- No competent relative or friend to accompany or drive patient home after surgery and/or to look after the patient at home for the first 24–48 hours post-operatively
- No access to a lift (for an upper-floor flat), telephone, or indoor toilet/ bathroom at home'

RISK ASSESSMENT AND SCORING SYSTEMS

What <u>use</u> are pre-operative scoring systems?
'Pre-operative scoring systems exist to allow the surgeon and anaesthetist to predict the morbidity and mortality of an individual patient. They can therefore be used to make decisions about:

- Whether surgery should proceed or whether the morbidity and mortality is too high and another management strategy should be followed (e.g. stenting an obstructed colonic cancer rather than an emergency operation)
- Where the patient should be operated on (day-case theatre, main theatre) and the seniority of the staff involved (consultant anaesthetist/surgeon required)
- Booking an appropriate level of care bed for the patient post-operatively:
  - Level 0   The ward
  - Level 1   Enhanced care
  - Level 2   HDU
  - Level 3   ICU
- Whether the surgery can be used to audit the outcomes of an individual surgeon or anaesthetist and allow comparison between units

A scoring system allows the patient to make a more informed decision about their consent to a procedure. However, no scoring system can predict with certainty outcomes in individual patients and they should not be used to influence clinical decision making.'

Can you give us an example, or indeed examples, of pre-assessment scoring systems?
'Yes. Firstly, the ASA (American Society of Anesthesiologists) grading. This is used commonly, mainly by anaesthetists, to classify patients. It is simple to use but fairly subjective. It divides patients into five groups depending on their co-morbidities (see overleaf).

ASA GRADING	
Class I	Normal healthy individual
Class II	Patient with mild systemic disease
Class III	Patient with severe systemic disease that limits activity but is not incapacitating
Class IV	Patient with incapacitating disease that is a constant threat to life
Class V	Moribund patient not expected to survive, with or without an operation

A more complex scoring system is the POSSUM score (Physiological and Operative Severity Score for the enUmeration of Mortality and Morbidity). This score uses individual patient parameters to predict operative morbidity and mortality. It requires 12 physiological and 6 operative parameters. These include:

POSSUM SCORE	
Physiological	**Operative**
• Age	• Operative severity
• Cardiac history	• Multiple procedures
• Respiratory history	• Total blood loss
• Blood pressure	• Peritoneal soiling
• Pulse rate	• Presence of malignancy
• GCS	• Mode of surgery
• Haemoglobin	
• White cell count	
• Serum urea	
• Serum sodium	
• Serum potassium	
• ECG	

Since its development in 1991 it has been adjusted, as it over-predicted mortality in low-risk procedures and the P-POSSUM was introduced. Subsequently, POSSUM has been altered to apply to specific groups of patients, for example CR-POSSUM for patients undergoing colorectal surgery.'

Moving on to different types of scoring systems... What can you tell us about early warning systems?

'Early warning systems are used to recognise ill patients on the ward early and institute critical care in a timely fashion. There are a variety of them and they include parameters such as:

- Airway compromise
- Respiratory rate and effort
- Heart rate
- BP
- Urine output
- GCS
- Anything that makes ward staff suspicious

An example in common usage is the MEWS (Medical Early Warning System). This system converts vital signs into a numerical score and nursing staff have a set threshold at which the doctor must be called to assess the patient. The MEWS score takes into consideration:

- Haemodynamic parameters (pulse and BP)
- Temperature
- Urine output
- Respiratory rate
- Level of consciousness'

There are lots of different scoring systems for critically ill patients. Do you know of any?

'Yes, an example of a scoring system for critical patients would be the APACHE II (Acute Physiology and Chronic Health Evaluation) scoring system. This is used to work out the severity of disease in patients admitted to ICU. It has three point-scoring components:

- Acute physiology (based on GCS, blood results, haemodynamic and urine output variables)
- Age
- Chronic health

It allows a comparison of different ICUs and also different treatments or new treatments. It has been seen to be particularly useful in predicting the severity and outcome of acute pancreatitis. An APACHE III score was formulated in 1991 to more accurately predicted patient outcome.

Another example of a scoring system for critically ill patients is SAPS II (Simplified Acute Physiology Score). This was also designed to calculate the severity of disease and predicted mortality in patients admitted to ICU. It is supposed to be better than the APACHE II score at comparing patients with different diseases. It is also particularly useful in comparing outcomes between different ICUs.'

What scoring systems would you use to grade the degree of reduced level of consciousness in a trauma patient?
'The Glasgow coma score (GCS) is used to work out the conscious level of patients with head injuries, or to monitor patients with a reduced level of consciousness. It is a 12-point score. Generally, brain injury is classified as severe if GCS $\leq$ 8, moderate if GCS 9–12, and minor if GCS $\geq$ 13. Arguably, the most important score is 8 as at this level it is thought a patient cannot protect their airway and therefore they may need airway protection. You cannot score less than 3. The score is based on the patient's best eye response, vocal response and movement response (EVM), see opposite.

The AVPU score is a simplified version of the GCS. You assess the patient's response to different stimuli and they score either A, V, P or U depending on which level they respond at:

- Alert (awake, although not necessarily orientated)
- Voice (makes any verbal response to speech)
- Pain (makes any response to pain)
- Unresponsive /unconscious (no response to any of the above)'

GLASGOW COMA SCORE

Best eye response (E)

1. No eye opening
2. Eyes open in response to pain
3. Eyes open to speech
4. Eyes open spontaneously

Best verbal response (V)

1. No verbal response
2. Incomprehensible sounds (moaning)
3. Inappropriate words (random words)
4. Confused (responds to questions but there is some disorientation and confusion)
5. Oriented (responds coherently and appropriately to questions)

Best motor response (M)

1. No motor response
2. Extension to pain
3. Abnormal flexion to pain
4. Flexion/withdrawal to pain
5. Localises to pain (purposeful movements towards changing a painful stimulus)
6. Obeys commands

DIATHERMY

Can you please explain how diathermy works and about the different settings available?

'The diathermy machine causes normal mains electricity to be transformed into high-frequency alternating current (HFAC) which passes through body tissues to generate heat to allow cutting of tissues and haemostasis. As it uses higher frequency current than that of mains electricity, it does not stimulate neuromuscular tissue (which would occur at frequencies below 50 kHz). Diathermy uses currents of 500 mA at frequencies of 400 kHz–10 MHz. Different diathermy settings are used for different purposes. The cutting setting is a continuous output that causes a high local temperature, leading to tissue disruption, some vessel coagulation and vaporisation of water. The coagulation setting is a pulsed-output of high-frequency current at short intervals. This causes tissue water vaporisation and vessel coagulation. There is a blend setting available which is a continuous sine-wave current with superimposed bursts of higher intensity.'

What is the difference between monopolar and bipolar diathermy?

'Monopolar diathermy is a high-power unit (400 W) which generates high-frequency current. The current passes from active electrode (HIGH current density), which is the tip of the pencil held by the surgeon, through the body, returning via the patient plate electrode (LOW current density) to the generator. A risk is that an alternative return pathway can occur if the patient touches earthed metal objects (which may cause burns in older machines); most modern diathermy machines do not have earth-referenced generators.

Bipolar diathermy uses a lower-power unit (50 W). The current passes between the two limbs of the diathermy forceps only and so there is no need for a patient plate electrode. It is inherently safer but you cannot use it for cutting or to touch other instruments to transfer current (buzzing). However, it is useful for surgery to extremities, e.g. digits, penis.'

What steps can be taken to maximise diathermy safety?

'This can be thought of in terms of maximising safety for staff and for patients. To improve safety for staff, smoke extraction should be used, as the smoke generated by diathermy has potential harmful effects. Newer monopolar diathermy pencils often come with a smoke extractor device; alternatively you can use the suction to remove the smoke.

There are several steps which can be taken to maximise diathermy safety for patients:

- Avoid pooling of inflammable agents (e.g. alcohol – I make sure I allow the skin preparation to dry) and avoid using diathermy near inflammable gases (e.g. in the colon).
- Ensure the patient is not touching earthed metals (for older machines).
- Use the lowest practicable power setting.
- Keep active electrode in contact with target tissue and in view.
- Don't use monopolar on narrow pedicles (e.g. penis, digits).
- Patients with pacemakers should have ECG monitoring throughout the operation. I would contact the cardiology team if I had concerns.
- Patients with implantable defibrillators will usually have this turned off pre-op and an external defibrillator should be available during surgery.
- Safe placement of the patient plate electrode.'

Can you expand on the safe placement of the patient plate electrode?
'The electrode should have good contact on dry, shaved skin and you should avoid kinking. The contact surface area should be at least 70 cm². When deciding where to place the electrode you must choose an area away from bony prominences and scar tissue, as poor blood supply means poor heat distribution. You should also avoid metal prostheses (e.g. hip). It is normally sited on the patient's thigh or back.'

What are some common causes of diathermy burns in patients?
'Causes of diathermy burns often involve careless technique, such as incorrect plate electrode placement or using spirit-based skin preparation fluid and not waiting for it to dry. Other risky practices include not replacing the electrode in a quiver after use or using diathermy on the large bowel (which should be avoided as explosions have been reported!). Diathermy should be used carefully on appendages (e.g. penis) where a high current can persist beyond the operative site; only bipolar diathermy should be used in these areas.'

LASER

Please can you tell us how lasers work?

'Laser stands for Light Amplification by the Stimulated Emission of Radiation. They produce light by high-voltage stimulation of a medium, causing it to emit photons that are then reflected around the medium, exciting other particles, which release further photons in phase with the initial photons. This process is repeated until a very high density of in-phase photons is achieved (coherent light), some of which is allowed to escape through a partially reflected mirror (the beam). At a cellular level, they vaporise tissue by evaporating water (for cutting or ablation) and coagulate proteins (for haemostasis).'

What types of different laser which are in use in surgery do you know?

'There are several different types of lasers used in surgery, including:

- Argon-beam laser used for endoscopic ablations
- CO_2 laser used in ENT ablation surgery and for removal of small skin lesions
- Nd-YAG laser used in laparoscopic surgery, endoscopic debulking surgery
- Holmium-YAG laser used in kidney stones, benign prostatic hyperplasia, arthroscopy'

What are the advantages of using lasers?

'Lasers can allow greater access as they can reach difficult areas: for instance, the beam can be projected through narrow spaces or down endoscopes. Lasers are very precise as they have very fine beams which can be used for cutting and/or coagulation. This means there is minimal damage to surrounding tissues. They also have selective effects – for instance, argon lasers selectively absorb red pigments (e.g. in blood vessels).'

What are the important issues around laser safety?

'Most hospitals using lasers will have a Laser Protection Advisor and a Laser Safety Policy to ensure their safe use. There are a variety of potential hazards associated with laser use which must be minimised, including eye hazards, fire hazard, damage to other structures and smoke.

1. <u>Eye hazards</u>
Lasers can cause damage to the retina or cornea. Safety precautions that must be considered include:

- All staff and the patient wear appropriate safety goggles
- A sign is placed on the operating theatre door warning of laser use
- Windows are covered
- Inform all present when laser about to be used
- All laser users must have undergone training

2. <u>Fire hazard</u>
Similarly to diathermy, there is a risk of fire with laser use. Precautions should be taken, for instance with skin prep.

3. <u>Damage to other structures</u>
There is potential to damage structures beyond the target if the laser burns through the target.

4. <u>Smoke</u>
Smoke from the laser has potential risks (as with diathermy). Safety precautions that must be considered include:

- Wearing masks
- Local ventilation systems to remove the smoke'

RADIATION USES AND RISKS

'When would you choose to perform a pre-operative CXR and AXR?
'I would perform a CXR in:

- All cases of cervical, thoracic or abdominal trauma
- Any patient with acute respiratory symptoms and signs
- Cases where there is suspicion of perforated intra-abdominal viscus
- All elective pre-op cases aged >60 undergoing major or major plus surgery
- ASA II (cardiovascular/respiratory disease), >40, undergoing any surgery
- All elective cardiothoracic surgery

I would perform an AXR when there is:

- Suspicion of obstruction
- Suspicion of perforated intra-abdominal viscus
- Suspicion of peritonitis
- Concern in inflammatory bowel disease of toxic megacolon'

Can you tell us how ultrasound scanning (USS) works and its risks and benefits?
'Ultrasound is the use of pulsed high-frequency sound waves emitted from the ultrasound probe that are differentially reflected by tissues of different densities (e.g. tissue, fluid, air). The higher the density of the object, the more sound is reflected. If all the sound is reflected (e.g. off a calcified object) then an acoustic shadow appears beyond that object. Reflected waves are identified by the same probe and are analysed by a machine into distance and intensity, producing a 2D image on the screen. USS is commonly used for imaging of the abdomen, pelvis, cardiac anatomy, thorax and vasculature. It is used for:

- Diagnosis, e.g. fluid collections, gallstones
- Monitoring, e.g. obstetrics, abdominal aortic aneurysm surveillance
- Treatment, e.g. guiding percutaneous procedures such as drain insertion or central venous line insertion

It is generally a very low-risk procedure and does not involve exposure to radiation. However, it is operator-dependent and can be limited by body habitus (obesity) and by dense structures (e.g. bone) which deflect sound waves.'

How does computed tomography (CT scanning) work and what are its common uses?

'CT images are created from the integration of X-ray images as the X-ray tube travels round the patient in a circle. The density of different tissues causes differential X-ray attenuation, which is recorded as an image with different levels of grey. The scan can be performed with or without IV contrast or oral/rectal contrast. Uses of CT include:

• Diagnosis, e.g. CTKUB is the gold standard for diagnosing renal/ureteric calculi, or CT-guided biopsy of a lesion
• Staging, e.g. CT thorax to look for evidence of metastases in colon cancer
• Trauma series. Whole-body CT scanning used to detect injuries in the trauma patient
• Treatment, e.g. CT-guided insertion of a drain into a collection'

What are the risks of CT and what safety precautions should be taken?

'The radiation dose is relatively high with CT scans as they represent multiple X-rays. The indication for a CT must be valid and other lower-risk interventions must be considered less useful. For instance, MRI is better at looking at the pelvis or spine and USS is better for looking for gallstones than CT.

Contrast used in CT scanning carries several risks. First, there is a risk of an anaphylactic reaction (usually with iodine-containing contrast). A thorough allergy history must be sought before contrast is given. Secondly, contrast can be nephrotoxic, particularly in those with pre-existing renal impairment (especially diabetics, and patients taking metformin must omit this around the time of CT). U&Es must be checked prior to contrast CT. It may be possible to still perform a scan if the renal function can be improved with rehydration or by stopping nephrotoxic drugs (e.g. NSAIDs). However, I would liaise with the radiologist.

CT is contraindicated in pregnancy and all female patients of childbearing age should have a negative pregnancy test prior to CT. If a patient is breastfeeding she should be advised not to for at least 24 hours following a contrast CT.

The CT scanner has been called the 'donut of death'. This is partly because resuscitation of an acutely ill patient is interrupted for a short period while the patient is being scanned. I would minimise this risk by being sure that the patient is fit for transfer to scan, going with the patient, and taking adequate monitoring and resuscitation equipment with me.'

How does magnetic resonance imaging (MRI) work?

'MRI uses a magnetic field to image tissues based on the movement of their hydrogen atoms in response to a radiofrequency pulse. The radiofrequency pulse can be altered to produce different responses from normal and abnormal tissues. This 'weights' the images, improving the visualisation of different aspects. For instance, in T1-weighted images the fat is white, other tissues shades of grey and liquid black and this gives good anatomical detail. Conversely, in T2-weighted images the fluids give the brightest signal.'

What are the risks and benefits of MRI scanning?

'The benefits of MRI scanning are that it involves no radiation and produces clear soft-tissue imaging. However it is expensive and is unsuitable for patients who are claustrophobic (it is more contained and takes longer than CT). It is also contraindicated in patients who have metal implants.'

How does intraoperative X-ray screening work and what are the safety risks which should be considered when using it?

'X-ray screening involves the production of a continuous image by an image intensifier. Bombardment with X-rays causes fluorescence of phosphor crystals within the machine translated into an image on screen. This allows a procedure to be guided by visualising the needle tip or contrast flow in real time.

Uses of screening include an on-table cholangiogram to exclude CBD stones during a laparoscopic cholecystectomy, assessing the reduction of a fracture or placement of fixation device in the orthopaedic theatre or intra-operative angiograms in vascular procedures. The main risk with screening is that, rather than a transient exposure to X-rays, screening delivers a higher radiation dose to the patient. Therefore, all personnel must wear protective shielding (lead aprons and thyroid collar). Indeed, some surgeons in addition have a special stand-alone screen. You must inform all staff when screening is initiated to allow those without protective shielding to leave. Contrast media might be used (for instance with a cholangiogram) and so the patient's allergy status should be checked as it is possible to have an anaphylactic reaction to contrast. In order to prevent contamination of the operative field the screening machine is covered with a sterile plastic sheet in case it accidentally comes into contact with anything sterile.'

TOURNIQUETS – INDICATIONS, APPLICATION AND COMPLICATIONS

When would you consider using a tourniquet in surgery and what would be the contraindications to using one?

'A tourniquet is an occlusive band temporarily applied to a limb to reduce blood flow. It is used to prevent excessive bleeding in limb surgery to allow a clear operative field (e.g. orthopaedic or vascular surgery). It is occasionally used for isolation of a limb for perfusion (e.g. Bier's block) but its use in trauma is controversial. Contraindications of using a tourniquet include the presence of cellulitis or wound infection in the same limb. In addition, careful consideration must be made before using a tourniquet in patients with peripheral vascular disease.'

Please talk us through the steps in the safe application and use of limb tourniquets.

'Prior to application of the limb tourniquet I would:

- Ensure the monitor or cuff was checked before application
- Ensure application to correct limb
- Ensure an adequate-breadth tourniquet (too thin can cause pressure necrosis)
- Get an assistant to help (it is easier/safer with two)

During application of the limb tourniquet I would:

- Avoid bony prominences
- Elevate the limb to allow blood flow out
- Place plenty of padding beneath the tourniquet
- Inflate to approximately 50 mmHg over systolic BP in the upper limb, 100 mmHg over systolic/or double the systolic BP in the lower limb for adults. Use the lowest pressure possible to achieve 'limb occlusion pressure'
- Note the time of application and record this somewhere in theatre

During surgery:

- The cuff should be deflated to allow reperfusion every 90 minutes (upper limbs) or 120 minutes (lower limb)

After surgery I would:

• **Check the site of the tourniquet after the cuff has been removed**
• **Record the 'tourniquet time' in the operation note'**

Thank you. Despite precautions, tourniquet use can have complications. Could you tell us about them?
'Complications due to tourniquet use include damage to skin, soft tissues or joints during application. Chemical burns can occur due to skin preparation getting under the tourniquet. During use of the tourniquet there may be pressure necrosis from an over-tight tourniquet and insufficient padding on prolonged application. Nerve damage has also been associated with tourniquet use, as has digital ischaemia, venous or arterial thrombosis. Following release of the tourniquet there is a risk of haemorrhage.'

THEATRE DESIGN, DRAPING, POSITIONING, SAFE HANDLING TECHNIQUES AND LIST ORDERING

Can you describe to us an ideal operating theatre design?
'Firstly, I would consider the ideal position of an operating theatre. It should be close to surgical wards to minimise the distance for patient transfer and maximise efficiency. It should also be near ICU/HDU and A&E so that acutely ill patients have minimum distance to travel. For convenience, radiology and sterile supplies departments should be close by.

The layout is also essential as clean areas must be kept separate from dirty areas. The anaesthetic rooms must be next to theatre. There should also be adequate space for staff recreation and stores.

Next, I would consider what is required for the ideal environment. Theatres need to be well heated, aiming for a temperature of 20–22°C to prevent patient hypothermia. There must be facilities to provide clean, filtered air flow (and laminar-flow ventilation in orthopaedic theatres). Other requirements include lighting, power, piped gas and suction facilities. In my ideal theatre there would also be a camera to provide recording facilities!'

What are the aims of draping in surgery and what tips would you give a junior to achieve a safe draping technique?
'The aim of draping is to provide a sterile area and prevent the spread of microorganisms into the operative field. Drapes should provide a barrier to fluid (to protect the patient from getting wet and to prevent a pool of fluid through which microorganisms can get through).

Tips I would give a junior are:

- Always drape with another scrubbed colleague.
- Handle the drapes as little as possible.
- Keep drapes held high so they do not come into contact with non-sterile areas.
- For a simple four-drape technique do the foot end first, then the head end, followed by the side drapes.
- Do not lean over the table to drape the opposite side.

- Secure drapes in place – some drapes have adhesive strips and some will require towel clips. Beware when removing drapes with adhesive strips as they can take skin off (especially in the elderly or in those on steroids) if they are not removed gently.
- If you are concerned a drape has become contaminated, either place another drape over it or, if this is not possible, discard the drape.
- Be aware of areas which might require additional drapes, such as arm boards.'

What are the risks associated with the transfer and positioning of patients in theatre?
'There are risks to the staff and to the patient. Injuries to staff commonly occur during transfers. It is important to have the table and trolley at the same height. I would use a slide board or sheet under the patient to allow easier transfer. I also would not move the patient until there were adequate people to help, at least four: one for the head (usually anaesthetist), one either side, one for the feet. If the patient is heavy more staff may be required. One person (usually the one with the head, i.e. the anaesthetist) coordinates the transfer.

Risks to the patient include risks to pressure areas, especially with the elderly, immobile, those on steroids or those with PVD. Particular areas at risk are the sacrum, heels and the back of the head. This can be prevented by the use of adequate padding and heel protectors. There is a chance of joint injury in positioning, for instance in placing patients in the lithotomy position or when 'breaking' the table. The limbs and cervical spine are particularly at risk. I would minimise this risk by employing coordinated lifting, head support, and taking care with transfers. There is the potential for nerve injuries when patients are placed in certain positions, such as to the brachial plexus in excessive arm abduction. Similarly, muscle injury is more likely in certain positions, for instance compartment syndrome has occurred after prolonged surgery in the lithotomy position. Eyes should also be closed and taped in the anaesthetised patient to minimise the risk of eye injury. It is important to preserve patient dignity during positioning and transfers and I always avoid unnecessary exposure of the patient.'

Your consultant has asked you to order his elective list for next week. Please place the patients listed below in order and explain your reasoning.

1. *Mrs Jones, DOB 01/01/1945, Laparoscopic right hemicolectomy for caecal carcinoma under GA*
2. *Miss Smith, DOB 01/01/2006, Open umbilical hernia repair under GA (latex allergy and diabetic)*
3. *Mr Peterson, DOB 01/01/1950, Excision biopsy of lipoma from back under LA (MRSA-positive)*
4. *Mr Todd, DOB 01/01/1960, Open right inguinal hernia repair*

'I would place the patients in the order 2, 1, 4, 3. There are three reasons why I would place Miss Smith (patient 2) first on the list. Firstly, she has a latex allergy and these patients should be first on the list so as to allow any latex dust to settle. This also reduces any delay caused by removing the latex-containing equipment from theatre impacting on the list. Secondly, she is diabetic and ideally these patients should also be first on the list as it reduces the amount of time they are left nil by mouth and allows quicker return to their normal glycaemic control. In addition, she is a child and to minimise upset caused by waiting, children should be operated on as early on the list as possible.

I would operate on Mrs Jones (patient 1) second as this is the most major case on the list and, as such, this is likely to be most variable in length and so this will avoid the list overrunning if it's placed last. In addition, it is a cancer operation which has targets and therefore cancellation should be avoided.

I would list Mr Todd (patient 4) third because I want to place Mr Peterson (patient 3) last on the list. The main reason to list Mr Peterson last is that he has MRSA and these patients should be placed last on the list if possible to reduce the risk of MRSA transmission to other patients. This also reduces any delay as: the patient should be recovered in theatre if they are having a GA, at least 15 minutes should be left after a patient with MRSA has left theatre to allow adequate air changes, and the theatre must be cleaned afterwards. The aim should be for all elective and where possible all emergency patients to be swabbed for MRSA pre-operatively. As Mr Peterson is having a local anaesthetic it is also more efficient for the anaesthetist to either place him at the beginning or end of the list as they will not be required during the operation and can do something else.'

INFECTION RISKS – BLOOD-BORNE VIRUSES, IMMUNISATION, UNIVERSAL PRECAUTIONS, PRECAUTIONS IN PATIENTS WITH HBV/HCV/HIV, MANAGEMENT OF SHARPS INJURIES

What immunisations do healthcare workers require?
'Healthcare professionals should be immunised against:

- Hepatitis B virus (HBV)
- Varicella zoster
- +/– mumps
- +/– rubella
- +/– measles'

What are universal precautions?
'These are precautions to protect staff from infection in all cases where there is a risk of contact with bodily fluids. They can be divided up into precautions which are barriers and those which are safe techniques. Barriers used in universal precautions include:

- Gloves (which reduce the amount of blood on a sharp by up to 86%)
- Gowns
- Masks
- Eye protection (goggles, face shields)

Safe sharps techniques which should be used in all cases are:

- Not re-sheathing needles
- Using sharps bin promptly
- Locating sharps bin as close to procedure as possible
- Transferring scalpel in a kidney dish
- Using a 'no touch' surgical technique'

Thank you. What special precautions would you employ when operating on patients known to have HBV/HCV/HIV?

'For high-risk surgical patients special precautions should be taken. In an ideal world these precautions would be taken with all cases but this is limited by time, expense etc. In addition to universal precautions I would use:

- Disposable drapes and gowns
- Double-gloving and 'indicator' glove systems
- Face shields
- Blunt suture needles
- Passing of instrument in a kidney dish
- Minimal theatre staff
- Only vital equipment in theatre'

Despite the measures you have described, sharps injuries can occur – what would you do if you sustained one?

'In the event of a sharps injury I would follow my unit's protocol, which includes:

- Encouraging bleeding by squeezing the wound
- Washing with water/soapy water (or alcohol wash if water not available)
- Reporting the incident (to occupational health in working hours or on-call microbiologist out of hours)
- Attending the appropriate department immediately (occupational health/ A&E)
- Counselling and testing of recipient and donor (for HBV, HCV, HIV status) if required
- Post-exposure prophylactic treatment (e.g. triple therapy started immediately in the event of high-risk exposure to HIV) – this should be discussed with a microbiologist or infectious diseases physician'

BLOOD PRODUCTS – APPROPRIATE USE

Please describe the types of blood products you are aware of and appropriate indications for their use.

'In the UK whole blood is rarely used now and it is usually separated into different components. I will deal with these one by one.

RBC concentrates (or packed cells)
This is whole blood from which plasma has been removed. The RBCs are suspended in SAG-M solution (sodium chloride, adenine, glucose and mannitol). The aim of transfusing packed cells is to increase the oxygen-carrying capacity of blood: 1 unit raises Hb by approx 1 g/dl and the volume of 1 unit is approx 180–350 ml. The indications for use include an Hb <7 (or Hb <10 if the patient has severe ischaemic heart disease).

Platelets
These are usually given as one adult dose and should be given within 30–60 minutes. The indications for using platelets are a significant haemorrhage (causing thrombocytopenia) or for prophylactic transfusion in patients with thrombocytopenia/primary platelet function disorder prior to a procedure.

Fresh frozen plasma (FFP)
This contains all coagulation factors but needs 30 minutes to thaw out. It is used in massive haemorrhage requiring large volumes of blood transfusion, DIC with haemorrhage, massive haemorrhage due to over anticoagulation with warfarin (although other treatments might be more effective) and in liver disease with prolonged PT prior to an invasive procedure.

Cryoprecipitate
This is used to replace factor VIII and fibrinogen. A low fibrinogen prolongs all clotting times and I would aim for fibrinogen > 1g/l. The main indication is DIC.

Thank you, I will stop you there. While most people will not have problems related to transfusion there are risks associated and therefore it is safest to minimise the use of blood products where possible. Can you tell us how this might be achieved?

'I think of minimising the quantity of blood products used pre-operatively, intraoperatively and post-operatively.

Pre-operatively

It is important to treat iron deficiency anaemia identified at the pre-assessment clinic with ferrous sulphate or equivalent to reduce the chance of the patient requiring a post-operative transfusion. I also consider carefully if/when to stop anticoagulants, e.g. warfarin or antiplatelet agents (e.g. aspirin/clopidogrel) pre-operatively as these can promote intraoperative blood loss. I would liaise with other specialties/senior colleagues regarding this. It is possible for a patient to pre-deposit blood. This is when the patient donates blood up to 5 weeks pre-operatively. However, it is contraindicated in patients with active infection, unstable angina, aortic stenosis or severe hypertension. Similarly, haemodilution is another technique available, when blood is taken immediately pre-operatively and replaced post-operatively. The contraindications are the same as with pre-depositing blood. There are several pharmacological means to reduce transfusion requirements, including:

- Erythropoetin (EPO). A renal hormone that induces red cell progenitor proliferation and differentiation
- Tranexamic acid. A lysine analogue that inhibits fibrinolysis which can be used for the prophylaxis and treatment of haemorrhage
- Aprotinin. An anti-fibrinolytic that reduces the need for transfusions in cardiac and hepatic surgery

Intraoperatively

A good surgical technique and haemostasis is essential. A cell-saver can also be used. It collects blood lost intraoperatively by suction which is processed and re-infused immediately. Contraindications include potential contamination of the blood with infection or malignant cells.

Post-operatively

It is possible to collect blood from surgical drains, which is then processed and replaced.'

'In order to minimise the risk of incompatibility reactions and infections associated with the use of blood products, strict safety precautions must be adhered to. What safety precautions are taken when using blood products?
'I divide the safety precautions into the different stages of a transfusion:

Blood donation
When blood is donated, high-risk donors are excluded. Then all blood donated is tested for HBV, HCV, HIV, HTLV and syphilis.

Pre-transfusion
Prior to transfusion all blood is grouped and screened so that it is ABO, rhesus D and other antibody compatible. Pre-transfusion it is important to educate the patient and explain the intended reason, risks and benefits, seek their consent and record this in the notes. When I am taking a sample for cross-matching I always check the patient's identity using their wristband, label the bottle at the bedside and provide adequate details on the request form, such as patient details, reason for transfusion, how much blood, when it is needed and requestor details. Next it is essential to prescribe the blood product clearly and secure timely, adequate IV access before the blood product arrives as the longer the blood product is out of the fridge the higher the risk of bacteria multiplying. All blood products are labelled with ABO/rhesus type, expiry date and details of the intended recipient, which must be checked against their wristband (at least two members of staff must check this). The nurses will record the blood pressure, pulse and temperature pre-transfusion.

During transfusion
It is important to use a sterile blood administration kit with a filter. Blood pressure, pulse and temperature should be checked and recorded 15 minutes after each unit is transfused and then at regular intervals, as per local guidelines (usually approximately every 30 minutes).

Post-transfusion
You must be wary of delayed reactions. If a second transfusion is required after 3 days a repeat sample to test must be sent to blood bank as there is a risk of new antibodies.'

We have heard about how you can avoid the risks of using blood products. Now we would like you to tell us what risks are associated with the use of blood products.

'The adverse effects of blood transfusion may be classified by time, type and severity of reaction. Massive transfusions carry their own complications and I will consider them separately.

Acute severe complications

There are acute severe immunological reactions such as an acute haemolytic transfusion reaction. This is due to an incompatible red cell transfusion, which is usually ABO incompatibility. It occurs after a small amount of blood product has been transfused. The symptoms include rigors, restlessness, chest tightness and joint pain. Treatment involves stopping the transfusion, resuscitation using the ABCD principles, sending blood cultures and cultures from the bag of blood and informing blood bank. You can also, rarely, see a bacterially contaminated blood reaction. It requires similar treatment to an acute haemolytic transfusion reaction together with antibiotics as per local protocols. Anaphylaxis can occur early in the transfusion. It is normally due to anti-IgA antibodies in the patient's plasma binding to normal IgA in the donor's plasma. I would stop the transfusion and treat as for any anaphylaxis. There are other acute severe complications such as fluid overload or a transfusion-related acute lung injury (TRALI). A TRALI usually occurs within 6 hours of transfusion and presents as SOB/non-productive cough. Patients may require non-invasive ventilation.

Less severe early complications

For instance, a febrile non-haemolytic transfusion reaction. This is manifested by a slight raise in temperature, likely to be due to the formation of cytokines during storage. It occurs later than acute haemolytic transfusion reactions and is treated by slowing/stopping the transfusion. It is possible to just get a mild allergic reaction rather than anaphylaxis. This is typically a reaction to plasma and it is therefore more common in components with large amounts of plasma, e.g. FFP.

Delayed complications

Include immunological reactions such as a delayed haemolytic transfusion reaction, which occurs > 24 hours post-transfusion. Transfusion-related graft-versus-host disease is rare and tends to occur in immunodeficient patients. It is thought the donor lymphocytes mount an immune response against the recipient's lymphoid tissue. Delayed complications of blood transfusions also include blood-borne infections. In the UK the risk of contracting HIV from a blood transfusion is now less than 1 in 2 million units and the risk of contracting HCV or HBV from a blood transfusion is 1 in 200 000. Variant Creutzfeldt–Jakob disease (vCJD) is a prion disease and the transmissible element has been found in leucocytes, so blood products are now leucocyte-depleted. Syphilis and HTLV can also be transmitted by blood product use.'

Thank you. You mentioned the complications of massive transfusion earlier – can you tell us about this?

'A massive transfusion is defined as transfusion of the total blood volume in < 24 hours. It can result in cardiac abnormalities, ARDS or acute lung injury and DIC.

One issue is hypothermia due to cold blood product infusion, which affects coagulation. This can be minimised by using a blood warmer. Electrolyte disturbances can occur with massive transfusion, such as hypocalcaemia, caused by the citrate used to store blood. However, citrate is rapidly metabolised and so this is a rare complication; it can occasionally be seen in neonates and hypothermic patients who can find it difficult to excrete citrate. The ECG should be monitored and, if abnormal, the hypocalcaemia should be treated with 10% calcium gluconate. Hyperkalaemia can also be a problem as cells lyse in stored blood, causing the plasma potassium content to rise. Therefore the potassium levels must be checked during massive transfusions. Clotting abnormalities will occur due in part to hypothermia and also because of the lack of platelets and clotting factors in stored blood. When giving a massive transfusion early consideration should be given to also giving FFP/platelets.'

VENOUS THROMBOEMBOLISM (VTE) PREVENTION

What is the aetiology of venous thromboembolism?
'Venous thrombosis occurs in response to factors described by Virchow's triad. This comprises endothelial damage (e.g. smoking, previous DVT), reduced venous flow or stasis (e.g. immobility, obstruction to flow) and hypercoagulability (e.g. inheredited coagulopathy, smoking, malignancy).'

What are the risk factors for VTE?
'NICE (National Institute for Health and Clinical Excellence) issued guidelines in 2010 regarding the prevention of VTE. Risk factors can be divided into patient factors, disease factors and surgical factors.

Patient factors include:

- Age > 60
- Obesity BMI > 30
- Known thrombophilia (e.g. protein C or S deficiency, lupus anticoagulant, factor V Leiden)
- HRT/oestrogen-containing OCP
- Previous medical history or first-degree relative family history of VTE
- Pregnancy
- Poor mobility

Disease factors include:

- Malignancy (especially pelvic or abdominal)
- Dehydration
- Critical care admission
- Acute abdominal pathology
- Acute admission with inflammatory pathology

Surgical factors include:

- Surgery of the pelvis or lower limb
- Length of surgery (e.g. total anaesthetic time and surgery time > 90 minutes or surgery involving the pelvis or lower limb and total anaesthetic time and surgery time > 60 minutes)'

What types of VTE prophylaxis do you know of? How would you decide what prophylaxis is most appropriate for a patient?

'Prophylaxis required depends on the risk of VTE. Prophylaxis can be divided into general preventative measures, mechanical prophylaxis and pharmacological prophylaxis. Occasionally in very high-risk patients a vena cava filter might be considered too.

General preventative measures are appropriate for all patients and include early mobilisation, preventing dehydration and avoiding calf pressure. For elective surgery other measures to consider are stopping HRT/ oestrogen-containing OCP 4 weeks prior to surgery (but advise alternative contraception). I would also consider whether regional anaesthesia could be used as this carries a lower risk of VTE than GA. In addition it is worth considering continuing any antiplatelet agents the patient takes (although this must be weighed against the risk of bleeding).

Mechanical VTE prophylaxis is also appropriate for most patients. Measures include graded elastic compression stockings. These must be properly fitted and applied pre-surgery. They are removed daily to inspect the skin for any damage and left on until the patient is mobile. They are contraindicated in peripheral vascular disease, recent lower limb skin grafts, ulceration, etc. An alternative is intermittent pneumatic calf compression devices but these are relatively expensive and prohibit mobilisation.

Pharmacological VTE prophylaxis protocols will vary between units. However, NICE guidelines suggest any patient undergoing surgery with an increased VTE risk and a low risk of major bleeding should have pharmacological VTE prophylaxis. All patients undergoing elective total hip or knee replacement or bariatric surgery need it. Different units may have different preferences as to what to use for pharmacological VTE prophylaxis. The 2010 NICE guidelines specifically state that aspirin or other antiplatelet agents are not adequate prophylaxis for VTE. Commonly used treatments include fondaparinux sodium, low-molecular-weight heparin, or unfractionated heparin (used in patients with renal failure). The duration of pharmacological VTE prophylaxis varies between patients. For non-orthopaedic surgery the VTE prophylaxis continues until the patient is mobile (usually 5–7 days) except in the case of major abdominal or pelvic cancer resections, in which case consider using prophylaxis for up to 28 days. For elective total hip replacement consider discharging the patient on 28–35 days of pharmacological VTE prophylaxis and for elective total knee replacement consider 10–14 days.'

What information would you give to your patient regarding the pharmacological prophylaxis of VTE?

'Before pharmacological VTE prophylaxis is given, patients should be offered written/verbal information on the risks of VTE and how to reduce these, together with the importance and side-effects of prophylaxis. If I were discharging a patient on VTE prophylaxis I would ensure they received written and verbal instructions on how to use it, side-effects to watch out for and advice on when to stop. Their GP must be informed too.'

SURGICAL SITE INFECTIONS, PRINCIPLES OF ASEPSIS AND ANTISEPSIS, APPROPRIATE USE OF ANTIBIOTICS

At least 5% of patients undergoing surgery develop a surgical site infection (SSI). What methods can be taken to reduce SSIs?

'Methods to reduce SSIs can be divided into pre-op, intraop and post-op.

Pre-operative methods

Include MRSA screening pre-admission and decontamination if necessary. On the day of surgery patients shower and are given a gown. If shaving is necessary this should take place just prior to surgery and an electric single-use shaver should be used (not a razor as these increase SSIs). Consider antibiotic prophylaxis pre-procedure. Use antiseptic skin preparation pre-op such as Betadine® (iodine-based) or chlorhexidine. This should be applied to the skin in a circular or sweeping motion, as friction on skin removes some bacterial colonisation. I would apply this several times to high-risk areas (e.g. perineum, groin). When scrubbing-up the aim is to decrease bacterial skin count. Stiff brushes damage the epidermis so are only used on fingernails.

Intraoperative methods

Include the use of sterilised equipment. In addition, surgical technique is vitally important in reducing SSIs. An aseptic technique should be used with thorough debridement of dirty wounds or thorough lavage, for instance in faecal peritonitis. The operation duration should be minimised, as should spillage (using suction and swabs). Careful haemostasis prevents post-op haematomas, which are a site for potential infection. It is important (especially in orthopaedic theatres) to control air quality. The aim is to decrease the number of airborne particles carrying bacteria from skin flora. Laminar flow plus ultra-clean air systems give a two-fold reduction in post-op wound infections Another means to control air quality is to reduce the movement of staff as a greater number of people in theatre and movement through doors has been associated with an increase in infection rates. Barrier methods to reduce microbial spread include gowns. Those gowns with bacteria-impermeable fabrics can reduce bacterial air counts by 40–70%.

Caps are worn to prevent hair from falling in the wound. Masks can deflect forceful expirations such as coughs and sneezes that carry bacteria, though they have no effect on SSI rates. Gloves are also used, although, interestingly, glove punctures or tears do not affect the incidence of SSIs.

Post-operatively

The incidence of SSIs can be reduced by using an aseptic technique to change dressings and using sterile water to clean wounds if < 48 hours post-op. If necessary, I would look at wounds at the end of the ward round, not in the middle.'

What is the aim of using prophylactic antibiotics in surgery? How would you decide what to use and when to use it?

'The aim of antibiotic prophylaxis is to obtain high systemic levels at the time of the procedure to prevent bacteria from multiplying. The use of prophylactic antibiotics in surgery depends on how 'clean' the procedure is. Surgical wounds can be classified by how 'clean' they are. NICE guidelines suggest using antibiotics in clean surgery only if using an implant or prosthesis. However, antibiotic use is recommended in clean-contaminated surgery, contaminated surgery and dirty or infected wounds. It may be necessary to give prophylaxis up to 30 minutes prior to induction, for instance when using a tourniquet or opening the bowel. In addition, if surgery is prolonged and lasts longer than the half-life of the antibiotic, then a further dose intra-operatively may be appropriate. I would consult local guidelines which antibiotics to use as well as taking into consideration any patient factors such as allergies or renal impairment (e.g. with gentamicin).'

You mentioned classifying wounds as to how 'clean' they are. Can you tell us more about this classification and how it affects the SSI rate?

'A clean wound is incised through non-inflamed tissue. There is no entry into the GI tract, respiratory tract or genitourinary tract. The contamination rate is <2%. Clean-contaminated wounds are those where there has been entry into the respiratory tract, gut or genitourinary tract but with minimal controlled contamination. The contamination rate is 8–10%. A contaminated wound is one where there is gross spillage from the gut, an acute, non-purulent inflammation, an open traumatic wound > 12–24 hours old, or a penetrating animal or human bite. The contamination rate is 12–20 %. A dirty or infected wound occurs when there is visceral perforation (e.g. faecal peritonitis) or an acute inflammation with pus, or in traumatic wounds where treatment is delayed and there is faecal contamination or devitalised tissue. The contamination rate is >25%.'

Thank you. What can you tell us about the use of prophylactic antibiotics in patients at risk of infective endocarditis?

'Patients at risk for infective endocarditis include patients with valve replacements or valvular heart disease and those who have previously had infective endocarditis. New guidance has changed practice considerably and now prophylaxis is not required for dental procedures or procedures on the genitourinary, upper and lower respiratory or upper/lower gastrointestinal tracts. However, if an at-risk patient is undergoing a gastrointestinal or genitourinary procedure at a site where there is a suspected infection and they are already receiving antibiotics, then they should receive antibiotics which cover organisms which cause infective endocarditis.'

What is the difference between asepsis and antisepsis?

'Asepsis is the prevention of the introduction of bacteria to the surgical field whereas antisepsis is the destruction of pre-existing bacteria in the surgical field.'

What is the difference between sterilisation and disinfection?

'Sterilisation means complete destruction of ALL viable microorganisms, including spores and viruses, by means of heat, chemicals or irradiation. Only inanimate objects can be sterilised (e.g. not skin because it damages tissues). Conversely, disinfection is the treatment of tissue or hard surfaces in an attempt to DECREASE the bacterial count – some viruses and bacterial spores remain active. Examples are scrubbing-up or prepping the patient.'

What methods of sterilisation do you know?

'Methods to sterilise medical equipment include steam (or autoclave) sterilisation. This is the most widely used method and is cheap and dependable. It uses saturated steam at high pressures and temperatures. It works by the moist heat denaturing the proteins in microorganisms. Holding times depend on temperature and pressure, e.g. 132°C for 4 minutes or 121°C for 30 minutes. As it uses damp heat, some materials such as plastics cannot be sterilised this way as they melt. 'Flash sterilisation' is similar to conventional steam sterilisation, except the item is placed either in an open tray or special container to allow rapid penetration of steam. It can be used if there is insufficient time to sterilise equipment by the preferred method.

Dry heat sterilisation is used for moisture-impenetrable items, e.g. powders and surgical instruments with fine-cutting edges. These are essentially hot-air ovens with little or no water vapour. They are effective but inefficient (160°C for 2 hours or 170°C for 1 hour). Ethylene oxide sterilisation uses a highly penetrative gas which is effective at ambient temperatures and pressures. It is therefore commonly used to sterilise equipment which is heat- or moisture-sensitive (e.g. rubber, plastics, electrical equipment). It has a limited availability, takes up to 6 hours, is an irritant and is expensive. Newer sterilisation techniques that may take the place of ethylene oxide include hydrogen peroxide gas plasma and liquid peracetic acid.

Irradiation sterilisation using gamma rays is limited to industry, for instance for large batches of single-use items, e.g. catheters or syringes.'

What types of disinfectant do you know?
'Disinfection of inanimate objects can be carried out with low-temperature steam or boiling water; disinfection of skin can be carried out with alcohols, chlorhexidine or iodine.

Alcohol has its broadest spectrum at 70% concentration. It is rapidly effective against Gram-positive and -negative bacteria and has some anti-viral activity. However, it is relatively inactive against spores and fungi and therefore is not effective against *Clostridium difficile*. It works by denaturing proteins.

Chlorhexidine has a good activity against *Staphylococcus aureus* but only moderate activity against Gram-negative bacteria and some activity against *Pseudomonas* with poor activity against spores, fungi and viruses. It works by causing bacterial cell-wall disruption.

Iodine has a broad spectrum of activity against bacteria, spores, fungi and viruses. However, it is easily inactivated by blood, faeces and pus. Other disadvantages are that it is an irritant and can cause local hypersensitivity.'

PRINCIPLES OF ANAESTHESIA – LOCAL, SEDATION, GENERAL, PAIN MANAGEMENT

If you were explaining to a junior how to use local anaesthetic safely what would you cover?

'Firstly, they should take an allergy history from the patient to ensure they are not allergic to LAs. Next, assess the procedure to be carried out under LA to ensure it is practicable. Then explain what the use of local involves to the patient: for instance 'You will feel a sting a bit like a bee-sting, the area will become numb to pain, but you will still be able to feel pushing and pulling. Let me know if you feel pain.' Check the maximum safe dose for that patient and only draw up that amount. You might want to use an LA combined with adrenaline/epinephrine. The advantages are that this slows systemic absorption, therefore prolonging length of action and meaning a larger dose can be given. It also reduces bleeding, making the operative field clearer. However, you should never use LAs containing adrenaline/epinephrine near end-arteries (e.g. digits/penis) as this could cause ischaemic necrosis. It is kinder to warm the LA to room temperature to decrease the pain of injection. Swab the area prior to infiltration. Be sure to aspirate before infiltrating to ensure you are not inadvertently in a blood vessel. Once you have infiltrated the area check it is numb with toothed forceps first. Watch out for the signs of LA toxicity.'

Thank you, if you could stop there... You have mentioned LA toxicity – what are the symptoms, signs and initial treatment of this?

'LA toxicity is due to an overdose of LA. This can occur with inadvertent IV administration or cuff failure in a Bier's block. The symptoms can be CNS symptoms and signs such as perioral tingling, anxiety, dizziness, tinnitus, drowsiness and muscle twitching, progressing to seizures and coma. There are also cardiac symptoms and signs, e.g. chest pain, SOB, hypotension and dysrhythmias. Initial treatment of LA toxicity is to stop administering LA and proceed with an ABCD approach to resuscitation – they might ultimately need inotropic response.'

We have heard about some of the risks with using LA – what benefits are there?

'Using LA has the advantage of avoiding the risks of a GA such as VTE and cardiorespiratory complications. The patient needs less recovery time. LA can also be used in conjunction with GA, which reduces opiate requirements and the level of GA required.'

Can you describe to us what sedation is and when a surgeon might use it?
'Sedation is the administration of drugs to alleviate discomfort and distress during procedures WITH maintenance of patient responsiveness and protective reflexes. Commonly used drugs include benzodiazepines (e.g. midazolam, temazepam, diazepam) and opioids, e.g. fentanyl. It can be used during invasive procedures such as endoscopy or as an amnesic/analgesic such as during relocation of a dislocated shoulder.'

Can you describe to us the safety precautions you might take when using sedation?
'It is important to check for allergies first. Secure IV access must be obtained before proceeding. The patient should be monitored before and throughout the procedure with pulse oximetry and ECG leads and monitored with regular checks for responsiveness and obeying commands. The patient should be given supplemental oxygen. I would be prepared for an adverse reaction by ensuring I had an assistant and resuscitation equipment nearby before starting. The drug should be titrated slowly against response (especially if combined with an opiate as this increases the risks of cardiorespiratory depression). The monitoring must continue until full consciousness is regained and the patient should be discharged home with a responsible adult.'

What are the complications of general anaesthesia?
'Complications of GAs can be divided into problems with intubation, problems with anaesthetic drugs and cardiorespiratory complications.

Problems with intubation
Range from a difficult airway and failed intubation to damage to structures in the mouth, down to a post-operative sore throat.

Problems with anaesthetic drugs
Include anaphylaxis, post-operative nausea and vomiting, and malignant hyperpyrexia.

Cardiorespiratory complications
Include MI, hypo/hypertension and arrhythmias. Possible respiratory complications are airway obstruction, hypoventilation and hypoxia. Gastric aspiration can occur, leading to chest infection, so patients are starved pre-operatively.'

You mentioned malignant hyperpyrexia – what is this?
'Malignant hyperpyrexia is a familial disorder which can by triggered by most inhalational anaesthetics and suxamethonium. Rapid influx of calcium into

muscle cells causes uncontrolled increase in skeletal muscle metabolism. Treatment includes dantrolene sodium, surface cooling and cool IV fluids. Family members must be counselled appropriately.'

What approach would you take to post-operative pain management?
'Pain post-operatively is usually managed with a combination of different drugs. I would use the analgesic ladder, as I would with any patient in pain:

Step 1 – simple analgesic (paracetamol, NSAIDs)
Step 2 – mild opiates (tramadol, codeine)
Step 3 – strong opiates (morphine, fentanyl)

Epidurals and patient-controlled analgesia are commonly used to deliver pain relief.'

You mentioned epidural analgesia. How does this work?
'A catheter is introduced via a large-bore needle into the extradural space. A combination of local anaesthetic and opiates is often used. The catheter is situated at the level of the nerve roots which supply the site being operated on (e.g. lumbar for pelvic surgery or thoracic for upper abdominal surgery). It causes blockage of segmental nerves. As sensory and sympathetic nerves are smaller in diameter they are blocked more than the motor fibres. The sympathetic blockade can also cause peripheral vasodilatation and hence hypotension. It can be used as a continuous infusion for several days so it is used for peri- and post-op analgesia.'

What would the contraindications be to an epidural?
'Contraindications to an epidural include local sepsis at the site of injection, anticoagulation, previous back surgery or congenital abnormality of the spine. In addition, uncorrected hypovolaemia is a contraindication due to the peripheral vasodilatation and hence hypotension caused by the sympathetic blockade. Aortic stenosis is similarly a contraindication as these patients cannot increase cardiac output to counteract the peripheral vasodilatation. Patient refusal is a fairly common contraindication.'

What are the advantages of epidural analgesia?
'Epidural analgesia reduces the need for systemic opioids and so the incidence of their side-effects. The incidence of post-op chest infections is reduced as is the stress response to surgery. As it is a continuous infusion it works while the patient is sleeping or unconscious. It is also useful in patients who cannot use patient-controlled analgesia.'

What are the complications of epidural analgesia?

'Complications related to insertion or removal of the epidural catheter include failure to site the epidural or accidental dural tap, which can induce headache. There is a risk of infection – the risk of epidural abscess increases if the catheter is left in situ > 72 hours. Haematoma formation can occur on insertion or removal. Therefore, catheters should not be removed when the patient is anticoagulated (they can be removed 12 hours post-LMWH). The blockage of segmental nerves carries complications too. The anaesthetic spreads caudally and cranially. A high block may cause respiratory depression, impair cough and deep inspiration. Level is controlled by initial placement level, patient positioning, and volume and concentration of anaesthetic. Loss of control of the sympathetic nervous system leads to peripheral vasodilatation and hence hypotension. There is also a risk of falling and urinary retention.'

How is patient-controlled analgesia (PCA) delivered?

'PCA is administered via a microprocessor-controlled pump connected to the patient via an IV line, which is triggered by the patient pressing a button in their hand. A pre-set bolus of drug (opiate) is delivered and then a timer prevents administration of another bolus for a 'lock-out interval'. A loading dose must be given at the start to achieve adequate analgesia. Patients must be educated how to use the PCA and the 'lock-out' which prevents overdose should be explained.'

What are the advantages and disadvantages of PCA?

'The advantages of PCA include the dose being matched to the patient's requirements. As the patient controls it, this leads to increased patient autonomy and decreased nurse workload (although the nurses need to monitor respiratory rate and level of sedation). It is also painless (no IM injections).

Disadvantages include side-effects of systemic opioids (unlike an epidural). PCA relies on several factors. Firstly, constant IV access is required and a dedicated IV line should be used for PCA to ensure that the drug does not accumulate retrogradely. Secondly, the patient must be able to use the button, which excludes patients who are not fully orientated or who do not understand how to use the system, or those with physical barriers to use such as rheumatoid hands. Technical error can be fatal (especially with background infusions) and the equipment is expensive.'

POST-OPERATIVE COMPLICATIONS

Which patients are at particular risk of post-operative complications?
'Patients at the extremes of age are at risk of post-operative complications. Pre-existing co-morbidities such as cardiovascular disease, respiratory disease, renal impairment, diabetes and liver disease also predispose to post-operative complications. In addition, some medications such as steroids and immunosuppressant drugs can increase the risk.'

What are the possible post-operative complications of an open-mesh inguinal hernia repair under GA?
'The complications of an operation can be divided up into immediate, early and late, as well as into complications specific to the operation or those general to any operation.

Immediate complications of an open-mesh inguinal hernia repair can be operation-specific such as damage to nearby structures (e.g. bowel, femoral vessels, testicular artery, vas deferens) or common to all operations, such as haemorrhage, acute pain, risks of GA (e.g. MI or aspiration).

Early complications of an open mesh inguinal hernia repair can also be operation-specific, such as haematoma or seroma formation, urinary retention, numbness over the area of skin supplied by the ilioinguinal nerve; or they can be general to any operation, e.g. chest or urinary (if catheter inserted), sepsis, wound infection, DVT/PE.

Late complications of an open mesh inguinal hernia repair which are operation-specific include recurrence of hernia, chronic pain secondary to ilioinguinal nerve entrapment or chronic infection of the mesh. Examples of late general complications would be a hypertrophic scar or a stitch abscess or sinus.'

You mentioned MI as a potential post-operative complication of an open inguinal hernia repair. What risk factors would be associated with an increased incidence of post-op MI?
'The patient's pre-existing medical conditions can significantly increase the risk of an MI post-operatively. For instance, an MI within 3 months increases the risk of peri-operative infarction to 25%. If the hernia repair was elective it should be delayed by at least 6 months. A history of hypertension, IHD,

LVF and tachyarrhythmias also increases the risk of a post-op MI. For example, hypertension can double the risk of a peri-operative MI and an elective hernia repair should be postponed until this is adequately treated. We have talked about inguinal hernia repair, which is an intermediate-grade procedure, but any more prolonged or complex surgery, especially vascular or cardiothoracic, would increase the risk of an MI.'

SECTION 4: SURGICAL SCIENCE, CRITICAL CARE, ANATOMY AND PATHOLOGY

CHAPTER 10 APPLIED SURGICAL SCIENCE AND CRITICAL CARE

A INTRODUCTION

This section of the book aims to give you an insight into the format of these OSCE stations. Some common cases, examples and model answers will be discussed but for more details you are directed towards the excellent critical care section in *Essential Revision Notes for Intercollegiate MRCS: Book 1* which covers all of the key topics for the Part B OSCE examination.

B EXAMPLE OSCE STATION

You are the surgical CT2 on call and you have been asked to go to A&E to see a 77-year-old gentleman with abdominal and back pain who has collapsed in the street. His vital signs are given below:

Pulse 124 bpm
BP 90/60 mmHg
RR 35/min
Sats 96% 15LO$_2$

Tell me how you're going to assess him?
'This gentleman is obviously critically ill and I would assess him using the CCrISP® system, while ensuring that he is simultaneously resuscitated and optimised according to the ABCDE priorities. I would perform a focused history and examination followed by review of charts and any initial investigations. The key decision I am aiming to make is whether the patient is stable enough for further assessment and investigation or whether I need to prepare him for transfer to theatre for any surgical treatment as soon as possible.'

What is your differential diagnosis?
'He has a ruptured AAA until proven otherwise.'

Good, if you think that he has got a ruptured AAA tell me what you are going to do next?

- **IV access – x2 wide bore cannulas in the antecubital fossae**
- **Bloods – FBC, U&Es, clotting, cross-match 6 units**
- **Fluid resuscitation with warmed crystalloid**
- **Urinary catheterisation**
- **Inform the anaesthetic team**
- **Inform the theatre staff**
- **Obtain consent**
- **Inform the next of kin**

What blood pressure are you happy with?
'In this situation there is a good argument for aiming for a systolic blood pressure of no greater than 100 mmHg in order not to remove any clot that may be acting as a tamponade if the patient has survived so far. Having said that, I would rely more on clinical markers of perfusion, in particular urinary output, rather than a nominal systolic blood pressure value.'

The patient goes to theatre and at the end of the case the anaesthetist takes a blood sample. Some of the results are printed on this card. What do you make of them?

Results	(Normal range)
Hb 8 g/dl	(12–18 g/dl)
HCT 41%	(40–52%)
WCC 12.4	(4–11 × 10⁹/l)
Plt 88	(150–400 × 10⁹/l)
PT 18.5 s	(10–14 s)
APPT 55 s	(30–45 s)
Fibrinogen 0.8 mg/ml	(1.5–4 mg/ml)
FDP 25 mg/ml	(<10 mg/ml)

Comment on the results in a logical manner.

What could you give the patient in order to correct some of the abnormalities you have commented on?

'I would liaise with my anaesthetic colleagues and the haematologists in order to ensure optimum treatment. In the first instance the patient requires transfusion of packed red cells and fresh frozen plasma (FFP). I would have a low threshold for using a platelet transfusion. In order to correct the fibrinogen deficit, cryoprecipitate could be used after discussion with the haematologists.'

On arrival to ICU his temperature is 34.9°C. Does this concern you?

'Yes. Any temperature below 36°C is hypothermia. Hypothermia has potentially serious consequences, which include:

- Arrhythmias
- Clotting abnormalities
- Enzymatic dysfunction, and
- CNS depression'

Do you know of any ways of preventing hypothermia in surgical patients?

'All surgical patients should have their temperature measured and recorded regularly. Pre-operative risk factors for hypothermia include ASA > II, combined general and regional anaesthesia, major surgery and cardiovascular disease. Simple measures to keep patients comfortably warm are important: these include the use of sheets, blankets and forced-air heaters. Intraoperatively, forced-air heaters, keeping the patient covered until surgical preparation and warming all IV fluids and irrigation solutions can help to ensure normothermia. Post-operatively, blankets and forced-air warmers can also be used to ensure temperatures remain above 36°C.'

The following day the ICU nurse is concerned because he is passing very dark brown urine via his catheter and asks you to review him. What do you think is the most likely cause of this?

'In this situation the dark urine is most likely due to myoglobinuria secondary to rhabdomyolysis.'

What other more serious consequence of rhabdomyolysis would you be concerned about?

'Acute renal failure due to acute tubular necrosis (ATN).'

What is the pathophysiological mechanism for acute renal failure in this situation?

'The myoglobin is toxic and causes damage to the cells of the proximal tubule, which results in debris and cells obliterating the lumen of the tubule, causing acute renal failure.'

What is the treatment for acute renal failure in this situation?

'The principles of managing any organ system failure apply to acute renal failure: supportive therapy in an attempt to correct physiology while addressing the underlying cause of injury. In general terms, optimising renal perfusion, meticulous fluid balance, nutritional support, treatment of sepsis, avoidance of renotoxic medication and exclusion of post-renal causes with renal USS are the priorities. Ultimately there may be a need to provide renal replacement therapy.'

On reviewing his charts you discover that his serum potassium is 6.1 mmol/l. How would you manage this?

'The first step is to repeat the sample to ensure that it isn't erroneous, while instituting emergency measures. I would assess and secure the ABCs, obtain an ECG and, if any changes are present, give 10 ml of 10% calcium gluconate IV. I would then administer 50 ml of 50% dextrose with 10 units of Actrapid insulin. I would ensure the patient is on a cardiac monitor and recheck the potassium level in 2–6 hours. Any medication that can cause or potentiate hyperkalaemia will need to be omitted.'

What are the indications for renal replacement therapy?

'The four main indications are:
- Fluid overload
- Hyperkalaemia
- Metabolic acidosis
- Uraemic complications'

What problems might you encounter in this patient on renal support in the ICU?

'Haemorrhage is an important problem which might be iatrogenic due to the anticoagulation required for dialysis/filtration or due to the coagulopathy commonly associated with acute renal failure. Sepsis is a serious problem associated with renal support and patients may mask a pyrexia while on a haemofilter. Vascular access may also be difficult.'

C EXAMPLES OF COMMONLY OCCURRING STATIONS

The table below gives some examples of common stations and where to look for detailed information.

Station	Questions	Where to go
BURNS	Definitions Classification Assessment of severity IV fluids Resuscitation Transfer to a regional burns centre	*Essential Revision Notes for Intercollegiate MRCS: Book 1; Chapter 5*
ACUTE PANCREATITIS	Aetiology Clinical features Scoring systems and prognostication CT scan interpretation Complications	*Essential Revision Notes for Intercollegiate MRCS: Book 2; Chapter 1; Biliary Tree and Pancreas*
SIRS, SEPSIS, MODS	Definitions Management principles Surviving sepsis	*Essential Revision Notes for Intercollegiate MRCS: Book 2; Chapters 2 & 7*
SHOCK	Definition Classification Assessment and management principles	*Essential Revision Notes for Intercollegiate MRCS: Book 1; Chapter 5*
RESPIRATORY FAILURE AND ARDS	Definition and classification Treatment Respiratory assessment and function Oxygen dissociation ARDS causes and treatment	*Essential Revision Notes for Intercollegiate MRCS: Book 1; Chapter 7*

Station	Questions	Where to go
CARDIOVASCULAR	CO/BP/MAP/CVP/SVR Starling's law Control of BP/CO Flow/resistance Cardiac cycle and pharmacology Inotropes	*Essential Revision Notes* *for Intercollegiate MRCS:* *Book 1; Chapter 7*
RENAL FAILURE	Definitions Pre/Renal/Post Renal causes Emergency management Renal replacement	*Essential Revision Notes* *for Intercollegiate MRCS:* *Book 1; Chapter 7*
COMPARTMENT SYNDROME	Definition and clinical assessment Measurement and interpretation of compartment pressures Abdominal compartment syndrome	*Essential Revision Notes* *for Intercollegiate MRCS:* *Book 1; Chapter 9;* and *Essential Revision Notes* *for Intercollegiate MRCS:* *Book 2; Chapter 2*
NUTRITION	Assessment Requirements Relevance to surgical practice and metabolic response to surgery Routes – enteral vs parenteral, complications	*Essential Revision Notes* *for Intercollegiate MRCS:* *Book 1; Chapter 6*
HEAD INJURY	ATLS Management in emergency department Physiology – autoregulation, Cerebral perfusion pressure, Monro–Kellie doctrine	*Essential Revision Notes* *for Intercollegiate MRCS:* *Book 1; Chapter 5*
FLUID BALANCE	Fluid requirements Body compartments Assessment of fluid status CVP monitoring Electrolyte disturbances – Na, K, Ca, Mg IV fluid types and uses	*Essential Revision Notes* *for Intercollegiate MRCS:* *Book 1; Chapter 7*
ACID BASE	Definitions – pH, BE, anion gap, buffers, Henderson–Hasselbalch Metabolic/Respiratory Acidosis – causes, consequences, treatment	*Essential Revision Notes* *for Intercollegiate MRCS:* *Book 1; Chapter 7*

Station	Questions	Where to go
THERMOREGULATION	Temperature regulation Hypothermia – definitions, prevention, management	*Essential Revision Notes* *for Intercollegiate MRCS:* *Book 1; Chapter 2*
PNEUMOTHORAX	Clinical signs and assessment Thoracocentesis Chest drain insertion	*Essential Revision Notes* *for Intercollegiate MRCS:* *Book 1; Chapter 5*
ANAESTHESIA	Principles Pre-operative assessment Safe use of LA	*Essential Revision Notes* *for Intercollegiate MRCS:* *Book 1; Chapter 6*

CHAPTER 11 ANATOMY AND SURGICAL PATHOLOGY

A INTRODUCTION

This section of the book aims to give you an insight into the format of the Anatomy and Surgical Pathology OSCE stations. Some common cases, examples and model answers will be discussed but for more details you are directed towards the excellent sections in *Essential Revision Notes for Intercollegiate MRCS: Books 1 and 2*, which cover all of the key topics for the Part B OSCE examination.

The topics for the anatomy stations remain unchanged in the new format Part B OSCE exam. The traditional anatomy texts, together with a high-quality atlas and time in the dissection room and operating theatre remain the key to success.

B EXAMPLE OSCE STATION

The following is a realistic example of an OSCE case.

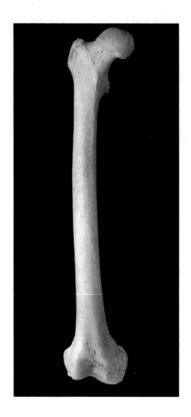

Which bone is this?
'This is a right femur.'

What is the blood supply to the head of the femur?
'There are three principal groups of vessels that supply the femoral head. The most important of these is from the trochanteric anastomosis, from which the nutrient vessels run along the neck of the femur to the head, bound under the retinacular fibres from the capsule. Some vessels also run in the ligamentum teres from the obturator artery, which is more important in childhood. The final supply comes from the vessels running up the medullary canal.'

Why is this relevant?

'In intracapsular fractures of the femoral neck the main retinacular vessels are commonly damaged, which can result in avascular necrosis of the femoral head and serious clinical consequences.'

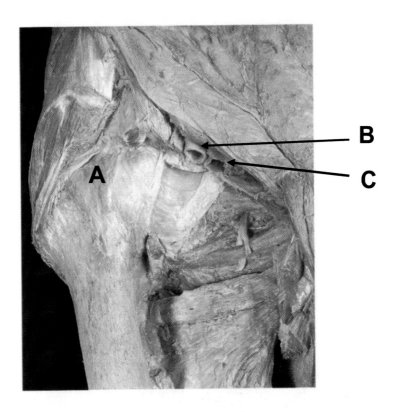

Regarding the hip joint, what is structure A?

'There are three ligaments of the hip joint. This one is the Y-shaped iliofemoral ligament and is the strongest and most important of these. It runs from the ilium to insert into the intertrochanteric line.'

What are structures B and C?

'B is the right femoral artery and C is the right femoral vein emerging from under the inguinal ligament.'

What is the surface landmark for the femoral artery?

'The femoral artery is located at the midinguinal point which lies at the mid-point between the ASIS and the symphysis pubis.'

693

Where then is the deep inguinal ring?

'This is located at the midpoint of the inguinal ligament, which runs between the ASIS and the pubic tubercle and is therefore located slightly lateral to the midinguinal point.'

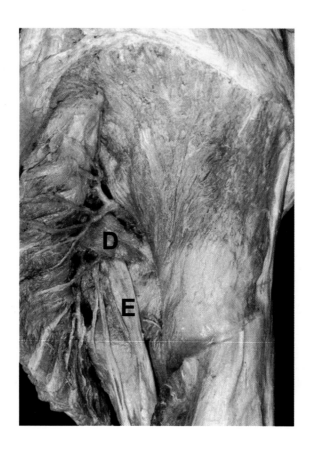

What structure is D?

'This is the right piriformis muscle.'

Which nerve is E? What is its root value and what are its main terminal branches?

'This is the right sciatic nerve. It originates from the lumbosacral trunk L4 and L5 and the sacral plexus S1, S2 and S3, which gives it the root value L4,5,S1,2,3. It has two terminal branches, the tibial and common peroneal nerves.'

Which nerve is at risk from a below-knee POP that is too tight? What are the clinical consequences of this?

'The common peroneal nerve is at risk with a below-knee POP where it winds around the head of the fibula. The clinical consequence of this is a patient presenting with foot drop due to paralysis of the dorsiflexor and evertor muscles supplied by this nerve.'

How, clinically, would you assess the integrity of the deep peroneal nerve?

'I would test for sensation in the first dorsal web space, between the hallux and second toe, which is an autonomous area for this nerve. I would expect decreased dorsiflexion and extension of the toes.'

Can you tell me why you might need to do this?

'A potential situation in which this may be necessary is when assessing a patient with a possible compartment syndrome.'

What is compartment syndrome?

'This is a progressive condition that develops when tissue pressure within a compartment exceeds capillary pressure and therefore compromises venous drainage and arterial inflow to that compartment. It is commonly seen within myofascial limb compartments but can also occur within the abdomen.'

If you found a palsy of the deep peroneal nerve, which compartment would this suggest has raised pressure?

'The deep peroneal nerve runs in the anterior compartment of the leg.'

CHAPTER 12
MOCK OSCE
EXAMINATIONS

A Examination 1

	STATION	QUESTION	COMMENTS
1. Anatomy and surgical pathology	Thyroid Thoracic inlet Brachial plexus	*'What is the blood supply to the thyroid? What surgical complications can occur post-thyroidectomy?'* *'What part of brachial plexus is this? What happens in an injury?'* *'Identify phrenic and vagus nerves.'*	Clear prosections. Examiner just asked direct questions and ticked boxes.
2. Anatomy and surgical pathology	Written 'Spot test'	Identify parts of the colon and appendix, abdominal wall muscles, branches of aorta.	Free text answers – difficult to know how much detail wanted. Abdominal wall dissection – difficult to work out layers.
3. Anatomy and surgical pathology	Thorax Lungs Pulmonary embolism	*'Describe the surface anatomy of the lungs and fissures.'* *'Identify lung hilar/root structures.'* *'Show me the left/right lungs from the specimens and explain your answer.'*	
4. Surgical skills and patient safety	Suturing skills Patient with a simulated injury on a pad attached to arm Range of sutures and instruments available	*'Please repair this laceration using non-absorbable suture in your usual manner.'*	Don't forget to confirm anaesthetic in situ and consented. Practice on the pads – more difficult than skin! Forgot tetanus.
5. REST			

	STATION	QUESTION	COMMENTS
6. Surgical skills and patient safety	Peri-operative care Surgical equipment	*'Discuss the problems and management of diabetes, allergies, MRSA in surgical patients on an elective list.'* *'What type of diathermy would you use for hernia/ amputation/with pacemaker?'* *'What skin prep do you use?'*	
7. Communication skills	Written communication	*'Your patient is on warfarin for a metallic MVR and needs an elective hernia repair. Please write to the GP about the plan for anticoagulation.'*	Time was limited – had to go through letters and then summarise and give instructions.
8. Applied surgical science and critical care	Data station Acute pancreatitis	History and initial assessment of patient with characteristic abdominal pain and associated symptoms. *'What is your differential diagnosis?' 'What do the blood results suggest?' 'What is the metabolic abnormality on the ABG result?'* *'Comment on the CXR/AXR/CT below.'* *'Describe your initial management in the emergency department.'*	Lots and lots of results and details to go through before even answering a question. Didn't finish a whole page of questions.
9. Applied surgical science and critical care	Fluid balance Fistulae Nutrition	*'How do you assess fluid needs post-laparotomy?'* *'How do you assess nutritional requirements?'* *'What methods of nutritional support available?'* *'What is a fistula?'*	Know the figures for weight-based fluid/electrolyte/nutritional needs.
10. Applied surgical science and critical care	Data station Acute abdomen	Written case presentation patient with RIF abdominal pain, anorexia and nausea. *'What is your differential diagnosis?'* *'What do the blood results suggest?' 'What does the ECG show?' – AF, 'and what steps do you need to take?'*	

STATION		QUESTION	COMMENTS
BREAK			
11. Communication skills **Preparation station**	A scenario detailing the case of a post-operative patient wanting to self-discharge from a ward is provided	*'Please read the details of the case provided and use the time to prepare to speak to the patient and discuss his/her decision.'*	
12. Communication skills	A scenario detailing the case of a post-operative patient wanting to self-discharge from a ward is provided An actor will play the role of the patient	*'Please discuss this and assess whether he is competent to make this decision.'*	Actor was enthusiastic and easy to talk to. Examiners didn't speak at all. Finished very early.
13. Communication skills **Preparation station**	A scenario about a patient requiring transfer to ICU with details of the history, examination and investigation results is provided	*'Read the information provided and use the time to prepare to discuss the case with an anaesthetist.'*	

	STATION	QUESTION	COMMENTS
14. Communication skills	Telephone the on-call ICU consultant using the provided telephone. An examiner will play the role of the consultant on the telephone	*'Please telephone the on-call ICU consultant about this patient, who underwent an anterior resection and now needs ICU care due to respiratory and acute renal failure.'*	Had to actually use the telephone. Lots of written info and results – only time to pick out and note down a few key ones. Consultant was difficult and I didn't get the bed. Had to argue my patient's corner as already had an A&E patient lined up for the last bed.
15. Clinical skills History	Dysphagia	*'Please take a history from this lady with difficulty swallowing.'*	Actor was friendly and allowed me to direct and focus the history.
16. REST			
17. Clinical skills History	Post-operative DVT/PE	*'Please take a history from this lady who had a THR 4 days ago and now feels SOB.'* *'What diagnostic tests do you want to do?'* *'What is your management plan?'*	
18. Clinical skills Physical examination	Osteoarthritis knee	*'This lady is complaining of pain in her right knee – please examine her and ask some questions.'* *'What are the treatment options?'*	
19. Clinical skills Physical examination	Large incisional hernia in previous laparotomy wound	*'Please examine this gentleman's abdomen and ask him some relevant questions.'* *'What problems could occur if you repaired it?'*	
20. Clinical skills Physical examination	Cardiovascular assessment patient with prosthetic aortic valve and CABG	*'This gentleman needs a right hemicolectomy for a descending colonic cancer. Please examine him and ask him some questions about his fitness for surgery.'* *'What tests do you want to do?'* *'Would you like to speak to anybody else?'* *'Would you operate on him?'*	

B Examination 2

	STATION	QUESTION	COMMENTS
1. Anatomy and surgical pathology	Carotid sheath – carotid arteries, jugular veins Salivary glands	*'Identify the carotid arteries and any visible branches.'* *'What structures are related to the parotid gland?'* *'Where are the salivary glands located and where do they open?'*	
2. Anatomy and surgical pathology	Written 'Spot test'	Lower limb major neurovascular structures, dermatomes, leg muscles and their actions	Difficult and detailed written answers.
3. Anatomy and surgical pathology	Carpal tunnel Upper limb nerves	*'Identify the carpal bones, flexor retinaculum and contents of the carpal tunnel.'* *'What is carpal tunnel syndrome?'* *'What would be the clinical presentation of median/ ulnar/radial nerve palsy?'*	
4. Surgical skills and patient safety	Hand washing	*'Please scrub, put on a surgical gown and gloves, as if you were about to start an operation.'*	
5. REST			
6. Surgical skills and patient safety	Trauma	*'Assess this patient who has just arrived in the emergency department following a motor vehicle collision.'* *'What different types of airway are you aware of?'* *'What are the options for intravenous access?'*	Had to insert a cannula into a simulated arm.
7. Communication skills	Written communication	*'Write a transfer letter to the regional neurosurgical centre for a patient with a head injury.'*	Not enough time.

STATION	QUESTION	COMMENTS
8. Applied surgical science and critical care	Data station Bowel obstruction AXR small-bowel obstruction Causes, investigations, management Metabolic acidosis ABG analysis	Ran out of time. Too much information to wade through.
9. Applied surgical science and critical care	Transfusions Intra-operative monitoring 'What parameters are measured during operations?' 'What are the complications of transfusions?' 'What blood products can be used in post-operative bleeding?'	
10. Applied surgical science and critical care	Data station Pancreatitis AXR, CT abdomen Haematology/biochemistry results ABG interpretation Complications	
BREAK		
11. Communication skills Preparation station	A scenario surrounding a critically ill patient deemed to be unfit for a surgical procedure is provided 'Please read the details of the case provided and use the time to prepare to speak to the patient's next of kin.'	
12. Communication skills	Communication skills with relatives An actor will play the role of the next of kin 'Please discuss with the patient's spouse the decision that has been taken not to offer further surgery to this patient with metastatic malignancy and, in the event of deterioration, not to attempt resuscitation.'	

	STATION	QUESTION	COMMENTS
13. Communication skills **Preparation station**	A scenario about a patient requiring transfer to ICU with details of the history, examination and investigation results is provided	*'Read the information provided and use the time to prepare to discuss the case with an anaesthetist.'*	Lots of information to read.
14. Communication skills	Telephone the on-call ICU consultant using the provided telephone An examiner will play the role of the consultant	*'Please telephone the on-call ICU consultant about this patient who needs HDU care for resuscitation prior to laparotomy.'*	
15. Clinical skills **History**	Post-operative patient with low mood	*'Please take a history from this patient who is feeling low following a prolonged stay in hospital.'* *'Any organic causes of depression?'* *'Any risk to herself or others?'* *'Who else would you involve?'*	Very convincing and upset actor. Non-verbal communication seemed important.
16. REST			
17. Clinical skills **History**	Mechanical back pain in a patient with potential cauda equina syndrome	*'Please take a history from this gentleman with back pain.'* *'What would you expect to find on examination?'* *'What further investigations would you request?'* *'What would be your management plan?'*	Actor was friendly but not sure he realised the significance of the neurological symptoms – I had to work hard to get the full story.

	STATION	QUESTION	COMMENTS
18. Clinical skills **Physical examination**	Post-operative patient DVT/PE	*'Please examine this patient who is day 5 following THR and is complaining of SOB.'* *'What is the diagnostic investigation?'* *'What is your treatment plan?'* *'What are the preventative strategies?'*	No physical signs on examination of the patient – I think it was an actor.
19. Clinical skills **Physical examination**	Recurrent inguinal hernia	*'Please examine this gentleman's right groin swelling.'* *'What are the management options?'* *'What do you need to warn him to look out for?'*	
20. Clinical skills **Physical examination**	Peripheral arterial disease History of intermittent claudication	*'Please examine this patient.'* *'What is your differential diagnosis?'* *'What investigations would you request?'* *'What are the treatment options?'*	No Doppler or equipment for ABPI provided.

C Examination 3

	STATION	QUESTION	COMMENTS
1. Anatomy and surgical pathology	Shoulder joint Rotator cuff	*'Identify the major anatomical structures on this scapula. Which side is it from?'* *'Is the shoulder joint a stable joint?'* *'Identify the muscles of the rotator cuff. What is their nerve supply and how do you test them clinically?'*	Clear prosections. Limited pathology questioning.
2. Anatomy and surgical pathology	Written 'Spot test'	Identification and osteology of femur Quadriceps origin/insertion/nerve supply/action Femoral artery Saphenous vein	
3. Anatomy and surgical pathology	Antecubital fossae Femoral triangle	*'What are the boundaries/contents of the antecubital fossa?'* *'What structures are found in the femoral triangle? What is the femoral sheath? Where do femoral herniae emerge?'*	
4. Surgical skills and patient safety	Suturing Simulated traumatic wound	*'Please repair this forearm laceration (sustained traumatically on glass from a smashed bottle) in your usual manner.'*	Issues around tetanus, X-ray imaging and scarring.
5. REST			
6. Surgical skills and patient safety	Intravenous access, venepuncture	Intravenous drug abuser with a groin abscess. Obtain intravenous access and obtain blood cultures. Discussion on blood-borne viruses and universal precautions for infection control.	

STATION	QUESTION	COMMENTS
7. Applied surgical science and critical care Regional anaesthesia Analgesia	Post-operative laparotomy patient with epidural in situ. *'Please assess this patient who is hypotensive on day 1 post-op. How may patients with epidurals become hypotensive? Discuss the options for analgesia if the epidural is turned off.'*	
8. Communication skills Written communication	*'Write to a patient's GP in order to arrange admission for a patient on warfarin for an elective procedure that necessitates peri-operative anti-coagulation due to a metallic valve replacement.'*	
9. Applied surgical science and critical care Pancreatitis	Clinical features, diagnosis, scoring and management Fluid balance Nutrition	
10. Applied surgical science and critical care Data station Acute abdomen	CXR/AXR interpretation ECG analysis ABG – metabolic acidosis causes and management	Lots and lots of results to deal with in limited time.
BREAK		
11. Communication skills Written station Informed consent Preparation station	*'Please read through the information and use this time to prepare to consent the patient for an anterior resection for a rectal cancer.'*	
12. Communication skills Communication skills with patients An actor will play the role of the patient	*'Please consent this patient for an anterior resection for rectal cancer.'*	Concerns regarding a stoma and a relative who died following a surgical procedure.

707

STATION	QUESTION	COMMENTS
13. Communication skills **Preparation station**	*'Read the information provided and use the time to prepare to discuss the case with the on-call neurosurgical consultant.'*	
A scenario about a patient requiring transfer to neurosurgical ICU with details of the history, examination and investigation results provided		
14. Communication skills	*'Please telephone the on call neurosurgical consultant about a patient who needs transfer to the regional neurosurgical centre following a traumatic head injury.'*	Difficult issues regarding beds and competing patients!
Communication skills with colleagues An examiner will play the role of the consultant		
15. Clinical skills **History**	*'Please make a full assessment of this lady who has a painful knee.'* *'What investigations would you like to do?'* *'What X-ray changes would you expect?'* *'What are the treatment options for this lady?'*	
Knee osteoarthritis		
16. REST		
17. Clinical skills **History**	*'Please take a history from this gentleman in the pre-assessment clinic prior to a hernia repair.'* *'What tests would you like to order?'*	
Shortness of breath COPD		

	STATION	QUESTION	COMMENTS
18. Clinical skills **Physical examination**	Cardiovascular examination Coronary artery bypass graft Pacemaker	'Please examine this lady who is scheduled to undergo a laparoscopic cholecystectomy.' 'What challenges does a pacemaker pose for surgeons?'	
19. Clinical skills **Physical examination**	Lower limb neurological examination	Young patient with mechanical back pain 'Please examine this patient's legs.'	No abnormal signs – actor I think.
20. Clinical skills **Physical examination**	Hip osteoarthritis	'Please assess this lady who has a painful hip.' 'What are the treatment options?'	

ABBREVIATIONS LIST

A&E	Accident and Emergency (Department)
AAA	Abdominal aortic aneurysm
ABCD(E)	Airway, breathing, circulation, disability (exposure)
ABG	Arterial blood gases
ABPI	Ankle–brachial pressure index
ACE(I)	Angiotensin-converting enzyme (inhibitor)
ADH	Antidiuretic hormone
ADLs	Activities of daily living
AF	Atrial fibrillation
AFB	Acid-fast bacilli
AFP	Alpha-fetoprotein
AIDS	Acquired immunodeficiency syndrome
AP	Anteroposterior (X-ray view)
APR	Abdominoperineal resection
APTT	Activated partial thromboplastin time
ARDS	Adult respiratory distress syndrome
AS	Ankylosing spondylitis
AS	Aortic stenosis
ASA	American Society of Anesthesiologists
ASD	Atrial septal defect
ASIS	Anterior superior iliac spine
ATLS	Advanced Trauma Life Support
ATN	Acute tubular necrosis
AXR	Abdominal X-ray
BCC	Basal cell carcinoma
BE	Base excess
BMI	Body mass index
BP	Blood pressure
BTA	British Thyroid Association
CABG	Coronary artery bypass graft
CBD	Common bile duct
CNS	Central nervous system
CO	Cardiac output
COPD	Chronic obstructive pulmonary disease
CREST	Calcinosis, Raynaud's, o(e)sophageal dysmotility, sclerodactyly, telangiectasia
CRP	C-reactive protein
CSF	Cerebrospinal fluid
CT	Computed tomography

CTA	CT angiography
CVA	Cerebrovascular accident
CVP	Central venous pressure
CXR	Chest X-ray
DCIS	Ductal carcinoma in situ
DIC	Disseminated intravascular coagulation
DIP(J)	Distal interphalangeal (joint)
DRE	Digital rectal examination
DU	Duodenal ulcer
DVT	Deep vein thrombosis
EBV	Epstein–Barr virus
ESR	Erythrocyte sedimentation rate
EUS	Endoscopic ultrasound
FBC	Full blood count
FDP	Fibrin/fibrinogen degradation products
FFP	Fresh frozen plasma
FNA	Fine-needle aspiration
FSH	Follicle-stimulating hormone
GA	General anaesthetic
GB	Gallbladder
GCS	Glasgow coma scale
GI	Gastrointestinal
GORD	Gastro-oesophageal reflux disease
GTN	Glyceryl trinitrate
GVHD	Graft-versus-host disease
Hb	Haemoglobin
HBV	Hepatitis B virus
HCG	Human chorionic gonadotropin
HCV	Hepatitis C virus
HCT	Haematocrit
HDU	High Dependency Unit
HIV	Human immunodeficiency virus
HOCM	Hypertrophic obstructive cardiomyopathy
HR	Heart rate
HRT	Hormone replacement therapy
HTLV	Human T-cell lymphotropic virus
IBD	Inflammatory bowel disease
ICP	Intracranial pressure
ICU	Intensive Care Unit
IHD	Ischaemic heart disease
IM	Intramuscular
IMA	Inferior mesenteric artery

IUCD	Intrauterine contraceptive device
IV	Intravenous
IVC	Inferior vena cava
IVDU	Intravenous drug user
IVU	Intravenous urethrography
JVP	Jugular venous pressure
KUB	Kidney, ureter, bladder (study)
LA	Local anaesthetic
LCIS	Lobular carcinoma in situ
LFT	Liver function test
LIF	Left iliac fossa
LMP	Last menstrual period
LMWH	Low-molecular-weight heparin
LN	Lymph node
LOC	Loss of consciousness
LP	Lumbar puncture
LUQ	Left upper quadrant
LVF	Left ventricular failure
MAP	Mean arterial pressure
MCP(J)	Metacarpophalangeal (joint)
MEN	Multiple endocrine neoplasia
MI	Myocardial infarction
MR	Mitral regurgitation
MRA	Magnetic resonance angiography
MRI	Magnetic resonance imaging
MRSA	Methicillin-resistant *Staphylococcus aureus*
MS	Multiple sclerosis
MVR	Mitral valve replacement
NG	Nasogastric
NICE	National Institute for Health and Clinical Excellence
NSAID	Non-steroidal anti-inflammatory drug
NSGCT	Non-seminomatous germ cell tumour
OA	Osteoarthritis
OCP	Oral contraceptive pill
OGD	Oesophagogastroduodenoscopy
ORIF	Open reduction with internal fixation
PCA	Patient-controlled analgesia
PCI	Percutaneous coronary intervention
PE	Pulmonary embolism
PEG	Percutaneous endoscopic gastrostomy
PET	Positron-emission tomography
PIP(J)	Proximal interphalangeal (joint)

Plt	Platelets
PND	Paroxysmal nocturnal dyspnoea
POP	Plaster of Paris
PR	Per rectum
PSIS	Posterior superior iliac spine
PT	Prothrombin time
PUD	Peptic ulcer disease
PUVA	Psoralen drugs with UV light
PV	Per vagina
PVD	Peripheral vascular disease
RA	Rheumatoid arthritis
RBC	Red blood cell
RIF	Right iliac fossa
RIG	Radiologically inserted gastrostomy
RLQ	Right lower quadrant
RR	Respiratory rate
RTA	Road traffic accident
RUQ	Right upper quadrant
SAH	Subarachnoid haemorrhage
SCC	Squamous cell carcinoma
SFJ	Sapheno-femoral junction
SIRS	Systemic inflammatory response syndrome
SOB(OE)	Short/shortness of breath (on exertion)
SOL	Space-occupying lesion
SSI	Surgical site infection
SVC	Superior vena cava
SVR	Systemic vascular resistance
T3	Triiodothyronine
T4	Thyroxine
TB	Tuberculosis
TEDS	Thromboembolic deterrent stockings
TFT(s)	Thyroid function test(s)
THR	Total hip replacement
TIA	Transient ischaemic attack
TNF(α)	Tumour necrosis factor (alpha)
TOE	Transoesophageal echocardiography
TPN	Total parenteral nutrition
TRAM	Transverse rectus abdominis myocutaneous (flap)
TRH	Thyrotropin-releasing hormone
TSH	Thyroid-stimulating hormone
TURP	Transurethral resection of the prostate
URTI	Upper respiratory tract infection

U&Es	Urea and electrolytes
UC	Ulcerative colitis
UGI	Upper gastrointestinal
UICC	Union Internationale Contre le Cancer
USS	Ultrasound scan
UTI	Urinary tract infection
VSD	Ventricular septal defect
VTE	Venous thromboembolism
WBC	White blood cell
WCC	White cell count

BIBLIOGRAPHY

ABC of Breast Disease: Dixon, 1st edition, BMJ Books, 1997.

ABC of Colorectal Disease: Jones D J, Irving MJ, 2nd edition, BMJ Books, 1999.

ABC of Urology: Dawson C, Whitfield H, 1st edition, BMJ Books, 1997.

An Aid to the MRCP Short Cases: Ryder, REJ et al., 1st edition, Blackwell Scientific Publications, 1992.

An Introduction to the Symptoms and Signs of Surgical Disease: Browse N, 3rd edition, Arnold Publishing (Hodder Headline), 1997.

Cash's Textbook of Orthopaedics and Rheumatology for Physiotherapists:

Tidswell, ME, Downie PA et al (editors) Mosby Year Book Europe Ltd., 1992.

Clinical Anatomy for Medical Students: Snell RS, 6th edition, Lippincott Williams & Williams, 2000.

Clinical Orthopaedic Examination: McRae R, 3rd edition, Churchill Livingstone, 1996.

Clinical Signs: Hayes C and Bell D, new edition, Churchill Livingstone, 1996.

Concise System of Orthopaedics and Fractures: Apley A G, and Solomon, L. 2nd edition Butterworth Heinemann, 1998.

Operative Surgery: Calne R and Pollard, S, Gower Medical Publishing, 1991.

Oxford textbook of Medicine: Weatherall, D.J. et al. 3rd edition, Oxford University Press, 1996.

Picture Tests in Surgery: Stiff et al, 1st edition, Churchill Livingstone, 1996.

Practice Exercise Therapy: Hollis M, Blackwell Scientific Publications, 1998.

Practical Fracture Treatment: McRae R, 2nd edition, Churchill Livingstone, 1989.

Spot diagnosis in General Surgery: Ellis H, 2nd edition, Blackwell Science Ltd., 1993.

The New Aird's Companion in Surgical Studies: Burnand K et al, 2nd edition, Churchill Livingstone, 1998.

INDEX

SUMMARY CARDS

Feeling in need of a helping hand towards success in your exams?
The following set of summary cards are to cut out and keep for handy
reference.

CONTENTS

EXAMINATION OF THE ISCHAEMIC OR DIABETIC LEG

Introduction
Lie down
Trousers and socks off

Inspection
General signs of:
  Cardiovascular disease
  Cigarette smoking
  Diabetes
Legs
  Pallor
  Guttering of veins
  Discoloration
  Ulcers
  Buerger's test (now or offer at the end)
    Raise leg slowly supporting heel
    Note angle at which foot blanches
    Swing leg over edge of bed
    Purple discoloration?
Feet
  Ulcers on pressure areas
  (heel, malleoli, head of fifth metatarsal,
  tips of toes, between toes, ball of foot)

Palpation
Temperature
Capillary refill
Pulses Femoral
    Popliteal
    Dorsalis pedis
    Posterior tibial
    Aortic aneurysm

continued overleaf

EXAMINATION OF VARICOSE VEINS

Introduction
Standing
Trousers off

Inspection
Visible dilated/tortuous veins
Venous stars
Signs of venous insufficiency in gaiter area:
  Oedema
  Haemosiderin deposition
  Lipodermatosclerosis
  Excema
  Ulceration

Palpation
Feel the veins
Test for pitting oedema
Defects in the deep fascia
Groins:
  Saphenofemoral junction (?varix)
  Cough impulse
  Tap test

Tourniquet test
Lie patient down
Lift leg, resting ankle on your shoulder
Empty veins
Apply tourniquet around upper thigh
Stand up
Do veins fill immediately?
  No – varicosities controlled at SFJ
  Yes – incompetence lower down

continued overleaf

EXAMINATION OF THE CRANIAL NERVE

Introduction
Smell
Eyes
  Visual acuity
  Pupil reflex
  Visual fields
  Eye movements
  Accommodation reflex
  Fundoscopy
Facial sensation
Facial muscle testing
Hearing
Taste and gag reflex
Palate
Head turning and shoulder shrug
Tongue
Summary sentence and diagnosis

Auscultation
Aorta and renal arteries
Femoral arteries
Adductor hiatus

Offer if appropriate
Examine rest of vascular tree including:
  Carotid arteries
  Heart murmurs
  Atrial fibrillation
  Blood pressure In both arms
Ankle-brachial pressure index
Summary sentence and diagnosis

Perthes test
Leave tourniquet on
Up and down on tiptoes working calf
  veins get better:
**'The deep venous system appears to be
functioning'**
  veins get worse and the patient develops severe
  discomfort:
**'There may be problems with the deep venous
system.'**

Offer if appropriate:
Abdominal and rectal examination
Doppler ultrasound assessment
Summary sentence and diagnosis

Introduction
  Tenderness
  Site
  Size
Define
  Shape
  Depth
Edges (sloping, punched out, undermined, rolled,
everted)
Base (healthy, sloughy, avascular, necrotic,
underlying structures)
Surrounding tissues (arterial, venous, neurological)

Offer if appropriate
Vascular examination
Neurological examination
Venous examination

Make a diagnosis
  Is the ulcer painless?
    Yes   No
(neurological)   Are foot pulses present?
        Yes   No
    (probably venous) (probably ischaemic)
Beware of multiple pathology especially in diabetics
Summary of findings and diagnosis

EXAMINATION OF THE ISCHAEMIC ARM

Introduction
Sitting
Shirt off

Inspection
General
  Signs of cardiovascular disease
  Short of breath
  Overweight
  Cyanosed
  Signs of cardiac surgery
Hands
  Cyanosis
  Nicotine staining
  Clubbing
  Vasculitic lesions
  Wasting of the pulp of the finger
  Skin changes
  Pallor
  Discoloration

Palpation
Temperature of the hands
Capillary refill
Radial pulse
Collapsing pulse? (raise wrist)
Radio-radial delay? (check other pulse)
Stretch thoracic inlet (pull on arm) – does pulse
  weaken?

continued overleaf

EXAMINATION OF THE ABDOMINAL AORTIC
ANEURYSM

Introduction
Lie flat with one pillow

Inspection
General (Shocked, pale, in pain, breathless)
Hands
  Pulse
  Pale palmar creases
  Nicotine staining
  Blood pressure in both arms
Eyes
  Arcus senilis
  Xanthomata
Neck
  Carotid pulse (character and bruit)
Abdomen
  Inspection
    Masses
    Scars
  Palpation of pulsatile mass
    Tender?site, size (transverse diameter)
    Shape, surface, edges
    Consistency (fluctuance, pulsatility,
    compressability, reducibility)
    Expansile?
    Upper and lower margins
    Femoral pulses
  Auscultate
    Aneurysm
    Renal arteries
    Femoral pulses

Offer if appropriate
Examine heart for cardiovascular disease
Examine legs for peripheral vascular disease
Summary sentence and diagnosis

continued overleaf

EXAMINATION OF THE HEART

Introduction
Sit at 45°
Shirt off

Inspection
General
  Breathlessness
  Cyanosis
  Palor
  Malar flush
  Scars
  Ankle oedema
Hands
  Clubbing
  Splinter haemorrhages
Pulses
  Rate
  Collapsing pulse
  Radio-radial delay
  Brachial pulses
  Blood pressure
Eyes
  Sclera pale?
Mouth
  Central cyanosis
Neck
  JVP
  Liver pressure
  Carotid pulse
Precordium
  Scars
  Pulsation

continued overleaf

SUMMARY CARD

MRCS PART B OSCEs
Essential Revision Notes

PASTEST
Dedicated to your success

EXAMINATION OF THE HEART (cont'd)

Palpation
Apex beat
Left sternal edge
Manubrium
Heaves or thrills?

Auscultation
Mitral area (left fourth intercostal space – rolled to left)
Tricuspid area (left fifth intercostal space – breathing out)
Pulmonary area (left second intercostal space – sitting up)
Aortic area (right second intercostal space – sitting up)
Carotid arteries
Lung bases

Check for sacral oedema

Offer if appropriate
Rest of vascular tree including peripheral vascular disease in legs

Summary sentence and diagnosis

SUMMARY CARD

MRCS PART B OSCEs
Essential Revision Notes

PASTEST
Dedicated to your success

EXAMINATION OF A THYROID LUMP

Introduction
Sitting on a chair away from the wall
Neck exposed

Inspection from the front
?Swelling, site, side.
Sip of water – moves with swallowing?
stick out tongue

Palpation from behind
Is it tender?
Left lobe – swallow
Right lobe – swallow

Describe the lump (see card)
Introduction: (tenderness, site, size)
Define: (shape, surface, edges)
Composition: (consistency, fluctuance, pulsatility, compressability, reducibility)
Layer of origin: (fixity, tethering)
Overlying and surrounding skin

Examine lymph nodes

Offer if appropriate:
Percuss for retrosternal extension
Auscultate for a Graves' bruit
Assess thyroid status

Summary of findings and diagnosis

SUMMARY CARD

MRCS PART B OSCEs
Essential Revision Notes

PASTEST
Dedicated to your success

EXAMINATION OF THE ISCHAEMIC ARM (cont'd)

Allen's test
Patient makes a fist
Occlude both ulnar and radial pulses
Patient opens palm (looks white)
Release ulnar artery – does palm pink up?
Patient makes a fist
Occlude both ulnar and radial pulses
Patient opens palm (looks white)
Release radial artery – does palm pink up?

Other pulses
Brachial (ask for BP in both arms)
Axillary
Subclavian
Carotid
Cervical rib

Auscultation
Carotid
Subclavian

Offer if appropriate
Examination of the heart
Vascular examination of lower limb
Neurological examination of arm

Summary sentence and diagnosis

MRCS PART B OSCEs
Essential Revision Notes

PASTEST

EXAMINATION OF A NECK LUMP

Introduction
Sit on a chair away from the wall
Neck exposed
Inspection
Face
    Myxoedema
    Hyperthyroidism
    Plethoric facies
Neck
    Neck lump
Offer the patient a drink
Moves with swallowing?
Stick out tongue
Moves with extending the tongue?
Palpate the neck from behind
Tender?
Obvious thyroid lump?
    Thyroid lump examination (see card)
Lump elsewhere?
    Describe the lump (see card)
    Introduction: (tenderness, site, size)
    Define: (shape, surface, edges)
    Composition: (consistency, fluctuance,
    pulsatility, compressability, reducibility)
    Layer of origin: (fixity, tethering)
    Overlying and surrounding skin
Examine lymph nodes
Summary sentence and differential diagnosis

www.pastest.co.uk

continued overleaf

MRCS PART B OSCEs
Essential Revision Notes

PASTEST

EXAMINATION OF THYROID STATUS

Introduction
Sit on a chair away from the wall
Neck exposed
Inspection
Signs of hyperthyroidism:
    tremor, restlessness, wasting
Signs of hypothyroidism:
    myxoedema facies, a dull aspect or periorbital
    puffiness
Goitre
Scars in the neck
Hands and pulse
Hyperthyroid
    sweaty, warm palms
    tachycardic/irregular pulse
    acropachy
Hypothyroid
    dry, cool and pale
    rough, inelastic skin
    non-pitting puffiness
    ?tingling or numbness in the hands
    ?bradycardic
Face: looking ahead
Graves' disease:
    Exophthalomus
    Lid retraction
    Signs of corneal irritation
    Lid lag
Hypothyroid:
    Thinning, dry, brittle hair
    Loss of the outer third of the eyebrows
    Sallow complexion

continued overleaf

MRCS PART B OSCEs
Essential Revision Notes

PASTEST

EXAMINATION OF A LUMP

Introduction
Patient comfortable, lump exposed.
Describe the lump in six separate sentences
1. Introduction
Tenderness
Site
Size
'There is a 3 cm non-tender lump on the right
shoulder'
2. Define
Shape
Surface
Edges
'It is hemispherical in shape with a smooth surface
and diffuse edges'
3. Composition
Consistency
Fluctuance
Pulsatility
Compressability
Reducibility
'It is rubbery and fluctuant, and is not pulsatile,
compressible or reducible'
4. Layer of origin
Fixity
Tethering
'It is not tethered to the overlying skin, which moves
over it,
and is not fixed to the underlying muscle,
so appears to arise from the subcutaneous tissues'
5. Overlying and surrounding skin
'The overlying skin is normal'

continued overleaf

733

SUMMARY CARD

MRCS PART B OSCEs
Essential Revision Notes

PASTEST

EXAMINATION OF THE PAROTID LUMP

Introduction
Patient seated

Inspection
Obvious swelling?
Tender at all?

Palpation
Describe the lump (see card).
Introduction: (tenderness, site, size)
Define: (shape, surface, edges)
Composition: (consistency, fluctuance, pulsatility, compressability, reducibility)
Layer of origin: (fixity, tethering)
Overlying and surrounding skin
Lymph nodes in neck
Any other lumps or sores on the scalp?

Inside the mouth
Inspect with pen torch
Lift tongue
Move it to the right
to the left
Ulcers or tonsilar swellings?
Palpate with glove
Inside of cheek
Stone in the duct?

Look at the face
Lesions on the face
Facial nerve palsy:
Show me your teeth
Raise your eyebrows
Scrunch your eyes tight closed

Make a diagnosis
Well circumscribed lump in the region of the parotid gland? (Adenoma)
Clinical evidence of malignancy, sialoadenitis or stones?

Summary sentence and diagnosis

SUMMARY CARD

MRCS PART B OSCEs
Essential Revision Notes

PASTEST

EXAMINATION OF THYROID STATUS (cont'd)

Examine the neck for a goitre or thyroid lump (see card)

Offer if appropriate
Check ankle reflexes
Ask the patient some questions

Summary of findings and diagnosis

SUMMARY CARD

MRCS PART B OSCEs
Essential Revision Notes

PASTEST

EXAMINATION OF A LUMP (cont'd)

6. Local lymph nodes
'The draining lymph nodes do not feel enlarged'

Offer if appropriate
Transillumination
Bruit
Distal arterial and nerve supply

Summary of findings and diagnosis

EXAMINATION OF THE BREAST

Introduction
Sit at 45°, shirt off
Hands on hips

Inspection
General(weight loss, SOB, pallor)
Breast asymmetry
    Skin changes (redness, puckering, peau d'orange, nodules, ulcer)
    Nipples and areolae (retraction, destruction, asymmetry, discharge)
Axillae and arms
    Swelling, nodes, veins, muscle wasting
Previous treatment
    Mastectomy, scarring, hair loss,
    Radiation burns, telangiectasia,
    lymphoedema,ink marks
Raise arms over head
    Look under breasts
    Look at axillae
    Look for tethering.

Palpate (hands behind head)
Ask: tender? any lumps?
Breast (normal side)
    All 4 quadrants, centre, nipple, axillary tail
Axilla (normal side)
    Take the elbow, relax the arm
    All 4 walls and apex

continued overleaf

EXAMINATION OF THE KNEE

Introduction
Lying flat on back

Look
Symmetry, swelling, scars, quads wasting

Feel
Is it tender?
Temperature
Extensor apparatus – quads, tendon, patella ligament, tubercle
Effusion – stroke test, patellar tap, feel synovium
Joint line

Move
Active + passive flexion and extension

Ligaments
Collateral (varus + valgus stress test)
Cruciates (anterior drawer/ Lachman's test, posterior drawer)
Rotational (Macintosh test)

Menisci
McMurray test

Patellae
Feel articular surface
Check mobility. Now test it pressing down hard against the femur.
Apprehension test

Offer if appropriate
Popliteal region
Inspect while standing
Gait
X-rays

Summary sentence and diagnosis

continued overleaf

EXAMINATION OF THE HIP

Introduction
Standing, trousers off

Look
From the front – pelvic tilting
    muscle wasting
    rotational deformity
From the side – scars
    lumbar lordosis
From behind – scoliosis
    gluteal muscle wasting
    sinus scars
Lie down to assess for shortening
    true length
    apparent length
    femur or tibia shortened? flex knees to see.

Feel
Greater trochanter
Head of femur
Adductor longus origin
Lesser trochanter

Move
Thomas' test (fixed flexion deformity/extension)
    –hand behind lumbar spine
    –flex good hip fully (knee to abdomen)
    –does lumbar spine flatten and bad hip stay on bed?
    No fixed flexion deformity
    –does bad hip rise from the bed?
    Fixed flexion deformity (loss of extension)
Flexion
Abduction and adduction (in extension)
Internal and external rotation (at 90°)

continued overleaf

MRCS PART B OSCEs
Essential Revision Notes

PASTEST

EXAMINATION OF THE HIP (cont'd)

Trendelenburg's test
Stand up
Stand on bad leg
Pelvis drops on opposite side? Test +ve.

Offer if appropriate
Gait
Neurological examination
Xrays

Summary sentence and diagnosis

MRCS PART B OSCEs
Essential Revision Notes

PASTEST

EXAMINATION OF RHEUMATOID HANDS

Introduction
Sleeves rolled up, hands on table

Look
Hands – symmetrical deforming polyarthropathy of joints
spindling of fingers
sparing of DIP joints
wasting of small muscles of hands
thin skin, bruising
ulnar deviation at MCP
radial deviation at wrist
Fingers – swan neck/buttonierre/Z thumb deformity
nail beds pale, vasculitic lesions present,
pitting, scaly rash absent
Palms – pale palmar creases, palmar erythema

Feel Joints
Rheumatoid nodules
Hebeden's nodes

Move Wrist
Grip
Finger pinch
Function

Sensation
Snuffbox
Thumb
Little finger

Elbow
Nodules
Psoriasis

Offer if appropriate
Examine other joints
Assess extra-articular manifestations
(eye, chest, cardiac, abdo, neuro, skin)
X-rays

Summary sentence and diagnosis

MRCS PART B OSCEs
Essential Revision Notes

PASTEST

EXAMINATION OF THE BREAST (cont'd)

Palpate (hands behind head) (cont'd)
Breast (side with lump)
All 4 quadrants, centre, nipple, axillary tail
Describe the lump (see card)
Introduction: (tenderness, site, size)
Define: (shape, surface, size)
Composition: (consistency, fluctuance,
pulsatility, compressability, reducibility)
Layer of origin: (fixity, tethering)
Overlying and surrounding skin
Assess fixity to pectoralis, hands on hips
Axilla (side with lump)
Take the elbow, relax the arm
All 4 walls and apex
Supraclavicular region both sides

Offer if appropriate
Listen to chest
Examine the abdomen

Summary sentence and diagnosis

EXAMINATION OF SHOULDER

Introduction
Patient sitting, shirt off
Look From in front
  sternoclavicular joint
  clavicle
  acromioclavicular joint
  asymmetry and wasting
  From the side
  From above – supraclavicular fossae
  Stand patient up
  look from behind
  winging of scapula
Feel Sternoclavicular joint
  Clavicle
  Acromioclavicular joint
  Glenohumeral joint
  Feel through axilla
Move (active then passive)
  Abduction
    initiation
    painful arc
    ability to hold arm up
  Adduction
    hand on opposite shoulder
  Forwards (flexion)
  Backwards (extension)
  Hands behind back
  Hands behind head
  Elbows by side (external rotation, internal rotation)
  Elbows abducted (external rotation, internal rotation)
  Feel for crepitations
  Deltoid power (and regimental badge sensation)

continued overleaf

EXAMINATION OF THE NECK

Introduction
Sitting on a chair
Inspection
Asymmetry, deformity, torticullis, muscle wasting, position of head
Scars, sinuses, localised tenderness
Palpation
Step deformity
Lateral masses and tenderness
Cervical rib
Tumour, nodes, masses, temperature
Movements
Forward flexion
Extension
Lateral flexion
Rotation
Feel for crepitations
Offer if appropriate
Neurological examination of arms
Lateral AP and peg X-rays
Summary sentence and diagnosis

EXAMINATION OF THE BACK

Introduction
Stand with trousers off, back to me
Inspection from the back
Scoliosis
Swellings
Scars
Abnormal pigmentation, hair, cafe au lait spots
Inspection from the side
Kyphosis
Gibbus
Lumbar curvature
Palpation
Vertebrae
Lumbar muscles
Sacroiliac joints
Step
Percussion
With patient bent forward
Movements
Forward flexion
Extension
Lateral flexion
Rotation
Lie down
Rotation at hip
Straight leg raise
Passive dorsiflexion

continued overleaf

737

SUMMARY CARD

MRCS PART B OSCEs
Essential Revision Notes

PASTEST

EXAMINATION OF THE BACK (cont'd)

Offer if appropriate
Reverse Lasègue test
Tests for functional overlay
Tests of sacroiliac joint
Neurological examination of leg
Femoral pulses
Abdominal examination
ESR
AP and lateral thoracic and lumbar spine X-rays.

Summary sentence and diagnosis

SUMMARY CARD

MRCS PART B OSCEs
Essential Revision Notes

PASTEST

EXAMINATION OF THE UPPER LIMB

Introduction
Shirt off, sitting or standing

Look
General inspection – face, neck
Arms: (front and back, arms out)
deformities
scars
tremor
muscle wasting
swollen joints

Feel
Tone

Move (power)
Deltoids (Push patient's elbows down)
Biceps (try to straighten patient's elbows)
Triceps (try to bend patient's elbows)
Squeeze fingers (C8, T1)
Finger extension (Radial nerve)
Spread fingers (ulnar nerve)
Paper between fingers (ulnar)
Thumb to ceiling (median nerve)

Coordination
Alternate movement clapping test
Finger to nose

Reflexes
Biceps, triceps, supinator

Sensation
Pinprick + light touch

Offer if appropriate
Joint position test, vibration sense, pulses
Range of movement neck, shoulder, elbow, wrist
Vascular examination

Summary sentence and diagnosis

SUMMARY CARD

MRCS PART B OSCEs
Essential Revision Notes

PASTEST

EXAMINATION OF SHOULDER (cont'd)

Offer if appropriate
Cervical spine examination (see card)
Neurological examination of upper limb (see card)
Drawer tests of Gerber and Ganz
Test for ruptured long head of biceps
X-rays

Summary sentence and diagnosis